DICTIONARY

ITALIAN•ENGLISH
ENGLISH•ITALIAN

DICTIONARY

ITALIAN • ENGLISH
ENGLISH • ITALIAN

TIGER BOOKS INTERNATIONAL
LONDON

© Geddes & Grosset Ltd 1994

This edition published in 1994 by
Tiger Books International PLC, London

ISBN 1-85501-374 6

Printed and bound in Slovenia

	Abbreviations	**Abbreviazioni**
abbr, abbrev	abbreviation	abbreviazione
adj	adjective	aggettivo
adv	adverb	avverbio
art	article	articolo
auto	automobile	automobile
aux	auxiliary	ausiliario
bot	botany	botanica
chem	chemistry	chimica
com	commerce	commercio
conj	conjunction	congiunzione
cul, culin	cooking term	espressione di cucina
dem	demonstrative	dimonstrativo
excl	exclamation	esclamazione
f	feminine noun	sostantivo feminile
fam	colloquial term	espressione familiare
fig	figurative use	uso figurato
gr	grammar	grammatica
interj	interjection	interiezione
inv, invar	invariable	invariabile
law	law term	giurisprudenza
m	masculine noun	sostantivo maschile
mar	marine term	termine marittimo
med	medicine	medicina
mus	music	musica
n	noun	sostantivo
pl	plural	plurale
poss	possessive	possessivo
pron	pronoun	pronome
prep	preposition	preposizione
rel	relative	relativo
relig	religious	religioso
sl	slang	gergo
vi	intransitive verb	verbo intransitivo
vr	reflexive verb	verbo riflessivo
vt	transitive verb	verbo transitivo
vulg	vulgar	volgare

A

a *prep* to; in; at; on; by; with; for.
abate *m* abbot.
abbagliante *adj* dazzling.
abbagliare *vt* to dazzle.
abbaiare *m* bark; * *vi* to bark.
abbaino *m* dormer window.
abbandonare *vt* to abandon; to leave; to forsake; to desert; to drop; * *vr* **~rsi** to give oneself up to.
abbandonato *adj* disused; marooned.
abbandono *m* desertion; neglect; retirement; withdrawal; abandon, abandonment; walkout.
abbassare *vt* to dim; to turn down; * *vi* to sink; * *vr* **~rsi** to abase oneself; to stoop; to abate.
abbastanza *adj*, enough; fairly; * *adv* enough; reasonably; relatively; **avere ~ di** to have a bellyful of.
abbattere *vt* to cull; to fell; to dash (hopes).
abbattimento *m* despondency, dejection.
abbattuto *adj* crestfallen, dejected, despondent.
abbellire *vt* to adorn; to beautify; to embellish.
abbiente *adj* well-to-do
abbigliamento *m* clothing; dress.
abbindolare *vt* to take in.
abbonamento *m* subscription; season ticket; * *vr* **~rsi** to subscribe.
abbonato *m* subscriber.
abbondante *adj* abundant; plentiful; copious; bountiful.
abbondanza *f* abundance; affluence; plenty; fullness.

abbondare *vi* to abound.
abbordare *vt* to accost.
abbreviare *vt* to abbreviate, to abridge.
abbreviazione *f* abbreviation.
abdicare (a) *vt* to abdicate.
abdicazione *f* abdication.
aberrazione *f* aberration.
abietto *adj* abject.
abile *adj* able, adept, adroit.
abilità *f* ability, aptitude.
abissale *adj* abysmal.
abisso *m* abyss.
abituare *vt* to accustom.
abituato *adj* accustomed.
abolire *vt* to abolish.
abolizione *f* abolition.
abominevole *adj* abominable.
a bordo *adv* aboard.
aborigeno *adj* aboriginal.
abortire *vi* to abort.
aborto *m* abortion.
aborrevole *adj* abhorrent.
aborrire *vt* to abhor.
abrasione *f* abrasion.
abrasivo *adj* abrasive.
abrogare *vt* to abrogate.
abside *f* apse.
abbozzare *vt* to draft.
abbozzo *m* draft.
abbozzo *m* sketch.
abbracciare *vt* to embrace; to hug; to span; to espouse.
abbraccio *m* cuddle; embrace; hug.
abbronzarsi *vr* to tan.
abbronzato *adj* tanned.
abbronzatura *f* suntan, tan.
abete *m* fir (tree), spruce; **legno di ~** *m* deal.
abile *adj* artful; deft; skilled, skilful.
abilità *f* ability; knack; skill; **~ artistica** artistry.

abisso *m* gulf.

abitabile *adj* habitable, inhabitable.

abitante *m/f* inhabitant.

abitare *vt* to inhabit; (ghost) to haunt; * *vi* to live.

abitazione *f* habitation.

abito *m* dress; gown; ~ **da sera** *m* evening dress.

abituale *adj* habitual; ordinary; routine.

abituato *adj* accustomed.

abitudine *f* habit; custom; practice; way.

abiurare *vi* to recant.

abnegazione *f* self-sacrifice.

abortire *vi* to abort, miscarry.

aborto *m* abortion, miscarriage.

abrogare *vt* to revoke, to repeal.

abrogazione *f* repeal.

abusare *vt* to misuse; ~ **di** to abuse.

abusivo *adj* unauthorized, unlawful.

abuso *m* abuse, misuse.

acacia *f* acacia.

acaro *m* mite.

accademia *f* academy.

accademico *adj* academic; * *m* academic, academician.

accadere *vt* to befall; * *vi* to befall; to happen; to occur; to pass.

accampamento *m* camp; encampment.

accampare *vt* to encamp.

accanitamente *adv* hotly.

accanito *adj* fierce.

accanto *prep* beside; ~ **a** next to.

accantonare *vt* to shelve.

accaparrarsi *vr* to hog; to scoop.

accappatoio *m* bathrobe.

accarezzare *vt* to fondle; to pet; to stroke.

accartocciare *vt* to crumple.

accatastare *vt* to stack.

accecare *vt* to blind.

accedere a *vi* to assent to; to attain (office); to adhere (to); to access.

accelerare *vt* to accelerate; to hasten; to precipitate; * *vi* to accelerate.

acceleratore *m* accelerator.

accelerazione *f* acceleration.

accendere *vt* to switch on; to turn on; to put on; to light; to strike (a match); to ignite; to kindle.

accendino *m* cigarette lighter.

accennare *vt* to mention.

accenno *m* allusion.

accensione *f* ignition; **chiave dell'~** *f* ignition key.

accentato *adj* stressed.

accento *m* accent; ~ **irlandese** *m* brogue; emphasis.

accentuare *vt* to accentuate.

accerchiare *vt* to circle; to ring.

accertare *vt* ascertain.

acceso *adj* on.

accessibile *adj* accessible.

accessione *f* accession.

accesso *m* access; **divieto d'~** no entry; fit.

accessori *mpl* fittings; trimmings

accessorio *n* accessory; attachment; fitment.

accetta *f* hatchet.

accettabile *adj* acceptable.

accettare *vt* to accept; to take.

accettazione *f* acceptance; reception.

acciaieria *f* steelworks.

acciaio *m* steel.

accidentato *adj* bumpy; rugged; uneven.

accidia *f* sloth.

accidioso *adj* slothful.

accigliarsi *vr* to scowl.

acciottolare *vt* to rattle.

acciottolio *m* rattle.

acciuffare *vt* to nab.

acciuga *f* anchovy.

acclamare *vt* to acclaim.

acclamazioni *fpl* acclaim.

acclimatare *vt* to acclimatize; * *vr* ~**rsi** to acclimatize oneself.

accoglienza *f* acceptance.

accompagnamento *m* accompaniment.

accompagnare *vt* to accompany.

accompagnatore *m* accompanist (*mus*).

acconsentire a *vi* to acquiesce in.

accorciare *vt* to abridge.

accordo *m* agreement; **essere d'~ con** to agree.

acclamare *vt* to hail.

accoccolarsi *vr* to nestle.

accogliente *adj* cosy, snug.

accoglienza *f* welcome.

accogliere *vt* to welcome.

accolito *m* henchman.

accollarsi *vr* to shoulder.

accomodante *adj* easy-going.

accomodare *vt* to mend.

accompagnare *vt* to accompany.

accompagnato *adj* accompanied.

accompagnatore *m* chaperone.

acconciatura *f* hairstyle.

accondiscendere *vi* to condescend.

acconsentire *vi* to consent.

accontentare *vt* to indulge; to humour; to please.

accoppiamento *m* copulation; mating.

accoppiare *vt* to mate; * *vr* ~**rsi** to copulate; to mate.

accorciare *vt* to shorten; to curtail.

accordare *vt* to grant; to tune; * *vi* to tune.

accordatore *m* tuner.

accordo *m* agreement; deal; settlement.

accorgersi *vr* to notice.

accortezza *f* shrewdness.

accorto *adj* astute; shrewd; politic.

accovacciarsi *vr* to crouch.

accozzaglia *f* jumble.

accreditare *vt* to credit.

accrescere *vt* to increase; * *vr* ~**rsi** to increase.

accucciarsi *vr* to duck.

accumulare *vt* to accumulate, to amass; to store; to hoard; * *vt* ~**rsi** to accumulate.

accumulo *m* accumulation.

accuratezza *f* accuracy.

accurato *adj* accurate; careful.

accusa *f* accusation, charge, prosecution (*law*); allegation; **mettere sotto ~** to impeach.

accusare *vt* to accuse; to charge.

accusativo *m* (*gr*) accusative.

accusato *m* accused.

accusatore *m* accuser.

acerbo *adj* unripe.

acero *m* maple.

acetato *m* acetate.

aceto *m* vinegar.

acetosa *f* sorrel.

acidità *f* acidity; sourness.

acido *adj* acid; caustic; sour; * *m* acid.

acme *m* acme.

acne *f* acne.

acqua *f* water; **~ dolce** fresh water; **tirare l'~** to flush.

acquaio *m* sink.

acquario *m* aquarium; **A~** Aquarius.

acquartieramento *m* billet.

acquatico *adj* aquatic.

acquattarsi *vr* to cower; to squat.

acquazzone *m* cloudburst; downpour; shower.

acquedotto *m* aquaduct.

acquerello *m* watercolour.

acquiescente *adj* acquiescent.

acquiescenza *f* acquiescence.

acquirente *m/f* purchaser.

acquisire *vt* to acquire.

acquistare *vt* to purchase.

acquisto *m* acquisition; purchase.

acquolina *f* drizzle; **che fa venire l'~ in bocca** *adj* mouth-watering

acquoso *adj* watery.

acre *adj* acrid; sour.

acrimonia *f* acrimony.

acro *m* acre.

acrobazia *f* stunt.

acustica *f* acoustics.

acute *adj* acute.

acutezza *f* smartness.

acuto *adj* sharp; keen; reedy.

adattamento *m* adaptation, adjustment.

adattare *vt* to adapt; * *vr* ~**rsi** to acclimatize.

adatto *adj* appropriate; right; fit; suitable; becoming.

adattare *vt* to suit.

addebitare *vt* to debit.

addebito *m* debit.

addestramento *m* training.

addestrare *vt* to train; to school.

addetto *m* attaché.

addio *m* farewell; goodbye; * *adj* **d'~** parting.

addirittura *adv* actually; even.

addirsi *vt* to befit.

additivo *m* additive.

addizionare *vt* to add.

addizione *f* addition.

addolcire *vt* to sweeten

addolcirsi *vr* to mellow

addolcito *adj* mellow

addolorare *vt* to distress; to grieve; to pain;

addolorato *adj* sorrowful; pained.

addome *m* abdomen.

addomesticare *vt* to domesticate; to tame.

addomesticato *adj* tame.

addomesticazione *f* domestication.

addominale *adj* abdominal.

addormentarsi *vr* to fall asleep

addormentato *adj* asleep; sleeping.

addossarsi *vr* to take on.

adeguatamente *adv* suitably.

adeguato *adj* adequate.

adenoidi *fpl* adenoids.

aderente *m/f* adherent.

aderire *vi* to adhere.

adesione *f* adhesion.

adesivo *m* adhesive; sticker.

adesso *adv*, *conj* now.

adiacente *adj* adjacent.

adiposo *adj* adipose.

adolescenza *f* adolescence.

adolescente *m/f* adolescent, teenager.

adolescenziale *adj* teenage.

adoperare *vt* to use.

adorabile *adj* adorable, lovable.

adorare *vt* to adore; to worship.

adorato *adj* beloved.

adorazione *f* adoration; worship.

adottare *vt* to adopt.

adottato *adj* adopted.

adozione *f* adoption.

adulare *vi* to crawl; * *vt* to fawn upon.

adulazione *f* adulation.

adulterare *vt* to adulterate; to doctor.

adultero *adj* adulterous; * *m* adulterer.

adultera *f* adulteress.

adulterio *m* adultery.

adulto *adj* adult; * *m* adult, grown-up.

adunare *vt* to mass; * *vr* ~**rsi** to mass.

aereo *adj* aerial.

aerobica *f* aerobics.

aeromobile *m* aircraft.

aeronatica *f* military air force.

aeroporto *m* airport.

aerosol *m* aerosol.

affabile *adj* affable, amiable, good-natured.

affaccendarsi *vr* to bustle.

affamato *adj* hungry; starving, famished.

affare *m* affair; deal; bargain; snip.

affari *mpl* business; **uomo d'~** *m* businessman; **donna d'~** *f* businesswoman.

affascinante *adj* fascinating; glamorous; intriguing.

affascinare *vt* to fascinate; to captivate, to charm; to enthral.

affaticare *vt* to fatigue; to strain.

affatto *adv* at all; **niente ~** not in the least.

affermare *vt* to affirm; to assert; to state.

affermativo *adj* affirmative.

affermato *adj* successful.

affermazione *f* assertion, claim, affirmation.

afferrare *vt* to catch, to clasp; to grasp; to grab, to snatch; to seize.

affettare *vt* to slice; to affect.

affettato *adj* affected.

affettatrice *f* slicer.

affetto *m* affection; fondness.

affettuoso *adj* loving, warm-hearted.

affezionato *adj* affectionate, fond.

affidabile *adj* dependable, reliable.

affidare *vt* to entrust; (actor) to cast.

affidatario *adj*: **genitore ~** *m* foster parent.

affidavit *m inv* affidavit.

affievolirsi *vr* to dwindle.

affiggere *vt* to post.

affilare *vt* to sharpen.

affilato *adj* sharp.

affiliare *vt* to affiliate.

affiliazione *f* affiliation.

affinché *conj* so that.

affine *adj* (*ling*) cognate; related.

affinità *f* affinity.

affittare *vt* to lease; to let; to rent.

affitto *m* rent; **proprietà in ~** *f* leasehold; **contratto d'~** *m* tenancy.

affliggere *vt* to afflict.

afflitto *adj* doleful.

affluente *m* tributary.

afflusso *m* influx; onrush.

affogare *vt, vi* to drown.

affollare *vt* to crowd; to throng; * *vr* **~rsi** to cram.

affondare *vi* to founder; to sink.

affrancare *vt* to stamp, to frank.

affrancato *adj* prepaid.

affrancatura *f* postage.

affresco *m* fresco.

affrettare *vt* to quicken; * *vr* **~rsi** to hurry, to make haste.

affrettato *adj* hasty.

affrontare *vt* to broach; to confront; to deal with, to tackle; to face.

affronto *m* affront, slur, snub, slight.

affumicare *vt* to smoke.

affumicato *adj* smoked.

affusto *m* gun carriage.

aforisma *m* aphorism.

afoso *adj* close, sultry, muggy.

afrodisiaco *m* aphrodisiac.

agenda *f* diary.

agente *m/f* agent; **~ immobiliare** *m* estate agent.

agenzia *f* agency; **~ viaggi** *f* travel agency.

agevolazione f concession; ~
  fiscale f tax relief.
agganciare vt to hook.
aggeggio m contraption; gadget.
aggettivo m adjective.
aggiungere vt to add.
agghiacciante adj gruesome,
  spine-chilling.
agghindarsi vr to preen.
aggiornare vt to update; to
  write up.
aggiornato adj up-to-date.
aggirare vt to circumvent; to
  skirt.
aggirarsi vr to prowl; ~ **furtivamente** vi to skulk; **chi si
  aggira furtivamente** m
  prowler.
aggiunta f addition, accession
  (to collection), adjunct.
aggiustare vt to adjust; to
  mend, to repair.
agglomerazione f agglomeration.
agglomerato m chipboard.
aggrapparsi vr to cling.
aggravamento m aggravation.
aggravare vt to aggravate.
aggraziato adj graceful.
aggredire vt to mug.
aggregare vt to affiliate.
aggressione f aggression.
aggressivo adj aggressive.
aggressore m aggressor; attacker.
aggrottare vt to contract; ~ **le
  sopracciglia** vi to knit one's
  brow, to frown.
aggrovigliare vt to tangle.
aggrumarsi vr to cake.
agguato m ambush; **stare in ~**
  to lie in ambush.
agile adj agile; lithe; nimble.
agilità f agility.
agio m ease; **sentirsi a proprio ~** to feel at one's ease.
agire vi to act.

agitare vt to agitate; to stir; to
  churn; to flail; * vr **~rsi** to fidget; to dither; to wriggle.
agitato adj flustered.
agitatore m agitator.
agitazione f agitation.
agitazione f fuss, flurry; state;
  unrest; **stato di ~** m fluster.
aglio m garlic; **spicchio d'~** m
  clove of garlic.
agnello m lamb.
ago m needle.
agonia f death throes.
agonistico adj competitive.
agosto m August.
agricolo adj agricultural.
agricoltore m farmer.
agricoltura f agriculture, farming.
agrifoglio m holly.
agrume m citrus.
aguzzino m slave-driver.
aguzzo adj sharp.
ahi! excl ouch!.
ahimè! excl alas!.
aia f farmyard.
AIDS m AIDS.
airone m heron.
aitante adj upstanding.
aiuola f (garden) border; flower bed.
aiutante m/f assistant; help; ~
  di campo aide-de-camp.
aiutare vt to assist, to aid, to
  help.
aiuto m aid, assistenza, help.
al di là prep beyond.
ala f wing; (sport) winger.
alabastro m alabaster.
alacremente adj busily.
alambicco m still.
alato adj winged.
alba f dawn, daybreak, sunrise.
albatro m albatross.
alberello m sapling.
albergatore m hotelier.
albergo m hotel.
albero m tree; ~ **da frutto** m

fruit tree; mast; (*mar*) spar; shaft; **~ a gomiti** *m* crankshaft; **~ a camme** *m* camshaft.

albicocca *f* apricot.

albicocco *m* apricot tree.

album *m* album.

alcali *m inv* alkali.

alcalino *adj* alkaline.

alce *m* elk, moose.

alchimia *f* alchemy.

alchimista *m* alchemist.

alcolico *adj* alcoholic.

alcolico *m* alcoholic; **bevande alcoliche** *fpl* liquor.

alcolismo *m* alcoholism.

alcolizzato *m* alcoholic.

alcool *m* alcohol, (*fam*) booze; **~ denaturato** *m* methylated spirits.

alcova *f* alcove.

alcuno *adj* some; * *pron* **alcuni** some.

alfabetico *adj* alphabetical; **in ordine ~** in alphabetical order.

alfabeto *m* alphabet; **~ Morse** *m* Morse code.

alfiere *m* (chess) bishop.

algebra *f* algebra.

alghe *fpl* algae; seaweed.

aliante *m* glider; **volo con l'~** *m* gliding.

alias *adv* alias.

alibi *m* alibi.

alienare *vt* to alienate.

alienazione *f* alienation.

alimentare *vt* to feed.

alimentari *m* grocery; **negoziante di ~** *m* grocer.

alimentazione *f* diet; input.

alimenti *mpl* alimony.

aliscafo *m* hydrofoil.

alito *m* breath.

alitosi *f* halitosis.

allacciare *vt* to tie; to lace; to buckle; * *vr* **~rsi** to buckle, to fasten.

allampanato *adj* weedy.

allargare *vt* to broaden.

allarmare *vt* to alarm.

allarme *m* alarm, alert; **falso ~** *m* false alarm.

allarmista *m/f* alarmist; scaremonger; * *adj* panicky.

allattare *vt* to suckle; to feed; **~ al seno** to breastfeed.

alleanza *f* alliance.

allearsi con *vr* to ally.

alleato *adj* allied; * *m* ally.

allegare *vt* to enclose; to append.

allegato *m* enclosure.

alleggerire *vt* to lighten; * *vr* **~rsi di** to jettison.

allegoria *f* allegory.

allegorico *adj* allegorical.

allegramente *adv* gaily.

allegria *f* gaiety; merriment.

allegro *m* cheerful, jolly, merry; perky.

allenamento *m* training.

allenare *vt* to train, to coach.

allenato *adj* trained.

allenatore *m* trainer, coach.

allentare *vt* to loosen; to slacken; to weaken; * *vt* **~rsi** to slacken.

allentato *adj* loose.

allergia *f* allergy.

allettante *adj* alluring; tantalizing; tempting.

allettare *vt* to allure; to entice.

allevamento *m* breeding; **~ di pesci** *m* fish farm.

allevare *vt* to breed; to bring up; to raise; to foster.

allevatore *m* breeder.

alleviare *vt* to alleviate; to ease; to relieve.

allibratore *m* bookmaker.

allievo *m* pupil.

alligatore *m* alligator.

allineare *vt* to align.

allineato *adj* aligned; **non ~** non-aligned.

allitterazione *f* alliteration.
allodola *f* lark, skylark.
alloggiamento *m* housing.
alloggiare *vt* to accommodate; to house; * *vi* to lodge; to stay.
alloggio *m* accommodation.
alludere a *vt* to allude.
allontanamento *m* estrangement.
allontanare *vt* to stave off.
allora *adv* then; **da ~** since.
alloro *m* bay, laurel.
allucinazione *f* hallucination.
alludere *vt* to hint.
alluminio *m* aluminium.
allungare *vt* to elongate; to lengthen.
allusione *f* allusion; hint.
alluvionale *adj* alluvial.
almanacco *m* almanac.
almeno *adv* at least.
alpinismo *m* climbing; mountaineering.
alpinista *m/f* climber; mountaineer.
alpino *adj* alpine.
alquanto *adv* somewhat.
altalena *f* swing; seesaw.
altare *m* altar.
alterco *m* wrangle.
alternante *adj* alternating.
alternare *vt* to alternate.
alternativa *f* alternative; **come ~** alternatively.
alternativo *adj* alternative.
alternato *adj* alternate.
alternatore *m* alternator.
altezza *f* height; headroom; highness; **essere all'~** to live up to.
altezzoso *adj* supercilious; snooty; lofty.
altitudine *f* altitude.
alto *adj* high; tall; treble; **in ~** aloft; **il più ~** topmost; **verso l'~** upwards; * *adv* **in ~** overhead; * *m* high.
altolocato *adj* grand.

altoparlante *m inv* loudspeaker; speaker.
altopiano *m* plateau.
altrettanto *adv* just as; likewise.
altrimenti *adv* else; otherwise.
altro *pron*: **un ~** another; other; **l'un l'~** one another; * *adj* other; more; * *adv* else.
altrove *adv* elsewhere.
altruista *adj* selfless; unselfish.
alveare *m* beehive, hive.
alzare *vt* to heighten; to raise; to turn up; * *vr* **~rsi** to rise; to stand up.
amaca *f* hammock.
amalgamare *vt* to amalgamate.
amante *m/f* lover; *f* mistress.
amare *vt* to love.
amaretto *m* macaroon.
amarezza *f* bitterness.
amarillide *f* amaryllis.
amaro *adj* bitter.
amazzone *f* horsewoman.
ambasciata *f* embassy.
ambasciatore *m* ambassador.
ambasciatrice *f* ambassadress.
ambedue *adj* both.
ambidestro *adj* ambidextrous.
ambientale *adj* environmental.
ambientalista *m/f* conservationist.
ambientarsi *vr* to find one's feet.
ambiente *m* environment; setting; **~ sociale** *m* milieu.
ambiguità *f inv* ambiguity.
ambiguo *adj* ambiguous; dubious.
ambito *m* scope.
ambizione *f* ambition.
ambizioso *adj* ambitious.
ambra *f*, *adj* amber.
ambulante *adj* itinerant.
ambulanza *f* ambulance.
ambulatorio *m* surgery.
ametista *f* amethyst.

amianto m asbestos.

amica f girlfriend.

amichevole adj amicable; friendly.

amicizia f friendship.

amico m friend; pal; ~ **del cuore** bosom friend.

amicone m chum, crony.

amido m starch.

ammaccare vt to dent.

ammaccatura f dent.

ammalarsi vr to sicken.

ammanettare vt to shackle.

ammassarsi vr to flock.

ammazzare vt to kill.

ammettere vt to accept, to admit; **bisogna ~ che** admittedly.

ammiccare vi to wink.

amministrare vt to administrate; ~ **male** to mismanage; to administer.

amministrativo adj administrative.

amministratore m administrator; trustee; ~ **delegato** managing director.

amministrazione f administration; ~ **della casa** f housekeeping; **cattiva ~** f mismanagement.

ammiragliato m admiralty.

ammiraglio m admiral.

ammirare vt to admire.

ammiratore m admirer; well-wisher.

ammirazione f admiration.

ammissibile adj admissible, allowable.

ammissione f acknowledgement, admission: entrance.

ammoniaca f ammonia.

ammettere vt to concede, to countenance, to brook; to grant; to own up.

ammissibile adj permissible.

ammobiliato adj furnished.

ammonimento m caveat.

ammonire vt to admonish; to caution.

ammontare vi to amount; ~ **a** to amount to; * vt to total.

ammonitorio adj cautionary.

ammorbidente m softener.

ammorbidire vt to soften.

ammortizzabile adj redeemable.

ammortizzare vt to absorb.

ammortizzatore m shock absorber

ammucchiare vt to heap, to pile.

ammuffito adj mouldy.

ammutinamento m mutiny.

ammutinarsi vr to mutiny.

ammutolito adj tongue-tied.

amnesia f amnesia.

amnistia f amnesty.

amorale adj amoral.

amore m love; **vero ~** true love; **storia d'~** f romance; **per ~** for the sake of; **malato d'~** adj lovesick.

amorfo adj amorphous.

amoroso adj amorous.

ampere m inv amp(ere).

ampiamente adv amply.

ampiamento m enlargement.

ampiezza f fullness.

ampio adj ample.

ampliare vt amplify; to enlarge; to widen.

amplificare vt amplify.

amplificatore m amplifier; ~ **di segnale** booster.

amplificazione f amplification; **impianto di ~** m public address system.

ampolla f cruet.

ampolloso adj turgid.

amputare vt amputate.

amputazione f amputation.

amuleto m amulet.

anacardio m cashew.

anacronismo m anachronism.

anagrafe f registry office.

anagramma *m* anagram.

analcolico *m* soft drink; * *adj* non-alcoholic.

analfabeta *m/f*, *adj* illiterate.

analisi *f inv* analysis; ~ **del sangue** blood test; ~ **infinitesimale** *f* calculus.

analista *m/f* analyst; ~ **sistemi** systems analyst.

analitico *adj* analytic(al).

analizzare *vt* to analyse.

analogia *f* analogy.

analogico *adj* analogue.

analogo *adj* analogous.

ananas *m inv* pineapple.

anarchia *f* anarchy.

anarchico *adj* anarchic; * *m* anarchist.

anatema *m* anathema.

anatomia *f* anatomy.

anatomico *adj* anatomical.

anatra *f* duck; **maschio dell'~** *m* drake.

anatroccolo *m* duckling.

anca *f* hip.

ancestrale *adj* ancestral.

anche *adv* also; too; as well.

ancheggiare *vt* to wiggle one's hips.

ancora *adv* again; another; even; still; already; * *adj* more.

àncora *f* anchor.

ancoraggio *m* anchorage.

andamento *m* trend.

andare *vi* to go; ~ **a gattoni** to crawl; ~ **furtivamente** to creep; ~ **a destra** to bear right; ~ **avanti** to lead; * *vt* ~ **bene a** to fit; ~ **sù e giù** to pace.

andarsene *vi* to go (away).

andata *f* **biglietto di** ~ *m* single ticket.

andatura *f* going, gait, walk.

aneddoto *m* anecdote.

anelito *m* gasp.

anello *m* ring; ~ **di fidanzamento** *m* engagement ring; link.

anemia *f* anaemia.

anemico *adj* anaemic.

anemone *m* (*bot*) anemone.

anestetico *m* anaesthetic.

anestetista *m/f* anaesthetist.

aneto *m* dill.

anfibio *m* amphibian; amphibious.

anfiteatro *m* amphitheatre.

angelico *adj* angelic.

angelo *m* angel.

anglicismo *m* anglicism.

anglicizzare *vt* anglicize.

angolino *m* nook.

angolo *m* angle; corner; ~ **sperduto** *m* backwater.

angoscia *f* anguish; distress; * *vr* ~**rsi** to agonize over.

anguilla *f* eel.

anguria *f* watermelon.

angusto *adj* cramped; poky.

anice *m* aniseed.

anima *f* soul.

animale *adj* animal; * *m* animal; ~ **domestico** *m* pet; **animali nocivi** *mpl* vermin.

animare *vt* to animate; to pep up.

animato *m* boisterous; * *adj* animate(d).

animazione *f* animation.

animelle *fpl* sweetbreads.

animosità *f inv* animosity.

annaffiatoio *m* watering can.

annali *mpl* annals; records.

annata *f* vintage; year.

annegare *vt*, *vi* to drown.

annerire *vt* to blacken; * *vr* ~**rsi** to blacken.

annesso *m* annex.

annettare *vt* to annex.

annientamento *m* annihilation.

annientare *vt* to annihilate.

anniversario *m* anniversary.

anno *m* year; session; ~ **nuovo** *m* New Year; ~ **luce** *m* light year; **all'~** per annum.

annodare *vt* to knot.

annoiare *vt* to bore.

annotare *vt* to annotate; to record.

annotazione *f* annotation.

annuale *adj* yearly.

annualità *f* annuity.

annuario *m* yearbook.

annullamento *m* annulment.

annullare *vt* to countermand; to abrogate, to annul; to invalidate; to nullify.

annunciare *vt* to announce.

annunciatore *m* newscaster.

annuncio *m* advertisement; accouncement; **annunci economici** *mpl* classified advertisements.

annuo *m* annual.

annusare *vt* to sniff.

anomalia *f* abnormality, anomaly.

anomalo *adj* anomalous.

anonimato *m* anonymity; obscurity.

anonimo *adj* anonymous; unnamed.

anoressia *f* anorexia.

anormale *adj* abnormal; freak.

anormalità *f* abnormality.

ansare *vi* to gasp.

ansia *f* anxiety.

ansimare *vi* to pant; to puff; to wheeze.

ansioso *adj* nervous; solicitous.

antagonismo *m* antagonism.

antagonista *m* antagonist.

antartico *adj* antarctic.

antecedente *adj* antecedent.

anteguerra *f* pre-war.

antenato *m* ancestor.

antenna *f* aerial, antenna; feeler.

anteprima *f* preview.

anteriore *adj* anterior; fore.

antiaderente *adj* non-stick.

antiaereo *adj* anti-aircraft.

antiappannante *m* demister.

antibiotico *m* antibiotic.

anticamera *f* antechamber.

antichità *f* antiquity.

anticiclone *m* anticyclone.

anticipare *vt* to advance; to forestall.

anticipo *m* andvance; down payment; **in ~** in advance or ahead; **dare un ~** to give an advance (loan); **pagato in ~** prepaid.

antico *adj* ancient, antique.

anticoncezionale *adj, m* contraceptive.

anticonformista *adj, m/f* nonconformist.

anticorpo *m* antibody.

antidolorifico *m* painkiller.

antidoto *m* antidote.

antieconomico *adj* uneconomic.

antifurto *m inv* burglar alarm.

antigelo *m* antifreeze.

antilope *f* antelope.

antincendio *adj*: **allarme ~** *f* fire alarm.

antiorario *adj*: **in senso ~** anticlockwise.

antipasto *m* hors d'oeuvres, starter.

antipatia *f* antipathy; dislike.

antipatico *adj* objectionable; unlovable.

antipodi *mpl* antipodes.

antiquariato *m* antiques; **pezzo d'~** *m* antique.

antiquario *m* antiquarian.

antiquato *adj* antiquated; dated; old-fashioned; stuffy.

antirrino *m* snapdragon.

antisemitico *adj* antisemitic.

antisettico *m, adj* antiseptic.

antisociale *adj* antisocial.

antistiminico *m* antihistamine.

antitesi *f inv* antithesis.

antologia *f* anthology; reader.

antracite *f* anthracite.

antropologia *f* anthropology.

anzianità *f* seniority.

anziano *adj* aged; elderly; old; * *m* elder.

aorta *f* aorta.

apartheid *f* apartheid.

apatia *f* apathy.

apatico *adj* apathetic; listless.

ape *f* bee.

aperitivo *m* aperitif.

aperto *adj* open; broad-minded; open-minded; gaping; **all'~** outdoor.

apertura *f* aperture; opening; spread.

apiario *m* apiary.

apice *m* prime.

apocalisse *f* Apocalypse.

apocrifo *adj* apocryphal.

apolide *adj* stateless.

apolitico *adj* apolitical.

apoplessia *f* apoplexy.

apoplettico *adj* apoplectic.

apostolico *adj* apostolic.

apostolo *m* apostle.

apostrofo *m* apostrophe.

apoteosi *f* apotheosis.

appagare *vt* to quench.

appaltatore *m* contractor.

appannarsi *vr* to mist up.

apparecchio *m* set; appliance; **~ acustico** *m* hearing aid; **~ ortodontico** *m* brace.

apparecchiare *vt* to lay (the table).

apparente *adj* outward; seeming.

apparentemente *adv* ostensibly.

apparenza *f* semblance.

apparire *vi* to appear; **~ indistintamente** to loom.

appariscente *adj* showy; **poco ~** inconspicuous.

appartamento *m* apartment; flat; suite.

appartato *adj* secluded.

appartenere *vi* to belong.

appassionante *adj* gripping.

appassionato *adj* devotee; enthusiastic; passionate; * *m* enthusiast.

appassire *vi* to droop; to fade; to wilt, to wither.

appellante *m/f* appellant; * *vt* **~rsi** (*law*) to appeal.

appello *m* appeal; muster.

appena *adv* barely; just; hardly; fresh, freshly; scarcely; **~ possibile** as soon as possible; * *conj* as soon as possible.

appendere *vt* to hang.

appendice *f* adjunct, appendage, appendix.

appetito *m* appetite.

appetitoso *adj* appetizing; luscious.

appezzamento *m* plot.

appianare *vt* to even; to settle; to patch up.

appiccicare *vt* to paste; * *vr* **~rsi** to stick.

appiccicoso *adj* clammy; sticky, glutinous.

applaudire *vt* to applaud; to clap.

applauso *m* applause, acclaim; clapping.

applicabile *adj* applicable.

applicare *vt* to enforce; * *vr* **~rsi** to apply.

applicato *adj* applied.

applicazione *f* application.

appoggiare *vt* to back; to lean; to support; to prop; to second; * *vr* **~rsi** to lean.

appoggio *m* backing; rest.

appollaiarsi *vr* to roost; to perch.

apporre *vt* affix, append.

apposito *adj* apposite.

apposizione *f* apposition.

apposta *adv* deliberately; on purpose.

apprendista *m/f* apprentice; trainee.

apprendistato *m* apprenticeship.

apprensione *f* apprehension; misgiving.

apprensivo *adj* apprehensive.

apprezzamento *m* appreciation.

apprezzare *vt* to appreciate.

approccio *m* approach.

approfittare *vi* to profit; **~ di** to take advantage of.

approfondire *vt* to deepen.

approfondito *adj* thorough; close.

appropriarsi *vr*; **~ di** to appropriate; **~ indebitamente** to embezzle.

appropriatamente *adv* aptly.

appropriato *adj* apt; proper; suitable.

appropriazione *f* appropriation; **~ indebita** embezzlement.

approssimativo *adj* approximate; rough.

approssimazione *f* approximation.

approvare *vt* to approve; to assent; to carry; to endorse; to subscribe; to pass.

approvazione *f* approbation, approval; endorsement.

approvvigionamento *m* procurement.

appuntamento *m* appointment; date; rendezvous.

appuntito *adj* pointed.

apribottiglie *m inv* bottle-opener.

aprile *m* April.

aprire *vt* to open; to unlock; **~ facendo leva** *vt* to prise.

apriscatole *m inv* tin-opener.

aquila *f* eagle.

aquilino *adj* aquiline; hooked (nose).

aquilone *m* kite.

aquilotto *m* eaglet.

arabesco *n* arabesque.

arabile *adj* arable.

arabo *adj*, *m* arab.

arachide *f* peanut.

aragosta *f* lobster.

araldica *f* heraldry.

araldo *m* herald.

arancia *f* orange.

aranciata *f* orangeade.

arancio *m* orange tree; *adj* orange.

arare *vi*, *vt* to plough.

aratro *m* plough.

arazzo *m* tapestry.

arbitrario *adj* arbitrary.

arbitrato *m* arbitration.

arbitro *m* arbitrator; referee; umpire; **fare da ~** to arbitrate.

arca *f* ark.

arcaico *adj* archaic.

arcangelo *m* archangel.

arcata *f* arcade.

archeologia *f* archeology.

archeologico *adj* archaeological.

archeologo *m* archaelogist.

architettare *vt* to engineer.

architetto *m* architect.

architettonico *adj* architectural.

architettura *f* architecture.

architrave *f* lintel.

archivi *mpl* records.

archiviare *vt* to file.

archivio *m* archives; file.

arciere *m* archer.

arcivescovado *m* archbishopric.

arcivescovo *m* archbishop.

arco *m* arch; bow; **tiro con l'~** archery; * *adj* **ad ~** arched.

arcobaleno *m* rainbow.

ardente *adj* ardent; aflame.

ardere *vi* to blaze; to glow.

ardesia *f* slate.

ardore *m* ardour.

arduo *adj* arduous.

area *f* area.

arena *f* arena, bullring.

arenaria *f* sandstone.

arenarsi *vr* run aground.

argano *m* winch.

argentato *adj* silvery.

argenteria *f* silver.

argentiere *m* silversmith.

argento *m* silver.

argilla *f* clay.

argine *m* embankment.

argomento *m* subject; topic.

arguto *adj* pithy; witty.

arguzia *f* wit, witticism.

aria *f* air; look; (*mus*) aria, (*auto*) choke; ~ **condizionata** *f* air-conditioning; **con ~ condizionata** *adj* air-conditioned; **senz' ~** *adj* airless.

aridità *f* dryness.

arido *adj* arid.

arieggiare *vt* air.

arieggiato *adj* airy.

ariete *m* ram; battering ram.

Ariete *m* Aries;

aringa *f* herring.

aristocratico *m* aristocrat; *adj* aristocratic.

aristocrazia *f* aristocracy.

aritmetica *f* arithmetic.

aritmetico *adj* arithmetical.

arlecchino *m* harlequin.

arma *f* weapon; ~ **da fuoco** firearm.

armadietto *m* cabinet; locker.

armadio *m* cupboard.

armaiolo *m* gunsmith.

armamentario *m* (*fig*) paraphernalia.

armamenti *mpl* armaments.

armare *vt* to arm.

armato *adj* armed; **uomo ~** gunman.

armatore *m* shipowner.

armatura *f* armour.

armeria *f* armoury.

armistizio *m* armistice.

armonia *f* concord; harmony.

armonica *f* harmonica; mouth-organ.

armonico *adj* harmonic.

armonioso *adj* harmonious.

armonizzare *vt*, *vi* to harmonize.

arnese *m* tool.

aroma *m* aroma.

aromatico *adj* aromatic.

arpa *f* harp.

arpione *m* harpoon.

arpista *f* harpist.

arrabbiare *vt* **far ~** to make someone angry; to enrage.

arrabbiatissimo *adj*: **essere ~** to fume.

arrabbiato *adj* angry.

arrampicarsi *vr* to climb, to clamber.

arrancare *vi* to plod.

arredamento *m* decor.

arredare *vt* to furnish.

arredatore *m* interior designer.

arrendersi *vr* to surrender.

arrestare *vt* to arrest; to apprehend; to stem; to stop, to stunt.

arresto *m* arrest; stop; ~ **cardiaco** *m* heart failure.

arretrati *mpl* arrears.

arretrato *adj* back; backward; **cumulo di lavoro ~** *m* backlog; **numero ~** *m* back number.

arricchimento *m* enrichment.

arricchire *vt* to enrich.

arricciare *vt* to curl.

arringa *f* harangue.

arringare *vt* to harangue.

arrivare *vi* to arrive; to go; to get; to turn up.

arrivederci *excl* goodbye.

arrivo *m* arrival; **in ~** *adj* incoming.

arrogante *adj* arrogant.

arroganza *f* arrogance.

arrossare *vt* to redden.

arrossire *vi* to blush, to flush, to redden.

arrostire *vt* to roast.

arrosto *adj inv*, *m* roast.

arrotondare *vt* to round.

arruffare *vt* to ruffle.

arruffato *adj* dishevelled.

arrugginire *vi, vt* to rust.

arruolamento *m* conscription; enlistment.

arruolare *vt* to conscript; to enlist.

arsenale *m* arsenal.

arsenico *m* arsenic.

arte *f* art; craft; **le belle arti** *fpl* the fine arts; **~ bellica** warfare.

arteria *f* artery.

arterioso *adj* (*anat*) arterial.

artico *adj* arctic.

articolare *vt* to articulate; **~ male** *vi* to slur one's speech.

articolazione *f* articulation; joint; enunciation.

articolo *m* article; item; story.

artificiale *adj* artificial; man-made.

artigianato *m* handicraft.

artigiano *m* craftsman; artisan.

artigliere *m* gunner.

artiglieria *f* artillery; ordnance.

artiglio *m* claw; talon.

artista *m/f* artist; entertainer; performer.

artistico *adj* artistic.

arto *m* limb.

artrite *f* arthritis.

arzillo *adj* spry.

ascella *f* armpit.

ascendente *m* ascendancy.

ascensione *f* ascent, ascension.

ascensore *m* lift.

ascesa *f* rise.

ascesso *m* abscess.

aspetto *m* appearance.

ascetico *adj* ascetic.

ascia *f* axe.

asciugacapelli *m inv* hair-dryer.

asciugamano *m* towel.

asciugare *vt* to dry; to blot (ink).

asciutissimo *adj* bone-dry.

asciutto *adj* dry; sere.

ascoltare *vi* to listen.

asfaltare *vt* to surface.

asfalto *m* asphalt.

asfissia *f* asphyxia.

asfissiare *vt* asphyxiate; **~ col gas** to gas.

asilo *m* asylum; **~ nido** *m* crèche; kindergarten; **~ infantile** *m* nursery school; playgroup.

asino *m* ass; donkey.

asma *f* asthma.

asmatico *adj* asthmatic.

asola *f* buttonhole.

asparago *m* asparagus.

aspettare *vt* to await; to expect; * *vi* to wait.

aspettativa *f* expectation.

aspetto *m* aspect; look; facet; **sotto certi ~** in some respects.

aspirante *adj* would-be.

aspirare *vt* to aspirate; to aspire.

aspirazione *f* aspiration; suction.

aspirina *f* aspirin.

asportabile *adj* removable.

asportare *vt* to remove.

asprezza *f* acrimony.

aspro *adj* acerbic, bitter; tart; sharp, sour; pungent; rugged; harsh; acrimonious.

assegnare *vt* allocate, allot.

assaggiare *vt* to taste; to sample.

assalire *vt* to assail.

assalitore *m* assailant.

assaltare *vt* to assault; to hold up (a bank).

assalto *m* assault; **prendere d'~** *vt* to storm.

assaporare *vt* to savour; to taste.

assassina *f* murderess.

assassinare *vt* to assassinate; to murder.

assassinio *m* assassination; murder; foul play.

assassino *m* assassin; murderer; killer.

asse *f* board; axis; **~ da stiro** ironing board; **~ di pavimento** floorboard.

assediare *vt* to besiege.

assedio *m* siege; **stato d'~** *m* martial law.

assegnare *vt* to assign; to award; to set.

assegno *m* cheque; **libretto degli assegni** *m* cheque book; **~ in bianco** *m* blank cheque.

assemblea *f* assembly.

assennato *adj* sensible.

assente *adj* absent; faraway; * *m/f* absentee.

assenteismo *m* absenteeism .

assenza *f* absence.

asserire *vt* to affirm; to allege.

assetato *adj* thirsty.

assicurare *vt* to assure; to insure; to secure.

assicuratore *m* insurer; underwriter.

assicurazione *f* assurance; insurance; undertaking.

assiduo *adj* assiduous; sedulous.

assillare *vt* to beset; to harass; to harry; to nag.

assimilare *vt* to assimilate; to absorb.

assimilazione *f* assimilation.

assioma *m* axiom.

assiomatico *adj* axiomatic.

assistente *m/f* helper; *m* auxiliary; **~ sociale** *m/f* social worker.

assistenza *f* help; aid; **~ postoperatoria** aftercare; **servizio ~ clienti** after-sales service; **~ sociale** social work.

assistenziale *adj* welfare; **stato ~** *m* welfare state.

assistere *vt* to help; to minister to.

asso *m* ace; **avere un ~ nella manica** to have an ace up one's sleeve.

associare *vt* to associate; to couple.

associazione *f* association; fellowship; partnership.

assodato *adj* cut-and-dried.

assoggettato *adj* subject.

assolato *adj* sunny.

assolo *m* solo.

assolutamente *adv* absolutely.

assoluto *adj* absolute; uncompromising; unmitigated.

assoluzione *f* acquittal; absolution.

assolvere *vt* to discharge; to absolve from; to acquit.

assomigliare *vi* to look like; to take after.

assonnato *adj* drowsy; sleepy; **con aria ~** *adv* sleepily.

assorbente *m* sanitary towel; * *adj* absorbent.

assorbimento *m* absorption; takeover.

assorbire *vt* to absorb.

assordante *adj* deafening.

assordare *vt* to deafen.

assortimento *m* assortment.

assortito *adj* assorted; mixed.

assorto *adj* intent.

assuefare *vt* to inure.

assuefazione *f* addiction.

assumere *vt* to employ, to engage; to take on; * *vr* **~rsi** to take upon oneself.

assurdità *f* absurdity.

assurdo *adj* absurd; preposterous; * *m* (an) absurdity.

asta *f* pole; shaft; **salto con l'~** pole vault; **~ dell'olio** *f* dipstick; auction.

astante *m/f* bystander.

astemio *adj* abstemious; teetotal; * *m* teetotaller.

astenersi *vr* to refrain; * *vi* to abstain.

astenzione *f* abstention.

asterisco *m* asterisk; star.

asticella *f* stick.

astinenza *f* abstinence; self-denial; **~ dall'alcool** *f* temperance.

astio *m* resentment; **guardare con ~** to glower.

astioso *adj* acrimonious.

astore *m* goshawk.

astratto *adj* abstract.

astrazione *f* abstraction.

astringente *adj, m* astringent.

astrologia *f* astrology.

astrologo *m* astrologer.

astronauta *m/f* astronaut; spaceman/woman.

astronomia *f* astronomy.

astronomico *adj* astronomical.

astronomo *m* astronomer.

astruso *adj* abstruse; recondite.

astuccio *m* case; **~ per matite** *m* pencil case.

astuto *adj* sly; wily.

astuzia *f* guile; trickery; ruse; slyness.

atavico *adj* ancestral.

ateismo *m* atheism.

ateo *m* atheist.

atipico *adj* unrepresentative.

atlante *m* atlas.

atleta *m/f* athlete.

atletico *adj* athletic.

atmosfera *f* atmosphere.

atmosferico *adj* atmospheric.

atomico *adj* atomic.

atomo *m* atom.

atout *m inv* trump.

atrio *m* lobby; concourse; vestibule.

atroce *adj* atrocious; excruciating; heinous.

atrocità *f inv* atrocity; enormity; outrage.

atrofia *f* atrophy.

attaccabrighe *m/f inv* troublemaker.

attaccamento *m* attachment.

attaccante *m* forward.

attaccare *vt* to affix; to charge (*mil*); to attach, to attack; to hitch up.

attacco *m* attack; strike; onslaught; fit; bout (illness); seizure; **~ improvviso** blitz; **~ massiccio** broadside.

attecchire *vi* to take; to root.

atteggiamento *m* attitude.

attendibile *adj* trustworthy; reputable.

attenersi *vr* to comply; to stick to.

attento *adj* careful; observant; watchful; **stare ~** to beware.

attenuante *adj* extenuating.

attenuare *vt* to attenuate; to assuage; extenuate; to tone down; * *vr* **~rsi** to moderate.

attenzione *f* attention; care; heed; caution.

atterraggio *m* landing; touchdown; **~ forzato** crash landing.

atterrare *vi* to land.

atterrire *vt* to appal.

attesa *f* wait; waiting; **lista d'~** waiting list; **sala d'~** waiting room; anticipation; expectancy, expectation; **in ~** *adj* expectant.

atteso *adj* due.

attestare *vt* to certify; to attest.

attestazione *f* certification.

attico *m* penthouse.

attiguo *adj* adjoining; **essere ~ a** to adjoin.

attinia *f* (*zool*) sea anemone.

attirare *vt* to attract; to draw;

~ con l'inganno to lure.

attivare *vt* activate.

attività *f* activity; business; pursuit.

attivo *adj* active; brisk.

attizzare *vt* to stoke.

attizzatoio *m* poker.

atto *m* act; **~ di proprietà** title deed.

attorcigliare *vt* to twist; * *vt* **~rsi** to coil; * *vr* to twist; to twine.

attorcigliato *adj* convoluted.

attore *m* actor; plaintiff.

attraente *adj* attractive; appealing; fetching; engaging.

attrattiva *f* attraction.

attraversare *vt* to cross; to span

attraverso *prep* across; through.

attrazione *f* attraction; pull.

attrezzare *vt* to equip.

attrezzatura *f* apparatus; equipment; gear; tackle; **~ da pesca** fishing tackle; (*pl*) amenities.

attrezzo *m* tool; **cassetta degli attrezzi** *f* toolbox.

attribuire *vt* attribute; ascribe; apportion; to give.

attributo *m* attribute.

attrice *f* actress.

attuabile *adj* viable

attuale *adj* current; present; prevailing; up-to-date.

attualità *f*: **problemi d'~** *mpl* current affairs.

attualmente *adv* just now; currently.

attuare *vt* to implement.

attutire *vt* to deaden; to cushion.

attutito *adj* muted.

audace *adj* audacious; daring; bold.

audacia *f* audacity; boldness; daring; temerity.

auditorio *m* auditorium.

augurare *vt* to wish.

augurio *m* wish.

augusto *adj* august.

aula *f* classroom.

aumentare *vt* to augment; to increase; to grow; to gain; to heighten; * *vi* increase; to heighten; to rise; to accrue.

aumento *m* raise; gain; increase; rise; **~ di valore** *m* appreciation.

aura *f* aura.

aureola *f* halo.

ausiliare *adj* auxiliary.

ausiliario *adj*, *m* ancillary.

auspicio *m* omen; **sotto gli auspici** under the auspices.

austerità *f* austerity.

austero *adj* austere; stark.

autenticare *vt* to witness.

autenticità *f* authenticity.

autentico *adj* authentic.

autista *m* chauffeur; *m/f* driver.

autoaffondare *vt* to scuttle.

autoarticolato *m* articulated lorry.

autobiografia *f* autobiography.

autoblinda *f* armoured car.

autobus *m* bus.

autocarro *m* lorry: **~ della nettezza urbana** *m* dustcart.

autocercante *adj* homing.

autocisterna *f* tanker.

autocommiserazione *f* self-pity.

autocontrollo *m* self-control.

autocrata *m* autocrat.

autocratico *adj* autocratic.

autodidatta *adj* self-taught.

autodifesa *f* self-defence.

autodisciplina *f* self-discipline.

autografo *m* autograph.

automatico *adj* automatic.

automazione *f* automation.

automobile *f* car; **~ sportiva** sports car.

automobilista *m/f* motorist.

autonoleggio *m* car hire.

autonomia *f* autonomy; range.

autonomo *adj* self-governing.

autopompa *f* fire engine.

autopsia *f* autopsy; post-mortem.

autore *m* author; writer.

autorespiratore *m* autolung.

autorevole *adj* authoritative.

autorimessa *f* garage.

autorità *f* authority.

autoritario *adj* authoritarian.

autoritario *adj* bossy.

autoritratto *m* self-portrait.

autorizzare *vt* to authorize.

autorizzazione *f* authorization; clearance; permit; licence; leave.

autostop *m* hitchhiking; **fare l'~** to hitch (a lift), to hitch-hike.

autostrada *f* motorway.

autosufficiente *adj* self-sufficient.

autotrasportatore *m* haulier.

autotrasporto *m* haulage.

autrice *f* authoress.

autunnale *adj* autumnal.

autunno *m* autumn.

avambraccio *m* forearm.

avamposto *m* outpost.

avances *fpl*: **fare delle ~ a** to make a pass at.

avanguardia *f* avant-garde; forefront; **d'~** *adj* avant-garde.

avanti *adv* ahead; forwards; **in ~** onwards; **in ~** *adj* forward; **più ~** further, farther.

avanzare *vi* advance; **~ a poco a poco** to edge forward.

avanzato *adj* advanced.

avanzi *mpl* leavings, leftovers, remains; dross

avanzo *m* remainder.

avarizia *f* avarice; meanness.

avaro *adj* avaricious; mean; * *m* miser.

avena *f* oats; **farina d'~** *f* oatmeal.

avere *vt* to have.

aviatore *m* flier.

aviazione *f* flying; aviation.

avidamente *adv* hungrily.

avidità *f* greed.

avido *adj* greedy, grasping; covetous.

aviofono *m* intercom.

aviorimessa *f* hangar.

avo *m* ancestor.

avocado *m* avocado.

avorio *m*, *adj* ivory.

avvalersi *vr*: **~ di** to avail oneself of.

avvallamento *m* subsidence.

avvallarsi *vr* to subside.

avvelenamento *m* poisoning; **~ del sangue** blood poisoning.

avvelenare *vt* to poison.

avvenimento *m* event; happening; incident.

avventarsi *vr* to go for.

avventato *adj* rash; unwise.

avvento *n* advent; coming.

avventura *f* adventure; affair.

avventuroso *adj* adventurous.

avverbio *m* adverb.

avversario *m* adversary; opponent; * *adj* opposing.

avversione *f* aversion; abomination, disgust.

avvertimento *m* warning.

avvertire *vt* to sense; to warn; alarm.

avviamento *m*; goodwill; **motorino d'~** *m* starter.

avviare *vt* to start.

avviato *adj*: **ben ~** going.

avvicinabile *adj* approachable.

avvicinare *vt* to approach; * *vr* **~rsi** to near.

avvilimento *m* abasement; humiliation; disheartenment.

avvilire *vt* to abase; to dishonour; to disgrace; to dishearten.

avvilito *adj* downcast; **essere ~** to mope.

avvincente *adj* absorbing; enthralling.

avvisare *vt* advise.

avviso *m* notice; advice.

avvitare *vt* to screw.

avvocato *m* advocate; lawyer; solicitor; attorney, barrister, counsel.

avvolgere *vt* to wind; to envelop; to coil; to swathe; to shroud.

avvoltoio *m* vulture.

azalea *f* azalea.

azienda *f* establishment.

azionare *vt* to drive; to power; to operate; to work.

azione *f* action; deed; share; **azioni** *fpl* holdings.

azionista *m/f* shareholder, stockholder.

azoto *m* nitrogen.

azzardo *m* gamble.

azzimato *adj* dapper; spruce.

azzuffarsi *vr* to brawl; to scuffle.

azzurro *adj* azure; blue.

B

babao *m* bogey man

babbo *m* pa(pa), dad(dy).

babbuino *m* baboon.

babordo *m* port.

bacca *f* berry.

baccano *m* hubbub; row.

baccello *m* pod.

bacchetta *f* baton; drumstick; wand; rod.

bacetto *m* peck.

baciare *vt* to kiss.

bacino *m* dock; pelvis; **~ carbonifero** coalfield; **~ idrico** reservoir.

bacio *m* kiss.

backgammon *m* backgammon.

baco *m* maggot.

badare *vt* to heed; to mind; **non ~ a** to discount.

badessa *f* abbess.

badia *f* abbey.

badminton *m* badminton

baffo *m*: **baffi** *mpl* moustache; whiskers.

bagaglio *m* baggage; **bagagli** *mpl* luggage.

bagliore *m* glare.

bagnante *m/f* bather.

bagnare *vt* to wet.

bagnato *adj* wet, soggy.

bagnino *m* lifeguard.

bagno *m* bath; **fare il ~** *vt* to bath; **fare il ~** *vt* to bathe; **stanza da ~** bathroom.

baia *f* bay; cove.

baionetta *f* bayonet.

baita *f* hut.

balaustrata *f* balustrade.

balbettare *vt, vi* to stutter, to stammer.

balbuzie *f* stammer, stutter.

balcone *m* balcony.

baldacchino *m* canopy; **letto a ~** four-poster (bed).

baldoria *f* spree; revelry; *vi* **far ~** to carouse; to revel.

balena *f* whale.

balestruccio *m* martin.

balia *f* wet nurse.

balistico *adj* ballistic.

balla *f* bale.

ballare *vt, vi* to dance.

ballata *f* ballad.

ballerina *f* ballerina.

ballerino *m* dancer.

ballo *m* dance; ball; **sala da ~** dance hall.

balsamico *adj* balmy.

balsamo *m* (hair) conditioner; balm.

baluardo *m* bulwark.

baluginare *vi* to glimmer.

balzare *vi* to pounce; to bound; to leap.

balzo *m* pounce; leap; bound.

bambinaia *f* nanny; baby-minder.

bambino *m* infant; baby; child (*pl* children); **~ che fa i primi passi** *m* toddler.

bambola *f* doll.

bambù *m* bamboo.

banale *adj* banal; mundane; commonplace; corny; run-of-the-mill.

banalità *f* platitude; *fpl* trivia.

banana *f* banana.

banano *m* banana tree.

banca *f* bank; **servirsi di una ~** *vi* to bank.

bancarella *f* stall.

bancarellista *m/f* stallholder.

bancaria *adj*; **attività ~** banking.

bancarotta *f* bankruptcy.

banchettare *vi* to feast.

banchetto *m* banquet; feast; spread.

banchiere *m* banker.

banchina *f* wharf.

banco *m* counter; pew; form; shoal; school (of fish); **~ degli imputati** *m* dock.

banconota *f* banknote.

banda *f* gang; band; bevy.

bandiera *f* flag; colours.

bandire *vt* to banish; to outlaw.

bandito *m* bandit.

banditore *m* auctioneer; town crier.

banjo *m inv* banjo.

bar *m* bar; café.

bara *f* coffin.

baracca *f* hut; shanty, shack.

baraonda *f* bedlam.

baratro *m* abyss.

barattare *vi, vt* to barter; to trade.

barattolo *m* jar; canister; **~ del tè** tea caddy.

barba *f* beard; **senza ~** *adj* clean-shaven; **~ corta** *f* stubble.

barbabietola *f* beet; beetroot; **~ da zucchero** *f* sugar beet.

barbaro *m* barbarian; * *adj* barbaric.

barbecue *m* barbecue.

barbiere *m* barber.

barbiturico *m* barbiturate.

barboncino *m* poodle.

barbuto *adj* bearded.

barca *f* boat.

barchino *m* punt.

barcollare *vi* to stagger; to reel.

bardare *vt* to harness.

bardatura *f* harness; trappings.

bardo *m* bard.

barella *f* stretcher.

barile *m* keg; barrel; cask.

barista *m/f* barman, barmaid, bartender.

baritono *m* baritone.

barlume *m* glimmer.

barmy *adj* suonato.

barocco *adj* baroque.

barometro *m* barometer.

barone *m* baron.

baronessa *f* baroness.

barra *f* tiller; **~ di comando** *f* joystick.

barricare *vt* to barricade.

barricata *f* barricade.

barriera *f* barrier.

baruffa *f* tussle; scrap.

basare *vt* to base.

base *f* base; basis; staple; grass roots; **buone basi** *fpl* good grounding.

baseball *m* baseball.

basilico *m* basil.

basilisco *m* basilisk.

bassifondi *mpl* slum area.

basso *adj* low; short; bass; * *m* (*mus*) bass.

bassopiano *m* lowland.

bassotto *m* dachshund.

bastardaggine *f* bastardy.

bastardo *m* bastard; (*sl*) sod; mongrel.

bastare *vi* to be enough; to suffice; **far ~** *vt* to eke out, to stretch.

bastione *m* rampart; **bastioni** *mpl* battlements.

bastoncino *m* stick; chopstick.

bastone *m* rod; club; cane; crook; staff; stick; **~ da passeggio** walking stick; **~ della tenda** *f* curtain rod.

battaglia *f* battle; **campo** *m* **di ~** battlefield.

battaglione *m* battalion.

battello *m* boat; **~ a ruote** *m* paddle steamer.

battente *m* knocker.

battere *vt* to hit; to beat; to flutter; **~ a macchina** to type; * *vi* to beat.

batteri *mpl* bacteria.

batteria *f* battery; drums; set.

batterista *m/f* drummer.

battesimo *m* baptism; christening.

battezzare *vt* to christen; to baptise.

battibecco *m* tiff; squabble.

battimano *m* clap.

battiscopa *m inv* skirting board.

battistero *m* baptistry.

battistrada *m inv* tread.

battito *m* beat; flutter; throb; **~ di ciglia** *m* blink.

battuta *f* quip; joke; sally.

batuffolo *m* wad.

baule *m* chest, trunk.

bauxite *f* bauxite.

bava *f* dribble; slime.

bavaglino *m* bib.

bavaglio *m* gag.

bazar *m* bazaar.

beatificare *vt* to beatify.

beatitudine *f* beatitude.

beccaccino *m* snipe.

beccare *vt* to peck.

beccata *f* peck.

becchino *m* gravedigger.

becco *m* bill, beak; spout.

becher *m* beaker.

befana *f* hag.

beffa *f* practical joke.

beffardo *adj* mocking; derisive; wry.

beffarsi *vr* to mock.

begonia *f* begonia.

beige *m inv* beige.

belare *vi* to baa, to bleat.

belato *m* bleat.

belladonna *f* deadly nightshade.

belletto *m* rouge.

bellezza *f* beauty.

bellicoso *adj* bellicose; truculent.

belligerante *adj* belligerent.

bello *adj* beautiful; handsome; good; good-looking, nice; nice-looking; lovely.

bemolle *adj* (*mus*) flat.

benché *conj* notwithstanding; though; although.

benda *f* blindfold.

bendare *vt* to blindfold.

bendato *adj* blindfold.

bendisposto *adj* well-disposed.

bene *m* good; welfare; * *excl* fine; * *adv* right; all right; well; * *adj* well; **voler ~ a** *vt* to love.

benedetto *adj* blessed.

benedicite *m* grace; **dire il ~** *vt* to say grace.

benedire *vt* to bless.

benedizione *f* benediction; blessing.

beneducato *adj* wellbred.

benefattore *m* benefactor.

beneficiario *m* beneficiary; payee.

beneficienza *f* charity.

benefico *adj* beneficient.

benessere *m* welfare, wellbeing.

benestante *adj* well-off.

benestare *m* assent; consent; **dare il ~ a qn** *vt* to give someone the go-ahead.

benevolenza *f* benevolence.

benevolo *adj* benevolent, benign.

beni *mpl* assets.

beniamino *m* pet, favourite.

benigno *adj* benign.

benino *adj*: **per ~** prim.

benvenuto *adj, m* welcome.

benvoluto *adj* popular.

benzina *f* petrol.

bere *m* drinking; * *vt* to drink; to imbibe; * *vi* to drink.

bernoccolo *m* bump.

berretto *m* cap; beret.

bersagliere *m* rifleman.

bersaglio *m* target; **~ per freccette** *m* dartboard.

bestemmia *f* curse; blasphemy.

bestemmiare *vi* o swear; to curse; to blaspheme.

bestemmiatore *m* blasphemer.

bestia *f* beast; **~ da soma** beast of burden.

bestiale *adj* bestial.

bestiame *m* livestock, cattle, stock.

bestiolina *f* creepy-crawly.

bestione *m* hulk.

betoniera *f* cement mixer.

bettola *f* dive.

betulla *f* birch.

bevanda *f* drink; **~ gasata** *f* pop.

bevitore *m* drinker.

biancastro *adj* whitish.

biancheria *f* laundry; **~ intima**

f lingerie, underwear.

bianco *adj* blank; white; * *m* white.

biancospino *m* hawthorn.

bibbia *f* bible.

bibita *f* drink.

biblico *adj* biblical.

bibliografia *f* bibliography.

biblioteca *f* library.

bibliotecario *m* librarian.

bicarbonato *m*: **~ di sodio** bicarbonate of soda.

bicchiere *m* glass; beaker; tumbler.

bicchierino *m* dram, nip.

bici *f inv* bike.

bicicletta *f* bicycle, cycle; **andare in ~** *vi* to cycle.

bicipite *m* biceps.

bidè *m inv* bidet.

bidello *m* janitor.

bidonata *f* raw deal.

bidone *m* drum; bin, dustbin.

bidonville *f inv* shanty town.

biennale *adj* biennial.

bifocali *adj* bifocal; **occhiali ~** *npl* bifocals.

biforcarsi *vr* to fork.

biforcazione *f* fork; bifurcation.

biforcuto *adj* forked.

bigamia *f* bigamy.

bigamo *m* bigamist.

bighellonare *vi* to loiter; to dawdle.

bighellone *m* loafer.

biglia *f* marble.

bigliardo *m* snooker.

bigliettaio *m* ticket collector.

biglietteria *f* ticket office.

biglietto *m* card; note; ticket.

bignè *m inv* éclair.

bigodino *m* curler, roller.

bikini *m inv* bikini.

bilancia *f* scales.

Bilancia *f* Libra.

bilanciare *vt* to offset.

bilancio *m* balance; budget; **~**

di esercizio balance sheet.

bilaterale *adj* bilateral.

bile *f* gall; bile.

biliardo *m* billiards; pool.

biliare *adj* bilious.

bilico *m*: **tenere in ~** to balance.

bilingue *adj* bilingual.

bilione *m* billion.

bimbo *m* baby.

binario *m* platform; track.

binocolo *m* binoculars.

biochimica *f* biochemistry.

biografia *f* biography.

biografico *adj* biographical.

biografo *m* biographer.

biologia *f* biology.

biologico *adj* biological.

biondo *m*, *adj* blond.

biossido *m* dioxide.

bipede *m* biped.

biposto *adj* two-seater.

birichinata *f* mischief.

birichino *adj* mischievous.

birillo *m* skittle.

birra *f* beer; ale; **~ bionda** *f* lager.

bis *excl*, *m inv* encore.

bisbetica *f* shrew.

bisbigliare *vt*, *vi* to whisper.

bisbiglio *m* whisper, whispering.

biscia *f* grass snake.

biscotto *m* biscuit.

bisecare *vt* to bisect.

bisestile *adj*: **anno ~** *m* leap year.

bisogno *m* need; want: **aver ~ di** *vt* to need.

bisognoso *adj* needy; deprived; impecunious.

bisonte *m* bison.

bistecca *f* steak; **~ di manzo** *f* steak; **~ di maiale** *f* porkchop.

bisticciare *vi* bicker; to spar; * *vt* **~rsi** to squabble.

bistrattare *vt* to mishandle.

bisturi *m inv* lancet; scalpel.

bitume *m* bitumen.

bivacco *m* bivouac.

bizzarria *f* quirk; oddity.

bizzarro *adj* droll; kinky; bizarre; weird.

blandire *vt* to wheedle.

blando *adj* bland.

blasé *adj* blasé.

blasfemo *adj* blasphemous.

blaterare *vi* to rattle on; * *vt* to prattle.

blatta *f* cockroach.

blazer *m* blazer.

bleso *adj*: **essere ~** *vi* to lisp; **pronuncia blesa** *f* lisp.

bloc-notes *m inv* notepad.

bloccare *vt* to block (up); to jam; to stop; * *vr* **~rsi** to stick; to stall.

bloccato *adj*: **~ dal ghiaccio** icebound.

blocchetto *m* pad.

blocco *m* bloc; block; blockade; freeze; **posto di ~** *m* checkpoint.

bluffare *vi* to bluff.

blusa *f* smock.

boa *f* buoy; boa.

bob *m inv* bobsleigh.

bobina *f* coil; spool; reel.

bocca *m* mouth; **guardare a ~ aperta** *vt* to gape.

boccaccia *f* trap.

boccale *m* mug.

boccaporto *m* hatch.

boccata *f* gulp.

bocchetta *f* nozzle.

bocchino *m* cigarette holder; mouthpiece.

boccia *f*: **le bocce** bowls; **campo da bocce** bowling green.

bocciare *vt* to fail.

bocciolo *m* bud.

boccolo *m* ringlet.

boccone *m* morsel; mouthful.

body *m inv* leotard.

boia *m* hangman, executioner.

boicottaggio *m* boycott.

boicottare *vt* to boycott, to black.

bolla *f* bubble.

bollettino *m* comuniqué; newsletter; bulletin.

bollire *vi* to boil; to seethe.

bollitore *m* kettle.

boma *m* boom.

bomba *f* bomb, bombshell; **~ incendiaria** *f* incendiary (bomb); **~ a orologieria** *f* time bomb.

bombardamento *m* bombardment.

bombardare *vt* to bomb; to bombard; to shell.

bombo *m* bumblebee.

bombola *f* gas cylinder.

bonificare *vt* to reclaim.

bontà *f* goodness.

boomerang *m inv* boomerang.

borbottare *vt, vi* to mutter; to mumble; to gabble.

borbottio *m* mutter.

bordare *vt* to edge.

bordeaux *adj* maroon.

bordeggiare *vi* to tack.

bordello *m* brothel.

bordo *m* edge, edging; surround; verge; (*mar*) tack; **fuori ~** *adj* overboard.

borghese *m* (*mil*) civilian; * *adj* bourgeois; **in ~** in plain clothes.

borghesia *f* bourgeosie; **dell'alta ~** *adj* upper-class.

borioso *m* prig.

borsa *f* handbag; pouch; bag; **~ di studio** bursary, grant, scholarship; **Borsa valori** *f* Stock Exchange.

borsaiolo *m* pickpocket.

borsellino *m* purse.

borsone *m* grip.

boscaglia *f* scrub; thicket.

boschetto *m* grove; coppice.

bosco *m* wood.

boscoso *adj* wooded; **zona boscosa** *f* woodland.

botanica *f* botany.

botanico *m* botanist; * *adj* botanic(al).

botola *f* trapdoor.

botta *f* bump; bash; **botte** *fpl* beating; hiding; butt.

botteghino *m* box office.

bottiglia *f* bottle.

bottino *m* loot; plunder; booty; spoil.

bottone *m* button; **~ automatico** *m* popper.

bouquet *m inv* bouquet.

boutique *f inv* boutique.

bovindo *m* bay window.

bovino *adj* bovine.

bowling *m* bowling; bowling alley.

box *m inv* playpen.

bozza *f* proof.

bozzolo *m* cocoon.

braccialetto *m* bracelet, bangle.

bracciante *m/f* farmhand.

bracciata *f* armful.

braccio *m* arm; jib; fathom.

bracciolo *m* armrest.

bracconaggio *m* poaching.

bracconiere *m* poacher.

brace *f* embers.

braciere *m* brazier.

bramare *vi* to yearn.

bramoso *adj* yearning.

branchia *f* gill.

branco *m* drove; gaggle (of geese); pride; pack.

brancolare *vi* to fumble.

brandello *m* shred.

brandire *vt* to flourish; to brandish; to swing.

brandy *m inv* brandy.

bravo *adj* good.

breccia *f* opening; breach.

breve *adj* brief; short.

brevettare *vt* to patent.

brevettato *adj* patented.

brevetto *m* patent.

brevità *f* brevity.

brezza *f* breeze; **~ marina** *f* sea breeze.

bric-a-brac *m* bric-a-brac.

briciola *f* breadcrumb; crumb.

briciolo *m* shred; scrap.

bricolage *m* do-it-yourself.

bridge *m* bridge.

brigata *f* brigade.

briglia *f* briglie; bridle; *fpl* harness.

brillante *adj* brilliant.

brillare *vi* to shine.

brillo *adj* merry; tipsy; tiddly.

brina *f* ftost; hoarfrost.

brindare *vt* to toast.

brindisi *m inv* toast; **qui ci vuole un ~!** this calls for a drink!

brio *m* liveliness.

brioso *adj* breezy.

brivido *m* shiver; thrill; shudder.

brocca *f* jug; pitcher.

broccato *m* brocade.

broccoli *mpl* broccoli.

brochure *f* brochure.

brodaglia *f* swill.

brodo *m* broth; stock; **~ ristretto** *m* consommé.

brodoso *adj* sloppy.

bronchiale *adj* bronchial.

bronchite *f* bronchitis.

broncio *m* pout; **tenere il ~** *vi* to sulk; **fare il ~** *vi* to pout.

brontolare *vi* to grumble; to grouse; to rumble.

brontolii *mpl* nagging.

brontolio *m* grumble.

brontolone *adj* nagging; * *m* nag.

bronzo *m* bronze.

brucare *vt* to crop.

bruciacchiare *vt* to singe; to scorch.

bruciacchiatura *f* scorch.

bruciapelo *adj*: **a ~** point-blank.

bruciare *vt* to burn; * *vi* to smart; to sting; to rankle.

bruciato *m* burning.

bruciatore *m* burner.

bruciatura *f* burn.

bruco *m* caterpillar.

brughiera *f* moor, heath.

brulicare *vi* to teem.

brumoso *adj* misty.

bruna *f* brunette.

bruscamente *adv* sharply; abruptly.

brusco *adj* abrupt, brusque, bluff, blunt, off-hand, curt; sharp; unceremonious; rude.

brutale *adj* brutal.

brutalità *f* brutality.

brutalmente *adv* roughly.

bruto *m*, brute; * *adj* brute; bad; ugly.

bruttezza *f* ugliness.

brutto *adj* bad; ugly.

bubble-gum *m inv* bubble gum.

buca *f* hole; pothole; pit; **~ di sabbia** *f* sandpit.

bucaneve *m inv* snowdrop.

bucare *vt* to hole; to prick.

bucato *m* washing.

buccia *f* peel; skin; rind; zest.

buco *m* hole.

bucolico *adj* bucolic.

buddismo *m* Buddhism.

budello *m* gut; **budella** *fpl* guts.

budino *m* pudding.

bue *m* ox.

bufalo *m* buffalo.

bufera *f* gale; **~ di neve** blizzard.

buffet *m inv* buffet.

buffo *adj* funny, comic.

buffone *m* buffoon; fool; jester.

buffoneria *f* antics.

bugia *f* lie; **~ pietosa** *f* white lie.

bugiardo *adj* lying; * *m m* liar, fibber.

buio *adj* dark; gloom; *m* dark, darkness; **~ pesto** pitch black.

bulbo *m* bulb; **~ oculare** *m* eyeball; **a forma di ~** *adj* bulbous.

bulldog *m inv* bulldog.

bulldozer *m inv* bulldozer.

bulletta *f* tack.

bullo *m* bully.

bullone *m* bolt.

bungalow *m inv* bungalow.

bunker *m inv* bunker.

buoi *mpl* oxen.

buongustaio *m* epicure; gourmet.

buono *m* coupon; token; **~ premio** *m* gift voucher; *adj* kind-hearted; good.

burattino *m* puppet.

burbero *adj* gruff; surly.

burla *f* prank.

burlone *m* joker; tease.

burocrate *m/f* bureaucrat.

burocrazia *f* bureaucracy; (*fig*) red tape.

burrasca *f* squall.

burrascoso *adj* rough; stormy; tempestuous.

burro *m* butter.

burrone *m* gully; ravine.

bussare *vi* to knock; to tap; * *vt* to rap.

bussata *f* rap.

bussola *f* compass.

busta *f* envelope.

bustarella *f* backhander; bribe.

bustina *f* sachet.

busto *m* bust; girdle, corset.

buttafuori *m inv* bouncer;

buttar *vt*: **~ fuori** to turf out; **~ via** to throw away.

byte *m* byte.

C

cabina *f* booth; (lorry) cab; (plane) cabin; cubicle; **~ di pilotaggio** cockpit, flight deck; **~ telefonica** *f* (tele)phone booth, callbox.

cacao *m* cocoa; **burro di ~** *m* lipsalve.

cacatoa *m inv* cockatoo.

caccia *f* hunt, hunting; chase; **una partita di ~** *f* shoot.

cacciare *vi* to hunt.

cacciatore *m* hunter, huntsman.

cacciatorpediniere *m* destroyer.

cacciavite *m inv* screwdriver.

cachemire *m inv* cashmere.

cachi *m* khaki, persimmon.

cactus *m inv* cactus.

cadavere *m* (dead) body, cadaver, corpse.

cadaverico *adj* cadaverous; deathly.

cadente *adj* tumble-down.

cadenza *f* cadence; **~ strascicata** *f* drawl.

cadere *vi* to fall; to topple over; to slump; * *vt* **lasciar ~** to drop.

cadetto *m* cadet.

caduta *f* fall; slump.

caffè *m* café; coffee; **pausa per il ~** *f* coffee break.

caffeina *f* caffeine.

caffettiera *f* coffee pot; **~ a filtro** *f* percolator.

cagionevole *adj* unsound.

cagliare *vi* to curdle.

caglio *m* rennet.

cagna *f* bitch.

cagnolino *m* puppy; **~ di lusso** *m* lapdog.

calabrone *m* hornet.

calamaro *m* squid.

calamità *f* calamity.

calamita *f* magnet.

calamitoso *adj* calamitous.

calare *vi* to drop; to wane; * *vt* to lower; to drop.

calca *f* squash.

calcagno *m* heel.

calcare *m* limestone.

calcatoio *m* ramrod.

calce *f* lime; **bianco di ~** *m* whitewash.

calcestruzzo *m* concrete; **rivestire di ~** *vt* to concrete.

calciatore *m* footballer.

calcificare *vt* to calcify.

calcio *m* kick; calcium; football; soccer; **dare un ~** *vt* to boot; to kick.

calcolabile *adj* calculable; computable.

calcolare *vt* to calculate; to compute; to reckon; **~ male** to misjudge; to miscalculate.

calcolatore *m* calculator.

calcoli *mpl* reckoning.

calcolo *m* calculation; computation; **~ biliare** *m* gallstone.

caldaia *f* boiler.

calderone *m* cauldron.

caldo *adj* hot, warm.

caleidoscopio *m* kaleidoscope.

calendario *m* calendar.

calendola *f* marigold.

calesse *m* trap.

calibrare *vt* to calibrate.

calibratura *f* calibration.

calibro *m* bore; calibre; gauge.

calice *m* chalice; goblet; glass.

calligra fia *f* calligraphy.

callista *m/f* chiropodist.

callo *m* corn.

calma *f* calm; cool; composure.

calmante *adj* soothing; sedative; * *m* sedative.

calmare *vt* to calm; to lull; to pacify; to steady; to soothe;

* *vr* **~rsi** *vr* to abate (storm); to simmer down, to calm down (person).

caloroso *adj* appreciative.

calmo *adj* calm; cool; untroubled.

calo *m* fall; drop.

calore *m* heat; warmth.

caloria *f* calorie.

calpestare *vt* to tread; to trample.

calunnia *f* aspersion; calumny; slander.

calunniare *vt* to slander; to malign.

calunnioso *adj* slanderous.

calvario *m* Calvary.

calvinista *m/f* calvinist.

calvizie *f* baldness.

calvo *adj* bald.

calza *f* stocking; **calze;** *fpl* hosiery.

calzante *m* shoehorn.

calzatura *f* footwear.

calzettone *m* sock.

calzino *m* sock, ankle sock.

calzolaio *m* cobbler; shoemaker.

calzoleria *f* shoeshop.

calzoncini *mpl* shorts.

camaleonte *m* chamaleon.

cambiamento *m* change; shift; **~ continuo** *m* flux.

cambiare *vt* to change; to switch; * *vi* to change.

cambio *m* change; exchange; **tasso di ~** *m* rate of exchange; **agente di ~** stockbroker; gear; **scatola del ~** *f* gearbox; **leva del ~** *f* gear lever.

camelia *f* camellia.

camera *f* room; chamber; (*pol*) house; **~ da letto** *f* bedroom; **~ degli ospiti** *f* guestroom; **~ dei bambini** *f* nursery; **~ oscura** *f* darkroom; **~ d'aria** *f* inner tube.

cameraman *m inv* cameraman.

cameratismo *m* companionship.

cameriera *f* waitress; maid, chambermaid.

cameriere *m* waiter; **~ personale** *m* valet.

camerino *m* dressing room.

camicetta *f* blouse.

camicia *f* shirt; **~ di forza** *f* straitjacket.

caminetto *m* fireplace.

camino *m* chimney.

camion *m inv* lorry, truck.

camioncino *m* pick-up truck.

camionista *m* truckdriver.

cammello *m* camel.

cammeo *m* cameo.

camminare *vi* walk; **~ senza fretta** amble; **~ su e giù** to pace; **~ in punta dei piedi** to tiptoe; **~ pesantemente** to tramp; **~ come una papera** to waddle; **~ a fatica** to wade; * *m* walking.

camminatore *m* walker.

camomilla *f* camomile.

camoscio *m* chamois; **pelle di ~** *f* chamois leather.

campagna *f* country, countryside; campaign; **~ di vendita** *f* sales drive; **fare una ~** *vi* to campaign.

campagnolo *m* countryman.

campana *f* bell; **sordo come una ~** *adj* stone-deaf.

campanello *m* bell; doorbell.

campanile *m* belfry; steeple.

campeggiare *vi* to camp.

campeggiatore *m* camper.

campeggio *m* camping; campsite.

campestre *adj* cross-country.

campionato *m* championship; league.

campione *m* champion; sample; specimen.

campo *m* ground, field; pitch; **lavoro sul ~** *m* fieldwork; **~**

da tennis tennis court.

campus *m inv* campus.

camuso *adj* snub-nosed.

canaglia *f* rabble.

canale *m* canal; channel.

canapa *f* hemp; **~ indiana** cannabis.

canarino *m* canary.

cancellare *vt* to cancel, to annul; to delete; to efface; to erase; to scratch; to obliterate; to scrub.

cancellata *f* railings.

cancellazione *f* cancellation.

cancelleria *f* stationery.

cancelletto girevole *m* turnstile.

cancelliere *m* chancellor.

cancello *m* gate.

Cancer *m* Cancer.

cancerogeno *adj* carcinogenic.

canceroso *adj* cancerous.

cancrena *f* gangrene.

cancro *m* cancer.

candeggiare *vt* to bleach.

candeggina *f* bleach.

candela *f* candle; sparking plug.

candelabro *m* candelabra.

candeliere *m* candlestick.

candida *f* thrush.

candidato *m* candidate; applicant; entrant; nominee.

candidatura *f* candidacy.

candito *adj* candied.

candore *m* candour; whiteness.

cane *m* dog; **~ per ciechi** *m* guide dog; **~ pastore** *m* sheepdog.

canfora *f* camphor.

canguro *m* kangaroo.

canile *m* kennel; **~ municipale** *m* dog pound.

canino *adj* canine; **~ superiore** *m* eyetooth.

canna *f* cane; crossbar; barrel (of gun); reed; **~ d'India** *f* rattan; **~ da pesca** *f* fishing rod;

~ **fumaria** f flue; ~ **da zuc-chero** f sugar cane.
cannella f cinnamon.
cannibale m/f cannibal.
cannibalismo m cannibalism.
cannone m canon.
cannoniera f gunboat.
cannuccia f straw.
canoa f canoe.
canone m canon; fee.
canonica f vicarage.
canonizzare vt to canonize.
canottiera f vest.
cantante m/f singer.
cantare vi to sing; to crow; * vt to sing; to chant.
canticchiare vt to hum.
cantiere m yard; ~ **navale** m dockyard, shipyard.
cantina f cellar; wine cellar.
canto m song; singing; crow; chant; ~ **funebre** m dirge.
cantone m canton.
canyon m inv canyon.
canzonatorio adj quizzical.
canzoncina f ditty.
canzone f song; ~ **folk** f folk-song.
caos m chaos.
caotico adj chaotic.
capace adj capable.
capacità f ability .
capo m head; **da ~ a** fresh.
capacità f capability; capacity; skill; fpl scope; power.
capanna f hut.
capanno m shed.
caparra f surety.
capelli mpl hair.
capezzale m bolster.
capezzolo m nipple.
capillare m capillary.
capire vt to understand; to com-prehend; to take in; to figure out, to fathom; **far ~** to inti-mate; * vi to understand.
capital f capital (city).
capitale m (fin) capital.

capitalismo m capitalism.
capitalista m/f capitalist.
capitalizzare vt to capitalize.
capitano m captain, skipper.
capitare vi to happen.
capite m: **pro ~ per** capita.
capitolare vi to capitulate.
capitolazione f sellout.
capitolo m chapter.
capitombolo m tumble.
capo m boss, chie f; command-er; leader; cape; head; head-land; **a ~ scoperto** adj bare-headed; **da ~** adv over again; **a tre capi** adj three-ply.
capobanda m ringleader.
capocameriere m head waiter.
Capodanno m New Year's Day.
capodoglio m sperm whale.
capofamiglia m/f householder.
capofitto: a ~ adv headlong.
capogiro m dizziness.
capolavoro m masterpiece.
capolinea m terminal, termi-nus.
caporale m corporal.
caposquadra m foreman.
capovolgere vt to invert; to overturn; * vr ~**rsi** to turn over.
capovolto adj, adv upside down.
cappa f cape; cloak.
cappella f chapel.
cappellaio m hatter.
cappellano m chaplain.
cappello m hat.
cappero m caper.
cappio m loop; noose.
cappotto m coat.
cappuccio m cowl; hood.
capra f goat.
capraio m goatherd.
capretto m kid.
capriccio m caprice; capriccio fancy; whim.
capriccioso adj capricious; temperamental.

Capricorno *m* Capricorn.
capri foglio *m* honeysuckle.
capriola *f* somersault.
capriolo *m* roebuck.
capro *m*: **~ espiatorio** *m* scapegoat.
caprone *m* billy goat.
capsula *f* capsule.
carabina *f* rifle.
caracollare *vi* to prance.
caraffa *f* carafe, decanter.
caramella *f* sweet; candy; **~ fondente** *f* fudge; **~ mou** *f inv* toffee.
caramello *m* caramel.
carato *m* carat.
carattere *m* character; type; **~ tipografico** *m* typeface.
caratteristica *f* feature; trait; * *adj* characteristic.
caratterizzare *vt* to characterize.
caratterizzazione *f* characterization.
carboidrato *m* carbohydrate.
carbonaio *m* coalman.
carboncino *m* charcoal.
carbone *m* coal; charcoal; **~ coke** *m* coke.
carbonio *m* carbon.
carbonizzare *vt* carbonize; to char.
carburante *m* fuel; **rifornirsi di ~** *vr* to refuel.
carburatore *m* carburettor.
carcassa *f* carcass.
carcerato *m* convict, jailbird.
carcere *m* jail, prison; **rimandere in ~** *vt* to remand.
carceriere *m* jailer.
carcio fo *m* artichoke.
cardiaco *adj* cardiac.
cardinale *adj*, *m* cardinal.
cardine *m* hinge.
cardio *m* cockle.
cardo *m* thistle.
carenza *f* shortage.
carestia *f* famine.

carezza *f* caress; stroke.
carezzare *vt* to caress.
carica *f* (*mil*) charge; **affrancatura a ~ del destinatario** *f* freepost.
caricabatterie *m inv* charger.
caricare *vt* to load; to wind.
caricatore *m* magazine.
caricatura *f* caricature; **fare una ~ di** *vt* to caricature.
carico *m* load; cargo; shipment; burden; **persona a ~** *f* dependant; * *adj* loaded.
carie *f* caries.
carino *adj* sweet, bonny, cute.
carisma *m* charisma.
carità *f* charity.
caritatevole *adj* beneficent; charitable.
carlino *m* pug.
carnagione *f* complexion.
carnale *adj* carnal.
carne *f* meat; flesh; **ben in ~** buxom; **pezzo di ~** *m* joint; **~ macinata** *f* mince; **di ~** *adj* meaty.
carne ficina *f* carnage.
carnevale *m* carnival.
carnivoro *adj* carnivorous.
carnoso *adj* fleshy.
caro *adj* dear; darling; expensive; **avere ~** *vt* to cherish; **rendere ~** *vt* to endear.
carogna *f* carrion.
carota *f* carrot.
carpa *f* carp.
carreggiata *f* carriageway.
carrello *m* trolley; **~ elevatore** *m* fork-lift truck; **~ d'atterraggio** *m* undercarriage.
carretto *m* cart.
carriera *f* career.
carriola *f* barrow, wheelbarrow.
carro *m* wagon; **~ armato** *m* tank.
carrozza *f* coach; carriage.
carrozzeria *f* bodywork.

carta *f* paper; charter; map; ~ **bianca** *f* carte blanche; ~ **carbone** *f* carbon paper; ~ **di credito** *f* credit card; ~ **d'imbarco** *f* boarding card; ~ **da gioco** *f* playing card; ~ **assorbente** *f* blotting paper; ~ **stagnola** *f* foil; ~ **protocollo** *f* foolscap; ~ **oleata** *f* greaseproof paper, wax paper; ~ **igienica** *f* toilet paper; ~ **da lettere** *f* notepaper, writing paper; ~ **da pareti** *f* wallpaper; ~ **straccia** *f* waste paper; ~ **vetrata** *f* sandpaper; **carte** *fpl* cards; *vt* **dare le carte** to deal.

cartella *f* briefcase; folder; file; satchel; portfolio.

cartellino *m* docket.

cartello *m* placard; cartel; ~ **stradale** *m* roadsign.

cartilagine *f* cartilage; gristle.

cartilaginoso *adj* gristly.

cartogra fia *f* cartography.

cartolaio *m* stationer.

cartolina *f* postcard; ~ **d'auguri** *f* greetings card.

cartone *m* cardboard; carton; ~ **animato** *m* cartoon.

cartuccia *f* cartridge.

casa *f* house; home; household; (*sl*) pad; **amore per la ~** *m* domesticity; ~ **colonica** *f* farmhouse; ~ **viaggiante** *f* mobile home; **fatto in ~** *adj* homemade; **verso ~** *adv* homeward(s).

casaccio *adj*: **a ~** at random.

casalinga *f* housewife.

casamento *m* tenement.

cascarci *vi* to fall for (a trick, etc).

cascata *f* cascade; water fall; **cascate** *fpl* (water)falls.

casco *m* helmet, crash helmet.

casella *f* pigeonhole.

casellario *m* filing cabinet.

caserma *f* barracks; ~ **dei pompieri** *f* fire station.

casinò *m inv* casino.

casino *m* carry-on.

caso *m* (*med*, *gr*) case; chance; **per caso** *adv* by accident, by chance; **a ~** *adj* at random.

caso mai *conj* in case.

cassa *f* case, crate; checkout; till; ~ **comune** *f* pool.

cassa forte *f* safe; strongbox.

casseruola *f* casserole.

cassetta *f* cassette; ~ **delle lettere** *f* postbox; ~ **per i fiori** *f* window box.

cassetto *m* drawer.

cassettone *m* chest of drawers.

cassiere *m* cashier; teller.

cast *m inv* cast.

casta *f* caste.

castagna *f* chestnut; ~ **d'ippocastano** *f* conker.

castagno *m* chestnut tree.

castano *adj* chestnut.

castello *m* castle.

castigare *vt* to castigate; to chasten; to discipline.

castità *f* chastity.

casto *adj* chaste.

castoro *m* beaver.

castrare *vt* to castrate; to neuter.

castrazione *f* castration.

casuale *adj* casual; haphazard.

cataclisma *m* cataclysm.

catacombe *fpl* catacombs.

catalizzatore *m* catalyst.

catalogo *m* catalogue.

catamarano *m* catamaran.

catapecchia *f* slum.

catarifrangente *m* cat's eye; reflector.

catarro *m* catarrh.

catastro fe *f* catastrophe.

catechismo *m* catechism.

categoria *f* category; class; grade.

categorico *adj* categoric(al);

absolute; downright;.

catena *f* chain; range; ~ **di montaggio** *f* production line.

cateratta *f* cataract.

catodo *m* cathode.

catrame *m* tar.

cattedrale *f* cathedral.

cattiveria *f* mischie *f*; wickedness.

cattività *f* captivity.

cattivo *adj* bad; ill; evil; nasty; malicious; wicked.

cattolicesimo *m* Catholicism.

cattolico *adj, m* Catholic, Roman Catholic.

cattura *f* capture.

caucciù *m* rubber.

causa *f* cause; law suit; ~ **giudiziaria** *f* litigation; **essere ~ di** *vt* to engender; **intentare ~** *vi* to sue; **a ~ di** *adj* due to. * *prep* owing to; on account of.

causare *vt* to cause; to bring about; to occasion.

caustico *adj* caustic; vitriolic.

cautamente *adv* warily.

cautela *f* wariness.

cauterizzare *vt* to cauterize; to sear.

cauto *adj* cautious; canny.

cauzione *f* bail.

cava *f* quarry; pit.

cavalcare *vt* to ride.

cavalcata *f* ride.

cavalcavia *m inv* overpass.

cavalcioni *prep*; **a ~ di** astride.

cavaliere *m* cavalier; horseman; knight.

cavalleresco *adj* chivalrous.

cavalleria *f* chivalry; cavalry.

cavallerizzo *m* rider.

cavalletta *f* grasshopper.

cavalletto *m* easel; trestle.

cavallina *f* leap frog.

cavallo *m* horse; horsepower; crotch; (chess) knight; **a ~** *adv* on horseback; **corse di cavalli** *fpl* horse-racing.

cavalloni *mpl* surf.

cavalluccio marino *m* seahorse.

cavarsela *vi* to cope; to pull through.

cavatappi *m inv* corkscrew.

caverna *f* cave, cavern.

cavia *f* guinea pig.

caviale *m* caviar.

caviglia *f* ankle.

cavillare *vi* to quibble.

cavillo *m* quibble.

cavità *f* hollow; pothole.

cavo *m* cable; **televisione via ~** cable television; * *adj* hollow.

cavolfiore *m* cauliflower.

cavolino *m*; **cavolini** *mpl* **di Bruxelles** Brussels sprouts.

cavolo *m* cabbage.

cazzo *m* prick.

cazzuola *f* trowel.

cece *m* chickpea.

cecità *f* blindness.

cedere *vt* to cede; to yield; * *vi* to give, to give in; to relent; to sink; to submit; to yield.

cediglia *f* cedilla.

cedro *m* cedar.

ce *f* fone *m* clout; slap.

celebrazione *f* celebration.

celebrità *f inv* celebrity; fame; stardom.

celeste *adj* blue, sky-blue; heavenly.

celestiale *adj* celestial.

celibato *m* celibacy.

celibe *adj* celibate (man); single.

cella *f* cell.

cello fan *m* cellophane.

cellulare *adj* cellular.

celluloide *f* celluloid.

cellulosa *f* cellulose.

cembalo *m* cymbal.

cementare *vt* to cement.

cemento *m* cement.

cena *f* dinner, supper.

cencio *m* rag.

cenere *f* ash.

cengia *f* ledge.

cenno *m* motion; wave; **~ del capo** *m* nod; **chiamare con un ~** *vt* to beckon; **salutare con un ~ della mano** *vt* to wave; **fare un ~ col capo** *vi* to nod.

cenotafio *m* cenotaph.

censimento *m* census.

censore *m* censor.

censorio *adj* censorious.

censura *f* censorship, censure.

censurare *vt* to censor, to censure.

centenario *m* centenary.

centenario *m*, *adj* centenarian.

centennale *adj* centennial.

centesimo *m* cent; hundredth; * *adj* hundredth.

centigrado *adj* centigrade.

centilitro *m* centilitre.

centimetro *m* centimetre.

cento *adj*, *m* hundred.

centrale *adj* central; middle; * *f* **~ elettrica** *f* power station.

centralinista *m/f* operator.

centralino *m* switchboard.

centralizzare *vt* to centralize.

centrifuga *f* centrifuge; spin-dryer.

centrifugo *adj* centrifugal.

centro *m* centre; middle; **~ civico rionale** *m* community centre; **~ del bersaglio** *m* bull's-eye; **~ commerciale** *m* shopping centre.

centurione *m* centurion.

cera *f* wax; polish; **~ d'api** *f* beeswax; **statua di ~** *f* waxwork; **museo delle cere** *m* waxworks; **dare la ~ a** *vt* to polish with wax.

ceralacca *f* sealing wax.

ceramica *f* ceramic; pottery.

cerata *m*; **cappello di ~** sou'wester.

cerbiatto *m* fawn.

cerbottana *f* blowpipe.

cercare *vt* to try; to look for; **~ a tastoni** to grope; to hunt for; * *vi* to search, to seek; to forage.

cerchio *m* circle; hoop; ring.

cereale *m* cereal.

cereali *mpl* grain.

cerebrale *adj* cerebral.

cerimonia *f* ceremony.

cerino *m* taper.

cerniera *f* hinge; zip.

cerotto *m* plaster.

certamente *adv* definitely.

certezza *f* certainty; sureness.

certificare *vt* to certify.

certificato *m* certificate; **~ di nascita** birth certificate; **~ di morte** death certificate.

certo *adj* certain; some; sure; * *pron* **certi** some.

certosino *m* Carthusian.

cerva *f* hind.

cervellata *f* saveloy.

cervello *m* brain; mastermind; **fare il lavaggio del ~ a** * *vt* to brainwash.

cervo *m* deer, stag; **carne di ~** *f* venison.

cesareo *adj* Caesarian.

cesoie *fpl* shears.

cespuglio *m* bush, shrub.

cessare *vt* to cease; * *vi* to cease, to stop.

cessazione *f* cessation.

cesso *m* (*Brit fam*) bog.

cestino *m* basket.

cesto *m* hamper.

cetra *f* zither.

cetriolino *m* gherkin.

cetriolo *m* cucumber.

champagne *m inv* champagne.

che *rel pron* that; which; who; whom; * *conj* that; then; * *adj* what

che *f m inv* che *f*.

cherosene *m* kerosene; paraffin.

cherubino *m* cherub.

chewing-gum *m inv* chewing gum.

chi *pron* who, whom; * *poss pron* **di** ~ whose.

chiacchierare *vi* to chat, to chatter; to gossip; to jabber.

chiacchierata *f* chat.

chiacchiere *fpl* chatter.

chiacchierio *m* jabber.

chiacchierone *m* chatterbox.

chiamare *vt* to call; to name; to term.

chiamata *f* call; ~ **alle armi** *f* (*mil*) call-up.

chiaramente *adv* clearly.

chiaretto *m* claret.

chiarezza *f* clarity; fairness.

chiarificazione *f* clarification.

chiarimento *m* explanation; **fornire un** ~ **a** *vt* to enlighten.

chiarire *vt* to clarify.

chiaro *adj* clear; articulate; fair; light; straightforward.

chiarore *m* flare.

chiaroveggente *m/f* clairvoyant.

chiasso *m* din.

chiassoso *adj* riotous.

chiatta *f* barge.

chiave *f* (mus) clef; wrench; **nota di** ~ *f* keynote; ~ **di sol** *f* treble clef; key; ~ **di volta** *f* keystone; ~ **fissa** *f* spanner; **chiudere a** ~ *vt* to lock.

chiavistello *m* bolt; latch.

chiazza *f* blotch.

chic *adj* chic, classy; smart.

chicche *fpl* goodies.

chicchirichi *m* cock-a-doodle-do.

chicco *m* grain; bean; ~ **di caffè** coffee bean.

chiedere *vt* to ask; ~ **notizie di** to ask after; * *vr* ~**rsi** to wonder; * *vi* ~ **a gran voce** to clamour; ~ **di** to inquire after.

chiesa *f* church.

chiffon *m* chiffon.

chiglia *f* keel.

chignon *m* bun.

chilo *m* kilo.

chilogrammo *m* kilogram(me).

chilometraggio *m* mileage.

chilometro *m* kilometre.

chimica *f* chemistry.

chimico *adj* chemical; * *m* chemist; **prodotto** ~ chemical.

chinare *vt* to bow; to incline; * *vr* **chinarsi** to droop; to stoop.

chinino *m* quinine.

chioccia *f* broody hen.

chiocciola *f* snail.

chiodo *m* nail; spike; ~ **fisso** *m* hobby-horse; **munire di chiodi** *vt* to spike.

chiodo *m* stud; nail.

chioma *f* hair.

chiosare *vt* to gloss.

chiosco *m* kiosk.

chiostro *m* cloister.

chip *m inv* silicon chip; microchip.

chiromante *m/f* fortune-teller.

chiromante *m/f* palmist.

chirurgia *f* surgery.

chirurgico *adj* surgical.

chirurgo *m* surgeon.

chitarra *f* guitar.

chitarrista *m/f* guitarist.

chiudere *vt* to close; to shut; * *vr* ~**si** to shut.

chiunque *pron* anybody; who.

chiurlo *m* curlew.

chiusa *f* lock; sluice.

chiuso *adj* closed.

chiusura *f* close-down; close; closing; fastener, fastening.

ci pers *pron* us.

cialda *f* waffle.

ciambella *f* doughnut.

ciance *fpl* drivel.

cianfrusaglie *fpl* junk.

cianografia *f* blueprint.

cianuro m cyanide.

ciao excl hullo, hi!

ciarlare vi to waffle.

ciarlatano m quack.

ciarliero adj chatty.

ciascuno adv apiece; * adj, pron, adv each.

cibernetica f cybernetics.

cibo m fare, food; (fam) grub.

cicala f cicada.

cicalino m bleeper, buzzer.

cicatrice f scar.

cicatrizzarsi vr to scar.

ciclamino m cyclamen.

ciclismo m cycling.

ciclista m/f cyclist.

ciclo m cycle.

ciclomotore m moped.

ciclone m cyclone.

cicogna f stork.

cicoria f chicory.

cicuta f hemlock.

ciecamente adv blindly.

cieco adj, m blind; **vicolo ~** m blind alley.

cielo m heaven; sky.

cifra f figure; digit.

cifrare vt to code.

ciglio m eyelash, lash; side.

cigno m swan; **giovane ~** m cygnet.

cigolare vi to grate; to squeak.

cigolio m squeak.

ciliegia f cherry.

ciliegio m cherry tree.

cilindrico adj cylindrical.

cilindro m cylinder; top hat.

cima f crown (of hill); peak; summit; top.

cimitero m cemetery; churchyard; graveyard.

cimurro m distemper.

cincia f tit.

cinegiornale m newsreel.

cinema m inv cinema.

cinepresa f cine camera, movie camera.

cinetico adj kinetic.

cinghia f belt, strap; **~ della ventola** f fanbelt.

cinghiale m boar.

cinguettare vi to chirp; to twitter.

cinguettio m chirp; twitter.

cinico adj cynic(al); * n cynic.

cinismo m cynicism.

cinquanta m, adj fifty.

cinquantesimo m, adj fiftieth.

cinque m, adj five.

cinto m; **~ erniario** truss.

cintura f belt; **~ di sicurezza** f seatbelt, safety belt.

cinturino m strap.

ciò dem pron that; * adv **con ~** thereby.

ciocca f lock; strand.

cioccolato m chocolate.

cioè adv i.e.; namely.

ciondolare vi to loll.

ciottoli mpl shingle.

ciottolo m cobblestone; pebble.

cipiglio m frown.

cipolla f onion; (med) bunion; rose (of watering can).

cipresso m cypress.

cipria f face powder.

circa adv around; some; somewhere.

circo m circus.

circolare adj, f circular; * vi to circulate.

circolazione f circulation; **~ del sangue** f bloodstream.

circolo m club; clubhouse.

circoncidere vt to circumcise.

circoncisione f circumcision.

circondare vt to encircle; to surround.

circonferenza f girth; circumference.

circonflesso adj circumflex.

circonlocuzione f circumlocution.

circonvallazione f by-pass.

circoscrivere vt to circumscribe.

circoscrizione f precinct.
circospetto adj circumspect; guarded.
circostanza f circumstance.
circostanziato adj circumstantial.
circuito m circuit; **televisione a ~ chiuso** f closed-circuit television; **~ di gara** m speedway.
cirripede m barnacle.
cirrosi f cirrhosis.
cisposo adj; **dagli occhi cisposi** bleary-eyed.
cisterna f tank.
cisti f inv cyst.
cistifellea f gall bladder.
citante m/f (law) claimant.
citare vt to cite; **~ in giudizio** to subpoena; to sue; to quote; * vi to quote.
citazione f quotation; subpoena.
cito fono m entry phone.
citrico adj citric.
citrullo m sucker.
città f inv city, town.
cittadella f citadel.
cittadino m citizen; national; **semplice ~** m commoner.
ciuffo m clump; tuft.
civetta f flirt; owl.
civettuolo adj coy.
civico adj civic.
civile adj civil; urbane; **protezione ~** f civil defence.
civilizzare vt to civilize.
civiltà f inv civilization.
clacson m inv hooter, horn; **suonare il ~** vt to toot.
clamore m clamour.
clamoroso adj resounding.
clan m inv clan.
clandestino adj clandestine; undercover.
clarinetto m clarinet.
classe f class, form; style; **prima ~** f first class.

classico adj classic(al); standard.
classificare vt to classify; to categorize; to grade; to sort.
classificatore m binder.
classificazione f classification.
classista m class consciousness.
clausola f clause; proviso; **~ addizionale** f rider.
claustrofobia f claustrophobia.
claustrofobico adj claustrophobic.
clavicembalo m harpsichord.
clavicola f collarbone.
clemente adj clement.
clemenza f clemency.
cleptomania f kleptomania.
clericale adj (rel) clerical.
clero m clergy.
clessidra f hourglass.
cliente m/f client, customer.
clientela f custom; clientele.
clima m climate.
climatico adj climatic.
climatizzato adj air-conditioned.
clinica f clinic; nursing home.
clipper m inv clipper.
clorare vt to chlorinate.
cloro m chlorine.
cloro filla f chlorophyll.
cloroformio m chloroform.
clou m inv highlight.
club m club.
coabitare vi to cohabit.
coagulare vt to coagulate; * vr **~rsi** to clot, to coagulate.
coalizione f coalition.
cobalto m cobalt.
cobra m inv cobra.
cocaina f cocaine.
coccarda f rosette.
coccinella f ladybird.
cocciuto adj pig-headed; stubborn.
coccò m; **noce di ~** f coconut.
coccodè m cackle (of hen);

fare ~ *vi* to cackle.

coccodrillo *m* crocodile.

coccolare *vt* to cosset; to cuddle; to mollycoddle.

cocktail *m inv* cocktail.

cocomero *m* watermelon.

coda *f* queue; tail; tailback; ~ **di cavallo** *f* ponytail.

codazzo *m* train.

codeina *f* codeine.

codice *m* code; cipher; ~ **a barre** bar code; ~ **di avviamento postale** *m* postcode.

codicillo *m* codicil.

coefficiente *m* coefficient.

coercizione *f* duress.

coerente *adj* consistent; coherent.

coerenza *f* coherence.

coesione *f* cohesion.

coesistenza *f* coexistence.

coesistere *vi* to coexist.

cofano *m* (*Brit*) bonnet.

cogliere *vt* to pluck; to pick; to seize.

cognac *m inv* cognac.

cognata *f* sister-in-law.

cognato *m* brother-in-law.

cognizione *f* cognition.

cognome *m* surname.

coincidenza *f* coincidence.

coincidere *vi* to coincide; to concur.

coinvolgere *vt* to involve.

colapasta *m inv* colander.

colare *vi* to run.

colazione *f*; **prima ~** breakfast; **seconda ~** lunch.

colera *f* cholera; **andare in ~** *vi* to throw a tantrum.

colesterolo *m* cholesterol.

colibrì *m inv* humming-bird.

colica *f* colic; gripe.

colla *f* gum; glue.

collaborare *vi* to collaborate.

collaboratore *m* (journal) contributor; collaborator.

collaborazione *f* collaboration.

collana *f* necklace; ~ **a girocollo** *m* choker.

collant *m inv* tights, pantyhose.

collasso *m* collapse.

collaudare *vt* to test.

collaudo *m* test.

collazionare *vt* to collate.

colle *m* hill.

collega *m/f* colleague, associate.

collegamento *m* connection.

collegare *vt* to connect, to link; * *vt* to join; to relate; ~ **a terra** (*elec*) to earth.

college *m* college; boarding school; ~ **elettorale** *m* constituency.

collegiale *m/f* boarder.

collera *f* rage; temper.

colletta *f* whip-round.

collettivo *m* collective; * *adj* collective; corporate.

collezionista *m* collector.

collie *m inv* collie (dog).

collina *f* hill; foothill.

collinoso *adj* hilly.

collirio *m* eyedrops.

collo *m* collar; neck; instep.

collocare *vt* to locate; to site.

colloquio *m* interview.

colloso *adj* gluey.

collusione *f* collusion.

collutorio *m* gargle; mouthwash.

colmare *vt*: ~ **qn di qc** *vt* to lavish something on somebody.

colombaia *f* dovecote.

colombo *m* dove.

colon *m inv* (*med*) colon.

colonnello *m* colonel.

colonia *f* colony; **acqua di ~** *f* eau de cologne.

coloniale *adj* colonial.

colonizzare *vt* to colonize; to settle.

colonizzatore *m* colonist.

colonna *f* column; pillar; ~ **sonora** *f* soundtrack; **met-**

tere in ~ *vt* to tabulate.
colonnina *f* bollard.
colono *m* settler.
colorante *m* dye; stain.
colorare *vt* to colour.
colorazione *f* colouring.
colore *m* colour; (cards) suit; **dai colori vivaci** *adj* colourful.
colossale *adj* colossal, mammoth, monstrous.
colpa *f* blame, fault; guilt; **senza ~** *adj* guiltless.
colpetto *m* dab; pat; tap; flick, flip; prod; poke; **dare un ~** *vt* to flick; **dare dei colpetti leggeri** *vt* to pat; **dare un ~ a** *vt* to poke.
colpevole *m* culprit; * *adj* guilty; culpable; * *vt* riconoscere ~ to convict.
colpevolezza *f* guilt, culpability.
colpire *vt* to hit; to knock; to smite; to strike; to clout; to impress; **~ violentemente** to batter.
colpo *m* bang; blow; knock; hit; slam; stroke; thump; whack; coup; **~ secco** chop; **~ di punta** jab; **fare un bel ~** to make a killing; **colpi d'arma a fuoco** *mpl* gun fire; **~ di grazia** *m* deathblow; **~ giornalistico** *m* scoop; **~ mancato** *m* miss; **che fa ~** *adj* striking.
coltellata *f* stab.
coltello *m* knife; **~ a serramanico** jack-knife.
coltivare *vt* to cultivate; to grow, to farm, to till.
coltivatore *m* grower.
coltivazione *f* crop; cultivation.
colto *adj* cultured, learned, educated.
coltura *f* (*agr*, *biol*) culture; growing.
coma *m inv* coma.

comandamento *m* commandment.
comandare *vt* to command.
comando *m* control; command; order.
comatoso *adj* comatose.
combattente *m/f* combatant; fighter.
combattere *vi* to battle; * *vt* to combat; to fight.
combattimento *m* combat, fight, fighting.
combinare *vt* to combine.
combinazione *f* combination.
combustibile *adj* combustible; * *m* fuel.
combustione *f* combustion.
come *conj* as; * *adv* how; * *prep* like; * *adj* such as.
cometa *f* comet.
comico *adj* comic; * *m* comedian.
comignolo *m* chimney stack.
cominciare *vt* to begin, to commence; to start; to take up; * *vi* to begin; to get; to start.
comitato *m* committee; **~ elettorale** *m* caucus.
comizio *m* rally; **comizi elettorali** *mpl* hustings.
commando *m* commando.
commedia *f* comedy; play.
commemorare *vt* to commemorate.
commemorativo *adj* memorial.
commemorazione *f* commemoration.
commentare *vt* to commentate.
commento *m* comment; commentary.
commerciale *adj* commercial; trading.
commercialista *m* chartered accountant.
commerciante *m/f* dealer, merchant, trader.
commerciare *vi* to trade.

commercio *m* commerce, trade, trading.

commessa *f* saleswoman.

commesso *m* salesman.

commestibile *adj* edible, eatable.

commettere *vt* to commit.

commiserazione *f* commiseration.

commissariato *m* commissariat.

commissario *m*; **~ di bordo** *m* purser.

commissionare *vt* to commission.

commissione *f* commision; board; errand.

commosso *adj* affected, touched.

commovente *adj* appealing, moving, touching, emotive.

commozione *f* emotion; **~ cerebrale** *f* concussion.

commuovere *vt* to move, to touch.

commutare *vt* to commute.

comodità *f* convenience.

comodo *adj* comfortable; convenient; handy.

compagnia *f* company, society.

compagno *m* companion; comrade; mate; **~ di classe** *m* classmate; **~ di studi** *m* fellow student; **~ di viaggio** *m* fellow traveller.

comparativo *adj* (*gr*) comparative.

comparire *vi* to appear.

comparsa *f* appearance.

compassione *f* compassion, pity.

compassionevole *adj* compassionate.

compasso *m* compass; **~ a punte fisse** *m* dividers.

compatibile *adj* compatible.

compatire *vt* to pity; * *vi* to sympathize.

compatriota *m/f* compatriot, fellow countryman.

compatto *adj* compact.

compendiare *vt* abridge.

compensare *vt* to compensate.

compensato *m* plywood.

compenso *m* compensation.

competente *adj* competent, proficient.

competenza *f* competence, proficiency.

competere *vi* to compete.

compiacente *adj* compliant.

compiacimento *m* complacency.

compiaciuto *adj* complacent; smug, self-righteous.

compiere *vt* to do; to accomplish; to fulfil.

compilare *vt* to compile.

compilazione *f* compilation.

compimento *m* fulfilment.

compito *m* homework; job; task.

compleanno *m* birthday.

complementare *adj* complementary; subsidiary.

complemento *m* complement.

complessità *f inv* complexity; intricacy; sophistication; involvement.

complessivo *adj* aggregate.

complesso *m* complex; ensemble, entirety; group; hang-up; **nel ~** by and large.

completamente *adv* fully; totally; wholly, utterly; absolutely; right.

completamento *m* completion; accomplishment.

completare *vt* to complete; to fill in (form, etc).

completo *adj* complete; absolute; whole; unidivided; suit; .

complicare *vt* to complicate.

complicato *adj* elaborate; involved.

complicazione *f* complication.

complice m/f accomplice, accessory; **essere ~ di** vt to aid and abet.

complicità f complicity.

complimentarsi vr to compliment.

complimento m compliment.

complottare vi, vt to plot.

complotto m plot.

componente adj component; * m component; constituent.

comporre vt to compose.

comportamento m behaviour.

comportare vt to entail; * vr **~rsi** to act; to behave; **~ male** to misbehave.

composito adj composite.

compositore m composer; compositor.

composizione f composition; make-up.

composto m compound; * adj self-possessed; composed; compound; (gr) **parola composta** f compound.

comprare vt to buy.

compratore m buyer.

comprendere vt to comprise; to comprehend; to encompass.

comprensibile adj comprehensible, understandable.

comprensione f comprehension, appreciation, understanding; sympathy.

comprensivo adj understanding, sympathetic.

compressa f compress; tablet.

comprimere vt to compress.

compromesso m compromise.

comprovare vt to substantiate.

computer m computer; **personal ~** m personal computer.

comune adj common; routine; ordinary; * m borough; municipality; **in ~** adj communal; **in ~** adv jointly.

comunemente adj commonly.

comunicare vt to communi-

cate; to impart; to commune.

comunicazione f communication; (road, etc); **di grande ~** arterial.

comunione f communion.

comunismo m communism.

comunista m/f communist.

comunità f inv community.

comunque adv anyhow; * conj however.

con prep with.

conato m; **avere dei conati di vomito** to retch.

concavo adj concave.

concedere vt allow.

concentramento m concentration; **campo di ~** m concentration camp.

concentrare vt to concentrate.

concentrato m concentrate; strong; **~ di frutta** m fruit squash.

concentrazione f concentration.

concentrico adj concentric.

concepibile adj conceivable.

concepimento m conception.

concepire vt to conceive.

concerto m concert, concerto, recital.

concessione f concession, franchise; **~ atta a placare** f sop.

concetto m concept.

conchiglia f shell.

conciare vt to cure.

conciliabile adj reconcilable.

conciliare vt to accommodate (differences).

conciliante adj accommodating, amenable .

concordare vt to agree, to conciliate; * vi to agree.

conciliatorio adj conciliatory.

conciliazione f conciliation.

concimare vt to manure.

concime m compost, manure.

conciso adj concise; crisp; terse.

concittadino *m* fellow citizen.

concludere *vt* to conclude; to clinch; * *vi* to conclude; to tie up.

conclusione *f* conclusion; **conclusioni** *fpl* findings.

conclusivo *adj* conclusive; closing.

concomitante *adj* concomitant.

concordanza *f* concordance.

concordare *vi* to settle.

concorrente *m/f* competitor; contestant, entrant.

concorrenza *f* competition.

concorrenziale *adj* competitive.

concorso *m* competition, contest.

concreto *adj* concrete.

concubina *f* concubine.

concupire *vt* to covet.

condanna *f* conviction, condemnation.

condannare *vt* to condemn; to sentence; to decry.

condensare *vt* to condense.

condensato *adj* potted.

condensazione *f* condensation.

condiglianze *fpl* condolences.

condimento *m* condiment, seasoning; dressing, relish; **~ per l'insalata** *m* salad dressing.

condire *vt* to dress, to season.

condiscendente *adj* condescending; acquiescent.

condiscendenza *f* compliance; **trattare con ~** *vt* to patronize

condividere *vt* to share.

condizionale *adj* conditional.

condizionare *vt* to condition.

condizionato *adj* qualified.

condizione *f* condition; state; **~ indispensabile** *f* precondition; **condizioni** *fpl* terms.

condotta *f* conduct; **cattiva ~** *f* misbehaviour, misconduct.

conducente *m* driver.

condurre *vt* to conduct; to lead; (ship) to sail.

conduttività *f* conductivity.

conduttore *m* (*phys*) conductor.

conduttura *f* conduit; pipeline; **~ principale** *f* main; **~ dell'acqua** *f* water main.

conduzione *f* conduction.

confederarsi *vr* to confederate.

confederato *adj* confederate.

confederazione *f* confederacy.

conferenza *f* talk; lecture; **~ stampa** *f* press conference; **tenere una ~** *vt* to lecture.

conferire *vt* to bestow, to confer.

conferma *f* confirmation.

confermare *vt* to confirm.

confessare *vt* to confess.

confessionale *m* confessional.

confessione *f* confession; denomination.

confessore *m* confessor.

confezionare *vt* to package; to tailor.

conficcare *vt* to stick; to plunge; to jab.

confidare *vt* to confide.

confidente *m* confidant.

confidenziale *adj* private.

configurazione *f* configuration.

confinante *adj* neighbouring.

confine *m* border, boundary, frontier,

confisca *f* confiscation; seizure.

confiscare *vt* to confiscate.

conflagrazione *f* conflagration.

conflitto *m* conflict; clash; strife.

confluenza *f* confluence.

confluire *vi* to merge; * *vt* to join.

confondere *vt* to confuse; to baffle.

conformarsi *vr* to conform.

conformità *f* conformity; compliance.

confortare *vt* to comfort.

conforto *m* comfort.

confusione *f* confusion, muddle; turmoil.

confuso *adj* confused; be fuddled; mixed-up.

confutare *vt* to disprove; to refute; to rebut.

congedare *vt* to dismiss.

congedo *m* dismissal; furlough.

congegno *m* device; contrivance.

congelamento *m* freezing, frostbite; **punto di ~** *m* freezing point

congelare *vt* to freeze; * *vr* **~rsi** to freeze.

congelato *adj* frozen, frostbitten.

congelatore *m* freezer, deep-freeze.

congenito *adj* congenital, in-bred.

congestionato *adj* congested.

congestione *f* congestion.

congettura *f* conjecture, surmise, guesswork.

congetturare *vt* to conjecture, to surmise.

congiuntive *adj*, *m* subjunctive.

congiuntura *f* conjuncture; juncture.

congiunzione *f* conjunction.

congiura *f* conspiracy.

congiurare *vi* to conspire.

conglomerato *m* conglomerate.

congratularsi *vr* to congratulate.

congratulazioni *fpl* congratulations.

congregazione *f* congregation.

congresso *m* congress.

congruità *f* congruity.

congruo *adj* congruous.

coniare *vt* to mint.

conico *adj* conic(al).

conifera *f* conifer.

conifero *adj* coniferous.

conigliera *f* rabbit hutch.

coniglio *m* rabbit.

coniugale *adj* conjugal, matrimonial, marital.

coniugare *vt* to conjugate.

coniugato *adj* married.

coniugazione *f* conjugation.

connivente *adj*; **essere ~ in** to connive.

connivenza *f* connivance.

cono *m* cone.

conoscente *m/f* acquaintance.

conoscenza *f* acquaintance; knowledge; consciousness; **privo di ~** *adj* insensible.

conoscere *vt* become acquainted with; to know.

conosciuto *adj* familiar.

conquista *f* conquest.

conquistare *vt* to conquer; to win.

conquistatore *m* conqueror.

consacrare *vt* to consecrate, to hallow.

consacrazione *f* consecration.

consapevole *adj* aware; mindful.

consapevolezza *f* awareness.

consapevolmente *adv* wittingly.

consciamente *adv* knowingly.

consecutivo *adj* consecutive; successive.

consegna *f* delivery.

consegnare *vt* to consign; to hand over; to deliver; to turn in.

conseguente *adj* consequent.

conseguenza *f* consequence; after-effect; **conseguenze** *fpl* aftermath; **di ~** *adv* consequently.

consenso *m* consensus; acquiescence; agreement.

conserva *f* preserve.

conservante *m* preservative.

conservare *vt* to conserve, to preserve; to retain.

conservatore *m* conservative; curator (of museum); * *adj* conservative.

conservatorio *m* conservatory.

conservazione *f* conservation, preservation.

considerare *vt* to consider; to regard; to deliberate; to treat.

considerazione *f* consideration.

considerevole *adj* considerable, handsome, sizeable.

consigliabile *adj* advisable.

consigliare *vt* advise; to recommend.

consigliere *m* adviser; councillor, counsellor.

consigli *mpl* guidance.

consiglio *m* advice; council, counsel; (*pol*) **C~ dei Ministri** The Cabinet.

consistenza *f* consistency; texture.

consistere *vi* to consist.

consociato *adj* associate.

consolare *adj* consular; * *vt* to console.

consolato *m* consulate.

consolazione *f* consolation, comfort, solace.

console *m* consul.

consolidare *vt* to consolidate; * *vr* ~**rsi** to strengthen.

consolidazione *f* consolidation.

consonante *f* consonant.

consorte *m/f* consort.

consorzio *m* consortium.

consueto *adj* customary.

consuetudine *f* custom.

consulente *m/f* adviser, consultant.

consulenza *f* consultancy.

consultare *vt* to consult; * *vi* to

refer; * *vr* to confer.

consultazione *f* consultation.

consultivo *adj* advisory.

consumare *vt* to consummate; to consume; to wear: * *vi* to fray; * *vr* ~**rsi** to wear away.

consumato *adj* threadbare, worn.

consumatore *m* consumer.

consumazione *f* consummation.

consumista *adj*; **società ~** consumer society.

consumo *m* consumption; **beni di ~** *mpl* consumer goods.

consunto *adj* worn-out.

consunzione *f* (*med*) tuberculosis, consumption.

contabile *m/f* accountant, bookkeeper.

contabilità *f* accountancy, bookkeeping.

contachilometri *m inv* mileometer.

contadino *m* peasant, rustic.

contagioso *adj* catching, contagious.

contagocce *m inv* dropper.

contaminare *vt* to contaminate.

contaminato *adj* tainted.

contaminazione *f* contamination.

contanti *mpl*; **in ~** in cash.

contare *vt* to count; ~ **su** to depend on, to rely on; to number; * *vi* to count.

contatore *m* meter; ~ **del gas** *m* gas meter.

contatto *m* contact; **lenti a ~** *fpl* contact lenses.

contattare *vt* to contact.

contatto *m* touch.

conte *m* count, earl.

contea *f* county, shire.

conteggio *m* count.

contegno *m* demeanour.

contegnoso *adj* demure.

contemplare *vt* to contemplate.

contemplativo *adj* contemplative.

contemplazione *f* contemplation.

contemporaneo *adj* contemporary, contemporaneous.

contendente *m/f* contender.

contendere *vi* to contend; * *vr* ~rsi to vie.

contenere *vt* to contain.

contenitore *m* container, holder.

contentare *vt* to suit.

contentezza *f* content, contentment.

contentissimo *adj* delighted.

contento *adj* content; contented; glad; happy; pleased; **tutto** ~ chuffed.

contenuto *m* contents.

contenzioso *adj* contentious.

contessa *f* countess.

contestare *vt* to contest; to dispute; to query.

contestatore *m* protestor.

contesto *m* context.

contiguo *adj* contiguous; adjoining; **essere** ~ **a** *vt* to adjoin.

continentale *adj* continental.

continente *m* continent; mainland.

contingente *m* contingent.

contingenza *f* contingency.

continuare *vt* to carry on, to continue; * *vi* to continue; to go on.

continuazione *f* continuance, continuation.

continuità *f* continuity.

continuo *adj* continual; continuous; constant; non-stop.

conto *m* account; bill; **dover rendere** ~ **a qn** to be answerable to someone; **non tenere** ~ **di** to override; **per** ~ **di** on

behalf of; ~ **in banca** *m* bank account; ~ **scoperto** overdraft; **estratto** ~ statement; ~ **spese** *m* expense account; **rendersi** ~ **di** *vr* to realize.

contorcere *vt* to contort; * *vr* ~rsi to squirm; to writhe.

contorno *m* contour, outline.

contorsione *f* contortion.

contrabbandare *vt* to smuggle.

contrabbandiere *m* smuggler.

contrabbando *m* contraband; smuggling.

contraccambiare *vt* to reciprocate; to requite.

contraccezione *f* contraception, birth control.

contraddire *vt* to contradict,

contraddittorio *adj* contradictory, conflicting; inconsistent.

contraddizione *f* contradiction.

contraereo *adj*; **fuoco** ~ *m* flak.

contrafatto *adj* counterfeit.

contraffare *vt* to counterfeit, to forge.

contraffattore *m* forger.

contraffazione *f* forgery.

contrafforte *m* buttress.

contrappeso *m* counterbalance.

contrariare *vt* to put out.

contrariato *adj* disgruntled.

contrario *m* contrary, opposite; * *adj* contrary; **al** ~ conversely.

contrarre *vt* to contract; to incur.

contrarsi *vr* to twitch.

contrastante *adj* contrasting.

contrastare *vi* to contrast.

contrasto *m* contrast.

contrattare *vi* to bargain, to haggle.

contrattempo *m* contretemps, upset.

contratto *m* contract; **~ d' affitto** *m* lease.

contrattuale *adj* contractual.

contravvenire *vt* to contravene; to flout.

contravvenzione *f* contravention.

contrazione *f* contraction.

contribuente *m/f* taxpayer.

contribuire *vi*, *vt* to contribute;
che contribuisce *adj* contributory.

contribuzione *f* contribution.

contro *prep* against, versus.

controbilanciare *vt* to counterbalance.

controcultura *f* underground.

controfigura *f* stand-in.

controfiletto *m* sirloin.

controfirmare *vt* countersign.

controllare *vt* to check; to inspect; to control; to test.

controllo *m* control; inspection;
~ delle nascite *m* birth control; **visita di ~** *f* (*med*) checkup.

controllore *m* inspector.

controproducente *adj* counterproductive.

controversia *f* controversy, dispute.

controverso *adj* controversial.

contumacia *f* default.

contusione *f* contusion.

conurbazione *f* conurbation.

convalescente *adj*, *m/f* convalescent.

convalescenza *f* convalescence; recuperation; **fare la ~**
to convalesce.

convalescenziario *m* sanatorium.

convalidare *vt* to authenticate;
to validate.

convegno *m* conference; **~
galante** *m* assignation.

convenire *vi* to convene.

convento *m* convent.

convenuto *adj* agreed; * *m* respondent.

convenzionale *adj* conventional.

convenzione *f* convention.

convergente *adj* convergent.

convergenza *f* convergence.

convergere *vi* to converge.

conversare *vi* to converse.

conversazione *f* talk; conversation; **~ mondana** *f* small
talk; **~ brillante** *f* repartee.

conversione *f* (*rel*) conversion.

convertibile *adj* convertible.

convertire *vt* to convert.

convertito *m* convert.

convertitore *m* converter.

convesso *adj* convex.

convettore *m* convector.

convezione *f* convection.

convincente *adj* convincing;
cogent; forcible.

convincere *vt* to convince; to
coax; **~ con le buone** to cajole.

convinto *adj* staunch.

convinzione *f* conviction; belief.

convocare *vt* to summon; to
convoke; to convene.

convoglio *m* convoy.

convulsione *f* convulsion.

convulso *adj* convulsive.

cooperare *vi* to cooperate.

cooperativa *f* cooperative.

cooperativo *adj* cooperative.

cooperazione *f* cooperation.

cooptare *vt* to coopt.

coordinamento *m* liaison; * *vt*
to coordinate.

coordinata *f* coordinate.

coordinatore *m* coordinator.

coordinazione *f* coordination.

coperchio *m* cover, lid.

coperta *f* blanket; deck; **coperte** *fpl* bedclothes; **~ termica** *f* electric blanket.

coperto *adj* cloudy, overcast; **~**

di vegetazione overgrown.
copertura f cover, covering.
copia f copy.
copiare vt to copy; to crib.
copiatrice f copier.
copione m scenario, script.
copioso adj profuse.
coppia f couple, pair, twosome.
copricapo m headdress.
copri fuoco m curfew.
copriletto m bedspread, counterpane.
coprimozzo m hubcap.
coprire vt to cover; to defray.
coraggio m courage, bravery; pluck; spirit; valour; ~ **dato da alcolici** m Dutch courage.
coraggioso adj brave, courageous, plucky, valiant.
corale adj choral.
corallino m coral reef.
corallo m coral.
corda f cord; string; rope; chord; ~ **del bucato** f clothes line: ~ **da acrobata** f tightrope.
cordame m rigging.
cordiale m cordial; * adj cordial, genial.
cordialità f friendliness.
cordicella f twine.
cordone m cord; ~ **ombelicale** m umbilical cord.
coreografia f choreography.
coreografo m choreographer.
coriaceo adj thick-skinned.
coriandoli mpl confetti.
coriandolo m coriander.
corista m/f chorister.
cornacchia f crow.
cornamusa f bagpipes; **suonatore di** ~ m piper.
cornea f cornea.
cornetta f cornet.
cornetto m croissant; cornet.
cornice f frame.
cornicione m cornice.
corno m horn.
coro m choir; chorus.

corollario m corollary.
corona f crown.
coronario adj cornoary.
coroncina f coronet.
coroner m inv coroner.
corpino m bodice.
corpo m body; corps.
corporale adj corporal, corporeal.
corporatura f build; frame.
corporazione f guild.
corpulento adj corpulent, portly.
corpulenza f corpulence.
corredino m layette.
correggere vt to correct; to emend; to right; to mark.
correlare vt to correlate.
correlativo adj correlative.
correlato adj interrelated.
correlazione f correlation.
corrente adj current; fluent; running; * f current; flow.
correo m co-respondent.
correre vi to race; to run; * vt to run.
correttezza f fair play.
correttivo adj corrective; remedial.
corretto adj correct; right.
correzione f correction; emendation.
corrida f bull fight.
corridoio m corridor.
corridore m runner; racer.
corriera f coach.
corriere m carrier; courier.
corrimano m handrail, rail.
corrispondente m/f correspondent; pen friend; * adj corrisponding.
corrispondenza f correspondence; **vendita per** ~ f mail order.
corrispondere vi to correspond; to match; to tally; * vt to correspond.
corroborare vt to corroborate.

corroborazione *f* corroboration.

corrodere *vt* to corrode; * *vr* ~rsi to corrode.

corrompere *vt* to corrupt; to bribe; to debauch.

corrosione *f* corrosion.

corrosivo *adj* corrosive.

corrotto *adj* corrupt.

corruttibile *adj* corruptible.

corruzione *f* corruption; bribery.

corsa *f* dash; race; run; racing.

corsia *f* ward.

corsivo *adj* italic.

corso *m* course; ~ **serale** *m* evening class; **moneta a ~ legale** *f* legal tender; **in ~** *adj* ongoing.

corte *f* court; ~ **marziale** *f* court-martial.

corteccia *f* bark.

corteggiamento *m* courtship.

corteggiare *vt* to court, to woo.

corteggiatore *m* suitor.

corteo *m* cortège; ~ **in maschera** *m* pageant.

cortese *adj* courteous, gracious.

cortesia *f* courtesy.

cortigiano *m* courtier.

cortile *m* courtyard; quadrangle; yard; backyard; ~ **per la ricreazione** *m* playground.

cortisone *m* cortisone.

corto *adj* short.

cortocircuito *m* short circuit.

corvo *m* crow; raven; rook.

cosa *pron* what; * *f* thing.

coscia *f* thigh; haunch; leg; ~ **di pollo** *f* drumstick.

cosciente *adj* conscious.

coscienza *f* conscience.

coscienzioso *adj* conscientious; painstaking.

coscritto *m* conscript.

così *adv* so; ~ ~ so-so; such; thus; that.

cosiddetto *adj* so-called.

cosmetico *adj, m* cosmetic.

cosmico *adj* cosmic.

cosmo *m* cosmos.

cosmonauta *m/f* cosmonaut, spaceman.

cosmopolita *adj, m/f* cosmopolitan.

cospargere *vt* to sprinkle; to spread; ~ **di sabbia** to sand.

cospicuo *adj* conspicuous.

cospiratore *m* conspirator.

costa *f* coast.

costante *adj* constant; steady; equable.

costantemente *adv* consistently.

costanza *f* constancy.

costare *vt* to cost.

costellazione *f* constellation.

costernazione *f* consternation.

costiero *adj* coastal; inshore.

costituire *vt* to constitute.

costituzionale *adj* constitutional.

costituzione *f* constitution.

costo *m* cost.

costola *f* rib.

costoletta *f* chop.

costoso *adj* costly, expensive.

costringere *vt* to constrain; to compel; to impel; to coerce; to constrict.

costrizione *f* compulsion; constraint; constriction.

costruire *vt* to construct, to build.

costruttore *m* builder.

costruzione *f* building, construction, edifice; ~ **annessa** *f* outhouse.

costume *m* costume; fancy dress; outfit; custom; wont; ~ **da bagno** bathing costume, swimsuit.

cotenna *f* rind; ~ **arrostita** *f* crackling.

cotogna *f* quince.

cotogno *m* quince tree.

cotoletta *f* cutlet.

cotonare *vt* to backcomb.

cotone *m* cotton; **~ idrofilo** *m* cotton wool.

cotonificio *m* cotton mill.

cotta *f* crush; surplice.

cottage *m* cottage.

cottimo *m*: **lavoro a ~** *m* piece-work.

cotto *adj* cooked; **poco ~** underdone.

cottura *f* baking.

coupé *m inv* (*auto*) coupé.

covare *vt* to brood; to incubate; to harbour; * *vi* **~ (sotto la cenere)** to smoulder.

covata *f* brood.

covo *m* den; haunt.

covone *m* sheaf.

cowboy *m inv* cowboy.

cozza *f* mussel.

cracker *m* cracker.

crampo *m* cramp.

cranio *m* skull.

crasso *adj* crass.

cratere *m* crater.

cravatta *f* tie.

creare *vt* to create.

creatività *f* creativity.

creativo *adj* creative.

creatore *m* creator.

creatura *f* creature.

creazione *f* creation; brain-child.

credente *m/f* believer.

credenza *f* dresser; sideboard; credence.

credenziali *vfpl* credentials.

credere *vt* to believe; to feel; to reckon; to understand; **non ~** to disbelieve; * *vi* to believe; to think.

credibile *adj* credible; believable.

credibilità *f* credibility.

credito *m* credit; **lettera di ~** *f* letter of credit.

creditore *m* creditor.

credo *m* creed.

credulità *f* credulity; gullibility.

credulo *adj* credulous.

credulone *adj* gullible.

crema *f* cream; **~ pasticcera** *f* custard; **color ~** *adj, f inv* cream; **~ per il viso** *f* face cream.

cremare *vt* cremate.

crematorio *m* crematorium.

cremazione *f* cremation.

cremisi *adj* crimson.

cremoso *adj* creamy.

creosoto *m* creosote.

crepa *f* crack; cleft.

crepaccio *m* crevasse; chasm.

crepuscolo *m* dusk, night fall, twilight.

crescente *adj* growing; increasing; rising.

crescere *vi* to grow.

crescione *m* cress.

crescita *f* growth.

cresima *f* confirmation.

cresimare *vt* to confirm.

crespo *m* crêpe; * *adj* fuzzy, frizzy.

cresta *f* crest; ridge.

cretino *m* cretin.

cric *m inv* jack.

cricca *f* clique.

criceto *m* hamster.

cricket *m* cricket.

criminale *m/f, adj* criminal, felon.

criminalità *f* crime.

crimine *m* felony.

crinale *m* ridge.

criniera *f* mane.

cripta *f* crypt.

crisi *f* crisis; turn.

cristalleria *f* glassware.

cristallino *adj* crystal-clear, cristalline.

cristallizzare *vt* to crystalize; * *vr* **~rsi** to crystallize.

cristallo *m* crystal.

cristianesimo *m* Christianity.

cristianità *f* Christianity, Christendom.

cristiano *m*, *adj* Christian.

Cristo *m* Christ.

criterio *m* criterion; yardstick.

critica *f* criticism.

criticare *vt* to criticize; to fault; to slate.

critico *m* critic, critique; * *adj* critical.

criticone *m* faultfinder.

crivellare *vt* to riddle.

croccante *adj* crisp, crunchy.

crocchetta *f* croquette.

croce *f* cross.

crociata *f* crusade.

crociato *m* crusader.

crociera *f* cruise.

crocifiggere *vt* to crucify.

crocifissione *f* crucifixion.

crocifisso *m* crucifix.

croco *m* crocus.

crogiolarsi *vr* to bask.

crogiolo *m* crucible.

crollare *vi* to collapse; to keel over; to slump.

crollo *m* collapse; slump.

cromatico *adj* chromatic.

cromato *adj*: **metallo ~** *m* chrome.

cronaca *f* chronicle.

cronico *adj* chronic.

cronista *m* reporter.

cronologia *f* chronology.

cronologico *adj* chronological.

cronometrare *vt* to time.

cronometro *m* chronometer; stopwatch.

croquet *m* croquet.

crosta *f* crust; scab.

crostaceo *m* crustacean, shellfish.

crostata *f* tart.

crotalo *m* rattlesnake.

cruciale *adj* crucial.

cruciverba *m inv* crossword.

crudele *adj* cruel; unkind

crudeltà *f* cruelty.

crudo *adj* raw; uncooked.

crumiro *m* blackleg; scab.

crup *m* croup.

crusca *f* bran.

cruscotto *m* dashboard.

cubico *adj* cubic.

cubo *m* cube.

cuccetta *f* couchette; bunk, berth; sleeper.

cucchiaiata *f* spoonful.

cucchiaino *m* teaspoon.

cucchiaio *m* spoon; **~ da portata** serving spoon.

cucciolata *f* litter.

cucciolo *m* pup, cub.

cucina *f* cooker, cookery; kitchen; **~ componibile** *f* fitted kitchen.

cucire *vt* to stitch, to sew; * *vi* to sew; **macchina da ~** *f* sewing machine.

cucito *m* needlework.

cucitrice *f* stapler.

cucitura *f* seam.

cuculo *m* cuckoo.

cuffia *f* earphones, headphones; bathing cap; bonnet.

cugino *m* cousin.

cui *rel pron* il **~** whose.

culinario *adj* culinary.

culla *f* crib, cradle, cot; **~ trasportabile** carrycot.

cullare *vt* to rock.

culminare *vi* to culminate.

culmine *m* culmination; acme; climax.

culo *m* (*sl*) bum, arse.

culto *m* cult.

cultura *f* culture, learning, edification.

culturale *adj* cultural.

cumino *m* caraway, cumin.

cumulativo *adj* cumulative.

cumulo *m* drift.

cuneo *m* wedge.

cunetta *f* dip; gutter.

cuocere *vt* to cook; **~ al forno**

to bake; **~ in bianco** to poach.

cuoco *m* cook.

cuoio *m* hide, leather; **~ capelluto** *m* scalp.

cuore *m* heart; **prendersi a ~** to befriend; **di ~** *adv* heartily; **dal ~ tenero** *adj* soft-hearted.

cupo *adj* gloomy, glum.

cupola *f* dome.

cura *f* cure; **aver ~ di** *vt* to groom.

curare *vt* to care for; to tend; to treat.

curato *m* curate.

curcuma *f* turmeric.

curiosare *vi* to browse; to snoop, to pry.

curiosità *f inv* curio; curiosity.

curioso *adj* curious; inquisitive, nos(e)y.

curriculum vitae *m inv* curriculum vitae.

curry *m* curry.

cursore *m* cursor.

curva *f* curve, bend, turn, turning.

curvare *vt* to curve.

curvatura *f* curvature; camber; warp.

cuscinetto *m* pad.

cuscino *m* cushion.

custode *m/f* custodian, attendant.

custodia *f* case; custody.

D

da *prep* to; out; off; since; from, by, for.

dado *m* die, dice; nut.

daino *m* deer; **femmina di ~** *f* doe; fallow deer.

dalia *f* dahlia.

daltonico *adj* colour-blind.

damigella *f* damsel; **~ d'onore** bridesmaid.

dandy *m* dandy.

dannazione *f* damnation.

danneggiare *vt* to harm, to hurt; to impair.

danno *m* harm; **danni** *mpl* breakage, havoc.

dannoso *adj* detrimental.

danza *f* dancing; **~ classica** ballet.

danzare *vi* to dance.

danze *f* dance.

dappertutto *adv* everywhere; throughout.

dapprima *adv* at first.

dardo *m* dart.

dare *vt* to give; **~ su** to overlook; * *vi* to give.

darsena *f* dock.

darsi *adv:* **può darsi** it may be.

data *f* date.

database *m* database.

datare *vt* to date.

dati *mpl* data.

dativo *m* dative.

datore *m:* **~ di lavoro** employer.

dattero *m* date.

dattilografia *f* typing.

dattilografo *m* typist.

dattiloscritto *m* typescript; * *adj* typewritten.

davanti *adv* ahead; * *prep* by; * *m* front, fore; * *adj* front.

davanzale *m* windowsill, sill, window ledge.

davvero *adv* really.

dazio *m* duty.

dea *f* goddess.

debilitare *vt* to debilitate.

debitamente *adv* duly.
debito *m* debt.
debitore *m* debtor.
debole *adj* weak, frail, feeble;
* *m* penchant; foible
debolezza *f* weakness, frailty,
feebleness.
debutto *m* debut.
decadente *adj* decadent.
decadenza *f* decadence.
decaffeinato *adj* decaffeinated.
decapitare *vt* to decapitate, to
behead.
decapitazione *f* decapitation.
decappottabile *adj, f* (*auto*)
convertible.
deceduto *adj* deceased.
decelerare *vt* to decelerate.
decennio *m* decade.
decente *adj* decent, proper.
decentramento *m* decentralization, devolution.
decenza *f* decency.
decesso *m* decease, demise.
decibel *m inv* decibel.
decidere *vt* to decide; to elect;
to resolve; **~ su** adjudicate.
deciduo *adj* deciduous.
decifrare *vt* to decipher.
decimale *adj, m* decimal.
decimare *vt* to decimate.
decimo *adj, m* tenth.
decisione *f* decision.
decisivo *adj* decisive.
deciso *adj* decided; set.
declamare *vt, vi* declaim.
declamazione *f* declamation.
declinare *vt, vi* to decline.
declinazione *f* declension.
declino *m* decline.
decodificare *vt* to decode.
decollare *vi* to take off.
decollato *adj* airborne.
decollo *m* takeoff
decomporre *vt* to decompose.
decomposizione *f* decomposition, decay.

decompressione *f* decompression.
decongestionante *m* decon-
gestant.
decorare *vt* to decorate, to
deck.
decorativo *adj* decorative.
decoratore *m* decorator.
decorazione *f* decoration; garnish.
decoro *m* decorum, propriety.
decoroso *adj* decorous, seemly.
decrepito *adj* decrepit.
decrescrere *vi* to decrease.
decretare *vt* to decree, to rule.
decreto *m* decree.
decurtare *vt* to dock.
dedica *f* dedication; inscription.
dedicare *vt* to dedicate, to devote; to give.
dedizione *f* dedication.
dedurre *vt* to deduce, to gather; to infer; to deduct.
deduzione *f* inference; deduction.
defecare *vi* to defecate.
deferente *adj* deferential, dutiful.
deferenza *f* deference.
defezionare *vi* to defect.
defezione *f* defection.
deficiente *adj* brainless.
deficit *m inv* deficit.
definibile *adj* definable.
definire *vt* to define; to class;
to settle; to finalize.
definitivo *adj* definitive, definite; firm.
definito *adj* defined; **ben ~**
clear-cut.
definizione *f* definition.
deflazione *f* deflation.
deflorare *vt* to deflower.
deformare *vt* to deform; to
warp.
deforme *adj* misshapen.
deformità *f* deformity.
defraudare *vt* to defraud.

defunto *adj* late.

degenerare *vi* to degenerate.

degenerato *adj, m* degenerate.

degenza *f* stay.

deglutizione *f* swallow.

degnarsi *vr* to deign, to condescend.

degradante *adj* degrading.

degradare *vt* to degrade, to demote.

degradazione *f* degradation.

degustazione *f* tasting; ~ **dei vini** *f* wine-tasting.

delegare *vt* to delegate, to depute.

delegato *m* delegate; commissioner.

delegazione *f* delegation.

delfino *m* dolphin.

deliberare *vi* to deliberate.

deliberazione *f* deliberation.

delicatezza *f* delicacy.

delicato *adj* delicate.

delimitare *vt* to delimit.

delineare *vt* to delineate.

delineazione *f* delineation.

delinquente *m* delinquent.

delinquenza *f* delinquency.

delinquenziale *adj* delinquent.

delirante *adj* delirious.

delirio *m* delirium.

delitto *m* crime.

delizia *f* delight.

delizioso *adj* charming, delightful, delicious, delectable, scrumptious.

delta *m inv* delta.

deltaplano *m* hang-gliding.

delucidare *vt* to elucidate.

deludente *adj* disappointing.

deludere *vt* to disappoint.

delusione *f* disappointment; comedown.

deluso *adj* disappointed.

demagogo *m* demagogue.

demarcazione *f* demarcation.

demistificare *vt* to debunk.

democratico *m, adj* democrat(ic).

democrazia *f* democracy.

demolire *vt* to demolish, to pull down, to knock down; to scrap.

demolizione *f* demolition.

demonio *m* demon, fiend.

demoralizzare *vt* to demoralize.

demoralizzato *adj* dispirited.

denaro *m* money; (stockings) denier.

denigrare *vt* to disparage.

denigratorio *adj* disparaging.

denominatore *m* denominator.

denotare *vt* to denote.

densità *f inv* density.

denso *adj* dense.

dente *m* tooth; cog; ~ **d'arresto** *m* ratchet; ~ **del giudizio** *m* wisdom tooth; **mal di denti** *m* toothache; ~ **di leone** *m* dandelion; **mettere i denti** *vi* to teethe.

dentiera *f* dentures.

dentifricio *m* toothpaste.

dentista *m/f* dentist.

dentistico *adj* dental.

dentro *prep* into; within; inside; * *adv* inside.

denudare *vt* to denude.

denuncia *f* denunciation.

denunciare *vt* to denounce; to report.

denutrito *adj* underfed, undernourished.

denutrizione *f* malnutrition.

deodorante *m* deodorant.

deodorare *vt* to deodorize.

deperibile *adj* perishable.

depilatore *m* hair remover.

depliant *m inv* brochure.

deplorare *vt* to deplore.

deplorevole *adj* deplorable; regrettable; sad.

deportare *vt* to deport.

deportazione *f* deportation.

depositante *m/f* depositor.

depositare *vt* to deposit; * *vr* ~**rsi** to settle.

deposito *m* deposit; depot; store; repository; warehouse; ~ **segreto** *m* cache, ~ **auto** *m* car pound.

deposizione *f* deposition; statement.

depravare *vt* to deprave.

depravato *adj* depraved.

depravazione *f* depravation.

deprecare *vt* to deprecate.

depredazione *f* depredation.

depressione *f* depression; low.

depresso *adj* depressed, downhearted.

deprezzamento *m* depreciation.

deprezzarsi *vr* to depreciate.

deprimente *adj* gloomy.

deprimere *vt* to depress.

depurare *vt* to purify.

depurazione *f* purification.

deputazione *f* deputation.

deragliare *vt*: **far** ~ to derail.

deretano *m* posterior.

deridere *vt* to deride.

derisione *f* derision.

deriva *f* drift; leeway; **alla** ~ *adj* adrift; **andare alla** ~ *vi* to drift.

derivare *vt* to derive; * *vi* ~ **da** to arise from.

derivato *adj*, *m* derivative.

derivazione *f* derivation.

dermatite *f* dermatitis.

dermatologia *f* dermatology.

derrick *m inv* derrick.

derubare *vt* to rob.

descrittivo *adj* descriptive.

descrivere *vt* to describe.

descrizione *f* description.

desertico *adj* desert.

deserto *m* desert; wilderness.

desiderabile *adj* desirable.

desiderare *vt* to desire; to wish; to want; to long for; to lust after; ~ **disperatamente** to crave; ~ **moltissimo** to hunger after; * *vi* to wish.

desiderio *m* desire; wish; longing; ~ **intenso** yearning; ~ **incontrollabile** *m* compulsion; **avere molto** ~ **di** *vt* to hanker after.

desideroso *adj* desirous, wishful.

designare *vt* to designate.

desinenza *f* ending.

desistere *vi* to desist.

desolato *adj* bleak, desolate, dreary.

desolazione *f* desolation.

despota *m* despot.

dessert *m inv* dessert, pudding.

destinare *vt* to intend; to earmark.

destinatario *m* recipient.

destinato *adj* destined.

destinazione *f* destination.

destino *m* destiny, fate, lot; doom.

destra *f* right.

destrezza *f* dexterity; ~ **di mano** *f* sleight of hand; **fare giochi di** ~ *vi* to juggle.

destro *adj* right; dext(e)rous.

detective *m*: ~ **privato** *m* private detective.

detenuto *m* inmate.

detenzione *f* detention; custody; ~ **preventiva** *f* remand.

deterioramento *m* deterioration.

deteriorarsi *vr* to deteriorate, to decay.

determinare *vt* to determine.

determinazione *f* determination, resolution.

deterrente *m* deterrent.

detersivo *m* detergent; soap powder.

detestabile *adj* detestable.

detestabile *adj* obnoxious, vile.

detestare *vt* to detest, to loathe.

detonare *vi* to detonate.

detonatore *m* detonator.

detonazione *f* detonation.

detrimento *m* detriment.

detriti *mpl* debris.

dettagliante *m* retailer.

dettagliare *vt* to detail.

dettaglio *m* detail; **al ~** *adj* (*com*) retail; **vendere al ~** *vt* to retail.

dettare *vt* to dictate.

dettatura *f* dictation.

detto *m* saying.

deturpare *vt* to blemish; to defile, to deface.

devastare *vt* to devastate; to ravage.

devastatore *adj* devastating.

devastazione *f* devastation; ravage.

deviare *vi* to deviate, to divert, to deflect.

deviatore *m* signalman.

deviazione *f* deviation, diversion, detour.

devolvere *vt* to devolve.

devoto *adj* devoted, devout.

devozione *f* devotion.

di *prep* of; any.

diabete *m* diabetes.

diabetico *adj, m* diabetic.

diabolico *adj* devilish, diabolical, fiendish.

diacono *m* deacon.

diadema *m* diadem, tiara.

diaframma *m* diaphragm; midriff.

diagnosi *f inv* diagnosis.

diagnosticare *vt* to diagnose.

diagnostico *adj* diagnostic.

diagonale *adj* diagonal.

diagramma *m* diagram.

dialetto *m* dialect.

dialisi *f* dialysis.

dialogo *m* dialogue.

diamantaio *m* diamond cutter.

diamante *m* diamond.

diametrale *adj* diametrical.

diametro *m* diameter.

diapason *m inv* tuning fork.

diapositiva *f* slide, transparency.

diario *m* diary.

diarrea *f* diarrhoea.

diavoletto *m* imp.

diavolo *m* devil.

dibattere *vt* to debate; * *vr* **~rsi** to flounder.

dibattito *m* debate.

dicembre *m* December.

diceria *f* hearsay.

dichiarare *vi* (cards) to bid; * *vt* to declare.

dichiarazione *f* declaration; pronouncement; statement; **~ dei redditi** *f* tax return.

diciannovesimo *adj, m* nineteenth.

diciassette *adj, m* seventeen.

diciassettesimo *adj, m* seventeenth.

diciottesimo *adj, m* eighteenth.

diciotto *adj, m* eighteen.

didattico *adj* educational, didactic.

dieci *adj, m inv* ten.

diesis *m* (*mus*) sharp; **in ~** *adv* (*mus*) sharp.

dieta *f* diet; **seguire una ~** *vi* to diet.

dietetico *adj* dietary.

dietro *prep* behind; * *m* back.

difendere *vt* to defend; to champion; to plead.

difensivo *adj* defensive.

difesa *f* defence.

difetto *m* defect; shortcoming; flaw, failing, fault.

difettoso *adj* defective, faulty, imperfect.

diffamare *vt* to libel, to vilify, to smear.

diffamatorio *adj* libellous.

diffamazione *f* defamation, libel.

differenza *f* difference.

differenziale *adj, m* differential.

differire *vi* to differ.

difficile *adj* difficult, hard, tricky, stiff.

difficoltà *f inv* difficulty.

diffidare *vt* to distrust, to mistrust.

diffidente *adj* distrustful, mistrustful, wary.

diffidenza *f* distrust, mistrust.

diffondere *vt* to diffuse; to popularize; * *vi* ~**rsi** to waft.

diffrazione *f* diffraction.

diffusione *f* diffusion.

diffuso *adj* widespread; prevalent; rife.

difterite *f* diphtheria.

diga *f* dyke.

digeribile *adj* digestible.

digerire *vt* to digest.

digestione *f* digestion.

digestivo *adj* digestive.

digitale *adj* digital; * *f* foxglove.

digiunare *vi* to fast.

digiuno *m* fast.

dignità *f* dignity.

dignitario *m* dignitary.

dignitoso *adj* dignified.

digressione *f* digression.

digrignare *vt:* ~ **i denti** to gnash one's teeth.

dilaniare *vt* to claw to pieces.

dilatare *vt* to dilate.

dilemma *m* dilemma.

dilettante *m/f* amateur.

dilettarsi *vr* to dabble.

diligente *adj* diligent, industrious.

diligenza *f* diligence.

diluire *vt* to dilute.

diluvio *m* deluge.

dimagrante *adj* slimming.

dimenare *vt* to wag; to waggle.

dimensione *f* dimension; **dimensioni** *fpl* size.

dimenticare *vi* to forget.

dimentico *adj* unmindful.

dimettersi *vr* to resign, to quit.

dimezzare *vt* to halve.

diminuire *vt* to diminish; to decrease; to lessen; to abate; * *vi* to decrease; to dwindle; to reduce; to lessen.

diminuzione *f* decrease.

dimissioni *fpl* resignation.

dimora *f* dwelling, abode.

dimorare *vi* to dwell.

dimostrabile *adj* demonstrable.

dimostrare *vt* to demonstrate; to prove.

dinamica *f* dynamics.

dinamico *adj* dynamic.

dinamismo *m* go, pep.

dinamitardo *m* bomber.

dinamite *f* dynamite.

dinamo *f inv* dynamo.

dinastia *f* dynasty.

dingo *m* dingo.

diniego *m* denial.

dinoccolato *adj* lanky; **camminare** ~ *vi* to slouch.

dinosauro *m* dinosaur.

dintorni *mpl* environs.

dio *m* god; **per amor di D~!** *excl* for God's sake!

diocesi *f inv* diocese.

dipanare *vt* to unravel.

dipendente *m/f* employee.

dipendenza *f* dependence, reliance.

dipendere *vi* to depend; ~ **da** to be contingent on.

dipingere *vt* to paint.

diploma *m* diploma.

diplomatico *m, adj* diplomat.

diplomato *adj* trained.

diplomazia *f* diplomacy.

dipsomania *f* dipsomania.

diradarsi *vr* to thin.

diramarsi *vr* to branch.

dire *vt* to speak; to tell; to say; **va detto che** *adv* admittedly; * *vi* to say.

direttamente *adv* directly; squarely; straight.

direttiva *f* directive.

direttive *fpl* guidelines.

diretto *adj* direct; first hand; non-stop; **~ a** *adv* bound for; **essere ~ a** *vi* to make for.

direttore *m* editor; (*mus*) conductor.

direttrice *f* manageress.

direzione *f* direction, way; leadership; administration.

dirigente *m/f* executive, director; * *adj* managerial.

dirigere *vt* to direct; to administer; (*mus*) to conduct; to run.

diritto *m* right; law; **~ civile** civil law; **~ comune** common law; **dare ~ a** *vt* to entitle; * *adj* right; straight; * *adv* straight.

diritti *mpl* dues; **~ d'autore** *mpl* copyright.

dirottamento *m* hijack.

dirottare *vt* to hijack.

dirottatore *m* hijacker.

dirotto *adj*: **piovere a ~** *vi* to pelt with rain; **sta piovendo a ~** it's pouring with rain.

disabitato *adj* uninhabited.

disaccordo *m* discord; **essere in ~** *vi* to disagree.

disadattato *m* misfit; maladjusted.

disadorno *adj* unadorned.

disagio *m* discomfort.

disamorato *adj* disaffected.

disapprovare *vi* to disapprove.

disapprovazione *f* disapproval, disfavour.

disarcionare *vt* to toss.

disarmante *adj* disarming.

disarmare *vt* to disarm.

disarmato *adj* unarmed.

disarmo *m* disarmament.

disastro *m* disaster; washout.

disastroso *adj* disastrous, dire, ruinous.

disattento *adj* inattentive, unheeding.

disattenzione *f* carelessness.

disavventura *f* misadventure.

discanto *m* descant.

discarica *f* dump, tip.

discendente *m/f* descendant.

discepolo *m* disciple.

discernere *vt* to discern.

discernimento *m* discrimination, discernment.

discesa *f* descent; **in ~** *adv* downhill.

dischetto *m* floppy disk.

disciplina *f* discipline.

disciplinare *adj* disciplinary.

disco *m* disc, discus; record; **~ volante** *m* flying saucer.

discolpa *f* exoneration.

discolpare *vt* to exonerate; to clear.

disconoscimento *m* disclaimer.

discordante *adj* discordant.

discordanza *f* disagreement; variance.

discordare *vi* to differ.

discordia *f*:**pomo della ~** *m* bone of contention.

discorsivo *m* discursive.

discorso *m* discourse, speech, address.

discoteca *f* disco.

discredito *m* discredit.

discrepanza *f* discrepancy.

discreto *adj* discreet; unobtrusive; fair.

discrezionale *adj* discretionary.

discrezione *f* discretion.

discriminazione *f* discrimination; **fare ~ tra** *vt* to discriminate.

discussione *f* discussion; argument.

discutere *vt* to discuss.

discutibile *adj* arguable, debatable, questionable.

disdegno *m* disdain.

disegnare *vt* to draw.

disegnatore *m* designer; **~ tecnico** *m* draughtsman.

disegno *m* drawing, design, picture, pattern.

diserbante *m* weedkiller.

diseredare *vt* to disinherit.

disertore *m* deserter.

diserzione *f* desertion.

disfare *vt* to undo, to unpack; * *vr* **~rsi di** to part with.

disfatta *f* rout.

disgelo *m* thaw.

disgrazia *f* misfortune.

disgraziato *adj* unlucky; wretched.

disgustare *vt* to disgust.

disgusto *m* disgust.

disgustoso *adj* disgusting; foul.

disidratare *vt* to dehydrate.

disidratato *adj* dehydrated.

disillusione *f* disenchantment.

disincantare *vt* to disenchant.

disincantato *adj* disenchanted.

disincarnato *adj* disembodied.

disinfettante *m* disinfectant.

disinfettare *vt* to disinfect.

disingannare *vt* to disillusion, to disabuse.

disinganno *m* disillusion.

disinnescare *vt* to defuse.

disinnestare *vt* to disengage.

disintegrarsi *vr* to disintegrate.

disinteressato *adj* disinterested.

disinvolto *adj* effortless; unconstrained; glib; nonchalant; **gioviale e ~** debonair.

disinvoltura *f* ease; aplomb.

dislessico *adj* word-blind.

disoccupato *adj* unemployed, jobless.

disoccupazione *f* unemployment.

disonestà *f* dishonesty.

disonesto *adj* dishonest; crooked.

disonorare *vt* to dishonour, to disgrace, to shame.

disonore *m* dishonour, disgrace.

disonorevole *adj* dishonourable, discreditable.

disordinato *adj* disorderly, untidy.

disordine *m* disorder, clutter, untidiness, mess; **in ~** in disarray.

disordini *mpl* (*pol*) disturbance, riot.

disorganizzato *adj* disorganized, unorganized.

disorganizzazione *f* disorganization.

disorientare *vt* to bewilder.

disorientato *adj* disorientated.

disossare *vt* to fillet.

dispari *adj inv* odd.

disparità *f inv* disparity.

dispendio *m* expenditure.

dispendioso *adj* extravagant, wasteful.

dispensa *f* dispensation; pantry, larder.

dispensare *vt* to dispense.

dispensario *m* dispensary.

dispepsia *f* dispepsia.

dispeptico *adj* dyspeptic.

disperare *vi* to despair.

disperato *adj* desperate, despairing, hopeless; **un caso ~** *m* a dead loss.

disperazione *f* despair, desperation.

disperdere *vt* to disperse; * *vr* **~rsi** to scatter.

dispersione *f* dispersal.

dispetto *m* spite; **far ~ a** *vt* to spite.

dispettoso *adj* spiteful.

dispiacente *adj* sorry.

dispiacere *vt* to displease; * *vr* **~rsi** to be sorry, to regret; * *m* chagrin, displeasure.

disponibile *adj* available; disposable.

disponibilità f willingness.

disporre vt to dispose; * vi ~ **di** to command.

dispositivo m device.

disposizione f arrangement; layout; ~ **naturale** f flair.

disposto adj disposed, willing; ~ **a fare** prepared to do.

dispotico adj domineering, despotic.

dispotismo m despotism.

disprezzare vt to despise; to scorn.

disprezzo m contempt, scorn.

disputa f dispute, contention.

disputarsi vr to dispute.

disquisizione f disquisition.

disseminare vt to disseminate.

dissenso m dissension, dissent.

dissenteria f dysentery.

dissentire vi to dissent.

dissertazione f dissertation.

dissidente m dissenter, dissident.

dissimile adj dissimilar, unlike.

dissimulazione f dissimulation.

dissipare vt to disssipate, to dispel; to allay.

dissipazione f dissipation.

dissociare vt to dissociate.

dissolutezza f debauchery.

dissoluto adj debauched, dissolute, loose, rakish.

dissolvere vt to dissolve.

dissomiglianza f dissimilarity.

dissonanza f dissonance.

dissotterrare vt to unearth.

dissuadere vt to deter, to dissuade.

distaccamento m detachment; secondment.

distaccare vt to second.

distaccato adj withdrawn, cool.

distacco m detachment.

distante adj distant; * adv off; * adj far.

distanza f distance; **a ~** adv apart.

distanziare vt to distance, to space.

distendersi vr to unwind.

distensione f detente.

distesa f expanse, stretch; tract.

disteso adj recumbent; outstretched.

distico m couplet.

distillare vt to distil.

distillazione f distillation.

distilleria f distillery.

distinguere vt to distinguish, to differentiate, to discriminate.

distintivo m badge.

distinto adj distinct.

distinzione f distinction; **senza distinzioni** adv regardless.

distogliere vt to remove; ~ **da** to avert from.

distorcere vt to distort.

distorsione f distortion.

distrarre vt to distract, to divert.

distratto adj distracted; forgetful; absent-minded.

distrazione f distraction; absent-mindedness, oversight; amusement.

distretto m district.

distribuire vt to distribute; to give out.

distributore m distributor; ~ **automatico** m vending machine.

distribuzione f distribution.

districare vt to extricate.

distruggere vt to destroy; to wreck.

distruttivo adj destructive.

distrutto adj destroyed; shattered, zonked.

distruzione f destruction.

disturbare vt to disturb; to trouble.

disturbo m disturbance; static; **fare azione di ~** vt to heckle.

disubbidiente adj disobedient, naughty.

disubbidienza f disobedience.

disubbidire vt to disobey.

disuguale adj unequal.

disuso m disuse; **essere in ~** vi to be in abeyance; **cadere in ~** vi to fall into disuse.

ditale m thimble.

dito m finger; **~ del piede** m toe.

ditta f firm.

dittatore m dictator.

dittatoriale adj dictatorial.

dittatura f dictatorship.

dittongo m diphthong.

diuretico adj diuretic.

divagare vi to digress, to ramble.

divampare vi to blaze, to flame.

divano m couch, settee.

divenire vi to become.

diventare vi to become; **~ grande** to grow up.

divergente adj divergent.

divergenza f divergence.

divergere vi to diverge.

diversamente adv otherwise, other than.

diversificare vi to diversify.

diversità f diversity.

diverso adj different; **diversi** adj sundry.

divertente adj amusing, entertaining.

divertimento m amusement, enjoyment, fun.

divertire vt amuse; * vr **~rsi** to enjoy oneself, to have a good time.

dividendo m dividend.

dividere vt to divide, to split, to share.

divieto m ban.

divinità f divinity, godhead, deity.

divino adj divine, heavenly, godlike.

divisa f uniform, strip.

divisibile adj divisible.

divisione f division.

diviso adj divided.

divisore m divisor.

divo m star; **~ del cinema** m film star.

divorare vt to devour, to wolf.

divorziare vt, vi to divorce.

divorziato adj divorced; * m divorcee.

divorzio m divorce.

divulgare vt to divulge; to leak.

dizionario m dictionary; **~ dei sinonimi** m thesaurus.

dizione f diction, elocution.

doccia f shower; **fare la ~** vi to shower.

docente adj teaching; * m **~ universitario** lecturer, don.

docile adj docile.

documentare vt to document.

documentario adj, m documentary.

documento m document; **documenti** mpl papers.

dodicesimo adj, m twelfth.

dodici adj, m inv twelve.

dogana f customs; **esente da ~** adj duty free.

doganiere m customs officer.

doglie fpl labour; **avere le ~** vi to be in labour.

dogma m dogma.

dogmatico adj dogmatic, opinionated.

dolce adj sweet; gentle; soft; **dalla voce ~** adv soft-spoken; * m sweet, pudding.

dolcemente adv gently.

dolcezza f sweetness.

dolcificante m sweetener.

dolciumi mpl confectionery.

dollaro m dollar.

dolore m ache, pain; grief, sorrow, woe; **~ acuto** m pang;

immenso ~ *m* heartbreak; ~ **atroce** *m* agony.

doloroso *adj* painful, sore.

domanda *f* question; inquiry; query; application; **fare una** ~ *vi* to ask a question.

domandarsi *vt* to wonder.

domani *adv*, *m inv* tomorrow.

domare *vt* to tame.

domenica *f* Sunday, Sabbath.

domestico *adj* domestic; * *m* servant.

domicilio *m* abode, domicile.

dominante *adj* dominant, uppermost.

dominare *vt* to dominate; to control; to subdue; to master.

dominazione *f* domination.

dominio *m* dominion, domain, domino.

donare *vt* to donate.

donatore *m* contributor; donor; ~ **di sangue** blood donor.

donazione *f* endowment, donation.

donchisciottesco *adj* quixotic.

dondolare *vt* to swing; to dangle; * *vi* to swing; to rock.

dondolo *adj*: **sedia a** ~ *f* rocking chair.

dongiovanni *m inv* ladykiller.

donna *f* woman; ~ **d'affari** *f* businesswoman.

donnaiolo *m* philanderer.

donnola *f* weasel.

dono *m* gift; ~ **del cielo** *m* godsend.

dopo *prep* after; * *adv* after; next; ~**tutto** after all; afterwards.

dopobarba *m inv* aftershave.

doppiamente *adv* doubly.

doppiare *vt* to dub.

doppio *adj* dual, double; twofold; **camera doppia** *f* double room; understudy.

dorare *vt* to gild.

doratura *f* gilding, gilt.

dormire *vi* to sleep, to slumber.

dormitorio *m* dormitory.

dorso *m* backstroke.

dosare *vt* to dose.

dose *f* dose.

dossier *m inv* dossier; (*law*) brief.

dotare *vt* to endow.

dotato *adj* gifted.

dote *f* dowry; accomplishment; **doti** *fpl* abilities.

dotto *adj* scholarly.

dottore *m* doctor; (*univ*) bachelor.

dottoressa *f* (*univ*) bachelor.

dottrina *f* doctrine.

dottrinale *m* doctrinal.

double-face *adj* reversible.

dove *adv* where, whereabouts; * *conj* where.

dovere *mod.vb* to have to; to owe; **io devo** I must; * *m* stint.

dovunque *conj* wherever.

dovuto *adj* due.

dozzina *f* dozen.

draga *f* dredge.

dragamine *m inv* minesweeper.

dragare *vt* to drag, to dredge.

drago *m* dragon.

dragoncello *m* tarragon.

dramatico *adj* dramatic.

dramma *m* drama.

drammatizzare *vt* to dramatize.

drammaturgo *m* playwright, dramatist.

drappeggiare *vt* to drape.

drappo *m* cloth; ~ **funebre** *m* pall.

drastico *adj* drastic.

drenaggio *m* drain, drainage.

drenare *vt* to drain.

dribbling *m* dribble.

dritto *adj* erect; * *adv* upright.

droga *f* drug, dope; spice.

drogare *vt* to drug; to spice.

drogato *m* addict, junkie.

dubbio *adj* dubious; * *m* doubt.
dubitare *vt* to doubt.
duca *m* duke.
duchessa *f* duchess.
due *m* two; * *adj* two; **tutti e ~** both; **a ~ porte** two-door; * *adv* **~ volte** twice.
duello *m* duel.
duetto *m* duet.
dumping *m* dumping.
duna *f* dune.
duodenale *adj* duodenal.
duodeno *m* duodenum.
duplicare *vt* to duplicate.

duplicato *m* duplicate.
duplice *adj* dual.
duplicità *f* duplicity.
durante *prep* during.
durare *vi* to last, to wear.
durata *f* length, duration.
duraturo *adj* enduring, lasting.
durevole *adj* durable.
durevolezza *f* durability.
durezza *f* hardness.
duro *adj* hard, stiff; trying; **~ d'orecchio** hard of hearing; **~ di cuore** hard-hearted.

E

e *conj* and.
ebanista *m/f* cabinet-maker.
ebano *m* ebony.
ebbrezza *f* intoxication.
ebollizione *f* boiling; **punto di ~** *m* boiling point.
ebraico *adj, m* Hebrew.
ebrea *f* Jewess.
ebreo *m* Jew, Hebrew; * *adj* Jewish, Hebrew.
eccedenza *f* excess; **~ di popolazione** *f* overspill.
eccedere *vt* to exceed.
eccellente *adj* excellent.
eccellenza *f* excellence; **la Sua E~** His Excellency.
eccentricità *f* eccentricity.
eccentrico *m* eccentric; crank; freak; * *adj* eccentric.
eccessivamente *adv* unduly.
eccessivo *adj* excessive, inordinate.
eccesso *m* excess.
eccetto *prep* except.
eccezionale *adj* grand; outstanding; exceptional; bumper; preeminent; swell.

eccezionalmente *adv* uniquely; extra.
eccezione *f* exception.
eccitabile *adj* excitable.
eccitare *vt* to excite.
eccitato *adj* excited.
eccitazione *f* excitement.
ecclesiastico *adj* ecclesiastical.
echeggiare *vi* to echo.
eclettico *adj* eclectic.
eclissare *vt* to eclipse; to outshine, to overshadow; to dwarf.
eclissi *f inv* eclipse.
eco *m/f* echo.
ecografia *f* ultrasound, scan.
ecologia *f* ecology.
economia *f* economy, economics; **fare ~** *vi* to economize.
economico *adj* economical, inexpensive.
economista *m/f* economist.
economo *m* bursar.
eczema *m* eczema.
edera *f* ivy.
edificare *vt* to edify.
edificio *m* building, edifice.

editore *m* publisher.
editoria *f* publishing.
editoriale *m* editorial.
editto *m* edict.
edizione *f* edition.
edonismo *m* hedonism.
educare *vt* to educate.
educato *adj* polite.
educazione *f* education; politeness; upbringing; **(buona)** ~ *f* breeding, good manners; ~ **fisica** *f* physical education.
effeminatezza *f* effeminacy.
effeminato *adj* effeminate.
effervescente *adj* effervescent, fizzy.
effervescenza *f* fizz.
effettivo *adj* actual; virtual.
effetto *m* effect; spin (of ball); ~ **sonoro** *m* sound effect; **effetti personali** *mpl* belongings; **non fare più** ~ *vi* to wear off;
effettuare *vt* to effect.
efficace *adj* effective, effectual.
efficacia *f* effectiveness, efficacy.
efficiente *adj* efficient; business-like.
efficienza *f* efficiency.
effigie *f* effigy.
effimero *adj* ephemeral.
eglefino *m* haddock.
egli *pron.*
ego *m* ego.
egocentrico *adj* self-centred.
egoismo *m* egoism, selfishness.
egoista *m/f* egoist; * *adj* selfish.
egotismo *m* egotism.
egotista *m/f* egotist.
egualitario *adj* egalitarian.
eiaculare *vt* to ejaculate.
eiaculazione *f* ejaculation.
elaborare *vt* to elaborate; to evolve; to hatch (a plot).
elaborato *adj* fancy.
elaboratore *m* computer.
elaborazione *f* elaboration; ~

dei dati *f* data processing; ~ **della parola** *f* word processing.
elasticità *f* elasticity, stretch.
elastico *adj* elastic; resilient; * *m* elastic; rubber band.
elefante *m* elephant.
elegante *adj* elegant; dressy; smart; snappy; stylish; posh; **abiti eleganti** *mpl* finery.
elegantemente *adv* smartly.
eleganza *f* elegance, smartness.
eleggere *vt* to elect.
eleggibile *adj* elegible.
eleggibilità *f* elegibility.
elegia *f* elegy.
elementare *adj* elementary.
elemento *m* element.
elemosina *f* alms.
elencare *vt* to list.
elenco *m* list; directory; ~ **telefonico** *m* telephone directory/book.
elettorale *adj* electoral; **fare un giro** ~ *vt* to canvass.
elettorato *m* electorate.
elettore *m* constituent, voter.
elettricista *m* electrician.
elettricità *f* electricity.
elettrico *adj* electric(al); * *m* **impianto** ~ wiring.
elettrificare *vt* to electrify.
elettrodo *m* electrode.
elettrolisi *f* electrolysis.
elettrone *m* electron.
elettronica *f* electronics.
elettronico *adj* electronic.
elevare *vt* to elevate.
elevazione *f* elevation.
elezione *f* election.
elezioni *fpl* elections; ~ **legislative** *fpl* general election; ~ **suppletive** *fpl* bye-election.
elica *f* screw, propeller.
elicottero *m* helicopter, chopper.
eliminare *vt* to eliminate; to remove.

eliminazione f elimination; disposal; removal.

elio m helium.

elisir m inv elixir.

élite f inv élite.

ella pron she.

ellittico adj elliptic(al).

elogio m eulogy; praise.

eloquente adj eloquent.

eloquenza f eloquence.

eludere vt to elude; to evade; to sidestep.

emaciato adj emaciated; gaunt.

emanare vt to exude; to shed.

emancipare vt to emancipate.

emancipazione f emancipation.

emarginato m drop-out; outcast.

ematologia f haematology.

embargo m embargo.

emblema m emblem.

emblematico adj emblematic.

embolia f bends.

embrione m embryo.

emendamento m amendment.

emendare vt amend.

emergenza f emergency.

emergere vi to emerge.

emetico m emetic.

emettere vt to emit; to issue; to release.

emicrania f migraine.

emigrante m/f emigrant.

emigrare vi to emigrate.

emigrazione f emigration.

eminente adj eminent; great; distinguished.

eminenza f eminence.

emirato m emirate.

emisfero m hemisphere.

emissario m emissary.

emissione f emission; issue; release.

emittente f transmitter.

emofilia f haemophilia.

emoglobia f haemaglobin.

emolumento m emolument.

emorragia f bleeding; haemorrhage; ~ **nasale** f nosebleed.

emorroidi fpl haemorrhoids, piles.

emotivo adj emotional (person), emotive (film, etc).

emozionante adj exciting.

emozionato adj excited; agog with excitement.

emozione f emotion.

empietà f impiety.

empio adj impious; godless.

empirico adj empirical.

emù m inv emu.

emulare vt to emulate.

emulsionare vt to emulsify.

emulsione f emulsion.

enciclica f encyclical.

enciclopedia f encyclopaedia.

encomio m commendation.

endemico adj endemic.

endovenoso adj intravenous.

energia f energy.

energico adj energetic, spirited; strenuous.

enfasi f emphasis, stress.

enfatico adj emphatic.

enigma m enigma.

enigmatico adj enigmatic, cryptic.

ennesimo adj umpteenth.

enorme adj enormous, huge, tremendous, terrific.

enormità f immensity.

ente m corporation.

enterite f entiritis.

entità f inv entity.

entourage m inv entourage.

entrambi adj both; either.

entrare vi to enter, to go in, to come in; **lasciare** ~ to admit; * vt to enter, to go in; **questo non c'entra** this doesn't enter into it.

entrata f entrance, entry, hall.

entroterra m (Australia) outback; **nell'**~ adv inland.

entusiasmare *vt* to thrill; * *vr* ~**rsi** to enthuse.

entusiasmo *m* enthusiasm, keenness, zest.

entusiasta *adj* keen.

enumerare *vt* to enumerate.

enunciare *vt* to enunciate.

enzima *m* enzyme.

epatite *f* hepatitis.

epico *adj* epic.

epidemia *f* epidemic.

epidemico *adj* epidemic.

Epifania *f* Epiphany.

epilessia *f* epilepsy.

epilettico *adj, m* epileptic

epilogo *m* epilogue.

episcopale *adj* episcopal.

episcopaliano *adj, m* Episcopalian.

episodio *m* episode, incident.

epistola *f* epistle.

epiteto *m* epithet.

epoca *f* epoch, day, age.

epopea *f* epic.

equatore *m* equator.

equatoriale *adj* equatorial.

equazione *f* equation.

equestre *adj* equestrian.

equidistante *adj* equidistant.

equilatero *adj* equilateral.

equilibrato *adj* level-headed.

equilibrio *m* equilibrium; balance; **tenere in** ~ *vt* to balance.

equinozio *m* equinox.

equipaggiamento *m* kit.

equipaggiare *vt* to fit out.

equipaggio *m* crew.

équipe *f inv* team; **lavoro d'**~ *m* teamwork.

equità *f* equity.

equitazione *f* riding; horsemanship; **scuola di** ~ *f* riding school.

equivalente *m/f* counterpart; * *adj* equivalent.

equivalere *vi* to be tantamount.

equivoco *m* misapprehension; * *adj* equivocal; underhand; **giocare sull'**~ *vi* to equivocate.

equo *adj* equitable.

era *f* era, age, time.

eradicare *vt* to root out.

erba *f* grass; (marijuana) pot; ~ **cipollina** chives; ~ **aromatica** *f* herb; **in** ~ budding.

erbaccia *f* weed.

erbaceo *adj* herbaceous.

erbivoro *adj, m* herbivorous.

erborista *m/f* herbalist.

erboso *adj* grassy.

erede *m* heir, heiress.

eredità *f* heredity, heritage; inheritance, legacy; **lasciare in** ~ *vt* to bequeath.

ereditare *vt* to inherit.

ereditario *adj* hereditary.

eremita *m* hermit.

eremitaggio *m* hermitage.

eresia *f* heresy.

eretico *adj, m* heretic.

erezione *f* erection.

ergastolo *m* life imprisonment.

erica *f* heather.

erigere *vt* to erect, to raise.

ermellino *m* ermine, stoat.

ermetico *adj* hermetic; airtight.

ernia *f* hernia.

erodere *vt* to erode.

eroe *m* hero.

eroico *adj* heroic.

eroina *f* heroin; heroine.

eroismo *m* heroism.

erotico *adj* erotic.

erpice *m* harrow.

erroneamente *adv* wrongly.

erroneo *adj* erroneous.

errore *m* error; mistake; fallacy; ~ **di stampa** *m* erratum, misprint; ~ **giudiziario** *m* miscarriage of justice;

erudito *adj* erudite.

erudizione *f* erudition, scholarship.

eruzione f eruption; **essere in ~** vi to erupt.

esacerbare vt to exacerbate.

esagerare vt to exaggerate; to overstate; to overdo; to stretch.

esagerato adj undue.

esagerazione f exaggeration.

esagonale adj hexagonal.

esagono m hexagon.

esalazione f fume.

esaltare vt to exalt.

esaltato adj exalted.

esame m examination; test; **~ di guida** m driving test; **~ di ammissione** m entrance examination.

esaminare vt to examine; to vet; to survey; **~ a fondo** to follow up.

esaminatore m examiner.

esangue adj bloodless.

esasperante adj aggravating.

esasperare vt to exasperate.

esasperazione f exasperation.

esattamente adv exactly.

esattezza f accuracy, exactness, exactitude.

esatto adj exact, accurate, spot-on.

esattore m (tax) collector; **~ delle imposte** m tax collector.

esauriente adj exhaustive, comprehensive.

esaurientemente adv at length.

esaurimento m exhaustion; **~ nervoso** m nervous breakdown.

esaurire vt to deplete; to exhaust.

esaurito adj exhausted; spent; out of print.

esca f bait.

eschimese adj Eskimo; **cane ~** m husky (dog).

esclamare vt to exclaim, to ejaculate.

esclamazione f exclamation, ejaculation.

escludere vt to exclude, to debar, to except.

esclusione f exclusion.

esclusivo adj exclusive, select; sole.

escogitare vt to devise; to contrive; to think up.

escrementi mpl excrement; (animals) droppings.

escursione f excursion; outing; ramble; **~ a piedi** f hike; **fare escursioni** vi to ramble.

escursionista m/f rambler.

esecrabile adj execrable.

esecutivo adj executive.

esecutore m executor.

esecuzione f execution.

eseguire vt to do, to execute; to perform.

esempio m example, instance.

esemplare adj exemplary.

esemplificare vt to exemplify.

esentare vt to exempt.

esente adj exempt.

esenzione f exemption.

esercitare vt to exercise; to drill; to exert; to ply; * vr **~rsi** to practise.

esercitazione f drill.

esercito m military, army.

esercizio m exercise, practice.

esibirsi vr to appear; to perform.

esibizionista m/f show-off.

esigente adj exacting, demanding.

esigenza f requirement.

esigere vt to expect; to demand; to exact.

esile adj slim.

esiliare vt to exile.

esilio m exile.

esistante adj halting.

esistente adj existent; extant.

esistenza f existence.

esistenziale adj existential.

esistenzialismo *m* existentialism.

esistere *vi* to exist.

esitante *adj* hesitant; tentative.

esitare *vi* to hestitate; to dither.

esitazione *f* hesitation.

esito *m* outcome.

esodo *m* exodus.

esofago *m* oesophagus.

esonerare *vt* to excuse.

esorbitante *adj* exorbitant; extortionate.

esorcismo *m* exorcism.

esorcizzare *vt* to exorcise.

esortare *vt* to exhort.

esoterico *adj* esoteric.

esotico *adj* exotic.

espandere *vt* to expand.

espansione *f* expansion.

espansivo *adj* expansive, effusive, gushing, demonstrative.

espatriato *adj, m* expatriate.

espediente *m* expedient.

espellere *vt* to expel; to eject.

esperienza *f* experience.

esperimentare *vt* to experience.

esperimento *m* experiment.

esperto *adj* accomplished; experienced; expert; * *m* expert; adept; troubleshooter; pundit.

espiare *vi* to atone for.

espiazione *f* atonement.

espirare *vt* to exhale.

esplicativo *adj* explanatory.

esplicitamente *adv* specifically.

esplicito *adj* explicit.

esplodere *vi* to explode; * *vt* to blow up.

esplorare *vt* to explore; to prospect.

esploratore *m* explorer.

esplorazione *f* exploration.

esplosione *f* explosion; blast.

esplosivo *adj, m* explosive.

esponente *m/f* exponent.

esporre *vt* to expose; to exhibit; to display; to show; to expound.

esportare *vt* to export.

esportatore *m* exporter.

esportazione *f* export.

esposimetro *m* exposure meter.

espositore *m* exhibitor.

esposizione *f* display, exposition; show; exposure.

esposto *adj* exposed.

espressione *f* expression.

espressivo *adj* expressive.

espresso *adj* express.

esprimere *vt* to express; to air; to phrase; to voice; * *vr* ~rsi to express oneself; **chi non sa** ~ *adj* inarticulate.

espropriare *vt* to expropriate.

esproprio *m* expropriation.

espulsione *f* expulsion, ejection.

espurgare *vt* to expurgate; to bowdlerize.

essenza *f* essence.

essenziale *adj* essential.

essenzialmente *adv* primarily.

essere *vi* to be; * *m* being.

essi *pers pron* they.

essiccare *vt* to dry.

essiccato *adj* dried; desiccated.

essistenza *f* being.

esso *m* it.

est *m* east; * *adv* verso ~ eastwards.

estasi *f inv* ecstasy; rapture; **mandare in** ~ *vt* to entrance.

estasiare *vt* to enrapture; to ravish.

estasiato *adj* rapturous.

estate *f* summer; **piena** ~ *f* midsummer.

estatico *adj* ecstatic.

estendersi *vr* to reach; to range; ~ **disordinatamente** to straggle.

estensione *f* extent.

estenuante *adj* gruelling; wearisome.

esterno *adj* external, exterior; outside; outward; outer; * *m* external, exterior; outside; **collaboratore ~** *m* freelance.

estero *adj* foreign; overseas; **all'~** *adv* overseas; **andare all'~** *vi* to go abroad.

esteso *adj* extensive.

estetico *adj* aesthetic.

estinguere *vt* to quench; to write off.

estinto *adj* extinct.

estintore *m* extinguisher; fire extinguisher.

estinzione *f* extinction.

estirpare *vt* to extirpate.

estorcere *vt* to extort.

estorsione *f* extortion.

estradare *vt* to extradite.

estradizione *f* extradition.

estramurale *adj* extramural.

estraneo *adj* foreign; alien; extraneous; * *m* outsider.

estrarre *vi* to abstract; * *vt* to mine; to draw; to extract.

estratto *m* excerpt.

estrazione *f* extraction; draw; **~ mineraria** *f* mining.

estremamente *adv* highly; exceedingly.

estremista *m/f* extremist.

estremità *f* end, extremity.

estremo *adj* far; extreme; utmost; * *m* extreme.

estrinseco *adj* extrinsic.

estrogeno *m* oestrogen.

estroverso *adj*, *m* extrovert.

estuario *m* estuary.

esuberante *adj* exuberant.

esuberanza *f* exuberance.

esule *m/f* exile.

esultante *adj* elated, jubilant.

esultanza *f* elation, jubilation.

esultare *vi* to exult.

esumare *vt* to exhume.

età *f inv* age.

etere *m* ether.

eternamente *adv* forever.

eternità *f* eternity.

eterno *adj* eternal; everlasting; timeless.

eterodosso *adj* unorthodox.

eterogeneo *adj* heterogeneous.

eterosessuale *adj*, straight; *m/f* heterosexual; *(fam)* straight.

etica *f* ethics.

etichetta *f* label; tag; etiquette.

etico *adj* ethical.

etimologia *f* etymology.

etimologico *adj* etymological.

etnico *adj* ethnic.

eucalipto *m* gum tree; eucalyptus.

Eucaristia *f* Eucharist.

eufemismo *m* euphemism.

euforia *f* euphoria.

eunuco *m* eunuch.

eutanasia *f* euthanasia.

evacuare *vt* to evacuate.

evacuazione *f* evacuation.

evadere *vi* to escape; to break out; to abscond; * *vt* to evade.

evidente *adj* apparent.

evangelico *adj* evangelic(al).

evangelista *m* evangelist.

evaporare *vi* to evaporate.

evaporazione *f* evaporation.

evasione *f* evasion; escape; breakout; escapism.

evasivo *adj* evasive; non-committal.

evento *m* occurrence.

eventuale *adj* eventual.

eventualità *f* eventuality.

evidente *adj* evident; plain; overt.

evitabile *adj* avoidable.

evitare *vt* to avoid; to shun; to miss; to eschew.

evocare *vt* to evoke.

evocativo *adj* evocative.

evoluzione *f* evolution.

evolversi *vr* to evolve.

extra *adj* extra.

extra-coniugale *adj* extramarital.

extrasensoriale *adj* extrasensory.

extraterrestre *m* alien.

F

fa *adv* ago; **quanto tempo ~?** how long ago?

fabbrica *f* factory; mill; works; **~ di birra** brewery.

fabbricante *m* manufacturer; **~ di birra** brewer.

fabbricare *vt* to manufacture; to make; to fabricate.

fabbricazione *f* manufacture; fabrication.

fabbro *m* smith; blacksmith; locksmith.

faccenda *f* chore; matter; affair; **faccende** *fpl* housework.

facchino *m* porter.

faccia *f* face; side; **~ tosta** *f* cheek (impudence); **a ~ in giù** *adj* prone.

facciale *adj* facial.

facciata *f* facade.

faceto *adj* facetious.

facile *adj* easy; effortless.

facilità *f* facility; easiness.

facilitare *vt* to facilitate; to ease.

facilmente *adv* easily.

facoltà *f inv* faculty; school.

facoltativo *adj* optional.

facsimile *m* facsimile; fax.

factotum *m* dogsbody.

faesite *f* hardboard.

faggio *m* beech.

fagiano *m* pheasant.

fagiolino *m* French bean.

fagiolo *m* bean; **~ bianco** *m* haricot.

faglia *f* (*geol*) fault.

fagotto *m* bassoon; bundle;

fare un ~ di *vt* to bundle.

fai da te *m* do-it-yourself.

faida *f* feud.

falce *f* scythe, sickle.

falciare *vt* to mow, to scythe.

falciatrice *f* mower.

falco *m* hawk, falcon; **~ pescatore** *m* osprey.

falconiera *f* falconry.

falegname *m* carpenter, joiner.

falegnameria *f* carpentry, joinery, woodwork.

falla *f* hole.

fallace *adj* fallacious.

fallibile *adj* fallible.

fallibilità *f* fallibility.

fallico *adj* phallic.

fallimento *m* failure.

fallire *vi* to fail, to abort, to backfire.

fallito *adj* abortive; bankrupt; * *m* bankrupt.

fallo *m* foul.

falò *m* bonfire.

falsificare *vt* to falsify, to fake, to fiddle; to cook (the books).

falsità *f* falsity, untruth.

falso *adj* false, fake, hollow, deceitful, dud, two-faced, untrue, spurious.

fama *f* fame.

fame *f* hunger; **sciopero della ~** *m* hunger strike; **aver ~** *vi* to be hungry; **morire di ~** *vi* to starve.

famelico *adj* ravenous.

famigerato *adj* notorious.

famiglia *f* family, household.

familiare *adj* familiar; homely; colloquial; **espressione ~** *f* colloquialism.

familiarità *f* familiarity.

familiarizzarsi *vr* to familiarize.

famoso *adj* famous, famed, noted.

fan *m* fan.

fanale *m* headlight.

fanatico *m* fanatic; buff; bigot; * *adj* fanatic; bigoted; hooked.

fanatismo *m* fanaticism.

fanciulla *f* maiden.

fanciullesco *adj* boyish.

fanciullo *m* boy.

fanello *m* linnet.

fanfara *f* fanfare.

fanfaronata *f* bluster.

fango *m* mud.

fangoso *adj* muddy.

fannullone *m* bum; layabout.

fantascienza *f* science fiction.

fantasia *f* fantasy.

fantasioso *adj* fanciful; whimsical.

fantasma *m* ghost, apparition, phantom; spook; * *adj* phantom; **abitato dai fantasmi** haunted.

fantasticare *vi* to fantasize.

fantasticheria *f* reverie.

fantastico *adj* fantastic, super.

fante *m* jack, knave.

fanteria *f* infantry.

fantino *m* jockey.

farabutto *m* scoundrel.

faraone *m* Pharoah.

farcire *vt* to stuff.

fare *vt* to do; to make; **~ lo stupido** to act the fool; * *vt, vi* **~ male** to hurt.

faretra *f* quiver.

farfalla *f* bow tie; butterfly.

farina *f* flour; meal.

farinoso *adj* powdery.

farmaceutico *adj* pharmaceutical.

farmacia *f* dispensary, pharmacy.

farmacista *m/f* chemist, pharmacist.

farneticare *vi* to rave.

faro *m* lighthouse; beacon; **~ antinebbia** *m* foglamp.

farsa *f* farce.

farsi *vr* to get.

fascia *f* bandage.

fascia *f* sling.

fasciare *vt* to strap.

fascino *m* glamour, fascination, allure, charm, mystique.

fascio *m* sheaf.

fascismo *m* fascism.

fascista *m/f* fascist.

fase *f* phase.

fastidio *m* annoyance.

fastidioso *adj* troublesome.

fasto *m* pomp.

fasullo *adj* bogus, fake, phoney.

fata *f* fairy.

fatale *adj* fatal; vital.

fatalismo *m* fatalism.

fatica *f* fatigue; toil.

faticare *vi* to labour, to toil, to slog.

faticata *f* slog.

faticoso *adj* strenuous, uphill, tough, tiring, laborious.

fatidico *adj* fateful.

fatiscente *adj* derelict.

fattibile *adj* workable.

fattibilità *f* feasibility.

fatto *pp* done; * *m* fact; * *adj* **ben ~** shapely.

fattore *m* bailiff; factor.

fattoria *f* farm; **piccola ~** (*Scot*) croft .

fattorino *m* errand boy.

fattura *f* bill, invoice; workmanship.

fatturare *vt* to invoice.

fatuo *adj* fatuous.

fauna *f* fauna.

fautore *m* campaigner.

fava *f* broad bean.

favo *m* honeycomb.

favola *f* fable.

favoloso *adj* fabulous.

favore *m* favour; **a ~ di** *prep* for.

favorevole *adj* favourable; auspicious.

favorire *vt* to favour, to further, to farther; to advance; to be conducive to.

favoritismo *m* favouritism.

favorito *adj* favoured, favourite.

fax *m* fax.

fazione *f* faction.

fazzolettino *m*: **~ di carta** tissue.

fazzoletto *m* handkerchief.

fazzolettone *m* bandanna.

febbraio *m* February.

febbre *f* fever.

febbrile *adj* feverish.

feccia *f* dregs, scum.

feci *fpl* faeces.

fecondare *vt* to fertilize.

fecondo *adj* fertile; **in età feconda** of childbearing age.

fede *f* faith, belief; wedding ring.

fedele *adj* faithful; true; regular; accurate; * *m/f* churchgoer, worshipper.

fedeltà *f* faithfulness, fidelity; accuracy.

federa *f* pillowcase, pillowslip.

federale *adj* federal.

federare *vt* to federate.

federazione *f* federation.

feed-back *m* feed-back.

fegato *m* liver; mettle.

felce *f* fern; bracken.

felice *adj* happy.

felicissimo *adj* overjoyed.

felicità *f* bliss, happiness.

felino *adj* feline.

felpa *f* plush; sweatshirt.

feltro *m* felt.

femmina *adj, f* female.

femminile *adj* feminine, womanly.

femminista *m/f* feminist; **movimento ~** *m* women's liberation.

femminuccia *f* cissy.

fendente *m* hack.

fenice *f* phoenix.

fenico *adj*; **acido ~** carbolic acid.

fenicottero *m* flamingo.

fenomenale *adj* phenomenal.

fenomeno *m* phenomenon.

feriale *adj*; **giorno ~** *m* weekday.

ferire *vt* to hurt, to injure, to wound.

ferita *f* wound; hurt; injury; **~ superficiale** *f* flesh wound.

ferito *adj* wounded.

fermabloc *m inv* clipboard.

fermacarte *m inv* paperweight.

fermaglio *m* clip, paperclip.

fermare *vt* to halt; to stop; to stay; to waylay; * *vi* to halt; * *vr* **~rsi** to stop; (car) to pull in, to pull up.

fermata *f* stop; halt; **~ d'autobus** bus stop.

fermentare *vi* to ferment; **mettere a ~** to brew.

fermentazione *f* brew.

fermento *m* ferment.

fermezza *f* firmness.

fermo *adj* firm; still; steady; stationary; **tenere ~** *vt* to steady.

feroce *adj* ferocious, fierce.

ferocia *f* ferocity, fierceness; savagery.

ferraglia *f* scrap.

ferramenta *fpl* hardware.

ferrare *vt* to shoe (a horse).

ferreo *adj* unswerving.

ferriera *f* ironworks.

ferro *m* iron; **~ di cavallo** *m* horseshoe; **~ da calza** *m* knitting needle; **minerale di ~** *m* iron ore.

ferrovia *f* railway.

ferroviere *m* railwayman.

fertile *adj* fertile.

fertilità *f* fertility.

fertilizzare *vt* to fertilize.

fervente *adj* fervent, fervid.

fervore *m* fervour.

fessura *f* fissure; chink; crepice; slot; slit; split.

festa *f* party, feast, festival, festivity, fête, gala; **di ~** *adj* festive.

festeggiamenti *mpl* rejoicings.

festeggiare *vt* to celebrate.

festival *m inv* festival.

fetale *adj* foetal.

fetente *m/f* stinker.

feticcio *m* fetish.

feticista *m/f* fetishist.

fetido *adj* fetid.

feto *m* foetus.

fetta *f* slice; **~ biscottata** *f* rusk.

fettuccia *f* tape.

feudale *adj* feudal.

feudalismo *m* feudalism.

fiaba *f* fairy tale.

fiaccare *vt* to wear down; to sap.

fiacco *adj* sluggish.

fiala *f* vial, phial.

fiamma *f* flame; pennant: **in fiamme** *adj* burning; ablaze, aflame, alight.

fiammeggiante *adj* lurid.

fiammella *f*: **di sicurezza** *f* pilot light.

fiammifero *m* match; **scatola per fiammiferi** *f* matchbox.

fiancheggiare *vt* to flank; to border.

fianco *m* side; flank; **fianchi** *mpl* loins; **di ~** *adv* edgeways, abreast.

fiaschetta *f* flask.

fiasco *m* flask, fiasco; flop.

fiato *m* wind; breath; **senza ~** *adj* breathless.

fibbia *f* buckle.

fibra *f* fibre; **~ di vetro** *f* fibreglass.

fibroso *adj* stringy.

ficcanaso *m/f inv* busy-body snooper.

ficcare *vt* to jam, to ram.

fico *m* fig.

fidanzamento *m* engagement betrothal.

fidanzare *vt* to betroth.

fidanzata *f* fiancée.

fidanzato *m* boyfriend; fiancé * *adj* engaged.

fidarsi *vr* to trust.

fidato *adj* trusted, trusty.

fiducia *f* trust, confidence.

fiducioso *adj* hopeful, trustful

fienile *m* hayloft.

fieno *m* hay; **raffreddore da ~** *m* hay fever.

fiera *f* fair; show; **~ campionaria** *f* trade fair.

fievole *adj* faint.

figlia *f* daughter.

figliare *vi* to calve.

figliastra *f* step-daughter.

figliastro *m* step-son.

figlio *m* son; **senza figli** *ad* childless.

figlioccia *f* goddaughter.

figlioccio *m* godchild, godson.

figura *f* figure; **~ rappresenta tiva** *f* figurehead.

figurare *vi* to figure.

figurativo *adj* figurative; **linguaggio ~** *m* imagery.

fila *f* line, row, tier, file.

filamento *m* filament.

filantropia *f* philanthropy.

filantropico *adj* philanthropic charitable.

filantropo *m* philanthropist.

filare *vi* to belt; * *vt* to spin.

filarmonico *adj* philharmonic

filastrocca *f* nursery rhyme.

filatelia *f* philately.

filato *m* yarn.

filatoio *m* spinning wheel.

filetto *m* fillet.

filiale *adj* filial.

filigrana *f* filigree; watermark.

film *m inv* film, motion picture, movie.

filmare *vt* to film.

filmina *f* filmstrip.

filo *m* thread; string; wire; flex; wisp; ~ **spinato** *m* barbed wire; ~ **elettrico** *m* lead; **fili argentati** *mpl* tinsel.

filocomunista *m* (*pol*) fellow traveller.

filologia *f* philology.

filologo *m* philologist.

filosofare *vi* to philosophize.

filosofia *f* philosophy.

filosofico *adj* philosophic(al).

filosofo *m* philosopher.

filtrare *vt* to percolate; to filter; * *vi* to percolate; to permeate; to seep.

filtro *m* filter; **con** ~ *adj* filtertipped.

finale *adj* final; eventual; finale; closing; ultimate; * *f* (*sport*) final.

finalista *m/f* finalist.

finalmente *adv* at last.

finanza *f* finance.

finanziare *vt* to finance; to fund.

finanziario *adj* financial.

finanziatore *m* financier.

finché *conj* until.

fine *adj* fine; acute; **senza** ~ endless; * *f* end; close; ending; finish; ~ **delle trasmissioni** *f* close-down; **porre** ~ **a** *vt* to end; **alla** ~ *adv* finally.

finemente *adv* finely.

finestra *f* window; ~ **a saliscendi** *f* sash window.

finestrino *m* window.

finezza *f* finesse.

fingere *vi* to fake, to pretend; to sham; * *vt* to pretend; to sham; ~ **di non vedere** to ignore.

finire *vt* to finish; * *vi* to finish, to end.

finito *adj* over; through; finite.

fino *adj* fine; * *prep* ~ **a** until.

finocchio *m* fennel; (*fam*) queer, poof.

finora *adv* hitherto; so far.

finto *adj* dummy, mock.

finzione *f* fiction, make-believe.

fioco *adj* dim.

fionda *f* catapult, sling.

fioraio *m* florist.

fiordo *m* fjord.

fiore *m* flower; bloom; **fiori** *mpl* (cards) clubs; blossom; **in fiore** *adj* flowery.

fiorente *adj* flourishing, thriving.

fioretto *m* foil.

fiorire *vi* to flower; to bloom.

firma *f* signature.

firmamento *m* firmament.

firmare *vt* to sign, to autograph; * *vi* to sign.

firmatario *m* signatory.

fisarmonica *f* accordion.

fiscale *adj* fiscal.

fischi *mpl* jeer.

fischiare *vt* to jeer, to boo; * *vi* to whistle.

fischiettare *vt* to whistle.

fischio *m* whistle; catcall.

fisica *f* physics.

fisicamente *adv* bodily.

fisico *adj* physical; * *m* physicist; physique.

fisiologia *f* physiology.

fisiologico *adj* physiological.

fisiologo *m* physiologist.

fisioterapia *f* physiotherapy.

fissare *vt* to fix; to peg; ~ **con chiodi** to tack.

fissazione *f* fixation.

fisso *adj* fixed; set; steady.

fitta *f* twinge, stab; ~ **al fianco** *f* stitch.

fittizio *adj* fictitious.

fitto *adj* close.

fiume *m* river, stream.
fiutare *vt* to scent.
fiuto *m* smell; ~ **negli affari** business acumen.
flaccido *adj* flabby, flaccid.
flagello *m* curse, scourge.
flagrante *adj* flagrant; **in** ~ red-handed.
flanella *f* flannel.
flash *m inv* flash, flash cube; newsflash.
flatulenza *f* flatulence, wind.
flautista *m/f* flautist.
flauto *m* flute, recorder.
fleboclisi *f* drip.
flemma *f* phlegm.
flemmatico *adj* phlegmatic.
flessibile *adj* flexible; supple, limber.
flessibilità *f* flexibility.
flipper *m* pinball machine.
flirt *m inv* flirtation.
flora *f* flora.
floreale *adj* floral.
florido *adj* florid.
floscio *adj* floppy.
floscio *adj* limp.
flotta *f* fleet.
flottiglia *f* flotilla.
fluidità *f* fluidity.
fluido *adj*, *m* fluid.
fluire *vi* to flow.
fluorescente *adj* fluorescent.
fluoruro *m* fluoride.
flusso *m* flow; ~ **di cassa** (*com*) cash flow.
fluttuare *vi* to fluctuate.
fluttuazione *f* fluctuation.
fobia *f* phobia.
foca *f* seal.
focale *adj* focal.
focena *f* porpoise.
focolaio *m* (*fig*) hotbed.
focolare *m* hearth; fireplace; **angolo del** ~ *m* fireside.
focoso *adj* hot.
fodera *f* lining.
foderare *vt* to line.

foderato *adj* lined.
fodero *m* scabbard.
foglia *f* leaf.
fogliame *m* foliage.
foglietto *m* slip.
foglio *m* folio, leaf (of paper), sheet.
fogna *f* sewer; **acque di** ~ *fpl* sewage.
fohn *m* hairdrier; **asciugare con il** ~ *vt* to blow-dry.
folata *f* gust.
folclore *m* folklore.
folla *f* crowd; mob.
folle *adj* crazy, insane; *vi* **andare in** ~ to coast; * *f* (*auto*) neutral; *m* madman.
follemente *adv* madly.
folletto *m* goblin, elf, pixie.
follia *f* insanity, madness.
folto *adj* bushy.
fomentare *vt* to foment.
fondale *m* backcloth.
fondamentale *adj* fundamental, basic; seminal.
fondamento *m* grounding.
fondare *vt* to establish, to found.
fondatore *m* founder.
fondazione *f* foundation, endowment.
fondente *m* fondant.
fondere *vi* to fuse; to melt; to smelt; * *vr* ~**rsi** to blend, to merge.
fonderia *f* foundry.
fondina *f* holster.
fondo *m* fund; bottom; sediment; ~ **per le piccole spese** *m* petty cash; **senza** ~ *adj* bottomless.
fondi *mpl* grounds.
fonema *m* phoneme.
fonetica *f* phonetics.
fonetico *adj* phonetic.
fontana *f* fountain.
fonte *m* spring, source; ~ **battesimale** *m* font.

footing *m* jogging; **fare ~** *vi* to jog.

foraggio *m* feed, fodder, forage, chaff.

forare *vt* to pierce; to punch.

forbici *fpl* scissors; **~ per potare** *fpl* secateurs.

forbicina *f* earwig.

forcella *f* crotch; wishbone.

forchetta *f* fork.

forcina *f* hairpin.

forcipe *m* forceps.

forcone *m* pitchfork.

foresta *f* forest.

forestale *adj* forest; **guardia ~** *f* forester.

forestiero *m* stranger.

forfora *f* dandruff.

forgiare *vt* to forge.

foriero *m* harbinger.

forma *f* shape; fitness; form; **in ~** *adj* fit.

formaggio *m* cheese; **piatto per il ~** *m* cheeseboard.

formale *adj* formal, ceremonial, ceremonious.

formalità *f inv* formality; **mancanza di ~** *f* informality.

formare *vt* to form, to shape.

formativo *adj* formative.

formato *m* format.

formattare *vt* to format.

formazione *f* formation; education; background.

formica *f* ant.

formicaio *m* anthill.

formichiere *m* anteater.

formicolare *vi* to tingle.

formicolio *m* tingle, tingling, pins and needles.

formidabile *adj* formidable.

formoso *adj* curvaceous.

formula *f* formula.

formulare *vt* to formulate; to word.

formulazione *f* wording.

fornace *f* forge; furnace; kiln.

fornaio *m* baker.

fornello *m* gas ring.

fornire *vt* to furnish, to provide, to supply.

fornitore *m* supplier, stockist, tradesman, purveyor

fornitura *f* supply, provision.

forno *m* oven.

foro *m* forum.

foro *m* hole, bore.

forse *adj* perhaps; * *adv* maybe.

forsennato *adj* frenzied; berserk.

forte *adj* forceful.

forte *m* (*mus*) forte; hard; loud; strong.

fortezza *f* fortress, stronghold.

fortificare *vt* to fortify.

fortificato *adj* walled.

fortificazione *f* fortification.

fortuito *adj* fortuitous.

fortuito *adj* accidental, incidental.

fortuna *f* luck; fortune; **colpo di ~** lucky break, fluke.

fortunatamente *adv* luckily.

fortunato *adj* fortunate, lucky.

foruncolo *m* spot, pimple, boil; **pieno di foruncoli** *adj* spotty.

forza *f* force; might; power; strength; coercion; leverage; **le forze armate** *fpl* the forces; **~ d'animo** *f* fortitude; **a ~ di** by dint of; **~ di volontà** *f* willpower.

forzare *vt* to force; to break into.

forzato *adj* forced.

foschia *f* haze, mist.

fosfato *m* phosphate.

fosforescente *adj* phosphorescent.

fosforo *m* phosphorus.

fossa *f* ditch.

fossato *m* moat.

fossetta *f* dimple.

fossile *adj, m* fossil

fosso *m* ditch, trench.

foto *f inv* shot.

fotocopia *f* photocopy.

fotocopiare *vt* to photocopy.

fotocopiatrice *f* photocopier.

fotogenico *adj* photogenic.

fotografare *vt* to photograph, to snap.

fotografia *f* picture; photograph, photography.

fotografico *adj* photographic.

fotografo *m* photographer.

fotomontaggio *m* photomontage.

fotosintesi *f* photosynthesis.

fottere *vt* to fuck.

foulard *m inv* scarf, cravat.

foyer *m inv* foyer.

fra *prep* between.

fracasso *m* crash, smash, noise, racket.

fradicio *adj* sodden.

fragile *adj* fragile, breakable, brittle.

fragilità *f* fragility.

fragola *f* strawberry.

fragoroso *adj* uproarious.

fragrante *adj* fragrant.

fragranza *f* fragrance.

fraintendere *vt* to be at cross-purposes.

fraintendere *vt* to misunderstand, to misconstrue.

frammentario *adj* fragmentary, piecemeal.

frammento *m* fragment; chip; snippet.

frammischiare *vt* to intermingle.

frana *f* landslide.

franchezza *f* frankness; openness; **brutale ~** bluntness.

franchigia *f* franchise.

franco *m* franc, frank; * *adj* candid; straightforward; outspoken; (*com*) free; **essere ~ con qn** to be open with somebody.

francobollo *m* stamp, postage stamp.

frangente *m* breaker (wave).

frangia *f* fringe.

frangiflutti *m inv* breakwater.

frangivento *m* windbreak.

frantumare *vt* to crush; to shatter, to smash.

frappé *m inv* milkshake.

frasario *m* phrase book.

frase *f* sentence; phrase; **~ di moda** catch phrase; **~ fatta** *f* cliché.

frassino *m* (*bot*) ash.

frastagliato *adj* rugged.

frate *m* friar.

fratellastro *m* step-brother.

fratello *m* brother.

fratello *m* brother, sibling.

fraternità *f* brotherhood, fraternity.

fraternizzare *vi* to fraternize.

fraterno *adj* fraternal, brotherly.

fratricida *adj*, *m/f* fratricide.

frattaglie *fpl* giblets; offal.

frattempo *adv*: **nel ~** in the meantime, in the meanwhile.

frattura *f* fracture.

fraudolento *adj* fraudulent.

frazione *f* fraction.

freccia *f* arrow; indicator; **mettere la freccia** *vi* to indicate

frecciata *f* gibe; **lanciare frecciate a** *vi* to gibe.

freddo *adj* cold, chill; stand-offish; * *m* cold, chill.

fregare *vt* to pinch, to nick.

fregata *f* frigate.

fregio *m* frieze.

fremere *vi* to thrill.

fremito *m* thrill.

frenare *vt* to curb; to control; * *vi* to brake.

frenesia *f* frenzy.

frenetico *adj* frenzied, frantic.

freno *m* brake; curb; **~ a mano** *m* handbrake; **agire da freno**

su *vi* to act as a disincentive; **porre ~ a** *vt* to crack down on; **tenere a ~** *vt* to restrain.

frequentare *vt* to attend; to frequent; to haunt; to consort (with); to patronize.

frequente *adj* frequent.

frequenza *f* frequency; attendance.

freschezza *f* freshness.

fresco *adj* fresh; crisp; cool; chilly; **mettere in ~** *vt* to chill.

frescura *f* cool.

fresia *f* freesia.

fretta *f* hurry, haste, rush; **in ~ e furia** *adv* hastily; **fare in ~** *vi* to hurry; **far ~** *vt* to rush; **fare ~ a** *vt* to hustle.

frettoloso *adj* hurried; cursory.

friggere *vt* to fry.

frigido *adj* frigid.

frignare *vi* to blubber.

frigo *m* fridge.

frigorifero *m* refrigerator.

fringuello *m* finch, chaffinch.

frittata *f* omelet(te).

frittella *f* fritter; pancake.

fritto *adj* fried.

frivolezza *f* frivolity; triviality; levity.

frivolo *adj* frivolous, flighty.

frizione *f* friction; clutch; **premere la ~** *vi* to declutch.

frizzante *adj* sparkling.

frizzare *vi* to fizz.

frocio *m* (*Amer fam*) fag.

frodo *m*: **cacciare di ~** *vt, vi* to poach.

fronda *f* frond.

frondoso *adj* leafy.

frontale *adj* frontal.

fronte *m* front; *f* forehead; *f* brow; **essere di ~ a** *vt* to face; **fare ~ a** *vt* to face up to; **di ~** *prep* facing; **di ~** *adv* opposite.

frontespizio *m* title page.

frontiera *f* frontier.

frontone *m* gable.

frottola *f* fib; cock-and-bull story.

frugale *adj* frugal; abstemious.

frugalmente *adv* sparingly.

frugare *vt* to delve; * *vi* to rummage; to rifle through.

frullare *vt* to whisk.

frullatore *m* mixer; blender; liquidizer; **passare al ~** *vt* to liquidize.

frullino *m* whisk.

frumento *m* corn; wheat.

frusciare *vi* to rustle.

fruscio *m* rustle.

frusta *f* whip.

frustare *vt* to flog, to lash, to whip.

frustata *f* lash.

frustino *m* riding crop.

frustrare *vt* to frustrate; to foil.

frustrato *adj* frustrated.

frustrazione *f* frustration.

frutta *f* fruit.

fruttare *vt* to yield.

frutteto *m* orchard.

fruttifero *adj* fruitful.

fruttivendolo *m* fruiterer, greengrocer.

frutto *m* fruit; **frutti di mare** *mpl* seafood.

fruttuoso *adj* fruitful.

fucilare *vt* to shoot.

fucilazione *f* shooting.

fucile *m* gun, rifle; **~ ad aria compressa** air gun; **~ da caccia** *m* shotgun.

fucina *f* smithy.

fuco *m* drone.

fucsia *f* fuchsia.

fuga *f* flight; escape; fugue; **~ romantica** *f* elopement; **~ precipitosa** *f* stampede.

fuggifuggi *m* debacle.

fuggire *vi* to abscond; to elope; to flee; * *vt* to flee.

fuggitivo *adj, m* fugitive, runaway.

fulcro *m* hub, fulcrum.

fuliggine *f* soot; **granellino di ~** *m* smut.

fulminare *vt* to electrocute; *vt* **~ con lo sguardo** to glare at.

fulmine *m* lightning, bolt of lightning, thunderbolt.

fulvo *m*, *adj* fawn.

fumante *adj* smoking.

fumare *vt* to smoke; * *vi* to smoke; to steam; **vietato ~** no smoking.

fumatore *m* smoker.

fumo *m* smoke, smoking; **senza ~** *adj* smokeless; **emettere ~** *vt* to fume.

fumoso *adj* smoky.

fune *f* rope.

funebre *adj*: **carro ~** *m* hearse.

funerale *m* funeral.

funereo *adj* funereal.

fungo *m* mushroom; **~ velenoso** *m* toadstool; **~ del legno** *m* dry rot.

funivia *f* cable-car.

funzionale *adj* functional.

funzionamento *m* function; **cattivo ~** *m* malfunction.

funzionare *vi* to operate; to work; to run; *vt* **far ~** to operate.

funzionario *m* official; **~ del fisco** assessor.

funzione *f* function; service.

fuoco *m* fire; focus; **~ incrociato** crossfire; **cessate il ~** ceasefire; **resistente al ~** *adj* fireproof; **fuochi d'artificio** *mpl* fireworks.

fuori *adv* outside; out; * *prep* out; **~ di** outside.

fuoribordo *adj* outboard.

fuorigioco *adj*; **in ~** offside.

fuorilegge *m* outlaw.

furberia *f* craftiness.

furbizia *f* cunning.

furbo *adj* crafty, cunning, artful, **essere più ~ di** *vt* to outwit

furetto *m* ferret.

furfante *m* knave.

furgone *m* van.

furia *f* fury, rage.

furibondo *adj* wild, livid; **rendere ~** *vt* to incense.

furiere *m* quartermaster.

furioso *adj* furious; raging; **rendere ~** *vt* to infuriate.

furtivamente *adv* by stealth; **procedere ~** *vi* to sidle.

furtivo *adj* furtive, stealthy, surreptitious.

furto *m* theft; snatch; larceny; **~ con scasso** burglary.

fusa *fpl* purr; **far le ~** *vi* to purr.

fusciacca *f* sash.

fusibile *m* fuse; **scatola dei fusibili** *f* fusebox.

fusione *f* fusion; merger; **punto di ~** *m* melting point.

fuso *m* spindle; * *adj* molten.

fusoliera *f* fuselage.

fustigazione *f* flogging.

fusto *m* he-man.

futile *adj* futile, self-defeating.

futilità *f* futility.

futuro *adj* future; prospective; coming; succeeding; elect; * *m* future.

G

gabardine *m inv* gabardine.

gabbia *f* cage; hutch; **mettere in ~** *vt* to cage.

gabbiano *m* (sea)gull.

gabinetto *m* lavatory, water closet, toilet, washroom.

gaffe *f inv* faux pas, blunder, clanger, boob.

gag *f inv* gag.

gaiamente *adv* merrily.

gala *m* gala.

galante *adj* gallant.

galassia *f* galaxy.

galea *f* galley.

galla *adv*: **a ~** afloat.

galleggiamento *m* floating; **linea di ~** *f* waterline.

galleggiante *m* float, ballcock; * *adj* buoyant.

galleggiare *vi* to float.

galleria *f* gallery, arcade; tunnel; **~ d'arte** art gallery.

galletto *m* cockerel.

gallina *f* hen.

gallo *m* cock, rooster.

gallone *m* gallon.

galoppare *vi* to gallop.

galoppo *m* gallop; **piccolo ~** *m* canter.

galvanizzare *vt* to galvanize.

gamba *f* leg.

gamberetto *m* shrimp.

gambero *m* prawn; crayfish.

gamberone *m*: **gamberoni** *mpl* scampi.

gambetto *m* gambit.

gambo *m* shank, stalk.

gamma *f* range, gamut.

gancio *m* hook; catch; clasp.

gangster *m inv* gangster.

gara *f* contest, competition.

garage *m inv* garage.

garantire *vt* to guarantee; to ensure; to secure; * *vi* to vouch.

garanzia *f* guarantee; warranty; *(fin)* collateral.

garbato *adj* graceful, suave,

garbo *m* grace.

gareggiare *vt* to race.

gargarismo *m* gargle; **fare i gargarismi** *vi* to gargle.

gargolla *f* gargoyle.

garitta *f* sentrybox.

garofano *m* carnation; **chiodo di ~** *m* clove.

garza *f* gauze, lint.

gas *m inv* gas; throttle; **impianto di produzione del ~** *m* gasworks.

gasolio *m* diesel.

gassato *adj* carbonated; **non ~** *adj* still.

gassoso *adj* gassy, gaseous.

gastrico *adj* gastric.

gastronomico *adj* gastronomic.

gattino *m* kitten.

gatto *m* cat, tomcat.

gazza *f* magpie.

gazzella *f* gazelle.

gazzetta *f* gazette.

gel *m inv* gel.

gelare *vt*, *vi* to freeze.

gelata *f* freeze.

gelatina *f* jelly; gelatine; **~ esplosiva** *f* gelignite.

gelato *m* ice, ice cream.

gelido *adj* frosty; freezing, raw.

gelo *m* frost.

gelone *m* chilblain.

gelosia *f* jealousy.

geloso *adj* jealous.

gelso *m* mulberry (tree); **mora di ~** mulberry fruit.

gelsomino *m* jasmine.

Gemelli *mpl* Gemini.

gemello *adj*, *m* twin.

gemere *vi* to moan, to groan, to wail.

gemito *m* moan, groan, wail.

gemma *f* gem.

gemogliare *vi* to sprout.

gene *m* gene.

genealogia *f* genealogy.

genealogico *adj* genealogical.

general *m* general; **~ di brigata** brigadier; * *adj* general, overall.

generalità *f inv* generality.

generalizzare *vi* to generalize.

generalizzazione *f* generalization.

generalmente *adv* in general, generally.

generare *vt* to generate; to sire.

generatore *m* generator.

generazione *f* generation.

genere *m* gender; kind, sort, genus.

generi *mpl*: ~ **alimentari** *mpl* foodstuffs.

generico *adj* generic; sweeping.

genero *m* son-in-law.

generosità *f* generosity.

generoso *adj* generous.

genetica *f* genetics.

gengiva *f* gum.

geniale *adj* brainy.

genio *m* genius.

genitali *mpl* genitals.

genitivo *m* genitive.

genitore *m* parent; ~ **affidatario** *m* foster parent; **dei genitori** *adj* parental.

gennaio *m* January.

gentaglia *f(fam)* hoi polloi, riffraff.

gente *f* people, folk.

gentile *adj* kind, nice, good, obliging, thoughtful; * *m* gentile.

gentilezza *f* kindness, civility.

gentiluomo *m* gentleman.

genuflettersi *vr* to genuflect.

genuino *adj* genuine, sterling.

geografia *f* geography.

geografico *adj* geographic(al).

geografo *m* geographer.

geologia *f* geology.

geologico *adj* geological.

geologo *m* geologist.

geometria *f* geometry.

geometrico *adj* geometric(al).

geranio *m* geranium.

gerarchia *f* hierarchy.

gergo *m* jargon, parlance, slang.

geriatrico *adj* geriatric.

germinare *vi* to germinate.

germoglio *m* shoot, sprout, off-

shoot; **germogli di soia** *mpl* beansprouts.

geroglifico *adj*, *m* hieroglyphic.

gessato *adj* pinstripe.

gesso *m* chalk; plaster; (*med*) cast.

gestazione *f* gestation.

gesticolare *vi* to gesticulate; to wave.

gestione *f* management, running, administration .

gestire *vt* to manage, to run, to administer.

gesto *m* gesture, sign; **ampio ~** *m* sweep.

gestore *m* manager; ~ **di un pub** *m* publican.

Gesù *m* Jesus.

gesuita *m* Jesuit.

gettare *vt* to throw; to chuck; to sprout; to cast.

getto *m* jet, spray.

geyser *m inv* geyser.

ghepardo *m* cheetah.

gheriglio *m* kernel.

gherone *m* gusset.

ghiacciaia *f* cooler.

ghiacciaio *m* glacier.

ghiacciato *adj* icy.

ghiaccio *m* ice; ~ **invisibile** *m* black ice.

ghiacciolo *m* icicle.

ghiaia *f* gravel.

ghianda *f* acorn.

ghiandaia *f* jay.

ghiandola *f* gland.

ghigliottina *f* guillotine.

ghigliottinare *vt* to guillotine.

ghiottone *m* glutton.

ghiottoneria *f* delicacy; gluttony.

ghirlanda *f* garland, wreath.

ghiro *m* dormouse.

ghisa *f* cast iron.

già *adv* already; yet.

giacca *f* jacket; ~ **a vento** *f* anorak, windcheater.

giacimento *m* deposit; **~ pe-trolifero** *m* oilfield.

giacinto *m* hyacinth; **~ dei boschi** bluebell.

giada *f* jade.

giaguaro *m* jaguar.

giaietto *m* jet.

giallastro *adj* yellowish; sallow.

giallo *adj*, * *m* yellow; (traffic lights) amber.

giardinaggio *m* gardening.

giardiniere *m* gardener.

giardino *m* garden.

giarrettiera *f* garter.

giavellotto *m* javelin.

gibbone *m* gibbon.

giga *f* jig.

gigante *m* giant.

gigantesco *adj* gigantic, monster.

giglio *m* lily.

gin *m inv* gin.

ginecologo *m* gynaecologist.

ginepro *m* juniper.

ginestra *f* broom; **~ spinosa** *f* gorse.

gingillarsi *vi* to dilly-dally.

ginnasta *m/f* gymnast.

ginnastica *f* gym, gymnastics.

ginnastico *adj* gymnastic.

ginocchio *m* knee.

giocare *vt*, *vi* to play; **~ chias-sosamente** *vi* to romp; **~ (d'azzardo)** *vt*, *vi* to gamble.

giocatore *m* player; **~ d'azzardo** gambler.

giocattolo *m* toy.

giocherellare *vt* to toy with, to fiddle.

giocherellone *adj* playful.

gioco *m* game; play; **~ chias-soso** *m* romp; **~ di carte** *m* card game; **doppio ~** *m* dou-ble-dealing; **~ d'azzardo** *m* gambling.

giocoliere *m* juggler.

giocoso *adj* frolicsome.

giogo *m* yoke.

gioia *f* joy, glee; *vt* **riempire di ~** to delight.

gioielliere *m* jeweller.

gioiello *m* jewel; **gioielli** *mpl* jewellery.

giornalaio *m* newsagent.

giornale *m* (news)paper; **~ra-dio** *m* news.

giornaliero *adj* daily.

giornalismo *m* journalism.

giornalista *m/f* journalist, col-umnist.

giornata *f* day.

giorno *m* day, daytime; **~ per ~** day by day; **di ~** by day; **buon ~** *excl* good morning; **un ~** *adv* sometime.

giostra *f* merry-go-round, roundabout, carousel.

giovane *adj* young; **più ~** jun-ior; * *m* youth.

giovanile *adj* juvenile, youth-ful.

giovanotto *m* youngster.

giovare *vt* to benefit.

giovedì *m inv* Thursday.

giovenca *f* heifer.

gioventù *f* youth.

gioviale *adj* jovial, hearty, joc-ular, convivial.

giovialità *f* heartiness.

giovinezza *f* youthfulness.

giraffa *f* giraffe.

giramondo *m/f* rover.

girare *vt* to revolve; to spin; to turn; (cheque) to endorse; * *vi* to revolve; to turn; **~ furtiva-mente** to lurk: **~ in cerca di clienti** (eg taxi) to cruise; * *vr* **~rsi** to turn round; to swivel.

girasole *m* sunflower.

girata *f* endorsement.

giretto *m* spin.

girevole *adj* revolving.

girino *m* tadpole.

giro *m* tour; round; circuit; turn; walk; ride; run; spin; tour; lap; **~ in macchina** *m* drive; ~ **d'affari** m turnover; **presa in** ~ f taunt; **in** ~ adv about, around; **prendere in** ~ vt to taunt.

gironzolare vi to roam; to stroll around; to wander.

girovagare vt per to wander.

gita f jaunt; excursion; trip.

giù adv down; **in** ~ downwards.

giubileo m jubilee.

giubilo m exultation.

giudicare vt to judge; to deem; to adjudicate.

giudice m judge.

giudiziario adj judicial; **azione giudiziaria** f prosecution.

giudizio m judgement; estimation.

giudizioso adj judicious.

giugno m June.

giumenta f mare.

giunca f junk.

giunco m rush.

giungla f jungle, wilderness.

giunta f junta.

giuntare vt to splice.

giuntura f join.

giuramento m oath.

giurare vt to swear, to vow; * vi to swear.

giurato m juror.

giuria f jury; panel.

giurisdizione f jurisdiction.

giurisprudenza f jurisprudence.

giustamente adv right.

giustapposizione f juxtaposition.

giustificabile adj justifiable.

giustificare vt to justify.

giustificazione f justification; warrant.

giustizia f justice.

giustiziare vt to execute.

giusto adj right; just; fair; proper.

glaciale adj glacial; frosty.

gladiatore m gladiator.

glassa f icing.

glassare vt to ice.

glicerina f glycerine.

globale adj global; comprehensive; blanket.

globo m globe.

globulo m corpuscle.

gloria f glory, kudos.

glorificare vt to glorify.

glorificazione f glorification.

glorioso adj glorious.

glossa f gloss.

glossario m glossary.

glucosio m glucose.

gnocco m dumpling.

gnomo m gnome.

gnu m inv gnu.

goal m inv goal.

gobba f hump.

gobbo adj hunch-backed; * m hunch-back.

goccia f drop, drip.

goccino m dash.

gocciolare vi to trickle.

gocciolina f droplet.

godere vt to enjoy.

godimento m enjoyment.

goffo adj clumsy, gauche, awkward, ungainly.

goffrare vt to emboss.

gola f throat, gullet; gorge.

golf m golf; **mazza da** ~ f golf club; **circolo di** ~ m golf club; **campo di** ~ m golf course; **giocatore di** ~ m golfer.

golfo m gulf.

goloso adj greedy.

gomitata f nudge, dig.

gomito m elbow; (tech) crank; **alzare il** ~ vi to booze.

gomma f rubber; tyre; ~ **a terra** f flat (tyre).

gommapiuma f foam rubber.

gommone m dinghy.

gondola f gondola.

gondoliere m gondolier.

gonfiabile adj inflatable.

gonfiare *vt* to inflate; to distend; * *vr* ~**rsi** to billow (sails); to swell.

gonfio *adj* swollen; puffy, bloated; **essere ~ di** *vi* to bulge.

gonfiore *m* swelling.

gong *m inv* gong.

gongolare *vi* to gloat.

gonna *f* skirt; ~ **pantalone** *f inv* culottes.

gonorrea *f* gonorrhoea.

gonzo *m* dupe.

gorgogliare *vi* to gurgle.

gorgoglio *m* gurgle.

gorilla *m inv* gorilla.

gormless *adj* tonto.

gotico *adj* gothic.

gotta *f* gout.

governante *f* governess; housekeeper.

governare *vt* to rule, to govern; (animals) to tend, to groom.

governatore *m* governor.

governo *m* government; administration.

gozzo *m* (*ornith*) crop.

gracchiare *vt* to rasp.

gracidare *vi* to croak.

gradazione *f* gradation; ~ **alcolica** *f* strength.

gradevole *adj* pleasant; ~ **al palato** palatable.

gradiente *m* gradient.

gradino *m* step.

gradito *adj* welcome; acceptable; **non ~** unwelcome.

grado *m* degree; grade; rank.

graduale *adj* gradual.

gradualmente *adv* little by little.

graduare *vt* to grade.

graffetta *f* staple.

graffiare *vt* to scratch; to claw.

graffio *m* scratch.

graffiti *mpl* graffiti.

grafica *f* graphics.

grafico *adj* graphic(al); * *m* graph.

grammatica *f* grammar.

grammaticale *adj* grammatical.

grammo *m* gram.

grammofono *m* gramophone.

grana *f* grain.

granaio *m* granary.

granata *f* grenade.

granatiere *m* grenadier.

granchio *m* crab.

grandangolare *adj* wide-angle.

grande *adj* big, large, great.

grandezza *f* greatness.

grandinare *vi* to hail.

grandine *f* hail; **chicco di ~** *m* hailstone.

grandiosità *f* grandeur.

grandioso *adj* grandiose.

granello *m* granule, grain.

granito *m* granite.

grano *m* corn, wheat; **campo di ~** *m* cornfield.

granturco *m* maize; **fiocchi di ~** *mpl* cornflakes; **farina finissima di ~** *f* cornflour.

granulare *vt* to granulate.

grappolo *m* bunch, cluster.

grassetto *adj* bold (type).

grasso *m* grease.

grasso *m* fat; ~ **dell'arrosto** *m* dripping; ~ **di balena** blubber; * *adj* fat, fatty; **piante grasse** *fpl* succulent plants.

grassoccio *adj* rotund.

grassotello *adj* podgy.

grata *f* grid, grate, grating.

graticcio *m* trellis.

graticola *f* gridiron.

gratifica *f* bonus.

gratis *adv* gratis.

gratitudine *f* gratitude, thankfulness.

grato *adj* grateful; appreciative; thankful.

grattacapo *m* (*fig*) headache.

grattacielo *m* skyscraper.

grattare *vt* to grate; * *vi* to scrape, to scratch.

gratuito *adj* free; gratuitous.
gravame *m* onus.
gravare *vt* to tax.
grave *adj* grave; serious; acute.
gravidanza *f* pregnancy.
gravido *adj* pregnant.
gravità *f* gravity.
gravitare *vi* to gravitate.
gravitazione *f* gravitation.
gravoso *adj* onerous.
grazia *f* grace; **grazie** *fpl* thanks;
grazioso *adj* pretty.
greco *adj* Greek.
gregge *m* flock, herd.
greggio *adj* unrefined, raw.
grembiule *m* apron, pinafore.
grembo *m* lap, womb.
grezzo *adj* crude.
grida *fpl* shouting.
gridare *vi*, *vt* to cry, to shout.
grido *m* cry; shout; **~ di incor-aggiamento** *m* cheer.
griffone *m* griffin.
grigio *m* grey; * *adj* grey, drab.
griglia *f* grill; **cuocere alla ~** *vt* to grill.
grilletto *m* trigger.
grillo *m* cricket.
grinta *f* drive.
gronda *f* eaves.
grondaia *f* gutter.
grondare *vt* to stream.
groppa *f* rump.
grossa *f* gross.
grossista *m/f* wholesaler.
grosso *adj* big; thick.
grossolanamente *adv* roughly.
grossolano *adj* gross; crude; earthy.
grotta *f* grotto; cave.
grottesco *adj* grotesque.
groviglio *m* entanglement, tan-gle.
gru *f inv* crane.
gruccia *f* (coat)hanger.
grugnire *vi* to grunt.
grugnito *m* grunt.
grumo *m* clot, lump.

gruppo *m* group; cluster; batch;
~ sanguigno blood group.
gruzzolo *m* hoard; nest egg.
guadagnare *vt* to earn; to gain.
guadagno *m* gain; return;
guadagni *mpl* earnings.
guadare *vt* to ford.
guado *m* ford.
guai *mpl* trouble.
guaina *f* sheath.
guaio *m* scrape, fix.
guaire *vi* to whine.
guaito *m* whine.
guancia *f* cheek.
guanciale *m* pillow.
guanto *m* glove; gauntlet.
guantoni *mpl* boxing gloves.
guardacaccia *m inv* game-keeper.
guardacoste *m inv* coastguard.
guardalinee *m inv* linesman.
guardare *vi* to look; to watch;
~ i bambini to baby sit; * *vt* to look; to survey; to watch; to view; **~ con occhi vogliosi** to leer.
guardaroba *m inv* wardrobe; cloakroom.
guardia *f* guard; watch; **~ del corpo** bodyguard; **corpo di ~** *m* guardroom; **~ forestale** *f* ranger; **cane da ~** watch-dog; **fare la ~ a** *vt* to guard.
guardiano *m* watchman; keep-er.
guaribile *adj* curable.
guarigione *f* cure.
guarire *vt* to cure; to heal.
guarnigione *f* garrison.
guarnire *vt* to garnish.
guarnizione *f* gasket.
guastafeste *m/f inv* spoilsport, kill-joy.
guastare *vt* to vitiate; * *vr* **~rsi** *vr* to go off, to spoil.
guasto *m* breakdown.
guerra *f* war; **~ civile** *f* civil war.

guerriero *m* warrior.

guerriglia *f* guerrilla warfare.

guerrigliero *m* guerrilla.

gufo *m* owl.

guglia *f* spire.

guida *f* leader; guide; guide-book; driving; guidance; runner.

guidare *vt* to drive; to guide; to steer; to lead.

guidatore *m* driver.

guinzaglio *m* leash, lead.

gulasch *m inv* goulash.

guru *m inv* guru.

guscio *m* shell; husk; ~ **d'uovo** *m* eggshell; ~ **di noce** *m* nutshell.

gustare *vt* to relish.

gusto *m* flavour; taste; relish; **di ~** *adv* heartily; **di ~** *adj* tasteful; **di cattivo ~** *adj* tasteless.

gutturale *adj* guttural.

H

habitat *m inv* habitat; home.

hamburger *m inv* hamburger.

handicap *m* handicap.

handicappato *adj* handicapped.

harem *m inv* harem.

hascisc *m* hash(ish).

herpes *m inv* cold sore; ~ **zoster** *m* (*med*) shingles.

hi-fi *m inv* hi-fi.

hobby *m inv* hobby.

hockey *m inv* hockey.

hostess *f inv* stewardess.

hostess *f inv* hostess.

hot dog *m inv* hot dog.

hotel *m inv* hotel.

house boat *f inv* houseboat.

I

ibrido *adj, m* hybrid.

iceberg *m inv* iceberg.

icona *f* icon.

iconoclasta *adj, m* iconoclast(ic).

idea *f* idea; notion; **mezza ~** *f* inkling; ~ **brillante** *f* brainwave; ~ **sbagliata** *f* misconception.

ideale *adj, m* ideal.

idealista *m/f* idealist.

idem *adv* ditto.

identico *adj* identical.

identificare *vt* to identify; to equate.

identità *f inv* identity.

ideologia *f* ideology.

idillico *adj* idyllic.

idillio *m* idyll.

idiomatico *adj* idiomatic(al); **frase idiomatica** *f* idiom.

idiota *m/f* idiot; moron.

idolatrare *vt* to idolize.

idolatria *f* idolatry.

idolo *m* idol.

idoneità *f* fitness.

idrante *m* hydrant.

idraulica *f* hydraulics.

idraulico *adj* hydraulic; * *m* plumber.

idrico *adj* water; **impianto ~** *m* waterworks.

idroelettrico *adj* hydroelectric.
idrofobia *f* hydrophobia.
idrofobo *adj* rabid.
idrogeno *m* hydrogen.
idrovolante *m* seaplane.
iena *f* hyena.
ieri *adv* yesterday.
iettatore *m* jinx.
igiene *f* hygiene.
igienico *adj* hygienic.
igloo *m inv* igloo.
ignaro *adj* oblivious, unaware.
ignizione *f* ignition.
ignobile *adj* ignoble, base.
ignominia *f* ignominy.
ignominioso *adj* ignominious.
ignorante *adj* ignorant; * *m/f* ignoramus.
ignoranza *f* ignorance.
gnorare *vt* to ignore; to disregard; to be unacquainted with.
ignoto *adj* nameless; unknown.
il *def art* the.
ilarità *f* hilarity, mirth.
illecito *adj* illicit, unlawful.
illegale *adj* illegal.
illegalità *f* illegality.
illeggibile *adj* illegible; unreadable; **grafia ~** *f* scrawl.
illegittimità *f* illegitimacy.
illegittimo *adj* illegitimate.
illeso *adj* unharmed.
illimitato *adj* limitless, boundless, unlimited.
illogico *adj* illogical.
illudere *vt* to delude.
illuminare *vt* to illuminate, to light.
illuminato *adj* enlightened.
illuminazione *f* lighting, illumination.
Illuminismo *m* Enlightenment.
illusione *f* illusion; delusion.
illusorio *adj* illusory; unrealistic.
illustrare *vt* to illustrate.
illustrativo *adj* illustrative.

illustrato *adj* pictorial; **libro ~** *m* picture book.
illustrazione *f* illustration.
illustre *adj* illustrious.
imbacuccare *vt* to muffle.
imballaggio *m* packing; **materiale da ~** *m* packing material.
imballare *vt* to pack.
imbalsamare *vt* to embalm.
imbarazzante *adj* embarrassing, awkward.
imbarazzato *adj* embarrassed; sheepish.
imbarazzo *m* embarrassment; **mettere in ~** *vt* to embarrass.
imbarcare *vt* to embark; to ship; * *vr* **~rsi** to board.
imbarco *m* embarkation.
imbastire *vt* (sewing) to baste, to tack.
imbastitura *f* tacking; **punto di ~** *m* tack.
imbattuto *adj* undefeated.
imbavagliare *vt* to gag.
imbecille *m* imbecile.
imbevere *vt* to imbue.
imbiancare *vt* to whitewash.
imbianchino *m* painter.
imboscata *f* ambush; **fare un'~a** *vt* to ambush.
imbottigliare *vt* to bottle.
imbottire *vt* to stuff, to pad.
imbottitura *f* stuffing, padding.
imbrattare *vt* to smudge, to daub.
imbrogliare *vt* to cheat, to embroil, to hoodwink.
imbroglio *m* cheat, fiddle.
imbroglione *m* cheat, swindler, fiddler.
imbronciato *adj* morose; sulky; in a huff.
imbuto *m* funnel.
imitare *vt* to imitate, to impersonate, to copy, to mimic.
imitativo *adj* imitative.

imitatore *m* mimic.

imitazione *f* imitation; fake; takeoff; **imitazioni** *fpl* mimicry.

immacolato *adj* pristine.

immagazzinamento *m* storage.

immagazzinare *vt* to store.

immaginabile *adj* imaginable.

immaginare *vt* to imagine; to picture; to visualize; **s'immagini!** *excl* think nothing of it!

immaginario *adj* imaginary, fictional.

immaginazione *f* imagination; **ricco di ~** *adj* imaginative.

immagine *f* image.

immancabile *adj* unfailing.

immangiabile *adj* inedible, unpalatable.

immatricolare *vt* to enrol, to register; * *vr* **~rsi** to matriculate.

immatricolazione *f* enrolment, matriculation.

immaturo *adj* immature; callow.

immediato *adj* immediate, instant.

immenso *adj* immense.

immergere *vt* to immerse, to duck, to dip, to steep, to plunge.

immeritato *adj* undeserved, unmerited.

immersione *f* immersion; **~ con autorespiratore** *f* skindiving.

immerso *adj* engrossed.

immigrato *m* immigrant.

immigrazione *f* immigration.

imminente *adj* imminent, forthcoming.

immischiarsi *vr* to meddle.

immissione *f* intake.

immobile *adj* immobile, motionless, still.

immobilità *f* immobility, stillness.

immondizie *fpl* rubbish.

immorale *adj* immoral.

immoralità *f* immorality.

immortalare *vt* to immortalize.

immortale *adj* immortal.

immortalità *f* immortality.

immotivato *adj* unmotivated.

immune *adj* immune.

immunità *f* immunity.

immunizzare *vt* to immunize.

immutabile *adj* unchanging, immutable.

impacchettare *vt* to parcel.

impacciato *adj* self-conscious, wooden.

impadronirsi *vr* to master (e.g. a language)

impalcatura *f* scaffolding.

impalpabile *adj* impalpable.

impappinarsi *vr* to flounder.

imparare *vt* to learn.

impareggiabile *adj* matchless, peerless.

imparentato *adj* related, kindred.

imparziale *adj* impartial, fair, unbiased, detached.

imparzialità *f* impartiality, fairness.

impasse *f* impasse.

impassibile *adj* impassive, unemotional; deadpan; stolid; **dalla faccia ~** poker-faced.

impastare *vt* to knead.

impasto *m* dough, paste.

impatto *m* impact.

impaurire *vt* to scare.

impaurito *adj* frightened.

impaziente *adj* impatient.

impazienza *f* impatience.

impazzire *vi* to go mad; **far ~ to** *vt* madden.

impeccabile *adj* impeccable; immaculate; faultless.

impedimento *m* impediment.

impedire *vt* to stop, to hinder.

impegnare *vt* to pledge, to pawn; * *vr* **~rsi** to covenant.

impegno *m* commitment; bond; engagement.

impellente *adj* compelling.

impenetrabile *adj* impenetrabile.

impenitente *adj* unrepentant.

impennarsi *vr* to rear.

impensabile *adj* unthinkable.

imperativo *adj* imperative.

imperatore *m* emperor.

imperatrice *f* empress.

impercettibile *adj* imperceptible.

imperdonabile *adj* unforgivable, inexcusable.

imperfetto *adj* imperfect.

imperfezione *f* imperfection, blemish.

imperiale *adj* imperial.

imperialismo *m* imperialism.

imperioso *adj* imperious.

imperituro *adj* undying.

impermeabile *adj* impermeable; mackintosh, raincoat.

impero *m* empire.

imperscrutabile *adj* inscrutable.

impersonale *adj* impersonal.

imperterrito *adj* undaunted, undismayed.

impertinente *adj* impertinent, pert, cocky.

impertinenza *f* impertinence, backchat.

imperturbabile *adj* imperturbable.

imperturbato *adj* undisturbed.

imperversare *vi* to be rife.

impervio *adj* impervious.

impestare *vt* to foul.

impetuosità *f* impetuosity.

impetuoso *adj* impetuous, hotheaded.

impiallacciatura *f* veneer.

impianto *m* plant; **impianti ~ elettrico** *m* wiring; *mpl* fixtures.

impiastro *m* poultice.

impiccare *vt* to hang.

impiccione *m* meddler.

impiegare *vt* to employ.

impiegato *m* clerk, office worker.

impiego *m* job, position; use.

impietrito *adj* petrified.

impigliare *vt* to entangle; to pile.

implacabile *adj* implacable, relentless, unrelenting.

implicare *vt* to implicate, to imply.

implicazione *f* implication.

implicito *adj* implicit.

implorare *vt* to implore, to entreat, to beseech; * *vi* to plead.

imponente *adj* imposing, impressive, awe-inspiring; towering.

imponibile *adj* taxable.

impopolare *adj* unpopular.

imporre *vt* to impose; to levy; * *vr* **imporsi che sa ~** to be assertive; to put one's foot down.

importante *adj* important; momentous; weighty; **il più ~** foremost.

importanza *f* importance; **avere più ~ di** *vt* to outweigh.

importare *vt* to import; * *vi* to matter; **non mi importa** I don't care.

importatore *m* importer.

importazione *f* import, importation.

importo *m* amount.

importunare *vt* to importune, to worry.

importuno *adj* importunate.

imposizione *f* imposition.

impossibile *adj* impossible; hopeless.

impossibilità *f* impossibility.

imposta *f* tax; levy; **~ sul reddito** *f* income tax; **~ indiret-**

ta *f* excise; **esente da ~** *adj* tax-free.

impostazione *f* layout.

imposto *adj* enforced.

impostore *m* impostor, sham.

impotente *adj* impotent, powerless.

impotenza *f* impotence.

impoverire *vt* to impoverish.

impoverito *adj* impoverished.

impraticabile *adj* impracticable.

imprecazione *f* expletive, imprecation.

impreciso *adj* imprecise.

impregnare *vt* to impregnate, to steep.

impregnato *adj* impregnated; **~ d'acqua** waterlogged.

impregnazione *f* impregnation.

imprenditore *m* entrepreneur.

impreparato *adj* unprepared.

impresa *f* concern; undertaking, venture; enterprise; exploit; feat; **imprese** *fpl* doings.

impressionabile *adj* impressionable.

impressione *f* impression, feeling, hunch; **fare ~ a** *vt* to impress.

imprevedibile *adj* unforeseeable, unpredictable.

imprevidente *adj* improvident.

imprevisto *adj* unforeseen.

imprigionare *vt* to imprison, to incarcerate.

imprimere *vt* to imprint.

improbabile *adj* improbable, unlikely.

improbabilità *f* improbability, unlikelihood.

improduttivo *adj* unproductive.

impronta *f* print; **~ digitale** *f* fingerprint.

impronunciabile *adj* unpronounceable.

improperi *mpl* abuse.

improvvisamente *adv* all at once.

improvvisare *vi* to improvise; * *vt* to improvise, to ad-lib, to extemporize.

improvvisato *adj* impromptu, ad-lib, makeshift, extempore

improvviso *adj* sudden, snap.

imprudente *adj* imprudent, ill-advised, injudicious.

imprudenza *f* imprudence.

impudico *adj* immodest.

impugnare *vt* to impugn.

impugnatura *f* hilt.

impulsivo *adj* impulsive.

impulso *m* impulse, urge.

impunemente *adv* with impunity.

impunito *adj* unpunished.

impurità *f inv* impurity.

impuro *adj* impure.

imputare *vt* to indict.

imputato *m* defendant, accused.

imputazione *f* charge, indictment.

incidente *m* accident.

incidere su *vt* affect.

in *prep* in; into; **~ vettura** *adv* aboard.

inabilità *f* inability.

inabitabile *adj* uninhabitable.

inaccessibile *adj* inaccessible.

inadatto *adj* inappropriate, unfit, unsuitable

inadeguato *adj* inadequate.

inadempiente *adj* defaulting; **risultare ~** *vi* to default.

inafferrabile *adj* elusive.

inalare *vt* to inhale.

inalterabile *adj* unalterable.

inalterato *adj* unaltered.

inamidare *vt* to starch.

inammissibile *adj* inadmissible.

inanimato *adj* inanimate.

inapplicabile *adj* inapplicable.

inaridire *vt* to parch.

inasprire *vt* to embitter.

inattaccabile *adj* impregnable, watertight.

inatteso *adj* unexpected.

inattività *f* inactivity.

inattivo *adj* inactive, idle.

inattuabile *adj* unworkable.

inaudito *adj* unheard-of.

inaugurale *adj* inaugural, maiden.

inaugurare *vt* to inaugurate.

inaugurazione *f* inauguration, opening.

inavvicinabile *adj* unapproachable.

inazione *f* inaction.

incagliarsi *vr* (*naut*) to ground.

incalcolabile *adj* incalculable.

incallito *adj* horny.

incalzare *vt* to ply.

incancrenito *adj* ingrained.

incandescente *adj* incandescent, white-hot.

incandescenza *f* glow.

incantare *vt* to enchant.

incantesimo *m* enchantment, spell, incantation.

incantevole *adj* enchanting, ravishing.

incanto *m* charm.

incapace *adj* incapable, unable, helpless; **rendere ~** *vt* to incapacitate.

incapacità *f* incapacity.

incaricare *vt* to commission.

incarico *m* assignment.

incarnare *vt* to embody, to epitomize.

incarnato *adj* incarnate.

incarnazione *f* incarnation, embodiment.

incartare *vt* to wrap.

incassare *vt* to cash.

incastellatura *f* housing.

incastrare *vt* to embed.

incatenare *vt* to chain, to fetter.

incauto *adj* incautious.

incavato *adj* cavernous.

incavolato *adj* ratty.

incendiario *adj* incendiary, inflamatory.

incendio *m* fire, blaze; **~ doloso** *m* arson.

inceneritore *m* incinerator.

incenso *m* incense.

incentivo *m* incentive, inducement.

incepparsi *vr* to jam, to stick.

incerato; telone ~ *m* tarpaulin.

incertezza *f* uncertainty, suspense.

incerto *adj* unsure, uncertain, touch-and-go.

incessante *adj* incessant, ceaseless, unremitting, unceasing.

incesto *m* incest.

incestuoso *adj* incestuous.

inchiesta *f* inquest, inquiry.

inchinarsi *vr* to bow.

inchino *m* curtsey; bow; **fare un ~** *vi* to curtsey.

inchiodare *vt* to nail.

inchiodato *adj* rooted.

inchiostro *m* ink.

inciampare *vi* to trip, to stumble.

incidente *m* accident; mishap; crash; **avere un ~** *vi* to crash.

incidenza *f* incidence.

incidere *vt* to incise; to engrave; to cut (a record); to carve; to inscribe; to lance; to score; **~ all'acquaforte** to etch.

incinta *adj* pregnant, expecting.

incipiente *adj* incipient.

incipriarsi *vr* to powder.

incisione *f* incision; cut; engraving; **~ all'acquaforte** *f* etching; **~ su legno** *f* woodcut.

incisivo *adj* incisive.

incitare *vt* to incite.

incivile *adj* uncivil.

inciviso *m* incisor.

inclemente *adj* inclement.

inclinare *vt* to tilt, to slant.

inclinato *adj* slanting, sloping; **essere ~** *vi* to slope.

inclinazione *f* inclination, bent.

includere *vt* to include.

inclusione *f* inclusion.

incluso *adj* including, inclusive.

incoerente *adj* incoherent.

incoerenza *f* incoherence, inconsistency.

incognito *m*: **in ~** *adj* incognito.

incollare *vt* to glue, to gum, to stick.

incolore *adj* colourless.

incolpare *vt* to blame.

incolto *adj* uncultivated, fallow; uneducated.

incolume *adj* uninjured, untouched.

incombente *adj* impending.

incominciare *vt*, *vi* to begin.

incommensurabile *adj* immeasurable.

incomodare *vt* to inconvenience.

incomparabile *adj* incomparable.

incompatibile *adj* incompatible.

incompatibilità *f* incompatibility.

incompetente *adj* incompetent.

incompetenza *f* incompetence.

incompiuto *adj* unfinished.

incompleto *adj* incomplete.

incomprensibile *adj* incomprehensible; **parole incomprensibili** *fpl* gibberish.

inconcludente *adj* inconclusive.

incondizionato *adj* unconditional, wholehearted, unqualified, unreserved.

inconfondibile *adj* unmistakable.

incongruo *adj* incongruous.

inconorazione *f* coronation.

inconsapevolmente *adv* unknowingly.

inconscio *adj*, *n* unconscious.

inconsolabile *adj* inconsolable.

incontestato *adj* unchallenged.

incontinente *adj* incontinent.

incontinenza *f* incontinence.

incontrare *vt* to meet, to encounter.

incontrastato *adj* undisputed.

incontro *m* encounter; meeting; match; (boxing) bout.

incontrollabile *adj* uncontrollable, compulsive.

incontrollato *adj* unchecked.

incontrovertibile *adj* incontrovertible, indisputable.

inconveniente *m* drawback.

incoraggiamento *m* encouragement.

incoraggiare *vt* to encourage.

incordare *vt* to string.

incornare *vt* to gore.

incorniciare *vt* to frame.

incoronare *vt* to crown.

incorporare *vt* to incorporate.

incorporazione *f* incorporation.

incorreggibile *adj* incorrigible, hopeless.

incorruttibile *adj* incorruptible.

incostante *adj* erratic.

incredibile *adj* incredible, unbelievable.

incredibilmente *adv* amazingly.

incredulità *f* incredulity, disbelief.

incredulo *adj* incredulous.

incremento *m* increment, increase; **forte ~** boom.

increscioso *adj* untoward.

increspare *vt* to pucker, to ripple.

increspatura *f* ripple.

incriminare *vt* to incriminate.

incrinare *vt* to crack.

incrociare *vt* to cross.

incrociatore *m* cruiser.

incrocio *m* crossing, crossroads, junction; crossbreed.

incrollabile *adj* unwavering.

incrostare *vt* to encrust, to cake.

incubatrice *f* incubator.

incubo *m* nightmare.

incudine *f* anvil.

inculcare *vt* to inculcate.

incurabile *adj* incurable, terminal.

incuriosire *vt* to intrigue.

incursione *f* incursion, inroad, foray, swoop; **fare un'~** *vi* to swoop.

incurvarsi *vi* to sag.

incustodito *adj* unattended.

indaco *m*, *adj* indigo.

indagare *vt* to investigate, to inquire (into).

indagine *f* investigation; survey.

indebolire *vt* to weaken, to enfeeble; * *vr* **~rsi** to weaken.

indecente *adj* indecent, rude.

indecenza *f* indecency.

indecisione *f* indecision.

indeciso *adj* undecided; indecisive; doubtful.

indecoroso *adj* unseemly.

indefinibile *adj* indefinable.

indefinito *adj* indefinite; undefined; nondescript.

indegno *adj* undeserving, unworthy.

indelebile *adj* indelible.

indelicato *adj* indelicate, tactless.

indenne *adj* unscathed.

indennità *f* allowance; compensation.

indennizzare *vt* to indemnify.

indennizzo *m* indemnity.

indentificazione *f* identification.

indescrivibile *adj* indescribable.

indeterminato *adj* indeterminate, undetermined.

indicare *vt* to indicate; to point; to state; to tell; to say; to quote; * *vi* to say.

indicativo *adj* indicative.

indicazione *f* indication; clue; **~ stradale** *f* signpost.

indice *m* index; forefinger, index finger.

indicibile *adj* unspeakable.

indietreggiare *vi* to recoil.

indietro *adv* behind; back, backwards; **fare marcia ~** *vi* to back, to reverse; **restare ~** *vi* to lag; **marcia indietra** *f* reverse (gear).

indifeso *adj* defenceless, unprotected.

indifferente *adj* indifferent, cold, uninterested, unmoved.

indifferenza *f* indifference, disregard.

indigeno *adj* indigenous, native, aboriginal, indigenous; * *m* native.

indigente *adj* destitute; * *m/f* pauper.

indigenza *f* destitution.

indigenza *f* penury.

indigestione *f* indigestion.

indignato *adj* indignant.

indignazione *f* indignation.

indimenticabile *adj* unforgettable.

indipendente *adj* independent; self-contained.

indipendenza *f* independence.

indire *vt* to call.

indiretto *adj* indirect, roundabout.

indirizzare *vt* to address; ~ **male** to misdirect.

indirizzario *m* mailing list.

indirizzo *m* address.

indisciplinato *adj* unruly, undisciplined.

indiscreto *adj* indiscreet.

indiscrezione *f* indiscretion.

indiscriminato *adj* indiscriminate.

indiscusso *adj* unquestioned.

indiscutibile *adj* unquestionable.

indispensabile *adj* indispensable.

indisposizione *f* indisposition, ailment.

indisposto *adj* indisposed, ill, unwell, poorly.

indistinguibile *adj* indistinguishable.

indistinto *adj* indistinct; **una massa indistinta** *f* blur.

indistruttibile *adj* indestructible.

indivia *f* endive.

individuale *adj* individual, one-man.

individualità *f* individuality.

individuare *vt* to detect, to pick out.

individuo *m* individual.

indivisibile *adj* indivisible.

indizio *m* clue, lead, pointer, sign.

indole *f* disposition, temper.

indolente *adj* indolent, workshy.

indolenza *f* indolence, lethargy.

indolenzito *adj* sore, stiff.

indolore *adj* painless.

indomabile *adj* indomitable.

indomato *adj* untamed.

indossare *vt* to wear; to model.

indossatore *m* model.

indottrinamento *m* indoctrination.

indottrinare *vt* to indoctrinate.

indovinare *vt, vi* to guess.

indovinello *m* riddle, conundrum.

indovino *m* soothsayer.

indubbiamente *adv* doubtless.

indubbio *adj* undoubted.

indubitabile *adj* indubitable.

indugiare *vi* to linger.

indulgente *adj* indulgent, lenient, soft.

indulgenza *f* indulgence.

indumento *m* garment.

indurire *vt* to harden; * *vr* ~**rsi** to set.

industria *f* industry, trade.

industriale *adj* industrial; **zona** ~ *f* industrial estate; * *m* industrialist.

industrializzare *vt* to industrialize.

induzione *f* induction.

inebetito *adj* dopey.

inebriante *adj* heady.

inebriare *vt* to intoxicate.

inedia *f* starvation.

inedito *adj* unpublished.

ineffabile *adj* ineffable.

inefficace *adj* ineffective, ineffectual.

inefficiente *adj* inefficient.

inefficienza *f* inefficiency.

ineguaglianza *f* inequality.

ineguale *adj* uneven.

ineleggibile *adj* ineligible.

inequivocabile *adj* unequivocal.

inerpicarsi *vr* to scramble.

inerte *adj* inert.

inerzia *f* inertia.

inesatezza *f* inaccuracy.

inesatto *adj* inaccurate.

inesauribile *adj* inexhaustible.

inesercitato *adj* unpractised.

inesistente *adj* non-existent.

inesorabile *adj* inexorable.

inesperienza *f* inexperience.

inesperto *adj* inexperienced; unskilful.

inesplicabile *adj* unaccountable.

inesplorato *adj* unexplored.

inesploso *adj* unexploded; live.

inespressivo *adj* expressionless.

inesprimibile *adj* inexpressable.

inestimabile *adj* inestimable, invaluable; **di valore ~** priceless.

inestricabile *adj* inextricable.

inettitudine *f* ineptitude.

inetto *adj* inept.

inevitabile *adj* inevitable, unavoidable, inescapable.

inevitabilmente *adv* inevitably.

infallibile *adj* infallible, foolproof, surefire, unerring.

infallibilità *f* infallibility.

infame *adj* infamous.

infamia *f* infamy.

infangare *vt* to soil; to taint.

infanticidio *m* infanticide.

infantile *adj* infantile, babyish, childish.

infanzia *f* infancy, childhood; **prima ~** *f* babyhood.

infarinatura *f* smattering.

infarto *m* heart attack.

infastidire *vt* to annoy, to bother.

infaticabile *adj* indefatigable, untiring.

infatti *adv* indeed.

infatuato *adj* infatuated.

infatuazione *f* infatuation.

infausto *adj* ill-fated, inauspicious, ominous.

infedele *adj* unfaithful, infidel; * *m* infidel.

infedeltà *f inv* unfaithfulness, infidelity.

infelice *adj* unhappy, miserable.

infelicità *f* unhappiness.

infeltrito *adj* matted.

inferiore *adj* inferior, lower.

inferiorità *f* inferiority.

infermeria *f* infirmary, sickbay.

infermiere *m* nurse.

infermità *f inv* affliction; **~ mentale** *f* insanity.

infermo *adj* infirm.

infernale *adj* infernal, hellish.

inferno *m* hell.

inferriata *f* grille.

infestare *vt* to infest.

infettare *vt* to infect.

infettivo *adj* infectious.

infezione *f* infection.

infiammabile *adj* flammable.

infiammare *vt* to inflame.

infiammazione *f* inflamation.

infilare *vt* to thread; to string; to tuck; to cram.

infiltrarsi *vr* to infiltrate.

infilzare *vt* to spike.

infine *adv* lastly.

infinità *f* infinity.

infinitivo *adj* infinitive.

infinito *adj* infinite; * *m* infinitive.

infittirsi *vi* to thicken.

inflazione *f* inflation.

inflessibile *adj* inflexible; adamant.

inflessibilità *f* inflexibility.

inflessione *f* inflection.

infliggere *vt* to inflict.

influente *adj* influential.

influenza *f* influence, influenza, sway, clout.

influenzare *vt* to influence, to sway, to swing.

influire su *vt* to affect.

infocato *adj* fiery.

infondato *adj* groundless, baseless, unfounded

infondere *vt* to infuse.

inforcatura *f* crotch.

informale *adj* informal, casual.

informare *vt* to acquaint, to apprise.

ingiurie *fpl* abuse

ingiurioso *adj* abusive.

ingresso *m* entrance; admission, admittance.

inimicarsi *vr* to antagonize.

informare *vt* to inform; ~ **male** to misinform; * *vr* ~**rsi** to inquire.

informatica *f* computer science.

informato *adj* knowledgeable.

informatore *m* informant.

informazioni *fpl* information.

informe *adj* shapeless.

infossato *adj* sunken.

infradiciare *vt* to douse.

inframmezzare *vt* to intersperse.

infrangere *vt* to infringe.

infrangibile *adj* unbreakable, shatter-proof.

infrarosso *adj* infra-red.

infrastruttura *f* infrastructure.

infrazione *f* offence, infraction.

infrequente *adj* infrequent.

infruttuoso *adj* unfruitful, barren.

infuriare *vi* to storm; * *vr* ~**rsi** to rage.

infusione *f* infusion; **lasciare in** ~ *vt* to infuse.

infuso *m* brew; **fare un** ~ **di** *vt* to brew.

ingaggiare *vt* to engage.

ingannare *vt* to deceive, to fool, to hoax, to trick, to dupe.

ingannevole *adj* deceptive.

inganno *m* trick, deceit, deception; **trarre in** ~ *vt* to mislead.

ingarbugliare *vt* to scramble.

ingarbugliato *adj* garbled.

ingegnere *m* engineer; ~ **civile** *m* civil engineer.

ingegneria *f* engineering.

ingegnosità *f* ingenuity.

ingegnoso *adj* ingenious.

ingenuo *adj* naïve, ingenuous, artless, simple, childlike.

inghiottire *vt* to swallow; to gulp (down); to engulf; * *vi* to swallow.

inginocchiarsi *vr* to kneel.

inginocchiatoio *m* hassock.

ingiunzione *f* injunction.

ingiurioso *adj* invidious; hurtful.

ingiustificato *adj* unjustified,

ingiustizia *f* injustice.

ingiusto *adj* wrong, wrongful, unfair, unjust.

inglorioso *adj* inglorious.

ingollare *vt* to bolt (food).

ingombrante *adj* cumbersome; * *vt* to clutter; to encumber.

ingorgo *f* blockage; bottleneck; traffic jam.

ingovernabile *adj* ungovernable.

ingozzare *vt* to guzzle.

ingrandimento *m* enlargement.

ingrandire *vt* to enlarge, to magnify.

ingrassare *vt* to fatten.

ingratitudine *f* ingratitude.

ingrato *adj* ungrateful, thankless.

ingraziarsi *vr* to ingratiate.

ingrediente *m* ingredient.

ingresso *m* entrance, entry.

ingrosso *adj*: **all'**~ *adv* wholesale.

ingualcibile *adj* crease-resistant.

inguine *m* groin.

inibire *vt* to inhibit.

inibito *adj* inhibited.

inibizione *f* inhibition.

iniettare *vt* to inject.

iniettato *adj* injected; ~ **di sangue** bloodshot.

iniezione *f* injection, shot.

inimicizia *f* enmity.

inimitabile *adj* inimitable.

inimmaginabile *adj* unimaginable, inconceivable.

inintelligibile *adj* unintelligible.

ininterrotto *adj* unbroken, uninterrupted.

iniquità *f* iniquity.

iniquo *adj* iniquitous, inequitable.

iniziale *f, adj* initial.

iniziare *vt* to begin, to start; to initiate; * *vi* to begin.

iniziativa *f* initiative, enterprise.

iniziazione *f* initiation.

inizio *m* beginning, commencement; onset; outset; start; **sapevo fin dall'~** I knew all along; **all'~** *adv* initially.

innaffiare *vt* to water.

innamorare *vt* to enamour; * *vr* **~rsi** to fall in love.

innanzi *adv* ahead; **d'ora ~** henceforth; **~ tutto** firstly.

innato *adj* innate, in-born.

innaturale *adj* unearthly, unnatural.

innegabile *adj* undeniable.

innervosire *vt* to fluster, to rattle.

innestare *vt* to graft, to implant; to engage.

innesto *m* graft.

inno *m* hymn, anthem.

innocente *adj* innocent.

innocenza *f* innocence.

innocuo *adj* innocuous, harmless.

innominabile *adj* unmentionable.

innovazione *f* innovation; **fare delle innovazioni** *vi* to innovate.

innumerevole *adj* innumerable, countless.

inoculare *vt* to inoculate.

inoculazione *f* inoculation.

inodore *adj* odourless, scentless.

inoffensivo *adj* unoffending, inoffensive.

inoltrare *vt* to forward.

inoltre *adv* furthermore, besides, moreover.

inondare *vt* to inundate, to flood, to swamp.

inondazione *f* inundation, flood.

inopportuno *adj* inopportune, unsuitable; ill-timed.

inorganico *adj* inorganic.

inorridire *vt* to horrify.

inorridito *adj* aghast.

inospitale *adj* inhospitable.

inosservato *adj* unnoticed, unobserved, unseen.

inossidabile *adj* stainless.

input *m* input.

inquietante *adj* disquieting.

inquieto *adj* uneasy.

inquietudine *f* disquiet.

inquilino *m* tenant, occupant, occupier.

inquinamento *m* pollution.

inquinare *vt* to pollute.

inquisizione *f* inquisition.

insalata *f* salad; **~ di cavolo bianco** coleslaw.

insalatiera *f* salad bowl.

insalubre *adj* unhygienic.

insaponare *vt* to soap.

insaponato *adj* soapy.

insaziabile *adj* insatiable, avid.

inscatolare *vt* to tin.

insediamento *m* settlement.

insediarsi *vr* to settle.

insegna *f* ensign.

insegna *f* standard.

insegne *fpl* insignia; **~ reali** *fpl* regalia.

insegnamento *m* teaching.

insegnante *m/f* teacher; *m* master, schoolmaster; *f* schoolmistress; **~ privato** *m* tutor.

insegnare vt, vi to teach.

inseguimento m chase, pursuit.

inseguire vt to chase, to pursue; to stalk.

inseminazione f insemination.

insenatura f inlet, creek.

insensato adj senseless, foolish, hare-brained; mindless.

insensibile adj insensitive, unfeeling, callous.

inseparabile adj inseparable.

inserire vt to insert.

inserto m insert.

inservibile adj dud; **arnese ~** m dud.

inserviente m orderly.

inserzione f insertion; advertisement.

insetticida m insecticide.

insetto m insect, bug; **~ nocivo** m pest.

insicurezza f insecurity.

insidioso adj insidious.

insieme adv, adj together; **mettere ~** vt to pool; * m aggregate.

insignificante adj insignificant; inconsequential; fiddling; niggling; trifling; petty.

insincerità f insincerity.

insincero adj insincere.

insinuare vt to insinuate; * vr **~rsi** to worm.

insinuazione f insinuation, innuendo.

insipido adj insipid, flavourless, tasteless.

insistente adj insistent; nagging (pain, etc).

insistenza f insistence.

insistere vi to insist; * vt to insist; to urge.

insoddisfacente adj unsatisfying.

insoddisfatto adj dissatisfied.

insoddisfazione f dissatisfaction.

insolazione f sunstroke.

insolente adj insolent.

insolenza f insolence.

insolito adj uncommon, unusual.

insolubile adj insoluble.

insoluto adj outstanding.

insolvente adj insolvent.

insolvenza f insolvency.

insondabile adj unfathomable.

insonne adj sleepless.

insonnia f insomnia.

insopportabile adj insufferable, unendurable, unbearable; beastly.

insormontabile adj insurmountable.

insorto m insurgent.

insostenibile adj untenable.

insostituibile adj irreplaceable.

insperato adj unhoped-for.

inspiegabile adj inexplicable.

inspiegato adj unexplained.

instabile adj unstable, unsettled.

instabilità f instability.

installare vt to install.

installatore m fitter.

installazione f installation.

instancabile adj tireless, unflagging.

instillare vt to instil.

insubordinato adj insubordinate.

insubordinazione f insubordination.

insuccesso m failure.

insufficiente adj insufficient, unsatisfactory.

insufficienza f insufficiency, deficiency.

insulare adj insular.

insulina f insulin.

insulso adj dull, inane.

insultante adj insulting.

insultare vt to insult, to abuse; to revile.

insulti *mpl* abuse.

insulto *m* insult.

insuperabile *adj* insuperable.

insuperato *adj* unbroken, un-equalled.

insurrezione *f* insurrection, uprising.

intaccare *vt* to notch.

intaglio *m* carving.

intarsiare *vt* to inlay.

intarsiato *adj* inlaid.

intasamento *m* snarl-up.

intasare *vt* to clog.

intascare *vt* to pocket.

intatto *adj* intact, unbroken, undamaged, unimpaired.

integrale *adj* wholemeal.

integrante *adj* integral.

integrare *vt* to integrate, to supplement, to eke out; * *vr* **~rsi** to fit in.

integrazione *f* integration.

integrità *f* integrity.

intelletto *m* intellect.

intellettuale *m/f, adj* intellectual.

intelligente *adj* intelligent, clever.

intelligenza *f* intelligence, cleverness, wit.

intellighenzia *f* intelligentsia.

intelligibile *adj* intelligible.

intendere *vt* to intend, to mean.

intenditore *m* connoisseur.

intensificare *vt* to intensify, to escalate.

intensificazione *f* escalation.

intensità *f inv*. intensity; brilliance.

intensivo *adj* intensive.

intenso *adj* intense, acute, heavy.

intento *adj, m* intent.

intenzionale *adj* intentional.

intenzionato *adj*: **ben ~** well-intentioned.

intenzione *f* intent, intention;

avere ~ di *vi* to intend.

interazione *f* interaction, inter-play.

intercedere *vi* to intercede.

intercessione *f* intercession.

intercettare *vt* to intercept; to tap.

interessante *adj* interesting.

interessare *vt* to interest; * *vr* **~rsi di** to care about.

interesse *m* interest; expediency; **tasso di ~** *m* interest rate; **~ personale** *m* self-interest.

interferenza *f* interference.

interferire *vt* to interfere.

interiezione *f* interjection.

interiora *fpl* entrails.

interiore *adj* inner, inward.

interlocutore *m* speaker.

intermediario *m* intermediary, go-between.

intermedio *adj* intermediate, in-between.

interminabile *adj* interminable, endless, unending, never-ending.

intermittente *adj* intermittent.

internazionale *adj* international.

interno *m* inside; interior; internal; (*tel*) extension; * *adj* interior; inland; *adv* **all'~** indoors, within.

intero *adj* entire, whole.

interporre *vt* to interpose.

interpretare *vt* to interpret; to render; to play; to act; to construe; **~ male** to misinterpret.

interpretazione *f* interpretation, performance.

interprete *m/f* interpreter.

interregno *m* interregnum.

interrogante *m/f* questioner.

interrogare *vt* to interrogate, to cross-examine; to quiz, to question.

interrogativo *adj* interrogative, quizzical; **punto ~** *m* question mark.

interrogatorio *m* interrogation.

interrompere *vt* to interrupt; to butt in; to discontinue; to abort; * *vi* to interrupt.

interruttore *m* switch.

interruzione *f* interruption, intermission.

intersecare *vt* to intersect.

intersezione *f* intersection.

interurbano *adj* long-distance.

intervallo *m* interval, interlude, break, recess, lapse, gap, half-time; **~ di tempo** *m* time-lag.

intervenire *vt* to intervene.

intervento *m* intervention; operation.

intervista *f* interview.

intervistatore *m* interviewer.

intesa *f* understanding.

intestato *adj* intestate.

intestinale *adj* intestinal.

intestino *m* intestine; bowels; gut.

intimidire *vt* to intimidate, to browbeat, to overawe, to cow.

intimità *f* intimacy.

intimo *adj* intimate, close; **più ~**, inmost, innermost.

intitolare *vt* to entitle.

intollerabile *adj* intolerable.

intollerante *adj* intolerant.

intolleranza *f* intolerance.

intonacare *vt* to plaster.

intonacatore *m* plasterer.

intonaco *m* plaster.

intonarsi *vr* to match, to tone.

intonazione *f* intonation, pitch.

intontimento *m* stupor.

intontire *vt* to stupefy.

intontito *adj* groggy.

intoppo *m* hitch, snag, hold-up.

intorbidire *vt* to cloud.

intorno a *prep* **about,** around; round; * *adv* around.

intorpidimento *m* numbness.

intorpidire *vt* to numb, to dull.

intorpidito *adj* torpid, numb, dead.

intossicazione *f* poisoning; **~ alimentare** *f* food poisoning.

intraducibile *adj* untranslatable.

intralcio *m* hindrance.

intransigenza *f* intransigence.

intransitabile *adj* impassable.

intransitivo *adj* intransitive.

intrappolare *vt* to trap, to corner.

intraprendente *adj* enterprising, go-ahead.

intraprendere *vt* to wage.

intrattabile *adj* unmanageable, intractable.

intrattenere *vt* to entertain, to regale.

intravedere *vt* to glimpse.

intrecciare *vt* to braid, to plait; to entwine; to intertwine; to weave; **intrecciati** *adj* crisscross; * *vr* **~rsi** to interlock.

intrepido *adj* intrepid, fearless.

intricato *adj* intricate.

intrigante *m* schemer; * *adj* scheming.

intrigo *m* intrigue.

intrinseco *adj* intrinsic, inherent.

introdurre *vt* to introduce.

introduttivo *adj* introductory.

introduzione *f* introduction.

introiti *mpl* takings.

intromettersi *vr* to intrude, to interfere.

intromissione *f* interference.

introspezione *f* introspection.

introvabile *adj* unobtainable.

introverso *m* introvert.

intrusione *f* intrusion.

intruso *m* intruder, interloper, gatecrasher.

intuire *vt* to sense, to divine.

intuitivo *adj* intuitive.

intuito *m* intuition.

inumanità *f* inhumanity.

inumano *adj* inhuman.

inumidire *vt* to damp, to dampen, to moisten.

inutile *adj* useless, unnecessary, worthless, pointless, needless.

inutilità *f* uselessness.

inutilizzato *adj* unused.

invadente *adj* obtrusive, officious.

invadere *vt* to invade; to overrun; * *vi* to encroach.

invalido *adj* disabled; invalid; * *m* invalid.

invano *adv* to no avail.

invariabile *adj* invariable.

invariato *adj* unchanged.

invasare *vt* to pot.

invasione *f* invasion.

invasore *m* invader.

invece *adv* instead; ~ **di** in lieu of.

invecchiare *vi* to age.

inveire *vi* to rail (against).

invendibile *adj* unsaleable.

invenduto *adj* unsold.

inventare *vt* to invent; to make up; to concoct (a story).

inventario *m* inventory, stocktaking.

inventivo *adj* inventive.

inventore *m* inventor.

invenzione *f* invention.

invernale *adj* winter, wintry.

inverno *m* winter; **pieno ~** *m* midwinter.

inverosimile *adj* unlikely.

inversione *f* inversion, reversal.

inverso *m* converse; * *adj* inverse, reverse.

invertebrato *m* invertebrate.

invertire *vt* to reverse; to switch.

investigatore *m* investigator, detective.

investimento *m* investment.

investire *vt* to invest.

inveterato *adj* inveterate, confirmed.

invettiva *f* invective.

inviare *vt* to send, to dispatch.

inviato *m* envoy.

invidia *f* envy.

invidiabile *adj* enviable; **poco ~** unenviable.

invidiare *vt* to grudge, to begrudge.

invidioso *adj* envious.

invincibile *adj* invincible, unconquerable.

invio *m* dispatch.

inviolabile *adj* inviolable.

invisibile *adj* invisible.

invitante *adj* inviting.

invitare *vt* to invite; to ask out; to take out.

invitato *m* guest.

invito *m* invitation.

invocare *vt* to invoke.

involontario *adj* involuntary.

involontario *adj* inadvertent, accidental, unwitting, unintentional.

involtino di fegato *m* faggot.

invulnerabile *adj* invulnerable.

inzuppare *vt* to drench, to soak, to dunk.

inzuppato *adj* waterlogged.

io *pron* I.

iodio *m* iodine.

iperbole *f* hyperbole.

ipermercato *m* hypermarket.

ipersensibile *adj* highly strung.

ipertensione *f* hypertension.

ipnosi *f* hypnosis.

ipnotico *adj* hypnotic.

ipnotismo *m* hypnotism.

ipnotizzare *vt* to hynotize, to mesmerize.

ipocondria *f* hypochondria.

ipocondriaco *m* hypochondriac.

ipocrisia *f* hypocrisy.
ipocrita *m/f* hypocrite;
ipocrito *adj* hypocritical; **discorsi ipocriti** *mpl* cant.
ipodermico *adj* hypodermic.
ipoteca *f* mortgage.
ipotecare *vt* to mortgage.
ipotesi *f inv* hypothesis.
ipotetico *adj* hypothetical.
ippocastano *m* horse chestnut.
ippoglosso *m* halibut.
ippopotamo *m* hippopotamus.
ira *f* wrath.
irascibile *adj* irascible, cantankerous, bad-tempered, sharp-tempered.
irato *adj* irate.
iride *f* iris.
iris *f inv* iris.
ironia *f* irony.
ironico *adj* ironic.
irradiare *vt* to irradiate.
irraggiare *vt* to radiate.
irraggiungibile *adj* unattainable.
irragionevole *adj* irrational.
irragionevole *adj* unreasonable.
irrazionale *adj* unreasonable.
irreale *adj* unreal.
irreconciliabile *adj* irreconcilable.
irrecuperabile *adj* irretrievable.
irrefrenabile *adj* irrepressible.
irrefutabile *adj* unanswerable.
irregolare *adj* irregular.
irregolarità *f inv* irregularity.
irreligioso *adj* irreligious.
irremovibile *adj* unshakable.
irreparabile *adj* irrepairable.
irreprensibile *adj* blameless
irreprensibile *adj* irreproachable, unimpeachable.
irrequieto *adj* restive, restless, fidgety; **persona irrequieta** *f* fidget.
irresistibile *adj* irresistible.

irresoluto *adj* irresolute.
irresponsabile *adj* irresponsible, feckless.
irrestringibile *adj* unshrinkable.
irriconoscibile *adj* unrecognizable.
irrigare *vt* to irrigate.
irrigazione *f* irrigation.
irrigidire *vt* to stiffen; * *vr* ~**rsi** to stiffen.
irriguardoso *adj* inconsiderate, unthinking.
irrilevante *adj* immaterial.
irripetibile *adj* unrepeatable.
irrisorio *adj* paltry.
irritabile *adj* irritable, petulant, testy.
irritante *adj* irritating, annoying, aggravating; **sostanza** ~ *f* irritant.
irritare *vt* to irritate, to aggravate, to vex.
irritato *adj* irritated, vexed.
irritazione *f* irritation.
irriverente *adj* irreverent, disrespectful, flippant.
irriverenza *f* irreverence.
irrompere *vi (fig)* to erupt.
irruvidire *vt* to roughen.
irruzione *f* raid; **fare** ~ **in** to raid *vt*.
iscrivere *vt* to enrol; * *vr* ~**rsi** to register; to enter for.
iscrizione *f* inscription; enrolment; membership; lettering.
Islam *m inv* Islam.
isola *f* island, isle.
isolamento *m* insulation; isolation, seclusion.
isolano *m* islander.
isolare *vt* to insulate; to isolate.
isolato *adj* insulated; marooned; ~ **acusticamente** soundproof.
ispessire *vt* to thicken.
ispettore *m* inspector.
ispezione *f* inspection.

ispido *adj* shaggy.
ispirare *vt* to inspire.
ispirazione *f* inspiration.
issare *vt* to hoist.
istantaneo *adj* instantaneous.
istante *m* instant.
isterectomia *f* hysterectomy.
isterico *adj* hysterical; **crisi isterica** *f inv* hysterics.
isterismo *m* hysteria.
istigare *vt* to instigate.
istigazione *f* instigation.
istintivo *adj* instinctive.
istinto *m* instinct.
istituire *vt* to institute, to establish.
istituto *m* institute, home; **~ superiore** *m* college.

istituzione *f* institution, establishment.
istmo *m* isthmus.
istrionico *adj* histrionic.
istruire *vt* to instruct, to educate.
istruttivo *adj* instructive.
istruttore *m* instructor.
istruzione *f* instruction, education, schooling; **~ superiore** *f* further education; **dare istruzioni a** *vt* to brief.
itinerante *adj* travelling.
itinerario *m* itinerary, route.
itterizia *f* jaundice.
iuta *f* jute.
IVA *f* VAT.

J

jazz *m* jazz.
jeans *mpl* jeans; **tessuto ~** *m* denim.
jeep *f inv* jeep.

jet *m inv* jet.
jolly *m* joker.
judo *m* judo.
juke-box *m inv* juke-box.

K

K.O. *m inv* knock-out.
karate *m* karate.
ketchup *m* ketchup.

kilt *m inv* kilt.
kolossal *m* spectacular.

L

la *pron* her.
là *adv* there.
labbro *m* lip.
labirinto *m* labyrinth, maze.
laboratorio *m* laboratory.

laburista *adj* labour.
lacca *f* lacquer, hairspray.
laccetto *m* tab.
lacchè *m inv* lackey, footman.
laccio *m* (shoe)lace; tether.

lacerante *adj* piercing.

lacerare *vt* to lacerate.

laconico *adj* laconic.

lacrima *f* tear; **in lacrime** *adj* tearful.

lacrimogeno *adj*; **gas ~** *m* teargas.

lacuna *f* hiatus.

ladro *m* thief, burglar, crook.

ladruncolo *m* filcher.

laggiù *adv* yonder.

laghetto *m* pond.

lagnanza *f* grievance.

lago *m* lake, (*Scot*) loch.

laguna *f* lagoon.

laico *m* layman; **laici** *mpl* laity; * *adj* lay, secular.

laim *m* lime.

lama *f* blade.

lamb's wool *m* lambswool.

lambire *vi* to lap; * *vt* to wash.

lamé *m inv* lamé.

lamentare *vt* to lament, to bewail, to bemoan; * *vr* **~rsi** to complain.

lamentela *f* complaint.

lamento *m* lament.

lamiera *f* sheet; **~ ondulata** *f* corrugated iron.

laminato *adj* laminated.

lampada *f* lamp; **~ a spirito** *f* blowlamp.

lampadario *m* chandelier.

lampadina *f* (light) bulb.

lampante *adj* self-evident.

lampeggiare *vi* to flash.

lampeggio *m*: **~ diffuso** sheet lightning.

lampo *m* flash; lightning.

lampone *m* raspberry, raspberry bush.

lana *f* wool; **di ~** *adj* woollen; **indumenti di ~** *mpl* woollens.

lancetta *f* pointer.

lancia *f* lance, spear.

lanciare *vt* to throw, to toss, to cast, to fling, to shoot, to bowl,

to pitch; * *vr* **~rsi** to dart, to dive.

lancinante *adj* stabbing, shooting.

lancio *m* throw; launch, blast-off; **rampa di ~** *f* launching pad.

languido *adj* languid; lackadaisical; **con gli occhi languidi** dewy-eyed.

languire *vi* to languish, to pine.

lanoso *adj* woolly.

lanterna *f* lantern.

lapidare *vt* to stone; to pelt with stones.

lapide *f* gravestone; tablet.

lapis *m* pencil.

lardo *m* lard.

larghezza *f* width, breadth, broadness; **nel senso della ~** *adv* breadthwise.

largo *adj* broad, wide; **al ~** offshore.

larice *m* larch.

laringe *f* larynx.

laringite *f* laryngitis.

larva *f* larva, grub.

lasciapassare *m inv* pass.

lasciare *vt* to leave, to let; to vacate, to quit; * *vr* **~rsi** to part.

lascito *m* bequest.

lascivo *adj* lascivious; lecherous; wanton.

laser *m inv* laser.

lassativo *m* laxative.

lasso *m*: **~ di tempo** *m* lag.

lastra *f* slab.

lastricare *vt* to pave.

latente *adj* latent, dormant.

laterale *adj* lateral, side, sideways.

latitudine *f* latitude.

lato *m* side.

latrare *vi* to bay.

latta *f* can, tinplate.

latte *m* milk; **~ in polvere** *m* dried milk; **~ cagliato** *m* curd(s); **~ concentrato** *m* evaporated milk; **~ detergente** *m* cleanser.

latteo *adj* milky; **Via Lattea** *f* Milky Way.

lattina *f* can, tin.

lattuga *f* lettuce.

laurea *f* degree; **consegna delle lauree** *f* graduation; * *vr* **~rsi** to graduate.

laureato *m* graduate.

lava *f* lava.

lavabile *adj* washable.

lavabo *m* washbasin.

lavacristallo *m* windscreen washer.

lavaggio *m* washing; **~ auto** car wash.

lavagna *f* blackboard.

lavanda *f* lavender.

lavanderia *f* laundry; **~ automatica** *f* launderette.

lavandino *m* basin.

lavare *vt* to wash; to bathe (a wound); to sluice; to launder; **~ a secco** to dry-clean; * *vi* **~ i piatti** to do the washing up; * *vr* **~rsi** to wash.

lavastoviglie *f inv* dishwasher.

lavata *f* wash.

lavativo *m* slacker.

lavatrice *f* washing machine.

lavello *m* sink; **piano del ~** *m* draining board.

lavorare *vi* to work; to labour; **~ troppo** to overwork.

lavoratore *m* worker; **~ accanito** *m* workaholic.

lavoretto *m* odd job.

lavoro *m* work; job; labour; **duro ~** *m* graft; **lavori stradali** *mpl* roadworks.

forza ~ *f* workforce; **~ eccessivo** *m* overwork; **~ preparatorio** *m* groundwork; **ora di ~** *f* manhour.

leader *m* leader.

leale *adj* loyal.

lealtà *f* loyalty, allegiance.

lebbra *f* leprosy.

lebbroso *m* leper.

lecca lecca *m inv* lollipop.

leccapiedi *m/f* sycophant.

leccare *vt* to lick, to lap.

leccata *f* lick.

leccornia *f* titbit.

ledere *vt* to impinge on.

lega *f* league; **~ per saldatura** *f* solder.

legale *adj* legal, lawful; * *f* **medicina ~** *f* forensic medicine.

legalità *f* legality.

legalizzare *vt* to legalize.

legalmente *adv* legally.

legame *m* link, bond.

legamento *m* ligament.

legare *vt* to tie, to fasten, to bind, to rope, to strap, to tether, to lash; **~ stretto** to truss.

legato *adj* bound.

legatura *f* slur.

legazione *f* legation.

legge *f* law; **senza leggi** *adj* lawless.

leggenda *f* legend.

leggendario *adj* legendary.

leggere *vt, vi* to read, to peruse.

leggermente *adv* lightly, slightly.

leggero *adj* light, flimsy, lightweight; faint; *vi* **prendere alla leggera** to trifle with.

leggibile *adj* legible; readable.

leggio *m* music stand.

legiferare *vt* to legislate.

legione *f* legion.

legislativo *adj* legislative; **corpo ~** *m* legislature.

legislatore *m* legislator.

legislazione *f* legislation.

legittimare *vt* to legitimize.

legittimità *f* legitimacy.

legittimo *adj* legitimate; rightful.

legna *f* wood; **~ da ardere** *f* firewood.

legname *m* timber.

legno *m* wood; **di ~** *adj* wooden; **legni** *mpl* (*mus*) woodwind.

lei *pron* her, she; **di ~** hers; * *pers pron* you.

lendine *f* nit.

lente *f* lens; **~ d'ingrandimento** *f* magnifying glass.

lentezza *f* slowness.

lenticchia *f* lentil.

lentiggine *f* freckle.

lentigginoso *adj* freckled.

lento *adj* slow, slugish; slack; backward (child).

lenza *f* fishing line.

lenzuolo *m* sheet.

leone *m* lion.

leonessa *f* lioness.

leopardo *m* leopard.

leporino *adj*: **labbro ~** *m* harelip.

lepre *f* hare.

lesbica *f* lesbian; (*sl*) dyke.

lesbico *adj* lesbian.

lesione *f* lesion; hurt.

lessare *vt* to boil.

lessico *m* lexicon.

letale *adj* lethal.

letame *m* muck.

letargico *adj* lethargic.

letargo *m* hibernation; **cadere in ~** *vi* to hibernate.

lettera *f* letter; **~ d'accompagnamento** *f* covering letter; **~ d'amore** *f* love letter; **lettere** *fpl* the arts; **dire** *or* **scrivere ~ per ~** *vi* to spell.

letterale *adj* literal.

letterario *adj* literary.

letteratura *f* literature.

lettino *m* cot.

letto *m* bed; **~ di piume** *m* feather bed; **~ di morte** *m* deathbed; **costretto a ~** *adj* bedridden.

lettore *m* reader.

lettura *f* reading; perusal; **sala di ~** *f* reading room.

leucemia *f* leukaemia.

leucisco *m*: **~ rosso** *m* roach.

leva *f* lever.

levatura *f* stature.

levigatezza *f* smoothness.

levriero *m* greyhound.

lezione *f* lesson.

lezioni *fpl* tuition.

li *pers pron* them.

lì *adv* there.

libbra *f* pound.

libellula *f* dragonfly.

liberale *adj* liberal.

liberalità *f* liberality; largesse.

liberamente *adv* freely.

liberare *vt* to liberate, to free, to unleash; to clear.

liberazione *f* liberation; deliverance; * *excl* **che ~!** good riddance!

libero *adj* free, unattached, unoccupied, vacant; **stanza libera** *f* vacancy; **segnale di ~** *m* dialling tone; **stile ~** (swim) crawl.

liberoscambismo *m* free trade.

libertà *f* liberty, freedom; **~ condizionale** *f* probation; **~ provvisoria** *f* parole; **in ~** *adv* at large.

libertino *m* libertine, rake.

libidine *f* lust.

libidinoso *adj* lustful, prurient; **espressione libidinosa** *f* leer.

libido *f inv* libido.

libraio *m* bookseller.

librarsi *vi* to soar; * *vr* to hover.

libreria *f* bookshop; bookcase.

libretto *m* libretto; booklet; **~ di circolazione** *m* logbook; **~ di risparmio** *m* passbook;

libro *m* book; **~ di testo** *m* textbook.

licenza *f* licence; leave.

licenziamento *m* dismissal; discharge; redundancy.

licenziare *vt* to dismiss, to sack, to fire, to discharge.

licenziato *adj* redundant.

licenzioso *adj* licentious.

lichene *m* lichen.

lieto *adj* pleased, glad, joyful, joyous.

lievitare *vi* to rise; **far ~** *vt* to leaven.

lievito *m* yeast; **~ in polvere** *m* baking powder.

ligneo *adj* ligneous.

ligustro *m* privet.

lilla *m inv* lilac.

lima *f* file.

limare *vt* to file.

limetta *f*: **~ di carta** *f* emery board; **~ per le unghie** *f* nail-file.

limetta *f* lime.

limitare *vt* to limit, to restrict, to confine.

limitazione *f* limitation, check.

limite *m* limit; **~ di velocità** *m* speed limit.

limiti *mpl* bounds.

limo *m* silt.

limonata *f* lemonade.

limone *m* lemon; **albero di ~** *m* lemon tree.

limousine *f inv* limousine.

limpido *adj* limpid.

lince *f* lynx; **dagli occhi di ~** *adj* eagle-eyed.

linciare *vt* to lynch.

linea *f* line; figure; **~ di demarcazione** *f* borderline; **~ secondaria** *f* (*rail*) branch line; **~ principale** *f* mainline.

lineare *adj* linear.

linfa *f* sap, lymph.

lingotto *m* ingot; **oro in lingotti** *m* bullion.

lingua *f* language; tongue; **~ madre** *f* mother tongue; **avere la ~ sciolta** *vt* to have the gift of the gab.

linguaggio *m* language, speech.

linguetta *f* flap, tab.

linguista *m/f* linguist.

linguistica *f* linguistics.

linguistico *adj* linguistic.

linimento *m* liniment.

lino *m* flax; linen; **seme di ~** *m* linseed.

linoleum *m* linoleum.

liofilizzato *adj* freeze-dried.

liquidare *vt* to liquidate; to clear; to sell off.

liquidazione *f* liquidation.

liquido *adj*, *m* liquid.

liquirizia *f* liquorice.

liquore *m* liqueur.

liquori *mpl* spirits.

lirico *adj* lyrical; operatic.

lisca *f* fishbone.

lisciare *vt* to smooth.

liscio *adj* smooth, smoothly, even, straight.

lista *f* list; roll; **~ nera** *f* blacklist; **~ dei vini** *f* wine list.

listino *m*: **~ prezzi** *m* price list.

litania *f* litany.

lite *f* row.

litigare *vi* to argue, to quarrel, to row, to wrangle, to fall out.

litigio *m* quarrel.

litigioso *adj* litigious, quarrelsome.

litografia *f* lithograph, lithography.

litorale *m* coast, coastline.

litre *m* litro.

liturgia *f* liturgy.

liuto *m* lute.

livellare *vt* to level; to equalize.

livello *m* level; **a ~ di** *adv* flush with; **ad alto ~** *adj* top level.

livido *m* bruise; * *adj* livid; **farsi un ~ a** *vt* to bruise.

livrea *f* livery.

lo *pron* him.

lobo *m* lobe.

locale *adj* local; **anestesia ~** *f* local anaesthetic; **amministrazione ~** *f* local government.

locali *mpl* premises.

località *f inv* locality.

localizzare *vt* to localize; **~ con esatezza** to pinpoint.

locanda *f* inn.

locandiere *m* innkeeper.

locomotiva *f* locomotive, engine.

locusta *f* locust.

lodare *vt* to praise, to commend.

lodevole *adj* laudable, praiseworthy, commendable, creditable, worthy.

loggia *f* lodge.

logica *f* logic.

logico *adk* logical.

logo *m inv* logo.

logoramento *m* wear.

logorarsi *vr* to wear out.

logoro *adj* effete.

lombaggine *f* lumbago.

lombata *f* loin.

lombrico *m* earthworm.

longevità *f* longevity.

longitudine *f* longitude.

lontananza *f* distance.

lontano *adj* distant, far, faraway; **più ~** farthest, furthest; *adv* farthest, furthest.

lontra *f* otter.

loquace *adj* loquacious, talkative, voluble, garrulous, comunicative.

loquacità *f* loquacity.

lordo *adj* gross.

loro pers *pron* you; them; * *poss adj* your(s), their; * *pron* your(s).

losanga *f* lozenge.

losco *adj* shifty.

lotta *f* fight; combat; battle; struggle; **~ libera** *f* wrestling.

lottare *vt* to fight, to struggle; * *vi* to struggle, to battle, to wrestle.

lottatore *m* wrestler.

lotteria *f* lottery, draw, sweepstake.

lotto *m* lot; **~ di terreno** *m* plot.

lozione *f* lotion.

lubrificante *m* lubricant.

lubrificare *vt* to lubricate, to grease.

lucchetto *m* padlock.

luccicare *vi* to glisten, to glitter, to gleam, to shimmer.

luccichio *m* gleam.

luccio *m* pike.

lucciola *f* firefly.

luce *f* light; **~ di giorno** *f* daylight; **~ di posizione** *f* sidelight.

lucente *adj* shining; gleaming; **~ e liscio** sleek.

lucentezza *f* gloss, shine, sheen.

lucernario *m* skylight.

lucertola *f* lizard.

lucidare *vt* to polish, to buff.

lucidato *adj* polished.

lucidata *f* polish.

lucido *adj* shiny, glossy; lucid; * *m* polish; **~ da scarpe** bootpolish.

lucrativo *adj* lucrative.

luglio *m* July.

lugubre *adj* lugubrious, mournful.

lui *pron* him, he.

lumaca *f* slug.

lume *m* **di candela** candlelight.

luminosità *f* brightness.

luminoso *adj* luminous, bright.

luna *f* moon; **~ piena** *f* full moon; **~ park** *m inv* funfair; **~ di miele** *f* honeymoon; **chiaro di ~** *f* moonlight.

lunare *adj* lunar.

lunatico *adj* moody.

lunedì *m inv* Monday.

lunga *f*: **di gran ~** far and away.

lunghezza *f* length; **per la ~** *adv* lengthways.

lungo *adj* long, lengthy, fulllength.

lungomare *m* esplanade, prom(enade), front, seafront.

lungometraggio *m*: **a ~** *adj* full-length.

luogo *m* place; scene; **~ d'incontro** *m* venue; **fuori ~** *adj* inappropriate.

lupo *m* wolf.

luppolo *m* hop.

lusinga *f* flattery; **persuadere con le lusinghe** *vt* to inveigle.

lusingare *vt* to flatter.

lusinghe *fpl* flattery.

lusinghiero *adj* flattering, complimentary.

lusso *m* luxury.

lussuoso *adj* luxurious.

lussureggiante *adj* lush, luxuriant.

lustrare *vt* to shine, to polish.

lustrino *m* sequin, spangle.

lustro *m* lustre.

lutto *m* mourning; bereavement; **in ~** *adj* bereaved.

M

ma *conj* but; yet.

macabro *adj* grim; sick.

macadam *m*: **~ al catrame** *m* tarmac.

maccheroni *mpl* macaroni.

macchia *f* spot, smudge, stain; blot; taint; slur; **~ d'olio** *f* oil slick; **senza ~** *adj* unblemished.

macchiare *vt* to mark, to stain, to spot, to blot.

macchiato *adj* spotted.

macchina *f* machine; car; **~ fotografica** *f* camera; **~ a tre porte** *f* hatchback; **~ da scrivere** *f* typewriter.

macchinari *mpl* machinery.

macchinazione *f* machination.

macchinista *m* engine driver.

macchiolina *f* fleck, speck.

macedonia *f* fruit salad.

macellaio *m* butcher.

macellare *vt* to butcher, to slaughter.

macellazione *f* slaughter.

macelleria *f* butcher's shop.

macello *m* shambles.

macerare *vt* to macerate.

macerie *fpl* rubble.

macigno *m* boulder.

macina *f* millstone.

macinare *vt* to grind, to mill.

macinino *m* grinder.

macis *m*, *f* mace.

madre *f* mother.

madrelingua *f* native language.

madreperla *f* mother-of-pearl.

madrina *f* godmother.

maestà *f* majesty.

maestoso *adj* majestic, stately.

maestra *f* teacher, schoolmistress.

maestria *f* craftsmanship.

maestro *m* maestro; teacher, schoolmaster.

maga *f* sorceress.

magazzino *m* warehouse, stockroom; **grande ~** *m* department store; **~ doganale** *m* bonded warehouse.

maggio *m* May.

maggiorana *f* marjoram.

maggioranza *f* majority.

maggiordomo *m* butler.

maggiore *adj* elder, eldest; senior; extra; major; **mia sorella ~** my big sister; ***** *m* major.

magia *f* magic.

magico *adj* magic.

magistrale *adj* masterly.

magistrato *m* magistrate.
magistratura *f* judiciary.
maglia *f* jersey; stitch; mesh; **lavorare a ~** *vi* to knit.
maglieria *f* knitwear.
maglietta *f* T-shirt.
maglione *m* jumper, sweater.
magnaccia *m inv* pimp.
magnanimità *f* magnanimity.
magnanimo *adj* magnanimous.
magnate *m* magnate, tycoon.
magnesia *f* magnesia.
magnesio *m* magnesium.
magnetico *adj* magnetic.
magnetismo *m* magnetism.
magnificare *vt* to extol.
magnificenza *f* magnificence.
magnifico *adj* magnificent, grand.
magniloquente *adj* bombastic.
mago *m* magician, wizard.
magro *adj* thin, lean, meagre; **~ e forte** wiry.
mai *adv* never, ever.
maiale *m* pig, pork.
maionese *f* mayonnaise.
maiuscolo *adj* capital.
mal *m*: **~ di mare** *m* seasickness; **~ d'auto** *m* carsickness; **avere il ~ di mare** *vi* to be seasick.
malaccorto *adj* misguided.
malandato *adj* shabby.
malaria *f* malaria.
malaticcio *adj* sickly, unhealthy.
malato *adj* ill, sick, diseased.
malattia *f* illness, sickness, disease, malady.
malavita *f* underworld.
malcontento *adj*, *m* malcontent.
male *m* harm, wrong, evil; **i mali** *mpl* the ills; **andato a ~** *adj* off; **far ~** *vi* to hurt.
maledetto *adj* damned, accursed, bloody.

maledire *vt* to curse.
maledizione *f* curse.
maleducato *adj* bad-mannered, ill-bred.
maleducazione *f* rudeness.
malefico *adj* malign.
malessere *m* malaise.
malevolenza *f* ill-will.
malevolo *adj* malevolent, acrimonious.
malfamato *adj* low, seamy.
malgrado *prep* despite; * *conj* in spite of.
maligno *adj* malignant, nasty, snide, spiteful, vicious.
malinconia *f* melancholy.
malinconico *adj* melancholy.
malincuore *adj*: **a ~** *adv* unwillingly.
malinteso *m* misunderstanding, mix-up.
malizia *f* malice.
malizioso *adj* mischievous, roguish.
malleabile *adj* malleable, pliable.
malmenare *vt* to manhandle.
malridotto *adj* tatty.
malsano *adj* unhealthy.
malsicuro *adj* insecure.
malto *m* malt.
maltrattare *vt* to maltreat, to mistreat, to ill-treat.
malva *f* mallow; * *adj* mauve.
malvagio *adj* evil, evil-minded, wicked.
malvolentieri *adv* unwillingly, grudgingly.
malvone *m* hollyhock.
mamma *f* (*inf*) mummy; **~ mia!** **futura ~** *f* mother-to-be; *excl* oh dear!
mammella *f* breast; udder.
mammifero *m* mammal.
mammut *m inv* mammoth.
manager *m inv* manager.
manata *f* slap; **dare una ~ a** *vt* to whack.

mancante *adj* missing, deficient.

mancanza *f* lack; deficiency; want; default; **in ~ di** *prep* failing.

mancare *vt* to miss; * *vi* to lack; to want; to fail; to pass away, to pass on.

mancia *f* tip; gratuity; **dare la ~ a** *vt* to tip.

manciata *f* handful.

mancino *adj* left-handed.

mandare *vt* to send; **~ tutto all'aria** to upset the apple cart.

mandarino *m* mandarin; mandarine, tangerine.

mandato *m* writ; warrant; mandate; **~ di morte** *m* death warrant; **~ di comparizione** *m* summons.

mandolino *m* mandolin.

mandorla *f* almond.

mandria *f* herd.

mandrillo *m* wolf.

maneggevole *adj* manageable, manoeuvrable; **poco ~** unwieldy.

maneggiare *vt* to handle; to wield; to ply.

maneggio *m* stables.

manetta *f* manacle.

manette *fpl* handcuffs.

manganello *m* cudgel, truncheon, cosh.

manganese *m* manganese.

mangiabile *adj* edible.

mangiare *vt* to eat; **dare da ~ a** *vt* to feed.

mangiata *f* feed.

mangiatoia *f* manger, crib, trough.

mangime *m* feed.

mango *m* mango.

mania *f* mania, craze.

maniaco *adj* manic; * *m* maniac.

manica *f* sleeve; **la M~** the English Channel; **giro della ~** armhole; **senza maniche** *adj* sleeveless.

manichino *m* dummy.

manico *m* handle.

manicomio *m* madhouse, asylum.

manicotto *m* muff.

manicure *f inv* manicure.

maniera *f* manner.

maniero *m* manor.

manifestante *m* demonstrator.

manifestare *vt* to demonstrate, to manifest, to evince.

manifestazione *f* demonstration, manifestation, show.

manifesto *m* manifesto, poster.

manigoldo *m* ruffian.

manipolare *vt* to manipulate.

manipolazione *f* manipulation.

manna *f* godsend.

mannaggia escl blast.

mannaia *f* chopper, cleaver.

mano *f* hand; coat (of paint); **lavorazione a ~** *f* handiwork; **stretta di ~** *f* handshake; **a portata di ~** *adj* at hand; **a mani vuote** empty-handed; **di seconda ~** second-hand.

manodopera *f* labour, manpower.

manomettere *vi* to tamper.

manopola *f* knob.

manoscritto *m* manuscript.

manovale *m* labourer.

manovra *f* manoeuvre.

manovrare *vi, vt* to manoeuvre.

mansarda *f* attic.

mantella *f* cloak.

mantello *m* cape.

mantenere *vt* to maintain; to support; to keep; to hold; **~ i contatti con** to liaise.

mantenimento *m* maintenance.

mantice *m* bellows.

manuale m handbook, guide, manual; * adj manual.

manubrio m handlebars; dumbbell.

manufatto m artefact.

manutenzione f maintenance; upkeep.

manzo m beef; steer.

mappa f map; **tracciare una ~** vt to map.

mappamondo m globe.

maratona f marathon.

marca f make, brand.

marcato adj pronounced; rugged.

marcatore m marker.

marchiare vt to brand.

marchio m hallmark, trademark.

marcia f gear; march.

marciapiede m pavement.

marciare vi to march.

marcio adj rotten.

marcire vi to rot.

marciume m rot.

marco m mark.

mare m sea; **~ lungo** m swell; **d'alto ~** adj ocean-going.

marea f tide; **alta ~** f high tide; **di ~** adj tidal.

maresciallo m marshall.

margarina f margarine.

marginale adj marginal.

margine m border, margin.

marijuana f marijuana.

marina f navy; marina, marine; **~ mercantile** f merchant navy.

marinaio m sailor, mariner, seaman.

marinare vt to marinate; **~ la scuola** to play truant.

marinaresco adj: **canzone marinaresca** f shanty.

marinata f marinade.

marino adj marine.

marito m husband.

marittimo adj maritime.

marketing m marketing.

marmellata f jam; **~ di arance** f marmalade.

marmo m marble.

marrone adj brown; **~ rossiccio** inv russet.

marsupiale m, adj marsupial.

marsupio m pouch.

martedì m inv Tuesday; **~ grasso** m Shrove Tuesday.

martellare vt to hammer.

martello m hammer; **~ da fabbro** m sledgehammer; **~ pneumatico** m pneumatic drill.

martin m inv: **~ pescatore** m kingfisher.

martire m martyr.

martirio m martyrdom.

martora f marten.

marzapane m marzipan.

marziale adj martial.

marzo m March.

mascalzone m rogue, rascal; villain.

mascara m inv mascara.

mascella f jaw.

maschera f mask; usherette; **festa in ~** f fancy dress party; **~ antigas** f gasmask.

mascherare vt to mask; to disguise; to gloss over.

mascherata f masquerade.

maschiaccio m tomboy.

maschile adj male, masculine; * m masculine.

maschilismo m chauvinism.

maschilista m chauvinist.

maschio adj, m male; (zool) buck.

masochista m/f masochist.

mass media m pl mass media.

massa f mass, body, bulk.

massacrare vt to massacre, to slaughter.

massacro m massacre, slaughter.

massaggiare vt to massage.

massaggiatore m masseur.

massaggiatrice *f* masseuse.

massaggio *m* massage.

massiccio *adj* massive.

massima *f* maxim.

massimizzare *vt* to maximize.

massimo *adj* utmost, maximum; * *m* utmost.

massone *m* mason; freemason.

massoneria *f* masonry; freemasonry.

mastello *m* tub.

masticare *vt* to masticate, to chew.

mastino *m* inglese *m* mastiff.

mastro *m* master; libro ~ *m* ledger.

masturbarsi *vr* to masturbate.

masturbatore *m* wanker.

masturbazione *f* masturbation.

matassa *f* skein.

matematica *f* mathematics, maths.

matematico *adj* mathematical; * *m* mathematician.

materasso *m* mattress.

materia *f* matter; subject.

materiale *adj* material; bodily; * *m* material.

materialismo *m* materialism.

maternità *f* motherhood, maternity.

materno *adj* motherly, maternal.

matinée *f inv* matinée.

matita *f* pencil.

matrice *f* stencil, counterfoil, stub.

matricola *f* fresher.

matrigna *f* step-mother.

matrimoniale *adj* matrimonial; letto ~ *m* double bed; camera ~ *f* double room.

matrimonio *m* marriage; wedding; certificato di ~ *m* marriage certificate.

mattatoio *m* slaughterhouse.

matterello *m* rolling pin.

mattina *f* morning, forenoon.

matto *adj* crazy, lunatic; * *m* lunatic, (*sl*) nut, nutcase.

mattone *m* brick.

mattonella *f* tile.

mattutino *m* matins.

maturare *vi* to ripen, to mellow; * *vr* ~**rsi** to mature.

maturità *f* maturity.

maturo *adj* mature, ripe, mellow.

matusa *m inv* old fogey, square.

mausoleo *m* mausoleum.

mazza *f* club (golf), bat; mace.

mazzo *m* bunch.

mazzolino *m* posy, spray.

mazzuolo *m* mallet.

me *pron* me.

meccanica *f* mechanics.

meccanico *m* mechanic, engineer; * *adj* mechanical.

meccanismo *m* mechanism, works.

meccanizzare *vt* to mechanize.

mecenate *m/f* patron.

medaglia *f* medal.

medaglione *m* medallion; locket.

media *mpl* media; * *f* average; sopra la ~ *adj* above par.

mediare *vt* to mediate.

mediatore *m* mediator; broker.

mediazione *f* mediation; brokerage.

medicare *vt* to medicate.

medicato *adj* medicated.

medicina *f* medicine; drug.

medicinale *adj* medicinal; * *m* drug.

medico *m* doctor; physician; ~ di famiglia *m* family doctor; * *adj* medical.

medievale *adj* medieval.

medio *adj* average, medium, mean, middling.

mediocre *adj* mediocre, middling, pedestrian.

mediocrità *f* mediocrity.

meditare *vi* to meditate, to cogitate.

meditativo *adj* meditative.

meditazione *f* meditation.

mediterraneo *adj* Mediterranean.

medusa *f* jellyfish.

megafono *m* megaphone.

megalomane *m/f* megalomaniac.

meglio *adv* better, best; **~ così** so much the better.

mela *f* apple; **~ selvatica** *f* crab apple.

melagrana *f* pomegranate.

melanzana *f* aubergine.

melassa *f* treacle, molasses.

melma *f* slime, ooze, mire.

melmoso *adj* slimy.

melo *m* apple tree.

melodia *f* melody, tune.

melodioso *adj* melodious, tuneful.

melodramma *m* melodrama.

melone *m* melon.

membrana *f* membrane.

membro *m* member, fellow.

memorabile *adj* memorable; **giorno ~** *m* red-letter day.

memorandum *m inv* memorandum.

memoria *f* memory; **imparare a ~** *vt* to memorize; **a ~** *adv* by rote.

mendicante *m/f* beggar.

mendicare *vt* to beg.

menestrello *m* minstrel.

meningite *f* meningitis.

meno *prep* less; minus; * *adj* fewer; less; * *adv* least; less; * *pron* less; * **a ~ che** *conj* unless.

menomazione *f* handicap, disability.

menopausa *f* menopause.

mensa *f* canteen.

mensile *adj* monthly.

mensola *f* bracket; cantilever;

~ del caminetto *f* mantelpiece.

menta *f* mint; **~ peperita** *f* peppermint.

mentale *adj* mental.

mentalità *f inv* mentality.

mentalmente *adv* mentally.

mente *f* mind; **di ~ aperta** *adj* open-minded.

mentire *vi* to lie.

mento *m* chin; **doppio ~** *m* double chin.

mentore *m* mentor.

mentre *conj* as, whereas, while.

menù *m inv* menu.

menzione *f* mention.

menzogna *f* lie, falsehood.

meraviglia *f* marvel.

meraviglioso *adj* marvellous, great, smashing.

mercantile *adj* mercantile.

mercato *m* market, marketplace; **~ nero** black market; **~ azionario** *m* stock market.

merce *f* merchandise.

mercenario *adj, m* mercenary.

merceria *f* haberdashery.

merciaio *m* haberdasher.

merci *fpl* goods.

mercoledì *m inv* Wednesday.

mercurio *m* mercury, quicksilver.

merda *f* shit.

meridiana *f* sundial; * *adj, m* meridian.

meridionale *adj* south.

meridione *m* south.

meringa *f* meringue.

meritare *vt* to merit, to deserve.

meritatamente *adv* deservedly.

meritato *adj* well-deserved.

meritevole *adj* deserving.

merito *m* merit.

meritocrazia *f* meritocracy.

meritorio *adj* meritorious.

merlango *m* whiting.

merlo *m* blackbird.

merluzzo *m* cod; **olio di fegato di ~** *m* cod-liver-oil.

meschinità *f* pettiness, narrow-mindedness;

meschino *adj* mean, narrow-minded, sordid.

mescolanza *f* mix.

mescolare *vt* to mix, to shuffle, to jumble, to mingle, to stir; * *vr* **~rsi** to hobnob.

mescolata *f* shuffle.

mese *m* month.

messa *f* mass.

messaggero *m* messenger.

messaggio *m* message.

messale *m* missal.

messinscena *f* act, sham.

mestiere *m* craft.

mestiere *m* occupation, trade.

mesto *adj* rueful.

mestolo *m* ladle, scoop.

mestruazione *f* menstruation.

mestruazioni *fpl* period.

meta *f* destination; (rugby) try.

metà *f inv* half; * *adj* half; mid; **a ~ prezzo** *adj, adv* half-price; **a ~ strada** *adj* halfway.

metabolismo *m* metabolism.

metafisica *f* metaphysics.

metafisico *adj* metaphysical.

metafora *f* metaphor.

metaforico *adj* metaphoric(al).

metallico *adj* metallic.

metallo *m* metal.

metallurgia *f* metallurgy.

metamorfosi *f inv* metamorphosis.

metano *m* methane.

metanolo *m* wood alcohol.

meteora *f* meteor.

meteorite *m* meteorite.

meteorologia *f* meteorology.

meteorologico *adj* meteorological.

meteorologo *m* weatherman.

meticcio *m* half-caste.

metodico *adj* methodical.

metodo *m* method.

metraggio *m* footage.

metrico *adj* metric.

metro *m* metre; **~ a nastro** *m* tape measure.

metrò *m inv* underground railway.

metropoli *f inv* metropolis.

metropolitana *f* underground railway.

metropolitano *adj* metropolitan.

mettere *vt* to put; **~ insieme** to lump together; to concoct; **~ via** to put away; to stand; to place; * *vr* **~rsi** to don.

mezz'ora *f* half-hour.

mezzaluna *f* half-moon, crescent.

mezzanino *m* mezzanine.

mezzanotte *f* midnight.

mezzo *m* middle, medium, mean ; *adj* half; **in ~ a** *prep* midst.

mezzi *mpl* wherewithal.

mezzogiorno *m* noon, midday.

mi *pron* me.

mia poss *adj* my.

miagolare *vi* to mew.

miagolio *m* mew.

micidiale *adj* deadly; murderous.

micio *m* pussy.

microbo *m* germ, microbe.

microfono *m* microphone.

microonda *f* microwave.

microscopico *adj* microscopic.

microscopio *m* microscope.

midollo *m* marrow.

miele *m* honey.

mietere *vt* to reap.

mietitore *m* reaper.

mietitrice *f* (combine) harvester.

miglio *m* mile; millet.

miglioramento *m* improvement.

migliorare *vt* to improve; to

better; * *vi* to improve.
migliore *adj* better, best, topmost; * *m* best.
migrare *vi* to migrate.
migratore *adj* migratory.
migrazione *f* migration.
milionario *m* millionaire.
milione *m* million.
milionesimo *m* millionth.
militante *m/f* militant.
militare *adj* military; * *vi* to militate.
milizia *f* militia.
mille *adj*, *m* thousand.
millennio *m* millennium.
millepiedi *m inv* centipede, millipede.
millesimo *adj*, *m* thousandth.
milligrammo *m* milligramme.
millilitro *m* millilitre.
millimetro *m* millimetre.
milza *f* spleen.
mimare *vt*, *vi* to mime.
mimetizzazione *f* camouflage.
mimo *m* mime.
mina *f* mine.
minaccia *f* threat, menace.
minacciare *vt* to threaten, to menace.
minaccioso *adj* menacing, forbidding.
minare *vt* to mine; to undermine.
minato *m*: **campo ~** minefield.
minatore *m* miner, coalminer.
minerale *m* mineral; **acqua ~** *f* mineral water; **~ grezzo** *m* ore; * *adj* mineral.
mineralogia *f* mineralogy.
minestra *f* soup.
mingherlino *m* weakling; * *adj* skinny.
miniatura *f* miniature.
miniera *f* mine; **~ di carbone** coalmine, colliery.
minima *f* minimum.
minimizzare *m* understatement; * *vt* to minimize; to play

down, to underplay, to soft-pedal.
minimo *adj* least; minimal; * *m* least; **andare al ~** *vi* to tick over.
ministeriale *adj* ministerial.
ministero *m* ministry.
ministro *m* minister; clergyman; **Primo ~** *m* Prime Minister.
minoranza *f* minority.
minore *adj* minor, lesser, younger.
minorenne *m/f* minor, juvenile; * under-age.
minorile *adj* juvenile.
minuetto *m* minuet.
minugia *f*: **corda di ~** catgut.
minuscolo *adj* tiny, minute, dainty, diminutive, slight.
minuto *adj* minute, tiny; fine; **minuta e graziosa** petite; * *m* minute.
minuzioso *adj* thorough.
mio *poss adj* my; *poss pron* mine.
miope *adj* short-sighted, near-sighted, myopic.
miopia *f* short-sightedness.
miracolo *m* miracle, wonder.
miracoloso *adj* miraculous.
miraggio *m* mirage.
miriade *f* myriad.
mirino *m* viewfinder, sight.
mirra *f* myrrh.
mirtillo *m* bilberry.
mirto *m* myrtle.
misantropo *m* misanthropist.
miscela *f* mixture, blend.
miscellanea *f* miscellany.
mischia *f* scrum.
mischiare *vt* to blend.
miscuglio *m* concoction.
miseria *f* poverty, want, misery; pittance.
misericordia *f* mercy.
misericordioso *adj* merciful.
misero *adj* poor.

misfatto *m* misdeed.

misogino *m* misogynist.

missile *m* missile.

missionario *m* missionary.

missione *f* mission.

misterioso *adj* mysterious.

mistero *m* mystery.

mistico *adj* mystic(al); * *m* mystic.

misto *adj* mixed.

mistura *f* mixture.

misura *f* size; measure, measurement; step; **fatto su ~** *adj* tailor-made.

misurare *vt* to measure; to gauge.

misurazione *f* measurement.

mite *adj* mild; meek.

mitigare *vt* to mitigate.

mitigazione *f* mitigation.

mito *m* myth.

mitologia *f* mythology.

mitra *f* mitre.

mitragliatore *m* submachine gun.

mitragliatrice *f* machine gun.

mittente *m/f* sender.

mobile *adj* mobile, moving.

mobili *mpl* furniture, furnishings.

mobilità *f* mobility.

mobilitare *vt* to mobilize.

mocassino *m* moccasin.

moccio *m* snot.

moccioso *m* brat; * *adj* snotty.

moda *f* fashion, vogue; **alla ~** *adj* fashionable; **fuori ~** *adj* unfashionable, out-of-date.

modanatura *f* moulding.

modellare *vt* to model, to fashion.

modello *m* pattern; model; mock-up.

moderare *vt* to temper.

moderato *adj* moderate; sparing; * *m* moderate.

moderazione *f* moderation.

modernizzare *vt* to modernize.

modernizzazione *f* modernization.

moderno *adj* modern.

modestia *f* modesty.

modesto *adj* modest, unassuming.

modifica *f* modification.

modificare *vt* to modify.

modista *f* milliner.

modo *m* way; mode; fashion; (*gr*) mood; **grosso ~** *adv* broadly; **in questo ~** so; **in qualche ~** somehow.

modulare *vt* to modulate.

modulazione *f* modulation.

modulo *m* form; module.

moffetta *f* skunk.

mogano *m* mahogany.

moglie *f* wife.

mohair *m* mohair.

molare *m* molar.

molecola *f* molecule.

molestare *vt* to molest.

molla *f* spring; **a ~** *adj* clockwork.

mollare *vt* to release; to ditch.

molle *adj* limp.

molleggiato *adj* springy.

molletta *f* clothes peg, peg; hairclip.

mollo *m*: **mettere a ~** *vt* to soak.

mollusco *m* mollusc.

molo *m* jetty, quay.

moltiplicare *vt* to multiply.

moltitudine *f* host, throng, multitude.

molto *adj* much; * *pron* much; **sto ~ meglio** I am a great deal better; * *adv* a lot; very; much.

molti *pron* many.

momentaneo *adj* momentary.

momento *m* moment; momentum; time; **dell'ultimo ~** *adj* last minute.

monaco *m* monk.

monarca *m* monarch.

monarchia *f* monarchy.

monastero *m* monastery.
monastico *adj* monastic.
mondano *adj* worldly.
mondiale *adj* world, world-wide.
mondo *m* world.
monello *m* urchin.
moneta *f* coin; currency.
monetario *adj* monetary.
mongolfiera *f* hot air balloon.
mongoloide *m/f* mongol.
monitor *m inv* monitor.
monocolo *m* monocle.
monocromatico *adj* monochrome.
monografico *adj*: **saggio ~** *m* memoir.
monografio *m* monograph.
monolocale *adj*: **appartamento ~** *m* studio apartment.
monologo *m* monologue.
monopattino *m* scooter.
monopolio *m* monopoly.
monopolizzare *vt* to monopolize.
monosillabo *m* monosyllable.
monossido *m* monoxide.
monotonia *f* monotony; sameness; flatness.
monotono *adj* monotonous, drab, humdrum, unvaried.
monouso *adj* disposable; throwaway.
monsone *m* monsoon.
montacarichi *m* lift, elevator, hoist.
montaggio *m* assembly; **catena di ~** assembly line.
montagna *f* mountain; **montagne russe** big dipper.
montagnoso *adj* mountainous.
montante *adj* rising; incoming (tide); * *m* upright.
montare *vt* to assemble; to mount.
montato *adj* assembled; big-headed.
montatura *f* frame.

monte *m* mount; **~ di pietà** *m* pawnshop.
monticello *m* knoll.
montone *m* ram; sheepskin; *m* mutton.
montuoso *adj* mountainous; **zona ~** *f* highlands.
monumentale *adj* monumental.
monumento *m* monument, memorial.
moquette *f* (fitted) carpet.
mora *f* bramble; blackberry.
morale *adj* moral; **principi morali** *mpl* morals; * *m* morale.
moraleggiante *adj* sanctimonious.
moraleggiare *vi* to moralize.
moralista *m* moralist.
moralità *f* morality.
morbidezza *f* softness.
morbido *adj* soft.
morbillo *m* measles.
morboso *adj* morbid.
mordere *vt* to bite.
morente *adj* dying.
morfina *f* morphine.
morire *vi* to die.
mormorare *vt*, *vi* to murmur.
mormorio *m* murmur; babbling.
moroso *m* defaulter.
morsa *f* vice.
morsetto *m* clamp; **stringere con un ~** *vt* to clamp.
morso *m* bite; bit (horse).
mortaio *m* mortar.
mortale *adj* mortal; deadly; killing; *m/f* mortal.
mortalità *f* mortality.
morte *f* death; dying.
mortificare *vt* to mortify.
mortificato *adj* contrite.
mortificazione *f* mortification, contrition.
morto *adj* dead.
mosaico *m* mosaic.

mosca *f* fly.

moscerino *m* midge.

moschea *f* mosque.

moscone *m* bluebottle.

mossa *f* move.

mostra *f* display; exhibition.

mostrare *vt* to show

mostro *m* monster.

mostruosità *f* monstruosity.

mostruoso *adj* monstrous.

motel *m inv* motel.

motivare *vt* to motivate.

motivazione *f* motivation.

motivo *m* reason, motive, grounds, cause, motif, score.

moto *m* motion.

moto *f inv.* (*fam*) motorbike.

motocicletta *f* motor-cycle.

motocross *m* motocross; **gara di ~** *f* scramble.

motolancia *f* launch.

motore *m* motor, engine.

motoscafo *m* motorboat; **~ da corsa** *m* speedboat.

motteggiare *vi* to quip.

motto *m* motto.

mousse *f inv* mousse.

movibile *adj* movable.

movimentato *adj* eventful, hectic; **una carriera movimentata** *f* a chequered career.

movimento *m* movement, motion.

mozzafiato *adj* breathtaking.

mozzare *vt* to dock.

mozzicone *m* cigarette end, cigarette butt, stub.

mozzo *m* hub.

mucca *f* cow.

mucchio *m* heap, pile, mound, stack.

muco *m* mucus.

mucoso *adj* mucous.

muffa *f* fungus, mildew, mould.

muffola *f* mitten.

muggire *vi* to bellow, to low, to moo.

muggito *m* bellow, moo.

mughetto *m* lily of the valley.

mugnaio *m* miller.

mugugnare *vi* to bellyache.

mugugno *m* grouse.

mulinello *m* eddy; reel.

mulino *m* mill; **~ a vento** *m* windmill.

mulo *m* mule.

multa *f* fine; **~ per sosta vietata** *f* parking ticket.

multare *vt* to fine.

multiplo *adj*, *m* multiple.

moltiplicazione *f* multiplication.

mummia *f* mummy.

municipale *adj* municipal.

municipio *m* town hall.

munificenza *f* munificence.

munifico *adj* bountiful.

munizioni *fpl* munitions.

muovere *vt* to move; to wriggle; * *vi* to move; * *vr* **~rsi** to stir.

murale *adj* mural; **pittura ~** *f* mural.

muratore *m* bricklayer, builder, mason.

muratura *f* masonry.

muro *m* wall.

musa *f* muse.

muschio *m* moss; musk; **bacca del ~** *f* cranberry.

muscolare *adj* muscular.

muscolo *m* muscle.

muscoli brawn.

muscoloso *adj* sinewy.

muscoso *adj* mossy.

museo *m* museum, gallery.

museruola *f* muzzle.

musica *f* music; **~ pop** *f* pop music.

musicale *adj* musical.

musicista *m/f* musician.

muso *m* muzzle, smout; face.

mussola *f* muslin.

mussolina *f* gossamer.

muta *f* moulting; **fare la ~** *vi* to moult.

mutabile *adj* fickle.

mutamento *m* switch.
mutande *fpl* pants, knickers.
mutandine *fpl* panties, briefs.
mutante *adj, m* mutant.
mutare *vi* to change.
mutazione *f* mutation; **subire una ~** *vi* to mutate.

mutevole *adj* changing.
mutilare *vt* to mutilate.
mutilato *m* cripple; **lasciare ~** *vt* to cripple.
mutilazione *f* mutilation.
mutismo *m* dumbness.
muto *adj* mute, dumb.

N

nacchere *fpl* castanets.
naftalina *f* naphthalene; **pallina di ~** *f* mothball.
nailon *m* nylon.
nano *m* midget, dwarf.
napalm *m* napalm.
nappa *f* tassel.
narciso *m* narcissus.
narcotico *adj, m* narcotic.
narice *f* nostril.
narrare *vt* to narrate.
narrativa *f* fiction.
narrativo *adj* narrative.
narrazione *f* narration, narrative.
nasale *adj* nasal.
nascita *f* birth; **luogo di ~** *m* birthplace; **diritto di ~** birthright.
nascondere *vt* to hide, to conceal, to cover, to screen, to secrete.
nascondiglio *m* hiding place, hideaway.
nascosto *adj* hidden, covert.
nasello *m* hake.
naso *m* nose.
nastro *m* ribbon; tape; **~ adesivo** *m* adhesive tape; **~ isolante** *m* insulating tape; **~ trasportatore** *m* conveyor belt.
nasturzio *m* nasturtium.
nata *adj* née; **~ Brown** née Brown.

Natale *m* Christmas, Xmas; * **biglietto di ~** *m* Christmas card; **canto di ~** *m* carol.
natale *adj* native.
natali *mpl* parentage.
natica *f* buttock.
Natività *f* Nativity
nativo *m* native
nato *adj* born; **~ morto** *adj* stillborn.
natura *f* nature; wildlife; **~ morta** *f* still life.
naturale *adj* natural; unaffected; **in grandezza ~** *adj* lifesized.
naturalista *m/ f* naturalist.
naturalizzare *vt* to naturalize.
naturalmente *adv* of course.
naufragio *m* (ship)wreck; sinking.
naufrago *m* castaway.
nausea *f* nausea; **fino alla ~** ad nauseam.
nauseabondo *adj* nauseous.
nauseare *vt* to nauseate, to sicken.
nauseato *adj* squeamish, queasy.
nautico *adj* nautical.
navale *adj* naval.
navata *f* nave, aisle.
nave *f* ship, boat; **~ traghetto** *f* car ferry; **~ ammiraglia** *f* flagship; **~ da guerra** battleship, warship; **~ cisterna** *f*

tanker; ~ **in disarmo** *f* hulk.

navetta *f* shuttle.

navigare *vt* to navigate; * *vi* to navigate, to sail.

navigazione *f* navigation, shipping; **tecnica di** ~ *f* seamanship.

nazionale *adj* national; **a livello** ~ nationwide.

nazionalismo *m* nationalism.

nazionalista *adj, m/ f* nationalist.

nazionalità *f inv* nationality.

nazionalizzare *vt* to nationalize.

nazione *f* nation.

nazista *adj, m/ f* Nazi.

né *conj* neither, nor; * *adv* nor, neither, either; * *adj* neither.

neanche *adv* either; * *conj* neither.

nebbia *f* fog.

nebbioso *adj* foggy.

nebuloso *adj* nebulous.

nécessaire *m* case, kit; ~ **da toilette** *m inv* toilet bag.

necessariamente *adv* necessarily.

necessario *adj* necessary; * **rendere** ~ *vt* to necessitate.

necessità *f* necessity, must.

necrofago *adj* necrophagous; **animale** ~ *m* scavenger.

necrologio *m* obituary.

nefasto *adj* fatal.

negare *vt* (deny).

negativa *f* (*gr*; *foto*) negative.

negativo *adj* negative.

negazione *f* negation, negative.

négligé *m inv* negligee.

negligente *adj* negligent, careless, remiss, slack.

negligenza *f* negligence, malpractice, slackness.

negoziante *m/ f* storekeeper.

negozio *m* shop.

negra *f* Negress.

negro *adj, m* Negro.

nemico *m* enemy, foe.

nemmeno *conj* neither.

neo *m* mole, beauty spot.

neon *m* neon; **insegna al** ~ *f* neon light.

neonato *adj* newborn, baby.

nepotismo *m* nepotism.

neppure *conj* neither.

nero *adj, m* black.

nervo *m* nerve.

nervoso *adj* nervous, jumpy.

nesso *m* relationship; **senza** ~ *adj* unrelated.

nessuno *pron* none, nobody.

nettamente *adv* outright.

nettare *m* nectar.

netto *adj* net, outright, pronounced.

netturbino *m* dustman.

neutrale *adj* neutral.

neutralità *f* neutrality.

neutralizzare *vt* to neutralize, to counteract.

neutro *adj* neuter, neutral.

neutrone *m* neutron; **bomba a** ~ *f* neutron bomb.

neve *f* snow; **palla di** ~ *f* snowball; **pupazzo di** ~ *m* snowman.

nevicare *vi* to snow.

nevischio *m* sleet.

nevoso *adj* snowy.

nevrosi *f inv* neurosis.

nevrotico *adj, m* neurotic.

nicchia *f* niche.

nichel *m* nickel.

nichilista *m/ f* nihilist.

nicotina *f* nicotine.

nidificare *vi* to nest.

nido *m* nest; ~ **d'aquila** *m* eyrie; ~ **d'ape** *m* honeycomb.

niente *pron* none; * *excl* non fa ~ never mind.

night *m inv* nightclub.

ninfea *f* waterlily.

ninfomane *adj, f* nymphomaniac.

ninnananna *f* lullaby.

ninnolo *m* trinket, bauble.

nipote *m* nephew, *f* niece; *m/ f* grandchild.

nipotina *f* granddaughter.

nipotino *m* grandson.

nitido *adj* clear, sharp.

nitrire *vi* to neigh, to whinny.

nitrito *m* neigh.

no *adv* no; * *adj* nessuno.

nobile *adj*, *m* noble.

nobiltà *f* nobility; **piccola ~** *f* gentry.

nobiluomo *m* nobleman.

nocca *f* knuckle.

nocciola *f* hazelnut; * *adj* hazel.

nocciolina *f* peanut.

nocciolo *m* hazel tree.

noce *f* walnut; *m* walnut tree; **~ moscata** *f* nutmeg.

nocivo *adj* noxious, harmful.

nodo *m* knot, crux.

nodoso *adj* knotty, gnarled.

nodulo *m* lump.

noi *pers pron* us, .we

noia *f* bore; boredom.

noioso *m* bore; * *adj* dull, boring, tedious; **diventare ~** *vi* to pall.

noleggiare *vt* to hire, to rent, to charter.

noleggio *m* hire, charter.

nolo *m* rental, freight.

nomade *m/ f* nomad.

nome *m* name, first name, forename; **secondo ~** *m* middle name; **~ da ragazza** *m* maiden name; **~ depositato** *m* trade name.

nomina *f* nomination.

nominale *adj* nominal.

nominare *vt* to name, to nominate.

nominativo *adj*, *m* nominative.

non *adv* not.

noncurante *adj* heedless.

nondimeno *adv* nonetheless.

nonna *f* grandmother, granny.

nonno *m* grandfather, granddad.

nonni *mpl* grandparents.

nono *adj*, *m* ninth.

nonostante *conj* in spite of; * *prep* notwithstanding; **ciò ~** *adv* nevertheless, notwithstanding.

nontiscordardimé *m inv* forget-me-not.

nord *adj* north; **del ~** northern, northerly; **verso ~** northerly; * *adv* northwards; * *m* north.

nordest *m* northeast.

nordovest *m* northwest.

norma *f* norm; **~ di vita** *f* ethos; **~ del regolamento comunale** *f* by-law.

normale *adj* normal.

normalmente *adv* ordinarily.

nostalgia *f* nostalgia; **avere la ~ di casa** *vt* to be homesick.

nostalgico *adj* wistful.

nostro *adj* our; * *pron* ours.

nostromo *m* boatswain.

nota *f* note.

notaio *m* notary; conveyancer.

notare *vt* to note, to spot.

notazione *f* notation.

notevole *adj* notable, substantial, remarkable.

notevolmente *adv* notably.

notifica *f* notification.

notificare *vt* to notify; to serve (warrant, etc).

notizia *f* news, word.

notiziario *m* news.

notizie *fpl* news.

noto *adj* well-known; distinguished.

notorietà *f* notoriety.

notte *f* night, night-time; **di ~** by night, overnight; * *excl* **buona ~** good night; * *adv* ogni ~ nightly; * *adj* di ogni ~ nightly.

notturno *adj* nocturnal.

novantesimo *adj*, *m* ninetieth.

nove *adj, m inv* nine.

diciannove *adj, m inv* nineteen.

novembre *m* November.

novità *f* novelty.

novizio *m* novice.

nozione *f* notion.

nozze *fpl* wedding.

nube *f* cloud.

nubile *adj* single or unmarried woman; celibate (woman).

nuca *f* nape.

nucleare *adj* nuclear.

nucleo *m* nucleus, core.

nudista *adj, m/ f* nudist.

nudità *f* nudity.

nudo *adj* nude, naked, bare.

nulla *m* nil, naught.

nullità *f* nonentity, nobody.

nullo *adj* null, void, invalid.

numerale *m* numeral.

numerare *vt* to number.

numerico *adj* numerical.

numero *m* number; size; issue; turn; ~ **di telefono** *m* telephone number.

numeroso *adj* numerous.

nunzio *m* nuncio; ~ **apostolico** *m* legate.

nuocere *vt* to harm.

nuora *f* daughter-in-law.

nuotare *vt, vi* to swim.

nuotata *f* swim.

nuotatina *f* dip.

nuoto *m* swimming.

nuovo *adj* new; ~ **arrivato** *m* newcomer; * **di ~** *adv* anew.

nutriente *adj* nourishing, nutritious.

nutrimento *m* nourishment, sustenance.

nutrire *vt* to nourish, to feed, to nurture, to foster, to cherish (a hope, etc).

nuvola *f* cloud.

nuvoloso *adj* cloudy.

nuziale *adj* nuptial, bridal.

O

o *conj* or, either.

oasi *f inv* oasis.

obbligare *vt* to oblige.

obbligato *adj* indebted.

obbligatorio *adj* mandatory, set, obligatory, compulsory.

obbligazione *f* debenture.

obbligo *m* obligation.

oberato *adj* overwhelmed; ~ **di debiti** burdened with debts.

obesità *f* obesity.

obeso *adj* obese, gross.

obiettare *vt* to object.

obiettivo *adj* objective, unprejudiced; * *m* target; lens.

obiezione *f* objection; * **sollevare ~ i** *vi* to demur.

obitorio *m* morgue, mortuary.

oblio *m* oblivion.

obliquo *adj* oblique.

oblò *m inv* porthole.

oblungo *adj* oblong.

oboe *m* oboe.

obsoleto *adj* obsolete.

oca *f* goose; **maschio dell'~** *m* gander; **pelle d'~** *f* goose pimples.

occasionale *adj* occasional.

occasione *f* occasion, chance, opportunity.

occhiali *mpl* glasses, spectacles, goggles; ~ **da sole** *mpl* dark glasses, sunglasses.

occhiata *f* look, glance; **dare un'~ a** *vt* to glance.

occhieggiare *vt* to ogle.

occhiello *m* buttonhole.

occhio *m* eye; **chiudere un ~ su** *vt* to overlook.

occidentale *adj* west, western.

occorrente *adj*, *m* requisite.

occultamento *m* cover-up.

occupare *vt* to take up, to occupy.

occuparsi *vr* to deal with, to look after, to attend to.

occupato *adj* busy.

occupatore *m* occupier; **~ abusivo** *m* squatter.

occupazione *f* occupation, employment.

oceanico *adj* oceanic.

oceano *m* ocean.

ocra *f* ochre.

oculista *m/f* oculist.

ode *f* ode.

odiare *vt* to hate.

odio *m* hatred, hate.

odioso *adj* hateful, horrid, odious.

odissea *f* odyssey.

odontoiatria *f* dentistry.

odore *m* odour, smell; **~ forte** *m* tang.

offendere *vt* to offend.

offensivo *adj* offensive.

offerta *f* bid, offer, contribution, tender; **~e** *fpl* bidding (auction).

offesa *f* offence.

offeso *adj* upset.

officina *f* garage, workshop.

offrire *vt* to offer, to treat, to bid, to tender, to stand; **~si** *vr* to volunteer.

offset *m inv* offset.

offuscare *vt* to blur.

oftalmico *adj* ophthalmic.

oggetto *m* object, (*comm*) re; **~ esposto** *m* exhibit.

oggi *adv*, *m inv* today.

oggigiorno *adv* nowadays.

ogni *adj* every, each.

ognuno *pron* each, everybody.

oleandro *m* oleander.

oleoso *adj* oily.

olfatto *m* smell.

oliare *vt* to oil.

oliatore *m* oilcan.

olio *m* oil; **quadro a ~** *m* oil painting; **~ d'oliva** *m* olive oil; **~ solare** *m* suntan oil; **~ di ricino** castor oil.

oliva *f* olive.

olmo *m* elm.

olocausto *m* holocaust.

oltraggiare *vt* to revile.

oltraggiare *vt* to outrage.

oltre *prep* besides, aside from, beyond, past;* *adv* farther; **andare ~** *vt* to overshoot.

oltremarino *adj*, *m* ultramarine.

oltrepassare *vt* to overstep.

omaggio *m* homage; **in ~** complimentary.

ombelico *m* navel.

ombra *f* shade, shadow.

ombrello *m* umbrella, brolly (*fam Brit*).

ombretto *m* eyeshadow.

ombroso *adj* shady, skittish.

omelia *f* homily.

omeopatia *f* homoeopathy.

omeopatico *m* homoeopath.

omeopatico *adj* homoeopathic.

omettere *vt* to omit.

omicida *adj* homicidal.

omicidio *m* murder, homicide; **~ colposo** *m* manslaughter.

omissione *f* omission.

omogeneità *f* homogeneity.

omogeneo *adj* smooth, homogeneous.

omonimo *m* homonym, namesake.

omosessuale *adj*, *m/f* homosexual, (*fam*) gay.

oncia *f* ounce.

onda *f* wave; **~ anomala** *f* tidal wave; **lunghezza d'~** *f* wavelength; * **a ~ lunga** *adj* long-wave; **a onde corte** adj short-wave; **a onde medie** adj medium-wave.

ondata f tide, wave, gush, surge; ~ **di caldo** f heatwave.

ondeggiamento m sway.

ondeggiare vi to sway.

ondulato adj corrugated, undulating, wavy.

onere m burden, onus.

onestà f honesty.

onesto adj honest, straight, square.

onisco m woodlouse.

onnipotente adj omnipotent.

onnipresente adj ubiquitous.

onnivoro adj omnivorous.

onorare vt to grace, to honour.

onorario adj honorary.

onorario m fee, retainer.

onore m honour, credit; **Vostro ~** m Your Worship.

onorevole adj honourable.

opaco adj opaque, matt.

opale m/f opal.

opera f work, opera.

operaio adj blue-collar; **classe ~ a** f working class; * m worker, workman.

operare vi to operate.

operativo adj operational, operative.

operazione f operation, transaction.

operoso adj industrious.

opinione f opinion, belief.

oppio m opium.

opporsi vr to oppose.

opportunista m/f opportunist.

opportuno adj fitting, timely, opportune, expedient.

opposizione f opposition.

opposto m, adj opposite.

oppressione f oppression.

oppressivo adj oppressive.

oppressore m oppressor.

opprimente adj oppressive, heavy.

opprimere vt to oppress, te burden.

optare vi to opt (for).

opulento adj opulent.

opuscolo m booklet, pamphlet

opzione f option.

ora adv, conj now; * f hour, time period; **ogni ~** hourly.

oracolo m oracle.

orale adj, m oral.

oralmente adv orally.

orario m timetable, schedule; **in senso ~** adv clockwise **fuso ~** m time zone.

oratore m speaker, orator.

orazione f oration.

orbettino m slowworm.

orbita f orbit; socket.

orbitare vi to orbit.

orchestra f orchestra.

orchestrale adj orchestral.

orchestrare vt to score music

orchidea f orchid.

orco m bogey man, ogre.

orda f horde.

ordinanza f odinance.

ordinare vt to order; to ordain

ordinario adj ordinary.

ordinato adj neat, orderly, tidy

ordinazione f order, orde form; ordination.

ordine m order, command; ti diness; ~ **gerarchico** m peck ing order; ~ **pubblico** m la and order; **di prim'~** adj firs rate; **mettere in ~** vt to tidy

orecchiabile adj catchword.

orecchino m earring.

orecchio m ear; **che non ha** adj tone-deaf; **suonare a ~** t to play by ear; **mal d'~i** m ear ache.

orecchioni mpl mumps.

orefice m goldsmith.

orfano adj, m orphan.

orfanotrofio m orphanage.

organetto m barrel organ.

organico adj organic.

organigramma *m* flow chart.
organismo *m* organism.
organista *m/f* organist
organizzare *vt* to organize, to arrange, to plan, to put on, to run.
organizzazione *f* organization, outfit.
organo *m* organ.
orgasmo *m* orgasm, climax.
orgia *f* orgy.
orgoglio *m* pride.
orgoglioso *adj* proud.
orientale *adj* oriental, easterly, eastern.
orientare *vt* to orientate.
oriente *m* east.
orifizio *m* orifice.
origano *m* oregano.
originale *adj, m* original.
originalità *f* originality.
origine *f* origin; **avere ~ in** *vi* to originate from.
origliare *vt* to eavesdrop.
orina *f* urine.
orinare *vi* to urinate.
orizzontale *adj* horizontal.
orizzonte *m* horizon.
orlo *m* rim, brim, brink, verge, edge; hem.
orma *f* trail, track, footprint.
ormeggiare *vi* to berth, to moor, to tie up.
ormeggio *m* berth.
ormone *m* hormone.
ornamentale *adj* ornamental.
ornamento *m* ornament.
ornare *vt* to ornament.
ornato *adj* ornate.
ornitologo *m* bird watcher.
oro *m* gold; **tempi d'~** *mpl* heyday; **d'~** *adj* golden.
orologiaio *m* watchmaker.
orologio *m* clock; **~ da polso** *m* wristwatch.
oroscopo *m* horoscope.
orrendo *adj* ghastly, horrendous, lurid.

orribile *adj* horrible, hideous.
orrore *m* horror; **film dell'~** *m inv* horror film.
orsacchiotto *m* teddy bear.
orso *m* bear.
ortaggio *m* vegetable.
ortensia *f* hydrangea.
ortica *f* nettle.
orticaria *f* rash.
orticoltore *m* horticulturist.
orticoltura *f* horticulture.
orto *m* vegetable garden, kitchen garden.
ortodossia *f* orthodoxy.
ortodosso *adj* orthodox.
ortografia *f* orthography.
ortografia *f* spelling.
ortopedia *f* orthopaedics.
ortopedico *adj* orthopaedic.
orzaiolo *m* sty(e).
orzo *m* barley.
osare *vt* to dare.
oscenità *f* obscenity.
osceno *adj* obscene, lewd.
oscillare *vi* to vacillate.
oscillare *vi* to sway, to oscillate, to waver, to seesaw.
oscillazione *f* swing.
oscurare *vt* to obscure, to darken.
oscurità *f* dark, darkness, blackness.
oscuro *adj* obscure.
ospedale *m* hospital.
ospitale *adj* hospitable.
ospitalità *f* hospitality.
ospitare *vt* to put up.
ospite *m/f* host, guest, visitor.
ospizio *m* hospice.
osseo *adj* bony.
osservanza *f* observance.
osservare *vt* to remark, to observe.
osservatore *m* observer.
osservatorio *m* observatory.
osservazione *f* remark, observation, comment; **punto d'~** *m* vantage point.

ossessionare *vt* to obsess.

ossessivo *adj* obsessive.

ossidare *vt* to tarnish, to oxidize.

ossificarsi *vr* to ossify.

ossigeno *m* oxygen.

osso *m* bone.

ostacolare *vt* to thwart, to hamper, to impede.

ostacolo *m* hurdle, stumbling block, obstacle.

ostaggio *m* hostage.

ostello *m* hostel.

ostentazione *f* flourish.

osteopatia *f* osteopathy.

osteria *f* (*fam*) boozer.

ostetrica *f* midwife.

ostetricia *f* midwifery.

ostia *f* host; wafer.

ostile *adj* hostile, unfriendly, inimical.

ostilità *f* hostility.

ostinato *adj* obstinate, wilful.

ostinazione *f* wilfulness.

ostracizzare *vt* to ostracize.

ostrica *f* oyster.

ostruire *vt* to obstruct.

ostruzione *f* obstruction.

ottagono *m* octagon.

ottano *m* octane.

ottanta *adj*, *m* eighty.

ottantesimo *adj* eightieth.

ottava *f* octave.

ottavino *m* piccolo.

ottavo *adj* eighth.

ottenere *vt* to gain, to get, to obtain.

ottenibile *adj* obtainable.

ottica *f* optics.

ottico *m* optician; * *adj* optic(al).

ottimale *adj* optimum.

ottimista *adj* optimistic, sanguine; * *m*/*f* optimist.

ottimistico *adj* optimistic.

ottimo *adj* fine.

otto *adj*, *m* eight; **oggi a ~** a week today.

ottobre *m* October.

ottone *m* brass.

ottundere *vt* to dull.

otturare *vt* to fill.

otturatore *m* shutter.

otturazione *f* filling.

ottuso *adj* obtuse, thick, dull.

ouverture *f inv* overture.

ovaia *f* ovary.

ovale *adj*, *m* oval.

overdose *f inv* overdose.

ovest *adj*, *m* west, westward.

ovile *m* sheepfold.

ovvio *adj* obvious.

oziare *vi* to laze.

ozono *m* ozone.

P

pacato *adj* subdued, sedate.

pacchiano *adj* tawdry.

pace *f* peace, calm.

pacificare *vt* to mollify.

padella *f* frying pan; bedpan.

padiglione *m* pavilion, summerhouse.

padre *m* father.

padrino *m* godfather.

padrona *f* mistress.

padronanza *f* mastery, grasp.

padrone *m* boss, master.

paesaggio *m* scenery, landscape.

paese *m* land, country, village **abitante di ~** *m* villager.

paesino *m* hamlet.

paffuto *adj* chubby.

paga *f* wages.

pagabile *adj* due.

pagamento *m* payment; **~ unico** *m* lump sum.

pagano *m* heathen.

pagare *vi*, *vt* to pay; **far ~** to charge; **pagherò** I.O.U.; **far ~ troppo** *vi* to overcharge; **da ~** *adj* owing.

pagella *f* report.

pagina *f* page; **prima ~** *f* front page.

paglia *f* straw; **copertura di ~** *f* thatch.

pagliaccio *m* clown.

pagliaio *m* haystack.

paglierino *adj* straw-coloured, buff.

paglietta *f* boater.

paio *m* pair.

pala *f* shovel.

palafreniere *m* groom.

palazzo *m* mansion; **~ per uffici** *m* office block.

palco *m* stage, dais, (theatre) box; (*zool*) antler; **~ dell'orchestra** *m* bandstand; **~ improvvisato** *m* soapbox.

palese *adj* glaring, manifest, undisguised.

palestra *f* gym.

paletta *f* spade, slice, scoop.

palio *m* contest; **mettere in ~** *vt* to raffle.

palissandro *m* rosewood.

palizzata *f* stockade.

palla *f* ball; **~ di canone** *f* cannonball; **~ di neve** *f* snowball.

pallacanestro *f* basketball.

pallavolo *f* volleyball.

pallido *adj* pale, wan.

palloncino *m* balloon; (**alcotest**) breathalyzer.

pallone *m* ball.

palo *m* stake, goalpost.

palpebra *f* eyelid.

palpitare *vi* to beat, to throb.

palude *f* swamp, bog, marsh.

paludoso *adj* marshy, swampy; **zona paludosa** *f* fen.

pancetta *f* bacon; **una fettina di ~** *f* rasher of bacon.

panchina *f* bench.

pancia *f* belly, tummy.

panciotto *m* waistcoat.

pane *m* bread, loaf; **~ tostato** *m* toast; **~ integrale** brown bread; **~ di Spagna** *m* sponge (cake).

pangrattato *m* breadcrumbs.

panico *m* flap.

panificio *m* bakery.

panino *m* roll, sandwich; **~ dolce** *m* bun.

panna *f* cream; **~ montata** *f* whipped cream.

panno *m* baize.

pannocchia *f* corn on the cob.

pantaloni *mpl* trousers.

pantano *m* morass.

pantofola *f* slipper.

papà *m* (*inf*) dad(dy).

papalina *f* skullcap.

pappa *f* mush, feed.

pappagallino *m* budgerigar.

papparsi *vr* to scoff.

parabrezza *m inv* windscreen.

paracenere *m* fender.

paradiso *m* heaven, paradise.

parafango *m* mudguard.

parafulmine *m* lightning conductor.

paragonare *vt* to liken, to compare.

paragone *m* comparison.

paralume *m* shade.

paralume *m* lampshade.

paramento *m* vestment.

paramontura *f* facing.

paranco *m* tackle.

paraocchi *mpl* blinkers.

parapiglia *f* scramble; **~ generale** *f* free-for-all.

parare *vt* to save.

parascolastico *adj* extracurricular.

parasole *m* sunshade.

parassita *m/f* hanger-on.

parata *f* parade; (*sport*) save; ~ **militare** *f* tattoo; ~ **aerea** *f* flypast.

paraurti *m inv* bumper.

paravento *m* screen.

parco *m* park; ~ **comunale** *m* common.

parecchio *adj* several; **parecchi** *adj* umpteen.

pareggiare *vi* to equalize, to draw, to tie.

pareggio *m* draw, tie, equalizer.

parente *m/f* relation, relative; ~ **più stretto** *m* next of kin; ~ **acquisito** *m* in-law; **parenti** *mpl* kin.

parentela *f* relationship.

parentesi *f inv* bracket.

parere *vi* to seem; **a quanto pare** *adv* seemingly, apparently; * ~ *m* opinion.

parete *f* wall.

pari *adj*, equal, even; **essere alla ~ con** *vi* to be level with; **ragazza alla ~** *f* au pair.

paria *m inv* untouchable.

parlamentare *m/f* member of parliament; ~ **di secondo piano** *m* backbencher.

parlare *vi* to talk, to tell, to speak; ~ **a vanvera** to babble.

parlata *f* speech.

parodia *f* travesty, burlesque.

parola *f* word; **parole** *fpl* lyrics; **senza ~** *adj* speechless; ~ **d'ordine** *f* watchword; ~ **per ~** *adj*, *adv* verbatim.

parolaccia *f* swearword, four-letter word; **parolaccie** *fpl* bad language.

parrucca *f* wig.

parrucchiere *m* hairdresser.

parrucchino *m* toupee.

parsimonia *f* thrift.

parsimonioso *adj* thrifty.

parte *f* part, share, side; **da qualche ~** *adv* somewhere;

da ~ *adv* aside; **da queste parti** *adv* hereabouts; **in gran ~** *adv* largely; **dall'altra ~** *adv*, *prep* across; **d'altra ~** then again; **a ~** *adj*, *adv* apart.

partecipare *vi* to participate; ~ **al dolore** *vi* to commiserate.

partecipazione *f* participation, involvement.

parteggiare *vi* to side.

partenza *f* departure.

particolare *adj* special, especial, distinctive; * *m* detail.

partire *vi* to leave, to depart, to start.

partita *f* lot, consignment; match, game; ~ **a quattro** *f* foursome; ~ **doppia** *adj* double-entry.

partitura *f* score.

parto *m* birth, confinement.

partorire *vt* to give birth, to bear.

parvenu *m inv* upstart.

pascolare *vi* to graze.

Pasqua *f* Easter.

passaggio *m* lift; ~ **pedonale** *m* walkway; **di ~** *adj* through.

passamontagna *m inv* balaclava.

passare *vi*, *vt* to pass, to go by; to relay; to strain.

passata *f* wipe.

passatempo *m* hobby.

passe-partout *m inv* skeleton key.

passeggero *adj* fleeting.

passeggiare *vi* to walk.

passeggiata *f* walk.

passeggiatina *f* stroll.

passera *f* flounder.

passerella *f* gangway, footbridge.

passero *m* sparrow.

passino *m* strainer.

passionale *adj* passionate, sultry.

passione *f* eagerness.

passo *m* step, pace, stride, tread, footstep; **fare un ~** *vi* to step; **~ lento** *m* crawl; **~ stretto** *m* defile; **camminare a grandi passi** *vi* to stride;

pastella *f* batter.

pastello *m* crayon.

pasticceria *f* cake shop.

pasticciere *m* confectioner.

pasticcino *m* cake.

pasticcio *m* pie; hash, mess, botch, *(fam)* cock-up; **fare un ~ di** *vt* to botch; to bungle.

pastiglia *f* lozenge.

pasto *m* meal; **~ a prezzo fisso** *m* table d'hôte.

pastoie *fpl* shackles.

pastone *m* mash.

pastorale *m* crook (bishop's).

pastore *m* shepherd; clergyman, vicar.

patata *f* potato, *(fam)* spud; **patate lesse** *fpl* boiled potatoes; **~ fritta** *f* chip.

patatina *f* crisp.

patella *f* limpet.

patente *f* licence; **~ di guida** *f* driving licence.

paternità *f* fatherhood.

paterno *adj* fatherly.

patibolo *m* scaffold, gallows.

patria *f* home, homeland, fatherland.

patrigno *m* step-father.

patrimonio *m* heritage, estate, wealth.

pattinaggio *m* skating; **~ sul ghiaccio** *m* ice-skating; **pista di ~** *f* rink.

pattinare *vi* to skate.

pattino *m* skate; **~ a rotelle** *m* roller skate.

pattumiera *f* dustpan.

paura *f* fear; **avere ~ di** *vt* to fear.

pauroso *adj* fearful.

pausa *f* stop, rest.

pavimentare *vt* to floor.

pavimento *m* floor.

pavoneggiarsi *vr* to swagger, to strut.

paziente *m*, *adj* patient; **~ esterno** *m* outpatient.

pazienza *f* forbearance.

pazzia *f* madness, folly, fad, lunacy.

pazzo *adj* demented, mad, insane, lunatic.

peccaminoso *adj* sinful.

peccare *vi* to sin.

peccato *m* shame, sin.

peccatore *m* sinner.

pecora *f* ewe, sheep; **~ nera** *f* black sheep.

peculiarità *f inv* idiosyncracy.

pedaggio *m* toll.

pedagogia *f* education.

pedinare *vt* to shadow, to tail, to trail,

peggio *adj*, *adv*, *m/f* worse, worst.

peggiorare *vt* to worsen, to compound.

peggiore *adj*, *m/f* worse, worst.

pelare *vt* to fleece, to rip off.

pelle *f* skin, leather; **~ di mucca** cowhide; **lasciarci la ~** *vi* to bite the dust.

pellerossa *m/f* redskin; **giovane guerriero ~** *m* brave.

pelliccia *f* fur, fur coat.

pellicciaio *m* furrier.

pellicina *f* cuticle.

pellicola *f* skin, film.

pelo *m* hair, fur, bristle, nap; **senza peli** *adj* hairless.

peloso *adj* hairy, furry.

peluche *f* plush; **di ~** *adj* fluffy.

peluria *f* fluff, fuzz.

pena *f* punishment; **~ capitale** *f* capital punishment; **~ di morte** death penalty.

pendenza *f* slant, incline; **essere in ~** *vi* to dip.

pendere *vi* to slant, to hang, to lean.

pendio m slope, tilt, hillside.

pendolare m commuter; **fare il ~** vi to commute.

penetrare vt to penetrate.

penitenza f forfeit.

penna f pen; feather; **~ a sfera** ballpoint pen.

pennarello m felt-tip pen.

pennellata f dab.

pennello m brush; **~ da barba** m shaving brush.

pennino m nib.

pennone m flagpole.

penoso adj distressing, lamentable, grievous.

pensare vi to think, to expect.

pensatore m thinker.

pensiero m thought, thinking.

pensieroso adj thoughtful.

pensionante m/f boarder, lodger.

pensionato adj retired; * m pensioner.

pensione f pension, retirement; superannuation; boarding house; **mandare in ~** vt to retire; **andare in ~** vi to retire; **~ familiare** f guesthouse; **essere a ~ da** to board.

pentagramma m staff.

Pentecoste f Whit.

pentimento m repentance.

pentirsi vr to repent, to rue.

pentito adj repentant.

pentola f saucepan.

penzolare vi to swing.

pepe m pepper; **~ della Giamaica** allspice.

per prep for, from, to, through.

percepibile adj discernible, noticeable.

perchè conj why, because, what for.

perciò adv thus.

percorrere vt to walk.

percorso m route.

percuotere vt to thrash.

perdente m underdog.

perdente m/f loser.

perdere vt to lose; to miss; to leak; to forfeit; to shed; to waste.

perdersi vt to go astray.

perdita f waste; leak; write-off; loss.

perdonabile adj excusable.

perdonare vt to forgive, to condone.

perdono m forgiveness.

perfetto adj perfect, flawless.

perfido adj wicked.

perfino adv even.

pergamena f scroll.

pericolo m danger, distress; **mettere in ~** vt to jeopardize, to endanger.

pericoloso adj dangerous, unsafe.

periferia f suburbia, outskirts.

periferico adj outlying.

periodico m journal.

periodo m period, spell, time.

perizia f expertise, survey.

perlina f bead.

perlustrare vt to search.

permaloso adj touchy.

permanente adj permanent.

permesso m leave.

permettere vt to allow, to enable; * vr **~rsi** afford.

permissività f laxity.

permissivo adj lax.

perno m swivel.

perplessità f bewilderment.

perplesso adj puzzled, bemused; **lasciare ~** vt to mystify, to fox.

perquisire vt to frisk, to search.

perquisizione f search.

perseguitare vt to dog, to hound; **~ ingiustamente** vt to victimize.

perseverare vi to soldier on.

persiana f shutter.

persistente adj lingering, niggling.

personaggio *m* character.
personale *m* staff.
personificazione *f* epitome.
perspicace *adj* discerning, acute.
perspicacia *f* acumen, insight.
pessimo *adj* abominable.
persuadere *vt* to persuade, to induce.
pertinente *adj* relevant; **non ~** *adj* irrelevant.
pertinenza *f* relevance.
pertosse *f* whooping cough.
pesante *adj* heavy, hefty.
pesantemente *adv* heavily.
pesare *vt*, *vi* to weigh.
pesca *f* fishing.
pescare *vi*, *vt* to fish.
pescatore *m* fisherman.
pesce *m* fish; **~ rosso** *m* gold fish.
pescecane *m* shark.
peschereccio *m* trawler.
pescivendolo *m* fishmonger.
pesciolino *m* small fish; **~ d'acqua dolce** *m* minnow.
pesista *m* weightlifter.
peso *m* weight, encumbrance; **~ leggero** *m* lightweight; **eccedenza di ~** *f* overweight; **~ medio** *m* middle weight; **sostenere il ~ di** *vt* to bear the brunt of.
pessimo *adj* wretched, lousy.
pestare *vi* to tread, to stamp.
peste *f* terror, scamp.
petardo *m* cracker, banger, squib.
petroliera *f* oil tanker.
petrolio *m* oil.
pettegolezze *fpl* gossip.
pettegolo *m* gossip.
pettinare *vt* to comb.
pettinato *m* worsted.
pettinatura *f* hairdo.
pettine *m* comb; (*zool*) scallop.
pettirosso *m* robin.
petto *m* breast, chest, bust, bos-

om; **~ a doppio ~** *adj* double-breasted.
pezzetto *m* scrap.
pezzo *m* piece, bit, snatch; **bel ~** *m* chunk; **venire in pezzi** *vi* to come apart; **~ grosso** *m* bigwig.
piacente *adj* good-looking.
piacere *vt* to please; **non ~** *vt* to dislike; * *m* pleasure; **~!** how do you do!; **mi fa molto ~ vedere**... I am glad to see....
piacevole *adj* nice, agreeable.
piaga *f* blight, sore.
piagnucolare *vi* to snivel, to whimper, to grizzle.
piagnucolio *m* whimper.
piagnucoloso *adj* snivelling.
pianerottolo *m* landing.
piangere *vt*, *vi* to cry, to weep, to howl, to mourn.
piano *m* floor, storey; scheme; **primo ~** *m* close-up, foreground; **al ~ inferiore** *adj* downstairs; * *adv* slowly; * *adj* slow; level.
pianta *f* map; plant; **~ del piede** *f* sole (of foot).
piantare *vt* to drop, to jilt.
piantato *adj* planted; **ben ~** *adj* strapping, burly.
pianterreno *m* ground floor.
piantime *m* seedling.
pianto *m* cry.
piastra *f* hotplate.
piastrella *f* tile; **a piastrelle** *adj* tiled.
piastrellare *vt* to tile.
piattino *m* saucer.
piatto *m* plate, dish; turntable; * *adj* flat, level.
piazza *f* square.
piazzale *m* forecourt.
piazzare *vt* to station.
piccante *adj* spicy, hot.
picche *fpl* spades.
picchiare *vt* to thump, to hit, to sock, to bash.

picchiata *f* nosedive, swoop; scendere in ~ *vi* to swoop.

picchio *m* woodpecker.

piccione *m* pigeon; ~ **viaggiatore** *m* carrier pigeon.

picco *m* peak; **a** ~ *adj* sheer.

piccolezza *f* smallness.

piccolino *adj* smallish.

piccolo *adj* small, little; **farsi ~ per la paura** *vi* to cringe.

piccozza *f* ice axe.

pidocchio *m* louse.

piede *m* foot; ~ **di porco** *m* crowbar; **a piedi** *adj* walking; **in piedi** *adj* standing.

piedestallo *m* mount.

piega *f* crease, fold, twist.

piegare *vt* to bend, to fold; * *vr* ~**rsi** to bend, to fold.

pieghevole *adj* collapsible, folding.

pieno *adj* full.

pietanza *f* dish.

pietoso *adj* sorry.

pietra *f* stone; ~ **miliare** *f* milestone; ~ **angolare** *f* cornerstone; ~ **tombale** *f* tombstone; **mettiamoci una ~ sopra** let bygones be bygones.

pietrisco *m* grit.

pigione *f* rent.

pigna *f* cone.

pignolo *adj* fastidious, fussy, finicky, niggling.

pigrizia *f* laziness, idleness.

pigro *adj* lazy, idle.

pila *f* battery, torch.

pilota *m* pilot; **secondo ~** *m* copilot; ~ **collaudatore** *m* test pilot.

pince *f inv* tuck, dart.

ping-pong *m* table tennis.

pinguedine *f* stoutness.

pinna *f* fin, flipper.

pinza *f* tongs.

pinzette *fpl* tweezers.

pio *adj* godly.

pioggerella *f* drizzle.

pioggia *f* rain.

piolo *m* rung.

piombo *m* lead.

piovano *adj* of rain; **acqua piovana** *f* rainwater.

piovere *vi* to rain.

piovigginare *vi* to drizzle.

piovoso *adj* wet, rainy.

piovra *f* octopus.

pipa *f* pipe; ~ **di radica** *f* briar pipe.

pipistrello *m* bat.

piroetta *f* twirl.

pirofilo *adj* ovenproof.

piroscafo *m* steamer; ~ **da carico** *m* freighter.

piscina *f* swimming pool, baths.

pisolino *m* doze, nap; **schiacciare un ~** *vi* to nap.

pista *f* scent; track; runway; ~ **d'atterraggio** *f* landing strip; ~ **di patinaggio** *f* ice rink, skating rink.

pistola *f* pistol, gun.

pitagorico *adj* Pythagoric; **tavola pitagorica** *f* multiplication table.

pittoresco *adj* scenic.

più *adv, adj* more, most; **in ~** *adj* extra, spare; **sempre di ~** more and more.

piuma *f* feather; **piume** *fpl* down.

piumone *m* duvet.

piuttosto *adv* sooner, somewhat, rather.

pizzicare *vt* to nip, to sting.

pizzico *m* nip, touch.

pizzo *m* lace.

placare *vt* to salve, to appease; * *vr* ~**rsi** to abate.

placenta *f* afterbirth.

plaid *m inv* rug.

planare *vi* to glide.

planata *f* glide.

plasmare *vt* to mould.

plastica *f* plastic; ~ **facciale** *f* face-lift.

platea f (teat) stalls.

plotone m squad; ~ **d'esecuzione** m firing squad.

poco m a little; **pochi** mpl few; **a ~ a ~** inch by inch.

podere m holding.

podio m rostrum.

poesia f verse.

poggiare vi to rest.

poggio m hillock.

poi adv then.

poiana f buzzard.

poiché conj inasmuch as, for.

pois m inv spot; **a ~** adj spotted.

polemico adj argumentative.

polena f (naut) figurehead.

polizia f police, (fam) fuzz; **agente di ~** (Brit) constable; **corpo di ~** m constabulary.

poliziotto m policemen, (fam) cop, bobby.

polizza f policy; ~ **d'assicurazione** f insurance policy.

pollaio m hen-house.

pollame m fowl.

pollice m inch; thumb.

pollo m chicken.

polmone m lung.

polo m pole; ~ **nord** m North Pole.

polpetta f rissole; ~ **di carne** f meatball.

polpettone m meatloaf.

polsino m cuff, wristband.

polso m wrist.

poltiglia f slush.

poltrona f armchair.

polvere f dust, powder; ~ **da sparo** f gunpowder.

polveroso adj dusty.

pomellato adj dappled.

pomeriggio m afternoon.

pomo m knob.

pomodoro m tomato.

pompa f pump; pomp; **impresario di pompe funebri** m undertaker.

pompelmo m grapefruit.

pompiere m fireman; **corpo dei pompieri** m fire brigade.

ponce m punch; **specie di ~** m toddy.

ponente m west; **di ~** adj westerly.

ponte m bridge; ~ **sospeso** m suspension bridge; ~ **aereo** m airlift.

popolo m people.

poppa f stern; **a ~** adj aft, astern.

porcellana f china.

porcellino m piglet; ~ **d'India** m guinea pig.

porcile m sty.

porco m pig, hog.

porre vt to lay, to set.

porro m wart; leek.

porta f door, gateway; ~ **d'ingresso** f front door; ~ **posteriore** backdoor; ~ **a vento** f swinging door.

portacenere m inv ashtray.

portachiavi m key-ring.

portacipria m inv compact.

portaerei f inv aircraft carrier.

portafinestra f French window.

portafoglio m wallet.

portafortuna m inv mascot.

portamento m carriage, bearing, deportment.

portaoggetti m inv **vano ~** m glove compartment.

portapane m inv **cassetta ~** f breadbin.

portare vt to carry, to get, to waft; ~ **a termine** to accomplish.

posta f post; ~ **aerea** airmail.

portare vt to wear, to carry, to take, to bring, to bear; ~ **avanti** vt to carry on.

portasciugamano m towel rail.

portasigarette m inv cigarette case.

portata f extent, range, reach, course; **di vasta ~** adj far-reaching.

portatore m bearer, carrier.

portauovo m eggcup.

portavoce m inv spokeman, mouthpiece.

portellone m door; **~ posteriore** m tailgate.

portiere m porter, doorman; goalkeeper; **~ in livrea** m commissionaire.

portinaio m caretaker,janitor.

portineria f lodge.

porto m port, harbour; **~ di mare** m seaport; **franco di ~** adj carriage-free.

portuale m docker.

porzione f helping.

posare vt to lay, to model.

posata f cutlery.

posato adj staid.

posatoio m roost.

posizione f position, viewpoint, stand, situation, setting.

posologia f dosage.

possedere vt to own, to have.

possente adj mighty.

possesso m tenure.

possessore m holder.

possibile adj possible

possibilità f inv possibility; **~** fpl scope.

posta f post, mail.

postagiro m giro.

posteggio m parking; **~ di taxi** m taxi rank.

posteriore adj hind, hindquarters, back, rear; **la parte ~** f the rear.

postilla f footnote.

posto m seat, room, spot; **in nessun ~** adv nowhere.

pot-pourri m inv (mus) medley.

potabile adj drinkable.

potere vt to be able to; * m power.

precedente m precedent; **sen-**

za precedenti adj all-time.

povero adj poor.

povertà f poverty.

pozzo m well; **~ nero** m cesspit; **~ petrolifero** m oil well.

pranzare vi to dine.

pranzo m lunch, feast.

prateria f grassland.

praticamente adv virtually.

pratico adj practical, sensible, down-to earth, versed; **privo di senso ~** impractical:

prato m meadow, lawn.

preannunciare vt to herald.

preavvertire vt to forewarn.

preavviso m notice.

precario adj precarious, uneasy.

precedente adj former, foregoing, old; **precedenti penali** mpl (criminal) record.

precedenza f precedence; **dare la ~** vt to give way.

precedere vt to antedate.

precipitare vi to crash (plane).

precipitarsi vr to rush.

precipitazioni fpl rainfall.

precisione f accuracy.

preciso adj accurate.

prego excl not at all.

precoce adj forward, early.

precursore m forerunner.

predilezione f fondness.

predire vt to pretell.

predisposto adj susceptible.

prefazione f foreword.

preferire vt to prefer.

preferito adj favourite.

prefisso m dialling code.

perforatrice f drill.

pregustamento m foretaste.

prelievo m withdrawal.

preliminare adj exploratory.

prematuro adj untimely, early.

premeditato adj deliberate.

premere vt to squeeze.

premiare vt to reward.

preminente *adj* leading.

premio *m* prize, award, bonus: **primo ~** *m* jackpot; **~ per il peggior contendente** *m* booby prize.

premunirsi *vr* to hedge one's bets.

premura *f* rush.

premuroso *adj* attentive, considerate.

prenatale *adj* antenatal.

prendere *vt* to take, to get, to acquire, to catch; **andare a ~** *vt* to fetch; **~ gusto a** *vt* to acquire a taste for; **~ freddo** *vi* to catch cold; **~ fuoco** *vi* to catch fire.

prenotare *vt* to reserve, to book.

prenotazione *f* reservation.

preoccupante *adj* worrying, disturbing.

preoccupare *vt* to worry, to trouble; * *vr* **~rsi** to mind, to worry, to fret.

preoccupato *adj* worried.

preoccupazione *f* worry, concern, care.

preponderante *adj* overriding.

prepotente *adj* overbearing, high-handed; **fare il ~** *vi* to bully.

prepuzio *m* foreskin.

presa *f* hold, grasp, grip; socket; **~ d'aria** vent; **~ multipla** *f* adaptor.

presagire *vi* to bode.

presentatore *m* announcer, TV host, compère.

presentare *vt* to introduce, to submit, to show, to table; * *vr* **~rsi** to arise, to stand.

presentazione *f* introduction.

presente *adj*, *m* present; **con la ~** *adv* herewith.

presentimento *m* foreboding.

preservativo *m* condom, sheath.

preside *m* headmaster, dean.

presidente *m* president, chairman.

presiedere *vt* to chair.

pressante *adj* urgent.

presso *adj* near, c/o; **nei pressi** *adv* thereabouts.

pressione *f* pressure, strain; **~ del sangue** blood pressure; **gruppo di ~** *m* lobby.

prestare *vt* to lend, to loan, to spare.

prestigiatore *m* conjurer.

prestigio *m* prestige; **fare giochi di ~** *vi* to conjure.

prestito *m* loan; **prendere in ~** *vt* to borrow.

presto *adv* early, soon.

presunto *adj* supposed.

presuntuoso *adj* overconfident.

pretendente *m/f* claimant.

pretendere *vt* to expect, to claim.

pretenzioso *adj* ostentatious.

pretesa *f* claim; **pretese** *fpl* affectation.

prevalere *vi* to prevail; **~ su** *vt* to get the better of, to overrule.

prevedere *vt* to foresee, to forecast, to envisage, to anticipate; **era da ~** it was bound to happen.

prevedibile *adj* foreseeable.

preventivare *vt* to estimate.

preventivo *m* estimate.

previdenza *f* foresight, forethought.

previsione *f* forecast; **previsioni del tempo** *fpl* weather forecast.

prezioso *adj* valuable.

prezzo *m* price; **a ~ ridotto** *adj* cut-rate; **a buon ~** *adj* cheap.

prigione *f* prison, jail, lock-up.

prigionia *f* captivity.

prigioniero *m*, *adj* captive.

prima *adv* before, beforehand, sooner; **sulle prime** *adv* at first; * *m* first.

primavera *f* spring, springtime.

primo *adj* first, early, former.

primula *f* cowslip.

principale *adj* main, chief, arch; **ruolo ~** *m* lead; **prodotto ~** *m* staple.

principalmente *adv* mainly.

principe *m* prince; **~ ereditario** *m* crown prince.

principiante *m/f* beginner, learner.

principio *m* beginning, inception; principle, tenet.

privare *vt* to deprive.

privazione *f* deprivation; **privazioni** *fpl* hardship.

privo *adj* wanting, devoid.

probabile *adj* probable, likely; **è ~ che si arrabbi** he's liable to get angry.

probabilità *f inv* probability, chance, likelihood; **~ fpl** odds.

problema *m* problem; **problemi** *mpl* trouble.

proboscide *f* trunk.

procedere *vi* to proceed; **~ velocemente** *vi* to speed along; **~ lentamente** *vi* to crawl.

processare *vt* to try.

processo *m* trial, process.

procione *m* raccoon.

procuratore *m* attorney.

prode *adj* stalwart.

prodezza *f* feat.

prodotto *m* product, comodity.

produzione *f* production, output, generation.

profanare *vt* to desecrate.

profanazione *f* desecration.

professionale *adj* professional, vocational.

professore *m* professor, teacher.

profondità *f* depth.

profondo *adj* deep, sound; **poco ~** *adj* shallow.

profugo *m* refugee.

profumare *vt* to scent.

profumato *adj* scented, redolent.

profumo *m* scent, smell.

profusione *f* profusion; **a ~** *adv* galore.

progenitori *mpl* forefathers.

progettare *vt* to design.

progetto *m* design.

programma *m* programme, syllabus, schedule.

programmare *vt* to time.

programmazione *f* programming.

progredire *vi* advance.

progresso *m* progress, advance; **fare ~** *vi* to make headway.

prontezza *f* alacrity.

proibire *vt* to forbid, to ban.

proiettare *vt* to screen.

proiettile *m* bullet; **a prova di ~** *adj* bulletproof.

prole *f* brood, young, issue, offspring.

prolisso *adj* long-winded.

prolunga *f* extension.

prolungare *vt* to lengthen, to extend.

promemoria *m inv* memo.

promotore *m* sponsor.

promozione *f* sponsorship.

promuovere *vt* to sponsor.

pronosticare *vt* to tip.

prontamente *adv* readily.

prontezza *f* readiness.

pronto *adj* ready; **~!** *excl (tel)* hullo.

pronunciare *vt* to pronounce, to utter.

propaganda *f* propaganda; **~ elettorale** *f* electioneering.

propagandista *m/f* canvasser.

propagare *vt* to spread.

propagazione *f* spread.

propenso *adj* inclined; **poco ~** *adj* disinclined

proporzionato *adj* commensurate.

proposito *m* intention; subject; **a ~ di** *prep* about, concerning; **a ~ ...** by the way....

pseudonimo *m* alias.

proposizione *f* clause (*gr*), proposition.

proprietà *f* ownership; **~ assoluta** *f* freehold.

proprietaria *f* landlady.

proprietario *m* owner, landlord; **~ terriero** *m* landowner.

proprio *adj* own; * *adv* just; **che lavora in ~** *adj* self-employed; **amor ~** *m* self-esteem.

prosperare *vi* to thrive, to flourish.

proroga *f* reprieve, grace; **concedere una ~** *vt* to reprieve.

prosciugamento *m* drainage.

prosciugare *vt* to drain.

prosciutto *m* ham; **~ affumicato** *m* gammon.

prossimamente *m inv* trailer.

prossimo *adj* next, forthcoming, coming.

proteggere *vt* to shield.

protesta *f* outcry.

protestare *vi* to protest, to remonstrate.

protezione *f* guard.

protrarsi *vi* to overrun.

prova *f* test, rehearsal, trial, fitting; **~ ardua** *f* ordeal.

provare *vt* to rehearse; to feel; to try.

provenire *vi* to emanate.

provetta *f* test-tube.

provino *m* audition.

provocante *adj* saucy.

provocare *vt* to provoke, to bring about, to spark.

provocatorio *adj* challenging.

provvedere *vt* to cater for.

provvedimento *m* measure.

provvisorio *adj* temporary, interim.

provvista *f* store, stock.

prua *f* fore, bow.

prudente *adj* careful, cautious.

prudenza *f* caution.

prudere *vi* to itch.

prugnola *f* sloe.

prugnolo *m* blackthorn.

prurito *m* itch.

pseudonimo *m* nom de plume.

puah *excl* ugh.

pubblicare *vt* to publish, to issue.

pubblicazione *f* publication; **pubblicazioni matrimoniali** *fpl* banns.

pubblicità *f* commercial, advertisement, advertising; **fare ~** *vi* to advertise.

pubblico *m* audience.

pugilato *m* boxing.

pugile *m* boxer; **fare il ~** *vi* to box.

pugnalare *vt* to stab.

pugnale *m* dagger.

pugno *m* fist.

pula *f* husk, chaff.

pulce *f* flea.

pulcino *m* chick.

puledra *f* filly.

puledro *m* foal, colt.

pulire *vt* to clean, to cleanse, to wipe.

pulitissimo *adj* spotless.

pulito *adj* clean.

pulizia *f* cleaning, cleanliness, cleanness.

pullman *m* coach.

pulsare *vi* to throb.

pungente *adj* cutting, nippy, acid, acrid.

pungere *vt* to bite (insect), to sting.

pungiglione *f* sting.

punire *vt* to chastise, to discipline.

punta *f* tip, tinge, bit (tool), barb, spike; **~ del dito** *f* fingertip.

puntare *vt* to aim; to back (a horse).

puntata *f* stake; instalment, episode; **opera a puntate** *f* serial.

punteggiare *vt* to dot.

punteggio *m* score.

punteruolo *m* awl.

puntina *f* stylus.

puntino *m* spot.

punto *m* dot, point, stop, stitch; **~ esclamativo** *m* exclamation mark; **~ morto** *m* deadlock; **~ e virgola** semi-colon; **due punti** (*typ*) colon; **~ morto** *m* standstill; **~ nero** blackhead; **~ cieco** *or* **~ debole** blind spot; **~ d'appoggio** *m* foothold; **a tal ~ che** *adv* insomuch.

puntone *m* rafter.

puntura *f* sting, bite (insect).

punzecchiare *vt* to needle.

pupazzo *m* puppet; **~ di neve** *m* snowman.

puré *m* mash.

pure *adv* also.

puro *adj* pure, sheer, mere, unadulterated.

purosangue *adj inv*, *m/f inv* thoroughbred.

purtroppo *adv* unluckily.

pusillanime *adj* fainthearted.

putiferio *m* rumpus, row, stink.

putrefarsi *vr* to decay.

puttana *f* prostitute, whore.

puzzare *vi* to smell, to stink, to reek.

puzzle *m* (jigsaw) puzzle.

puzzo *m* stench, reek, stink, smell.

puzzolente *adj* smelly, rank

Q

qua *adv* here.

qua qua *m* quack; **fare ~** *vi* to quack.

quacchero *adj*, *m* Quaker.

quaderno *m* exercise book.

quadrangolo *m* quadrangle.

quadrante *m* dial, face (of watch, etc), quadrant.

quadrato *adj*, *m* square.

quadrigemino *adj*: **gemello ~** *m* quadruplet.

quadrilatero *adj* quadrilateral.

quadro *m* square; painting, picture; **~ di comando** *m* console; **quadri** *mpl* (cards) diamonds.

quadrupede *m* quadruped.

quadruplo *adj* quadruple, fourfold.

quaglia *f* quail.

qualche *adj* some.

qualcosa *pron* something.

qualcuno *pron* anybody, somebody.

quei *dem adj* those.

quale *adj* what, which.

qualifica *f* qualification.

qualificare *vt* to qualify.

qualificato *adj* qualified.

qualità *f* quality.

qualsiasi *adj* any; **~ cosa** *pron* whatever; **in ~ momento** *conj* whenever.

quando *adv*, *conj* when.

quantità *f inv* quantity; **piccola ~** *f* modicum; **comprare in grande ~** *vt* to buy in bulk.

quantitativo *adj* quantitative.

quanto *adj* how much; **quanti**

adj how many; tanti **quanti** as many as; **~ a** *adv* as to, as for; **~ a me** as for me.

quaranta *m inv* forty.

quarantena *f* quarantine.

quarantesimo *adj, m* fortieth.

quartetto *m* quartet.

quartier *m* quarter; **~ generale** *m* headquarters; **~ residenziale** *m* housing estate.

quarto *m* quarter, fourth; * *adj* fourth; **un ~ d'ora** *m* a quarter of an hour.

quarzo *m* quartz.

quasi *adv* almost, nearly; **~ tutto** *pron* most.

quattordicesimo *adj, m* fourteenth.

quattordici *adj, m* fourteen.

quattro *adj, m* four; **dividere in ~** *vt* to quarter.

quel *adj* that; **quelli** *pron* those.

quercia *f* oak.

questo *dem adj, dem pron* this;

questi *dem adj, dem pron* these; **con ~** *adv* hereby.

questionario *m* questionnaire.

questione *f* question.

questore *m* commissioner of police.

qui *adv* here; **da ~ in avanti** *adv* hereafter.

quietare *vt* to hush.

quindi *adv* therefore, consequently.

quindicesimo *adj* fifteenth.

quindici *m, adj* fifteen; **~ giorni** *m* fortnight.

quinte *fpl* wings; **dietro le ~** *adj, adv* offstage.

quintetto *m* quintet.

quinto *adj, m* fifth.

quiz *m inv* quiz.

quorum *m inv* quorum.

quota *f* quota, dues; **~ di ammissione** *f* entrance fee.

quotidiano *adj, m* daily.

quoziente *m* quotient.

quadrare *vi* to square.

R

abarbaro *m* rhubarb.

abbia *f* anger; rabies; **con ~** *adv* angrily.

abbino *m* rabbi.

abbrividire *vi* to shiver, to wince, to shudder; **che fa ~** creepy.

accapricciante *adj* grisly, bloodcurdling.

acchetta *f* racket; **~ da tennis** *f* tennis racket.

acchiudere *vt* to encase.

accogliere *vt* to collect, to pick up, to gather.

accolta *f* collection, set:

accolto *m* crop, harvest; **fare il ~ di** *vt* to harvest.

raccomandabile *adj* advisable; **poco ~** *adj* disreputable.

raccomandare *vt* to recommend; **mi raccomando!** be sure!.

raccomandata *f* registered letter.

raccomandazione *f* recommendation.

raccontare *vt* to relate, to tell, to recount.

racconto *m* story, yarn.

raccordo *m* connection; **binario di ~** *m* siding.

rachitismo *m* rickets.

racimolare *vt* to glean.

racket *m inv* racket.

radar *m* radar.

raddobbare *vt* to refit.

raddobbo *m* refit.

raddoppiare *vt* to double, to redouble.

raddrizzare *vt* to straighten, to right, to unbend.

radere *vt* to shave; to raze.

radersi *vr* to shave.

radiale *adj* radial.

radiante *adj* radiant.

radiatore *m* radiator.

radiazione *f* radiation.

radicale *adj* radical, sweeping * *m/f* radical.

radicare *vi* to root.

radicato *adj* entrenched.

radice *f* root.

radio *f* radio; * *m* radium.

radioamatore *m* radio ham.

radioattività *f* radioactivity.

radioattivo *adj* radioactive; **pioggia radioattiva** *f* fallout.

radiografia *f* X-ray, radiography.

radiologo *m* radiographer.

radioso *adj* sunny.

rado *adj* sparse.

radunare *vt* to assemble, to rally, to gather, to muster.

radunarsi *vr* to congregate, to collect.

raduno *m* gathering, rally, meeting.

radura *f* clearing.

rafano *m* horseradish.

raffermo *adj* stale.

raffica *f* gust, volley, flurry; ~ **di vento** *f* blast of wind; ~ **di domande** *f* barrage of questions.

raffinare *vt* to refine.

raffinatezza *f* refinement, polish.

raffinato *adj* polished, cultured, sophisticated.

raffineria *f* refinery.

rafforzare *vt* to fortify.

raffreddare *vt* to cool.

raffreddore *m* cold.

rafia *f* raffia.

raganella *f* rattle.

ragazza *f* girl; **di** ~ *adj* girlish

ragazzino *m* kid.

ragazzo *m* boy, lad; boyfriend.

raggelante *adj* withering.

raggio *m* spoke; radius; ray, beam; ~ **di luna** *m* moonbeam; **a lungo** ~ *adj* long-range.

raggirare *vt* to bamboozle.

raggiro *m* swindle; **indurre con raggiri** *vt* to con.

raggiungere *vt* to hit, to attain to reach.

raggiungibile *adj* attainable.

raggruppare *vt* to group.

ragionamento *m* reasoning.

ragionare *vi* to reason.

ragione *f* reason, sense; **aver** ~ *vi* to be right.

ragionevole *adj* reasonable, thinking, rational.

ragioniere *m/f* accountant

ragioneria *f* accountancy

ragliare *vi* to bray.

raglio *m* bray.

ragnatela *f* web, spider-web cobweb.

ragno *m* spider.

rallegrare *vt* to gladden.

rallegrarsi *vr* to rejoice, to brighten.

rallentare *vt, vi* to slow (down).

rally *m inv* rally.

ramato *adj* auburn.

rame *m* copper.

ramificare *vi* to ramify.

ramificazione *f* ramification.

rammarico *m* regret.

rammendare *vt* to darn.

rammendo *m* mending. darn.

rammentare *vt* to recollect.

ramo *m* branch, bough.

ramoscello *m* sprig, twig.

rampa *f* ramp, flight (of stairs) ~ **di lancio** *f* launch pad.

rampante *adj* rampant.

rampicante *f* creeper.

rana *f* frog; **nuoto a ~** *m* breast-stroke.

ranch *m inv* ranch.

rancido *adj* rancid, rank.

rancore *m* grudge, ill feeling, rancour.

randagio *adj* stray.

randello *m* club, bludgeon.

rango *m* standing.

rantolo *m* rattle.

ranuncolo *m* buttercup.

rapa *f* turnip.

rapace *adj* predatory.

rapare *vt* to crop.

rapida *f* rapids.

rapire *vt* to abduct, to kidnap.

rapitore *m* abductor, kidnapper.

rapporti *mpl* dealings.

rapporto *m* report, relation, rapport, ratio; **rapporti** *mpl* intercourse; **rapporti sessuali** *mpl* sex.

rapprendersi *vr* to congeal.

rappresaglie *fpl* reprisals, retaliation.

rappresentante *m* representative.

rappresentare *vt* to represent, to enact, to depict, to perform.

rappresentativo *adj* representative.

rappresentazione *f* performance, representation.

rapsodia *f* rhapsody.

raramente *adv* seldom.

rarità *f* rarity.

raro *adj* rare; **sono rari** they are few and far between.

raschiare *vt* to scrape.

raschiatura *f* scrape.

raschietto *m* scraper.

raso *m* satin.

rasoio *m* razor; **~ elettrico** *m* shaver.

raspa *f* rasp.

raspare *vt* to rasp.

rassegnato *adj* resigned.

rassicurante *adj* reassuring, soothing.

rassicurare *vt* to reassure.

rastrellare *vt* to rake.

rastrelliera *f* rack.

rastrello *m* rake.

rata *f* instalment.

ratifica *f* ratification.

ratificare *vt* to ratify.

ratto *m* rat.

rattoppare *vt* to patch (up).

rattristare *vt* to sadden.

rauco *adj* hoarse, husky, rough, raucous.

ravanello *m* radish.

ravvivare *vt* to liven up, to enliven, to brighten.

razionale *adj* rational.

razionalità *f* rationality.

razionalizzare *vt* to rationalize.

razionare *vt* to ration.

razione *f* ration.

razza *f* race, strain, breed; skate; (fish) razza, ray.

razziale *adj* racial.

razzismo *m* racism.

razzista *m/f* racialist.

razzo *m* rocket.

re *m inv* king.

reagire *vi* to react.

reale *adj* real, actual, royal.

reali *mpl* royalty.

realismo *m* realism.

realista *m/f* realist; royalist.

realistico *adj* realistic, lifelike.

realizzabile *adj* feasible.

realizzare *vt* to realize, accomplish, to achieve; * **~rsi** to come to fruition.

realizzazione *f* accomplishment, achievement, realization.

realtà *f* reality; **in ~** in fact.

reattore *m* reactor; **~ autofertilizzante** *m* breeder.

reazionario *m* reactionary, die-hard; * *adj* reactionary.

reazione *f* reaction, after-effect; **~ a catena** *f* chain reaction; **motore a ~** *m* jet engine; **~ violenta** *f* backlash.

rebbio *m* prong.

rebus *m* puzzle.

recalcitrante *adj* recalcitrant.

recalcitrare *vt* to balk.

recensione *f* notice.

recensire *vt* to review.

recensore *m* reviewer.

recente *adj* recent.

reception *f inv* reception.

recessione *f* recession.

recintare *vt* to enclose, to fence.

recinto *m* fence, compound, enclosure, paddock, pen.

recipiente *m* vessel, receptacle.

reciproco *adj* mutual, reciprocal.

reciso *adj* cut.

recita *f* recital.

recitare *vt, vi* to recite.

reclamizzare *vt* to publicize.

reclusione *f* imprisonment, confinement.

recluso *adj* recluse.

recluta *f* recruit.

reclutamento *m* recruitment.

reclutare *vt* to recruit.

record *m inv* record.

recriminare *vt* to recriminate.

recriminazione *f* recrimination.

redazionale *adj* editorial.

redditività *f* profitability.

redditizio *adj* profitable.

reddito *m* income, revenue.

Redentore *m* Redeemer.

redenzione *f* redemption.

redigere *vt* to edit.

redimere *vt* to redeem.

redine *f* rein.

referendum *m inv* referendum.

referenza *f* reference; **referenze** *fpl* credentials, testimonial.

refettorio *m* refectory.

refrigerante *m* coolant.

refrigerare *vt* to refrigerate.

regalare *vt* to give.

regale *adj* regal.

regalo *m* gift.

regata *f* regatta.

reggente *m/f* regent.

reggenza *f* regency.

reggere a *vt* to stand.

reggimento *m* regiment.

reggiseno *m* bra; brassiere.

regime *m* régime.

regina *f* queen.

regionale *adj* regional.

regione *f* region.

regista *m* producer.

registrare *vt* to register, to record, to tape, to enter.

registratore *m* tape recorder, recorder; **~ a cassette** *m* cassette recorder.

registrazione *f* registration.

registro *m* record, register.

regnare *vi* to rule, to reign.

regno *m* kingdom, reign, realm.

regola *f* rule; **~ principale** *f* golden rule.

regolamento *m* rule; settlement, regulation.

regolare *vt* to regulate, to set, to readjust; * *adj* regular, even.

regolarità *f* regularity.

regolatore *m* regulator; **~ luminoso** *m* dimmer switch.

regredire *vi* to regress.

regressivo *adj* regressive.

regresso *m* regression.

reincarnazione *f* reincarnation.

reintegrare *vt* to reinstate.

reinvestire *vt* to plough back.

reiterare *vt* to reiterate.

reiterazione *f* reiteration.

relativo *adj* relative, pertaining, comparative.

relax *m* relaxation.

relazione *f* paper; relation, relationship.

relè *m* relay.

relegare *vt* to relegate.

relegazione *f* relegation.

religione *f* religion.

religioso *adj* religious, holy.

reliquia *f* relic.

relitto *m* wreck; **relitti** *mpl* wreckage.

remare *vi* to row, to scull.

rematore *m* rower.

reminiscenza *f* reminiscence.

remissione *f* remission.

remissivo *adj* subservient.

remo *m* oar.

remoto *adj* remote.

remunerativo *adj* gainful.

renale *adj* renal.

rendere *vt* to render.

rendimento *m* performance, output.

rene *m* kidney.

renna *f* reindeer.

reparto *m* unit, department.

reperto *m* exhibit.

repertorio *m* repertory, repertoire.

replica *f* repeat, replica.

reportage *m inv* report.

repressione *f* suppression, repression.

repressivo *adj* repressive.

represso *adj* pent-up.

reprimere *vt* to suppress, to repress, to quell, to clamp down.

repubblica *f* republic.

repubblicano *m* republican.

reputazione *f* reputation, repute

requisire *vt* to comandeer, to requisition.

requisizione *f* requisition.

resa *f* surrender; yield, return.

rescindere *vt* to rescind.

rescissione *f* termination

residente *adj*, *m* resident.

residenza *f* residence.

residuo *m* residue; * *adj* residual.

resina *f* resin.

resinoso *adj* resinous.

resistente *adj* tough, hard-wearing, strong.

resistenza *f* resistance, endurance, strength, stamina.

resistere *vt* to resist, to withstand.

respingente *m* buffer.

respingere *vt* to repulse, to repel, to spurn, to quash.

respirare *vt* to breathe.

respiratore *m* respirator; ~ **a tubo** *m* snorkel.

respiratorio *adj* respiratory.

respirazione *f* breathing, respiration.

respiro *m* breath, breathing; **dare ~ a** *vt* to give respite to; **attimo di ~** breathing space.

responsabile *adj* responsible, liable.

responsabilità *f* responsibility, liability.

ressa *f* crush, rush.

restare *vt* to stay, to remain.

restaurare *vt* to restore.

Restaurazione *f* Restoration.

restauro *m* renovation, restoration.

resti *mpl* remains.

restio *adj* reluctant.

restituire *vt* to give back, to repay, to return, to restore.

restituzione *f* restitution.

resto *m* rest, change, remainder, remnant.

restringere *vt* to narrow; * *vr* ~**rsi** to shrink.

restrittivo *adj* restrictive.

restrizione *f* restriction, restraint.

retata *f* roundup, catch, haul.

rete *f* net, network, grid; ~ **metallica** *f* netting.

reticella *f* hairnet.
reticenze *f* reticence.
reticolato *m* lattice.
retina *f* retina.
retorica *f* rhetoric.
retorico *adj* rhetorical.
retribuzione *f* retribution.
retro *m* back.
retrocucina *m inv* scullery.
retrodatare *vt* to backdate.
retrogrado *adj* retrograde.
retromarcia *f* reverse.
retroscena *f* backstage.
retrospettiva *f* retrospective.
retrospettivo *adj* retrospective; **giudizio ~** *m* hindsight.
retrovisore *m* rear-view mirror.
rettangolare *adj* rectangular.
rettangolo *m* rectangle, oblong.
rettifica *f* rectification.
rettificare *vt* to rectify.
rettile *m* reptile.
rettilineo *adj* rectilinear.
rettitudine *f* righteousness,
rectitude.
retto *m* upright; rectum; * *adj*
right.
rettore *m* vice-chancellor, rector.
reumatico *adj* rheumatic.
reumatismo *m* rheumatism.
reverendo *m* Reverend.
reverente *adj* reverent, reverential.
revisionare *vt* to service, to
overhaul.
revisione *f* review, service, revision, overhaul; **fare una ~
di** *vt* to review; **~ dei conti** *f*
audit; **fare una ~ di** *vt* to audit.
revisore *m* reviser; **~ dei conti** auditor.
revocare *vt* to revoke, to lift.
riabilitare *vt* to rehabilitate.
riabilitazione *f* rehabilitation.
riadattarsi *vr* to readjust.

rianimare *vt* to revive.
rianimazione *f* reanimation;
centro di ~ *m* intensive care
unit.
riaprire *vt* to reopen.
riarmo *m* rearmament.
riarso *adj* parched.
riassicurare *vt* to reinsure.
riassumere *vt* to sum up, to
outline.
riassunto *m* summary, résumé.
ribalta *f* flap; **luci della ~** *fpl*
footlights.
ribaltabile *adj* reclining.
ribaltare *vt* to capsize.
ribattere *vt* to retort.
ribattino *m* rivet.
ribellarsi *vr* to revolt, to rebel.
ribelle *adj* rebel, rebellious,
wayward, defiant, insurgent;
* *m/f* rebel.
ribellione *f* rebellion.
ribes *m inv* currant.
ribrezzo *m* loathing.
ricadere *vi* to relapse.
ricaduta *f* relapse.
ricamare *vt* to embroider.
ricambiare *vt* to repay.
ricambio *m* relay, refill; **pezzo
di ~** *m* spare part.
ricamo *m* embroidery; **saggio
di ~** *m* sampler.
ricapitolare *vt, vi* to recapitulate.
ricaricare *vt* to recharge.
ricattare *vt* to blackmail.
ricatto *m* blackmail.
ricavato *m* proceeds.
ricchezza *f* wealth, richness;
ricchezze *fpl* riches.
riccio *m* hedgehog; * *adj* curly.
ricciolo *m* curl.
ricco *adj* wealthy, rich.
ricerca *f* research, search,
quest, hunt; **fare ~** *vi* to research; **andare alla ~ di** *vi* to
scout around for; **~ di mercato** *f* market research.

ricercato *adj* elaborate.

ricetta *f* prescription, recipe.

ricettario *m* cookery book.

ricevere *vt* to receive, to get.

ricevimento *m* reception.

ricevitore *m* receiver.

ricevuta *f* receipt.

richiamare *vt* to phone back, to retrieve, to recall.

richiamo *m* recall, catchword, (*med*) booster, lure; **uccello di ~ m** decoy.

richiedere *vt* to request, to require.

richiesta *f* request, demand.

richiesto *adj* sought-after.

ricognitore *m* scout.

ricognizione *f* reconnaissance; **fare una ~** *vi*, *vt* to reconnoitre.

ricomparire *vi* to reappear.

ricompensa *f* recompense, reward.

ricompensare *vt* to recompense.

riconciliare *vt* to reconcile.

riconciliazione *f* reconciliation.

riconoscente *adj* thankful.

riconoscenza *f* gratefulness.

riconoscere *vt* to recognize, to know.

riconoscimento *m* recognition.

riconsiderare *vt* to reconsider.

ricoprire *vt* to recover, to coat.

ricordare *vt* to recall, to remember, to remind.

ricordo *m* souvenir, recollection, keepsake, memory; **~ di famiglia** *m* heirloom.

ricorrente *adj* recurrent.

ricorrenza *f* recurrence.

ricorrere to return; ~ in giudizio *vi* to prosecute.

ricorso *m* recourse, resort; **far ~ a** *vt* to resort to.

ricostituente *m* tonic.

ricostruire *vt* to rebuild, to reconstruct.

ricoverato *m* inpatient.

ricreazione *f* recreation.

ricuperare *vt* to salvage, to recover, to retrieve, to repossess.

ricupero *m* retrieval, recovery.

ridacchiare *vi* to chuckle, to titter, to snigger, to cackle, to giggle.

ridere *vi* to laugh, to scoff.

ridicolo *m* ridicule; **mettere in ~** *vt* to ridicule; * *adj* laughable, ridiculous.

ridondante *adj* redundant.

ridondanza *f* redundancy.

ridotto *adj* diminished.

ridurre *vt* to reduce, to cut, to lower, to whittle away; **~ drasticamente** *vt* to axe.

riduzione *f* cut, cutback, reduction.

rielezione *f* reelection.

riempire *vt* to fill, to refill to stuff.

rientranza *f* recess.

rientro *m* reentry.

rievocare *vt* to conjure up.

riferimento *m* reference; **punto di ~ m** landmark; **con ~ a** with reference to.

riferirsi *vr* to refer; **~ a** to pertain to.

riffa *f* raffle; **di ~** *or* **di raffa** by hook or by crook.

rifinitura *f* finish.

rifiutare *vt* to refuse, to turn down, to rebuff.

rifiuto *m* refusal, rebuff, denial; **rifiuti** *mpl* litter.

riflessione *f* reflection.

riflessivo *adj* reflexive.

riflesso *m* reflection, reflex.

riflettere *vt* to mirror, to think over, to reflect.

riflettore *m* searchlight, floodlight, spotlight.

rifluire *vi* to ebb.

riflusso *m* ebb.

riforma *f* reform.

Riforma f Reformation.
riformare vt to reform.
riformatore m reformer.
riformatorio m borstal.
riformista m/f reformist.
rifornire vt to stock, to replenish.
rifrangere vt to refract.
rifrazione f refraction.
rifugiato m refugee; ~ **politico** m defector.
rifugio m shelter, haven, refuge, retreat; ~ antiatomico m fallout shelter.
riga f stripe, line, (hair) parting.
rigare vt to streak, to rule.
rigato adj lined.
rigenerare vt to regenerate.
rigenerato adj regenerate.
rigenerazione f regeneration.
rigetto m rejection.
righello m ruler.
rigidezza f rigidity.
rigidità f stiffness.
rigido adj rigid, stiff, hard, strict, intemperate.
rigonfiamento m bulge.
rigore m rigour; **a ~ di termini** adv strictly speaking.
rigoroso adj stringent, rigorous.
riguadagnare vt to regain.
riguardante prep respecting.
riguardare vt to regard, to concern.
riguardo m regard; ~ **a** prep regarding, concerning; **senza ~** adv regardless.
rilanciare vt to reflate.
rilasciare vt to release, to issue.
rilascio m release, issue.
rilassare vt to relax; * vr ~**rsi** to relax.
rilassato adj relaxed, (fam) laid-back.
rilegare vt to bind.

rilegato adj bound.
rilegatore m bookbinder.
rilegatura f binding.
rilevamento m survey.
rilievo m relief; **mettere in ~** vt to stress.
riluttante adj unwilling.
riluttanza f reluctance, disinclination.
rima f rhyme; **far ~ con** vi to rhyme.
rimandare vt to postpone, to put off, to defer, to delay, to refer.
rimando m cross-reference.
rimanere vi to stay, to remain.
rimbalzare vi to bounce, to rebound, to ricochet.
rimbalzo m bounce, ricochet; **di ~** adv on the rebound.
rimbombare vi to reverberate.
rimbombo m reverberation.
rimborsare vt to refund, to reimburse, to pay back.
rimborso m reimbursement, repayment, refund, rebate.
rimediare vt to remedy, to make up for.
rimedio m remedy.
rimessa f remittance.
rimettere vt to remit.
rimodellare vt to remodel.
rimorchiare vt to tow, to pick up.
rimorchiatore m tug.
rimorchio m tow, trailer; **cavo per ~** m towrope.
rimorso m remorse.
rimostrare vi to expostulate.
rimozione f removal.
rimpatriare vt to repatriate.
rimpiangere vt to regret.
rimpianto m regret.
rimpiazzare vt to replace.
rimpinzarsi vr to gorge.
rimproverare vt to reprimand, to reproach, to blame, to reprehend.

rimprovero *m* rebuke, reprimand, reproach; **di ~** *adj* reproachful.

rimuginare *vt* to mull over; * *vi* to brood.

rimunerare *vt* to rimunerate.

rimunerazione *f* remuneration.

rimuovere *vt* to remove, to dislodge.

Rinascimento *m* Renaissance.

rinchiudere *vt* to confine, to pen.

rinforzare *vt* to strengthen, to toughen, to boost, to brace, to reinforce.

rinforzo *m* brace.

rinfrescante *adj* cooling.

rinfrescare *vi*, *vt* to freshen, to refresh.

rinfusa *f*: **alla ~** *adj* higgledy-piggledy.

ring *m inv* boxing ring.

ringhiare *vi* to growl, to snarl.

ringhiera *f* banisters.

ringhio *m* snarl, growl.

ringiovanire *vt* to rejuvenate.

ringraziamento *m* thanksgiving.

ringraziare *vt* to thank.

rinnegare *vt* to disown.

rinnegato *m* renegade.

rinnovare *vt* to refurbish, to renovate, to renew.

rinnovo *m* renewal.

rinoceronte *m* rhinoceros.

rinomanza *f* renown.

rinomato *adj* renowned.

rinsecchirsi *vr* to shrivel.

rintoccare *vi* to strike.

rintocco *m* stroke, chime; **~ funebre** *m* knell.

rintracciare *vt* to trace.

rinuncia *f* renunciation.

rinunciare *vt* to renounce, to surrender, to relinquish, to waive, to give up, to forgo.

rinvigorire *vt* to exhilarate.

riorganizzare *vt* to reorganize.

riorganizzazione *f* reorganization.

riparabile *adj* reparable.

riparare *vt* to repair, to fix, to redress; to shelter, to shade.

riparazione *f* reparation, repair, redress.

riparo *m* cover, refuge, shelter.

ripartire *vt* to mete out.

ripassare *vt* to revise.

ripasso *m* revision.

ripensare *vi* to think over; **ripensandoci** in retrospect.

ripercorrere *vt* to retrace.

ripercussioni *fpl* repercussions.

ripetere *vt* to repeat; * *vr* **~rsi** to recur.

ripetizione *f* repetition.

ripetutamente *adv* repeatedly.

ripiano *m* shelf.

ripicca *f* pique.

ripido *adj* steep.

ripiegare *vt* to refold; **~ su** to fall back on.

ripieno *m* stuffing, filling.

riportare *vt* to report, (*math*) to carry.

riporto *m* carry-over; **cane da ~** *m* retriever.

riposante *adj* restful.

riposare *vi* to rest, to stand, to repose; * *vr* **~rsi** to rest.

riposo *m* rest, repose.

ripostiglio *m* boxroom.

riprendere *vt* to recapture, to retake, to resume.

riprendersi *vi* to recover.

ripresa *f* resumption, take, upturn, recovery.

ripristino *m* revival.

riprodurre *vt* to reproduce ; * *vr* **~rsi** to breed.

riproduzione *f* reproduction.

riprovevole *adj* reprehensible.

ripudiare *vt* to repudiate.

ripugnante *adj* repulsive, loathsome, repugnant.

ripugnanza *f* distaste, repugnance, repulsion.

ripulsione *f* repulsion.

riqualificare *vi, vt* to retrain.

riqualificazione *f* retraining.

risaia *f* paddy field.

risalire *vi* to reascend; **~ a** *vi* to date from.

risalto *m* prominence; **dare ~ a** *vt* to feature.

risata *f* laugh, laughter; **~ fragorosa** *f* guffaw.

risatina *f* snigger; **~ stupida** *f* titter.

riscaldamento *m* heating.

riscattare *vt* to ransom.

riscatto *m* ransom.

rischiare *vt* to risk, to venture, to hazard, to chance.

rischio *m* risk, hazard, chance.

rischioso *adj* risky, hazardous.

risciacquare *vt* to rinse, to swill.

risciò *m inv* rickshaw.

risentimento *m* resentment; **pieno di ~** *adj* resentful.

risentirsi *vr* to resent.

riserbo *m* reserve.

riserva *f* reservation, reserve, qualification; **di ~** *adj* spare.

riservare *vt* to reserve, to book.

riservato *adj* confidential, secretive, cagey, classified.

risiedere *vi* to reside.

risma *f* ream.

riso *m* rice.

risolare *vt* to sole.

risolino *m* giggle, snigger; **~ stridulo** cackle.

risolutezza *f* resolve.

risoluto *adj* resolute, unfaltering, determined, purposeful, steadfast.

risoluzione *f* resolution.

risolvere *vt* to resolve, to solve, to sort out.

risonante *adj* resonant.

risonanza *f* resonance.

risonare *vi* to resound.

risorsa *f* resource.

risparmiare *vt* to spare, to save.

risparmiatore *m* saver.

risparmio *m* saving; **libretto di ~** *m* savings account; **cassa di ~** *f* savings bank.

rispecchiare *vt* to reflect.

rispettabile *adj* respectable.

rispettabilità *f* respectability.

rispettare *vt* to respect; **far ~** *vt* to enforce.

rispettivo *adj* respective.

rispetto *m* respect; **~ a** *prep* vis-à-vis; **~ di sé** *m* self-respect; **mancanza di ~** *f* disrespect.

rispettoso *adj* respectful, dutiful; **~ delle leggi** *adj* law-abiding.

risplendente *adj* resplendent.

rispondere *vi* to answer, to respond, to reply, to counter; **~ male a qn** *vi* to snap somebody's head off.

risposarsi *vr* to remarry.

risposta *f* reply, response, retort.

rissa *f* brawl, fracas.

ristabilire *vt* to reestablish; * *vr* **~rsi** to recuperate.

ristagno *m* stagnation.

ristampa *f* reprint, reissue.

ristorante *m* restaurant.

ristoro *m* refreshment.

ristrutturare *vt* to convert.

ristrutturazione *f* conversion.

risultare *vi* to result, to emerge, to ensue.

risultato *m* result, upshot; **avere come ~** *vi* to result.

risuonare *vi* to ring.

risurrezione *f* resurrection.

risuscitare *vt* to resuscitate.

risvegliare *vt* to stir.

risveglio *m* awakening, revival.

risvolto *m* lapel.

ritagliare *vt* to clip.

ritaglio *m* snip, cutting, clipping.

ritardare *vt* to hold up, to delay.

ritardatario *m* latecomer.

ritardato *adj* retarded.

ritardo *m* delay; **in ~** *adj* late.

ritenere *vt* to rank, to opine.

ritentivo *adj* retentive.

ritenuto *adj*: **essere ~ ricco** *vi* to be reputed to be rich.

ritenzione *f* retention.

ritirare *vt* to withdraw, to retract, to take back; * *vr* **~rsi** to retire, to retreat, to secede.

ritiro *m* withdrawal.

ritmico *adj* rhythmical.

ritmo *m* rhythm, beat, swing.

rito *m* rite, ceremonial.

ritoccare *vt* to retouch, touch up.

ritornare *vi* to revert, to go back.

ritornello *m* chorus, refrain.

ritorno *m* return; **biglietto andata e ~** *m* return ticket; **essere di ~** to be back.

ritrarre *vt* to portray; * *vr* **~rsi** to recede.

ritrasmettere *vt* to relay.

ritrattare *vt* to retract.

ritrattazione *f* recantation.

ritratto *m* portrait.

ritrovarsi *vr* to rendezvous.

ritto *adj* upright.

rituale *adj*, *m* ritual.

riunione *f* meeting, reunion.

riunire *vt* to rally, to reunite, to reunite; * *vr* **~rsi** to riunite, to sit.

riuscire *vi* to succeed.

riuscita *f* success.

riuscito *adj* successful; **non ~** *adj* unsuccessful.

riva *f* bank (river); **~ del mare** *f* seashore.

rivale *adj*, *m* rival.

rivaleggiare *vt* to rival.

rivalità *f* rivalry.

rivalutare *vt* to revalue.

rivedere *vt* to revise.

rivelare *vt* to give away, to disclose, to reveal; * *vr* **~rsi** to turn out, to prove.

rivelato *adj* revealed; **mai ~** *adj* untold.

rivelatore *m* detector, indicator; * *adj* revealing, telltale.

rivelazione *f* revelation, disclosure.

rivendicare *vt* to stake, to claim.

riversare *vt* to disgorge; * *vr* **~rsi** to surge.

rivestimento *m* facing, casing.

rivestire *vt* to cover; **~ con materiale isolante** *vt* to lag.

rivettare *vt* to rivet.

rivista *f* magazine, review.

rivolo *m* trickle.

rivolta *f* revolt.

rivoltante *adj* revolting.

rivoltare *vt* to revolt.

rivoltella *f* gun, revolver.

rivoltoso *m* rioter.

rivoluzionario *adj*, *m* revolutionary.

rivoluzione *f* revolution.

rizzarsi *vi* to bristle.

roano *m* roan.

roba *f* stuff, things.

robbia *f* madder.

robot *m inv* robot.

robustezza *f* sturdiness.

robusto *adj* stout, sturdy, robust, hardy.

roccia *f* rock.

roccioso *adj* rocky.

rock *m* rock.

roditore *m* rodent.

rododendro *m* rhododendrum.

rognone *m* kidney.

rognoso *adj* mangy.

romantico *adj* romantic.

romanziere *m* novelist.

romanzo *m* novel.

rombo *m* rhombus; boom, rumble; **~ di tuono** *m* thunderclap.

romice *m* dock.

rompere *vt* to snap, to break, to rupture; * *vr* **~rsi** to break.

rompicapo *m* puzzle.

rondella *f* washer.

rondine *f* swallow.

rondone *m* swift.

ronzare *vi* to drone, to hum, to buzz.

ronzino *m* nag.

ronzio *m* drone, buzz, hum.

rosa *f* rose; * *adj, m inv* pink; **~ selvatica** brier.

rosaio *m* rosebed.

rosario *m* rosary.

rosato *adj* rosy; **vino ~** *m* rosé wine.

rosbif *m* roast beef.

roseo *adj* rosy.

rosicchiare *vt* to gnaw, to nibble.

rosmarino *m* rosemary.

rosolare *vt* to brown.

rosone *m* rose.

rospo *m* toad.

rosseggiare *vi* to glow.

rossetto *m* lipstick.

rossiccio *adj* reddish, ginger.

rosso *adj, m* red.

rossore *m* redness, blush, flush.

rosticceria *f* takeaway.

rotaia *f* rail.

rotare *vi* to rotate.

rotatoria *f* roundabout.

rotazione *f* rotation.

roteare *vi* to gyrate, to wheel; **far ~** *vt* to twirl.

rotella *f* caster, roller.

rotolare *vi, vt* to roll; * *vr* **~rsi** to wallow.

rotolo *m* scroll, coil, roll.

rotondo *adj* round.

rotta *f* course, route.

rottame *m* write-off.

rotto *adj* broken.

rottura *f* severance, rupture, break.

rotula *f* knee-cap.

roulette *f* roulette.

roulotte *f inv* caravan.

round *m inv* round.

routine *f* routine.

rovente *adj* red-hot.

rovescia *f* lapel; **alla ~** *adj* inside out; **conto alla ~** *m* countdown.

rovesciamento *m* overthrow.

rovesciare *vt* to tip, to topple, to spill, to upset, to overthrow: * *vr* **~rsi** to tip.

rovescio *m* reverse, (*sport*) backhand, purl.

rovina *f* ruin, undoing, downfall.

rovinare *vt* to spoil, to ruin.

rovistare *vi* to rummage, to ransack.

rovo *m* bramble bush.

royalty *m inv* royalty.

rozzo *adj* boorish, uncouth, rough.

rubacchiare *vt* to pilfer, to filch.

rubamazzo *m* snap.

rubare *vt* to steal.

rubicondo *adj* ruddy.

rubinetto *m* tap, (water) cock.

rubino *adj, m* ruby.

rublo *m* rouble.

rubrica *f* rubric.

rudere *m* ruin.

rudimentale *adj* rough and ready.

rudimento *m* rudiment.

ruga *f* wrinkle, line.

rugby *m* rugby.

ruggine *f* rust.

rugginoso *adj* rusty.

ruggire *vi* to roar.

ruggito *m* roar.

rugiada *f* dew.

rullare *vi* to taxi.

rullino *m* film, roll.

rullo *m* roller; **~ compressore** *m* steamroller.

rum *m inv* rum.

ruminare *vi* to ruminate, to chew over.

rumore *m* noise, sound; **~ metallico** *m* clank, clang; **~ secco** *m* rattle; **produrre un ~ metallico** *vi* to jangle.

rumorosamente *adv* noisily.

rumoroso *adj* vociferous, noisy.

ruolo *m* role.

ruota *f* wheel; **~ di scorta** *f* spare wheel; **andare a ~ libera** *vi* to freewheel; **~ dentata** *f* gearwheel.

rupe *f* crag.

rurale *adj* rural.

ruscelletto *m* rivulet.

ruscello *m* stream, brook.

ruspante *adj* free-range.

russare *vi* to snore.

rustico *adj* rustic.

rusticone *m* bumpkin.

ruta *f* rue.

ruttare *vi* to belch, to burp.

rutto *m* burp, belch.

ruvidità *f* roughness.

ruvido *adj* rough, coarse.

ruzzolare *vi* to tumble.

S

sabato *m* Saturday, Sabbath.

sabbia *f* sand; **sacco di ~** *m* sandbag; **sabbie mobili** *fpl* quicksand.

sabbiare *vt* to sandblast.

sabbioso *adj* sandy.

sabotaggio *m* sabotage.

sabotare *vt* to sabotage.

saccarina *f* saccharin.

saccheggiare *vt* to sack, to raid, to pillage, to loot.

saccheggiatore *m* marauder.

saccheggio *m* sack, plunder.

sacchetto *m* carrier bag, bag.

sacco *m* sack; **~ a pelo** *m* sleeping bag.

sacerdotale *adj* priestly.

sacerdote *m* clergyman.

sacerdotessa *f* priestess.

sacerdozio *m* priesthood.

sacramento *m* sacrament.

sacrificale *adj* sacrificial.

sacrificare *vt* to sacrifice.

sacrificio *m* sacrifice.

sacrilegio *m* sacrilege.

sacrilego *adj* sacrilegious.

sacro *adj* sacred.

sacrosanto *adj* sacrosanct.

sadico *m* sadist.

sadico *adj* sadistic.

sadismo *m* sadism.

safari *m inv* safari.

saga *f* saga.

saggezza *f* wisdom.

saggio *adj* wise; * *m* essay; sage.

Sagittario *m* Sagittarius.

sagoma *f* silhouette, template.

sagrestano *m* sexton.

sagrestia *f* vestry.

sagù *m* sago.

sala *f* room, hall; **~ da ballo** *f* ballroom; **~ d'udienza** *f* courtroom; **~ di regia** (*TV, radio*) *f* control room; **~ di comando** (*naut, mil*) *f* control room; **~ d'attesa** *f* departure lounge; airport lounge.

salamandra *f* salamander.

salame *m* salami, sausage.

salamoia *f* brine; **mettere in ~** *vt* to souse.

salare *vt* to salt, to cure.

salariato *m* wage earner.

salato *adj* savoury, salty; **piatto ~** *m* savoury.

saldamente *adv* steadily, fast.

saldare *vt* to weld, to solder; to settle, to pay off; **lampada a benzina per ~** *f* blowlamp.

saldarsi *vr* to set.

saldatura *f* weld.

saldo *adj* steady, firm; * *m* balance.

sale *m* salt.

salgemma *m* rock salt.

salice *m* willow; **~ piangente** *m* weeping willow.

salicone *m* pussy willow.

saliente *adj* salient.

saliera *f* salt cellar.

salina *f* saltworks.

salino *adj* saline.

salire *vt, vi* to ascend, to mount, to climb, to go up ; **~ su** to board.

salita *f* rise, climb, slope, ascension; **in ~** *adj* uphill.

saliva *f* saliva.

salivare *vi* to salivate.

salma *f* corpse.

salmo *m* psalm.

salmone *m* salmon.

salnitro *m* saltpeter.

salone *m* salon, saloon, lounge, hall.

saloon *m inv* saloon.

salopette *f inv* dungarees.

salotto *m* parlour, drawing room, sitting room.

salpare *vi* to set sail.

salsa *f* sauce; **~ indiana** *f* chutney.

salsetta *f* dip.

salsiccia *f* sausage, banger.

saltare *vi, vt* to jump; * *vi* to spring, to skip; **~ con un balzo** *vi* to vault; **far ~** *vt* to blast.

saltatore *m* jumper.

saltellare *vi* to skip, to caper, to hop, to cavort.

saltello *m* skip, hop.

salto *m* jump, spring; **fare un ~** *vi* to pop in; **~ mortale** *m* somersault.

saltuario *adj* casual (labour).

salubre *adj* wholesome, salubrious.

salumeria *f* delicatessen.

salutare *adj* salutary; * *vt* to salute, to greet.

salute *f* health.

saluto *m* greeting, salute; **distinti saluti** *mpl* yours sincerely.

salva *f* salvo.

salvacondotto *m* safe-conduct.

salvadanaio *m* piggy bank.

salvaguardare *vt* to safeguard.

salvaguardia *f* safeguard.

salvare *vt* to save, to rescue.

salvataggio *m* salvage, rescue; **lancia di ~** *f* lifeboat; **giubbotto di ~** *m* life jacket; **sagola di ~** *f* lifeline.

salvatore *m* saviour.

salvezza *f* salvation, boon.

salvia *f* sage.

salvo *prep* save; * *adj* safe.

sambuco *m* elder; **bacca di ~** *f* elderberry.

San Silvestro *m*: **la notte di ~** *f* New Year's Eve.

sancire *vt* to sanction.

sandalo *m* sandal.

sandwich *m* sandwich.

sangue *m* blood; **~ freddo** *m* sangfroid; **al ~** *adj* rare.

sanguinaccio *m* black pudding.

sanguinante *adj* bleeding, bloody.

sanguinare *vi* to bleed.

sanguinario *adj* bloodthirsty.

sanguinoso *adj* gory.

sanguisuga *f* leech, bloodsucker.

sanità *f* soundness; ~ **mentale** *f* sanity.

sano *adj* healthy, sound; ~ **e salvo** *adj* safe and sound, unhurt; ~ **di mente** *adj* sane.

santificare *vt* to sanctify.

santità *f* sanctity, godliness, holiness.

santo *m* saint; * *adj* saintly, holy; **lo Spirito S~** *m* the Holy Ghost.

santuario *m* sanctuary, shrine.

sanzione *f* sanction.

sapere *vi* to know, to smell (of), to hear; **io non so nuotare** I can't swim; * *m* knowledge.

sapientone *m* smart aleck, know-all.

saponata *f* soap suds.

sapone *m* soap.

sapore *m* taste, flavour, savour; ~ **forte** *m* tang.

saporito *adj* tasty.

saracinesca *f* shutter.

sarcasmo *m* sarcasm.

sarcastico *adj* sarcastic.

sarcofago *m* sarcophagus.

sardina *f* sardine, pilchard.

sardonico *adj* sardonic.

sarta *f* seamstress.

sarto *m* tailor, dressmaker.

sassofono *m* saxophone.

sassoso *adj* stony.

Satana *m* Satan.

satanico *adj* satanic.

satellite *m* satellite.

satira *f* satire, lampoon.

satireggiare *vi* to satirize.

satirico *adj* satirical; **scrittore** ~ *m* satirist.

satiro *m* satyr.

saturare *vt* to saturate.

savana *f* savannah.

saziare *vt* to satiate.

sazio *adj* replete.

sbaciucchiarsi *vr* to smooch.

sbadigliare *vi* to yawn.

sbadiglio *m* yawn.

sbagliare *vt* to make a mistake, to err; * *vr* ~**rsi** to slip up, to mistake.

sbagliato *adj* wrong.

sbaglio *m* mistake, slip.

sballottare *vt* to toss, to jostle, to buffet.

sbalordire *vt* to stagger, to astound.

sbalorditivo *adj* staggering.

sbalordito *adj* flabbergasted.

sbaragliare *vt* to rout.

sbarazzare *vt* to rid.

sbarazzarsi *vr* to throw off.

sbarcare *vi* to disembark, to land.

sbarco *m* landing, disembarkation.

sbarra *f* rail, bar.

sbarramento *m* barrage.

sbarrare *vt* to bar, to cross; ~ **gli occhi** *vi* to goggle; ~ **contro** *vt* to strike.

sbattere *vt*, *vi* to bang, to slam, to flap, to bump; ~ **le palpebre** *vt* to blink; **andare a ~ contro** *vt* to blunder into.

sbavare *vi* to slaver, to drool, to slobber.

sbiadirsi *vr* to fade.

sbiancare *vt* to whiten; ~ **in viso** *vi* to blanch.

sbigottire *vt* to dumbfound.

sbigottito *adj* aghast.

sbilanciarsi *vr* to overbalance.

sbilenco *adj* lop-sided.

sbirciare *vi* to peek, to peep.

sbloccare *vt* to unblock.

sbornia *f* drunkenness; **postumi di una** ~ *mpl* hangover.

sborsare *vt* to disburse, to fork out.

sbottonare *vt* to unbutton.

sbranare *vt* to savage, to maul.

sbriciolare *vt* to crumble; * *vr* ~**rsi** to crumble.

sbrigare *vt* to deal with, to polish off.

sbrigativo *adj* brisk.

sbrinare *vt* to defrost.

sbrindellato *adj* bedraggled.

sbrodolare *vt* to dribble.

sbrogliare *vt* to untangle, to disentangle.

sbronzo *adj* drunk, tight.

sbucciapatate *m* potato peeler.

sbucciare *vt* to peel, to skin.

sbuffare *vi* to snort, to chug.

sbuffata *f* snort.

scacchi *mpl* chess; **pezzo degli ~** *m* chessman.

scacchiera *f* chessboard.

scacciare *vt* to oust.

scacco *m* check (chess); **~ matto** *m* checkmate.

scadente *adj* shoddy, third-rate, ropy.

scadenza *f* expiry, deadline.

scadere *vi* to fall due, to lapse, to expire.

scaduto *adj* out-of-date, overdue.

scaffalature *fpl* shelving.

scafo *m* hull.

scagionare *vt* to vindicate; * *m* vindication.

scaglia *f* scale, flake.

scagliare *vt* to sling, to hurl.

scaglionare *vt* to stagger.

scala *f* scale, ladder, staircase; **~ di sicurezza** *f* fire escape; **su vasta ~** *adj* full-scale; **~ cronologica** *f* timescale; **in grande ~** *adj* large scale; **~ mobile** *f* escalator.

scalare *vt* to scale, to climb.

scalata *f* climb.

scaldabagno *m* water-heater, geyser.

scaldare *vt* to warm, to heat; **~ con aromi** *vt* to mull; * *vr* **~rsi** to warm up.

scaldavivande *m inv* hotplate.

scaletta *f* stile.

scalfittura *f* score.

scalino *m* stair.

scalo *m* slipway.

scalogno *m* shallot.

scalpello *m* chisel.

scalpitare *vt* to paw the ground.

scalpore *m* sensation, stir, furore.

scaltrezza *f* wiliness.

scaltro *adj* knowing, wily.

scalzo *adj* barefoot(ed).

scambiare *vt* to swap, to exchange.

scambio *m* exchange, swap, interchange; **libero ~** *m* free trade.

scamosciata *adj* oil-tanned; **pelle ~** *f* suede.

scampanellata *f* ring.

scampanio *m* peal.

scampare *vt* to escape.

scampolo *m* remnant.

scanalatura *f* slot.

scandagliare *vt* to plumb.

scandaglio *m* sounding, sounding line.

scandalizzare *vt* to scandalize, to shock.

scandalo *m* scandal.

scandaloso *adj* shocking, outrageous, scandalous.

scandire *vi* to scan.

scansafatiche *m/f* shirker.

scansare *vt* to shirk.

scapolo *adj* unmarried; * *m* bachelor.

scappare *vi* to escape, to abscond; **lasciarsi ~** *vr* to blurt out.

scappatella *f* escapade.

scappatoia *f* loophole.

scarabeo *m* beetle.

scarabocchiare *vt* to scribble, to doodle.

scarabocchio *m* scribble, doodle.

scarafaggio *m* cockroach.

scaramuccia *f* skirmish.

scaraventare *vt* to dash.

scardinare *vt* to unhinge.

scarica *f* discharge.

scaricare *vt* to dump, to unload, to discharge.

scaricatore *m* unloader; **~ di porto** *m* stevedore.

scarico *m* drain, plughole, outlet; **tubazione di ~** *f* wastepipe: **tubo di ~** *m* drainpipe; **gas di ~** *m* exhaust; * *adj* flat battery).

scarlattina *f* scarlet fever.

scarlatto *adj, m* scarlet.

scarmigliato *adj* unkempt.

scarpa *f* shoe; **scarpe da ginnastica** *fpl* trainers.

scarpata *f* scarp, escarpment.

scarpetta *f* bootee.

scarpone *m* boot, brogue; **~ da sci** *m* ski boot.

scarsità *f* dearth, scarcity, scarceness.

scarso *adj* slender, scant, scarce, sparse.

scartare *vt* to push aside, to unwrap, to discard, to reject.

scartavetrare *vt* to sand.

scarto *m* reject; **di ~** *adj* waste, trashy.

scartoffie *fpl* bumf.

scassato *adj* dilapidated.

scassinatore *m* housebreaker.

scatenare *vt* to trigger (off); * *vr* **~rsi** to go on the rampage, to let rip.

scatola *f* tin, box.

scattare *vi* to click.

scatto *m* click; **muoversi a scatti** *vr* to jerk; **a scatti** *adj* jerky.

scavare *vt* to excavate, to dig, to sink, to channel, to gouge, to hollow; **~ gallerie** to burrow.

scavatore *m* digger.

scavezzacollo *m* daredevil.

scavo *m* excavation, dig, cutting (railway, etc).

scegliere *vt* to single out, to select, to cull (fruit), to choose, to pick.

sceicco *m* sheik.

scellerato *m* miscreant.

scellino *m* shilling.

scelta *f* selection, pick, option, choice; * *adj* select.

scemo *m* nit, twit.

scena *f* scene.

scendere *vt, vi* to come down, to descend.

sceneggiatura *f* screenplay.

sceriffo *m* sheriff.

scervellarsi *vr* to rack one's brains.

scervellato *m* scatterbrain.

scetticismo *m* scepticism.

scettico *m* sceptic; * *adj* sceptical.

scettro *m* sceptre.

scheda *f* index card.

scheggia *f* sliver, splinter.

scheggiare *vt* to chip; * *vr* **~rsi** to splinter.

scheggiatura *f* chip.

scheletrico *adj* scraggy.

scheletro *m* skeleton.

schematico *adj* schematic.

scherma *f* fencing.

schermo *m* screen.

scherno *m* mockery.

scherzare *vi* to joke, to kid, to jest.

scherzetto *m* caper.

scherzo *m* joke, lark, trick, jest, hoax.

schiaccianoci *m inv* nutcrackers.

schiacciante *adj* damning, overwhelming.

schiacciare *vt* to swat, to squash, to mash, to crush.

schiaffeggiare *vt* to smack.

schiaffo *m* slap, smack, buffet; **dare uno ~ a** *vt* to slap.

schiarirsi *vr* to brighten.

schiavitù *f* slavery.

schiavo *m* slave; **rendere ~** *vt* to enslave.

schiena *f* back.

schiera *f* array.

schieramento *m* array.

schierare *vt* to deploy, to marshall.

schietto *adj* frank, outright, forthright.

schiffo *m* cuff.

schifoso *adj* lousy, rotten.

schioccare *vt* to snap.

schiocco *m* snap, pop, smack.

schiudersi *vr* to unfold, to hatch (egg).

schiuma *f* froth, foam, lather.

schiumare *vt* to skim; * *vi* to froth.

schiumeggiare *vi* to foam.

schiumoso *adj* frothy.

schivare *vt* to dodge.

schivata *f* dodge; **fare una ~** *vi* to duck.

schizofrenia *f* schizophrenia.

schizzare *vt* to splash, to squirt; to sketch.

schizzinoso *adj* choosy, fussy.

schizzo *m* squirt; sketch.

schooner *m inv* schooner.

sci *m inv* ski, skiing.

scia *f* wake, trail.

sciacallo *m* jackal.

sciacquare *vt* to rinse.

sciacquatura *f* rinse.

sciacquone *m* flush.

sciagurato *m* wretch.

scialbo *m* dowdy.

scialle *m* wrap, shawl.

scialuppa *f* sloop.

sciamare *vi* to swarm.

sciame *m* swarm.

sciarada *f* charade.

sciare *vi* to ski.

sciarlatano *m* charlatan.

sciarpa *f* scarf.

sciatica *f* sciatica.

sciatore *m* skier.

sciatto *adj* slipshod, slovenly.

sciattone *m* slob.

scientifico *adj* scientific.

scienza *f* science.

scienziato *m* scientist.

scimitarra *f* scimitar.

scimmia *f* monkey, ape.

scimpanzé *m inv* chimpanzee

scintilla *f* spark.

scintillante *adj* scintillating.

scintillare *vi* to twinkle, to sparkle, to glint.

scintillio *m* twinkle, glint sparkle.

scioccare *vt* to shock.

sciocchezza *f* silliness, trifle.

sciocco *m* fool; * *adj* silly, soppy, daft, nonsensical.

sciogliere *vt* to melt, to dissolve, to disband, to untie; **~ da** *vt* to absolve from.

scioglilingua *m inv* tongue twister.

scioglimento *m* dissolution.

scioltezza *f* fluency.

sciolto *adj* loose, runny.

scioperante *m/f* striker.

scioperare *vi* to strike.

sciopero *m* strike, stoppage.

sciovinismo *m* chauvinism.

sciovinista *m/f* chauvinist.

scipito *adj* vapid.

scippatore *m* bag-snatcher.

scisma *m* schism.

scissione *f* split.

scissionista *adj* breakaway.

sciupare *vt* to mar.

scivolare *vi* to slide, to slip.

scivolata *f* slip.

scivolo *m* slide, chute; **~ a spirale** *m* helter skelter.

scivolone *m* slide.

scivoloso *adj* slippery.

sclerosi *f* sclerosis.

scocciato *adj* narked.

scocciatura *f* drag.

scodella *f* bowl.

scodinzolare *vi* to wag.

scogliera *f* reef, cliff.

scoiato *adj* skinned.

scoiattolo *m* squirrel.

scolara *f* schoolgirl.

scolaro *m* schoolboy.

scolastico *adj* scholastic.

scollato *adj* low-cut.

scollatura *f* cleavage.

scolorimento *m* discoloration.

scolorire *vt* to discolour.

scolpare *vt* to exculpate.

scolpire *vi, vt* to sculpt, to carve.

scombussolamento *m* disruption.

scombussolare *vt* to disrupt, to upset, to unsettle.

scombussolato *adj* upset.

scommessa *f* wager, bet.

scommettere *vi, vt* to bet, to wager.

scomodità *f* inconvenience.

scomodo *adj* uncomfortable, inconvenient.

scompagnato *adj* odd.

scomparire *vi* to die out, to disappear.

scomparsa *f* disappearance.

scomparso *adj* defunct.

scompartimento *m* compartment.

scompigliare *vt* to mess up.

scomposto *adj* dishevelled; **sdraiarsi/sedersi in modo ~** *vr* to sprawl.

scomunica *f* excommunication.

scomunicare *vt* to excommunicate.

sconcertante *adj* uncanny, puzzling, confusing.

sconcertare *vt* to abash, to disconcert, to nonplus.

sconcertato *adj* abashed; embarrassed.

sconcezze *fpl* smut.

sconcio *adj* smutty.

sconfiggere *vt* to vanquish, to defeat.

sconfinato *adj* unbounded.

sconfitta *f* defeat, beating.

scongelare *vt* to thaw.

sconnesso *adj* unconnected, desultory.

sconosciuto *adj* strange, unknown, unfamiliar; * *m* stranger.

sconsiderato *adj* thoughtless.

sconsigliabile *adj* inadvisable.

sconsolato *adj* disconsolate, forlorn.

scontato *adj* discounted, foreseen; **un risultato ~** *m* a foregone conclusion; **dare per ~** *vi* to take for granted.

scontentezza *f* discontent.

scontento *adj* discontent, discontented.

sconto *m* discount.

scontrarsi *vr* to crash, to collide, to clash.

scontro *m* clash, smash, collision, confrontation.

scontroso *adj* sullen, bloody-minded.

sconveniente *adj* unbecoming.

sconvolgere *vt* to convulse.

sconvolgimento *m* upheaval.

sconvolto *adj* deranged, shattered.

scooter *m inv* scooter.

scopa *f* broom; **~ di filacce** *f* mop.

scopare *vt, vi* to sweep, to brush.

scopata *f* sweep.

scoperta *f* discovery, detection, find: **~ decisiva** *f* breakthrough.

scoperto *adj* exposed.

scopo *m* purpose, point, end, goal; **senza ~** *adj* aimless.

scoppiare *vi* to burst, to break out; **far ~** *vt* to pop, to burst; **~ a piangere** *vi* to burst into tears.

scoppiettare *vi* to sputter, to crackle.

scoppiettio *m* crackle.

scoppio *m* blowout, outbreak, outburst.

scoprire *vt* to uncover, to find out, to rumble, to discover.

scoraggiamento *m* discouragement.

scoraggiante *adj* discouraging, daunting.

scoraggiare *vt* to discourage, to dishearten.

scorbutico *adj* grumpy.

scorbuto *m* scurvy.

scoreggia *f* fart.

scoreggiare *vi* to fart.

scorgere *vt* to spy, to descry.

scorie *fpl* slag.

Scorpione *m* Scorpio.

scorpione *m* scorpion.

scorrere *vi* to run, to stream, to course.

scorrettezza *f* impropriety.

scorretto *adj* incorrect, improper; **gioco ~** *m* foul play.

scorrevole *adj* sliding, fluent.

scorso *adj* last.

scorta *f* stockpile, escort.

scortare *vt* to escort.

scortese *adj* discourteous, unkind, impolite.

scortesia *f* impoliteness, discourtesy.

scorticare *vt* to scrape, to graze.

scorticatura *f* graze.

scossa *f* jolt, tremor, shake, shock.

scotch *m inv* adhesive tape, sellotape.

scotennare *vt* to scalp.

scottare *vt* to scald, to blanch.

scottato *adj* sunburnt.

scottatura *f* scald, sunburn.

scovolino *m* pipe cleaner.

scozzese *adj* Scottish; **tessuto ~** *m* plaid.

screditare *vt* to discredit; * *vr* **~rsi** to cheapen oneself.

scremare *vt* to skim.

scremato *adj* skimmed.

screpolatura *f* chap.

screziato *adj* speckled.

scriba *m* scribe.

scribacchiare *vt* to scrawl.

scribacchino *m* hack.

scricchiolare *vi* to crunch, t creak.

scricchiolio *m* creak, crunch.

scricciolo *m* wren.

scrigno *m* casket.

scrittore *m* writer.

scrittura *f* writing, handwri ing, script; **Sacre scrittur** *fpl* Scripture.

scrivania *f* desk, writing desk

scrivere *vt, vi* to write, to per * *m* writing.

scroccare *vi* to sponge, t scrounge, to cadge.

scroccone *m/f* scrounge sponger, cadger.

scrofa *f* sow.

scrollata *f* shaking.

scrostarsi *vr* to flake.

scrostato *adj* flakey.

scroto *m* scrotum.

scrupolo *m* scruple, qualm compunction; **senza scrupo li** *adj* unscrupulous.

scrupoloso *adj* scrupulous.

scrutare *vt* to scan, to peer, eye, to scrutinize.

scrutinio *m* scrutiny.

scuderia *f* stable.

scudo *m* shield.

sculacciare *vt* to spank, t smack.

scultore *m* sculptor.

scultura *f* sculpture; **~ in leg no** *f* woodcarving.

scuola *f* school; **~ superior privata** *f* public school; **~ se rale** *f* night school; **~ di per fezionamento** *f* finishin school; **~ guida** *f* drivin school; **~ d'arte** *f* art school.

scuotere vt to shake, to rouse.
scuro adj dark; di colorito ~ adj swarthy.
scurrile adj scurrilous.
scusa f excuse; scuse fpl apology; di ~ adj apologetic; ~! scusi! excl sorry!.
scusare vt to excuse; * vr ~rsi to apologize.
sdegnare vt to disdain.
sdegno m outrage.
sdegnoso adj disdainful.
sdentato adj toothless.
sdoganamento m clearance.
sdolcinato adj sloppy.
sdraiarsi vr to lie down.
sdraiato adj lying; essere ~ vi to recline.
sdrucciolevole adj slippery.
se conj if, whether.
se stessi pers pron themselves.
secca f shallow; in ~ adv aground.
seccante adj tiresome, irksome.
seccare vt to dry.
seccato adj cross.
seccatura f bother, nuisance.
secchezza f dryness.
secchio m pail, (coal) scuttle, bucket.
secco adj dry.
secernare vt to secrete.
secessione f secession.
secolare adj secular.
secolo m century.
secondario adj secondary, incidental; prodotto ~ m spin-off; scuola ~ f secondary school.
secondino m screw.
secondo prep according to, under; * adj, m second.
secretaire m bureau.
secrezione f secretion, discharge.
sedano m celery.
sedativo m, adj sedative.
sede f seat, head office; ~ vescovile f see.

sedentario adj sedentary.
sedere vi to sit; far ~ vt to seat; * m bottom, backside; * vr ~rsi to sit.
sedia f chair, seat; ~ a rotelle f wheelchair; ~ a sdraio f deckchair.
sedicente adj self-styled.
sedicesimo adj, m sixteenth.
sedici adj, m sixteen.
sedile m seat.
sedimento m sediment, lees.
sedizione f sedition.
sedizioso adj seditious.
seducente adj glamorous, seductive.
sedurre vt to seduce.
seduta f sitting, session.
seduttore m seducer.
seduzione f seduction.
sega f saw.
segale f rye.
segare vt to saw.
segatura f sawdust.
seggio m seat.
seggiolino m seat; ~ eiettabile m ejector seat.
seggiolone m high chair.
segheria f sawmill.
seghettato adj serrated, jagged.
seghetto m hacksaw.
segmento m segment.
segnalare vt, vi to signal.
segnale m signal, sign; ~ acustico m bleep.
segnalibro m bookmark.
segnare vt to show, to write down, to score, to mark.
segnato adj marked; ~ dalle intemperie adj weather-beaten.
segnatura f signature.
segnavento m inv weathervane.
segno m indicator, token, tick, sign, mark.
segregare vt to segregate, to sequester.

segregazione f segregation.
segreta f dungeon.
segretariato m secretariate.
segretario m secretary; ~ **comunale** m town clerk.
segreteria telefonica f answering machine.
segretezza f secrecy.
segretissimo adj top-secret.
segreto adj secret, sneaking; * m secret.
seguace m/f follower.
seguente adj following.
segugio m bloodhound, sleuth, hound.
seguire vt to follow; * vi to ensue.
seguito m retinue, sequel, following; **in ~** adv thereafter, afterwards.
sei adj, m six.
selezionare vt to select.
selezione f selection.
self-service adj inv self-service.
sella f saddle; **senza ~** adj bareback.
sellaio m sadler.
sellare vt to saddle.
sellino m seat; ~ **posteriore** m pillion.
seltz m inv soda.
selvaggina f game.
selvaggio adj uncivilized, wild, savage; * m savage.
selvatico adj wild.
semaforo m traffic lights.
semantica f semantics.
sembianza f guise.
sembrare vi to seem, to appear, to look; **voler ~** vt to purport.
seme m seed, pip.
semestrale adj half-yearly.
semiasse m axle.
semicerchio m semicircle.
semicircolare adj semicircular.
semiconduttore m semiconductor.

semifinale f semifinal.
semina f sowing.
seminare vt to sow, to seed.
seminario m seminar, semi nary.
seminterrato m basement.
semiprezioso adj semipre cious.
semolino m semolina.
semplice adj simple, plain easy.
semplicemente adv simply merely.
sempliciotto m simpleton.
semplicità f simplicity.
semplificare vt to simplify.
semplificazione f simplifica tion.
sempre adv always, ever; **pe ~** adv forever; **~ più veloce** adv faster and faster.
sempreverde m/f evergreen.
senape f mustard.
senato m senate.
senatore m senator.
senile adj senile.
senilità f senility.
senna f senna.
senno m sense.
seno m bosom, breast; sinus; a **~ scoperto** adj topless.
sensale m/f middleman; ~ **d matrimoni** m matchmaker.
sensazione f sensation, feel feeling.
sensibile adj tender, sensitive
sensibilità f sensitivity.
senso m sense, feeling; **priv di sensi** adj senseless; **senza ~** adj meaningless; **buon ~** m common sense.
sensuale adj sensual.
sensualità f sensuality.
sentenza f sentence.
sentenzioso adj sententious.
sentiero m track, trail, path.
sentimentale adj sentimental
sentimento m sentiment, feel

ing; ~ **falso** *m* bathos.
sentinella *f* sentry, look-out.
sentire *vt* to feel, to hear, to catch; ~ **odore di** *vt* to smell; ~ **per caso** *vt* to overhear.
sentito *adj* warm.
senza *prep* without, apart from.
separabile *adj* separable.
separare *vt* to separate, to part.
separatamente *adv* separately.
separato *adj* separate, estranged, discrete; **vivere separati** to live apart.
separazione *f* separation, parting.
sepolcro *m* sepulchre.
sepoltura *f* burial.
seppellimento *m* interment.
seppellire *vt* to bury, to inter.
seppia *f* cuttlefish.
sequenza *f* sequence, clip.
sequestrare *vt* to impound, to sequestrate.
sequestro *m* attachment; ~ **di persona** *m* kidnapping.
sera *f* evening.
serata *f* evening.
serbatoio *m* tank, cistern; ~ **del carburante** *m* fuel tank.
serenata *f* serenade; **fare la ~ a** *vt* to serenade.
serenità *f* serenity, equanimity.
sereno *adj* serene, halcyon, calm.
serge *f* serge.
sergente *m* sergeant.
serie *f inv* succession, series, run.
serigrafia *f* silk-screen printing.
serio *adj* serious, earnest.
sermone *m* sermon.
serpeggiante *adj* winding.
serpeggiare *vi* to meander.
serpente *m* snake, serpent.
serpentina *f* serpentine.

serra *f* hot-house, greenhouse, conservatory.
serraglio *m* seraglio; menagerie.
serrata *f* lockout.
serratura *f* lock; **buco della ~** *m* keyhole.
servile *adj* servile; menial.
servire *vi* to wait, to serve, to dish.
servizio *m* service, (press, radio, TV) coverage; ~ **da tè** *m* tea service.
servo *m* servant; ~ **favorito** *m* minion.
sessanta *adj, m* sixty.
sessantesimo *adj, m* sixtieth.
sessismo *m* sexism.
sessista *adj* sexist.
sesso *m* sex.
sessuale *adj* sexual.
sessualità *f* sexuality.
sestante *m* sextant.
sestetto *m* sextet.
sesto *adj, m* sixth.
set *m inv* set.
seta *f* silk; **baco da ~** *m* silkworm.
setacciare *vt* to scour, to sieve, to sift.
setaccio *m* sieve, riddle.
sete *f* thirst.
setola *f* bristle.
setoloso *adj* bristly.
setta *f* sect.
settanta *adj, m* seventy.
settantesimo *adj, m* seventieth.
settario *adj* sectarian.
sette *adj, m* seven.
settembre *m* September.
settentrionale *adj* northern.
settentrione *m* north.
setter *m inv* setter.
setticemia *f* septicaemia.
settico *adj* septic.
settimana *f* week; **fine ~** *m inv* weekend.

settimanale *adj, m* weekly.

settimo *adj, m* seventh.

settore *m* sector.

severità *f* strictness, harshness, severity.

severo *adj* severe, harsh, strict.

sexy *adj inv* sexy.

sezionamento *m* dissection.

sezionare *vt* to dissect.

sezione *f* section, department; ~ trasversale *f* cross-section.

sfaccettatura *f* facet.

sfacchinata *f* drudgery.

sfacciataggine *f* forwardness.

sfacciato *adj* blatant, brazen, barefaced.

sfacelo *m* dilapidation.

sfarzo *m* pageantry.

sfavorevole *adj* unfavourable, adverse.

sfortuna *f* adversity.

simile *adj* alike.

sfera *f* sphere.

sferico *adj* spherical.

sferragliare *vi* to clatter, to rattle.

sfibrato *adj* jaded.

sfida *f* dare, defiance, challenge.

sfidante *m/f* challenger.

sfidare *vt* to defy to brave, to dare, to challenge.

sfigurare *vt* to disfigure.

sfilare *vt* to unthread; * *vi* to parade; ~ davanti *vi* to file past.

sfilata *f* parade, marchpast; ~ di moda fashion show.

sfinge *f* sphinx.

sfiorare *vi* to touch on, to brush.

sfocato *adj* fuzzy, hazy.

sfoderato *adj* unlined.

sfogare *vt* to vent.

sfoggiare *vt* to flaunt.

sfogliare *vt* to flip through.

sfogo *m* rash.

sfolgorare *vi* to glare, to flare.

sfondo *m* background.

sformato *adj* baggy.

sfortunatamente *adv* unfortunately, unhappily.

sfortunato *adj* hapless, unlucky, unfortunate.

sforzarsi *vr* to strive, to exert oneself.

sforzo *m* stress, exertion, effort

sfrattare *vt* to evict.

sfratto *m* eviction.

sfrecciare *vi* to zoom off.

sfregare *vt* to rub, to chafe, to scour.

sfregiare *vt* to deface, to slash, to scar.

sfrenato *adj* unrestrained.

sfrigolare *vi* to sizzle.

sfrontatezza *f* effrontery, impudence.

sfrontato *adj* unashamed, brash, impudent.

sfruttamento *m* exploitation.

sfruttare *vt* to tap, to exploit.

sfruttato *adj* exploited; non ~ *adj* untapped.

sfuggire *vi* to slip, to escape.

sfumatura *f* tint, nuance, overtone.

sgabello *m* stool.

sgambettare *vi* to scamper, to frolic.

sganciare *vt* to unhook, to uncouple.

sgangherato *adj* ramshackle.

sgarbato *adj* churlish, bad-mannered.

sgargiante *adj* garish.

sgarrare *vi* to lapse.

sgattaiolare *vi* to sneak; ~ via *vi* to scuttle off.

sgobbare *vi* to slave, to plod.

sgobbone *m* slogger.

sgocciolare *vi* to drip.

sgombero *m* clearance.

sgombrare *vt* to clear.

sgombro *adj* clear; * *m* mackerel.

sgomentare *vt* to dismay.

sgomento *m* dismay; * *adj* dismayed.

sgonfiare *vt* to deflate.

sgonfio *adj* flat.

sgorgante *adj* gushing.

sgorgare *vi* to well up, to gush.

sgradevole *adj* undesirable, distasteful, nasty; **oggetto ~ alla vista** *adj* eyesore.

sgradevolezza *f* unpleasantness.

sgranare *vt* to shell.

sgranocchiare *vt* to munch, to crunch.

sgridare *vt* to scold.

sguaiato *adj* ribald.

sgualcire *vt* to crease.

sgualdrina *f* tart, slut.

sguardo *m* look, gaze; **~ fisso** *m* stare; **~ passeggero** *m* glimpse.

sguazzare *vi* to paddle, to dabble.

shampoo *m inv* shampoo.

shearling *m* sheepskin.

sherry *m inv* sherry.

shock *m inv* shock.

show-room *m inv* showroom.

si *pers pron* itself, themselves.

sì *adv*, *m* yes, yeah.

sibilare *vi* to hiss.

sibilo *m* hiss.

siccità *f* drought.

siccome *conj* since.

sicomoro *m* sycamore.

sicurezza *f* safety, security; **di massima ~** *adj* gilt-edged (stocks, etc).

sicuro *adj* sure, safe, secure, confident; **~ di se** *adj* self-confident; **una cosa ~** *f* a cinch.

sidro *m* cider.

siepe *f* hedge.

siero *m* serum.

sifilide *f* syphilis.

sifone *m* siphon.

sigaretta *f* cigarette, (*fam*) fag.

sigaro *m* cigar; **~ spuntato** *m* cheroot.

sigillare *vt* to seal.

sigillo *m* seal.

sigla *f* abbreviation; **~ editoriale** *f* imprint.

significare *vt* to signify, to mean.

significativo *adj* meaningful, significant.

significato *m* meaning, significance, purport.

signora *f* lady, madam, Mrs.; **da ~** *adj* ladylike.

signore *m* sir, gentleman, lord, Mr.

signorina *f* Miss.

silenziatore *m* silencer.

silenzio *m* silence, quiet, hush.

silenziosamente *adv* softly.

silenzioso *adj* quiet, silent.

silfo *m* sylph.

silice *f* flint.

sillaba *f* syllable.

sillogismo *m* syllogism.

silo *m* silo.

siluro *m* torpedo.

silvicoltura *f* forestry.

simboleggiare *vt* to symbolize.

simbolico *adj* symbolic, token.

simbolo *m* symbol.

simile *adj* similar, comparable, like; **simili** *mpl* fellow men.

similitudine *f* simile.

simmetria *f* symmetry.

simmetrico *adj* symmetrical.

simpatia *f* liking, fellow feeling; **prendere in ~** *vt* to take to.

simpatico *adj* likeable, nice, congenial.

simposio *m* symposium.

simulare *vt* to simulate, to feign.

simulato *adj* sham.

simulazione *f* simulation.

simultaneo *adj* simultaneous, concurrent.

sinagoga *m* sinagogue.

sincerità *f* sincerity.

sincero *adj* sincere, true, heart-felt.

sincronizzare *vt* to synchronize.

sindaca *f* mayoress.

sindacalismo *m* trade unionism.

sindacalista *m/f* trade unionist, unionist.

sindacalizzare *vt* to unionize.

sindacato *m* syndicate, trade union, union.

sindaco *m* mayor.

sindrome *f* syndrome.

sinecura *f* sinecure.

sinfonia *f* symphony.

singhiozzare *vi* to sob.

singhiozzo *m* sob, hiccup; **avere il ~** *vi* to hiccup.

singolare *adj* singular, quaint.

singolarità *f* singularity.

singolo *adj* single; * *m* singles (tennis).

sinistra *f* left hand; **a ~** *adv* on the left.

sinistro *adj* left, eerie, sinister, spooky.

sinodo *m* synod.

sinonimo *m* synonym, byword; * *adj* synonymous.

sinossi *f inv* synopsis.

sintassi *f* syntax.

sintesi *f inv* synthesis.

sintomo *m* symptom.

sintonizzatore *m* tuner.

sinuoso *adj* sinuous.

sirena *f* siren, hooter, mermaid.

siringa *f* syringe.

siringare *vt* to syringe.

sistema *m* system.

sistemare *vt* to settle, to position, to fix, to arrange.

sistematico *adj* systematic.

sistemazione *f* accommodation, arrangement.

sit-in *m inv* sit-in.

situare *vt* to place.

situato *adj* situated.

situazione *f* situation; **~ critica** *f* plight.

skate-board *m inv* skateboard.

sketch *m inv* sketch; **~ satirico** *m* skit.

slacciare *vt* to undo, to unfasten.

slam *m inv* slam.

slang *m* slang.

sleale *adj* treacherous, disloyal.

slealtà *f* treachery, disloyalty.

slegato *adj* disjointed.

slip *m inv* pants, underpants, briefs.

slitta *f* sled, sledge, sleigh.

slittamento *m* skid.

slittare *vi* to skid.

slittino *m* toboggan.

slogan *m inv* slogan.

slogare *vt* to wrench, to strain, to dislocate; * *vr* **~rsi** to twist, to sprain.

slogatura *f* dislocation, sprain.

smagliare *vt* to ladder.

smagliatura *f* run.

smaltare *vt* to enamel.

smalto *m* enamel, glaze; **~ per unghie** *m* nail varnish.

smammare *vi* to push off.

smarrire *vt* to mislay, to misplace; * *vr* **~rsi** to stray.

smarrito *adj* lost; **ufficio oggetti smarriti** *m* lost property office.

smascherare *vt* to unmask, to expose.

smembrare *vt* to dismember.

smemoratezza *f* forgetfulness.

smentire *vt* to belie, to deny, to disclaim.

smentita *f* disclaimer.

smeraldo *m* emerald.

smeriglio *m* emery.

smerlare *vt* to scallop.

smerlo *m* scallop.

smettere *vt* to quit, to stop.

smidollato *adj* spineless.

sminuire *vt* to understate, to detract, to belittle.

smistare *vt* to sort, to shunt.

smisurato *adj* immense.

smoderato *adj* immoderate.

smog *m inv* smog.

smontare *vt* to take down, to dismantle, to dismount.

smorfia *f* grimace.

smorto *adj* pasty.

smottamento *m* landslip.

smussare *vt* to dull, to bevel.

smussatura *f* bevel.

snazionalizzare *vt* to denationalize.

snellezza *f* slenderness.

snello *adj* trim, slender.

snervante *adj* nerve-racking.

snervare *vt* to enervate.

snidare *vt* to ferret out.

sniffare *vt* to sniff.

snob *m/f inv* snob; * *adj* snobbish, snob, genteel.

snobbare *vt* to snub, to slight.

snobismo *m* snobbery.

sobbalzare *vi* to lurch, to jolt.

sobbalzo *m* lurch, start, jerk.

sobbollire *vi* to simmer.

sobborgo *m* suburb.

sobrietà *f* sobriety.

sobrio *adj* sober.

socchiuso *adj* ajar.

soccombere *vi* to succumb.

soccorrere *vt* to help, to aid.

soccorso *m* help; **pronto ~** *m* first aid.

socialismo *m* socialism.

socialista *m/f* socialist.

società *f inv* society, company, corporation; ~ **per azioni** *f* joint stock company.

socievole *adj* sociable; **poco ~** *adj* unsociable.

socio *m* partner, member.

sociologia *f* sociology.

sociologico *adj* sociological.

sociologo *m* sociologist.

soda *f* soda.

soddisfacente *adj* satisfactory, gratifying.

soddisfare *vt* to satisfy, to content, to gratify, to meet.

soddisfatto *adj* satisfied; ~ **di sé** *adj* self-satisfied.

soddisfazione *f* satisfaction, gratification, fulfilment.

sodio *m* sodium.

sodo *adj* hard-boiled.

sofà *m inv* sofa.

sofferente *adj* ailing.

sofferenza *f* affliction, suffering.

soffiare *vi* to puff, to blow.

soffiata *f* tip-off.

soffice *adj* soft.

soffietto *m* bellows.

soffio *m* puff.

soffitta *f* attic, garret, loft.

soffitto *m* ceiling.

soffocamento *m* asphyxiation.

soffocante *adj* sweltering, overpowering, stifling.

soffocare *vt* to suffocate, to stifle, to choke, to cramp.

soffocazione *f* suffocation.

soffrire *vt, vi* to suffer.

sofisticare *vt* to adulterate.

sofisticato *adj* sophisticated.

software *m* software.

soggettivo *adj* subjective.

soggetto *m* subject; **~ a** *adj* subject to, prone to, liable to.

sogghignare *vi* to sneer.

sogghigno *m* sneer.

soggiogare *vt* to subjugate.

soggiorno *m* living room; stay.

soglia *f* threshold, doorstep.

sogliola *f* sole.

sognare *vt, vi* to dream, to muse; **~ ad occhi aperti** *vi* to daydream.

sognatore *m* dreamer.

sogno *m* dream, fantasy; **mondo dei sogni** *m* cloud-cuckooland; **di ~** *adj* dreamy.

soia *f* soya.

solamente *adv* only.

solare *adj* solar.

solarium *m inv* solarium.

solcare *vt* to furrow.

solco *m* rut, groove, furrow.

soldato *m* soldier; **~ semplice** *m* private.

soldo *m* penny, cent; **soldi** *mpl* money, cash; **senza un ~** *adj* penniless.

sole *m* sun; **prendere il ~** *vi* to sunbathe; **senza ~** *adj* sunless; **luce del ~** *f* sunlight, sunshine.

solecismo *m* solecism.

soleggiato *adj* sunny.

solenne *adj* solemn.

solennità *f inv* solemnity.

solennizzare *vt* to solemnize.

soletta *f* insole.

solfato *m* sulphate.

solforico *adj* sulphuric.

solfuro *m* sulphide.

solidarietà *f* solidarity.

solidificare *vt* to solidify.

solidità *f* solidity.

solido *adj* solid, sturdy; * *m* solid.

soliloquio *m* soliloquy.

solista *m/f* soloist.

solitario *adj* solitary, lonely; * *m* solitaire.

solito *adj* stock, usual, accustomed; **di ~** *adv* usually.

solitudine *f* solitude, loneliness.

sollecitare *vt* to solicit, to invite.

sollecito *m* reminder; * *adj* expeditious.

sollecitudine *f* solicitude.

solletico *m* tickle; **far il ~ a** *vt* to tickle; **che soffre il ~** *adj* ticklish.

sollevare *vt* to raise, to lift, to uplift, to bring up; **~ con una leva** *vt* to pry.

sollievo *m* relief.

solo *adj* alone, single, very; * *conj* but, only.

solstizio *m* solstice.

soltanto *adv* only, just.

solubile *adj* soluble, (coffee) instant.

soluzione *f* solution.

solvente *adj, m* solvent.

solvenza *f* solvency.

somaro *m* dunce.

somiglianza *f* similarity, resemblance, likeness.

somigliare *vt* to resemble.

somma *f* sum, amount.

sommare *vt* to add.

sommario *m* abstract.

sommergere *vt* to submerge, to overwhelm; * *vr* **~rsi** to sink.

sommergibile *m* submarine.

sommersione *f* submersion.

somministrare *vt* to dose, to administer.

somministrazione *f* administration.

sommo *adj* supreme, paramount.

sommossa *f* riot, rising.

sonaglio *m* rattle.

sonata *f* sonata.

sonda *f* probe.

sondaggio *m* poll; **~ di opinioni** *m* opinion poll.

sondare *vt* to sound, to probe.

sonetto *m* sonnet.

sonico *adj* sonic.

sonnambulismo *m* sleepwalking, somnambulism.

sonnambulo *m* sleepwalker, somnambulist.

sonnecchiare *vi* to snooze, to doze, to drowse.

sonnellino *m* snooze.

sonnifero *m* sleeping pill.

sonno *m* slumber, sleep.

sonnolento *adj* sleepy, dozy.

sonnolenza *f* sleepiness, somnolence, drowsiness.

sonoro *adj* sonorous.

sontuoso *adj* palatial, sumptuous, plush.

soporifero *adj* soporific.

soppiantare *vt* to supplant, to supersede.

soppiatto; di ~ *adv* stealthily.

sopportabile *adj* bearable, endurable.

sopportare *vt* to bear, to stand, to endure.

sopportazione *f* tolerance.

sopprimere *vt* to suppress, to put down.

sopra *prep* over, above, on; **di ~** *adj* upstairs; **piano di ~** *m* upstairs.

soprabito *m* overcoat.

sopracciglio *m* eyebrow.

sopraelevato *adj* overhead.

sopraffare *vt* to overpower, to overwhelm.

sopraggiungere *vi* to intervene.

soprammenzionato *adj* abovementioned.

soprannaturale *adj*, *m* supernatural.

soprannome *m* nickname.

soprannominare *vt* to nickname.

soprano *m/f* soprano.

sopratetto *m* flysheet.

soprattutto *adv* above all.

sopravvalutare *vt* to overrate, to overestimate.

sopravvenire *vi* to supervene.

sopravvivenza *f* subsistence.

sopravvivere *vt*, *vi* to survive; **~ a** *vt* to outlive.

soprintendente *m/f* superintendent.

sorbetto *m* sorbet, sherbet.

sordido *adj* sordid.

sordità *f* deafness.

sordo *adj* deaf.

sordomuto *adj* deaf-and-dumb.

sorella *f* sister, sibling; **da ~** *adv* sisterly.

sorellastra *f* step-sister.

sorgente *f* spring, source, fount.

sorgere *vi* to rise, to spring; * *m* rise.

soriano *m* tabby cat.

sormontabile *adj* surmountable.

sormontare *vt* to surmount, to top.

sorpassare *vt*, *vi* to pass, to outstrip.

sorpassato *adj* outdated, outmoded.

sorprendente *adj* surprising, startling, astonishing

sorprendere *vt* to surprise, to catch.

sorpresa *f* surprise; **bella ~** *f* windfall.

sorpresina *f* treat.

sorridere *vi* to smile; **~ in modo sciocco** *vi* to simper; **~ radiosamente** *vi* to beam; **~ compiaciuto** *vi* to smirk.

sorrisetto *m* smile; **~ sciocco** *m* simper.

sorriso *m* smile; **~ compiaciuto** *m* smirk; **largo ~** *m* grin; **fare un largo ~** *vi* to grin.

sorsata *f* draught.

sorseggiare *vt* to sip.

sorso *m* sip.

sorte *f* fate, lot.

sorteggio *m* draw.

sorvegliante *m/f* supervisor, overseer.

sorveglianza *f* supervision, watch.

sorvegliare *vt* to supervise, to invigilate, to oversee.

S.O.S. *m* S.O.S.

sosia *m inv* double.

sospendere *vt* to suspend, to stay, to adjourn.

sospensione *f* suspension, stoppage, adjournment; **~ dell'esecuzione** *f* stay of execution.

sospeso *adj* suspended; **in ~** *adj*

pending; **essere in ~** *vi* to be in abeyance.

sospettare *vt* to suspect.

sospetto *m* suspicion; * *adj* suspect, fishy.

sospettoso *adj* suspicious.

sospirare *vi* to sigh.

sospiro *m* sigh.

sosta *f* stop, stopover, halt.

sostantivo *adj* substantive; * *m* noun, substantive.

sostanza *f* substance.

sostanziale *adj* substantial.

sostanzioso *adj* substantial, filling.

sostegno *m* support, prop, mainstay.

sostenere *vt* to support, to sustain, to contend, to uphold.

sostenibile *adj* tenable.

sostenitore *m* supporter, backer, campaigner, advocate.

sostentamento *m* livelihood.

sostituire *vt* to substitute, to deputize, to replace.

sostituto *m* replacement, substitute; * *adj* deputy.

sostituzione *f* substitution.

sottaceti *mpl* pickles; **mettere sottaceto** *vt* to pickle.

sotterfugio *m* subterfuge.

sotterraneo *adj* subterranean, underground.

sottigliezza *f* subtlety.

sottile *adj* subtle, thin, fine.

sottilmente *adv* subtly.

sotto *adv*, *prep* under, underneath, below, beneath.

sottobicchiere *m* coaster.

sottobosco *m* undergrowth.

sottoesposto *adj* underexposed.

sottolineare *vt* to underline, to emphasize.

sottomano *adj* handy.

sottomarino *adj* underwater.

sottomesso *adj* submissive.

sottomettere *vt* to subdue.

sottomissione *f* submission, subjection.

sottopassaggio *m* subway, underpass.

sottopeso *adj* underweight.

sottoporre *vt* to subject.

sottoprodotto *m* by-product.

sottoscritto *adj*, *m* undersigned.

sottoscrivere *vt* to sign, to underwrite.

sottosegretario *m* undersecretary.

sottosopra *adj*, *adv* topsy-turvy, upside down.

sottosviluppato *adj* underdeveloped.

sottotitolo *m* subtitle, caption.

sottovalutare *vt* to undervalue, to underestimate, to underrate.

sottovento *adj* lee, leeward.

sottoveste *f* slip, petticoat.

sottrarre *vt* to subtract.

sottrazione *f* subtraction.

sottufficiale *m* non-commissioned officer; **~ di marina** *m* petty officer.

soufflé *m inv* soufflé.

souvenir *m inv* souvenir.

soviet *m inv* soviet.

sovietico *adj* soviet.

sovrabbondanza *f* surfeit, glut.

sovraccaricare *vt* to overload.

sovraffollato *adj* overcrowded.

sovranità *f* sovereignty.

sovrano *m* ruler, sovereign; * *adj* sovereign.

sovrappiù: *m* **di ~** *adj* surplus.

sovrapporsi *vr* to overlap.

sovrapposizione *f* overlap.

sovrapprezzo *m* surcharge.

sovrastruttura *f* superstructure.

sovrumano *adj* superhuman.

sovvenzionare *vt* to subsidize.

sovvenzione *f* grant, subsidy.

sovversione *f* subversion.

sovversivo *adj*, *m* subversive.

sovvertire *vt* to subvert.

spaccare *vt* to split, to chop; * *vr* ~**rsi** to split.

spaccatura *f* rift.

spacciare *vt* to peddle.

spacciatore *m* (drug) pusher; pedlar.

spacco *m* slit, vent, split.

spaccone *m* braggart.

spada *f* sword; **pesce** ~ *m* swordfish.

spadaccino *m* swordsman.

spadino *m* rapier.

spadroneggiare *vt* to domineer.

spaghetti *mpl* spaghetti.

spago *m* string.

spalancarsi *vr* to gape.

spalancato *adj* yawning, wide open.

spalare *vt* to shovel.

spalla *f* shoulder; **alzata di spalle** *f* shrug.

spallina *f* strap.

spalmare *vt* to smear, to spread.

spandersi *vr* to spread.

spaniel *m inv* spaniel.

spanna *f* span.

sparare *vt* to fire, to shoot.

sparatoria *f* shooting.

spareggio *m* disparity; **partita di** ~ *f* play-off.

spargere *vt* to strew.

spargimento *m* scattering; ~ **di sangue** *m* bloodshed.

sparlare *vi* to backbite.

sparo *m* shot, gunshot.

sparpagliare *vt* to scatter.

spartano *adj* spartan.

spartiacque *m* watershed.

spartizione *f* share-out.

sparviero *m* sparrowhawk.

spasmo *m* spasm.

spasmodico *adj* spasmodic.

spassionato *adj* dispassionate.

spassosissimo *adj* hilarious.

spastico *m*, *adj* spastic.

spatola *f* spatula.

spauracchio *m* bugbear.

spavalderia *f* bravado.

spaventapasseri *m inv* scarecrow.

spaventare *vt* to frighten, to startle, to scare.

spaventato *adj* frightened.

spavento *m* scare, fright.

spaventoso *adj* frightening, abysmal, horrific.

spaziale *adj* spatial; **veicolo** ~ *m* spacecraft.

spazio *m* room, space, gap; ~ **cosmico** *m* outer space.

spazioso *adj* spacious, roomy.

spazzacamino *m* chimney sweep.

spazzaneve *m inv* snowplough.

spazzare *vt*, *vi* to sweep.

spazzatura *f* trash, rubbish.

spazzola *f* brush; ~ **per capelli** *f* hairbrush.

spazzolare *vt* to brush.

spazzolino *m* small brush; ~ **da denti** *m* toothbrush; ~ **da unghie** *m* nailbrush.

specchio *m* mirror, looking glass.

speciale *adj* special.

specialista *m/f* (*med*) consultant, specialist.

specialità *f inv* speciality.

specializzato *adj* specialist, skilled.

specializzazione *f* specialization; **di** ~ **dopo la laurea** *adj* post-graduate.

specie *f inv* sort, species.

specificare *vt* to specify; ~ **uno per uno** *vt* to itemize.

specificazione *f* specification.

specifico *adj* specific.

specioso *adj* specious.

speculare *vi* to speculate, to profiteer.

speculativo *adj* speculative.

speculatore *m* profiteer.

spedire *vt* to ship, to send, to dispatch; ~ **per posta** *vt* to post, to mail.

spedizione *f* trek, expedition, dispatch.

spedizioniere *m* shipper.

spegnere *vt* to switch off, to extinguish, to blow out (candle); * *vr* ~**rsi** to die down.

spellare *vt* to skin; ~**rsi** to peel.

spendaccione *m* spendthrift.

spendere *vt* to spend, to expend.

spennare *vt* to pluck.

spensierato *adj* happy-go-lucky, light hearted, carefree.

spento *adj* dull, off.

speranza *f* hope.

sperare *vt* to hope.

sperduto *adj* godforsaken.

spergiurare *vt* to perjure.

spergiuro *m* perjury.

spericolato *adj* reckless.

sperimentale *adj* experimental.

sperimentare *vt* to test.

sperma *m* sperm, semen.

speronare *vt* to ram.

sperone *m* spur.

sperperare *vt* to squander.

spesa *f* expense, shopping, groceries, outlay; **fare la** ~ *vi* to shop.

spesso *adj* thick; * *adv* often.

spessore *m* thickness.

spettacolo *m* spectacle, show, entertainment; **il mondo dello** ~ *m* show business.

spettare *vi* to be due, to appertain.

spettatore *m* spectator, onlooker.

spettinato *adj* uncombed.

spettrale *adj* spectral.

spettro *m* spectre.

spezie *fpl* spice.

spezzato *adj* broken.

spezzone *m* extract.

spia *f* spy; **fare la** ~ **a** *vi* to sneak on; ~ **luminosa** *f* warning light.

spiacevole *adj* unpleasant, disagreeable.

spiaggia *f* seaside, beach.

spianare *vt* to smooth, to level, to flatten.

spiare *vi* to peep, to spy.

spicchio *m* gore (in skirt), segment.

spiccioli *m pl* small change.

spiedino *m* kebab.

spiedo *m* spit, skewer.

spiegabile *adj* explicable.

spiegare *vt* to unfold, to spread, to explain.

spiegazione *f* explanation, elucidation.

spiegazzare *vt* to screw up, to crinkle.

spietato *adj* pitiless, ruthless, remorseless.

spifferare *vt* to blab.

spiffero *m* draught.

spigliato *adj* racy, jaunty.

spigoloso *adj* angular.

spilla *f* brooch; ~ **di balia** *f* safety pin.

spillo *m* pin; **fissare con uno** ~ *vt* to pin.

spilorcio *adj* stingy.

spilungone *adj* lanky.

spina *f* plug, thorn, prickle; ~ **dorsale** *f* spine, backbone; **alla** ~ *adj* on draught.

spinaci *mpl* spinach.

spinale *adj* spinal.

spinello *m* joint.

spinetta *f* spinet.

spingere *vt* to push, to propel, to shove, to drive; ~ **con forza** *vt* to thrust.

spinoso *adj* thorny, prickly, spiky.

spinta *f* push, impetus, boost.

spinto *adj* suggestive, risqué, bawdy, naughty.

spintone *m* thrust, shove.

spionaggio *m* spying, espionage.

spioncino *m* peephole.

spione *m* telltale, sneak.

spirale *adj* spiral; * *f* spiral, (contraceptive) coil.

spirare *vi* to expire.

spiritista *m/f* spiritualist.

spirito *m* spirit.

spiritosaggine *f* wisecrack.

spiritoso *adj* humorous.

spirituale *adj* spiritual.

spiritualità *f* spirituality.

splendido *adj* splendid, stunning, gorgeous.

splendore *m* radiance, splendour.

spogliare *vt* to undress, to despoil, to divest, to strip; * *vr* ~rsi to strip.

spogliarellista *m/f* stripper.

spogliarello *m* striptease.

spoglio *adj* bare.

spola *f* shuttle; **fare la ~ tra** *vi* to ply between, to shuttle.

spolverare *vt, vi* to dust.

sponda *f* shore.

sponsor *m/f inv*.

sponsorizzare *vt* to sponsor.

sponsorizzazione *f* sponsorship.

spontaneamente *adv* voluntarily.

spontaneità *f* spontaneity.

spontaneo *adj* unstudied, spontaneous.

spopolamento *m* depopulation.

spopolare *vt* to depopulate.

sporadico *adj* sporadic.

sporcare *vt* to soil, to foul, to smear.

sporcizia *f* dirtiness.

sporco *adj* dirty, smutty; * *m* dirt.

sporgente *adj* overhanging.

sporgenza *f* ledge.

sporgere *vi* to protrude, to stick out, to jut (out), to overhang.

sport *m inv* sport; **~ invernali** *mpl* winter sports.

sportello *m* door; **~ automatico** *m* cash dispenser.

sportiva *f* sportswoman.

sportivo *m* sportsman.

sposa *f* bride.

sposare *vt* to wed, to marry; * *vr* ~rsi to marry.

sposato *adj* married.

sposo *m* spouse, bridegroom.

spossessare *vt* to dispossess.

spostare *vt* to budge, to shift, to move, to displace.

spot *m inv* spotlight.

spratto *m* sprat.

spray *m inv* spray.

sprecare *vt* to fritter (away), to waste.

sprecato *adj* misspent.

spreco *m* wastage, waste.

sprecone *adj* wasteful.

spregevole *adj* contemptible, despicable.

spregiativo *adj* derogatory.

spremere *vt* to squeeze.

sprezzante *adj* scornful, scathing, contemptuous.

sprigionare *vt* to give off.

sprint *m inv* sprint.

spronare *vt* to spur, to urge on, to goad.

sprone *m* yoke, boost, spur.

sproporzionato *adj* disproportionate.

sprovvisto *adj* lacking; **essere colto (preso) alla ~** to be taken aback, unawares.

spruzzare *vt* to spray, to squirt.

spruzzatina *f* sprinkling.

spruzzo *m* splash, spray.

spudorato *adj* shameless.

spugna *f* towelling, sponge; **lavare con una ~** *vt* to sponge.

spugnoso *adj* spongy.

spumoso *adj* foamy.

spuntare *vt* to tick, to trim; ~ denti *vt* to cut teeth; * *vi* to dawn (day).

spuntata *f* trim.

spuntino *m* snack.

spurgare *vt* to bleed (radiators, etc).

sputacchiare *vi* to splutter.

sputare *vt*, *vi* to spit.

sputo *m* spit, spittle.

squadra *f* team, side; ~ di armati *f* posse.

squadrare *vt* to square.

squadrone *m* troop, squadron.

squalificare *vt* to disqualify.

squallido *adj* seedy, sleazy, squalid, dingy.

squallore *m* squalor.

squalo *m* shark.

squama *f* scale.

squamare *vt* to scale.

squarciare *vt* to gash.

squarcio *m* gash.

squash *m* squash.

squaw *f inv* squaw.

squilibrato *adj* unbalanced.

squilibrio *m* imbalance.

squillo *m* ring.

squisito *adj* exquisite.

squittio *m* squeak.

squittire *vi* to peep, to squeak.

sradicare *vt* to eradicate, to uproot.

srotolare *vt* to unwind, to unroll.

stabile *adj* stable.

stabilimento *m* plant.

stabilire *vt* to establish, to set, to stipulate, to name.

stabilità *f* stability.

stabilito *adj* set.

stabilizzare *vt* to stabilize.

staccabile *adj* detachable.

staccare *vt* to unplug, to disconnect, to detach; * *vr* ~**rsi** to come off.

staccato *adj* unattached, detached, loose.

stadera *f* steelyard.

stadio *m* stage.

staffa *f* stirrup.

stagionare *vt* to season.

stagionato *adj* ripe.

stagione *f* season; **di ~** *adj* seasonable; **bassa ~** *f* off season.

stagnante *adj* slack, stagnant.

stagnare *vi* to stagnate.

stagno *adj* watertight; * *m* tin.

stalagmite *f* stalagmite.

stalattite *f* stalactite.

stalla *f* stable, stall, barn, cowshed.

stallo *m* stalemate; **andare in ~** *vi* to stall.

stallone *m* stud, stallion.

stame *m* stamen.

stampa *f* press, print, printing; **stampe** *fpl* printed matter; **agenzia ~** *f* news agency.

stampante *m* printer.

stampare *vt* to print.

stampatello *m* printing.

stampato *m* print.

stampella *f* crutch.

stampo *m* cast, mould.

stancare *vt* to tire; * *vr* ~**rsi** to flag.

stanchezza *f* tiredness, weariness, fatigue.

stanco *adj* weary, tired; ~ **morto** *adj* dead tired.

stand *m inv* stall, stand.

standard *adj*, *m inv* standard.

standing *m* financial standing.

stantio *adj* stale, musty.

stantuffo *m* piston.

stanza *f* room.

stanziamento *m* allocation.

stanziare *vt* to station.

stappare *vt* to uncork.

stare *vi* to stay, to stand; ~ **in piedi** *vi* to stand; ~ **per (fare qc)** *vi* to be about to (do something).

starnutire *vi* to sneeze.
starnuto *m* sneeze.
starter *m inv* starter.
stasera *adv* tonight.
statico *adj* static.
statista *m* statesman.
statistica *f* statistics.
statistico *adj* statistical.
stato *m* status, state.
statua *f* statue.
statuario *adj* statuesque, statuary.
statura *f* stature.
status *m* status.
statuto *m* statute, charter.
stazionario *adj* stationary,
stazione *f* station; **~ di servizio** *f* service station.
stecca *f* slat, splint, cue.
steeplechase *m inv* steeplechase.
stella *f* star; **~ filante** *f* streamer; **~ di mare** *f* starfish.
stellato *adj* starry.
stelo *m* stem.
stendardo *m* banner.
stendere *vt* to stretch, to lay.
stendibiancheria *m inv* clothes horse.
stenografia *f* stenography, shorthand.
stenografo *m* stenographer.
stentato *adj* laboured; **parlare un inglese ~** *vt* to speak broken English.
sterco *m* dung.
stereo *m inv* stereo, hi-fi.
stereofonia *f* stereo.
stereotipo *m* stereotype.
sterile *adj* barren, sterile.
sterilità *f* sterility.
sterilizzare *vt* to sterilize.
sterlina *f* pound (sterling).
sterminare *vt* to exterminate.
sterminio *m* extermination.
sterno *m* sternum, breastbone.
sterzare *vi* to swerve, to steer.
sterzata *f* swerve.

sterzo *m* lock.
stesso *adj* self, same, self-same, very, own * *pron* same * *adv* anyhow.
stetoscopio *m* stethoscope.
steward *m inv* steward.
stia *f* coop.
stigma *m* stigma.
stigmatizzare *vt* to stigmatize.
stile *m* style, panache.
stiletto *m* stiletto.
stima *f* esteem, valuation, estimation.
stimabile *adj* reputable.
stimare *vt* to treasure, to esteem.
stimato *adj* valued.
stimolante *m* stimulant; *adj* stimulating, piquant, challenging.
stimolare *vt* to stimulate, to whet, to arouse.
stimolazione *f* stimulation.
stimolo *m* stimulus, fillip; **essere di ~ a** *vi* to prod.
stinco *m* shank, shin.
stipare *vt* to cram; **~ di** *vt* to pack.
stipato *adj* crammed.
stipendio *m* wages, salary.
stipulazione *f* stipulation.
stiracchiarsi *vr* to stretch.
stirare *vt* to press, to iron; (muscles) to flex; * *m* ironing.
stirpe *f* stock, lineage, ancestry.
stitichezza *f* constipation.
stitico *adj* constipated.
stiva *f* hold.
stivale *m* boot.
stivare *vt* to stow.
stizzito *adj* peeved.
stizzoso *adj* peevish.
stock *m* stock.
stoffa *f* fabric, cloth, material; **negoziante di ~** *m* draper.
stoicismo *m* stoicism.
stoico *n* stoic; * *adj* stoical.
stola *f* stole.

stomaco *m* stomach; **bruciore di ~** *m* heartburn.

stonare *vt* to jar.

stonato *adj* flat, off-key.

stop *m* stop sign; **il fanalino dello ~** *m* brakelight.

stoppia *f* stubble.

stoppino *m* wick.

stordire *vt* to daze.

stordito *adj* light headed, in a daze, dazed.

storia *f* story, history; **storie** *fpl* fuss.

storico *adj* historic(al); * *m* historian.

storione *m* sturgeon.

storno *adj* starling.

storpiare *vt* to maim.

storta *f* retort.

storto *adj* crooked, awry; **guardare qn ~** *vt* to look askance at somebody; **con le gambe storte** *adj* bandy-legged.

strabico *adj* cross-eyed; **essere ~** *vi* to squint.

strabismo *m* squint, cast.

stracciare *vt* to shred.

stracciato *adj* ragged.

straccio *m* duster, rag; **passare lo ~** *vt* to mop.

strada *f* street, road, way; **~ transitabile** *f* thoroughfare; **portare qn su una brutta ~** to lead astray; **~ secondaria** *f* byway; **~ principale** *f* main road; **a metà ~** *adv* midway.

stradina *f* lane.

strafare *m* overkill.

strage *f* slaughter.

strambo *adj* rum.

stramoderno *adj* new-fangled.

strangolamento *m* strangulation.

strangolare *vt* to strangle.

straniero *m* alien, foreigner; * *adj* alien, foreign.

strano *adj* strange, peculiar, odd.

straordinario *adj* extraordinary; * *m* overtime.

strapazzare *vt* to overwork, (*culin*) to scramble.

strappare *vt* to tear, to rip, to wrench, to snatch;

strappo *m* strain, rip, tear.

straripare *vi* to flood.

strascicare *vt* to shuffle, to drawl.

strascicato *adj* trailing; **un passo ~** *m* shuffle.

stratagemma *m* stratagem, ploy.

strategia *f* strategy.

strategico *adj* strategic.

strato *m* stratum, ply, layer; **~ sottile** *m* film.

strattone *m* tug, wrench; **dare uno ~ a** *vt* to tug.

stravagante *adj* extravagant, outlandish, flamboyant.

stravaganze *f* extravagance.

stravedere *vi* to dote.

stravolto *adj* distraught.

straziante *adj* harrowing.

strega *f* witch; **caccia alle streghe** *f* witch-hunt.

stregare *vt* to bewitch.

stregone *m* sorcerer.

stregoneria *f* witchcraft, sorcery.

stremare *vt* to exhaust.

strepitoso *adj* roaring.

stress *m* stress.

stressante *adj* stressful.

stretta *f* squeeze.

strettamente *adv* closely.

stretto *adj* tight, strict, narrow; * *m* strait, sound.

striare *vt* to streak.

stricnina *f* strychnine.

stridere *vi* to screech.

stridio *m* rasp.

strido *m* screech.

stridulo *adj* shrill, grating.

strillare *vi* to yell, to bawl, to screech, to shriek.

strillo *m* scream, shriek, squeal.

striminzito *adj* stunted, puny.

strimpellare *vt* to strum.

stringa *f* shoelace.

stringente *adj* stringent.

stringere *vt* to tighten, to grip, to clench; * *vr* ~**rsi** to narrow.

striscia *f* streak, strip, band; **striscie pedonali** *fpl* pedestrian crossing.

strisciare *vi* to creep, to trail; ~ **di fronte a** *vi* to grovel.

striscio *m* smear; **di** ~ *adj* glancing.

striscione *m* banner.

stritolare *vt* to mangle.

strizzare *vt* to squeeze, to wring.

strizzata *f* squeeze.

strizzatina *f*: **una** ~ **d'occhio** *f* wink.

strizzatoio *m* mangle.

strofinaccio *m* dishcloth.

strofinamento *m* rub.

strofinare *vt* to scrub, to rub.

strofinata *f* scrub.

strombettare *vi* to blare.

stroncare *vt* to scotch, to quash.

stronza *f* bitch.

stronzio *m* strontium.

stronzo *m* turd, pig.

stropicciare *vt* to wrinkle.

strozzare *vt* to throttle, to strangle.

strozzatore *m* strangler.

struggente *adj* poignant.

strumentale *adj* instrumental.

strumento *m* instrument, tool.

struttura *f* structure, shell, framework.

strutturare *vt* to structure.

struzzo *m* ostrich.

stucchevole *adj* sickly.

stucco *m* stucco, putty.

studente *m* student; ~ **universitario** *m* undergraduate.

studiare *vt, vi* to study, to read.

studio *m* studio, study, practice.

studioso *adj* studious; * *m* scholar.

stufa *f* fire, heater, stove; ~ **a gas** *f* gasfire; ~ **elettrica** *f* electric fire.

stufare *vt* to stew.

stufato *m* stew.

stufo *adj* fed-up.

stunt-man *m inv* stuntman.

stupefacente *m* drug.

stupendo *adj* stupendous, wonderful, terrific.

stupidità *f* stupidity.

stupido *adj* stupid, witless, idiotic.

stupire *vt* to stupefy, to amaze, to astonish; * *vr* ~**rsi** to wonder, to marvel.

stupore *m* wonder, astonishment, amazement.

stuprare *vt* to rape.

stupratore *m* rapist.

stupro *m* rape.

sturalavandini *m inv* plunger.

stuzzicadenti *m inv* toothpick.

stuzzicare *vt* to tease, to bait.

su *adv* up, above; * *prep* over, on.

subacqueo *adj* underwater.

subaffittare *vt, vi* to sublet.

subalterno *adj, m* subordinate.

subappaltare *vt* to subcontract.

subconscio *m* subconscious.

subcosciente *adj* subconscious.

subdolo *adj* devious.

subentrante *adj* incoming.

subire *vt* to undergo, to sustain.

subito *adv* at once, straight away, forthwith.

sublimare *vt* to sublimate.

sublime *adj* sublime.

subliminale *adj* subliminal.

subnormale *adj* subnormal.

subordinare *vt* to subordinate.

subordinato *adj, m* subordinate.

subordinazione *f* subordination.

suburbano *adj* suburban.

succedere *vi* to happen, to transpire, to succeed.

successione *f* succession, sequence.

successivo *adj* subsequent, succeeding, next.

successo *m* success, hit.

successone *m* smash.

successore *m* successor.

succhiare *vt, vi* to suck.

succinto *adj* succinct, scanty.

succo *m* juice, gist; **~ di frutta** *m* fruit juice.

succoso *adj* juicy.

succulento *adj* succulent.

sud *adj, m* south; **del ~** *adj* southerly, southern; **verso ~** *adv* southward(s).

sudare *vt, vi* to sweat.

sudario *m* shroud.

suddetto *adj* aforementioned.

suddito *m* subject.

suddividere *vt* to subdivide.

sudicio *m* filth; * *adj* grimy, grubby.

sudiciume *m* grime, filth.

sudore *m* sweat.

sufficiente *adj* sufficient, enough, adequate.

sufficienza *f* enough; (*scol*) pass mark.

suffragetta *f* suffragette.

suffragio *m* suffrage.

suffumicare *vt* to fumigate.

suggerimento *m* tip, suggestion.

suggerire *vt* to suggest, to prompt.

suggeritore *m* prompter.

sughero *m* cork.

sugo *m* sauce; **~ dell'arrosto** *m* gravy.

suicida *adj* suicidal; * *m/f* suicide.

suicidio *m* suicide.

suini *mpl* swine.

suite *f inv* suite.

sultanina *f* sultana; **uva ~** *f* sultana.

sultano *m* sultan.

suo poss *adj, pron* your(s), her(s), his, its.

suocera *f* mother-in-law.

suocero *m* father-in-law.

suola *f* sole.

suonare *vt, vi* to sound, to play, to ring, to blow (trumpet, etc).

suono *m* sound; **~ acuto** *m* twang

suora *f* nun, sister.

superare *vt* to pass, to top, to excel, to surpass, to weather, to exceed, to clear, to overtake; **~ numericamente** *vt* to outnumber.

superbo *adj* superb, haughty.

superficiale *adj* superficial, perfunctory, facile.

superficie *f* top, surface; **risalire in ~** *vi* to surface.

superfluo *adj* superfluous.

superiore *adj* upper, senior, advanced; * *m/f* superior.

superiorità *f* superiority.

superlativo *adj, m* superlative.

supermercato *m* supermarket.

superpetroliera *f* supertanker.

superpotenza *f* superpower.

supersonico *adj* supersonic.

superstite *m/f* survivor.

superstizione *f* superstition.

superstizioso *adj* superstitious.

superuomo *m* superman.

supino *adj* supine.

supplementare *adj* supplementary, additional, backup, extra.

supplemento *m* supplement.

supplica *f* supplication, plea, entreaty.

supplicare *vt* to beg, to appeal.

supporre *vt* to presume, to suppose, to guess, to assume.

supportabile *adj* tolerable, bearable.

supportare *vt* to bear.

supporto *m* strut.

supposizione *f* assumption, supposition, guess.

supposta *f* suppository.

suppurare *vi* to fester.

supremazia *f* supremacy.

supremo *adj* ultimate, crowning.

surf *m* surfboard.

surgelare *vt* to freeze.

surgelato *adj* frozen.

surplus *m inv* surplus.

surreale *adj* surrealistic.

surrealismo *m* surrealism.

surrogato *adj, m* surrogate.

suscettibilità *f* susceptibility, sensibility.

susina *f* plum, damson.

susino *m* plum tree.

suspense *m* suspense.

sussidiario *m* subsidiary.

sussidio *m* help; **~ di disoccupazione** *m* dole.

sutura *f* suture.

svago *m* leisure.

svaligiare *vt* to rifle, to burgle.

svalutazione *f* devaluation.

svanire *vi* to vanish.

svantaggiato *adj* underprivileged.

svantaggio *m* disadvantage.

svantaggioso *adj* disadvantageous.

svariato *adj* diverse, multifarious.

svasato *adj* flared.

svastica *f* swastika.

sveglia *f* alarm.

svegliare *vt* to awake, to rouse; * *vr* **~rsi** to wake; **~ troppo tardi** to oversleep.

sveglio *adj* awake, smart, alert, quick-witted; **completamente ~** *adj* wide-awake.

svelare *vt* to unveil.

svelto *adj* agile, smart.

svendita *f* sale.

svenimento *m* swoon, faint.

svenire *vi* to swoon, to faint.

sventolare *vt* to wave.

sventrare *vt* to gut.

sventurato *adj* luckless.

sverniciare *vt* to strip.

svestire *vt* to disrobe.

svezzare *vt* to wean.

sviare *vt* to sidetrack.

svignarsela *vi* to skive off, to slink away, to bolt.

svilire *vt* to debase.

sviluppare *vt* to develop; * *vr* **~rsi** to develop; **~ rapidamente** to mushroom.

sviluppo *m* development, twist.

svista *f* oversight, lapse.

svitare *vt* to unscrew.

svogliato *adj* half-hearted.

svolazzare *vi* to flit, to flutter.

svolazzo *m* flourish.

svolgere *vt* to perform.

svuotare *vt* to drain.

swing *m* swing.

T

tabaccaio *m* tobacconist.

tabacchiera *f* snuffbox.

tabacco *m* tobacco; **~ da fiuto** *m* snuff.

tabella *f* chart, schedule, table.

tabellone *m* billboard, scoreboard.

tabernacolo *m* tabernacle.

tabù *m inv* taboo.

tabulatore *m* tabulator.

tacca *f* notch.

taccagno *adj* miserly.

taccheggiare *vi* to shoplift.

taccheggiatore *m* shoplifter.

tacchino *m* turkey.

tacco *m* heel.

taccola *f* jackdaw.

taccuino *m* notebook.

tacere *vi* to keep quiet; **far ~** *vt* to silence.

tachimetro *m* speedometer.

tacito *adj* tacit, unwritten.

taciturno *adj* taciturn.

tafano *m* horsefly.

tafferuglio *m* scuffle, scrimmage.

taffettà *m* taffeta.

taglia *f* size; **~ forte** *f* outsize.

tagliaboschi *m inv* woodcutter, woodsman.

tagliaerba *m inv* lawnmower.

taglialegna *m inv* lumberjack.

tagliare *vt* to cut, to slice, to sever, to hack, to chop, to carve.

tagliatelle *fpl* noodles.

tagliaunghie *m* clippers.

tagliente *adj* cutting, sharp, keen; **non ~** *adj* blunt.

tagliere *m* chopping board, breadboard.

taglietto *m* nick.

taglio *m* cut, cutback, slash; **a doppio ~** *adj* double-edged; **~ di capelli** *m* haircut.

tailleur *m inv* suit.

talco *m* talc, talcum powder.

tale *adj* such.

talea *f* cutting.

talento *m* talent; **di ~** *adj* talented.

talismano *m* talisman.

talmente *adv* such.

talpa *f* mole.

tamburellare *vt* to drum.

tamburino *m* tambourine.

tamburo *m* drum.

tamponamento *m* plugging; **~ a catena** *m* pile-up.

tamponare *vt* to dab.

tampone *m* tampon, wad, swab.

tana *f* warren, hole (fox, etc), burrow, den, lair.

tanga *m inv* G-string.

tangente *f* tangent.

tangibile *adj* tangible.

tanto *adj, pron* much, many; **ogni ~** *adv* now and then.

tappa *f* stage, leg.

tappare *vt* to bung, to cap, to cork, to plug.

tappetino *m* mat; **~ da bagno** bathmat.

tappeto *m* carpet, rug.

tappezzare *vt* to paper.

tappezzeria *f* upholstery.

tappo *m* top, bung, stopper, spigot, plug.

tarantola *f* tarantula.

tarchiato *adj* squat.

tardi *adj* late.

targa *f* plate.

tariffa *f* rate, tariff, fare, charge; **~ ridotta** *f* off-peak rate.

tarlo *m* woodworm.

tarma *f* moth.

tartan *m inv* tartan.

tartaro *m* tartar.

tartaruga *f* tortoise; **guscio di ~** *m* tortoiseshell; **~ acquatica** *f* turtle.

tartufo *m* truffle.

tasca *f* pocket.

tascabile *m* paperback.

tassa *f* duty, tax; **~ doganale** *f* customs duty.

tassare *vt* to tax.

tassativo *adj* imperative.

tassazione *f* taxation.

tassista *m/f* taxi-driver.

tasso *m* rate; badger; yew.

tastare *vt* to feel, to finger.

tastiera *f* keyboard.

tasto *m* key.

tattica *f* tactic, tactics.

tattico *adj* tactical.

tatto *m* touch, tact, feel.

tatuaggio *m* tattoo.

tatuare *vt* to tattoo.

tautologia *f* tautology.

tautologico *adj* tautological.

taverna *f* tavern.

tavola *f* table, plank; ~ **calda** *f* snack-bar.

tavolino *m* coffee table.

tavolo *m* table; ~ **da carte** card table.

tavolozza *f* palette.

taxi *m inv* taxi, cab.

tazza *f* cup; ~ **da tè** *f* teacup.

tazzone *m* mug.

tè *m inv* tea; ~ **al limone** *m inv* lemon tea.

teatrale *adj* theatrical.

teatro *m* theatre; **abitué del ~** *m/f* theatregoer; ~ **lirico** *m* opera house.

tecnica *f* skill, technique.

tecnicità *f* technicality.

tecnico *m* technician; * *adj* technical.

tecnologia *f* technology.

tecnologico *adj* technological.

tedio *m* tedium.

tee *m inv* tee.

teenager *m/f inv* teenager.

tegola *f* tile.

teiera *f* teapot.

tek *m* teak.

tela *f* web, canvas; ~ **indiana** *f* cheesecloth; ~ **grezza** calico.

telaio *m* frame, loom, chassis.

telecomando *m* remote control.

telecomunicazioni *fpl* telecommunications.

telecronaca *f* commentary.

telecronista *m/f* commentator.

telefonare *vi* to phone, to ring, to call.

telefonata *f* telephone call.

telefonista *m/f* telephonist.

telefono *m* telephone, phone; ~ **pubblico** *m* payphone; ~ **rosso** *m* hotline.

telegiornale *m* TV news.

telegrafico *adj* telegraphic.

telegrafo *m* telegraph.

telegramma *m* telegram.

telenovella *f* soap opera.

telepatia *f* telepathy.

telescopio *m* telescope.

telespettatore *m* viewer.

televisione *f* television; **trasmettere per ~** *vt* to televise.

televisore *m* television set.

telex *m inv* telex.

telone *m* tarpaulin; ~ **impermeabile** *m* groundsheet.

tema *m* theme.

temerario *adj* foolhardy.

temere *vt vi* to fear, to dread.

tempera *f* distemper.

temperamatite *m inv* sharpener.

temperamento *m* temperament, temper.

temperare *vt* to sharpen.

temperato *adj* temperate.

temperatura *f* temperature.

temperino *m* penknife.

tempesta *f* tempest, storm.

tempestare *vt* to pelt.

tempestivo *adj* prompt.

tempia *f* temple.

tempio *m* temple.

tempismo *m* timing.

tempo *m* time; weather; tense; ~ **libero** *m* spare time, leisure; **appena in ~** in the nick of time; **a ~ pieno** *adj, adv* full-time.

temporale *m* storm, thunderstorm; **da ~** *adj* thundery.

temporaneamente *adv* temporarily.

tenace *adj* tenacious, dogged.

tenacia *f* tenacity.

tenda *f* tent, curtain; **grande ~** *f* marquee; **~ avvolgibile** *f* blind.

tendenza *f* tendency, inclination, drift, bias.

tendenziosa *adj* tendentious; **una domanda ~** *f* a leading question.

tender *m inv* tender.

tendere *vt* to tend, to stretch, to strain, to tense, to extend; **tendere a** *vi* to be inclined to.

tendine *m* tendon, sinew; **~ del ginocchio** *m* hamstring.

tendone *m* awning; **~ del circo** *m* big top.

tenente *m* lieutenant.

tenere *vt* to keep, to stock, to retain, to carry, to hold, to have; **~ stretto** *vt* to clutch; **~ fede a** *vt* to abide by.

tenerezza *f* tenderness, gentleness, endearment.

tenero *adj* tender, endearing.

tenia *f* tapeworm.

tennis *m* tennis.

tennista *m/f* tennis player.

tenore *m* tenor.

tenorile *adj* tenor.

tensione *f* tension, stress, strain; **mancanza di ~** *f* slackness.

tentacolo *m* tentacle.

tentare *vt* to tempt, to attempt, to endeavour.

tentativo *m* endeavour, go, bid, try, attempt.

tentazione *f* temptation.

tentoni *adv* gropingly; **andare a ~** *vi* to fumble.

tenue *adj* tenuous, subdued.

tenuta *f* attire, estate.

teologia *f* theology.

teologico *adj* theological.

teologo *m* theologian.

teorema *m* theorem.

teoretico *adj* theoretical.

teoria *f* theory; **in ~** in theory, in the abstract.

teorico *m* theorist.

teorizzare *vi* to theorize.

teppista *m/f* hooligan, thug, hoodlum.

terapeutica *f* therapeutics.

terapeutico *adj* therapeutic.

terapia *f* therapy.

terapista *m/f* therapist.

tergicristallo *m* windscreen wiper.

tergiversare *vi* to prevaricate, to hedge.

tergo *m* back; **a ~** *adv* overleaf.

termale *adj* thermal; **stazione ~** *f* spa.

terminal *m* air terminal

terminale *adj*, *m* terminal.

terminare *vi*, *vt* to end, to terminate.

termine *m* term, limit, end; **portare a ~** *vt* to pull off; **a lungo ~** *adj* long-term; **~ improprio** *m* misnomer; **senza mezzi termini** *adv* bluntly.

termite *f* termite.

termometro *m* thermometer.

termoresistente *adj* heat-resistant.

termosifone *m* radiator.

termostato *m* thermostat.

terra *f* land, ground, earth; **per via di ~** *adv*, *adj* overland; **di ~ cotta** *adj* earthen; **a ~** *adj* ashore; **scendere a ~** *vi* to go ashore.

terraglie *fpl* earthenware.

terraiolo *m* landlubber.

terrazza *f* patio, terrace.

terremoto *m* earthquake.

terreno *m* ground, land, terrain, soil; **~ coltivabile** *m* farmland.

terrestre *adj* terrestrial; **forze terrestri** *fpl* land forces.

terribile *adj* terrible, frightful, awful, appalling.

terriccio *m* loam.

terrier *m inv* terrier.

terrificare *vt* to terrify.
territoriale *adj* territorial.
territorio *m* territory.
terrore *m* terror, dread.
terrorismo *m* terrorism.
terrorista *m/f* terrorist.
terrorizzare *vt* to terrorize.
terzo *adj*, *m* third.
teschio *m* skull.
tesi *f inv* thesis, contention.
teso *adj* tense, fraught, uptight, taut, edgy.
tesoriere *m* treasurer.
tesoro *m* treasure; exchequer; darling, sweetheart.
tessera *f* card.
tessere *vt*, *vi* to weave.
tessile *adj* textile.
tessitore *m* spinner.
tessitura *f* weaving.
tessuti *mpl* textiles.
tessuto *f* fabric, cloth, tissue, material.
test *m* test; **Pap ~** *m* cervical smear.
testa *f* head; **essere in ~** *vi* to be in the lead; **in ~** *adj* leading; **mal di ~** *m* headache.
testamento *m* testament, will.
testardaggine *f* stubbornness.
testardo *adj* headstrong.
testata *f* warhead; butt; **dare una ~** *vt* to butt.
testicolo *m* testicle.
testimone *m* witness; **banco dei testimoni** *m* witness box; **~ oculare** *m* eyewitness.
testimonianza *f* evidence, testimony.
testimoniare *vi* to testify, to witness.
testo *m* text.
testuale *adj* textual.
tetano *m* tetanus.
tetro *adj* bleak, dismal, sombre.
tetta *f* tit, boob.
tettarella *f* teat.
tetto *m* roof; **senza ~** *adj* home-

less; **~ apribile** *m* sunroof; **mettere il ~** *vi* to roof.
thermos *m inv* vacuum flask, thermos flask.
thriller *m inv* thriller.
tibia *f* shinbone.
tic *m inv* tic, twitch; **~ tac** *m inv* tick.
ticchettare *vi* to tick.
tiepido *adj* tepid, lukewarm.
tifo *m* typhus.
tifone *m* typhoon.
tifoso *m* fan, supporter.
tiglio *m* lime.
tigre *f* tiger, tigress.
timbrare *vt* to stamp.
timbro *m* stamp; **~ postale** *m* postmark.
timer *m inv* timer.
timidezza *f* timidity, shyness, diffidence.
timido *adj* shy, diffident, bashful, timid.
timo *m* thyme.
timone *m* rudder, helm.
timoniere *m* cox.
timore *m* fear; **~ reverenziale** *m* awe; **nel ~ che** *conj* lest.
timoroso *adj* apprehensive.
timpano *m* eardrum.
tingere *vt* to stain, to tint, to dye, to colour.
tino *m* vat.
tinta *f* paint, hue.
tintarella *f* suntan.
tintinnare *vi* to tinkle, to clink, to chink.
tintinnio *m* clink, ping, clatter.
tintore *m* dyer.
tintoria *f* dye-works.
tintura *f* dye.
tipico *adj* typical.
tipo *m* type, fellow, class, sort.
tipografo *m* printer, typographer.
tirannia *f* tyranny.
tirannico *adj* tyrannical.
tiranno *m* tyrant.

tirante *m* guy rope.

tirare *vi* to pull, to strain, to draw; **~ avanti** *vi* to go ahead; **~ su** *vt* to hitch up.

tirata *f* pull, tirade.

tirato *adj* haggard.

tiratore *m* shot; **franco ~** *m* sniper; **~ scelto** *m* marksman.

tirchio *adj* tight-fisted.

tirocinante *m/f* trainee.

tirocinio *m* apprenticeship; **fare ~** *vi* to train.

tiroide *f* thyroid.

titillare *vt* to titillate.

titolare *m* bearer, occupant, occupier.

titolo *m* title, designation, stock; bond; **titoli di testa** *mpl* credits.

tizio *m* chap, bloke, guy.

tizzone *m* cinder.

toccare *vt* to touch.

tocco *adj* touched; * *m* touch.

toga *f* gown.

togliere *vi* to take away, to remove.

toilette *f inv* toilet, dressing table; **~ per uomini** *f* gents; **articoli da ~** *mpl* toiletries.

tollerante *adj* tolerant.

tolleranza *f* tolerance.

tollerare *vt* to tolerate, to suffer.

tomaia *f* upper.

tomba *f* tomb, grave.

tombola *f* bingo.

tomo *m* tome.

tonaca *f* cassock, habit, frock.

tonalità *f* shade.

tonare *vi* to thunder.

tonfo *m* splash, thud, thump.

tonica *f* tonic; **acqua ~** *f* tonic water.

tonificante *adj* invigorating, bracing.

tonnellaggio *m* tonnage.

tonnellata *f* ton.

tonno *m* tuna.

tono *m* tone.

tonsilla *f* tonsil.

tonsillite *f* tonsillitis.

tonsura *f* tonsure.

tonto *adj* stupid; * *m* fool, jerk

topazio *m* topaz.

topo *m* mouse; **~ campagnolo** *m* field mouse; **~ di bibliote ca** *m* bookworm.

topografia *f* topography.

toporagno *m* shrew.

toppa *f* patch.

torace *m* thorax.

torba *f* peat.

torbido *adj* murky.

torchio *m* press.

torcia *f* torch.

torcicollo *m* crick in the neck, stiff neck.

tordo *m* thrush.

torello *m* bullock.

torero *m* bullfighter.

tormentare *vt* to torment, to badger, to pester, to plague.

tormento *m* torment.

tornado *m inv* tornado.

tornante *m* hairpin bend.

tornare *vi* to return; **~ indietro** *vi* to turn back.

torneo *m* tournament.

tornio *m* lathe.

tornire *vt* to turn.

toro *m* bull.

Toro *m* Taurus.

torre *f* tower, (chess) rook; **~ di guardia** *f* watchtower; **~ di controllo** *f* control tower.

torrefare *vt* to roast (coffee).

torrente *m* torrent.

torrenziale *adj* torrential.

torretta *f* turret.

torrido *adj* torrid.

torrione *m* keep.

torrone *m* nougat.

torso *m* torso.

torsolo *m* stalk, core.

torta *f* pie, cake.

torto *m* wrong; **far ~ a** *vt* to wrong.

tortora *f* turtledove.

tortuoso *adj* circuitous, tortuous.

tortura *f* torture.

torturare *vt* to torture.

torvo *adj* grim; **sguardo ~** *m* scowl.

tosare *vt* to shear, to clip (dog, etc).

tosasiepi *m* hedge clippers.

tosse *f* cough.

tossico *adj* toxic.

tossicodipendente *m/f* drug addict.

tossicodipendenza *f* addiction.

tossicomane *m/f* addict.

tossina *f* toxin.

tossire *vi* to cough.

tostapane *m inv* toaster.

tostare *vt* to toast.

totale *adj* total, utter; * *m* total.

totalità *f* totality.

totalitario *adj* totalitarian.

tournée *f* tour.

tovaglia *f* tablecloth.

tovagliolo *m* napkin, serviette.

tozzo *adj* thickset.

tra *prep* between; **~ poco** *adv* shortly.

traballante *adj* rickety, shaky.

traballare *vi* to wobble.

traboccare *vi* to overflow, to slop, to brim over.

trabocchetto *m* booby trap.

tracagnotto *adj* dumpy.

tracannare *vt* to swill.

traccia *f* smear, trace; **essere sulle traccie di** *vt* to track.

tracciare *vt* to chart, to trace, to plot.

trachea *f* trachea, windpipe.

tracolla *f* strap.

tradimento *m* betrayal, treason.

tradire *vt* to betray, to shop.

traditore *m* traitor.

tradizionale *adj* traditional.

tradizione *f* tradition; **tradizioni** *fpl* lore.

tradurre *vt, vi* to translate.

traduttore *m* translator.

traduzione *f* translation.

trafficante *m/f* trafficker.

trafficare *vi* to traffic.

traffico *m* traffic.

trafficone *m* wheeler-dealer.

trafiggere *vt* to transfix, to spear, to impale.

trafila *f* rigmarole.

tragedia *f* tragedy.

traghetto *m* ferry.

tragicamente *adv* tragically.

tragico *adj* tragic.

tragicommedia *f* tragicomedy.

tragitto *m* haul, run.

traguardo *m* finishing line, finish, winning post.

tram *m inv* tram.

trama *f* story, plot, weave.

tramare *vi* to scheme.

trambusto *m* commotion, bustle, uproar, palaver.

tramezzino *m* sandwich.

tramontare *vi* to set.

tramonto *m* sundown, sunset.

tramortire *vt* to stun.

trampolino *m* springboard, diving board.

trampolo *m* stilt.

tran tran *m* routine.

trance *f inv* trance.

tranello *m* catch, decoy, pitfall.

trangugiare *vt* to gobble.

tranne *prep* except, but, bar.

tranquillamente *adv* happily.

tranquillante *m* tranquillizer.

tranquillità *f* ease.

tranquillo *adj* leisurely, quiet, tranquil.

transatlantico *m* liner.

transatlantico *adj* transatlantic.

transistor *m inv* transistor.

transitivo *adj* transitive.

transito *m* transit.
transitorio *adj* transient.
transizione *f* transition.
trantran *m* grind.
trapanare *vt* to drill.
trapano *m* drill.
trapezio *m* trapeze.
trapiantare *vt* to transplant.
trapianto *m* transplant.
trappola *f* trap, snare; **~ mortale** *f* deathtrap.
trapunta *f* quilt; **~ di piuma** *f* eiderdown.
trasalire *vi* to start, to flinch.
trasandatezza *f* shabbiness.
trasandato *adj* scruffy, sloppy.
trascendere *vt* to transcend.
trascinante *adj* rousing.
trascinare *vt* to haul, to drag, to lug; **~ a fatica** to heave; * *vr* **~rsi** to trudge.
trascorrere *vi* to elapse, to spend.
trascrizione *f* transcription.
trascurabile *adj* unimportant, negligible.
trascurare *vt* to neglect, to overlook, to disregard.
trascuratezza *f* neglect.
trasferibile *adj* transferable.
trasferimento *m* transfer.
trasferire *vt* to shift, to transfer.
trasferta *f* transfer; **giocare in ~** *vi* (*sport*) to play away.
trasformare *vt* adapt, to turn, to transform, to change.
trasformatore *m* transformer.
trasformazione *f* transformation.
trasfusione *f* transfusion; **~ di sangue** *f* blood transfusion.
trasgredire *vt* to transgress.
trasgressione *f* misdemeanour.
trasgressore *m* offender.
traslocare *vt*, *vi* to move.
trasloco *m* removal, move.
trasmettere *vt* to transmit, to

convey, to broadcast; * *vr* **~rs** (sound) to carry.
trasmissione *f* transmission, drive, broadcast; **~ anteriore** *f* front-wheel drive.
trasparente *adj* transparent, see-through, clear, sheer.
trasparenza *f* transparency.
traspirare *vi* to perspire, t transpire.
traspirazione *f* perspiration.
trasportare *vt* to convey, t transport.
trasporto *m* transport, trans portation, conveyance.
trastullarsi *vr* to tinker.
trasudare *vt* to ooze.
tratta *f* (bank) draft.
trattamento *m* treatment; **~ del viso** *m* facial.
trattare *vt* to treat, to process to transact, to handle, to negotiate.
trattatello *m* tract.
trattativa *f* negotiation.
trattato *m* treaty, treatise.
trattenere *vt* to detain, to withhold, to restrain, to keep.
trattenimento *m* entertainment.
trattenuta *f* stoppage.
trattino *m* dash, hyphen.
tratto *m* stretch, reach, section, line; **tutto d'un ~** all at once.
trattore *m* tractor.
trauma *m* trauma.
traumatizzante *adj* traumatic.
travagliato *adj* troubled.
travasare *vt* to siphon, to decant.
trave *f* beam, girder.
traveller's cheque *m inv* traveller's cheque.
traversa *f* rung.
traversata *f* crossing.
traversina *f* sleeper.
traverso *adj* cross; **di ~** *adj*,

adv askew, sidelong.
travestimento *m* disguise.
travestire *vt* to disguise.
travestito *m* transvestite; * *adj* (in) drag.
travisare *vt* to misrepresent.
trazione *f* traction.
tre *adj, m* three; **vincere per ~ volte** consecutive to get a hat-trick.
trebbiare *vt* to thresh.
treccia *f* plait, braid.
treccina *f* pigtail.
tredicesimo *adj, m* thirteenth.
tredici *adj, m inv* thirteen.
tredimensionale *adj* three-dimensional.
tregua *f* respite, lull, truce.
tremare *vi* to quiver, to tremble, to quake.
tremendo *adj* dreadful, tremendous.
trementina *f* turpentine.
tremito *m* tremble, trembling.
tremolare *vi* to flicker.
tremolio *m* flicker.
trench *m inv* trench coat.
treno *m* train; **~ postale** *m* mail train.
trenta *adj, m* thirty.
trentesimo *adj, m* thirtieth.
trepidazione *f* trepidation.
treppiede *m* tripod.
tresca *f* intrigue.
triangolare *adj* triangular.
triangolo *m* triangle.
tribale *adj* tribal.
tribolazione *f* tribulation.
tribordo *m* starboard.
tribù *f* tribe.
tribuna *f* gallery; **~ coperta** *f* grandstand.
tribunale *m* law court, tribunal.
tributo *m* tribute.
tricheco *m* walrus.
triciclo *m* tricycle.
tricofizia *f* ringworm.

trifoglio *m* shamrock, clover.
trigonometria *f* trigonometry.
trillare *vi* to trill.
trillo *m* trill.
trilogia *f* trilogy.
trimestrale *adj* quarterly.
trimestre *m* term.
trincea *f* trench.
trinciante *m* carving knife.
trinciare *vt* to shred.
Trinità *f* Trinity.
trio *m* trio.
trionfale *adj* triumphal.
trionfante *adj* triumphant.
trionfo *m* triumph.
trip *m inv* trip.
triplicare *vt* to treble.
triplice *adj* triple; **in ~ copia** *adj* triplicate.
triplo *adj* triple, treble.
trippa *f* tripe.
triste *adj* sad, woeful.
tristezza *f* misery, sadness.
tritacarne *m inv* mincer.
tritare *vt* to mince.
trito *adj* hackneyed, trite.
tritone *m* newt.
trivellare *vt* to bore.
trivellazione *f* drilling; **impianto di ~** *m* oil rig.
trofeo *m* trophy.
tromba *f* trumpet, bugle; **~ d'aria** *f* whirlwind.
trombone *m* trombone; daffodil.
trombosi *f* thrombosis; **~ coronarica** *f* coronary.
troncare *vt* to sever.
tronco *m* log, trunk.
troncone *m* stump.
trono *m* throne.
tropicale *adj* tropical.
troppo *adv* too.
troppopieno *m* overflow.
trota *f* trout; **~ salmonata** *f* salmon trout.
trottare *vi* to trot.
trotto *m* trot.

trottola f top.

troupe f troupe.

trovare vt to find; **venire a ~** * vi to come round; * vr **~rsi** to stand.

trovata f gimmick.

trovatello m foundling.

truccare vt to rig.

trucchetto m dodge.

trucco m trick, hocus-pocus, make-up.

trucidare vt to slaughter.

truciolo m (wood) shaving.

truffa f fraud, confidence trick, swindle.

truffare vt to swindle.

truffatore m con man.

truppe fpl troops.

trust m inv trust.

tu pers pron you.

tuba f tuba.

tubare vi to coo.

tubature fpl piping.

tubazione f tubing.

tubercolosi f tuberculosis.

tubo m tube, pipe; **~ di gomma** m hose(pipe); **~ a raggi catodici** m cathode-ray tube.

tuffarsi vr to plunge, to dive.

tuffatore m diver.

tuffo m plunge, dive; **tuffi** mpl diving.

tugurio m hovel.

tulipano m tulip.

tumore m tumour, growth.

tumultuare vi riot.

tumultuoso adj tumultuous.

tunica f robe, tunic.

tunnel m inv tunnel.

tuo poss adj, pron your(s).

tuonare vi to rant.

tuono m thunder.

tuorlo m yolk.

turbante m turban.

turbare vt to agitate, to upset, to perturb.

turbato adj upset, disturbed.

turbina f turbine.

turbinare vi to eddy.

turbinio m swirl.

turbolento adj turbulent, rowdy, obstreperous.

turbolenza f turbulence.

turchese adj, m turquoise.

turismo m sightseeing, tourism, touring; **ufficio del ~** m tourist office.

turista m/f tourist.

turistico adj tourist; **attrazioni turistiche** fpl sights.

turno m shift, turn; **~ di notte** m nightshift.

tuta f overalls; **~ da ginnastica** f tracksuit.

tutela f guardianship.

tutina f rompers.

tutore m guardian.

tuttavia conj however, yet, all the same, nevertheless; * adv though.

tutto adj all, every, any; * pron everything, everybody; * m whole; **ci sedemmo tutti quanti** we all sat down; **~ sommato** altogether; **in ~** prep throughout.

tuttofare m handyman.

twist m twist.

U

ubbidiente adj obedient.

ubbidienza f obedience.

ubbidire vi, vt to obey.

ubicazione f site.

ubriachezza f drunkenness.

ubriaco adj drunk, inebriated,

(*fam*) plastered, (*fam*) pissed; ~ **fradicio** *adj* dead drunk; * *m* drunk.

ubriacone *m* drunkard.

uccelliera *f* aviary.

uccellino *m* fledgling.

uccello *m* bird.

uccidere *vt* to kill, to slay.

uccisione *f* killing.

udibile *adj* audible; **non** ~ *adj* inaudible.

udienza *f* hearing, audience.

udito *m* hearing.

ufficiale *adj* official; * *m* officer; ~ **giudiziario** *m* bailiff; ~ **di stato civile** *m* registrar.

ufficiare *vi* to officiate.

ufficio *m* office, bureau; ~ **postale** *m* post office; **orario d'~** *m* office hours; **d'~** *adj* clerical; **lavoro d'~** *m* paperwork.

ufficioso *adj* unofficial.

uguaglianza *f* equality.

uguagliare *vt* to touch, to match, to equal.

uguale *m/f* match; * *adj* equal.

ugualmente *adv* equally.

ulcera *f* ulcer.

ulivo *m* olive tree.

ulteriore *adj* ulterior, further, farther.

ultimamente *adv* lately.

ultimatum *m inv* ultimatum.

ultimo *adj* last, latter, final; **negli ultimi ultimi** *adv* latterly.

ululare *vi* to howl.

ululato *m* howl.

umanamente *adv* humanly.

umanista *m/f* humanist.

umanità *f* humanity, mankind.

umanitario *adj* humanitarian, humane.

umano *adj* human; **essere** ~ *m* human (being).

umidità *f* humidity, wet, moisture, dampness.

umido *adj* damp, humid, moist,

wet; ~ **e freddo** *adj* dank.

umile *adj* lowly, humble.

umiliare *vt* to demean, to humiliate, to humble.

umiliazione *f* indignity, humiliation.

umilmente *adv* humbly.

umiltà *f* humility.

umore *m* mood, frame of mind, humour.

umorismo *m* humour.

umorista *m/f* humorist.

unanime *adj* unamity.

unanimità *f* unanimity.

uncinetto *m* crochet.

undicesimo *adj, m* eleventh.

undici *adj, m* eleven.

ungere *vt* to anoint, to grease, (*culin*) to baste.

unghia *f* fingernail, nail, claw.

unguento *m* ointment, salve.

unico *adj* sole, unique, one, single; **a senso** ~ *adj* one-way.

unicorno *m* unicorn.

unificante *adj* cohesive.

unificare *vt* to unify, to unite.

unificazione *f* unification.

uniforme *adj* uniform.

uniformemente *adv* evenly.

uniformità *f* uniformity.

unilaterale *adj* one-sided, unilateral.

unione *f* union, unity.

unire *vt* to join, to unify, to unite; * *vr* ~**rsi** to join, to coalesce.

unisono *m* unison.

unità *f inv* unit, unity.

unito *adj* united; **in tinta unita** *adj* plain.

universale *adj* universal.

università *f* university.

universo *m* universe.

univoco *adj* one-to-one.

uno *adj, m* one; **l'~ o l'altro** *adj* either; **a** ~ **a** ~ *adv* singly.

unto *m* grease; * *adj* greasy.

untuoso *adj* greasy, smarmy.

unzione f unction.

uomo m (pl **uomini**) man, fellow; ~ **d'affari** m businessman; **da** ~ adj men's.

uovo m egg; ~ **in camicia** m poached egg; ~ **sodo** m boiled egg; **uova di pesce** fpl roe, spawn; **deporre le uova** vi to spawn; ~ **di Pasqua** m Easter egg.

uragano m hurricane.

uranio m uranium.

urbano adj urban.

urgente adj urgent.

urgenza f urgency.

urlare vi, vt to howl, to bellow, to yell, to scream.

urlo m scream, yell, wail, bellow.

urna f urn.

urogallo m grouse.

urtare vt to bang against, to jar, to impinge on.

usabile adj expendabile.

usanza f usage.

usare vt to use.

usato adj used, spent.

uscente adj outgoing.

usciere m usher.

uscire vi to go out.

uscita f exit, release; ~ **di sicurezza** f emergency exit.

usignolo m nightingale.

uso m usage, use, wear; **a doppio** ~ adj dual purpose.

ustione f burn.

usura f wear, usury; ~ **per attrito** f attrition.

usuraio m usurer.

usurpare vt to usurp, to encroach.

utensile m utensil, implement.

utero m uterus, womb; ~ **collo dell'utero** m cervix.

utile adj useful, helpful; **essere** ~ **a qn** vi to stand somebody in good stead.

utilità f usefulness, utility.

utilizzabile adj usable.

utilizzare vt to utilize.

uva f grapes; ~ **passa** f currant; **una chicca d'**~ f grape; ~ **un grappolo d'**~ m a bunch of grapes; ~ **spina** f gooseberry.

uvetta f raisin.

V

vacanza f vacation, holiday; ~ **organizzata** f package holiday.

vacca f cow.

vaccinare vt to vaccinate.

vaccinazione f vaccination.

vaccino m vaccine.

vacillante adj rocky, shaky, wavering, unsteady.

vacillare vi to totter, to falter.

vacuo adj blank, vacant, vacuous.

vagabondo m tramp, vagabond, vagrant;* adj roving.

vagamente adj dimly.

vagare vi to rove, to drift.

vagina f vagina.

vaglia m draft; ~ **postale** f money order.

vagliare vt to screen.

vago adj faint, woolly, vague, remote, shadowy.

vagone m carriage, wagon.

vaiolo m smallpox.

valanga f spate, avalanche.

valere vi to be worth.

validità f validity, soundness.

valido adj valid, sound, worthwhile; **non ~** *adj* invalid.

alutare *f* to appraise.

aligia *f* suitcase, case; **fare le valigie** *vt* to pack.

alle *f* valley, dale.

allone *m* glen.

alore *m* value, worth; **~ nominale** *m* face value.

alorizzare *vt* to enhance.

aloroso *adj* manful.

aluta *f* currency; **~ estera** *f* foreign currency, exchange.

alutare *vt* to assess, to evaluate, to value, to estimate.

alutazione *f* valuation, appraisal, assessment, estimate.

alvola *f* valve.

alzer *m inv* waltz.

ampiro *m* vampire.

andalismo *m* vandalism.

andalizzare *vt* to vandalize.

andalo *m* vandal.

anga *f* spade.

angare *vt* to dig.

angelo *m* gospel.

aniglia *f* vanilla.

anità *f inv* vanity, conceit.

anitoso *adj* vain, conceited.

ano *m* space; **~ della porta** *m* doorway; * *adj* vain, fruitless.

antaggio *m* advantage, perk, benefit; **vantaggi** *mpl* fringe benefits; **trarre ~** *vi* to benefit, to capitalize on; **vantaggioso** *adj* advantageous.

antare *vt* to boast; **che si vanta sempre** *adj* boastful; *vr* **~rsi** to brag.

anteria *f* boast.

apore *m* vapour, steam; **cuocere a ~** *vt* to steam.

aporizzare *vt* to vapourize.

arare *vt* to launch.

ariabile *adj* changeable, variable.

ariante *f* variant.

ariare *vt, vi* to vary, to range.

ariazione *f* variation.

varicella *f* chickenpox.

varietà *f inv* variety.

vario *adj* varied, various, miscellaneous.

variopinto *adj* mottled, motley.

varo *m* launch, launching.

vasaio *m* potter.

vasca *f* basin; **~ da bagno** bathtub.

vascello *m* vessel.

vaschetta *f* tub.

vasectomia *f* vasectomy.

vaselina *f* vaseline.

vasellame *m* crockery.

vasetto *m* pot.

vasino *m* potty.

vaso *m* vase; **~ sanguino** blood vessel; **~ del gabinetto** *m* toilet bowl; **(conservato) in ~** *adj* potted; **~ da fiori** *m* flowerpot.

vassoio *m* tray, salver.

vastità *f* magnitude.

vasto *adj* vast.

vecchiaia *f* old age.

vecchio *adj* old.

veci *f* duties; **fa le ~ del direttore** he is the acting manager.

vedere *vi, vt* to see, to view; **non ~ l'ora di fare qc** to look forward to doing something; * *vr* **~rsi** to show.

vedova *f* widow.

vedovo *m* widower.

veduta *f* outlook, view.

veemente *adj* vehement.

veemenza *f* vehemence.

vegetare *vi* to vegetate.

vegetariano *adj, m* vegetarian.

vegetazione *f* vegetation; **~ densa** *f* overgrowth.

veggente *m/f* seer.

veglia *f* wake, vigil.

veicolo *m* vehicle.

vela *f* sail, sailing; **andare a gonfie vele** *vi* to be successful.

velare *vt* to veil.

veleno *m* poison, venom.

velenoso *adj* poisonous, venomous.

velina *f* tissue; **carta ~** *f* tissue paper.

velismo *m* yachting.

vello *m* fleece.

vellutato *adj* silky.

velluto *m* velvet; **~ a coste** *m* corduroy.

velo *m* veil, ply.

veloce *adj* quick, fast, speedy.

velocemente *adv* fast.

velocità *f* speed, velocity; **eccesso di ~** *m* speeding; **andare a ~ eccessiva** *vi* to speed.

vena *f* vein, seam, streak; **~ nascosta** *f* undercurrent; **~ varicosa** *f* varicose vein.

venale *adj* venal.

vendere *vt* to sell; **~ per strada** *vt* to hawk.

vendetta *f* vendetta, revenge, vengeance.

vendibile *adj* saleable, marketable.

vendicare *vt* to avenge; * *vr* **~rsi** to retaliate.

vendicativo *adj* revengeful, vindictive.

vendita *f* sale; **punto ~** *m* outlet.

venditore *m* seller, vendor.

venerabile *adj* venerable.

venerare *vt* to venerate, to revere.

venerazione *f* veneration, reverence.

venerdì *m* Friday ; **V~ Santo** *m* Good Friday.

venereo *adj* venereal; **malattia venerea** *f* venereal disease.

venial *adj* veniale.

venire *vi* to come; **~ incontro a** *vt* to accommodate.

ventaglio *m* fan.

ventesimo *adj, m* twentieth.

venti *adj, m* twenty.

venticello *m* breeze.

ventilare *vt* to ventilate.

ventilato *adj* ventilated; **mal ~** *adj* stuffy.

ventilatore *m* fan, ventilator.

ventilazione *f* ventilation.

vento *m* wind; **~ in coda** *m* tail-wind; **far ~** *vt* to fan.

ventosa *f* sucker.

ventoso *adj* windy, breezy, blustery, gusty.

ventre *m* stomach.

ventriglio *m* gizzard.

ventriloquo *m* ventriloquist.

ventuno *m* blackjack, pontoon.

veramente *adv* truly, really, actually.

veranda *f* veranda(h), porch.

verbale *m* minutes; *adj* verbal.

verbo *m* verb.

verboso *adj* wordy, verbose.

verdastro *adj* greenish.

verde *adj, m* green; **essere al ~** *vi* to be hard-up.

verdetto *m* verdict.

verdura *f* greens; **verdure** *fpl* vegetables.

vergine *adj, f* virgin.

Vergine *f* Virgo.

verginità *f* virginity.

vergogna *f* shame, disgrace; **pieno di ~** *adj* ashamed.

vergognare *vt* to shame.

vergognoso *adj* shameful, shame-faced, disgraceful, damnable.

verifica *f* verification.

verificare *vt* to verify, to try, to check.

verita *f inv* truth; **per la ~** as a matter of fact.

veritiero *adj* truthful.

verme *m* worm.

vermut *m inv* vermouth.

vernice *f* paint, paintwork; **~**

trasparente f varnish.
verniciare vt to paint.
vero adj true, real, veritable.
versante m slope.
versare vt to spill, to shed, to pour.
versatile adj versatile, adaptable, all-round.
versato adj conversant.
versione f version.
verso prep toward(s); * m verse.
vertebra f vertebra.
vertebrato adj, m vertebrate.
verticale adj, f vertical.
vertice m apex, vertex, summit.
vertigine f dizziness, giddiness, vertigo.
vertiginoso adj giddy, dizzy.
verve f verve.
vescica, blister, bladder.
vescovo m bishop.
vespa f wasp.
vespasiano m urinal.
vestaglia f dressing gown.
vestiario m apparel.
vestigio m vestige.
vestire m dressing; * vt to clothe, to dress.
vestito m dress, frock; **vestiti** mpl clothes; * adj clad .
veterano m veteran.
veterinario adj veterinary; * m vet, veterinary surgeon.
veto m veto; **porre il ~ a** vt to veto.
vetraio m glazier.
vetrina f showcase, window.
vetro m glass, windowpane; **~ smerigliato** m frosted glass; **~ piano** m plate glass.
vetta f summit.
via f road; **~ a mezzaluna** f crescent.
via prep via, by.
viadotto m viaduct.
viaggiare vi to travel.
viaggiatore m traveller.
viaggio m journey, trip, **viaggi**

mpl travel; **~ per mare** m voyage; **in ~** adv en route; **di/da ~** adj travelling.
viale m avenue, mall, drive.
vibrante adj vibrant.
vibrare vi to vibrate, to shudder.
vibrazione f vibration, shudder.
vicepresidente m vice-chairman.
viceversa adv vice versa.
vicinanza f proximity, closeness, **vicinanze** fpl vicinity, neighbourhood; **nelle vicinanze** adj locally.
vicinato m neighbourhood.
vicino m neighbour; **da buon ~** adj neighbourly;* adj, adv close, near, nearby; * prep near.
vicolo m alley; **~ cieco** m cul-de-sac.
video m inv video.
videotape m inv videotape.
vietare vt to prohibit.
vigilanza f vigilance.
vigile adj vigilant, alert.
vigilia f eve ; **la ~ di Natale** f Christmas Eve.
vigliaccheria f cowardice.
vigliacco m, adj coward.
vigna f vineyard.
vigneto m vineyard.
vignetta f cartoon.
vignettista m/f cartoonist.
vigore m vigour.
vigoroso adj vigorous, pithy, lusty.
vile adj base.
villa f villa, hall, country house.
villano adj rude.
villeggiante m holiday-maker.
villeggiatura f holiday; **località di ~** f holiday resort.
viltà f baseness.
vimine m wicker; **di vimini** adj wicker.

vincere *vt*, *vi* to win.
vincitore *m* winner, victor.
vinile *m* vinyl.
vino *m* wine; ~ **bianco/rosso** white/red wine; ~ **ordinario** *m* plonk.
viola *m*, *adj* purple; * *f* viola, violet.
violaciocca *f* wallflower.
violare *vt* to violate.
violazione *f* breach, infringement, violation.
violentare *vt* to rape.
violentatore *m* rapist.
violentemente *adv* wildly.
violento *adj* violent.
violenza *f* violence.
violetto *adj*, *m* violet.
violinista *m/f* violinist, fiddler.
violino *m* violin, fiddle.
violoncello *m* violoncello, cello.
vipera *f* viper, adder.
virare *vi* to turn, to veer.
virgola *f* comma, point.
virgoletta *f* inverted comma; **virgolette** *fpl* quotation marks.
virile *adj* manly, virile.
virilità *f* virility, manliness, manhood.
virtù *f inv* virtue.
virtuoso *adj* virtuous, righteous.
virulento *adj* virulent.
virus *m inv* virus.
vischio *m* mistletoe.
viscido *adj* slimy; **un tipo ~** *m* creep.
viscoso *adj* viscous.
visibile *adj* visible.
visibilità *f* visibility.
visiera *f* visor.
visione *f* vision.
visita *f* visit, examination, tour; ~ **medica** *f* medical; **orario delle visite** *m* visiting hours.
visitare *vt* to visit, to examine.

visitatore *m* visitor, caller.
visivo *adj* visual; **sussidi vi sivi** *mpl* visual aids.
viso *m* face.
visone *m* mink.
vispo *adj* frisky, bright.
vista *f* sight, vista, vision, view eyesight; **punto di ~** *m* view
visto *adj* seen; ~ **che** *conj* see ing that, considering; * *m* visa
vistoso *adj* showy, flashy gaudy.
vita *f* life, lieftime, living; waist waistline; ~ **dell'al di là** *f* af terlife; **privo di ~** *adj* lifeless ~ **sentimentale** *f* love life; l€ **durata della ~** *f* lifespan.
vitale *adj* vital.
vitalità *f* vitality.
vitamina *f* vitamin.
vite *f* vine, grapevine; screw.
vitello *m* calf, veal.
vitreo *adj* glassy.
vittima *f* victim, fatality, casu alty.
vitto *m* board; ~ **e alloggio** *m* keep.
vittoria *f* victory, win; **una ~ €** **pari merito** *f* a dead heat; ~ **facile** *f* walkover.
vittorioso *adj* victorious.
vivace *adj* sprightly, lively, skit tish, vivacious.
vivacità *f* liveliness.
vivaio *m* nursery.
vivente *adj* living.
vivere *vi* to live, to subsist; ~ **di** to live on.
vivido *adj* vivid.
vivisezione *f* vivisection.
vivo *m* quick; * *adj* alive, live.
viziare *vt* to indulge, to pam per.
viziato *adj* spoilt.
vizio *m* vice; **che induce al ~** *adj* addictive.
vocabolario *m* vocabulary, dic tionary.

vocale *f* vowel; * *adj* vocal.
vocativo *adj* vocative.
vocazione *f* vocation, calling.
voce *f* voice, rumour, entry, item; **ad alta** ~ *adv* aloud.
vodka *f inv* vodka.
voglia *f* fancy, inclination, craving, birthmark.
voi *pers pron* you.
volano *m* shuttlecock.
volante *adj* flying; * *m* steering wheel.
volantino *m* leaflet.
volare *m* flying; * *vi* to fly.
volatile *adj* volatile.
volente *adv* wanting; ~ **o nolente** *adv* willy-nilly.
volenteroso *adj* willing.
volere *vt* to want, to wish; * *m* will, wish(es); **senza** ~ *adv* accidentally.
volgare *adj* coarse, vulgar.
volgarità *f* vulgarity, crudity.
volizione *f* volition.
volo *m* flight; ~ **charter** *m* charter flight; **in** ~ *adj* airborne; ~ **di linea** *m* scheduled flight.
volontà *f* will; **spontanea** ~ *f* free will; **buona** ~ *f* goodwill.
volontario *m* volunteer; * *adj* volontary.
volpe *f* fox.
volt *m inv* volt.
volta *f* time; vault; **passaggio a** ~ *m* archway; **un' altra** ~ *adv* again, once more; **qualche** ~ *adv* sometimes; **mille**

volte *adv* over and over; **più volte** *adv* many a time; **una** ~ *adv* once; **ancora una** ~ *adv* once more.
voltagabbana *m/f inv* turncoat.
voltaggio *m* voltage.
voltare *vt* to turn, to turn over.
volteggiare *vi* to whirl, to twirl.
volto *m* countenance.
volume *m* volume, sound, bulk.
voluminoso *adj* bulky.
voluttuoso *adj* sensuous, voluptuous.
vomitare *vi* to vomit, to be sick, (*fam*) to puke, (*fam*) to throw up.
vomito *m* vomit.
vongola *f* clam.
vorace *adj* voracious.
vortice *m* whirl, whirlpool, vortex.
vostro poss *adj*, *pron* your(s).
votare *vt*, *vi* to vote.
votazione *f* poll, vote, voting, ballot; **consultare tramite** ~ *vt* to ballot.
voto *m* mark, grade, vow, vote; ~ **decisivo** *m* casting vote; **concedere il diritto di** ~ **a** *vt* to enfranchise;
vulcanico *adj* volcanic.
vulcano *m* volcano.
vulnerabile *adj* vulnerable.
vuotare *vt* to empty, to bale out.
vuoto *m* vacuum, vacancy, void, emptiness, gap, blank; * *adj* unoccupied, empty.

W

wagon-lit *m inv* sleeping car.
walzer *m inv* waltz.
WC *m inv* WC, toilet.

weekend *m inv* weekend.
western *m inv* western (film).
würstel *m inv* frankfurter.

XYZ

xilofono *m* xylophone.
yacht *m inv* yacht.
yankee *m/f inv* yankee.
yard *f inv* yard.
yearling *m inv* yearling.
yen *m inv* yen.
yoga *m* yoga.
yogurt *m inv* yoghurt.
yuppy *m/f* yuppie.
zaffata *f* whiff.
zafferano *m* saffron.
zaffiro *m* sapphire.
zaino *m* rucksack, haversack, knapsack, backpack.
zampa *f* paw; **~ anteriore** *f* foreleg.
zampata *f* kick; **dare una ~** *vt* to paw.
zampogna *f* bagpipes.
zangola *f* churn.
zanna *f* fang, tusk.
zanzara *f* mosquito, gnat.
zanzarone *m* daddy-long-legs.
zappa *f* hoe.
zappare *vt* to hoe.
zar *m inv* czar, tsar.
zarina *f* czarina.
zattera *f* raft.
zavorra *f* ballast.
zebra *f* zebra.
zecca *f* mint; tick, louse; **nuovo di ~** *adj* brand-new.
zelante *adj* zealous.
zelo *m* zeal.
zenit *m inv* zenith.
zenzero *m* ginger.
zeppa *f* wedge; **pieno ~** *adj* chock-full.
zerbino *m* doormat.
zero *m* nought, zero, nil.
zia *f* aunt.
zibellino *m* sable.
zigomo *m* cheekbone.
zigzag *m inv* zigzag.
zimbello *m* laughing stock.

zinco *m* zinc.
zingaro *m* gypsy.
zio *m* uncle.
zip *m inv* zip.
zitella *f* spinster.
zoccolo *m* hoof, clog.
zodiaco *m* zodiac.
zolfo *m* sulphur.
zolla *f* clod, sod; **~ erbosa** *f* turf.
zolletta *f* lump; **~ di zucchero** *f* sugar lump.
zona *f* zone; **~ di competenza** *f* catchment area (school); **~ verde** *f* green belt.
zonzo *m*: **andare a ~** *vi* to saunter.
zoo *m inv* zoo.
zoologico *adj* zoological.
zoologo *m* zoologist.
zoologia *f* zoology.
zoom *m inv* zoom.
zoppicamento *m* limp.
zoppicare *vi* to hobble, to limp.
zoppo *m* cripple; * *adj* lame.
zoster *m*: **herpes zoster** *m* (*med*) shingles.
zotico *m* lout.
zoticone *m* oaf, boor.
zucca *f* pumpkin, marrow, gourd.
zuccherare *vt* to sugar, to sweeten.
zuccherato *adj* sugary.
zucchero *m* sugar; **~ semolato** *m* caster sugar; **~ filato** *m* candyfloss; **~ greggio** *m* brown sugar.
zucchetto *m* skullcap.
zucchina *f* courgette.
zuccone *m* blockhead.
zuffa *f* fray, dust-up, set-to, rough and tumble.
zumare *vi* to zoom.
zuppa *f* soup; **~ inglese** *f* (*culin*) trifle.
zuppiera *f* tureen.

English-Italian
Dictionary

A

a *art* un, uno, una, un'; * *prep* a, per.

aback *adv* **to be taken ~** sconcertato; essere colto (preso) alla sprovvista.

abandon *vt* abbandonare; * *n* disinvoltura *f*; brio *m*.

abandonment *n* abbandono *m*.

abase *vt* umiliare, mortificare; * *vi* umiliarsi, abbassarsi.

abash *vt* sconcertare, imbarazzare.

abashed *adj* sconcertato, imbarazzato.

abate *vi* placcarsi, calmarsi, abbassarsi.

abbess *n* badessa *f*.

abbey *n* badia *f*.

abbot *n* abate *m*.

abbreviate *vt* abbreviare.

abbreviation *n* abbreviazione *f*.

abdicate *vt* abdicare a, rinunciare a.

abdication *n* abdicazione *f*.

abdomen *n* addome *m*.

abdominal *adj* addominale.

abduct *vt* rapire.

abduction *n* rapimento *m*; sequestro *m* di persona.

abductor *n* rapitore *m*.

aberration *n* aberrazione *f*.

abet *vt* **to aid and ~** essere complice di.

abeyance, to be in *vi* essere in disuso; essere in sospeso.

abhor *vt* aborrire, provare orrore per, detestare.

abhorrence *n* orrore *m*.

abhorrent *adj* ripugnante, aborrevole.

abide, by *vi* attenersi a, rispettare, tener fede a.

ability *n* capacità *f*, abilità *f*;

abilities *npl* doti *fpl*.

abject *adj* abietto; umiliante.

ablaze *adj* in fiamme.

able *adj* capace, abile, intelligente; **to be ~ to do** poter fare.

able-bodied *adj* robusto, valido.

abnormal *adj* anormale.

abnormality *n* anormalità *f*, anomalia *f*.

aboard *adv* a bordo, in vettura.

abode *n* domicilio *m*, dimora *f*.

abolish *vt* abolire.

abolition *n* abolizione *f*.

abominable *adj* abominevole; pessimo, orrendo, orribile.

abomination *n* avversione *f*, disgusto *m*; cosa orrenda *f*.

aboriginal *adj* aborigeno.

abort *vi* abortire, fallire; *vt* interrompere.

abortion *n* aborto *m*.

abortive *adj* fallito, mancato.

abound *vi* abbondare.

about *prep* intorno a; **somewhere ~ here** qui intorno da qualche parte; a proposito di; **we talked ~ it** ne abbiamo parlato; * *adv* in giro, qua e là; **to look ~** guardarsi intorno; circa; **~ 20 cars** una ventina di macchine; **to be ~ to** stare per.

above *prep* sopra; * *adv* al di sopra; **~ all** soprattutto; **~mentioned** sopra menzionato.

abrasion *n* abrasione *f*.

abrasive *adj* abrasivo.

abreast *adv* di fianco.

abridge *vt* accorciare, abbreviare, riassumere, compendiare.

abridged *adj* ridotto; ~ **edition** edizione ridotta.

abroad *adv* all'estero; **to go ~** andare all'estero.

abrogate *vt* abrogare, annullare.

abrupt *adj* brusco.

abscess *n* ascesso *m*.

abscond *vi* evadere, scappare, fuggire.

absence *n* assenza *f*, mancanza *f*.

absent *adj* assente; ~ **minded** distratto; mancante.

absentee *n* assente *m/f*.

absenteeism *n* assenteismo *m*.

absolute *adj* assoluto; totale; categorico. ~ **ly** *adv* assolutamente, completamente.

absolution *n* assoluzione *f*.

absolve *vt* scogliere da, assolvere da.

absorb *vt* assorbire, ammortizzare, assimilare.

absorbent *adj* assorbente;.

absorbing *adj* avvincente, molto interessante.

absorption *n* assorbimento *m*.

abstain *vi* astenersi.

abstemious *adj* moderato, frugale; astemio.

abstention *n* astensione *f*.

abstinence *n* astinenza *f*.

abstract *adj* astratto; * *n* riassunto *m*; **in the ~** in teoria, in estratto; sommario *m*; * *vt* estrarre, riassumere.

abstraction *n* astrazione *f*, distrazione *f*.

abstruse *adj* astruso, recondito, oscuro.

absurd *adj* assurdo, ridicolo.

absurdity *n* assurdità *f*, assurdo *m*.

abundance *n* abbondanza *f*, gran quantità *f*.

abundant *adj* abbondante; ~ **in** ricco di.

abuse *vt* insultare; abusare di;

* *n* insulti *mpl*, ingiurie *fpl*, improperi *mpl*; abuso *m*.

abusive *adj* offensivo, ingiurioso.

abysmal *adj* abissale, spaventoso.

abyss *n* abisso *m*, baratro *m*.

acacia *n* acacia *f*.

academic *adj* accademico, universitario, intellettuale; * *n* accademico *m*.

academician *n* accademico *m*.

academy *n* accademia *f*.

accede *vi* acconsentire a; salire a; aderire a.

accelerate *vt, vi* accelerare.

acceleration *n* accelerazione *f*.

accelerator *n* acceleratore *m*.

accent *n* accento *m*.

accentuate *vt* accentuare; mettere in risalto.

accept *vt* accettare, ammettere.

acceptable *adj* accettabile; gradito.

acceptance *n* accettazione *f*; accoglienza *f*.

access *vt* accedere a * *n* accesso *m*.

accessible *adj* accessibile; facilmente reperibile.

accession *n* aggiunta *f*; accessione *f*; ~ **to throne** salita *f*.

accessory *n* accessorio *m*; (*law*) complice *m/f*.

accident *n* incidente *m*, disgrazia *f*; caso *m*.

accidental *adj* fortuito; involontario; ~ **ly** *adv* per caso; senza volere.

acclaim *vt* acclamare * *n* acclamazioni *fpl*; applauso *m*.

acclimatize *vt* acclimatare; * *vi* acclimatarsi, adattarsi.

accommodate *vt* ospitare, alloggiare; venire in contro a; (*differences*) conciliare.

accomodating *adj* conciliante; premuroso.

accommodation n sistemazione f, alloggio m.

accompaniment n accompagnamento m.

accompanist n (mus) accompagnatore m, accompagnatrice f.

accompany vt accompagnare.

accomplice n complice m/f.

accomplish vt compiere, portare a termine, realizzare.

accomplished adj esperto.

accomplishment n completamento m, realizzazione f; talento m, dote f.

accord n accordo m; **with one ~** all'unanimità; **of one's own ~** spontaneamente.

accordance: n **in ~ with** secondo m, in conformità di/a.

according to prep secondo, stando a; conforme a; **~ ly** adv di conseguenza.

accordion n (mus) fisarmonica.

accost vt abbordare.

account n conto m; relazione f, resoconto m; considerazione f; **on no ~** per nessun motivo; in nessun caso; **on ~** in acconto; **on ~ of** a causa di; * vt **to ~ for** rendere conto di; spiegare.

accountancy n ragioneria f, contabilità f.

accountant n ragioniere m, ragioneria f, contabile m/f.

account book n libro m di conti.

account number n numero m di conto.

accrue vi aumentare; maturare.

accumulate vt accumulare; vi accumularsi.

accumulation n accumulo m, mucchio m.

accuracy n esattezza f; accuratezza f; precisione f; fedeltà f.

accurate adj accurato, esatto, preciso; corretto; fedele.

accursed adj maledetto.

accusation n accusa f.

accusative n (gram) accusativo m.

accuse vt accusare.

accused n accusato m, imputato m.

accuser n accusatore m, accusatrice f.

accustom vt abituare.

accustomed adj abituato; solito.

ace n asso m **to have an ~ up one's sleave** avere un asso nella manica.

acerbic adj aspro.

acetate n (chem) acetato m.

ache n dolore m; * vi far male.

achieve vt raggiungere; realizzare.

achievement n realizzazione f; raggiungimento m.

acid adj acido, caustico; * n acido m.

acidity n acidità f.

acknowledge vt riconoscere, ammettere; ricambiare.

acknowledgement n riconoscimento m, ammissione f; (of letter, etc) riscontro m.

acme n culmine m.

acne n acne f.

acorn n ghianda f.

acoustics n acustica f.

acquaint vt informare; **to be ~ed with** conoscere.

acquaintance n conoscenza f; conoscente m/f.

acquiesce vi acconsentire a.

acquiescence n acquiescenza f, consenso m.

acquiescent adj acquiescente, remissivo, condiscendente.

acquire vt acquisire; prendere; **to ~ a taste for** prendere gusto a.

acquisition n acquisto m.

acquit vt assolvere.

acquittal n assoluzione f.

acre n acro m.

acrid adj acre, pungente.

acrimonious adj aspro, astioso, malevolo.

acrimony n acrimonia f, asprezza f.

across adv dall'altra parte; * prep attraverso.

act vt interpretare **to ~ the fool** fare lo stupido; * vi recitare; agire; vr comportarsi * n (deed) atto m; (law) legge f; (theatre) atto m.

acting adj **he is the ~ manager** fa le veci del direttore.

action n azione f.

activate vt attivare.

activity n attività f.

actor n attore m.

actress n attrice f.

actual adj reale, effettivo; ~ ly adv veramente, addirittura.

acumen n perspicacia f **business ~** fiuto negli affari.

acute adj acuto; fine; intenso; grave; perspicace.

adamant adj inflessibile.

adapt vt modificare; trasformare; adattare.

adaptable adj versatile.

adaptation n adattamento m.

adaptor n presa multipla f, riduttore m.

add vt aggiungere, sommare, addizionare.

adder n vipera f.

addict n tossicomane m/f, drogato m.

addiction n assuefazione f, tossicodipendenza f.

addictive adj che induce al vizio.

addition n aggiunta f, addizione f, **there has been an ~ to the family** la famiglia si è accre-

sciuta.

additional adj supplementare.

additive n additivo m.

address vt indirizzare; rivolgere * n indirizzo m, recapito m; discorso m.

adenoids n adenoidi fpl.

adept adj abile; * n esperto m.

adequate adj sufficiente; adeguato.

adhere vi aderire.

adherent n aderente m/f.

adhesion n adesione f.

adhesive n adesivo m.

adhesive tape n nastro adesivo m.

adipose adj adiposo.

adjacent adj adiacente.

adjective n aggettivo m.

adjoin vt essere attiguo/contiguo a.

adjoining adj attiguo, contiguo.

adjourn vt rinviare; sospendere.

adjournment n rinvio m; sospensione f.

adjudicate vt giudicare; decidere su.

adjunct n aggiunta f, appendice f.

adjust vt regolare; modificare; aggiustare.

adjustable adj regolabile.

adjustment n regolazione f, modifica f, adattamento m.

ad-lib vt improvvisare; * adj improvvisato.

administer vt dirigere, gestire; amministrare; somministrare.

administration n direzione f, gestione f, amministrazione f; somministrazione f; governo m.

administrative adj amministrativo.

administrator n amministratore m, amministratrice f.

admirable *adj* ammirevole.

admiral *n* ammiraglio *m*.

admiralty *m* ammiragliato *m*, (*GB*) ministero *m* della marina.

admiration *n* ammirazione *f*.

admire *vt* ammirare.

admirer *n* ammiratore *m*, ammiratrice *f*.

admissible *adj* ammissibile.

admission *adj* ammissione, ingresso.

admit *vt* lasciar entrare; ammettere.

admittance *n* ingresso *m*.

admittedly *adj* bisogna ammettere che; va detto che.

admonish *vt* ammonire.

ad nauseam *adv* fino alla nausea.

adolescence *n* adolescenza *f*.

adolescent *n* adolescente *m/f*.

adopt *vt* adottare.

adopted *adj* adottato.

adoption *n* adozione *f*.

adorable *adj* adorabile.

adoration *n* adorazione *f*.

adore *vt* adorare.

adorn *vt* abbellire, ornare.

adrift *adv* alla deriva.

adroit *adj* abile.

adulation *n* adulazione *f*.

adult *adj* adulto; * *n* adulto *m*, adulta *f*.

adulterate *vt* adulterare.

adulterer *n* adultero *m*.

adulteress *n* adultera *f*.

adulterous *adj* adultero.

adultery *n* adulterio *m*.

advance *vt* anticipare; favorire; *vi* avanzare; progredire; * *n* progresso *m*; in anticipo *m*; dare un anticipo *m*.

advanced *adj* avanzato, superiore.

advantage *n* vantaggio *m*; **to take ~ of** approfittare di.

advantageous *adj* vantaggioso.

advent *n* avvento *m*.

adventure *n* avventura *f*.

adventurous *adj* avventuroso.

adverb *n* avverbio *m*.

adversary *n* avversario *m*.

adverse *adj* sfavorevole.

adversity *n* sfortuna *f*.

advertise *vt* fare pubblicità, reclamizzare.

advertisement *n* pubblicità *f*, inserzione *f*, annuncio *m*.

advertising *n* pubblicità *f*.

advice *n* consiglio *m*; avviso *m*.

advisable *adj* consigliabile; raccomandabile.

advise *vt* consigliare; avvisare.

adviser *n* consigliere *m*, consulente *m/f*.

advisory *adj* consultivo.

advocate *n* avvocato *m*; sostenitore *m* * *vt* sostenere la validità di.

aerial *n* antenna *f*; * *adj* aereo.

aerobics *npl* aerobica *f*.

aerosol *n* aerosol *m*.

aesthetic *adj* estetico.

afar *adv* lontano; **from ~** da lontano.

affable *adj* affabile.

affair *n* faccenda *f*, affare *m*; relazione *f*, avventura *f*.

affect *vt* influire su, incidere su.

affectation *n* ostentazione *f*, pretese *fpl*.

affected *adj* affettato; commosso.

affection *n* affetto *m*.

affectionate *adj* affezionato.

affidavit *n* affidavit *m invar*.

affiliate *vt* affiliare, aggregare.

affiliation *n* affiliazione *f*.

affinity *n* affinità *f*.

affirm *vt* affermare, asserire.

affirmation *n* affermazione *f*.

affirmative *adj* affermativo.

affix *vt* apporre, attaccare.

afflict *vt* affliggere.

affliction n sofferenza f, infermità f.

affluence n ricchezza f, abbondanza f.

affluent adj ricco.

afford vt permettersi.

affray n rissa f.

affront n affronto m, offesa f.

aflame adv in fiamme adj ardente.

afloat adv a galla.

aforementioned adj suddetto.

afraid adj aver paura; temere.

afresh adv da capo, di nuovo.

aft adv a poppa.

after prep dopo * adv ~ **all** dopotutto; malgrado tutto.

afterbirth n placenta f.

aftercare n assistenza f postoperatoria.

after-effects npl ripercussione f, conseguenza f; reazione f.

afterlife n vita f dell'aldilà.

aftermath n conseguenze fpl.

afternoon n pomeriggio m.

after-sales service n servizio m assistenza f cliente.

aftershave n dopobarba m.

aftertaste n sapore m che rimane in bocca.

afterwards adv dopo, più tardi, in seguito.

again adv ancora, di nuovo, un'altra volta; ~ **and** ~ ripetutamente; **then** ~ d'altra parte.

against prep contro.

age n età f, epoca f, era f; * adj **under** ~ minorenne; * vi invecchiare.

aged adj anziano.

agency n agenzia f.

agenda n ordine del giorno m.

agent n agente m/f.

agglomeration n agglomerazione f.

aggravate vt aggravare; irritare.

aggravation n aggravamento m.

aggravating adj esasperante, irritante.

aggregate n insieme m; * adj complessivo.

aggression n aggressione f.

aggressive adj aggressivo.

aggressor n aggressore m.

aggrieved adj offeso.

aghast adj spigottito, inorridito.

agile adj agile, svelto.

agility n agilità f.

agitate vt turbare, agitare.

agitation n agitazione f.

agitator n agitatore/trice m/f.

ago adv fa; **how long** ~? quanto tempo fa?

agog adj impaziente; ~ **with excitement** emozionato.

agonize over vi angosciarsi.

agony n dolore m atroce.

agree vt essere d'accordo con; (gram) concordare.

agreeable adj piacevole.

agreed adj convenuto.

agreement n accordo m, consenso m.

agricultural adj agricolo.

agriculture n agricoltura f.

aground adv (mar) in secca * vi **to run** ~ arenarsi.

ahead adv avanti; davanti; in anticipo.

aid vt aiuto m; assistenza f.

aide-de-camp n aiutante m di campo.

AIDS n AIDS m.

ailing adj sofferente.

ailment n indisposizione f.

aim vt puntare, mirare; * n mira f; scopo m.

aimless adj senza scopo.

air n aria f; * vt arieggiare; esprimere.

airborne adj decollato, in volo.

air-conditioned adj ad/con aria condizionata, climatizzato.

air-conditioning *n* aria *f* condizionata.

aircraft *n* aeromobile *m*.

air force *n* aeronautica *f* militare.

air freshener *n* deodorante *m* per l'ambiente.

air gun *n* fucile *m* ad aria compressa.

airless *adj* senz'aria.

airlift *n* ponte *m* aereo.

airline *n* linea *f* aerea.

airmail *n* posta *f* aerea.

airport *n* aeroporto *m*.

airstrip *n* pista *f* di atterraggio.

air terminal *n* terminal *m*.

airtight *adj* ermetico.

airy *adj* arieggiato.

aisle *n* navata *f*.

ajar *adj* socchiuso.

alabaster *n* alabastro *m*.

alacrity *n* prontezza *f*.

alarm *n* allarme *m*, sveglia *f*; * *vt* allarmare.

alarmist *n* allarmista *m/f*.

alas *adv* ahimè.

albatross *n* albatro *m*.

album *n* album *m*.

alchemist *n* alchimista *m*.

alchemy *n* alchimia *f*.

alcohol *n* alcool *m*.

alcoholic *adj* alcolico; * *n* alcolizzato *m*.

alcoholism *n* alcolismo *m*.

alcove *n* alcova *f*.

alder *n* (*bot*) ontano *m*.

ale *n* birra *f*.

alert *adj* sveglio; vigile; * *n* allarme *m*; * *vt* avvertire.

algae *npl* alghe *fpl*.

algebra *n* algebra *f*.

alias *n* pseudonimo *m*; * *adv* alias, altrimenti detto.

alibi *n* alibi *m*.

alien *adj* estraneo, straniero; * *n* straniero, extraterrestre.

alienate *vt* alienare.

alienation *n* alienazione *f*.

alight *adj* essere in fiamme; * *vi* scendere.

align *vt* allineare.

alike *adj* simile.

alimony *n* alimenti *mpl*.

alive *adj* vivo.

alkali *n* alcali *m*.

alkaline *adj* alcalino.

all *adj* tutto; * *adv* ~ **at once** tutto d'un tratto; ~ **the same** tuttavia; **not at ~!** prego! * *pron* **we ~ sat down** ci sedemmo tutti quanti.

allay *vt* dissipare.

allegation *n* accusa *f*.

allege *vt* asserire.

allegiance *n* lealtà *f*.

allegorical *adj* allegorico.

allegory *n* allegoria *f*.

allergy *n* allergia *f*.

alleviate *vt* alleviare.

alley *n* vicolo *m*.

alliance *n* alleanza *f*.

allied *adj* alleato.

alligator *n* alligatore *m*.

alliteration *n* allitterazione *f*.

all-night *adj* aperto/che dura tutta la notte.

allocate *vt* assegnare.

allocation *n* stanziamento *m*.

allot *vt* assegnare.

allow *vt* permettere; concedere.

allowable *adj* ammissibile.

allowance *n* indennità *f*.

alloy *n* lega *f*.

all-right *adv* bene.

all-round *adj* versatile.

allspice *n* pepe *m* della Giamaica.

all-time *adj* senza precedente.

allude *vt* alludere a.

allure *vt* allettare * *n* fascino *m*.

alluring *adj* allettante.

allusion *n* accenno *m*; allusione *f*.

alluvial *adj* alluvionale.

ally *n* alleato *m*; * *vt* allearsi.

almanac *n* almanacco *m*.

almighty *adj* onnipotente *m*.

almond *n* mandorla *f*.

almond tree *n* mandorlo *m*.

almost *adv* quasi.

alms *n* elemosina *f*.

aloft *prep* in alto.

alone *adj* solo; * *adv* da solo; **to leave ~** lasciare in pace.

along *prep* lungo; * *adv* **take it ~** prendilo con te; **I knew all ~** sapevo fin dall'inizio.

aloof *adj* distaccato; * *adv* a distanza.

aloud *adj* a voce alta.

alphabet *n* alfabeto *m*.

alphabetical *adj* alfabetico; **~ly** *adv* in ordine alfabetico.

alpine *n* alpino *m*.

already *adv* già.

also *adv* anche, pure.

altar *n* altare *m*.

alter *vt* modificare.

alteration *n* modifica *f*.

altercation *n* lite *f*.

alternate *adj* alternato; * *vt* alternare.

alternating *adj* alternante.

alternative *n* alternativa *f*; * *adj* alternativo; **~ly** *adv* come alternativa.

alternator *n* alternatore *m*.

although *conj* benché.

altitude *n* altitudine *f*.

altogether *adv* tutto sommato.

aluminium *n* alluminio *m*.

always *adv* sempre.

a.m. *adv* del mattino.

amalgamate *vt* amalgamare.

amaryllis *n* (*bot*) amarillide *f*.

amass *vt* accumulare.

amateur *n* dilettante *m/f*.

amaze *vt* stupire.

amazement *n* stupore *m*.

amazing *adj* sorprendente; **~ly** *adv* incredibilmente.

ambassador *n* ambasciatore *m*.

ambassadress *n* ambasciatrice *f*.

amber *n* ambra *f*; * *adj* ambra.

ambidextrous *adj* ambidestro.

ambiguity *n* ambiguità *f*.

ambiguous *adj* ambiguo.

ambition *n* ambizione *f*.

ambitious *adj* ambizioso.

amble *vi* camminare senza fretta.

ambulance *n* ambulanza *f*.

ambush *n* imboscata *f*; **to lie in ~** stare in agguato * *vt* fare un'imboscata a.

amenable *adj* conciliante.

amend *vt* (*law*) emendare.

amendment *n* emendamento *m*.

amends *npl* risarcimento *m*.

amenities *npl* attrezzatura *f*.

America *n* America *f*.

American *adj* americano.

amethyst *n* ametista *f*.

ambiable *adj* affabile.

amicable *adj* amichevole.

amid(st) *prep* in mezzo a, tra.

amiss *adv* male; **don't take it ~** non ti offendere.

ammonia *n* (*chem*) ammoniaca *f*.

ammunition *n* munizioni *fpl*.

amnesia *n* amnesia *f*.

amnesty *n* amnistia *f*.

among(st) *prep* tra, in mezzo a.

amoral *adv* amorale.

amorous *adj* amoroso.

amorphous *adj* amorfo.

amount *n* somma *f*, importo *m*; * *vi* ammontare a.

amp(ere) *n* ampere *m*.

amphibian *n* anfibio *m*;.

amphibious *adj* anfibio.

amphitheatre *n* anfiteatro *f*.

ample *adj* ampio.

amplification *n* amplificazione *f*.

amplifier *n* amplificatore *m*.

amplify *vt* (*sound*) amplificare; (*statement*) ampliare.

amply *adv* ampiamente.

amputate *vt* amputare.
amputation *n* amputazione *f.*
amulet *n* amuleto *m.*
amuse *vt* divertire.
amusement *n* divertimento *m.*
amusing *adj* divertente.
an *art* un, uno, una.
anachronism *n* anacronismo *m.*
anaemia *n* anemia *f.*
anaemic *adj* anemico.
anaesthetic *n* anestetico *m.*
anaesthetist *n* anestetista *m/f.*
anagram *n* anagramma *m.*
analogue *adj* analogico.
analogous *adj* analogo.
analogy *n* analogia *f.*
analysis *n* analisi *f.*
analyst *n* analista *m/f.*
analytical *adj* analitico.
analyze *vt* analizzare.
anarchic *adj* anarchico.
anarchist *n* anarchico *m.*
anarchy *n* anarchia *n.*
anathema *n* anatema *m.*
anatomical *adj* anatomico.
anatomy *n* anatomia *f.*
ancestor *n* antenato *m,* avo *m.*
ancestral *adj* ancestrale, atavico.
ancestry *n* stirpe *f.*
anchor *n* ancora *f.*
anchorage *n* ancoraggio *m.*
anchovy *n* acciuga *f.*
ancient *adj* antico.
ancillary *adj* ausiliario.
and *conj* e; **faster ~ faster** sempre più veloce.
anecdote *n* aneddoto *m.*
anemone *n* (*bot*) anemone *m;* (*zool*) **sea ~** attinia *f.*
anew *adv* di nuovo.
angel *n* angelo *m.*
angelic *adj* angelico.
anger *n* rabbia *f;* * *vt* far arrabbiare.
angle *n* angolo *m;* * *vt* pescare con la lenza.
angler *n* pescatore *m.*

anglicism *n* anglicismo *m.*
anglicize *vt* anglicizzare.
angling *n* pesca *f* con la lenza.
angrily *adv* con rabbia.
angry *adj* arrabbiato.
anguish *n* angoscia *f.*
angular *adj* spigoloso.
animal *adj, n* animale *m;.*
animate *vt* animare; * *adj* animato.
animated *adj* animato.
animation *n* animazione *f.*
animosity *n* animosità *f.*
aniseed *n* anice *m.*
ankle *n* caviglia *f;* **~ socks** calzini *mpl.*
annals *n* annali *mpl.*
annex *vt* annettere.
annexe *n* annesso *m.*
annihilate *vt* annientare.
annihilation *n* annientamento *m.*
anniversary *n* anniversario *m.*
annotate *vt* annotare.
annotation *n* annotazione *f.*
announce *vt* annunciare.
announcement *n* annuncio *m.*
announcer *n* presentatore *m.*
annoy *vt* infastidire.
annoyance *n* fastidio *m.*
annoying *adj* irritante.
annual *adj* annuo.
annuity *n* annualità *f.*
annul *vt* annullare.
annulment *n* annullamento *m.*
anodyne *adj, n* sedativo *m.*
anoint *vt* ungere.
anomalous *adj* anomalo.
anomaly *n* anomalia *f.*
anonymity *n* anonimato *m.*
anonymous *adj* anonimo.
anorak *n* giacca *f* a vento.
anorexia *n* anoressia *f.*
another *adj* un altro, ancora; **one ~** l'un l'altro.
answer *vt* rispondere; **to ~ for** rispondere di; **to ~ to** rispondere a; * *n* risposta *f.*

answerable *adj* responsabile; dover rendere conto di.

answering machine *n* segreteria *f* telefonica.

ant *n* formica *f.*

antagonism *n* antagonismo *m.*

antagonist *n* antagonista *m/f.*

antagonize *vt* inimicarsi.

antarctic *adj* antartico.

anteater *n* formichiere *m.*

antecedent *n* antecedente *m.*

antechamber *n* anticamera *f.*

antedate *vt* precedere; retrodatare.

antelope *n* antilope *f.*

antenatal *adj* prenatale.

antenna *n* antenna *f.*

anterior *adj* anteriore.

anthem *n* inno *m.*

ant-hill *n* formicaio *m.*

anthology *n* antologia *f.*

anthracite *n* antracite *f.*

anthropology *n* antropologia *f.*

anti-aircraft *adj* antiaereo.

antibiotic *n* antibiotico *m.*

antibody *n* anticorpo *m.*

anticipate *vt* prevedere.

anticipation *n* attesa *f.*

anticlockwise *adj* antiorario; * *adv* in senso antiorario.

antics *n* buffoneria *f.*

anticyclone *n* anticiclone *m.*

antidote *n* antidoto *m.*

antifreeze *n* antigelo *m.*

antihistamene *n* antistaminico *m.*

antipathy *n* antipatia *f.*

antipodes *n* antipodi *mpl.*

antiquarian *n* antiquario *m.*

antiquated *adj* antiquato.

antique *adj* antico * *n* pezzo *m* di antiquariato.

antiquity *n* antichità *f.*

antisemitic *adj* antisemitico.

antiseptic *adj, n* antisettico *m.*

antisocial *adj* antisociale.

antithesis *n* antitesi *f.*

antler *n* (*zool*) palco *m.*

anvil *n* incudine *m.*

anxiety *n* ansia *f.*

anxious *adj* preoccupato.

any *adj* del, dello, della, dei, degli, delle, qualche, un po', ogni, qualsiasi, qualunque, tutto; * *pron* qualcuno, nessuno, chiunque; **~thing** qualcosa; niente; * *adv* **~how** comunque, in ogni modo.

aorta *n* aorta *f.*

apace *adv* velocemente.

apart *adv* a distanza; separatamente; a pezzi; a parte.

apartheid *n* apartheid *f.*

apartment *n* appartamento *m.*

apathetic *adj* apatico.

apathy *n* apatia *f.*

ape *n* scimmia *f.*

aperitif *n* aperitivo *m.*

aperture *n* apertura *f.*

apex *n* vertice *m.*

aphorism *n* aforisma *m.*

aphrodisiac *adj* afrodisiaco.

apiary *n* apiario *m.*

apiece *adv* ciascuno.

aplomb *n* disinvoltura *m.*

Apocalypse *n* apocalisse *f.*

apocryphal *adj* apocrifo.

apolitical *adj* apolitico.

apologetic *adj* (pieno) di scuse.

apologize *vt* scusarsi.

apology *n* scuse *fpl.*

apoplectic *adj* apoplettico.

apoplexy *n* apoplessia *f.*

apostle *n* apostolo *m.*

apostolic *adj* apostolico.

apostrophe *n* apostrofo *m.*

apotheosis *n* apoteosi *f.*

appal *vt* atterrire.

appalling *adj* terribile.

apparatus *n* attrezzatura *f.*

apparel *n* vestiario *m.*

apparent *adj* evidente; * **~ly** *adv* a quanto pare.

apparition *n* fantasma *m.*

appeal *vi* supplicare; (*law*) appellarsi; * *n* (*law*) appello *m.*

appealing *adj* attraente; commovente.

appear *vi* apparire; comparire; sembrare; esibirsi.

appearance *n* aspetto *m*; comparsa *f*.

appease *vt* placare.

appellant *n* (*law*) appellante *m/f*.

append *vt* apporre; allegare.

appendage *n* appendice *f*.

appendix *n* appendice *f*.

appertain *vi* spettare.

appetite *n* appetito *m*.

appetizing *adj* appetitoso.

applaud *vi* applaudire.

applause *n* applauso *m*.

apple *n* mela *f*; **to upset the ~ cart** mandare tutto all'aria.

apple tree *n* melo *m*.

appliance *n* apparecchio *m*.

applicable *adj* applicabile.

applicant *n* candidato *m*.

application *n* applicazione *f*; domanda *f*.

applied *adj* applicato.

apply *vt* applicare; applicarsi; rivolgersi.

appoint *vt* nominare.

appointment *n* appuntamento *m*; nomina *f*.

apportion *vt* attribuire.

apposite *adj* apposito.

apposition *n* apposizione *f*.

appraisal *n* valutazione *f*.

appraise *vt* valutare.

appreciable *adj* notevole.

appreciate *vt* apprezzare; * *vi* aumentare di valore.

appreciation *n* apprezzamento *m*; comprensione *f*; aumento *m* di valore.

appreciative *adj* grato; caloroso.

apprehend *vt* arrestare.

apprehension *n* apprensione *f*.

apprehensive *adj* apprensivo, timoroso.

apprentice *n* apprendista *m/f*.

apprenticeship *n* apprendistato *m*.

apprise *vt* informare.

approach *vt, vi* avvicinar(si) a; * *n* approccio *m*.

approachable *adj* avvicinabile.

approbation *n* approvazione *f*.

appropriate *vt* appropriarsi di; * *adj* adatto.

approval *n* approvazione *f*.

approve (of) *vt* approvare.

approximate *adj* approssimativo.

approximation *n* approssimazione *f*.

apricot *n* albicocca *f*; **~ tree** albicocco *m*.

April *n* aprile *m*.

apron *n* grembiule *m*.

apse *n* abside *f*.

apt *adj* appropriato; **~ly** *adv* appropriatamente.

aptitude *n* abilità *f*.

aqualung *n* autorespiratore *m*.

aquarium *n* acquario *m*.

Aquarius *n* Acquario *m*.

aquatic *adj* acquatico.

aqueduct *n* acquedotto *m*.

aquiline *adj* aquilino.

Arab *n*, *adj* arabo *m*.

arabesque *n* arabesco *m*.

arable *adj* arabile.

arbitrary *adj* arbitrario.

arbitrate *vt* fare da arbitro.

arbitration *n* arbitrato *m*.

arbitrator *n* arbitro *m*.

arcade *n* arcata *f*; galleria *f*.

arch *n* arco *m*; * *adj* principale; malizioso.

archaeological *adj* archeologico.

archaeologist *n* archeologo *m*.

archaeology *n* archeologia *m*.

archaic *adj* arcaico.

archangel *n* arcangelo *m*.

archbishop *n* arcivescovo *m*.

archbishopric n arcivescovado m.

arched adj ad arco.

archer n arciere m.

archery n tiro m con l'arco.

architect n architetto m.

architectural adj architettonico.

architecture n architettura f.

archives npl archivio m.

archway n passaggio m a volta.

artic adj artico.

ardent adj ardente.

ardour n ardore m.

arduous adj arduo.

area n area f.

arena n arena f.

arguable adj discutibile.

argue vi litigare.

argument n discussione f.

argumentative adj polemico.

aria n (mus) aria f.

arid adj arido.

Aries n Ariete m.

arise vi presentarsi; derivare da.

aristocracy n aristocrazia f.

aristocrat n, adj aristocratico m.

arithmetic n aritmetica f.

arithmetical adj aritmetico.

ark n arca f.

arm n braccio m; * vt armare.

armament n armamenti mpl.

armchair n poltrona f.

armed adj armato.

armful n bracciata f.

armhole n giro m della manica.

armistice n armistizio m.

armour n armatura f.

armoured car n autoblinda f.

armoury n armeria f.

armpit n ascella f.

armrest n bracciolo m.

army n esercito m.

aroma n aroma m.

aromatico adj aromatico m.

around prep intorno; * adv circa.

arouse vt svegliare; stimolare.

arrange vt sistemare; organizzare.

arrangement n sistemazione f disposizione f.

array n schieramento m, schiera f.

arrears npl arretrati mpl.

arrest n arresto m; * vt arrestare.

arrival n arrivo m.

arrive vt arrivare.

arrogance n arroganza f.

arrogant adj arrogante.

arrow n freccia f.

arse n culo m.

arsenal n arsenale m.

arsenic n arsenico m.

arson n incendio m doloso.

art n arte f; ~s npl lettere fpl, studi mpl umanistici.

artefact n manufatto m.

arterial adj (anat) arterioso; di grande comunicazione.

artery n arteria f.

artful adj furbo; abile.

art gallery n galleria n d'arte.

arthritis n artrite f.

artichoke n carciofo m.

article n articolo m.

articulate vt articolare; * adj chiaro.

articulated lorry n autoarticolato m.

articulation n articolazione f.

artificial adj artificiale.

artillery n artiglieria f.

artisan n artigiano m.

artist m artista m/f.

artistic adj artistico.

artistry n abilità f artistica.

artless adj ingenuo.

art school n scuola f d'arte.

as conj mentre; come; ~ to, ~ for quanto a.

asbestos n amianto m.

ascend vt salire.

ascendancy n ascendente m.

ascension n ascensione f.

ascent n ascensione f.

ascertain vt accertare.

ascetic adj ascetico.

ascribe vt attribuire.

ash n (bot) frassino m; cenere f.

ashamed adj pieno di vergogna.

ashore adv a terra; **to go ~** scendere a terra.

ashtray n portacenere m.

Ash Wednesday n mercoledì m delle cenere.

aside adv da parte; **~ from** oltre a.

ask vt chiedere; **to ~ after** chiedere notizie; **to ~ a question** fare una domanda; **to ~ out** invitare.

askance adv **to look ~** guardare qualcuno storto.

askew adv di traverso.

asleep adj addormentato.

asparagus n asparago m.

aspect n aspetto m.

aspersion n calunnia f.

asphalt n asfalto m.

asphyxia n asfissia f.

asphyxiate vt asfissiare.

asphyxiation n soffocamento m.

aspirate vt aspirare.

aspiration n aspirazione f.

aspire vt aspirare.

aspirin n aspirina f.

ass n asino m.

assail vt assalire.

assailant n assalitore m.

assassin n assassino m.

assassinate vt assassinare.

assassination n assassinio m.

assault n assalto m; * vt assaltare.

assemble vt radunare; montare.

assembly n assemblea f; montaggio m.

assembly line n catena f di montaggio.

assent n benestare m; * vi approvare.

assert vt affermare.

assertion n affermazione f.

assertive adj che sa imporsi.

assess vt valutare.

assessment n valutazione f.

assessor n funzionario m del fisco.

assets npl beni mpl.

assiduous adj assiduo.

assign vt assegnare.

assignation n convegno m gallante.

assignemnt n incarico m.

assimilate vt assimilare.

assimilation n assimilazione f.

assist vt aiutare.

assistance n aiuto m.

assistant n aiutante m/f.

associate vt associare; * adj consociato; * n collega m/f.

association n associazione f.

assorted adj assortito.

assortment n assortimento.

assuage vt attenuare.

assume vt supporre.

assumption n supposizione f.

assurance n assicurazione f.

assure vt assicurare.

asterisk n asterisco m.

astern adv (mar) a poppa.

asthma n asma f.

asthmatic adj asmatico.

astonish vt stupire.

astonishing adj sorprendente.

astonishment n stupore m.

astound vt sbalordire.

astray adv **to go ~** perdersi; **to lead ~** portare qualcuno su una brutta strada.

astride adj a cavalcioni.

astringent n, adj astringente m.

astrologer n astrologo m.

astrology n astrologia f.

astronaut n astronauta m/f.

astronomer n astronomo m.

astronomical adj astronomico.

astronomy n astronomia f.
astute adj accorto.
asylum n asilo m; manicomio m.
at prep a; ~ once subito; ~ all affatto; ~ first dapprima; ~ last finalmente.
atheism n ateismo m.
atheist n ateo m.
athlete n atleta m/f.
athletic adj atletico.
atlas n atlante m.
atmosphere n atmosfera f.
atmospheric adj atmosferico.
atom n atomo m.
atomic adj atomico.
atone vi espiare.
atonement n espiazione f.
atrocious adv atroce.
atrocity n atrocità f.
atrophy n atrofia f.
attach vt attaccare.
attaché n addetto m.
attachment n accessorio m; attaccamento m.
attack vt attaccare; * n attacco m.
attacker n aggressore m.
attain vt raggiungere.
attainable adj raggiungibile.
attempt vt tentare; * n tentativo m.
attend vt frequentare; to ~ to occuparsi di.
attendance n frequenza f.
attendant n custode m/f.
attention n attenzione f.
attentive adj premuroso.
attenuate vt attenuare.
attest vt attestare.
attic n soffitta f, mansarda f.
attire n tenuta f.
attitude n atteggiamento m.
attorney n avvocato m, procuratore m.
attract vt attirare.
attraction n attrazione f; attrattiva f.
attractive adj attraente.

attribute vt attribuire; * n attributo m.
attrition n usura f (per attrito).
aubergine n melanzana f.
auburn adj ramato.
auction n asta f.
auctioneer n banditore m.
audacious adj audace.
audacity n audacia f.
audible adj udibile.
audience n pubblico m; udienza f.
audit n revisione f dei conti; * vt fare una revisione di.
audition n provino m.
auditor n revisore m dei conti.
auditorium n auditorio m.
augment vt aumentare.
August n agosto m.
august adj augusto.
aunt n zia f.
au pair n ragazza f alla pari.
aura n aura f.
auspices npl auspici mpl.
auspicious adj favorevole.
austere adj austero.
austerity n austerità f.
authentic adj autentico.
authenticate vt convalidare.
authenticity n autenticità f.
author n autore m.
authoress n autrice f.
authoritarian adj autoritario.
authoritative adj autorevole.
authority n autorità f.
authorization n autorizzazione f.
authorize vt autorizzare.
autobiography n autobiografia f.
autocrat n autocrata m.
autocratic adj autocratico.
autograph n autografo; * vt firmare.
automatic adj automatico.
automation n automazione f.
autonomy n autonomia f.
autopsy n autopsia f.

autumn *n* autunno *m*.
autumnal *adj* autunnale.
auxiliary *adj* ausiliario; *(gram)* ausiliare; * *n* assistente.
avail *vt* **to ~ oneself of** avvalersi di; * *n* **to no ~** in vano.
available *adj* disponibile.
avalanche *n* valanga *f*.
avant-garde *n* avanguardia *f*; * *adj* d'avanguardia.
avarice *n* avarizia *f*.
avaricious *adj* avaro.
avenge *vt* vendicare.
avenue *n* viale *m*.
average *n* media *f*; * *adj* medio.
aversion *n* avversione *f*.
avert *vt* distogliere da.
aviary *n* uccelliera *f*.
aviation *n* aviazione *f*.
avid *adj* insaziabile.
avocado *n* avocado *m*.
avoid *vt* evitare.
avoidable *adj* evitabile.
await *vt* aspettare.
awake *vt* svegliare; * *adj* sveglio.

awakening *n* risveglio *m*.
award *vt* assegnare; * *n* premio *m*.
aware *adj* consapevole.
awareness *n* consapevolezza *f*.
away *adv* lontano; **far and ~** di gran lunga.
away game *n* partita *f* in trasferta.
awe *n* timore *m* riverenziale.
awe-inspiring *adj* imponente.
awful *adj* terribile.
awkward *adj* imbarazzante; goffo.
awl *n* punteruolo *m*.
awning *n* tendone *m*.
awry *adv* storto.
axe *n* ascia; * *vt* ridurre drasticamente.
axiom *n* assioma *m*.
axiomatic *adj* assiomatico.
axis *n* asse *m*.
axle *n* semiasse *m*.
azalea *n* azalea *f*.
azure *n* azzurro.

B

baa *vi* belare.
babble *vi* parlare a vanvera.
babbling *n* mormorio *m*.
baboon *n* babbuino *m*.
baby *n* bambino *m*, bimbo *m*, neonato *m*.
babyhood *n* prima *f* infanzia.
babyish *adj* infantile.
baby-minder *n* bambinaia *f*.
baby-sit *vi* guardare i bambini.
baby-sitter *n* baby sitter *m/f*.
bachelor *n* scapolo *m*; *(univ)* dottore *m*, dottoressa *f*.
back *n* schiena *f*; dietro *m*; retro *m*; * *adj* posteriore; arre-

trato; * *adv* indietro; **I'll be ~ soon** sarò di ritorno fra poco; * *vt* appoggiare; puntare su; * *vi* fare marcia indietro.
backbencher *n (GB)* parlamentare *m/f* di secondo piano.
backbite *vt* sparlare.
backbone *n* spina *f* dorsale.
backchat *n* impertinenza *f*.
backcloth *n* fondale *m*.
backcomb *vt* cotonare.
backdate *vt* retrodatare.
backdoor *n* porta *f* posteriore.
backer *n* sostenitore *m*.

backfire *vi* fallire. .

backgammon *n* backgammon *m*.

background *n* sfondo *m*; formazione *f*.

backhand *n* rovescio *m*.

backhander *n* bustarella *f*.

backing *n* appoggio *m*.

backlash *n* reazione *f* violenta.

backlog *n* cumulo *m* di lavoro arretrato.

backnumber *n* numero *m* arretrato.

backpack *n* zaino *m*.

backside *n* sedere *m*.

back stage *n* nel retroscena *f*.

back stroke *n* dorso *m*.

backup *adj* supplementare.

backward *adj* all'indietro; lento; arretrato.

backwards *adv* indietro.

backwater *n* angolo *m* sperduto.

backyard *n* cortile *m*.

bacon *n* pancetta *f*.

bacteria *n* batteri *mpl*.

bad *adj* cattivo; brutto; ~ **language** parolacce.

badge *n* distintivo *m*.

badger *n* tasso *m*; * *vt* **to ~** tormentare.

bad-mannered *adj* maleducato, sgarbato.

badminton *n* badminton *m*.

bad tempered *adj* irascibile.

baffle *vt* confondere.

bag *n* borsa *f*, sacchetto *m*.

baggage *n* bagaglio *m*.

baggy *adj* sformato.

bagpipes *n* cornamusa *f*, zampogna *f*.

bag-snatcher *n* scippatore *m*.

bail *n* cauzione *f*.

bailiff *n* ufficiale *m/f* giudiziario; fattore *m*.

bait *vt* stuzzicare; * *n* esca *f*.

baize *n* panno *m*.

bake *vt* cuocere (al forno).

baker *n* fornaio *m*.

bakery *n* panificio *m*.

baking *n* cottura *f*.

baking powder *n* lievito *m* in polvere.

balaclava *n* passamontagna *m*.

balance *n* equilibrio *m*; bilancio *m*; saldo *m*; * *vt* tenere in equilibrio/in bilico.

balance sheet *n* bilancio *m* di esercizio.

balcony *n* balcone *m*.

bald *adj* calvo.

baldness *n* calvizie *f*.

bale *n* balla *f*; * *vi* vuotare.

baleful *adj* maligno.

balk *vi* recalcitrare.

ball *n* palla *f*; ballo *m*.

ballad *n* ballata *f*.

ballast *n* zavorra *f*.

ballcock *n* galleggiante *m*.

ballerina *n* ballerina *f*.

ballet *n* danza *f* classica.

ballistic *adj* balistico.

balloon *n* palloncino *m*; **hot air ~** mongolfiera *f*.

ballot *n* votazione *f*; * *vt* consultare tramite votazione.

ballpoint (pen) *n* penna *f* a sfera.

ballroom *n* sala *f* da ballo.

balm *n* balsamo *m*.

balmy *adj* balsamico.

balustrade *n* balaustrata *f*.

bamboo *n* bambù *m*.

bamboozle *vt* raggirare.

ban *n* divieto *m*; * *vt* proibire.

banal *adj* banale.

banana *n* banana *f*; ~ **tree** banano *m*.

band *n* banda *f*; striscia *f*.

bandage *n* fascia *f*.

bandanna *n* fazzolettone *m*.

bandit *n* bandito *m*.

bandstand *n* palco *m* dell'orchestra.

bandy-legged *adj* con le gambe storte.

bang n colpo m * vt, vi sbattere.
banger n salsiccia f; petardo m.
bangle n braccialetto m.
banish vt bandire.
banisters npl ringhiera f.
banjo n banjo m.
bank n riva f; banca f; * vi to ~ servirsi di una banca.
bank account n conto m in banca.
banker n banchiere m.
banking n attività f bancaria.
banknote n banconota f.
bankrupt adj fallito; * n fallito m.
bankruptcy n bancarotta f.
bank statement n estratto m conto.
banner n stendardo m; striscione m.
bans npl pubblicazioni fpl matrimoniali.
banquet n banchetto m.
baptism n battesimo m.
baptistery n battistero m.
baptize vt battezzare.
bar n bar m; sbarra f; * vt sbarrare; * prep tranne.
barb n punta f.
barbarian n barbaro m.
barbaric adj barbaro.
barbecue n barbecue m.
barbed wire n filo m spinato.
barber n barbiere m.
bar code n codice m a barre.
barbiturate n barbiturico m.
bard n bardo m.
bare adj nudo; spoglio; semplice.
bareback adj senza sella.
barefaced adj sfacciato.
barefoot(ed) adj scalzo.
bareheaded adj a capo scoperto.
barely adv appena.
bargain n affare m; * vi contrattare.
barge n chiatta f.
baritone n baritono m.

bark n corteccia f; abbaiare m; * vi abbaiare.
barley n orzo m.
barmaid n barista f.
barman n barista m.
barmy adj suonato.
barn n stalla f.
barnacle n cirripedi m.
barometer n barometro m.
baron n barone m.
baroness n baronessa f.
baroque adj barocco.
barracks n caserma f.
barrage n sbarramento m; a ~ of questions una raffica di domande.
barrel n barile m; canna f.
barrel organ n organetto m.
barren adj infruttuoso; sterile.
barricade n barricata; * vt barricare.
barrier n barriera f.
barrister n avvocato m.
barrow n carriola f.
bartender n barista m.
barter vi, vt barattare.
base n base f; * vt basare * adj ignobile, vile.
baseball n baseball m.
baseless adj infondato.
basement n seminterrato m.
baseness n viltà f.
bash n botta; * vt picchiare.
bashful adj timido.
basic adj fondamentale.
basil n basilico m.
basilisk n basilisco m.
basin n lavandino m.
basis n base f.
bask vt crogiolarsi.
basket n cestino m.
basketball n pallacanestro f.
bass adj basso.
bassoon n fagotto m.
bastard adj bastardo.
bastardy n bastardaggine f.
baste vt (culin) ungere; (sewing) imbastire.

bat n (zool) pipistrello m; (sport) mazza f.

batch n gruppo m.

bath n bagno m; * vt fare il bagno.

bathe vt lavare; * vi fare il bagno.

bather n bagnante m/f.

bathing cap n cuffia f.

bathing costume n costume m.

bath mat n tappetino m da bagno.

bathos n sentimento m falso.

bathrobe n accappatoio m.

bathroom n (stanza da) bagno m.

baths npl piscina f.

bathtub n vasca f da bagno.

baton n bacchetta f.

battalion n battaglione m.

batter vt colpire violentemente; * n pastella f.

battering ram n ariete m.

battery n pila f, batteria f.

battle n battaglia f, lotta f; * vi lottare, combattere.

battlefield n campo m di battaglia.

battlements npl bastioni mpl.

battleship n nave f da guerra.

bauble n ninnolo m.

bauxite n bauxite f.

bawdy adj spinto.

bawl vi strillare.

bay n baia f; alloro m; * vt latrare.

bayonet n baionetta f.

bay window n bovindo m.

bazaar n bazar m.

be vi essere.

beach n spiaggia f.

beacon n faro m.

bead n perlina f.

beak n becco m.

beaker n (chem) bicchiere m, becher m.

beam n trave f; raggio m; * vi sorridere radiosamente.

bean n fagiolo m; chicco m.

beansprouts npl germogli mpl di soia.

bear[1] vt portare; sopportare; partorire; * vi to ~ right andare a destra.

bear[2] n orso m.

bearable adj sopportabile.

beard n barba f.

bearded adj barbuto.

bearer n portatore m; titolare m/f.

bearing n portamento m.

beast n bestia f; ~ of burden bestia da soma.

beastly adj insopportabile.

beat vt battere; * vi palpitare * n battito m; ritmo m.

beatify vt beatificare.

beating n botte fpl; sconfitta f.

beatitude n beatitudine f.

beautiful adj bello; splendido.

beautify vt abbellire.

beauty n bellezza f; ~ spot neo m.

beaver n castoro m.

because conj perché.

beckon vi chiamare con un cenno.

become vi diventare; divenire.

becoming adj adatto.

bed n letto m.

bedclothes npl coperte fpl.

bedlam n baraonda f.

bedpan n padella f.

bedraggled adj sbrindellato.

bedridden adj costretto a letto.

bedroom n camera f da letto.

bedspread n copriletto m.

bee n ape f.

beech n faggio m.

beef n manzo m.

beefsteak n bistecca (di manzo) f.

beehive n alveare m.

beer n birra f.

beeswax n cera f d'api.

beet(root) n barbabietola f.

beetle n scarabeo m.
befall vt, vi accadere.
befit vt adirsi.
before adv prima di.
beforehand adv prima.
befriend vt prendersi a cuore.
befuddled adj confuso.
beg vt mendicare; supplicare.
beggar n mendicante m/f.
begin vt, vi cominciare, incominciare, iniziare.
beginner n principiante m/f.
beginning n inizio m, principio m.
begonia n begonia f.
begrudge vt invidiare.
behalf n per conto di.
behave vi comportarsi.
behaviour n comportamento m.
behead vt decapitare.
behind prep dietro.
beige adj beige.
being n essere m, esistenza f.
belated adj in ritardo.
belch vi ruttare; * n rutto m.
belfry n campanile m.
belie vt smentire.
belief n fede f; convinzione f; opinione f.
believable adj credibile.
believe vt, vi credere a.
believer n credente m/f.
belittle vt sminuire.
bell n campanello m.
bellicose adj bellicoso.
belligerent adj belligerante.
bellow vi muggire; * n muggito m; urlo m.
bellows n mantice m, soffietto m.
belly n pancia f.
bellyache vi mugugnare.
bellyful n: **to have a ~ of** avere abbastanza di.
belong vi appartenere.
belongings npl effetti mpl personali.
beloved adj adorato.

below prep, adv sotto.
belt n cintura f; * vi filare.
bemoan vt lamentare.
bemused adj perplesso.
bench n panchina f.
bend vt piegare; * vi piegarsi; * n curva f.
bends n embolia f.
beneath adv, prep sotto.
benediction n benedizione f.
benefactor n benefattore m.
beneficent adj caritatevole.
beneficial adj benefico.
beneficiary n beneficiario m.
benefit n vantaggio m; * vt giovare; * vi trarre vantaggio.
benvolence n benevolenza f.
benevolent adj benevolo.
benign adj benevolo; benigno.
bent n inclinazione f.
bequeath vt lasciare in eredità.
bequest n lascito m.
berrate vt rimproverare.
bereaved adj in lutto.
bereavement n lutto.
beret n berretto m.
berry n bacca f.
berserk adj forsennato.
berth n cuccetta f; ormeggio m; * vi ormeggiare.
beseech vt implorare.
beset vt assillare.
beside prep a canto a.
besides prep oltre a; * adv inoltre.
besiege vt assediare.
best adj migliore; * adv meglio; * n il migliore.
bestial adj bestiale.
bestow vt conferire.
bestseller n bestseller m.
bet vt, vi scommettere * n scommessa f.
betray vt tradire.
betrayal n tradimento m.
betroth vt fidanzare.
bethrothal n fidanzamento m.
better adj migliore; **so much**

the ~ meglio così; * *adv* meglio; * *vt* migliorare.

between *prep* tra, fra.

bevel *n* smussatura *f*; *vt* smussare.

beverage *n* bevanda *f*.

bevy *n* banda *f*.

bewale *vt* lamentare.

beware *vi* stare attento.

bewilder *vt* disorientare.

bewilderment *n* perplessità *f*.

bewitch *vt* stregare.

beyond *prep* oltre; al di là.

bias *n* tendenza *f*.

bib *n* bavaglino *m*.

Bible *n* bibbia *f*.

biblical *adj* biblico.

bibliography *n* bibliografia *f*.

bicarbonate of soda *n* bicarbonato *m* di sodio.

biceps *n* bicipite *m*.

bicker *vi* bisticciare.

bicycle *n* bicicletta *f*.

bid *vt* offrire; * *vi* dichiarare; * *n*
offerto *m*; tentativo *m*.

bidding *n* offerte *fpl*.

bidet *n* bidè *m*.

biennial *adj* biennale.

bifocals *npl* occhiali *mpl* bifocali.

bifurcation *n* biforcazione *f*.

big *adj* grande; grosso; **my ~
sister** mia sorella maggiore.

bigamist *n* bigamo *m*.

bigamy *n* bigamia *f*.

big dipper *n* montagne *fpl*
russe.

big-headed *adj* montato.

bigot *n* fanatico *m*.

bigoted *adj* fanatico.

bigwig *n* pezzo *m* grosso.

bike *n* bici *f*.

bikini *n* bikini *m*.

bilateral *adj* bilaterale.

bilberry *n* mirtillo *m*.

bile *n* bile *f*.

bilingual *adj* bilingue.

bilious *adj* biliare.

bill *n* becco *m*; fattura *f*; conto *m*.

billboard *n* tabellone *m*.

billet *n* acquartieramento *m*.

billiards *npl* biliardo *m*.

billion *n* bilione *m*.

billow *vi* gonfiarsi.

billy *n* caprone *m*.

bin *n* bidone *m*.

bind *vt* legare; rilegare.

binder *n* classificatore *m*.

binding *n* rilegatura *f*.

bingo *n* tombola *f*.

binoculars *n* binocolo *m*.

biochemistry *n* biochimica *f*.

biographer *n* biografo *m*.

biographical *adj* biografico.

biography *n* biografia *f*.

biological *adj* biologico.

biology *n* biologia *f*.

biped *n* bipede *m*.

birch *n* betulla *f*.

bird *n* uccello *m*.

bird watcher *n* ornitologo *m*.

birth *n* nascita *f*; parto *m*.

birth certificate *n* certificato
m di nascita.

birth control *n* controllo *m*
delle nascite, contraccezione *f*.

birthday *n* compleanno *m*.

birthmark *n* voglia *f*.

birthplace *n* luogo *m* di nascita.

birthright *n* diritto *m* di nascita.

biscuit *n* biscotto *m*.

bisect *vt* bisecare.

bishop *n* vescovo *m*; (*chess*) alfiere *m*.

bison *n* bisonte *m*.

bit *n* punta *f*; pezzo *m*; morso *m*.

bitch *n* cagna *f*; (*fam*) stronza *f*.

bite *vt* mordere; pungere; **~ the
dust** lasciarci la pelle; * *n*
morso *m*; puntura *f*.

bitter *adj* amaro; aspro.

bitterness *n* amarezza *f*.

bitumen *n* bitume *m*.

bivouac *n* bivacco *m*.

bizarre *adj* bizzarro.

blab *vt* spifferare.

black *adj* nero; * *n* nero; * *vt* boicottare.

blackberry *n* mora *f*.

blackbird *n* merlo *m*.

blackboard *n* lavagna *f*.

blacken *vi* annerirsi; * *vt* annerire.

blackhead *n* punto *m* nero.

black ice *n* ghiaccio *m* invisibile.

backjack *n* ventuno *m*.

blackleg *n* crumiro *m*.

blacklist *n* lista *f* nera.

blackmail *n* ricatto *m*; * *vt* ricattare.

black market *n* mercato *m* nero.

blackness *n* oscurità *f*.

black pudding *n* sanguinaccio *m*.

black sheep *n* pecora *f* nera.

blacksmith *n* fabbro *m*.

blackthorn *n* prugnolo *m*.

bladder *n* vescica *f*.

blade *n* lama *f*.

blame *vt* incolpare; rimproverare; * *n* colpa *f*.

blameless *adj* irreprensibile.

blanch *vt* (*culin*) scottare; * *vi* sbiancare.

bland *adj* blando.

blank *adj* bianco; vacuo; * *n* vuoto *m*.

blank cheque *n* assegno *m* in bianco.

blanket *n* coperta *f*; * *adj* globale.

blare *vi* strombettare.

blasé *adj* blasé.

blaspheme *vi* bestemmiare.

blasphemer *n* bestemmiatore *m*.

blasphemous *adj* blasfemo.

blasphemy *n* bestemmia *f*.

blast *n* esplosione *f*; raffica *f*; * *vt* far saltare; * *excl* ~! mannaggia!

blast-off *n* lancio *m*.

blatant *adj* sfacciato.

blaze *n* incendio *m*; * *vi* ardere; divampare.

blazer *n* blazer *m*.

bleach *vt* candeggiare; * *n* candeggina *f*.

bleak *adj* tetro; desolato.

bleary(-eyed) *adj* dagli occhi cisposi.

bleat *n* belato *m*; * *vt* belare.

bleed *vi* sanguinare; * *vt* spurgare.

bleeding *n* emorragia *f*; * *adj* sanguinante.

bleep *n* segnale *m* acustico.

bleeper *n* cicalino *m*.

blemish *vt* deturpare; * *n* imperfezione *f*.

blend *vt* mischiare; * *vi* fondersi; * *n* miscela *f*.

blender *n* frullatore *m*.

bless *vt* benedire.

blessed *adj* benedetto.

blessing *n* benedizione *f*.

blight *n* piaga *f*.

blind *adj*, *n* cieco *m*; ~ **alley** vicolo *m* cieco; * *vt* accecare; **Venetian** ~ tenda *f* avvolgibile.

blindfold *vt* bendare; * *n* benda *m*; * *adj* bendato.

blindly *adv* ciecamente.

blindness *n* cecità *f*.

blind spot *n* punto *m* cieco; punto *m* debole.

blink *vt* sbattere le palpebre; * *n* battito *m* di ciglia.

blinkers *npl* paraocchi *mpl*.

bliss *n* felicità *f*.

blissful *adj* stupendo.

blister *n* vescica *f*.

blitz *n* attacco *m* improvviso.

blizzard *n* bufera *f* di neve.

bloated *adj* gonfio.

bloc *n* blocco *m*; * *vt* bloccare.

block *n* blocco *m*.

blockade *n* blocco *m*.

blockage *n* ingorgo *m*.

blockbuster *n* cosa *f* sensazionale.

blockhead n zuccone m.

bloke n tizio m.

blonde adj, n biondo m.

blood n sangue m.

bloodcurdling adj raccapricciante.

blood donor n donatore m di sangue.

blood group n gruppo m sanguino.

bloodhound n segugio m.

bloodless adj esangue.

blood poisoning n avvelenamento m del sangue.

blood pressure n pressione f del sangue.

bloodshed n spargimento m di sangue.

bloodshot adj iniettato di sangue.

bloodstream n circolazione f del sangue.

bloodsucker n sanguisuga f.

blood test n analisi f del sangue.

bloodthirsty adj sanguinario.

blood transfusion n trasfusione f di sangue.

blood vessel n vaso m sanguino.

bloody adj sanguinante; maledetto; ~ minded scontroso.

bloom n fiore m; * vi sfiorire.

blossom n fiori mpl.

blot vt macchiare; asciugare; * n macchia f.

blotch n chiazza f.

blotting paper n carta f assorbente.

blouse n camicetta f.

blow vi soffiare; * vt suonare; esplodere; * n colpo m.

blow-dry vt asciugare con il fohn.

blowlamp n lampada f a benzina per saldare.

blow out vt spegnere.

blowout n scoppio m.

blowpipe n cerbottana f.

blubber n grasso m di balena; * vi frignare.

bludgeon n randello m.

blue adj azzurro, celeste.

bluebell n giacinto m dei boschi.

bluebottle n moscone m.

blue-collar adj operaio.

blueprint n cianografia f.

bluff adj brusco; a picco; * vi bluffare.

blunder n gaffe f; * vi ~ into andare a sbattere contro.

blunt adj non tagliente; brusco.

bluntly adv senza mezzi termini.

bluntness n brutale franchezza f.

blur n massa f indistinta; * vt offuscare.

blurt out vt lasciarsi scappare.

blush n rossore m; * vi arrossire.

bluster n fanfaronata f.

blustery adj ventoso.

B.O. n odore m sgradevole.

boa n boa m.

boar n cinghiale m.

board n asse f; (chess) scacchiera f; vitto m; commissione f; * vt imbarcarsi su; salire su; * vi essere a pensione da.

boarder n pensionante m/f; collegiale m/f.

boarding card n carta f d'imbarco.

boarding house n pensione f.

boarding school n collegio m.

boast vt vantare; * n vanteria f.

boastful adj si vanta sempre.

boat n barca f; nave f.

boater n paglietta f.

boatswain n nostromo m.

bobby n poliziotto m.

bobsleigh n bob m.

bode vt presagire.

bodice *n* corpino *m*.

bodily *adj* materiale; * *adv* fisicamente.

body *n* corpo *m*; cadavere *m*; massa *f*; * *pron* **any~** qualcuno.

bodyguard *n* guardia *f* del corpo.

bodywork *n* carrozzeria *f*.

bog *n* palude *f*; cesso *m*.

bogey man *n* orco *m*, babau *m*.

bogus *adj* fasullo.

boil *vi* bollire; * *vt* (far) lessare; * *n* foruncolo *m*.

boiled egg *n* uovo *m* sodo.

boiled potatoes *npl* patate *fpl* lesse.

boiler *n* caldaia *f*.

boiling point *n* punto *m* di ebollizione.

boisterous *adj* animato.

bold *adj* audace; **~ type** grassetto.

boldness *n* audacia *f*.

bollard *n* colonnina *f*.

bolster *n* capezzale *m*; * *vt* sostenere.

bolt *n* chiavistello *m*; bullone *m*; fulmine *m*; * *vi* svignarsela; * *vt* ingollare.

bomb *n* bomba *f*; *vt* bombardare.

bombardment *n* bombardamento *m*.

bombastic *adj* magniloquente.

bomber *n* dinamitardo *m*.

bombshell *n* bomba *f*.

bond *n* impegno *m*; legame *m*; titolo *m*.

bonded warehouse *n* magazzino *m* doganale.

bone *n* osso *m*; (*fish*) lisca *f*.

bone-dry *adj* asciuttissimo.

bonfire *n* falò *m*.

bonnet *n* cuffia *f*; cofano *m*.

bonny *adj* carino.

bonus *n* gratifica *f*; premio *m*.

bony *adj* osseo.

boo *vt* fischiare.

boob *n* gaffe *f*; tetta *f*.

booby prize *n* premio per il peggior contendente.

booby trap *n* trabocchetto *m*.

book *n* libro *m*; quaderno *m*; * *vt* prenotare, riservare.

bookbinder *n* rilegatore *m*.

bookcase *n* libreria *f*.

bookkeeper *n* contabile *m/f*.

bookkeeping *n* contabilità *f*.

booklet *n* opuscolo *m*.

bookmaker *n* allibratore *m/f*.

bookmark *n* segnalibro *m*.

bookseller *n* libraio *m*.

bookshop *n* libreria *f*.

bookstall *n* bancarella *f*.

bookworm *n* topo *m* di biblioteca.

boom *n* boma *f*; rombo *m*; forte incremento *m*; * *vi* andare a gonfie vele.

boomerang *n* boomerang *m*.

boon *n* salvezza *f*.

boor *n* zoticone *m*.

boorish *adj* rozzo.

boost *n* spinta *f*; sprone *m*; * *vt* rinforzare.

booster *n* (*med*) richiamo *m*; amplificatore di segnale *m*.

boot *n* stivale *m*; **to ~** dare un calcio.

bootee *n* scarpetta *f*.

booth *n* cabina *f*.

bootleg *adj* di contrabbando.

boot polish *n* lucido *m* da scarpe.

booty *n* bottino *m*.

booze *vi* alzare il gomito; * *n* alcol *m*.

boozer *n* osteria *f*.

border *n* confine *m*; margine *m*; aiuola *f*; * *vt* fiancheggiare.

borderline *n* linea *f* di demarcazione.

bore *vt* trivellare; annoiare; * *n* foro *m*; calibro *m*; noia *f*; noioso *m*.

boredom *n* noia *f*.

boring *adj* noioso.
born *adj* nato.
borough *n* comune *m*.
borrow *vt* prendere in presti-to.
borstal *n* riformatorio *m*.
bosom *n* petto *m*, seno *m*.
bosom friend amico/ca *m/f* del cuore.
boss *n* capo *m*, padrone *m*.
bossy *adj* autoritario.
botanic(al) *adj* botanico.
botanist *n* botanico *m*.
botany *n* botanica *f*.
botch *vt* fare un pasticcio; * *n* pasticcio *m*.
both *adj* entrambi; ambedue; tutti e due.
bother *vt* infastidire; **a ~** una seccatura.
bottle *n* bottiglia *f*; * *vt* imbot-tigliare.
bottleneck *n* ingorgo *m*.
bottle-opener *n* apribottiglie *m*.
bottom *n* fondo *m*; sedere *m*.
bottomless *adj* senza fondo.
bough *n* ramo *m*.
boulder *n* macigno *m*.
bounce *vi* rimbalzare * *n* rim-balzo *m*.
bouncer *n* buttafuori *m*.
bound(s) *n* limiti *mpl*; balzo *m*; * *vi* balzare; * *adj* legato; rile-gato; **~ for** diretto a; **it was ~ to happen** era da prevedersi.
boundary *n* confine *m*.
boundless *adj* illimitato.
bountiful *adj* abbondante; mu-nifico.
bouquet *n* bouquet *m*.
bourgeois *adj* borghese.
bourgeoisie *n* borghesia *f*.
bout *n* attacco *m*; incontro *m*.
boutique *n* boutique *f*.
bovine *adj* bovino.
bow *vt* chinare; * *vi* inchinarsi; * *n* inchino *m*; prua *f*.

bow *n* arco *m*.
bowdlerize *vt* espurgare.
bowels *npl* intestino *m*.
bowl *n* scodella *f*; * *vt* lanciare.
bowling *n* bocce *fpl*; bowling *m*.
bowling alley *n* bowling *m*.
bowling green *n* campo *m* da bocce.
bow tie *n* farfalla *f*.
box *n* scatola *f*; palco *m*; * *vi* fare il pugile.
boxing *n* pugilato *m*.
boxer *n* pugile *m*.
boxing gloves *npl* guantoni *mpl*.
boxing ring *n* ring *m*.
box office *n* botteghino *m*.
boxroom *n* ripostiglio *m*.
boy *n* ragazzo *m*; fanciullo *m*.
boycott *vt* boicottare; * *n* boi-cottaggio *m*.
boyfriend *n* ragazzo *m*; fidan-zato *m*.
boyish *adj* fanciullesco.
bra *n* reggiseno *m*.
brace *n* apparecchio *m* ortodon-tico; rinforzo *m*; * *vt* rinforza-re.
bracelet *n* braccialetto *m*.
bracing *adj* tonificante.
bracken *n* felce *f*.
bracket *n* mensola *f*; parentesi *f*.
brag *vt*, *vi* vantarsi.
braggart *n* spaccone *m*.
braid *n* treccia *f*; * *vt* intrecciare.
brain *n* cervello *m*.
brainchild *n* creazione *f*.
brainless *adj* deficiente.
brainwash *vt* fare il lavaggio del cervello.
brainwave *n* idea *f* brillante.
brainy *adj* geniale.
brake *n* freno *vi* frenare.
brake light *n* fanalino *m* dello stop.
bramble *n* mora *f*.
bramble bush *n* rovo *m*.

bran n crusca f.

branch n ramo m; * vi diramarsi.

branch line n linea f secondaria.

brand n marca f; * vt marchiare.

brandish vt brandire.

brand-new adj nuovo di zecca.

brandy n brandy m.

brash adj sfrontato.

brass n ottone m.

brassiere n reggiseno m.

brat n moccioso m.

bravado n spavalderia f.

brave adj coraggioso; * vt sfidare; * n giovane guerriero m pellerossa.

bravery n coraggio m.

brawl n rissa f; * vi azzuffarsi.

brawn n muscoli mpl.

bray vi ragliare; * n raglio m.

brazen adj sfacciato.

brazier n bracciere m.

breach n violazione f; breccia f.

bread n pane m.

breadbin n cassetta f portapane.

breadboard n tagliere m.

breadcrumb n briciola f.

breadcrumbs n pangrattato m.

breadth n larghezza f.

breadwinner n chi mantiene la famiglia.

break vt rompere; * vi rompersi; **to ~ into** forzare; **to ~ out** scoppiare; evadere; **to ~ up** andare in vacanza; * n rottura f; intervallo m; **a lucky ~** un colpo di fortuna.

breakable adj fragile.

breakage n danni mpl.

breakaway adj scissionista.

breakdown n guasto m; esaurimento m nervoso.

breaker n frangente m.

breakfast n prima colazione f.

breakthrough n scoperta f decisiva.

breakwater n frangiflutti m.

breast n petto m; seno m; mammella f.

breastbone n sterno m.

breast-feed vt allattare (al seno).

breaststroke n nuoto m a rana.

breath n fiato n; alito m.

breathe vt respirare.

breathing n respiro m, respirazione f.

breathalyzer n palloncino m.

breathing space n attimo m di respiro.

breathless adj senza fiato.

breathtaking adj mozzafiato.

breed n razza f; * vt allevare; * vi riprodursi.

breeder n allevatore m; reattore m autofertilizzante.

breeding n allevamento m; buona educazione f.

breeze n brezza f, venticello m.

breezy adj ventoso; brioso.

brevity n brevità f.

brew vt mettere a fermentare; fare un infuso di; * n fermentazione f; infuso m.

brewer n fabbricante m di birra.

brewery n fabbrica f di birra.

briar n pipa f di radica.

bribe n bustarella f; * vt corrompere.

bribery n corruzione f.

bric-à-brac n bric-à-brac m.

brick n mattone m.

bricklayer n muratore m.

bridal adj nuziale.

bride n sposa f.

bridegroom n sposo m.

bridesmaid n damigella f d'onore.

bridge n ponte m; bridge m.

bridle n briglia f.

brief adj breve; * n dossier; * vt dare istruzioni a.

briefcase n cartella f.

briefs *n* slip; mutandine *fpl*.

brier *n* rosa *f* selvatica.

brigade *n* brigata *f*.

brigadier *n* generale *m* di brigata.

bright *adj* luminoso; vispo.

brighten *vt* ravvivare; * *vi* schiarirsi; rallegrarsi.

brightness *n* luminosità *f*.

brilliance *n* intensità *f*; intelligenza *f* scintillante.

brilliant *adj* brillante.

brim *n* orlo *m*; * *vi* traboccare di.

bring *vt* portare; **to ~ about** causare, provocare; **to ~ up** allevare; sollevare.

brink *n* orlo *m*.

brisk *adj* sbrigativo; attivo.

bristle *n* setola *f*; pelo *m*; * *vi* rizzarsi.

bristly *adj* setoloso.

brittle *adj* fragile.

broach *vt* affrontare.

broad *adj* largo.

broadbean *n* fava *f*.

broadcast *n* trasmissione *f*; * *vt* trasmettere.

broaden *vt* allargare.

broadly *adv* grosso modo.

broad-minded *adj* aperto.

broadside *n* attacco *m* massiccio.

broadways *adv* nel senso della larghezza.

brocade *n* braccato *m*.

broccoli *n* broccoli *mpl*.

brochure *n* depliant *m*; brochure *f*.

brogue *n* scarpone *m*; accento *m* irlandese.

broken *adj* rotto, spezzato; ~ **English** parlare un inglese stentato.

broker *n* mediatore *m*, agente *m* di cambio.

brokerage *n* mediazione *f*.

brolly *n* ombrello *m*.

bronchial *adj* bronchiale.

bronchitis *n* bronchite *f*.

bronze *n* bronzo *m*.

brooch *n* spilla *f*.

brood *vi* covare, rimuginare; * *n* covata *f*; prole *f*.

broody hen *n* chioccia *f*.

brook *n* ruscello *m*; * *vt* ammettere.

broom *n* scopa *f*; (*bot*) ginestra *f*.

broth *n* brodo *m*.

brothel *n* bordello *m*.

brother *n* fratello *m*.

brotherhood *n* fraternità *f*.

brother-in-law *n* cognato *m*.

brotherly *adj* fraterno.

brow *n* fronte *f*; **eye~** sopracciglio *m*.

browbeat *vt* intimidire.

brown *adj* marrone; ~ **sugar** zucchero greggio; ~**bread** pane integrale; * *vt* (*culin*) rosolare.

browse *vi* curiosare.

bruise *vt* farsi un livido a; * *n* livido *m*.

brunette *n* bruna *f*.

brunt *n*: **to bear the ~ of** sostenere il peso di.

brush *n* spazzola *f*; * *vt* spazzolare; scopare; sfiorare.

brusque *adj* brusco.

Brussels sprout *n* cavolino *m* di Bruxelles.

brutal *adj* brutale.

brutality *n* brutalità *f*.

brute *n* bruto *m*; *adj* bruto.

bubble *n* bolla *f*.

bubblegum *n* bubblegum *m*.

buck *n* (*zool*) maschio *m*.

bucket *n* secchio *m*.

buckle *n* fibbia *f*; * *vt* allacciare; * *vi* allacciarsi.

bucolic *adj* bucolico.

bud *n* bocciolo *m*.

Buddhism *m* buddismo *m*.

budding *adj* in erba.

budge *vt* spostare.

budgerigar *n* pappagallino *m*.

budget *n* bilancio *m*.

buff *n* fanatico *m*; * *adj* color paglierino; * *vt* lucidare.

buffalo *n* bufalo *m*.

buffer *n* respingente *m*.

buffet *n* schiaffo; buffet *m*; * *vt* sballottare.

buffoon *m* buffone *m*.

bug *n* insetto *m*.

bugbear *n* spauracchio *m*.

bugle *n* tromba *f*.

build *n* corporatura *f*; * *vt* costruire.

builder *n* costruttore *m*; muratore *m*.

building *n* costruzione *f*; edificio *m*.

bulb *n* bulbo *m*; lampadina *f*.

bulbous *adj* a forma di bulbo.

bulge *vi* essere gonfio; * *n* rigonfiamento *m*.

bulk *n* volume *m*; massa *f*; **in ~** comprare in grandi quantità.

bulky *adj* voluminoso.

bull *n* toro *m*.

bulldog *n* bulldog *m*.

bulldozer *n* bulldozer *m*.

bullet *n* proiettile *m*.

bulletin *n* bollettino *m*.

bulletproof *adj* a prova di proiettile.

bullfight *n* corrida *f*.

bullfighter *n* torero *m*.

bullion *n* oro *m* in lingotti.

bullock *n* torello *m*.

bullring *n* arena *f*.

bull's-eye *n* centro *m* (del bersaglio).

bully *n* bullo *m*; * *vt* fare il prepotente.

bullwark *n* baluardo *m*.

bum *n* culo *m*; fannullone *m*; * *adj* scadente.

bumblebee *n* bombo *m*.

bumpf *n* scartoffie *fpl*.

bump *n* botta *f*; bernoccolo *m*; * *vt* sbattere.

bumper *n* paraurti *mpl*; * *adj* eccezionale.

bumpkin *n* rusticone *m*.

bumpy *adj* accidentato.

bun *n* panino *m* dolce; chignon *m*.

bunch *n* mazzo *m*; grappolo *m*.

bundle *n* fagotto *m*; * *vt* fare un fagotto.

bung *n* tappo *m*; * *vt* tappare.

bungalow *n* bungalow *m*.

bungle *vt* fare un pasticcio; * *vi* fare pasticci.

bunion *n* (*med*) cipolla *f*.

bunk *n* cuccetta *f*.

bunker *n* bunker *m*.

buoy *n* (*mar*) boa *f*.

buoyant *adj* galleggiante.

burden *n* carico *m*; onere *m*; * *vt* opprimere; oberare.

bureau *n* ufficio *m*; secrétaire *m*.

bureaucracy *n* burocrazia *f*.

bureaucrat *n* burocrate *m/f*.

burglar *n* ladro *m*.

burglar alarm *n* antifurto *m*.

burglary *n* furto *m*.

burgle *vt* svaligiare.

burial *n* sepoltura *f*.

burlesque *n* parodia *f*.

burly *adj* ben piantato.

burn *vt* bruciare; * *n* bruciatura *f*, ustione *f*.

burner *n* bruciatore *m*.

burning *n* bruciato *m*; * *adj* in fiamme.

burp *n* rutto *m*; * *vi* ruttare.

burrow *n* tana *f*; * *vt* scavare.

bursar *n* economo *m*.

bursary *n* borsa *f* di studio.

burst *vi* scoppiare; **to ~ into tears** scoppiare a piangere; * *vt* fare scoppiare.

bury *vt* seppellire.

bus *n* autobus *m*.

bush *n* cespuglio *m*.

bushy *adj* folto.

busily *adv* alacremente.
business *n* affari *mpl*; attività *f*.
businesslike *adj* efficiente.
businessman *n* uomo *m* d'affari.
businesswoman *n* donna *f* d'affari.
bus-stop *n* fermata *f* d'autobus.
bust *n* busto *m*; petto *m*.
bustle *vi* affaccendarsi; * *n* trambusto *m*.
busy *adj* occupato.
busybody *n* ficcanaso *m/f*.
but *conj* ma; * *adv* solo; * *prep* tranne.
butcher *n* macellaio *m*; * *vt* macellare.
butcher's shop *n* macelleria *f*.
butler *n* maggiordomo *m*.
butt *n* botte *f*; mozzicone *m*; * *vt* dare una testata; * *vi* **to ~ in** interrompere.
butter *n* burro *m*.
buttercup *n* (*bot*) ranuncolo *m*.
butterfly *n* farfalla *f*.

buttock *n* natica *f*.
button *n* bottone *m*.
buttonhole *n* asola *f*, occhiello *m*.
buttress *n* contrafforte *m*.
buxom *adj* ben in carne.
buy *vt* comprare.
buyer *n* compratore *m*.
buzz *n* ronzio; * *vi* ronzare.
buzzard *n* poiana *f*.
buzzer *n* cicalino *m*.
by *adv* vicino; * *prep* vicino; via; davanti; **~ and large** nel complesso.
bye-election *n* elezioni *fpl* suppletive.
bygone *adj* passato; **let ~s be ~s** mettiamoci una pietra sopra.
by-law *n* norma *f* di regolamento comunale.
bypass *n* circonvallazione *f*.
by-product *n* sottoprodotto *m*.
bystander *n* astante *m/f*.
byte *n* (*comput*) byte *m*.
byway *n* strada *f* secondaria.
byword *n* sinonimo *m*.

C

cab *n* taxi *m*; cabina *f*.
cabbage *n* cavolo *m*.
cabin *n* capanna *f*; cabina *f*.
cabinet *n* armadietto *m*; Consiglio *m* dei Ministri.
cabinet-maker *n* ebanista *m/f*.
cable *n* cavo *m*.
cable car *n* funivia *f*.
cable television *n* televisione *f* via cavo.
cache *n* deposito *m* segreto.
cackle *vi* fare coccodè; ridacchiare; * *n* coccodè; risolino *m* stridulo;.
cactus *n* cactus *m*.
cadaver *n* cadavere *m*.

cadaverous *adj* cadaverico.
caddy *n* (*tea*) barattolo *m* del tè.
cadence *n* cadenza *f*.
cadet *n* cadetto *m*.
cadge *vt* scroccare.
cadger *n* scroccone *m*.
Caesarean *n* cesareo *m*.
café *n* caffè *m*; bar *m*.
caffeine *n* caffeina *f*.
cage *n* gabbia *f*; * *vt* mettere in gabbia.
cagey *adj* riservato.
cajole *vt* convincere con le buone.
cake *n* torta *f*; pasticcino *m*; * *vt* incrostare; * *vi* aggrumarsi.

cake shop n pasticceria f.
calamitous adj calamitoso.
calamity n calamità f.
calcify vt calcificare.
calceum n calcio m.
calculable adj calcolabile.
calculate vt calcolare.
calculation n calcolo m.
calculator n calcolatore m.
calculus n analisi f infinitesimale.
calendar n calendario m.
calf n vitello m.
calibrate vt calibrare.
calibration n calibratura f.
caliber n calibro m.
calico n tela f grezza.
call vt chiamare; telefonare a; indire; * vi **this ~s for a drink** qui ci vuole un brindisi; **I now ~ on Mr Smith to speak** invito Mr Smith a parlare; * n richiamo m; telefonata f; chiamata f.
call box n cabina f telefonica.
caller n visitatore m.
calligraphy n calligrafia f.
calling n vocazione f.
callous adj insensibile.
callow adj immaturo.
call-up n chiamata f alle armi.
calm n calma f; pace f; * adj calmo m; sereno m; * vt calmare.
calorie n caloria f.
calumny n calunnia f.
Calvary n Calvario m.
calve vi figliare.
Calvinist n calvinista m/f.
camber n curvatura f.
camel n camello m.
camellia n camelia f.
cameo n cammeo m.
camera n macchina f fotografica.
cameraman n cameraman m.
camomile n camomilla f.
camouflage n mimetizzazione f.

camp n accampamento m; * vi campeggiare.
campaign n campagna f; * vi fare una campagna.
campaigner n fautore m, sostenitore m.
camper n campeggiatore m.
camping n campeggio m.
camphor n canfora f.
campsite n campeggio m.
campus n campus m.
camshaft n albero m a camme.
can vi potere; **I ~'t swim** non so nuotare; * n latta f; lattina f.
canal n canale m.
canary n canarino m.
cancel vt cancellare.
cancellation n cancellazione f.
cancer n cancro m.
Cancer n Cancro m.
cancerous adj canceroso.
candelabra n candelabro m.
candid adj franco.
candidacy n candidatura f.
candidate n candidato m.
candied adj candito.
candle n candela f.
candlelight n lume m di candela.
candlestick n candeliere m.
candor n candore m.
candy n caramella f.
candyfloss n zucchero m filato.
cane n canna f; bastone m.
canine adj canino.
canister n barattolo m.
cannabis n canapa f indiana.
cannibal n cannibale m/f.
cannibalism n cannibalismo m.
canny adj cauto.
cannon n cannone m.
cannonball n palla f di canone.
canoe n canoa f.
canon n canone m.
cononize vt canonizzare.

canopy n baldacchino m.
cant n discorsi mpl ipocriti.
cantankerous adj irascibile.
canteen n mensa f.
canter n piccolo galoppo m.
cantilever n mensola f.
canton n cantone m.
canvas n tela f.
canvass vt fare un giro elettorale.
canvasser n propagandista m/f.
canyon n canyon m.
cap n berretto m; * vt tappare; superare.
capability n capacità f.
capable adj capace.
capacity n capacità f.
cape n capo m; cappa f; mantello m.
caper n cappero m; scherzetto m; * vt saltellare.
capillary adj capillare.
capital n lettera maiuscola; capitale f; capitale m.
capitalism n capitalismo m.
capitalist n capitalista m/f.
capitalize vt capitalizzare; * vi **to ~ on** trarre vantaggio da.
capital punishment n pena f capitale.
capitulate vi capitolare.
caprice n capriccio m.
capricious adj capriccioso.
Capricorn n Capricorno.
capsize vt ribaltare; * vi ribaltarsi.
capsule n capsula f.
captain n capitano m.
caption n sottotitolo m.
captivate vt affascinare.
captive adj, n prigioniero m.
captivity n prigionia f; cattività f.
captor n rapitore m.
capture n cattura f.
car n macchina f, automobile f.
carafe n caraffa f.
caramel n caramello m.

carat n carato m.
caravan n roulotte f.
caraway n (bot) cumino m.
carbohydrate n carboidrato m.
carbolic acid n acido m fenico.
carbon n carbonio m.
carbonated adj gassato.
carbonize vt carbonizzare.
carbon paper n carta f carbone.
carbuncle n foruncolo m.
carburettor n carburatore m.
carcass n carcassa f.
carcinogenic adj cancerogeno.
card n biglietto m; tessera f; carta f.
cardboard n cartone m.
card game n gioco m di carte.
cardiac adj cardiaco.
cardinal adj cardinale; * n cardinale m.
card table n tavolo m da carte.
care n preoccupazione f; attenzione f; * vi interessarsi; **I don't ~** non mi importa.
career n carriera f.
carefree n spensierato m.
careful adj attento; accurato; prudente.
careless adj distratto; negligente.
carelessness n disattenzione f.
caress n carezza f; * vt carezzare.
caretaker n portinaio m.
car-ferry n nave f traghetto.
cargo n carico m.
carhire n autonoleggio m.
caricature n caricatura f; * vt fare una caricatura di.
caries n carie f.
carnage n carneficina f.
carnal adj carnale.
carnation n garofano m.
carnival n carnevale m.
carniverous adj carnivoro.
carol n canto m di Natale.
carouse vi fare baldoria.

carousel n giostra f.

carp n carpa f.

carpenter n falegname m.

carpentry n falegnameria f.

carpet n tappeto m; moquette f.

carriage n carrozza f; vagone m; portamento m.

carriage-free adj franco di porto.

carriageway n carreggiata f.

carrier n corriere m; (med) portatore; portaerei f; sacchetto m.

carrier pigeon n piccione m viaggiatore.

carrion n carogna f.

carrot n carota f.

carry vt portare; tenere; riportare; approvare; **to ~ on** portare avanti; continuare; * vi trasmettersi.

carrycot n culla f trasportabile.

carry-on n casino m.

carsick n mal m d'auto.

cart n carretto m.

carte blanche n carta f bianca.

cartel n cartello m.

Carthusian n certosino m.

cartilage n cartilagine f.

cartography n cartografia f.

carton n cartone m.

cartoon n vignetta f; cartone m animato.

cartoonist n vignettista m/f.

cartridge n cartuccia f.

carve vt tagliere; incidere; scolpire.

carving n intaglio m.

carving knife n trinciante m.

car wash n lavaggio m auto.

cascade n cascata f.

case n valigia f; custodia f; astuccio m; cassa f; (gram, med) caso m; **in ~** caso mai.

cash n soldi mpl; **in ~** in contanti; * vt incassare.

cash dispenser n sportello m automatico.

cashew n anacardio m.

cashier n cassiere m.

cashmere n cachemire m.

casing n rivestimento m.

casino n casinò m.

cask n barile m.

casket n scrigno m.

casserole n casseruola f.

cassette n cassetta f.

cassette recorder n registratore m a cassette.

cassock n tonaca f.

cast vt gettare; lanciare; affidare; * n gesso m; cast m; stampo m; strabismo m.

castanets n nacchere fpl.

castaway n naufrago m.

caste n casta f.

caster n rotella f.

caster sugar n zucchero m semolato.

castigate vt castigare.

casting vote n voto m decisivo.

cast iron n ghisa f.

castle n castello m.

castor oil n olio m di ricino.

castrate vt castrare.

castration n castrazione f.

casual adj casuale; informale; saltuario; indifferente.

casualty n vittima f.

cat n gatto m.

cataclysm n cataclisma m.

catacombs npl catacombe fpl.

catalogue n catalogo m.

catalyst n catalizzatore m.

catamaran n catamarano m.

catapult n fionda f.

cataract n cataratta f.

catarrh n catarro m.

catastrophe n catastrofe f.

catcall n fischio m.

catch vt afferrare; prendere; sorprendere; sentire; **to ~ cold** prendere freddo; * vi **to ~ fire** prendere fuoco; * n

tranello *m*; gancio *m*; retata *f*.
catching *adj* contagioso.
catch phrase *n* frase *f* di moda.
catchment area *n* (*school*) zona *f* di competenza.
catchword *n* richiamo *m*.
catchy *adj* orecchiabile.
catechism *n* catechismo *m*.
categorical *adj* categorico.
categorize *vt* classificare.
category *n* categoria *f*.
cater *vi* provvedere a.
caterpillar *n* bruco *m*.
catgut *n* corda *f* di minugia.
cathedral *n* cattedrale *f*; duomo *m*.
cathode *adj* catodo; ~ **ray tube** tubo a raggi catodici.
catholic *adj* cattolico; ampio.
Catholicism *n* cattolicesimo *m*.
cat's eye *n* catarifrangente *m*.
cattle *n* bestiame *m*.
caucus *n* comitato *m* elettorale.
cauldron *n* calderone *m*.
cauliflower *n* cavolfiore *m*.
cause *n* causa *f*; motivo *m*; * *vt* causare.
causeway *n* strada *f* rialzata.
caustic *adj* caustico.
cauterize *vt* cauterizzare.
caution *n* attenzione; prudenza *f*; * *vt* ammonire.
cautionary *adj* ammonitorio.
cautious *adj* cauto; prudente.
cavalier *n* cavaliere *m*; * *adj* brusco.
cavalry *n* cavalleria *f*.
cave *n* brocca *f*; caverna *f*.
caveat *n* ammonimento *m*.
cavern *n* caverna *f*.
cavernous *adj* incavato.
caviar *n* caviale *m*.
cavity *n* cavità *f*.
cavort *vt* saltellare.
cease *vt, vi* cessare.
ceasefire *n* cessate il fuoco *m*.
ceaseless *adj* incessante.

cedar *n* cedro *m*.
cede *vt* cedere.
cedilla *n* cediglia *f*.
ceiling *n* soffitto *m*.
celebrate *vt* festeggiare.
celebration *n* celebrazione *f*.
celebrity *n* celebrità *f*.
celery *n* sedano *m*.
celestial *adj* celestiale.
celibacy *n* celibato *m*.
celibate *adj* celibe (*man*); nubile (*woman*).
cell *n* cella *f*.
cellar *n* cantina *f*.
cello *n* violoncello *m*.
cellophane *n* cellofan *m*.
cellular *adj* cellulare.
celluloide *n* celluloide *f*.
cellulose *n* cellulosa *f*.
cement *n* cemento *m*; * *vt* cementare.
cemetery *n* cimitero *m*.
cenotaph *n* cenotafio *m*.
censor *n* censore *m*; * *vt* censurare.
censorious *adj* censorio.
censorship *n* censura *f*.
censure *n* censura *f*; * *vt* censurare.
census *n* censimento *m*.
cent *n* centesimo *m*.
centenarian *n* centenario *m*.
centenary *n* centenario *m*.
centennial *adj* centennale.
centigrade *n* centigrado *m*.
centilitre *n* centilitro *m*.
centimetre *n* centimetro *m*.
centipede *n* millepiedi *m*.
central *adj* centrale.
centralize *vt* centralizzare.
centrifugal *adj* centrifugo.
centrifuge *n* centrifuga *f*.
centurian *n* centurione *m*.
century *n* secolo *m*.
ceramic *adj* di ceramica; ~**s** *npl* ceramica *f*.
cereal *n* cereale *m*.
cerebral *adj* cerebrale.

ceremonial *adj* formale; * *n* rito *m*.

ceremonious *adj* formale.

ceremony *n* cerimonia *f*.

certain *adj* certo; sicuro.

certainty *n* certezza *f*.

certificate *n* certificato *m*.

certification *n* attestazione *f*.

certify *vt* certificare; attestare.

cervical *adj* cervicale; * *n* ~ smear Pap-test *m*.

cervix *n* collo *m* dell'utero.

cessation *n* cessazione *f*.

cesspit *n* pozzo *m* nero.

chafe *vt* sfregare.

chaff *n* foraggio *m*; pula *f*.

chaffinch *n* fringuello *m*.

chagrin *n* dispiacere *m*.

chain *n* catena *f*; * *vt* incatenare.

chain reaction *n* reazione *f* a catena.

chair *n* sedia *f*, poltrona *f*; * *vt* presiedere.

chairman *n* presidente *m*.

chalice *n* calice *m*.

chalk *n* gesso *m*.

challenge *n* sfida *f*; * *vt* sfidare.

challenger *n* sfidante *m/f*.

challenging *adj* provocatorio; stimolante.

chamber *n* camera *f*.

chambermaid *n* cameriera *f*.

chameleon *n* camaleonte *m*.

chamois leather *n* pelle *f* di camoscio.

champagne *n* champagne *m*.

champion *n* campione *m*; * *vt* difendere.

championship *n* campionato *m*.

chance *n* caso *m*; occasione *f*; probabilità *f*; rischio *m*; * *vt* rischiare.

chancellor *n* cancelliere *m*.

chandelier *n* lampadario *m*.

change *vt* cambiare; trasformare; * *vi* mutare; * *n* cambia-

mento *m*; resto *m*; spiccioli *mpl*.

changeable *adj* variabile.

changing *adj* mutevole.

channel *n* canale *m*; * *vt* scavare.

chant *n* canto *m*; * *vt* cantare.

chaos *n* caos *m*.

chaotic *adj* caotico.

chap *n* screpolatura *f*; (*fam*) tizio *m*.

chapel *n* cappella *f*.

chaperone *n* accompagnatore *m*.

chaplain *n* cappellano *m*.

chapter *n* capitolo *m*.

char *vt* carbonizzare.

character *n* carattere *m*; personaggio *m*.

characteristic *adj* caratteristico.

characterization *n* caratterizzazione *f*.

characterize *vt* caratterizzare.

charade *n* sciarada *f*.

charcoal *n* carbone *m*, carboncino *m*.

charge *vt* accusare; (*mil*) attaccare; far pagare; * *n* imputazione *f*; (*mil*) carica *f*; tariffa *f*.

chargé d'affaires *n* incaricato *m* d'affari.

charger *n* caricabatteria *m*.

charisma *n* carisma *m*.

charitable *adj* filantropico; caritatevole.

charity *n* carità *f*; beneficenza *f*.

charlatan *n* ciarlatano *m*.

charm *n* fascino *m*; incanto *m*; * *vt* affascinare.

charming *adj* delizioso.

chart *n* tabella; * *vt* tracciare.

charter *n* carta *f*; statuto *m*; noleggio *m*; * *vt* noleggiare.

charter flight *n* volo *m* charter.

chartered accountant *n* commercialista m/f.

chase vt inseguire; * n inseguimento m; caccia f.

chasm n crepaccio m.

chassis n telaio m.

chaste adj casto.

chasten vt castigare.

chastise vt punire.

chastity n castità f.

chat vi chiacchierare; * n chiacchierata f.

chatter vi chiacchierare; * n chiacchiere fpl.

chatterbox n chiacchierone m.

chatty adj ciarliero.

chauffeur n autista m.

chauvinism n maschilismo m; sciovinismo m.

chauvinist n maschilista m; sciovinista m/f.

cheap adj a buon prezzo.

cheapen vt screditarsi.

cheat vt imbrogliare; * n imbroglione m.

check vt verificare; controllare; * n limitazione f; controllo m; (chess) scacco m.

checkmate n scacco m matto.

checkout n cassa f.

checkpoint n posto m di blocco.

checkup n visita f di controllo.

cheek n guancia f; (fam) faccia f tosta.

cheekbone n zigomo m.

cheer n grido m di incoraggiamento.

cheerful adj allegro.

cheese n formaggio m.

cheeseboard n piatto m per il formaggio.

cheesecloth n tela f indiana.

cheetah n ghepardo m.

chef n chef m.

chemical adj chimico; * n prodotto m chimico.

chemist n chimico m; farmacista m/f.

chemistry n chimica f.

cheque n assegno m.

cheque-book n libretto m degli assegni.

chequered adj a quadretti; **a ~ career** una carriera movimentata.

cherish vt nutrire; avere caro.

cheroot n sigaro m spuntato.

cherry n ciliegia f.

cherrytree n ciliegio m.

cherub n cherubino m.

chess n scacchi mpl.

chessboard n scacchiera f.

chessman n pezzo m degli scacchi.

chest n petto m; baule m; **~ of drawers** cassettone m.

chestnut n castagna f; adj castano.

chestnut tree n castagno m.

chew vt masticare.

chewing gum n chewing-gum m.

chic adj chic.

chick n pulcino m.

chicken n pollo m.

chickenpox n varicella f.

chickpea n cece m.

chicory n cicoria f.

chief adj principale; * n capo m.

chiffon n chiffon m.

chilblain n gelone m.

child n bambino m; **~bearing age** in età feconda.

childhood n infanzia f.

childish adj infantile.

childless adj senza figli.

childlike adj ingenuo.

children npl bambini mpl.

chill adj freddo; * n freddo; * vt mettere in fresco.

chilly adj fresco.

chime n rintocco m; * vi suonare.

chimney n camino m.

chimpanzee n scimpanzé m.

chin n mento m.

china(ware) *n* porcellana *f*.

chink *n* fessura *f*; * *vt* tintinnare.

chip *vt* scheggiare; * *n* frammento *m*; patatina *f* fritta; scheggiatura *f*.

chipboard *n* agglomerato *m*.

chiropodist *n* callista *m/f*.

chirp *vi* cinguettare; * *n* cinguettio *m*;.

chisel *n* scalpello *m*.

chivalrous *adj* cavalleresco.

chivalry *n* cavalleria *f*.

chives *npl* erba *f* cipollina.

chlorinate *vt* clorare.

chlorine *n* cloro *m*.

chloroform *n* cloroformio *m*.

chlorophyll *n* clorofilla *f*.

chock-full *adj* pieno zeppo.

chocolate *n* cioccolato *m*.

choice *n* scelta *f*; * *adj* di prima scelta.

choir *n* coro *m*.

choke *vt* soffocare; * *n* aria *f*.

choker *n* collana *f* a girocollo.

cholera *n* colera *m*.

cholesterol *n* colesterolo *m*.

choose *vt* scegliere.

choosey *adj* schizzinoso.

chop *vt* tagliare; spaccare; * *n* colpo *m* secco; costoletta *f*.

chopper *n* mannaia *f*; elicottero *m*.

chopping board *n* tagliere *m*.

chopsticks *npl* bastoncini *mpl*.

choral *adj* corale.

chord *n* corda *f*.

chore *n* faccenda *f*.

choreographer *n* coreografo *m*.

choreography *n* coreografia *f*.

chorister *n* corista *m/f*.

chorus *n* coro *m*; ritornello *m*.

Christ *n* Cristo *m*.

christen *vt* battezzare.

Christendom *n* cristianità *f*.

christening *n* battesimo *m*.

Christian *adj*, *n* cristiano *m*.

Christianity *n* cristianesimo *m*.

Christmas *n* Natale *m*.

Christmas card *n* biglietto *m* di Natale.

Christmas Eve *n* vigilia *f* di Natale.

chromatic *adj* cromatico.

chrome *n* metallo *m* cromato.

chronic *adj* cronico.

chronicle *n* cronaca *f*.

chronological *adj* cronologico.

chronology *n* cronologia *f*.

chronometer *n* cronometro *m*.

chubby *adj* paffuto.

chuck *vt* gettare.

chuckle *vi* ridacchiare.

chuffed *adj* tutto contento.

chug *vi* sbuffare.

chum *n* amicone *m*.

chunk *n* bel pezzo *m*.

church *n* chiesa *f*.

churchgoer *n* fedele *m/f*.

churchyard *n* cimitero *m*.

churlish *adj* sgarbato.

churn *n* zangola *f*; * *vt* agitare.

chute *n* scivolo *m*.

chutney *n* salsa *f* indiana.

cicada *n* cicala *f*.

cider *n* sidro *m*.

cigar *n* sigaro *m*.

cigarette *n* sigaretta *f*.

cigarette case *n* portasigarette *m*.

cigarette end *n* mozzicone *m*.

cigarette holder *n* bocchino *m*.

cigarette lighter *n* accendino *m*.

cinch *n* una cosa *f* sicura.

cinder *n* tizzone *m*.

cinecamera *n* cinepresa *f*.

cinema *n* cinema *m*.

cinnamon *n* cannella *f*.

cipher *n* codice *m*.

circle *n* cerchio *m*; * *vt* accerchiare.

circuit *n* giro *m*; circuito *m*.

circuitous *adj* tortuoso.

circular *adj* circolare; * *n* circolare *f*.

circulate *vi* circolare.

circulation *n* circolazione *f*.

circumcise *vt* circoncidere.

circumcision *n* circoncisione *f*.

circumference *n* circonferenza *f*.

circumflex *n* accento *m* circonflesso.

circumlocution *n* circonlocuzione *f*.

circumscribe *vt* circoscrivere.

circumspect *adj* circospetto.

circumstance *n* circostanza *f*.

circumstantial *adj* circostanziato.

circumvent *vt* aggirare.

circus *n* circo *m*.

cirrhosis *n* cirrosi *f*.

cissy *n* femminuccia *f*.

cistern *n* serbatoio *m*.

citadel *n* cittadella *f*.

cite *vt* citare.

citizen *n* cittadino *m*.

citric *adj* citrico.

citrus *n* agrume *m*.

city *n* città *f*.

civic *adj* civico.

civil *adj* civile.

civil defence *n* protezione *f* civile.

civil engineer *n* ingegnere *m* civile.

civilian *n* (*mil*) borghese *m*.

civility *n* gentilezza *f*.

civilization *n* civiltà *f*.

civilize *vt* civilizzare.

civil law *n* diritto *m* civile.

civil war *n* guerra *f* civile.

clad *adj* vestito.

claim *vt* rivendicare; pretendere; * *n* pretesa *f*; affermazione *f*.

claimant *n* (*law*) citante *m/f*; pretendente *m/f*.

clairvoyant *n* chiaroveggente *m/f*.

clam *n* vongola *f*.

clamber *vi* arrampicarsi.

clammy *adj* appiccicoso.

clamour *n* clamore *m*; * *vi* chiedere a gran voce.

clamp *n* morsetto *m*; * *vt* stringere; * *vi* **to ~ down (on)** riprimere.

clan *n* clan *m*.

clandestine *adj* clandestino.

clang *n* rumore *m* metallico.

clanger *n* gaffe *f*.

clap *vt* applaudire; * *n* battimano *m*.

clapping *n* applauso *m*.

claptrap *n* sciocchezze *fpl*.

claret *n* chiaretto *m*.

clarification *n* chiarificazione *f*.

clarify *vt* chiarire.

clarinet *n* clarinetto *m*.

clarity *n* chiarezza *f*.

clash *vi* scontrarsi; * *n* conflitto *m*; scontro *m*.

clasp *n* gancio *m*; * *vt* afferrare.

class *n* tipo *m*; categoria *f*; classe *f*; * *vt* definire.

class conscious *adj* classista.

classic(al) *adj* classico.

classification *n* classificazione *f*.

classified *adj* riservato.

classified advertisements *n* annunci *mpl* economici.

classify *vt* classificare.

classmate *n* compagno *m* di classe.

classroom *n* aula *f*.

classy *adj* chic.

clatter *vi* sferragliare; * *n* tintinnio *m*.

clause *n* proposizione *f*; clausola *f*.

claustrophobia *n* claustrofobia *f*.

claustrophobic *adj* claustrofobico.

claw *n* unghia *f*; artiglio *m*; * *vt* graffiare; **to ~ to pieces** dilaniare.

```
            JOLLY'S BOOKS
             PO BOX 132
        LYNDONVILLE, VT  05851


TIME  5:26 PM    DATE 06/27/97
TERM# 00332425   MER# 000161202853990
TRAN TYPE SALE
#4512109116475
EXP DATE 11/97    CARD TYPE VISA
TICKET # 000199
AUTH CODE 072564   SEQ #    001


TOTAL                        $8.30



SIGN X_____


   I AGREE TO PAY ABOVE TOTAL AMOUNT
   ACCORDING TO CARD ISSUER AGGREEMENT
```

clay n argilla f.

clean adj pulito; corretto m; * vt
 pulire.

cleaning n pulizia f.

cleanliness n pulizia f.

cleanness n pulizia f.

cleanse vt pulire.

cleanser n latte m detergente.

clean-shaven adj senza barba.

clear adj chiaro; trasparente;
 nitido; sgombro; * vt liberare;
 sgombrare; superare; (law)
 discolpare; liquidare.

clearance n sdoganamento m;
 autorizzazione f; sgombro m.

clear-cut adj ben definito.

clearing n radura f.

clearly adv chiaramente.

cleavage n scolatura f.

cleaver n mannaia f.

clef n chiave f.

cleft n crepa f.

clemency n clemenza f.

clement adj clemente.

clench vt stringere.

clergy n clero m.

clergyman n sacerdote m; pastore m; ministro m.

clerical adj (rel) clericale; (com)
 d'ufficio.

clerk n impiegato m.

clever adj intelligente.

cleverness n intelligenza f.

cliché n frase f fatta.

click vi scattare; * n scatto m.

client n cliente m/f.

clientele n clientela f.

cliff n scogliera f.

climate n clima m.

climatic adj climatico.

climax n culmine m; orgasmo m.

climb vt, vi salire; arrampicarsi; * n salita f; scalata f.

climber n alpinista m/f.

climbing n alpinismo m.

clinch vt concludere.

cling vi aggrapparsi.

clinic n clinica f.

clink vi tintinnare; * n tintinnio m.

clip n (cin) sequenza f; fermaglio m; moletta f; * vt tosare;
 ritagliare.

clipboard n fermabloc m.

clipper n clipper m.

clippers npl tagliaunghie m;
 tosasiepi m.

clipping n ritaglio m.

clique n cricca n.

cloak n cappa f; mantella f.

cloakroom n guardaroba m.

clock n orologio m.

clockwise adv in senso orario.

clockwork adj a molla.

clod n zolla f.

clog n zoccolo m; * vt intasare.

cloister n chiostro m.

close vt chiudere; * adv vicino;
 * adj vicino; intimo; approfondito; fitto; afoso; * n fine f;
 chiusura f.

closed adj chiuso.

closed-circuit n circuito m
 chiuso.

close-down n chiusura f; fine f
 delle trasmissioni.

closely adv strettamente.

closeness n vicinanza f.

close-up n primo m piano.

closing adj conclusivo; finale.

closure n chiusura f.

clot n grumo m; * vi coagularsi.

cloth n tessuto m, stoffa f.

clothe vt vestire.

clothes npl vestiti mpl.

clothes basket n cesto m per il
 bucato.

clotheshorse n stendibiancheria m.

clothesline n corda f del bucato.

clothes peg n moletta f.

clothing n abbigliamento m.

cloud n nuvola f; nube f; * vt intorbidire.

cloudburst n acquazzone m.

cloud-cuckoo-land *n* mondo *m* dei sogni.

cloudy *adj* nuvoloso; coperto.

clout *n* ceffone *m*; influenza *f*; * *vt* colpire.

clove *n* chiodo *m* di garofano; ~ **of garlic** spicchio *m* d'aglio.

clover *n* trifoglio *m*.

clown *n* pagliaccio *m*.

club *n* randello *m*; mazza *f*; bastone *m*; circolo *m*; club *m*; (*cards*) fiori *mpl*.

clubhouse *n* circolo *m*.

clue *n* indicazione *f*; indizio *m*.

clump *n* ciuffo *m*.

clumsy *adj* goffo.

cluster *n* grappolo *m*; gruppo *m*.

clutch *n* frizione *f*; * *vt* tenere stretto.

clutter *n* disordine *m*; * *vt* ingombrare.

coach *n* corriera *f*; pullman *m*; carrozza *f*; allenatore *m*; * *vt* allenare.

coagulate *vt* coagulare.

coal *n* carbone *m*.

coalesce *vi* unirsi.

coalfield *n* bacino *m* carbonifero.

coalition *n* coalizione *f*.

coalman *n* carbonaio *m*.

coalmine *n* miniera *f* di carbone.

coalminer *n* minatore *m*.

coarse *adj* ruvido; volgare.

coast *n* costa *f*; litorale *m*; * *vt* andare in folle.

coastal *adj* costiero.

coaster *n* sottobicchiere *m*.

coastguard *n* guardacoste *m*.

coastline *n* litorale *m*.

coat *n* capotto *m*; mano *f*; * *vt* ricoprire.

coathanger *n* gruccia *f*.

coax *vt* convincere.

cobalt *n* cobalto *m*.

cobble *n* ciottolo *m*.

cobbler *n* calzolaio *m*.

cobra *n* cobra *m*.

cobweb *n* ragnatela *f*.

cocaine *n* cocaina *f*.

cock *n* gallo *m*; rubinetto *m*.

cock-a-doodle-doo *n* chicchirichì *mpl*.

cock-and-bull story *n* frottola *f*.

cockatoo *n* cacatoa *m*.

cockerel *n* galletto *m*.

cockle *n* cardio *m*.

cockpit *n* cabina *f* di pilotaggio.

cockroach *n* scarafaggio *m*.

cocktail *n* cocktail *m*.

cock-up *n* pasticcio *m*.

cocky *adj* impertinente.

cocoa *n* cacao *m*.

coconut *n* noce *f* di cocco.

cocoon *n* bozzolo *m*.

cod *n* merluzzo *m*.

code *n* codice *m*; * *vt* cifrare.

codeine *n* codeina *f*.

codicil *n* codicillo *m*.

cod-liver oil *n* olio *m* di fegato di merluzzo.

coerce *vt* costringere.

coefficient *n* coefficiente *m*.

coercion *n* forza *f*.

coexist *vi* coesistere.

coexistence *n* coesistenza *f*.

coffee *n* caffè *m*.

coffee break *n* pausa *f* per il caffè.

coffee pot *n* caffettiera *f*.

coffee table *n* tavolino *m*.

coffin *n* barra *f*.

cog *n* dente *m*.

cogent *adj* convincente.

cogitate *vi* meditare.

cognac *n* cognac *m*.

cognate *adj* (*ling*) affine.

cognition *n* cognizione *f*.

cohabit *vi* coabitare.

coherence *n* coerenza *f*.

coherent *adj* coerente.

cohesion *n* coesione *f*.

cohesive *adj* unificante.

coil *n* rotolo *m*; bobina *f*; spirale

f; * *vt* avvolgere; * *vi* attorcigliarsi.

coin *n* moneta *f.*

coincide *vi* coincidere.

coincidence *n* coincidenza *f.*

coke *n* carbone *m* coke.

colander *n* colapasta *m.*

cold *adj* freddo; indifferente; * *n*
freddo *m;* raffreddore *m;.*

cold-blooded *adj* spietato.

cold sore *n* herpes *m.*

coleslaw *n* insalata *f* di cavolo
bianco.

colic *n* colica *f.*

collaborate *vt* collaborare.

collaboration *n* collaborazione
f.

collaborator *n* collaboratore *m.*

collapse *n* crollo *m;* collasso *m;*
* *vi* crollare.

collapsible *adj* pieghevole.

collar *n* collo *m.*

collarbone *n* clavicola *f.*

collate *vt* collazionare.

collateral *n* (*fin*) garanzia *f.*

colleague *n* collega *m/f.*

collect *vt* raccogliere; * *vi* radunarsi.

collection *n* raccolta *f.*

collective *adj, n* collettivo *m;.*

collector *n* esattore *m;* collezionista *m/f.*

college *n* college *m;* collegio *m;*
istituto *m* superiore.

collide *vi* scontrarsi.

collie *n* collie *m.*

colliery *n* miniera *f* di carbone.

collision *n* scontro *m.*

colloquial *adj* familiare.

colloquialism *n* espressione *f*
familiare.

collusion *n* collusione *f.*

colon *n* (*med*) colon *m;* (*gram*)
due punti *mpl.*

colonel *n* colonnello *m.*

colonial *adj* coloniale.

colonist *n* colonizzatore *m.*

colonize *vt* colonizzare.

colony *n* colonia *f.*

colossal *adj* colossale.

colour *n* colore *m;* ~s bandiera
f; * *vt* colorare; tingere.

colour-blind *adj* daltonico.

colourful *adj* dai colori vivaci.

colouring *n* colorazione *f.*

colourless *adj* incolore.

colt *n* puledro *m.*

column *n* colonna *f.*

columnist *n* giornalista *m/f.*

coma *n* coma *m.*

comatose *adj* comatoso.

comb *n* pettine *m;* * *vt* pettinare.

combat *n* lotta *f;* combattimento *m;* * *vt* combattere.

combatant *n* combattente *m/f.*

combination *n* combinazione *f.*

combine *vt* combinare.

combustible *adj* combustibile.

combustion *n* combustione *f.*

come *vi* venire; **to ~ apart** andare in pezzi; **to ~ round** venire; **to ~ in** entrare; **to ~ off**
staccarsi.

comedian *n* comico *m.*

comedienne *n* attrice *f* comica.

comedown *n* delusione *f.*

comedy *n* commedia *f.*

comet *n* cometa *f.*

comfort *n* consolazione *f;* conforto *m;* * *vt* confortare.

comfortable *adj* comodo.

comic(al) *adj* comico; buffo.

coming *adj* prossimo; futuro;
* *n* avvento *m.*

comma *n* virgola *f.*

command *vt* comandare; disporre di; * *n* ordine *m;* commando *m.*

commandeer *vt* requisire.

commander *n* capo *m.*

commandment *n* comandamento *m.*

commando *n* commando *m.*

commemorate *vt* commemorare.

commemoration n commemorazione f.

commence vt cominciare.

commencement n inizio m.

commend vt lodare.

commendable adj lodevole.

commendation n encomio m.

commensurate adj proporzionato.

comment n commento m; osservazione f.

commentary n commento m; telecronaca f.

commentate vt commentare.

commentator n telecronista m/f.

commerce n commercio m.

commercial adj commerciale; * n pubblicità f.

commiserate vt partecipare al dolore di.

commiseration n commiserazione f.

commisariat n commissariato m.

commission n commissione f; * vt commissionare; incaricare.

commissionaire n portiere m in livrea.

commissioner n delegato m; (police) questore m.

commit vt commettere.

commitment n impegno m.

committee n comitato m.

commodity n prodotto m.

common adj comune; * n parco comunale.

commoner n semplice cittadino m.

common law n diritto m comune.

commonly adv comunemente.

commonplace adj banale.

common sense n buon senso m.

commotion n trambusto m.

communal adj in comune.

commune vt comunicare.

communicate vt comunicare.

communication n comunicazione f.

communicative adj loquace.

communion n comunione f.

communiqué n bollettino m.

communism n comunismo m.

communist n comunista m/f.

community n comunità f.

community centre n centro m civico rionale.

commute vt commutare; * vi fare il pendolare.

compact adj compatto; * n portacipria m.

companion n compagno m.

companionship n cameratismo m.

company n compagnia f; società f.

comparable adj simile.

comparative adj relativo; (gram) comparativo.

compare vt paragonare.

comparison n paragone m.

compartment n scompartimento m.

compass n bussola f; compasso m.

compassion n compassione f.

compassionate adj compassionevole.

compatible adj compatibile.

compatriot n compatriota m.

compel vt costringere.

compelling adj impellente.

compensate vt compensare.

compensation n compenso m; indennità f.

compére n presentatore m.

compete vt competere.

competence n competenza f.

competent adj competente.

competition n concorrenza f; concorso m; gara f.

competitive adj agonistico; concorrenziale.

competitor n concorrente m/f.
compilation n compilazione f.
compile vt compilare.
complacency n compiacimento m.
complacent adj compiaciuto.
complain vi lamentarsi.
complaint n lamentela f.
complement n complemento m.
complementary adj complementare.
complete adj completo; * vt completare.
completion n completamento m.
complex adj complesso.
complexion n carnagione f.
complexity n complessità f.
compliance n conformità f.
compliant adj compiacente.
complicate vt complicare.
complication n complicazione f.
complicity n complicità.
compliment n complimento m; * vi complimentarsi.
complimentary adj lusinghiero; in omaggio.
comply vi attenersi a.
component adj, n componente m.
compose vt comporre.
composed adj composto.
composer n compositore m.
composite adj composito.
composition n composizione f.
compositor n compositore m.
compost n concime m.
composure n calma f.
compound vt peggiorare; * n composto m; (gram) parola f composta; recinto m; * adj composto.
comprehend vt capire, comprendere.
comprehensible adj comprensibile.
comprehension n comprensione f.
comprehensive adj esauriente; globale.
compress vt comprimere; * n compressa f.
comprise vt comprendere.
compromise n compromesso m.
compulsion n costrizione f; desiderio m incontrollabile.
compulsive adj incontrollabile.
compulsory adj obbligatorio.
compunction n scrupolo m.
computable adj calcolabile.
computation n calcolo m.
compute vt calcolare.
computer n elaboratore m; computer m.
computer programming n programmazione f.
computer science n informatica f.
comrade n compagno m.
con vt (fam) indurre con raggiri.
concave adj concavo.
conceal vt nascondere.
concede vt ammettere.
conceit n vanità f.
conceited adj vanitoso.
conceivable adj concepibile.
conceive vt concepire.
concentrate vt concentrare.
concentration n concentrazione f.
concentration camp n campo m di concentramento.
concentric adj concentrico.
concept n concetto m.
conception n concepimento m.
concern vt riguardare; * n preoccupazione f; impresa f.
concerning prep riguardo a.
concert n concerto m.
concerto n concerto m.
concession n concessione f.
conciliate vt conciliare.
conciliation n conciliazione f.
conciliatory adj conciliatorio.

concise *adj* conciso.

conclude *vt, vi* concludere.

conclusion *n* conclusione *f*.

conclusive *adj* conclusivo.

concoct *vt* mettere insieme; inventare.

concoction *n* miscuglio *m*.

concomitant *adj* concomitante.

concord *n* armonia *f*; accordo *m*.

concordance *n* concordanza *f*.

concourse *n* atrio *m*.

concrete *n* calcestruzzo *m*; * *adj* concreto; di calcestruzzo *m*; * *vt* rivestire di calcestruzzo.

concubine *n* concubina *f*.

concur *vi* coincidere.

concurrent *adj* simultaneo.

concussion *n* commozione *f* cerebrale.

condemn *vt* condannare.

condemnation *n* condanna *f*.

condensation *n* condensazione *f*.

condense *vt* condensare.

condescend *vi* accondiscendere; degnarsi.

condescending *adj* condiscendente.

condiment *n* condimento *m*.

condition *vt* condizionare; * *n* condizione *f*.

conditional *adj* condizionale.

coditioner *n* balsamo *m*.

condolences *npl* condoglianze *fpl*.

condom *n* preservativo *m*.

condone *vt* perdonare.

conducive *vi* favorire.

conduct *vt* condurre; (*mus*) dirigere; * *n* condotta *f*.

conduction *n* conduzione *f*.

conductivity *n* conduttività *f*.

conductor *n* (*mus*) direttore; (*elect*) conduttore *m*.

conduit *n* conduttura *f*.

cone *n* cono *m*; pigna *f*.

confectioner *n* pasticciere *m*.

confectionery *n* dolciumi *mpl*.

confederacy *n* confederazione *f*.

confederate *adj* confederato; * *vi* confederarsi.

confer *vt* conferire; * *vi* consultarsi.

conference *n* convegno *m*.

confess *vt* confessare.

confession *n* confessione *f*.

confessional *n* confessionale *m*.

confessor *n* confessore *m*.

confetti *n* coriandoli *mpl*.

confidant *n* confidente *m*.

confide *vt* confidare.

confidence *n* fiducia *f*.

confidence trick *n* truffa *f*.

confident *adj* sicuro.

confidential *adj* riservato.

configuration *n* configurazione *f*.

confine *vt* rinchiudere; limitare.

confinement *n* reclusione *f*; parto *m*.

confirm *vt* confermare; (*rel*) cresimare.

confirmation *n* conferma *f*; (*rel*) cresima *f*.

confirmed *adj* inveterato.

confiscate *vt* confiscare.

confiscation *n* confisca *f*.

conflagration *n* conflagrazione *f*.

conflict *n* conflitto *m*.

conflicting *adj* contraddittorio.

confluence *n* confluenza *f*.

conform *vi* conformarsi.

conformity *n* conformità *f*.

confound *vt* sconcertare.

confront *vt* affrontare.

confrontation *n* scontro *m*.

confuse *vt* confondere.

confused *adj* confuso.

confusing *adj* sconcertante.

confusion n confusione f.
congeal vi rapprendersi.
congenial adj simpatico.
congenital adj congenito.
congested adj congestionato.
congestion n congestione f.
conglomerate n conglomerato m.
congratulate vt congratularsi con.
congratulations npl congratulazioni fpl.
congregate vi radunarsi.
congregation n congregazione f.
congress n congresso m.
congruity n congruità f.
congruous adj congruo.
conical adj conico.
conifer n conifera f.
coniferous adj (bot) conifero.
conjecture n congettura f; * vt, vi congetturare.
conjugal adj coniugale.
conjugate vt coniugare.
conjugation n coniugazione f.
conjunction n congiunzione f.
conjuncture n congiuntura f.
conjure vi rievocare; fare giochi di prestigio.
conjurer n prestigiatore m.
conker n castagna f d'ippocastano.
con man n truffatore m.
connect vt collegare.
connection n collegamento m.
connivance n connivenza f.
connive vi essere connivente in.
connoisseur n intenditore m.
conquer vt conquistare.
conqueror n conquistatore m.
conquest n conquista f.
conscience n coscienza f.
conscientious adj coscienzioso.
conscious adj cosciente.
consciousness n conoscenza f.

conscript n coscritto m; * vt arruolare.
conscription n arruolamento m.
consecrate vt consacrare.
consecration n consacrazione f.
consecutive adj consecutivo.
consensus n consenso m.
consent n benestare m; * vi acconsentire a.
consequence n conseguenza f.
consequent adj conseguente; * adv ~ly di conseguenza; quindi.
conservation n conservazione f.
conservationist n ambientalista m/f.
conservative adj, n conservatore m.
conservatory n serra f; (mus) conservatore m.
conserve vt conservare.
consider vt considerare.
considerable adj considerevole.
considerate adj premuroso.
consideration n considerazione f.
considering conj visto che; * adv tutto sommato.
consign vt consegnare.
consignment n partita f.
consist vi consistere.
consistency n consistenza f.
consistent adj coerente; * adv ~ly costantemente.
consolation n consolazione f.
console vt consolare; * n quadro m di comando.
consolidate vt consolidare.
consolidation n consolidazione f.
consommé n brodo m ristretto.
consonant n (gram) consonante f.
consort n consorte m/f; * vt frequentare.

consortium n consorzio m.

conspicuous adj cospicuo.

conspiracy n congiura f.

conspirator n cospiratore m.

conspire vi congiurare.

constable n (Brit) agente m/f di polizia.

constabulary n (Brit) corpo m di polizia.

constancy n costanza f.

constant adj continuo; costante.

constellation n costellazione f.

consternation n costernazione f.

constipated adj stitico.

constipation n stitichezza f.

constituency n collegio m elettorale.

const.tuent n componente m; elettore m.

constitute vt costituire.

constitution n costituzione f.

constitutional adj costituzionale.

constrain vt costringere.

constraint n costrizione f.

constrict vt costringere.

constriction n costrizione f.

construct vt costruire.

construction n costruzione f.

construe vt interpretare.

consul n console m.

consular adj consolare.

consulate n consolato m.

consult vt consultare.

consultancy n consulenza f.

consultant n consulente m/f; (med) specialista m/f.

consultation n consultazione f.

consume vt consumare.

consumer n consumatore m.

consumer goods npl beni mpl di consumo.

consumer society n società f consumista.

consummate vt consumare; * adj consumato.

consummation n consumazione f.

consumption n consumo m; (med) consunzione f.

contact n contatto; * vt contattare.

contact lenses npl lenti fpl a contatto.

contagious adj contagioso.

contain vt contenere.

container n contenitore m.

contaminate vt contaminare.

contamination n contaminazione f.

contemplate vt contemplare.

contemplation n contemplazione f.

contemplative adj contemplativo.

contemporaneous adj contemporaneo.

contemporary adj contemporaneo.

contempt n disprezzo m.

contemptible adj spregevole.

contemptuous adj sprezzante.

contend vt sostenere; * vi contendere.

contender n contendente m/f.

content adj contento; * n contentezza; * vt soddisfare.

contents npl contenuto m.

contended adj contento.

contention n tesi f; disputa f; **bone of ~** pomo della discordia.

contentious adj contenzioso.

contentment n contentezza f.

contest vt contestare; * n gara f; concorso m.

contestant n concorrente m/f.

context n contesto m.

contiguous adj contiguo.

continent n continente m.

continental adj continentale.

contingency n contingenza f.

contingent adj, n contingente m; * vi dipendere da.

continual adj continuo.
continuance n continuazione f.
continuation n continuazione f.
continue vt, vi continuare.
continuity n continuità f.
continuous adj continuo.
contort vt contorcere.
contortion n contorsione f.
contour n contorno m.
contraband adj, n contrabbando m.
contraception n contraccezione f.
contraceptive adj, n anticoncezionale f.
contract vt contrarre; * n contratto m.
contraction n contrazione f.
contractor n appaltatore m.
contractual adj contrattuale.
contradict vt contraddire.
contradiction n contraddizione f.
contradictory adj contraddittorio.
contraption n aggeggio m.
contrary adj contrario; * n contrario m.
contrast n contrasto; * vi contrastare.
contrasting adj contrastante.
contravene vt contravvenire.
contravention n contravvenzione f.
contretemps n contrattempo m.
contribute vt, vi contribuire.
contribution n offerta f; contribuzione f.
contributor n donatore m; collaboratore m.
contributory adj che contribuisce.
contrite adj mortificato.
contrition n mortificazione f.
contrivance n congegno m.
contrive vt escogitare.

control n controllo m, comando m; * vt controllare, frenare, dominare.
control room n (TV/radio) sala f di reggia; (mil) sala f di comando.
control tower n torre f di controllo.
controversial adj controverso.
controversy n controversia f.
contusion n contusione f.
conundrum n indovinello m.
conurbation n conurbazione f.
convalesce vi fare la convalescenza.
convalescence n convalescenza f.
convalescent adj, n convalescente m/f.
convection n convezione f.
convector n convettore m.
convene vt convocare; * vi convenire.
convenience n comodità f.
convenient adj comodo.
convent n convento m.
convention n convenzione f.
conventional adj convenzionale.
converge vi convergere.
convergence n convergenza f.
convergent adj convergente.
conversant adj versato.
conversation n conversazione f.
converse vi conversare; * n inverso m; * adj apposto.
conversely adv al contrario.
conversion n (rel) conversione f; ristrutturazione f.
convert vt convertire; ristrutturare; * n convertito m.
converter n convertitore m.
convertible adj convertibile; * n auto f decappottabile.
convex adj convesso.
convey vt trasportare; trasmettere.

conveyance n trasporto m.

conveyancer n notaio m.

conveyer belt n nastro m trasportatore.

convict vt riconoscere colpevole; * n carcerato m.

conviction n condanna f; convinzione f.

convince vt convincere.

convincing adj convincente.

convivial adj gioviale.

convoke vt convocare.

convoluted adj attorcigliato.

convoy n convoglio m.

convulse vt sconvolgere.

convulsion n convulsione f.

convulsive adj convulso.

coo vi tubare.

cook n cuoco m; * vt cuocere; (fam) falsificare.

cooker n cucina f.

cookery n cucina f.

cookerybook n ricettario m.

cool adj fresco; calmo; distaccato; * n frescura f; calma f; * vt raffreddare.

coolant n refrigerante m.

cooler n ghiacciaia f.

cooling adj rinfrescante.

coop n stia f.

cooperate vi cooperare.

cooperation n cooperazione f.

cooperative adj cooperativo; * n cooperativa f.

coopt vt cooptare.

coordinate vt coordinare; * n coordinata f.

coordination n coordinazione f.

coordinator n coordinatore m.

cop n poliziotto m.

cope vi cavarsela.

copier n copiatrice f.

copilot n secondo pilota m.

copious adj abbondante.

copper n rame m.

coppice n boschetto m.

copulate vi accoppiarsi.

copulation n accoppiamento m.

copy n copia; * vt imitare, copiare.

copyright n diritti mpl d'autore.

coral n corallo m.

coral reef n corallino m.

cord n corda f.

cordial adj, n cordiale m.

corduroy n velluto m a coste.

core n torsolo m; nucleo m.

co-respondent n correo m.

coriander n coriandolo m.

cork n sughero m; * vt tappare.

corkscrew n cavatappi m.

corn n grano m; frumento m; callo m.

corn on the cob n pannocchia f.

cornea n cornea f.

corner n angolo m; * vt intrappolare.

cornerstone n pietra f angolare.

cornet n (mus) cornetta f; cornetto m.

cornfield n campo m di grano.

cornflakes npl fiochi mpl di granturco.

cornflour n farina f finissima di granturco.

cornice n cornicione m.

corny adj banale.

corollary n corollario m.

coronary adj coronario; * n trombosi f coronarica.

coronation n incoronazione f.

coroner n coroner m.

coronet n coroncina f.

corporal adj corporale; * n caporale m.

corporate adj collettivo.

corporation n società f; ente m.

corporeal adj corporale.

corps n corpo m.

corpse n cadavere m.

corpulence n corpulenza f.

corpulent adj corpulento.

corpuscle n globulo m.

correct vt correggere; * adj corretto.

correction n correzione f.

corrective adj correttivo.

correlate vt correlare.

correlation n correlazione f.

correlative adj correlativo.

correspond vi corrispondere.

correspondence n corrispondenza f.

correspondent n corrispondente m/f.

corridor n corridoio m.

corroborate vt corroborare.

corroboration n corroborazione f.

corrode vt corrodere.

corrosion n corrosione f.

corrosive adj corrosivo.

corrugated adj ondulato; * n ~ iron lamiera f ondulata.

corrupt vt corrompere; * adj corrotto.

corruptible adj corruttibile.

corruption n corruzione f.

corset n busto m.

cortège n corteo m.

cortisone n cortisone m.

cosh n manganello m.

cosmetic adj, n cosmetico m.

cosmic adj cosmico.

cosmonaut n cosmonauta m/f.

cosmopolitan adj, n cosmopolita m/f.

cosmos n cosmo m.

cosset vt coccolare.

cost n costo; * vt costare.

costly adj costoso.

costume n costume m.

cosy adj accogliente.

cot n lettino m.

cottage n cottage m.

cotton n cotone m.

cotton mill n cotonificio m.

cotton wool n cotone m idrofilo.

couch n divano m.

couchette n cuccetta f.

cough n tosse f; * vi tossire.

council n consiglio m.

councillor n consigliere m.

counsel n consiglio; avvocato m.

counsellor n consigliere m.

count vt, vi contare; * n conteggio m; conte m.

countdown n conto m alla rovescia.

countenance n volto m; * vt ammettere.

counter n banco m; * vt rispondere.

counteract vt neutralizzare.

counterbalance vt controbilanciare; * n contrappeso m.

counterfeit vt contraffare; * adj contraffatto.

counterfoil n matrice f.

countermand vt annullare.

counterpane n copriletto m.

counterpart n equivalente m/f.

counterproductive adj controproducente.

countersign vt controfirmare.

countess n contessa f.

countless adj innumerevole.

country n paese m; campagna f.

country house n villa f.

countryman n campagnolo m.

countryside n campagna f.

county n contea f.

coup n colpo m.

coupé n coupé m.

couple n coppia f; * vt associare.

couplet n distico m.

coupon n buono m.

courage n coraggio m.

courageous adj coraggioso.

courgette n zucchino m.

courier n corriere m.

course n corso m; rotta f; portata f; of ~ naturalmente; * vi scorrere.

court n corte f; * vt corteggiare.

courteous adj cortese.

courtesy n cortesia f.

courtier n corteggiano m.

court-martial *n* corte *f* marziale.

courtroom *n* sala *f* d'udienza.

courtship *n* corteggiamento *m*.

courtyard *n* cortile *m*.

cousin *n* cugino *m*.

cove *n* baia *f*.

covenant *n* accordo *m*; * *vi* impegnarsi.

cover *n* copertura; coperchio *m*; riparo *m*; * *vt* coprire; nascondere.

coverage *n* (*press, TV, radio*) servizio *m*.

covering *n* copertura *f*.

covering letter *n* lettera *f* di accompagnamento.

covert *adj* nascosto.

cover-up *n* occultamento *m*.

covet *vt* concupire.

covetous *adj* avido.

cow *n* mucca *f*; vacca *f*; * *vt* intimidire.

coward *n* vigliacco *m*.

cowardice *n* vigliaccheria *f*.

cowardly *adj* vigliacco.

cowboy *n* cowboy *m*.

cower *vi* acquattarsi.

cowhide *n* pelle *f* di mucca.

cowl *n* cappuccio *n*.

cowshed *n* stalla *f*.

cowslip *n* primula *f*.

cox *n* timoniere *m*.

coy *adj* civettuolo.

crab *n* granchio *m*.

crab apple *n* mela *f* selvatica.

crack *n* crepa *f*; * *vt* incrinare; *vi* **to ~ down on** porre freno a.

cracker *n* petardo *m*; cracker *m*.

crackle *vi* scoppiettare; * *n* scoppiettio *m*.

crackling *n* cotenna *f* arrostita.

cradle *n* culla *f*.

craft *n* mestiere *m*; arte *f*.

craftiness *n* furberia *f*.

craftsman *n* artigiano *m*.

craftsmanship *n* maestria *f*.

crafty *adj* furbo.

crag *n* rupe *f*.

cram *vt* infilare; stipare; * *vi* affollarsi.

crammed *adj* stipato.

cramp *n* crampo *m*; * *vt* soffocare.

cramped *adj* angusto.

cranberry *n* bacca *f* del muschio.

crane *n* gru *f*.

crank *n* gomito *m*; eccentrico *m*.

crankshaft *n* albero *m* a gomiti.

crash *vt* avere un'incidente con; * *vi* precipitare; scontrarsi; * *n* fracasso *m*; incidente *m*.

crash helmet *n* casco *m*.

crash landing *n* atterraggio *m* forzato.

crass *adj* crasso.

crate *n* cassa *f*.

crater *n* cratere *m*.

cravat *n* foulard *m*.

crave *vt* desiderare disperatamente.

craving *n* voglia *f*.

crawl *vi* andare a gattone; procedere lentamente; adulare; * *n* passo *m* lento; stile *m* libero.

crayfish *n* gambero *m*.

crayon *n* pastello *m*.

craze *n* mania *f*.

crazy *adj* matto; folle.

creak *vi* scricchiolare; * *n* scricchiolio *m*.

cream *n* crema *f*; panna *f*; * *adj* color crema.

creamy *adj* cremoso.

crease *n* piega *f*; * *vt* sgualcire.

crease-resistant *adj* ingualcibile.

create *vt* creare.

creation *n* creazione *f*.

creative *adj* creativo.

creativity *n* creatività *f*.

creator n creatore m.

creature n creatura f.

crèche n asilo m nido.

credence n credenza f.

credentials npl credenziali fpl; referenze fpl.

credibility n credibilità f.

credible adj credibile.

credit n credito m; onore m; ~s (TV, etc) titoli mpl di testa/coda; * vt credere; accreditare.

creditable adj lodevole.

credit card n carta f di credito.

creditor n creditore m.

credulity n credulità f.

credulous adj credulo.

creed n credo m.

creek n insenatura f.

creep vi strisciare; andare furtivamente; * n tipo m viscido.

creeper n (bot) rampicante f.

creepy adj che fa rabbrividire.

creepy-crawly n bestiolina f.

cremate vt cremare.

cremation n cremazione f.

crematorium n crematorio m.

creosote n creosoto m.

crêpe n crespo m.

crescent n mezzaluna f; via f.

cress n crescione m.

crest n cresta f.

crestfallen adj abbattuto.

cretin n cretino m.

crevasse n crepaccio m.

crevice n fessura f.

crew n equipaggio m.

crib n culla f; mangiatoia f; * vt copiare.

crick n torcicollo m.

cricket n grillo m; cricket m.

crime n criminalità f; delitto m.

criminal adj, n criminale m/f.

crimson adj cremisi.

cringe vi farsi piccolo dalla paura.

crinkle vt spiegazzare.

cripple n zoppo m; mutilato m; * vt lasciare mutilato.

crisis n crisi f.

crisp adj croccante; fresco; conciso; * n patatina f.

criss-cross adj intrecciati.

criterion n criterio m.

critic n critico m.

critical adj critico.

criticism n critica f.

criticize vt criticare.

critique n assaggio m critico.

croak vi gracidare.

crochet n uncinetto m.

crockery n vasellame m.

crocodile n coccodrillo m.

crocus n croco m.

croft n piccola fattoria f.

croissant n cornetto m.

crony n amicone m.

crook n bastone m; pastorale m; (fam) ladro m.

crooked adj storto; disonesto.

crop n coltivazione f; raccolto m; (ornith) gozzo m; (riding) frustino m; * vt brucare; rapare.

croquet n croquet m.

croquette n crocchetta f.

cross n croce f; incrocio m; * adj seccato; * vt attraversare; sbarrare; incrociare.

crossbar n canna f.

crossbreed n incrocio m.

cross-country n campestre f.

cross-examine vt interrogare.

cross-eyed adj strabico.

crossfire n fuoco m incrociato.

crossing n traversata f; incrocio m; strisce fpl pedonali.

cross-purposes npl fraintendere.

cross-reference n rimando m.

crossroad n incrocio m.

cross-section n sezione f trasversale.

crossword n cruciverba m.

crotch n forcella f; (anat) inforcatura f; (garment) cavallo m.

crouch vi accovacciarsi.

croup n crup m.

crow n corvo m; cornacchia f; canto m; * vi cantare.

crowbar n piede m di porco.

crowd n folla f; * vt affollare.

crown n corona f; cima f; * vt incoronare.

crown prince n principe m ereditario.

crowning adj supremo.

crucial adj cruciale.

crucible n crogiolo m.

crucifix n crocefisso m.

crucifixion n crocifissione f.

crucify vt crocifiggere.

crude adj grezzo; grossolano.

crudity n volgarità f.

cruel adj crudele.

cruelty n crudeltà f.

cruet n ampolla f.

cruise n crociera f; * vi (taxi) girare in cerca di clienti.

cruiser n incrociatore m.

crumb n briciola f.

crumble vt sbriciolare; * vi sbriciolarsi.

crumple vt accartocciare.

crunch vt sgranocchiare; * vi scricchiolare; * n scricchiolio m.

crunchy adj croccante.

crusade n crociata f.

crusader n crociato m.

crush vt schiacciare; frantumare; * n ressa f; cotta f.

crust n crosta f;.

crustacean n crostaceo m.

crutch n stampella f.

crux n nodo m.

cry vi gridare; piangere; * vt gridare; * n grido m; pianto m.

crypt n cripta f.

cryptic adj enigmatico.

crystal n cristallo m.

crystal-clear adj cristallino.

crystallize vt cristallizzare; * vi cristallizzarsi.

cub n cucciolo m.

cube n cubo m.

cubic adj cubico.

cubicle n cabina f.

cuckoo n cucullo m.

cucumber n cetriolo m.

cud n ruminatura f; **to chew the ~** ruminare.

cuddle n abbraccio m; * vt coccolare.

cudgel n manganello m.

cue n stecca f.

cuff n schiaffo m; polsino m.

cul-de-sac n vicolo m cieco.

culinary adj culinario.

cull vt scegliere; selezionare e abbattere.

culminate vi culminare.

culmination n culmine m.

culottes npl gonna f pantalone.

culpability n colpevolezza f.

culpable adj colpevole.

culprit n colpevole m/f.

cult n culto m.

cultivate vt coltivare.

cultivation n coltivazione f.

cultural adj culturale.

culture n cultura f; (agric) coltura f.

cultured adj colto, raffinato.

cumbersome adj ingombrante.

cumin n cumino m.

cumulative adj cumulativo.

cunning adj furbo; * n furbizia f.

cup n tazza f.

cupboard n armadio m.

curable adj guaribile.

curate n curato m.

curator n conservatore m.

curb n freno m; * vt frenare.

curds npl latte m cagliato.

curdle vt far cagliare.

cure n cura f; guarigione m; * vt guarire; salare; conciare.

curfew n coprifuoco m.

curio n curiosità f.

curiosity n curiosità f.

curious adj curioso.

curl n ricciolo m; * vt arricciare.

curler n bigodino m.

curlew n chiurlo m.

curly adj riccio.

currant n uva f passa; ribes m.

currency n moneta f; valuta f estera.

current adj attuale; corrente; * n corrente f.

current affairs npl problemi mpl d'attualità.

currently adv attualmente.

curriculum vitae n curriculum vitae m.

curry n curry m.

curse vt maledire; * vi bestemmiare; * n maledizione f; flagello m; bestemmia f.

cursor n cursore m.

cursory adj frettoloso.

curt adj brusco.

curtail vt accorciare.

curtain n tenda f.

curtain rod n bastone m della tenda.

curtsy n inchino; * vi fare un inchino.

curvaceous adj formosa.

curvature n curvatura f.

curve vt curvare; * vi curvarsi; * n curva f.

cushion n cuscino m; * vt attutire.

custard n crema f pasticcera.

custodian n custode m/f.

custody n custodia f; detenzione f.

custom n costume m; consuetudine f; abitudine f; clientela f.

customary adj consueto.

customer n cliente m/f.

customs npl dogana f.

customs duty n tassa f doganale.

customs officer n doganiere m.

cut vt tagliare; ridurre; **to ~ a record** incidere; * vi tagliare; **to ~ teeth** spuntare; * adj reciso; **~ and dried** assodato; * n taglio m; incisione f; riduzione f.

cutback n taglio m; riduzione f.

cute adj carino.

cuticle n pellicina f.

cutlery n posate fpl.

cutlet n cotoletta f.

cut-rate adj a prezzo ridotto.

cut-throat n assassino m; * adj spietato.

cutting n talea f; ritaglio m; scavo m; * adj tagliente; pungente.

cuttlefish n seppia f.

cyanide n cianuro m.

cybernetics n cibernetica f.

cyclamen n ciclamino m.

cycle n bicicletta f; ciclo m; * vi andare in bicicletta.

cycling n ciclismo m.

cyclist ciclista m/f.

cyclone n ciclone m.

cygnet n giovane cigno m.

cylinder n cilindro m.

cylindric(al) adj cilindrico.

cymbal n cembalo m.

cynic(al) adj cinico; * n cinico m.

cynicism n cinismo m.

cypress n cipresso m.

cyst n cisti f.

czar n zar m.

czarina n zarina f.

D

dab n colpetto m; pennellata f; * vt tamponare.

dabble vt sguazzare; * vi dilettarsi.

dachshund n bassotto m.

dad(dy) n papà m, babbo m.

daddy-long-legs n zanzarone m.

daffodil n trombone m.

daft adj sciocco.

dagger n pugnale m.

dahlia n dalia f.

daily adj quotidiano; giornaliero; * n quotidiano m.

dainty adj minuto; delicato.

dairy n latteria f.

dairy farm n caseificio m.

dairy produce n latticini mpl.

dais n palco m.

daisy n margherita f.

daisy wheel n margherita f.

dale n valle f.

dally vi dilungarsi.

dam n diga f; * vt arginare.

damage n danno m.

damaging adj nocivo.

damask n damasco m.

dame n (nob) gentildonna f; (teat) vecchia signora f.

damn vt dannare; maledire; * interj accidenti!

damnable adj vergognoso.

damnation n dannazione f.

damning adj schiacciante.

damp adj umido; * n umidità f; * vt inumidire.

dampen vt inumidire.

dampness n umidità f.

damson n susina f.

dance n ballo m; danza f; * vt ballare; * vi danzare.

dance hall n sala f da ballo.

dancer n ballerino m.

dandelion n dente m di leone.

dandruff n forfora f.

dandy n dandy m.

danger n pericolo m.

dangerous adj pericoloso.

dangle vi dondolare.

dank adj freddo e umido.

dapper adj azzimato.

dappled adj pomellato.

dare vt sfidare; osare; * n sfida f.

daredevil n scavezzacollo m.

daring adj audace; * n audacia f.

dark adj scuro; buio; * n buio m; oscurità f.

darken vt oscurare.

dark glasses npl occhiali mpl da sole.

darkness n oscurità f.

darkroom n camera f oscura.

darling adj caro; * n tesoro m.

darn n rammendo m; * vt rammendare.

dart n dardo m; pince f; * vi lanciarsi.

dartboard n bersaglio m per freccette.

dash n goccino m; trattino m; corsa f; * vt scaraventare; abbattere.

dashboard n cruscotto m.

dashing adj affascinante.

data npl dati mpl.

database n database m.

data processing n elaborazione f dei dati.

date n data f; appuntamento m; dattero m; * vt datare; * vi risalire a.

dated adj antiquato.

dative n dativo m.

daub vt imbrattare.

daughter n figlia f.

daughter-in-law n nuora f.

daunting adj scoraggiante.

dawdle *vi* bighellonare.

dawn *n* alba *f*; * *vi* spuntare.

day *n* giorno *m*; giornata *f*; epoca *f*; **by ~** di giorno; **~ by ~** giorno per giorno.

daybreak *n* alba *f*.

daydream *vi* sognare ad occhi aperti.

daylight *n* luce *f* del giorno.

daytime *n* giorno *m*.

daze *vt* stordire; * *n* **in a ~** stordito.

dazed *adj* stordito.

dazzle *vt* abbagliare.

dazzling *adj* abbagliante.

deacon *n* diacono *m*.

dead *adj* morto; intorpidito; scarico; assoluto; **~ tired** stanco morto; **~ loss** caso disperato.

dead drunk *adj* ubriaco fradicio.

deaden *vt* attutire.

dead heat *n* vittoria *f* a pare merito.

deadline *n* scadenza *f*.

deadlock *n* punto *m* morto.

deadly *adj* mortale; micidiale.

deadpan *adj* impassibile.

deaf *adj* sordo.

deaf-and-dumb *adj* sordomuto.

deafen *vt* assordare.

deafening *adj* assordante.

deafness *n* sordità *f*.

deal *n* affare *m*; accordo *m*; legno *m* di abete; **I am a great ~ better** sto molto meglio; * *vi* **to ~ with** occuparsi di; affrontare; sbrigare; * *vt* dare le carte.

dealer *n* commerciante *m/f*.

dealings *npl* rapporti *mpl*.

dean *n* preside *m/f*.

dear *adj* caro; **oh ~!** mamma mia!.

dearth *n* scarsità *f*.

death *n* morte *f*.

deathbed *n* letto *m* di morte.

deathblow *n* colpo *m* di grazia.

death certificate *n* certificato *m* di morte.

deathly *adj* cadaverico.

death penalty *n* pena *f* di morte.

death throes *npl* agonia *f*.

death trap *n* trappola *f* mortale.

death warrant *n* mandato *m* di morte.

debacle *n* fuggi fuggi *m*.

debar *vt* escludere.

debase *vt* svilire.

debatable *adj* discutibile.

debate *n* dibattito *m*; * *vt* dibattere.

debauch *vt* corrompere.

debauched *adj* dissoluto.

debauchery *n* dissolutezza *f*.

debenture *n* obbligazione *f*.

debilitate *vt* debilitare.

debit *n* addebito; * *vt* addebitare.

debonair(e) *adj* gioviale e disinvolto.

debris *n* detriti *mpl*.

debt *n* debito *m*.

debtor *n* debitore *m*.

debunk *vt* demistificare.

debut *n* debutto *m*.

decade *n* decennio *m*.

decadence *n* decadenza *f*.

decadent *adj* decadente.

decaffeinated *adj* decaffeinato.

decant *vt* travasare.

decanter *n* caraffa *f*.

decapitate *vt* decapitare.

decapitation *n* decapitazione *f*.

decay *vi* putrefarsi; deteriorarsi; * *n* decomposizione *f*.

decease *n* decesso *m*.

deceased *adj* deceduto; * *n* defunto *m*.

deceit *n* inganno *m*.

deceitful *adj* falso.

deceive *vt* ingannare.

decelerate *vt* decelerare.

December *n* dicembre *m*.

decency *n* decenza *f*.

decent *adj* decente.

decentralization *n* decentramento *m*.

deception *n* inganno *m*.

deceptive *adj* ingannevole.

decibel *n* decibel *m*.

decide *vt* decidere.

decided *adj* deciso.

deciduous *adj* deciduo.

decimal *adj, n* decimale *m*.

decimate *vt* decimare.

decipher *vt* decifrare.

decision *n* decisione *f*.

decisive *adj* decisivo.

deck *n* coperta *f*; * *vt* decorare.

deckchair *n* sedia *f* a sdraio.

declaim *vi* declamare.

declamation *n* declamazione *f*.

declaration *n* dichiarazione *f*.

declare *vt* dichiarare.

declension *n* declinazione *f*.

decline *vt, vi* declinare; * *n* declino *m*.

declutch *vi* premere la frizione.

decode *vt* decodificare.

decompose *vt* decomporre.

decomposition *n* decomposizione *f*.

decompression *n* decompressione *f*.

dicongestant *adj* decongestionante.

decor *n* arredamento *m*.

decorate *vt* decorare.

decoration *n* decorazione *f*.

decorative *adj* decorativo.

decorator *n* decoratore *m*.

decorous *adj* decoroso.

decorum *n* decoro *m*.

decoy *n* uccello *m* da richiamo; tranello *m*.

decrease *vt, vi* diminuire; * *n* diminuzione *f*.

decree *n* decreto *m*; * *vt* decretare.

decrepit *adj* decrepito.

decry *vt* condannare.

dedicate *vt* dedicare.

dedication *n* dedizione *f*; dedica *f*.

deduce *vt* dedurre.

deduct *vt* dedurre.

deduction *n* deduzione *f*.

deed *n* azione *f*.

deem *vt* giudicare.

deep *adj* profondo.

deepen *vt* approfondire.

deep-freeze *n* congelatore *m*.

deer *n* cervo *m*.

deface *vt* deturpare.

defamation *n* diffamazione *f*.

default *n* mancanza *f*; contumacia *f*; * *vi* risultare inadempiente.

defaulter *n* moroso *m*.

defeat *n* sconfitta *f*; * *vt* sconfiggere.

defecate *vi* defecare.

defect *n* difetto *m*; * *vi* defezionare.

defection *n* defezione *f*.

defective *adj* difettoso.

defector *n* rifugiato *m* politico.

defence *n* difesa *f*.

defenceless *adj* indifeso.

defend *vt* difendere.

defendant *n* imputato *m*.

defensive *adj* difensivo.

defer *vt* rimandare.

deference *n* deferenza *f*.

deferential *adj* deferente.

defiance *n* sfida *f*.

defiant *adj* ribelle.

deficiency *n* mancanza *f*; insufficienza *f*.

deficient *adj* mancante.

deficit *n* deficit *m*.

defile *vt* deturpare; * *n* passo *m* stretto.

definable *adj* definibile.

define *vt* definire.

definite *adj* definitivo; **~ly** *adv* certamente.

definition *n* definizione *f*.

definitive *adj* definitivo.

deflate *vt* sgonfiare.

deflation *n* deflazione *f*.

deflect *vt* deviare.

deflower *vt* deflorare.

deform *vt* deformare.

deformity *n* deformità *f*.

defraud *vt* defraudare.

defray *vt* coprire.

defrost *vt* sbrinare.

deft *adj* abile.

defunct *adj* scomparso.

defuse *vt* disinnescare.

defy *vt* sfidare.

degenerate *vi* degenerare; * *adj*, *n* degenerato *m*.

degradation *n* degradazione *f*.

degrade *vt* degradare.

degrading *adj* degradante.

degree *n* grado *m*; laurea *f*.

dehydrate *vt* disidratare.

dehydrated *adj* disidratato.

deign *vt* degnarsi.

deity *n* divinità *f*.

dejected *adj* abbattuto.

dejection *n* abbattimento *m*.

delay *vt* rimandare; * *vi* ritardare; * *n* ritardo *m*.

delectable *adj* delizioso.

delegate *vt* delegare; * *n* delegato *m*.

delegation *n* delegazione *f*.

delete *vt* cancellare.

deliberate *vt* considerare; * *vi* deliberare; * *adj* premeditato; **~ly** * *adv* apposta.

deliberation *n* deliberazione *f*.

delicacy *n* delicatezza *f*; ghiottoneria *f*.

delicate *adj* delicato.

delicatessen *n* salumeria *f*.

delicious *adj* delizioso.

delight *n* delizia *f*; * *vt* riempire di gioia.

delighted *adj* contentissimo.

delightful *adj* delizioso.

delimit *vt* delimitare.

delineate *vt* delineare.

delineation *n* delineazione *f*.

delinquency *n* delinquenza *f*.

delinquent *n* delinquente; * *adj* delinquenziale.

delirious *adj* delirante.

delirium *n* delirio *m*.

deliver *vt* consegnare.

deliverance *n* liberazione *f*.

delivery *n* consegna *f*.

delta *n* delta *m*.

delude *vt* illudere.

deluge *n* diluvio *m*.

delusion *n* illusione *f*.

delve *vi* frugare.

demagogue *n* demagogo *m*.

demand *n* richiesta *f*; * *vt* esigere.

demanding *adj* esigente.

demarcation *n* demarcazione *f*.

demean *vt* umiliare.

demeanour *n* contegno *m*.

demented *adj* pazzo.

demise *n* decesso *m*.

demister *n* antiappannante *m*.

democracy *n* democrazia *f*.

democrat *n* democratico *m*.

democratic *adj* democratico.

demolish *vt* demolire.

demolition *n* demolizione *f*.

demon *n* demonio *m*.

demonstrable *adj* dimostrabile.

demonstrate *vt* manifestare; dimostrare.

demonstration *n* manifestazione *f*.

demonstrative *adj* espansivo.

demonstrator *n* manifestante *m/f*.

demoralize *vt* demoralizzare.

demote *vt* degradare.

demur *vi* sollevare obiezione.

demure *adj* contegnoso.

den *n* tana *f*, covo *m*.

denationalize *vt* snazionalizzare.

denial *n* rifiuto *m*; diniego *m*.

denier *n* denaro *m*.

denim *n* tessuto *m* jeans.

denomination *n* confessione *f*.

denominator *n* denominatore *m*.

denote *vt* denotare.

denounce *vt* denunciare.

dense *adj* denso.

density *n* densità *f*.

dent *n* ammaccatura *f*; * *vt* ammaccare.

dental *adj* dentistico.

dentist *n* dentista *m/f*.

dentistry *n* odontoiatria *f*.

dentures *npl* dentiera *f*.

denude *vt* denudare.

denunciation *n* denuncia *f*.

deny *vt* negare; smentire.

deodorant *n* deodorante *m*.

deodorize *vt* deodorare.

depart *vi* partire.

department *n* reparto *m*; sezione *f*.

department store *n* grande magazzino *m*.

departure *n* partenza *f*.

departure lounge *n* sala *f* d'attesa.

depend *vi* dipendere; ~ **on** contare su.

dependable *adj* affidabile.

dependant *n* persona *f* a carico.

dependence *n* dipendenza *f*.

dependent *adj*: **to be** ~ **on** dipendere da.

depict *vt* rappresentare.

deplete *vt* esaurire.

deplorable *adj* deplorevole.

deplore *vt* deplorare.

deploy *vt* schierare.

depopulate *vt* spopolare.

depopulation *n* spopolamento *m*.

deport *vt* deportare.

deportation *n* deportazione *f*.

deportment *n* portamento *m*.

deposit *vt* depositare; * *n* deposito *m*.

deposition *n* deposizione *f*.

depositor *n* depositante *m/f*.

depot *n* deposito *m*.

deprave *vt* depravare.

depraved *adj* depravato.

depravity *n* depravazione *f*.

deprecate *vt* deprecare.

depreciate *vi* deprezzarsi.

depreciation *n* deprezzamento *m*.

depredation *n* depredazione *f*.

depress *vt* deprimere.

depressed *adj* depresso.

depression *n* depressione *f*.

deprivation *n* privazione *f*.

deprive *vt* privare.

deprived *adj* bisognoso.

depth *n* profondità *f*.

deputation *n* deputazione *f*.

depute *vt* delegare.

deputize *vi* sostituire.

deputy *n* sostituto *m*.

derail *vt* far deragliare.

deranged *adj* sconvolto.

derelict *adj* fatiscente.

deride *vt* deridere.

derision *n* derisione *f*.

derisive *adj* beffardo.

derivation *n* derivazione *f*.

derivative *adj*, *n* derivato *m*.

derive *vt* derivare.

dermatitis *n* dermatite *f*.

dermatology *n* dermatologia *f*.

derogatory *adj* spregiativo.

derrick *n* derrick *m*.

descant *n* discanto *m*.

descend *vt* scendere.

descendant *n* discendente *m/f*.

descent *n* discesa *f*.

describe *vt* descrivere.

description *n* descrizione *f*.

descriptive *adj* descrittivo.

descry *vt* scorgere.

desecrate *vt* profanare.

desecration *n* profanazione *f*.

desert[1] *n* deserto; * *adj* desertico.

desert[2] *vt* abbandonare.

deserter *n* disertore *m*.

desertion *n* diserzione *f*.

deserve *vt* meritare.

deservedly *adv* meritatamente.

deserving *adj* meritevole.

desiccated *adj* essiccato.

design *vt* progettare; * *n* progetto *m*; disegno *m*.

designate *vt* designare.

designation *n* titolo *m*.

designer *n* disegnatore *m*.

desirable *adj* desiderabile.

desire *n* desiderio *m*; * *vt* desiderare.

desirous *adj* desideroso.

desist *vi* desistere.

desk *n* scrivania *f*.

desolate *adj* desolato.

desolation *n* desolazione *f*.

despair *n* disperazione *f*; * *vi*
disperare.

despairing *adj* disperato.

desperado *n* disperato *m*.

desperate *adj* disperato.

desperation *n* disperazione *f*.

despicable *adj* spregevole.

despise *vt* disprezzare.

despite *prep* malgrado.

despoil *vt* spogliare.

despondency *n* abbattimento *m*.

despondent *adj* abbattuto.

despot *n* despota *m*.

despotic *adj* dispotico.

despotism *n* dispotismo *m*.

dessert *n* dessert *m*.

destination *n* destinazione *f*.

destined *adj* destinato.

destiny *n* destino *m*.

destitute *adj* indigente.

destitution *n* indigenza *f*.

destroy *vt* distruggere.

destroyer *n* cacciatorpediniere
m.

destruction *n* distruzione *f*.

destructive *adj* distruttivo.

desultory *adj* sconnesso.

detach *vt* staccare.

detachable *adj* staccabile.

detached *adj* staccato; imparziale.

detachment *n* distacco *m*; distaccamento *m*.

detail *n* particolare *m*; dettaglio *m*; * *vt* dettagliare.

detain *vt* trattenere.

detect *vt* individuare.

detection *n* scoperta *f*.

detective *n* investigatore *m*.

detector *n* rivelatore *m*.

detente *n* distensione *f*.

detention *n* detenzione *f*.

deter *vt* dissuadere.

detergent *n* detersivo *m*.

deteriorate *vi* deteriorarsi.

deterioration *n* deterioramento *m*.

determination *n* determinazione *f*.

determine *vt* determinare.

determined *adj* risoluto.

deterrent *n* deterrente *m*.

detest *vt* detestare.

detestable *adj* detestabile.

detonate *vi* detonare.

detonation *n* detonazione *f*.

detonator *n* detonatore *m*.

detour *n* deviazione *f*.

detract *vi* sminuire.

detriment *n* detrimento *m*.

detrimental *adj* dannoso.

deuce *n* quaranta pari *m*.

devaluation *n* svalutazione *f*.

devastate *vt* devastare.

devastating *adj* devastatore.

devastation *n* devastazione *f*.

develop *vt* sviluppare.

development *n* sviluppo *m*.

deviate *vi* deviare.

deviation *n* deviazione *f*.

device *n* congegno *m*; dispositivo *m*.

devil n diavolo m.

devilish adj diabolico.

devious adj subdolo.

devise vt escogitare.

devoid adj; ~ **of** privo di.

devolution n decentramento m.

devolve vt devolvere.

devote vt dedicare.

devoted adj devoto.

devotee n appassionato m.

devotion n devozione f.

devour vt divorare.

devout adj devoto.

dew n rugiada f.

dewy-eyed adj con gli occhi languidi.

dexterity n destrezza f.

dexterous adj destro.

diabetes n diabete m.

diabetic adj, n diabetico m.

diabolic adj diabolico.

diadem n diadema m.

diagnose vt diagnosticare.

diagnosis n diagnosi f.

diagnostic adj diagnostico.

diagonal adj diagonale.

diagram n diagramma m.

dial n quadrante m.

dialect n dialetto m.

dialogue n dialogo m.

dialling code n prefisso m.

dialling tone n segnale m di libero.

dialysis n dialisi f.

diameter n diametro m.

diametric(al) adj diametrale.

diamond n diamante m.

diamond-cutter n diamantaio m.

diamonds npl quadri mpl.

diaphragm n diaframma m.

diarrhoea n diarrea f.

diary n diario m; agenda f.

dice npl dado m.

dictate vt, vi dettare.

dictation n dettatura f.

dictator n dittatore m.

dictatorial adj dittatoriale.

dictatorship n dittatura f.

diction n dizione f.

dictionary n vocabolario m.

didactic adj didattico.

die vi morire; **to ~ down** spegnersi; **to ~ out** scomparire.

die n dado m.

diehard n reazionario m.

diesel n gasolio m.

diet n dieta f; alimentazione f; * vi seguire una dieta.

dietary adj dietetico.

differ vi differire; discordare.

difference n differenza f.

different adj diverso.

differential adj, n differenziale m.

differentiate vt distinguere.

difficult adj difficile.

difficulty n difficoltà f.

diffidence n timidezza f.

diffident adj timido.

diffraction n diffrazione f.

diffuse vt diffondere; * adj diffuso.

diffusion n diffusione f.

dig vt vangare; scavare; * n gomitata f; scavo m.

digest vt digerire.

digestible adj digeribile.

digestion n digestione f.

digestive adj digestivo.

digger n scavatore m.

digit n cifra f.

digital adj digitale.

dignified adj dignitoso.

dignitary n dignitario m.

dignity n dignità f.

digress vi divagare.

digression n digressione f.

dilapidated adj scassato.

dilapidation n sfacelo m.

dilate vt dilatare.

dilemma n dilemma m.

diligence n diligenza f.

diligent adj diligente.

dill n aneto m.

dilly-dally *vi* gingillarsi.

dilute *vt* diluire.

dim *adj* fioco; * *vt* abbassare.

dimension *n* dimenzione *f.*

diminish *vt* diminuire.

diminished *adj* ridotto.

diminutive *adj* minuto.

dimly *adv* vagamente.

dimmer *n* regolatore *m* luminoso.

dimple *n* fossetta *f.*

din *n* chiasso *m.*

dine *vi* pranzare.

dinghy *n* gommone *m.*

dingy *adj* squallido.

dingo *n* dingo *m.*

dinner *n* cena *f.*

dinosaur *n* dinosauro *m.*

dint *n*; **by ~ of** a forza di.

diocese *n* diocesi *f.*

dioxide *n* biossido *m.*

dip *vt* immergere; * *vi* essere in pendenza; * *n* nuotatina *f*; (*culin*) salsetta *f*; cunetta *f.*

diphtheria *n* difterite *f.*

diphthong *n* dittongo *m.*

diploma *n* diploma *m.*

diplomacy *n* diplomazia *f.*

diplomat *n* diplomatico *m.*

diplomatic *adj* diplomatico.

dipsomania *n* dipsomania *f.*

dipstick *n* asta *f* dell'olio.

dire *adj* disastroso.

direct *adj* diretto; * *vt* dirigere a.

direction *n* direzione *f.*

directive *n* direttiva *f.*

directly *adj* direttamente.

director *n* dirigente *m/f.*

directory *n* elenco *m.*

dirge *n* canto *m* funebre.

dirt *n* sporco *m.*

dirtiness *n* sporcizia *f.*

dirty *adj* sporco.

disability *n* menomazione *f.*

disabled *adj* invalido.

disabuse *vt* disingannare.

disadvantage *n* svantaggio *m.*

disadvantageous *adj* svantaggioso.

disaffected *adj* disamorato.

disagree *vi* essere in disaccordo.

disagreeable *adj* spiacevole.

disagreement *n* discordanza *f.*

disallow *vt* respingere.

disappear *vi* scomparire.

disappearance *n* scomparsa *f.*

disappoint *vt* deludere.

disappointed *adj* deluso.

disappointing *adj* deludente.

disappointment *n* delusione *f.*

disapproval *n* disapprovazione *f.*

disapprove *vi* disapprovare.

disarm *vt* disarmare.

disarmament *n* disarmo *m.*

disarming *adj* disarmante.

disarray *n* disordine *m.*

disaster *n* disastro *m.*

disastrous *adj* disastroso.

disband *vt* sciogliere.

disbelief *n* incredulità *f.*

disbelieve *vt* non credere a.

disburse *vt* sborsare.

disc *n* disco *m.*

discard *vt* scartare.

discern *vt* discernere.

discernible *adj* percepibile.

discerning *adj* perspicace.

discernment *n* discernimento *m.*

discharge *vt* scaricare; licenziare; assolvere; * *n* scarica *f*; licenziamento *m*; secrezione *f.*

disciple *n* discepolo *m.*

disciplinary *adj* disciplinare.

discipline *n* disciplina *f*; * *vt* castigare; punire.

disclaim *vt* smentire.

disclaimer *n* smentita *f*; disconoscimento *m.*

disclose *vt* rivelare.

disclosure *n* rivelazione *f.*

disco *n* discoteca *f.*

discolour *vt* scolorire.

discolouration n scolorimento m.

discomfort n disaggio m.

disconcert vt sconcertare.

disconnect vt staccare.

disconsolate adj sconsolato.

discontent n scontentezza f; scontento m.

discontented adj scontento.

discontinue vt interrompere.

discord n disaccordo m.

discordant adj discordante.

discount n sconto; * vt non badare a.

discourage vt scoraggiare.

discouragement n scoraggiamento m.

discouraging adj scoraggiante.

discourse n discorso m.

discourteous adj scortese.

discourtesy n scortesia f.

discover vt scoprire.

discovery n scoperta f.

discredit vt screditare; * n discredito m.

discreditable adj disonorevole.

discreet adj discreto.

discrepancy n discrepanza f.

discrete adj separato.

discretion n discrezione f.

discretionary adj discrezionale.

discriminate vi distinguere; fare discriminazione tra.

discrimination n discriminazione f; discernimento m.

discursive adj discorsivo.

discus n disco m.

discuss vt discutere.

discussion n discussione f.

disdain vt sdegnare; * n disdegno m.

disdainful adj sdegnoso.

disease n malattia f.

diseased adj malato.

disembark vi sbarcare.

disembarkation n sbarco m.

disembodied adj disincarnato.

disenchant vt disincantare.

disenchanted adj disincantato.

disenchantment n disillusione f.

disengage vt disinnestare.

disentangle vt sbrogliare.

disfavour n disapprovazione f.

disfigure vt sfigurare.

disgorge vt riversare.

disgrace n vergogna f; disonore m; * vt disonorare.

disgraceful adj vergognoso.

disgruntled adj contrariato.

disguise vt travestire; mascherare; * n travestimento m.

disgust n disgusto m; * vt disgustare.

disgusting adj disgustoso.

dish n piatto m; pietanza f; * vt servire.

dishcloth n strofinaccio m.

dishearten vt scoraggiare.

dishevelled adj arruffato; tutto in disordine.

dishonest adj disonesto.

dishonesty n disonestà f.

dishonour n disonore m; * vt disonorare.

dishonourable adj disonorevole.

dishwasher n lavastoviglie f.

disillusion vt disingannare; * n disinganno m.

disincentive n: to act as a ~ to agire da freno su.

disinclination n riluttanza f.

disinclined adj poco propenso.

disinfect vt disinfettare.

disinfectant n disinfettante m.

disinherit vt diseredare.

disintegrate vi disintegrarsi.

disinterested adj disinteressato.

disjointed adj slegato.

disk n dischetto m.

dislike n antipatia f; * vt non piacere.

dislocate *vt* slogare.

dislocation *n* slogatura *f*.

dislodge *vt* rimuovere.

disloyal *adj* sleale.

disloyalty *n* slealtà *f*.

dismal *adj* tetro.

dismantle *vt* smontare.

dismay *n* sgomento; * *vt* sgomentare.

dismember *vt* smembrare.

dismiss *vt* congedare; licenziare.

dismissal *n* licenziamento *m*; congedo *m*:

dismount *vi* smontare; scendere.

disobedience *n* disubbidienza *f*.

disobedient *adj* disubbidiente.

disobey *vt* disubbidire.

disorder *n* disordine *m*.

disorderly *avv* disordinato.

disorganization *n* disorganizzazione *f*.

disorganized *adj* disorganizzato.

disorientated *adj* disorientato.

disown *vt* rinnegare.

disparage *vt* denigrare.

disparaging *adj* denigratorio.

disparity *n* disparità *f*.

dispassionate *adj* spassionato.

dispatch *vt* spedire; inviare; * *n* invio *m*, spedizione *f*.

dispel *vt* dissipare.

dispensary *n* farmacia *f*; dispensario *m*.

dispensation *n* dispensa *f*.

dispersal *n* dispersione *f*.

dispense *vt* dispensare.

disperse *vt* disperdere.

dispirited *adj* demoralizzato.

displace *vt* spostare.

display *vt* esporre; * *n* mostra *f*; esposizione *f*:

displeased *adj* dispiacere.

displeasure *n* dispiacere *m*.

disposable *adj* disponibile; monouso.

disposal *n* eliminazione *f*.

dispose *vt* disporre.

disposed *adj* disposto.

disposition *n* indole *f*.

dispossess *vt* spossessare.

disproportionate *adj* sproporzionato.

disprove *vt* confutare.

dispute *n* disputa *f*; controversia *f*; * *vt* contestare; disputarsi.

disqualify *vt* squalificare.

disquiet *n* inquietudine *f*.

disquieting *adj* inquietante.

disquisition *n* disquisizione *f*.

disregard *vt* ignorare; trascurare; * *n* indifferenza *f*.

disreputable *adj* poco raccomandabile.

disrespect *n* mancanza di rispetto *m*.

disrespectful *adj* irriverente.

disrobe *vt* svestire.

disrupt *vt* scombussolare.

disruption *n* scombussolamento *m*.

dissatisfaction *n* insoddisfazione *f*.

dissatisfied *adj* insoddisfatto.

dissect *vt* sezionare.

dissection *n* sezionamento *m*.

disseminate *vt* disseminare.

dissension *n* dissenso *m*.

dissent *vi* dissentire; * *n* dissenso *m*.

dissenter *n* dissidente *m/f*.

dissertation *n* dissertazione *f*.

dissident *n* dissidente *m/f*.

dissimilar *adj* dissimile.

dissimilarity *n* dissomiglianza *f*.

dissimulation *n* dissimulazione *f*.

dissipate *vt* dissipare.

dissipation *n* dissipazione *f*.

dissociate *vt* dissociare.

dissolute *adj* dissoluto.

dissolution *n* scioglimento *m*.

dissolve *vt* sciogliere; dissolvere.

dissonance *n* dissonanza *f*.

dissuade *vt* dissuadere.

distance *n* distanza *f*; lontananza *f*; * *vt* distanziare.

distant *adj* lontano; distante.

distaste *n* ripugnanza *f*.

distasteful *adj* sgradevole.

distemper *n* tempera *f*; cimurro *m*.

distend *vt* gonfiare.

distil *vt* distillare.

distillation *n* distillazione *f*.

distillery *n* distilleria *f*.

distinct *adj* distinto.

distinction *n* distinzione *f*.

distinctive *adj* particolare.

distinguish *vt* distinguere.

distinguished *adj* eminente; noto

distort *vt* distorcere.

distortion *n* distorsione *f*.

distract *vt* distrarre.

distracted *adj* distratto.

distraction *n* distrazione *f*.

distraught *adj* stravolto.

distress *n* angoscia *f*; pericolo *m*; * *vt* addolorare.

distressing *adj* penoso.

distribute *vt* distribuire.

distribution *n* distribuzione *f*.

distributor *n* distributore *m*.

district *n* distretto *m*.

distrust *n* diffidenza *f*; * *vt* diffidare.

distrustful *adj* diffidente.

disturb *vt* disturbare.

disturbance *n* disturbo *m*; disordini *mpl*.

disturbed *adj* turbato.

disturbing *adj* preoccupante.

disuse *n* disuso *m*.

disused *adj* abbandonato.

ditch *n* fosso *m*; * *vt* mollare.

dither *vi* agitarsi; esitare.

ditto *adv* idem.

ditty *n* canzoncina *f*.

diuretic *adj* diuretico.

dive *vi* tuffarsi; lanciarsi; * *n* tuffo *m*; bettola *f*.

diver *n* tuffatore *m*.

diverge *vi* divergere.

divergence *n* divergenza *f*.

divergent *adj* divergente.

diverse *adj* svariato.

diversify *vt* diversificare.

diversion *n* deviazione *f*.

diversity *n* diversità *f*.

divert *vt* deviare; distrarre.

divest *vt* spogliare.

divide *vt* dividere.

divided *adj* diviso.

dividend *n* dividendo *m*.

dividers *npl* compasso *m* a punte fisse.

divine *adj* divino; * *vt* intuire.

diving *n* tuffi *mpl*.

diving board *n* trampolino *m*.

divinity *n* divinità *f*.

divisible *adj* divisibile.

division *n* divisione *f*.

divisor *n* divisore *m*.

divorce *n* divorzio *m*; * *vi* divorziare.

divorced *adj* divorziato.

divulge *vt* divulgare.

dizziness *n* capogiro *m*; vertigine *f*.

dizzy *adj* vertiginoso.

do *vt* fare; compiere; eseguire.

docile *adj* docile.

dock *n* (*bot*) romice *m*; bacino *m*; darsena *f*; banco degli imputati; * *vt* mozzare; decurtare; * *vi* entrare in bacino.

docker *n* portuale *m*.

docket *n* cartellino *m*.

dockyard *n* cantiere *m* navale.

doctor *n* dottore *m*; medico *m*; * *vt* adulterare.

doctrinal *adj* dottrinale.

doctrine *n* dottrina *f*.

document *n* documento *m*; * *vt* documentare.

documentary *adj*, *n* documentario *m*.

dodge vt schivare; * n trucchetto m.

doe n femmina di daino.

dog n cane m; * vt perseguitare.

dogged adj tenace.

dogma n dogma m.

dogmatic adj dogmatico.

dogsbody n factotum m.

doings npl imprese fpl.

do-it-yourself n bricolage m, fai da te m.

dole n sussidio m di disoccupazione.

doleful adj afflitto.

doll n bambola f.

dollar n dollaro m.

dolphin n delfino m.

domain n dominio m.

dome n cupola f.

domestic adj domestico.

domesticate vt addomesticare.

domesticity n amore m per la casa.

domicile n domicilio m.

dominant adj dominante.

dominate vt, vi dominare.

domination n dominazione f.

domineer vt spadroneggiare.

domineering adj despotico.

dominion n dominio m.

domino n domino m.

don n docente m universitario; * vi mettersi.

donate vt donare.

donation n donazione f.

done adj fatto; cotto.

donkey n asino m.

donor n donatore m.

doodle vi scarabocchiare.

doom n destino m.

door n porta f.

doorbell n campanello m.

doorman n portiere m.

doormat n zerbino m.

doorstep n soglia f.

doorway n vano m della porta.

dope n droga f.

dopey adj inebetito.

dormant adj latente.

dormer window n abbaino m.

dormitory n dormitorio m.

dormouse n ghiro m.

dosage n posologia f.

dose n dose f; * vt somministrare; dosare.

dossier n dossier m.

dot n punto m; * vi punteggiare.

dote vi stravedere.

double adj doppio; * vt raddoppiare; * n sosia m.

double bed n letto m matrimoniale.

double-breasted adj a doppio petto.

double chin n doppio mento m.

double-dealing n doppio gioco m.

double-edged adj a doppio taglio.

double entry n (fin) partita f doppia.

double room n camera f matrimoniale, camera f doppia.

doubly adj doppiamente.

doubt n dubbio m; * vt dubitare di.

doubtful adj indeciso.

doubtless adv indubbiamente.

dough n impasto m.

doughnut n ciambella f.

douse vt infradiciare.

dove n colombo m.

dovecot n colombaia f.

dowdy adj scialbo.

down n piume fpl; * adv giù; * adj upside ~ capovolto.

downcast adj avvilito.

downfall n rovina f.

downhearted adj depresso.

downhill adv in discesa.

down payment n anticipo m.

downpour n acquazzone m.

downright adj categorico.

downstairs adj al piano inferiore.

down-to-earth adj pratico.

downwards *adv* in giù.

dowry *n* dote *f*.

doze *vi* sonnecchiare; * *n* pisolino *m*.

dozen *n* dozzina *f*.

dozy *adj* sonnolento.

drab *adj* grigio; monotono.

draft *n* abbozzo *m*; tratta *f*; * *vt* abbozzare.

drag *n* resistenza *f*; scocciatura *f*; * *vt* trascinare; dragare; * *adj* in ~ travestito.

dragon *n* drago *m*.

dragonfly *n* libellula *f*.

drain *vt* prosciugare; drenare; svuotare; * *n* scarico *m*; drenaggio *m*.

drainage *n* drenaggio *m*; prosciugamento *m*.

draining board *n* piano *m* del lavello.

drainpipe *n* tubo *m* di scarico.

drake *n* maschio dell'anatra.

dram *n* bicchierino *m*.

drama *n* dramma *m*.

dramatic *adj* drammatico.

dramatist *n* drammaturgo *m*.

dramatize *vt* drammatizzare.

drape *vt* drappeggiare.

draper *n* negoziante *m/f* di stoffe.

drastic *adj* drastico.

draught *n* spiffero *m*; sorsata *f*; * *adj* on ~ alla spina.

draughtsman *n* disegnatore *m* tecnico.

draw *vt* disegnare; tirare; attirare; pareggiare; estrarre; * *n* sorteggio *m*; lotteria *f*; estrazione *f*; pareggio *m*.

drawback *n* inconveniente *m*.

drawer *n* cassetto *m*.

drawing *n* disegno *m*.

drawing room *n* salotto *m*.

drawl *n* cadenza *f* strascicata; * *vt* strascicare.

dread *n* terrore *m*; * *vt* temere.

dreadful *adj* tremendo.

dream *n* sogno *m*; * *vt*, *vi* sognare.

dreamer *n* sognatore *m*.

dreamy *adj* di sogno.

dreary *adj* desolato.

dredge *n* draga *f*; * *vt* dragare.

dregs *npl* feccia *f*.

drench *vt* inzuppare.

dress *vt* vestire; condire; * *n* vestito *m*, abito *m*; abbigliamento *m*.

dresser *n* credenza *f*.

dressing *n* vestire *m*; (*med*) fasciatura *f*; (*culin*) condimento *m*.

dressing gown *n* vestaglia *f*.

dressing room *n* camerino *m*.

dressing table *n* toilette *f*.

dressmaker *n* sarto *m*.

dressy *adj* elegante.

dribble *n* bava *f*; (*sport*) dribbling *m*; * *vt* sbrodolare.

dried *adj* secco; essiccato.

drift *n* deriva *f*; tendenza *f*; cumulo *m*; * *vi* andare alla deriva; vagare.

drill *n* trapano *m*; perforatrice *f*; esercitazione *f*; * *vt* trapanare; esercitare.

drink *vt*, *vi* bere; * *n* bevanda *f*; bibita *f*.

drinkable *adj* potabile.

drinker *n* bevitore *m*.

drinking *n* bere *m*.

drip *vi* sgocciolare; * *n* goccia *f*; (*med*) fleboclisi *f*.

dripping *n* grasso *m* dell'arrosto.

drive *vt* spingere; guidare; azionare; * *n* giro *m* in macchina; viale *m*; grinta *f*; **sales** ~ campagna *f* di vendita; trasmissione *f*.

drivel *n* ciance *fpl*.

driver *n* guidatore *m*; autista *m/f*; conducente *m/f*.

driving *n* guida *f*.

driving licence *n* patente *m* di guida.

driving school n scuola f guida.

driving test n esame m per la patente.

drizzle vi piovigginare; * n pioggerella f.

droll adj bizzarro.

drone n fuco m; ronzio m; * vi ronzare.

drool vi sbavare.

droop vi chinarsi; appassire.

drop n goccia f; calo m; * vi lasciar cadere; abbandonare; piantare; calare.

droplet n gocciolina f.

drop-out n emarginato m.

dropper n contagocce m.

droppings npl escrementi mpl.

dross n avanzi mpl.

drought n siccità f.

drove n branco m.

drown vt, vi affogare, annegare.

drowsiness n sonnolenza f.

drowse vi sonnecchiare.

drowsy adj assonnato.

drudgery n sfacchinata f.

drug n medicina f; medicinale f; droga f; stupefacente; * vt drogare.

drug addict n tossicodipendente m/f.

drug pusher n spacciatore m.

drum n tamburo m; ~s batteria f; bidone m; timpano m; * vt, vi tamburellare.

drummer n batterista m/f.

drumstick n bacchetta f; coscia f di pollo.

drunk adj, n ubriaco m.

drunkard n ubriacone m.

drunken adj ubriaco.

drunkenness n ubriachezza f.

dry adj secco; asciutto; * vt seccare; essiccare; asciugare.

dry-clean vt lavare a secco.

dryness n secchezza f; aridità f.

dry rot n fungo m del legno.

dual adj doppio; duplice.

dual-purpose adj a doppio uso.

dub vt doppiare.

dubious adj dubbio; ambiguo.

duchess n duchessa f.

duck n anatra f; * vt immergere; * vi fare una schivata; accucciarsi.

duckling n anatroccolo m.

dud adj inservibile; * n arnese m inservibile.

due adj pagabile; dovuto; atteso; * vi **to fall** ~ scadere; ~ **to** a causa di; * n ~s quota f; diritti mpl.

duel n duello m.

duet n duetto m.

duke n duca m.

dull adj ottuso; noioso; spento; * vt ottundere; intorpidire; smussare.

duly adv debitamente.

dumb adj muto.

dumbbell n manubrio m.

dumbfound vt sbigottire.

dumness n mutismo m.

dummy adj finto; * n manichino m.

dump vt scaricare; * n discarica f.

dumping n dumping m.

dumpling n gnocco m di pasta.

dumpy adj tracagnotto.

dunce n somaro m.

dune n duna f.

dung n sterco m.

dungarees npl salopette f.

dungeon n segreta f.

dunk vt inzuppare.

duodenal adj duodenale.

duodenum n duodeno m.

dupe n gonzo m; * vt ingannare.

duplicate n duplicato m; * vt duplicare.

duplicity n duplicità f.

durability n durevolezza f.

durable adj durevole.

duration n durata f.

duress n coercizione f.

during prep durante.
dusk n crepuscolo m.
dust n polvere f; * vt, vi spolverare.
dustbin n bidone m.
dustcart n autocarro m della nettezza urbana.
duster n straccio m.
dustman n netturbino m.
dustpan n pattumiera f.
dust-up n zuffa f.
dusty adj polveroso.
dutch courage n coraggio m dato da alcolici.
dutiful adj deferente; rispettoso.
duty n dovere m; tassa f; dazio m.
duty-free adj esente da dogana.
duvet n piumone m.

dwarf n nano m; * vt eclissare.
dwell vi dimorare.
dwelling n dimora f.
dwindle vi diminuire; affievolirsi.
dye vt tingere; * n colorante m; tintura f.
dyer n tintore m.
dye-works n tintoria f
dying adj morente; * n morte f.
dyke n diga f; (fam) lesbica f.
dynamic adj dinamico.
dynamics n dinamica f.
dynamite n dinamite f.
dynamo n dinamo f.
dynasty n dinastia f.
dysentery n dissenteria f.
dyspepsia n dispepsia f.
dyspeptic adj dispeptico.

E

each adj ogni; ciascuno, * pron ognuno; ciascuno; * adv ciascuno.
eager adj appassionato.
eagerness n passione f.
eagle n aquila f.
eagle-eyed adj dagli occhi di lince.
eaglet n aquilotto m.
ear n orecchio m; **by ~** a orecchio.
earache n mal m d'orecchi.
eardrum n timpano m.
earl n conte m.
early adj primo; precoce; prematuro; * adv presto.
earmark vt destinare.
earn vt guadagnare.
earnest adj serio.
earnings npl guadagni mpl.
earphones npl cuffia f.
earring n orecchino m.

earth n terra f; * vt collegare a terra.
earthen adj di terracotta.
earthenware n terraglie fpl.
earthquake n terremoto m.
earthworm n lombrico m.
earthy adj grossolano.
earwig n forbicina f.
ease n disinvoltura f; tranquillità; **at ~** sentirsi a proprio agio; * vt facilitare; alleviare.
easel n cavalletto m.
easily adv facilmente.
easiness n facilità f.
east n est m; oriente m.
Easter n Pasqua f.
Easter egg n uovo m di Pasqua.
easterly adj orientale.
eastern adj orientale.
eastwards adv verso est.
easy adj facile; **~ going** accomodante.

easy chair n poltrona f.

eat vt mangiare.

eatable adj commestibile.

eau de Cologne n acqua f di Colonia.

eaves npl gronda f.

eavesdrop vi origliare.

ebb n riflusso m; * vi rifluire.

ebony n ebano m.

eccentric adj, n eccentrico m.

eccentricity n eccentricità f.

ecclesiastic adj ecclesiastico.

echo n eco m/f; * vi echeggiare.

éclair n bignè n.

eclectic adj eclettico.

eclipse n ecclissi f; * vt eclissare.

ecology n ecologia f.

economic(al) adj economico.

economics npl economia f.

economist n economista m/f.

economize vi fare economia.

economy n economia f.

ecstasy n estasi f.

ecstatic adj estatico.

eczema n eczema m.

eddy n mulinello m; * vi turbinare.

edge n orlo m; bordo m; * vt bordare; * vi **to ~ forward** avanzare a poco a poco.

edgeways adv di fianco.

edging n bordo m.

edgy adj teso.

edible adj mangiabile; commestibile.

edict n editto m.

edification n cultura f.

edifice n edificio m; costruzione f.

edify vt edificare.

edit vt dirigere; redigere.

edition n edizione f.

editor n direttore m.

editorial adj redazionale; * n editoriale.

educate vt istruire; educare.

educated adj colto.

education n istruzione f; formazione f; pedagogia f.

educational adj didattico.

eel n anguilla f.

eerie adj sinistro.

efface vt cancellare.

effect n effetto m; **~s** effetti mpl; * vt effettuare.

effective adj efficace.

effectiveness n efficacia f.

effectual adj efficace.

effeminacy n effeminatezza f.

effeminate adj effeminato.

effervescent adj effervescente.

effete adj logoro.

efficacy n efficacia f.

efficiency n efficenza f.

efficient adj efficiente.

effigy n effigie f.

effort n sforzo m.

effortless adj facile; disinvolto.

effrontery n sfrontatezza f.

effusive adj espansivo.

egalitarian adj egualitario.

egg n uovo m; * vt **to ~ on** spingere.

eggcup n portauovo m.

eggshell n guscio m d'uovo.

ego n ego m.

egoism n egoismo m.

egoist n egoista m/f.

egotism n egotismo m.

egotist n egotista m/f.

eiderdown n trapunta f di piuma.

eight adj, n otto m.

eighteen adj, n diciotto m.

eighteenth adj, n diciottesimo m.

eighth adj, n ottavo m.

eightieth adj, n ottantesimo m.

eighty adj, n ottanta m.

either pron, adj l'uno o l'altro; * adj entrambi; * conj **~ ... or** o ... o; * adv neanche.

ejaculate vt, vi esclamare; eiaculare.

ejaculation n esclamazione f;

eiaculazione f.

eject vt espellere.

ejection n espulsione f.

ejector seat n seggiolino m eiettabile.

eke vt integrare; far bastare.

elaborate vt elaborare; * adj complicato; ricercato.

elapse vi trascorrere.

elastic adj, n elastico m.

elasticity n elasticità f.

elated adj esultante.

elation n esultanza f.

elbow n gomito m.

elbow-room n spazio m.

elder n anziano m; (bot) sambuco m; * adj maggiore.

elderberry n bacca di sambuco.

elder!y adj anziano.

eldest adj maggiore.

elect vt eleggere; decidere; * adj futuro.

election n elezione f.

electioneering n propaganda f elettorale.

electoral adj elettorale.

electorate n elettorato m.

electric(al) adj elettrico.

electric blanket n coperta f termica.

electric fire n stufa f elettrica.

electrician n elettricista m/f.

electricity n elettricità f.

electrify vt elettrificare.

electrocute vt fulminare.

electrode n elettrodo m.

electrolysis n elettrolisi f.

electron n elettrone m.

electronic adj elettronico; ~s npl elettronica f.

elegance n eleganza f.

elegant adj elegante.

elegy n elegia f.

element n elemento m.

elementary adj elementare.

elephant n elefante m.

elevate vt elevare.

elevation n elevazione f.

elevator n montacarichi m.

eleven adj, n undici m.

eleventh adj, n undicesimo m.

elf n folletto m.

elicit vt strappare.

eligibility n eleggibilità f.

eligible adj eleggibile.

eliminate vt eliminare.

elimination n eliminazione f.

élite n élite f.

elixir n elisir m.

elk n alce m.

eliptic(al) ellittico.

elm n olmo m.

elocution n dizione f.

elongate vt allungare.

elope vi fuggire.

elopement n fuga (romantica) f.

eloquence n eloquenza f.

eloquent adj eloquente.

else adv altro; altrimenti.

elsewhere adv altrove.

elucidate vt delucidare.

elucidation n spiegazione f.

elude vt eludere.

elusive adj inafferrabile.

emaciated adj emaciato.

emanate vi provenire.

emancipate vt emancipare.

emancipation n emancipazione f.

embalm vt imbalsamare.

embankment n argine m.

embargo n embargo m.

embark vt imbarcare.

embarkation n imbarco m.

embarrass vt mettere in imbarazzo.

embarrassing adj imbarazzante.

embarrassment n imbarazzo m.

embassy n ambasciata f.

embed vt incastrare.

embellish vt abbellire.

embers npl brace f.

embezzle vt appropriarsi indebitamente.

embezzlement n appropriazione f indebita.

embitter vt inasprire.

emblem n emblema m.

emblematic(al) adj emblematico.

embodiment n incarnazione f.

embody vt incarnare.

emboss vt goffrare.

embrace vt abbracciare; * n abbraccio m.

embroider vt ricamare.

embroidery n ricamo m.

embroil vt imbrogliare.

embryo n embrione m.

emend vt correggere.

emendation n correzione f.

emerald n smeraldo m.

emerge vi emergere.

emergency n emergenza f.

emergency exit n uscita f di sicurezza.

emery n smeriglio m

emery board n limetta f di carta.

emetic n emetico m.

emigrant n emigrante m/f.

emigrate vi emigrare.

emigration n emigrazione f.

eminence n eminenza f; reputazione f.

eminent adj eminente.

emirate n emirato m.

emissary n emissario m.

emission n emissione f.

emit vt emettere.

emolument n emolumento m.

emotion n emozione f.

emotional adj emotivo.

emotive adj emotivo; commovente.

emperor n imperatore m.

emphasis n accento m; enfasi f.

emphasize vt sottolineare.

emphatic adj enfatico.

empire n impero m.

empirical adj empirico.

employ vt impiegare; assumere.

employee n dipendente m/f.

employer n datore m di lavoro.

employment n occupazione f.

empress n imperatrice f.

emptiness n vuoto m.

empty adj vuoto; * vt vuotare.

empty-handed adj a mani vuote.

emu n emù m.

emulate vt emulare.

emulsify vt emulsionare.

emulsion n emulsione f.

enable vt permettere.

enact vt rappresentare.

enamel n smalto; * vt smaltare.

enamour vt innamorare.

encamp vi accampare.

encampment n accampamento m.

encase vt racchiudere.

enchant vt incantare.

enchanting adj incantevole.

enchantment n incantesimo m.

encircle vt circondare.

enclose vt allegare; recintare.

enclosure n allegato m; recinto m;

encompass vt comprendere.

encore excl, n bis m.

encounter n incontro m; * vt incontrare.

encourage vt incoraggiare.

encouragement n incoraggiamento m.

encroach vi usurpare; invadere.

encrust vt incrostare.

encumber vt ingombrare.

encumbrance n peso m.

encyclical n enciclica f

encyclopaedia n enciclopedia f.

end n fine f; estremità f; scopo

m; * *vi* finire; terminare; * *vt* porre fine a.

endanger *vt* mettere in pericolo.

endear *vt* rendere caro.

endearing *adj* tenero.

endearment *n* tenerezza *f*.

endeavour *vt* tentare; * *n* tentativo *m*.

endemic *adj* endemico.

ending *n* fine *f*; (*gram*) desinenza *f*.

endive *n* (*bot*) indivia *f*.

endless *adj* senza fine; interminabile.

endorse *vt* girare; approvare.

endorsement *n* girata *f*; approvazione *f*.

endow *vt* dotare.

endowment *n* fondazione *f*; donazione *f*.

endurable *adj* sopportabile.

endurance *n* resistenza *f*.

endure *vt* sopportare.

enduring *adj* duraturo.

enemy *n* nemico *m*.

energetic *adj* energico.

energy *n* energia *f*.

enervate *vt* snervare.

enfeeble *vt* indebolire.

enforce *vt* applicare; far rispettare.

enforced *adj* imposto.

enfranchise *vt* concedere il diritto di voto a.

engage *vt* assumere; innestare; ingaggiare.

engaged *adj* fidanzato.

engagement *n* fidanzamento *m*; impegno *m*.

engagement ring *n* anello *m* di fidanzamento.

engaging *adj* attraente.

engender *vt* essere causa di.

engine *n* motore *m*; locomotivo *m*.

engine driver *n* macchinista *m*.

engineer *n* ingegnere *m*, meccanico *m*; * *vt* architettare.

engineering *n* ingegneria *f*.

engrave *vt* incidere.

engraving *n* incisione *f*.

engrossed *adj* immerso.

engulf *vt* inghiottire.

enhance *vt* valorizzare.

enigma *n* enigma *m*.

enigmatic *adj* enigmatico.

enjoy *vt* godere; divertirsi.

enjoyment *m* godimento *m*; divertimento *m*.

enlarge *vt* ingrandire; ampliare.

enlargement *n* ingrandimento *m*; ampliamento *m*.

enlighten *vt* fornire chiarimento a.

enlightened *adj* illuminato.

Enlightenment *n* l'Illuminismo *m*.

enlist *vt* arruolare.

enlistment *n* arruolamento *m*.

enliven *vt* ravvivare.

enmity *n* inimicizia *f*.

enormity *n* atrocità *f*.

enormous *adj* enorme.

enough *adj*, sufficiente; *adj*, * *adv* abbastanza; * *vi* **to be ~** bastare.

enquire *vt* = inquire.

enrage *vt* fare arrabbiare.

enrapture *vt* estasiare.

enrich *vt* arricchire.

enrichment *n* arricchimento *m*.

enrol *vt* iscrivere; immatricolare.

enrolment *n* iscrizione *f*; immatricolazione *f*.

en route *adv* in viaggio.

ensemble *n* complesso *m*.

ensign *n* insegne *f*.

enslave *vt* rendere schiavo.

ensue *vi* seguire; risultare.

ensure *vt* garantire.

entail *vt* comportare.

entangle *vt* impigliare.

entanglement n groviglio m.

enter vt registrare; **to ~ for** iscriversi; * vi entrare; **this does not ~ into it** questo non c'entra.

enteritis n enterite f.

enterprise n impresa f; iniziativa f.

enterprising adj intraprendente.

entertain vt intrattenere.

entertainer n artista m/f.

entertaining adj divertente.

entertainment n trattenimento m; spettacolo m.

enthral vt affascinare.

enthralling adj avvincente.

enthuse vi entusiasmarsi.

enthusiasm n entusiasmo m.

enthusiast n appassionato m.

enthusiastic adj appassionato.

entice vt allettare.

entire adj intero.

entirety n complesso m.

entitle vt intitolare; dare diritto a.

entity n entità f.

entourage n entourage m.

entrails npl interiora fpl.

entrance n entrata f, ingresso m, ammissione f; * vt mandare in estasi.

entrance examination n esame m di ammissione.

entrance fee n quota f di ammissione.

entrant n concorrente m/f; candidato m.

entreat vt implorare.

entreaty n supplica f.

entrenched adj radicato.

entrepreneur n imprenditore m.

entrust vt affidare.

entry n ingresso m, entrata f; accesso m; voce f.

entry phone n citofono m.

entwine vt intrecciare.

enumerate vt enumerare.

enunciate vt enunciare.

enunciation n articolazione f.

envelop vt avvolgere.

envelope n busta f.

enviable adj invidiabile.

envious adj invidioso.

environment n ambiente m.

environmental adj ambientale.

environs npl dintorni mpl.

envisage vt prevedere.

envoy n inviato m.

envy n invidia f.

enzyme n enzima m.

ephemeral adj effimero.

epic adj epico; * n epopea f.

epicure n buongustaio m.

epidemic adj epidemico; * n epidemia f.

epilepsy n epilessia f.

epileptic adj, n epilettico m.

epilogue n epilogo m.

Epiphany n Epifania f.

episcopal adj episcopale.

episcopalian adj, n episcopaliano m.

episode n episodio m.

epistle n epistola f.

epithet n epiteto m.

epitome n personificazione f.

epitomize vt incarnare.

epoch n epoca f.

equable adj costante.

equal adj uguale; * n pari m; * vt uguagliare.

equalize vt livellare; * vi pareggiare

equalizer n pareggio m.

equality n uguaglianza f.

equally adv ugualmente.

equanimity n serenità f.

equate vt identificare.

equation n equazione f.

equator n equatore m.

equatorial adj equatoriale.

equestrian adj equestre.

equidistant adj equidistante.

equilateral adj equilatero.

equilibrium n equilibrio m.

equinox n equinozio m.

equip vt attrezzare.

equipment n attrezzatura f.

equitable adj equo.

equity n equità f.

equivalent adj equivalente.

equivocal adj equivoco.

equivocate vi giocare sull'equivoco.

era n era f.

eradicate vt sradicare.

erase vt cancellare.

erect vt erigere; * adj diritto.

erection n erezione f.

ermine n ermellino m.

erode vt erodere.

erotic adj erotico.

err vi sbagliare.

errand n commissione f.

errand boy n fattorino m.

erratic adj incostante.

erratum n errore m di stampa.

erroneous adj erroneo.

error n errore m.

erudite adj erudito.

erudition n erudizione f.

erupt vi essere in eruzione; erompere.

eruption n eruzione f.

escalate vt intensificare; * vi intensificarsi.

escalation n intensificazione f.

escalator n scala f mobile.

escapade n scappatella f.

escape vt sfuggire a; scampare; * vi scappare; evadere; * n fuga f; evasione f.

escapism n evasione f.

escarpment n scarpata f.

eschew vt evitare.

escort n scorta f; * vt scortare.

esoteric adj esoterico.

especial adj particolare.

espionage n spionaggio m.

esplanade n lungomare m.

espouse vt abbracciare.

essay n saggio m.

essence n essenza f.

essential adj essenziale.

establish vt stabilire; istituire; fondare.

establishment n istituzione f; azienda f.

estate n tenuta f; patrimonio m.

estate agent n agente m/f immobiliare.

esteem vt stimare; * n stima f.

estimate vt valutare; preventivare; * n preventivo m; valutazione f.

estimation n giudizio m; stima f.

estranged adj separato.

estrangement n allontanamento m.

estuary n estuario m.

etch vt incidere all'acquaforte.

etching n incisione f all'acquaforte.

eternal adj eterno.

eternity n eternità f.

ether n etere m.

ethical adj etico.

ethics npl etica f.

ethnic adj etnico.

ethos n norma f di vita.

etiquette n etichetta f.

etymological adj etimologico.

etymology n etimologia f.

eucalyptus n eucalipto m.

Eucharist n eucarestia f.

eulogy n elogio m.

eunuch n eunuco m.

euphemism n eufemismo.

euphoria n euforia f.

euthanasia n eutanasia f.

evacuate vt evacuare.

evacuation n evacuazione f.

evade vt eludere; evadere.

evaluate vt valutare.

evaluation n valutazione f.

evangelic(al) adj evangelico.

evangelist n evangelista m.

evaporate vi evaporare.

evaporated milk n latte m concentrato.
evaporation n evaporazione f.
evasion n evasione f.
evasive adj evasivo.
eve n vigilia f.
even adj liscio; regolare; pari; * adv perfino; addirittura; ancora; * vt appianare.
evening n sera f, serata f.
evening class n corso m serale.
evening dress n abito m da sera.
evenly adv uniformemente.
event n avvenimento m.
eventful adj movimentato.
eventual adj finale; eventuale.
eventuality n eventualità f.
ever adv sempre; mai; **for ~** per sempre.
evergreen n sempreverde m/f.
everlasting adj eterno.
every adj ogni, tutti; * pron **~body** ognuno, tutti; **~thing** tutto; * adv **~where** dappertutto.
evict vt sfrattare.
eviction n sfratto m.
evidence n testimonianza f; prove fpl.
evident adj evidente.
evil adj cattivo; malvagio; * n male m.
evil-minded adj malvagio.
evince vt manifestare.
evocative adj evocativo.
evoke vt evocare.
evolution n evoluzione f.
evolve vt elaborare; * vi evolversi.
ewe n pecora f.
exacerbate vt esacerbare.
exact adj esatto; * vt esigere.
exacting adj esigente.
exactly adj esattamente.
exactness, exactitude n esattezza f.
exaggerate vt esagerare.
exaggeration n esagerazione f.

exalt vt esaltare.
exalted adj esaltato.
examination n esame m; visita f.
examine vt esaminare; visitare.
examiner n esaminatore m.
example n esempio m.
exasperate vt esasperare.
exasperation n esasperazione f.
excavate vt scavare.
excavation n scavo m.
exceed vt eccedere; superare.
exceedingly adv estremamente.
excel vt superare.
excellence n eccellenza f.
Excellency n Eccellenza f.
excellent adj eccellente.
except vt escludere; * prep tranne, eccetto.
exception n eccezione f.
exceptional adj eccezionale.
excerpt n estratto m.
excess n eccesso m.
excessive adj eccessivo.
exchange vt scambiare; * n scambio m.
exchange rate n tasso m di cambio.
exchequer n tesoro m.
excise n imposta f indiretta.
excitable adj eccitabile.
excite vt eccitare.
excited adj emozionato; eccitato.
excitement n eccitazione f.
exciting adj emozionante.
exclaim vt esclamare.
exclamation n esclamazione f.
exclamation mark n punto m esclamativo.
exclude vt escludere.
exclusion n esclusione f.
exclusive adj esclusivo.
excommunicate vt scomunicare.
excommunication n scomunica f.

excrement n escrementi mpl.

excruciating adj atroce.

exculpate vt scolpare.

excursion n gita f, escursione f.

excusable adj perdonabile.

excuse vt scusare; esonerare; * n scusa f.

execrable adj esecrabile.

execute vt giustiziare; eseguire.

execution n esecuzione f.

executioner n boia m.

executive adj esecutivo; * n dirigente m/f.

executor n esecutore m.

exemplary adj esemplare.

exemplify vt esemplificare.

exempt adj esente; * vt esentare.

exemption n esenzione f.

exercise n esercizio m; * vt esercitare.

exercise book m quaderno m.

exert vt esercitare; **to ~ oneself** sforzarsi.

exertion n sforzo m.

exhale vt, vi espirare.

exhaust n gas m di scarico; * vt stremare; esaurire.

exhausted adj esausto.

exhaustion n esaurimento m.

exhaustive adj esauriente.

exhibit vt esporre; * n oggetto m esposto; reperto m.

exhibitor n espositore m.

exhibition n mostra f.

exhilarate vt rinvigorire.

exhort vt esortare.

exhume vt esumare.

exile n esilio m; esule m/f; * vt esiliare.

exist vi esistere.

existence n esistenza f.

existent adj esistente.

existential adj esistenziale.

existentialism n esistenzialismo m.

exit n uscita f.

exodus n esodo m.

exonerate vt discolpare.

exoneration n discolpa f.

exhorbitant adj esorbitante.

exorcise vt esorcizzare.

exorcism n esorcismo m.

exotic adj esotico.

expand vt espandere.

expanse n distesa f.

expansion n espansione f.

expansive adj espansivo.

expatriate adj, n espatriato m.

expect vt aspettare; pensare; pretendere; esigere.

expectancy n attesa f.

expectant adj in attesa.

expectant mother n donna f incinta.

expectation n aspettativa f; attesa f.

expediency n interesse m.

expedient adj opportuno; * n espediente m.

expedite vt accelerare.

expedition n spedizione f.

expeditious adj sollecito.

expel vt espellere.

expend vt spendere.

expendable adj usabile.

expenditure n dispendio m.

expense n spesa f.

expense account n conto m spese.

expensive adj costoso, caro.

experience n esperienza f; * vt sperimentare.

experienced adj esperto.

experiment n esperimento m.

experimental adj sperimentale.

expert adj, n esperto m.

expertise n perizia f.

expire vi scadere; spirare.

expiry n scadenza f.

explain vt spiegare.

explanation n spiegazione f.

explanatory adj esplicativo.

expletive n imprecazione f.

explicable *adj* spiegabile.

explicit *adj* esplicito.

explode *vi* esplodere.

exploit *vt* sfruttare; * *n* impresa *f*.

exploitation *n* sfruttamento *m*.

exploration *n* esplorazione *f*.

exploratory *adj* preliminare.

explore *vt* esplorare.

explorer *n* esploratore *m*.

explosion *n* esplosione *f*.

explosive *adj, n* esplosivo *m*.

exponent *n* esponente *m/f*.

export *vt* esportare; * *n* esportazione *f*.

exporter *n* esportatore *m*.

expose *vt* esporre; smascherare.

exposed *adj* esposto; scoperto.

exposition *n* esposizione *f*.

expostulate *vi* rimostrare.

exposure *n* esposizione *f*.

exposure meter *n* esposimetro *m*.

expound *vt* esporre.

express *vt* esprimere; * *adj* espresso.

expression *n* espressione *f*.

expressionless *adj* inespressivo.

expressive *adj* espressivo.

expropriate *vt* espropriare.

expropriation *n* esproprio *m*.

expulsion *n* espulsione *f*.

expurgate *vt* espurgare.

exquisite *adj* squisito.

extant *adj* esistente.

extempore *adj* improvvisato.

extemporize *vi* improvvisare.

extend *vt* tendere; prolungare.

extension *n* prolunga *f*; (numero) interno.

extensive *adj* esteso.

extent *n* estensione *f*; portata *f*.

extenuate *vt* attenuare.

extenuating *adj* attenuante.

exterior *adj, n* esterno *m*.

exterminate *vt* sterminare.

extermination *n* sterminio *m*.

external *adj* esterno.

extinct *adj* estinto.

extinction *n* estinzione *f*.

extinguish *vt* spegnere.

extinguisher *n* estintore *m*.

extirpate *vt* estirpare.

extol *vt* magnificare.

extort *vt* estorcere.

extortion *n* estorsione *f*.

extortionate *adj* esorbitante.

extra *adj* in più; supplementare; maggiore; * *adv* extra; eccezionalmente.

extract *vt* estrarre; * *n* spezzone *m*.

extraction *n* estrazione *f*.

extracurricular *adj* parascolastico.

extradite *vt* estradare.

extradition *n* estradizione *f*.

extramarital *adj* extraconiugale.

extramural *adj* estramurale.

extraneous *adj* estraneo.

extraordinary *adj* straordinario.

extrasensory *adj* extrasensoriale.

extravagance *n* stravaganza *f*.

extravagant *adj* dispendioso; stravagante.

extreme *adj, n* estremo *m*.

extremist *n* estremista *m/f*.

extremity *n* estremità *f*.

extricate *vt* districare.

extrinsic(al) *adj* estrinseco.

extrovert *adj, n* estroverso *m*.

exuberance *n* esuberanza *f*.

exuberant *adj* esuberante.

exude *vt* emanare.

exult *vi* esultare.

exultation *n* giubilo *m*.

eye *n* occhio *m*; * *vt* scrutare.

eyeball *n* bulbo *m* oculare.

eyebrow *n* sopracciglio *m*.

eyedrops *npl* collirio *m*.

eyelash *n* ciglio *m*.

eyelid n palpebra f.
eyeshadow n ombretto m.
eyesight n vista f.
eyesore n oggetto m sgradevole
   alla vista.

eyetooth n canino m superiore.
eyewitness n testimone m/f
   oculare.
eyrie n nido m d'aquila.

F

fable n favola f.
fabric n stoffa f, tessuto m.
fabricate vt fabbricare.
fabrication n fabbricazione f.
fabulous adj favoloso.
facade n facciata f.
face n faccia f, viso m; muso m;
   quadrante m; * vt affrontare;
   essere di fronte a; * vi **to ~ up
   to** fare fronte a.
face cream n crema f per il viso.
face-lift n plastica f facciale.
face powder n cipria f.
facet n sfaccettatura f; aspetto
   m.
facetious adj faceto.
face value n valore m nominale.
facial adj faciale; * n trattamento m del viso.
facile adj superficiale.
facilitate vt facilitare.
facility n facilità f.
facing n rivestimento m; paramontura f; * adj di fronte
facsimile n facsimile m.
fact n fatto m; **in ~** in realtà.
faction n fazione f.
factor n fattore m.
factory n fabbrica f.
factual adj che riguarda i fatti.
faculty n facoltà f.
fad n pazzia f.
fade vi appassire; sbiadirsi.
faeces feci fpl.
fag n (fam) sigaretta f; (Amer
   fam) frocio m.

faggot n (culin) involtino m di
   fegato.
fail vi fallire; mancare; * vt bocciare.
failing n difetto m; * prep in
   mancanza di.
failure n fallimento m; insuccesso m.
faint vi svenire; * n svenimento; * adj leggero; fievole; vago.
fainthearted adj pusillanime.
fair adj giusto; imparziale; discreto; chiaro; * n fiera f.
fairly adv in modo imparziale;
   abbastanza.
fairness n imparzialità f; chiarezza f.
fair play n correttezza f.
fairy n fata f.
fairy tale n fiaba f.
faith n fede f.
faithful adj fedele.
faithfulness n fedeltà f.
fake n falso m; imitazione f;
   * adj fasullo; * vt falsificare;
   * vi fingere.
falcon n falco m.
falconry n falconiera f.
fall vi cadere; **to ~ asleep** addormentarsi; **to ~ in love** innamorarsi; **to ~ back on** ripiegare su; **to ~ for** cascarci; **to
   ~ out** litigare; * n caduta f;
   calo m.
fallacious adj fallace.
fallacy n errore m.
fallibility n fallibilità f.

fallible adj fallibile.

fallout n pioggia f radioattiva.

fallout shelter n rifugio m antiatomico.

fallow adj incolto; **~ deer** n daino m.

false adj falso.

false alarm n falso allarme m.

falsehood n menzogna f.

falsify vt falsificare.

falsity n falsità f.

falter vi vacillare.

fame n fama f, celebrità f.

famed adj famoso.

familiar adj conosciuto, familiare.

familiarity n familiarità f.

familiarize vt familiarizzarsi.

family n famiglia f.

family doctor n medico m di famiglia.

famine n carestia f.

famished adj affamato.

famous adj famoso.

fan n ventaglio m; ventilatore m; fan m/f, tifoso m; * vt fare vento.

fanatic adj, n fanatico m.

fanaticism n fanatismo m.

fan belt n cinghia f della ventola.

fanciful adj fantasioso.

fancy n voglia f, capriccio m; * adj elaborato.

fancy dress n costume m; **~ party** festa f in maschera.

fanfare n fanfara f.

fang n zanna f.

fantasize vi fantasticare.

fantastic adj fantastico.

fantasy n fantasia f, sogno m.

far adv lontano; **so ~** finora; * adj lontano; di gran lunga; estremo.

faraway adj lontano; assente.

farce n farsa f.

farcical adj ridicolo.

fare n tariffa f; cibo m.

farewell excl, n addio m.

farm n fattoria f; * vt coltivare.

farmer n agricoltore m.

farmhand n bracciante m/f.

farmhouse n casa f colonica.

farming n agricoltura f.

farmland n terreno m coltivabile.

farmyard n aia f.

far-reaching adj di vasta portata.

fart n (sl) scoreggia; * vi scoreggiare.

farther adv più avanti; oltre; * adj ulteriore; * vt favorire.

farthest adv, adj più lontano.

fascinate vt affascinare.

fascinating adj affascinante.

fascination n fascino m.

fascism n fascismo m.

fascist n fascista m/f.

fashion n moda f; modo m; * vt modellare.

fashionable adj alla moda.

fashion show n sfilata f di moda.

fast vi digiunare; * adj veloce, rapido; * adv velocemente; saldamente; * n digiuno m.

fasten vt legare.

fastener, fastening n chiusura f.

fast food n fast food m.

fastidious adj pignolo; difficile.

fat adj, n grasso m.

fatal adj fatale; nefasto.

fatalism n fatalismo m.

fatality n vittima f.

fate n destino m; sorte f.

fateful adj fatidico.

father n padre m.

fatherhood n paternità f.

father-in-law n suocero m.

fatherland n patria f.

fatherly adj paterno.

fathom n braccio m; * vt capire.

fatigue n fatica f, stanchezza f; * vt affaticare.

fatten vt ingrassare.

fatty adj grasso.

fatuous adj fatuo.

fault n difetto m; colpa f; faglia f; * vt criticare.

faultfinder n criticone m/f.

faultless adj impeccabile.

faulty adj difettoso.

fauna n fauna f.

faux pas n gaffe f.

favour n favore m; * vt favorire.

favourable adj favorevole.

favoured adj favorito.

favourite n preferito m.

favouritism n favoritismo m.

fawn n cerbiatto m; * adj, n fulvo m; * vi adulare.

fax n fax m.

fear vi temere, avere paura di; * n paura f.

fearful adj pauroso.

fearless adj intrepido.

feasibility n fattibilità f.

feasible adj realizzabile.

feast n pranzo m; banchetto m; festa f; * vi banchettare.

feat n impresa f; prodezza f.

feather n penna f, piuma f.

feather bed n letto m di piume.

feature n caratteristica f; * vt dare risalto a.

February n febbraio m.

feckless adj irresponsabile.

federal adj federale.

federate vt federare.

federation n federazione f.

fed-up adj stufo.

fee n onorario m.

feeble adj debole.

feebleness n debolezza f.

feed vt nutrire; alimentare; dar da mangiare a; * n pappa f; mangiata f; mangime m; foraggio m.

feedback n feedback m.

feel vt tastare, sentire; credere; provare; * n tatto m; sensazione f.

feeler n antenna f.

feeling n senso m, sensazione f; sentimento m; impressione f.

feign vt simulare, fingere.

feline adj felino.

fell vt abbattere.

fellow n uomo m; tipo m; membro m.

fellow citizen n concittadino m.

fellow countryman n compatriota m/f.

fellow feeling n simpatia f.

fellow men npl simili mpl.

fellowhsip n associazione f; borsa f di studio.

fellow student n compagno m di studi.

fellow traveller n compagno m di viaggio; filocomunista m/f.

felon n criminale m/f.

felony n crimine m.

felt n feltro m.

felt-tip pen n pennarello m.

female adj, n femmina f.

feminine adj femminile.

feminist n femminista m/f.

fen n zona f paludosa.

fence n recinto m; * vt recintare.

fencing n scherma f.

fender n paracenere m.

fennel n (bot) finocchio m.

ferment n fermento; * vi fermentare.

fern n (bot) felce f.

ferocious adj feroce.

ferocity n ferocia f.

ferret n furetto m; * vt to ~ out snidare.

ferry n traghetto m.

fertile adj fertile.

fertility n fertilità f.

fertilize vt fecondare; (agric) fertilizzare.

fervent adj fervente.

fervid adj fervente.

fervour n fervore m.

fester vi suppurare.
festival n festa f, festival m.
festive adj di festa.
festivity n festa f.
fetch vt andare a prendere.
fetching adj attraente.
fête n festa f.
fetid adj fetido.
fetish n feticcio f.
fettishist n feticista m/f.
fetter vt incatenare.
feud n faida f.
feudal adj feudale.
feudalism n feudalismo m.
fever n febbre f.
feverish adj febbrile.
few n poco m; * adj pochi; ~ **and far between** rari.
fewer adj meno.
fewest adj il minor numero di.
fiancé n fidanzato m.
fiancée n fidanzata f.
fiasco n fiasco m.
fib n frottola f.
fibber n bugiardo m.
fibre n fibra f.
fibreglass n fibra f di vetro.
fickle adj mutabile.
fiction n narrativa f; finzione f.
fictional adj immaginario.
fictitious adj fittizio.
fiddle n violino m; imbroglio m; * vi giocherellare; * vt falsificare.
fiddler n violinista m/f; imbroglione m/f.
fiddling adj insignificante.
fidelity n fedeltà f.
fidget n persona f irrequieta; * vi agitarsi.
fidgety adj irrequieto.
field n campo m.
fieldmouse n topo m campagnolo.
fieldwork n lavoro m sul campo.
fiend n demonio m.
fiendish adj diabolico.

fierce adj feroce; accanito.
fierceness n ferocia f
fiery adj infocato.
fifteen adj, n quindici m.
fifteenth adj, n quindicesimo m.
fifth adj, n quinto m.
fiftieth adj, n cinquantesimo m.
fifty adj, n cinquanta f.
fig n fico m.
fight vt combattere; lottare; * n combattimento m; lotta f.
fighter n combattente m/f.
fighting n combattimento m.
figurative adj figurativo.
figure n figura f; cifra f; linea f; * vi figurare; * vt to ~ **out** capire.
figurehead n (naut) polena f; figura f rappresentativa.
filament n filamento m.
filch vt rubacchiare.
filcher n ladruncolo m.
file n lima f; cartella f; archivio m; fila f; * vt limare; archiviare; * vi to ~ **past** sfilare davanti.
filial adj filiale.
filigree n filigrana f.
filing cabinet n casellario m.
fill vt riempire; orturare; to ~ **in** completare.
fillet n filetto m; * vt disossare.
filling n otturazione f; ripieno m; * adj sostanzioso.
fillip n stimolo m.
filly n puledra f.
film n film m, pellicola f; rullino m; strato m sottile; * vi filmare.
film star n divo m del cinema.
film strip n filmina f.
filter n filtro m; * vt filtrare.
filter-tipped adj con filtro.
filth n sudiciume f.
filthy adj sudicio.
fin n pinna f.
final adj ultimo, finale; * n finale f.

finale n finale m.

finalist n finalista m/f.

finalize vt definire.

finally n alla fine.

finance n finanza f; * vt finanziare.

financial adj finanziario.

financier n finanziatore m.

finch n fringuello m.

find vt trovare; **to ~ out** scoprire; **to ~ ones feet** ambientarsi; * n scoperta f.

findings npl conclusioni fpl.

fine adj fine, sottile, fino; ottimo; * excl bene; * n multa f; * vt multare.

fine arts npl belle arti fpl.

finely adv finemente.

finery n abiti mpl eleganti.

finesse n finezza f.

finger n dito m; * vt tastare.

fingernail n unghia f.

fingerprint n impronta f digitale.

fingertip n punta f del dito.

finicky adj pignolo.

finish vt, vi finire; * n fine f; traguardo m.

finishing line n traguardo m.

finishing school n scuola f di perfezionamento.

finite adj finito.

fir (tree) n abete m.

fire n fuoco m; incendio m; stufa f; * vt sparare; licenziare.

fire alarm n allarme m antincendio.

firearm n arma f da fuoco.

fire brigade n corpo m dei pompieri.

fire engine n autopompa f antincendio.

fire escape n scala f di sicurezza.

fire extinguisher n estintore m.

firefly n lucciola f.

fireman n pompiere m.

fireplace n caminetto m.

fireproof adj resistente al fuoco.

fireside n angolo m del focolare.

fire station n caserma f dei pompieri.

firewood n legna f da ardere.

fireworks n fuochi d'artificio.

firing n spari mpl.

firing squad n plotone m d'esecuzione.

firm adj saldo; fermo; definitivo; * n ditta f.

firmament n firmamento m.

firmness n fermezza f.

first adj, n primo m; * adv prima; **at ~** sulle prime; **~ly** innanzi tutto.

first aid n pronto soccorso m.

first-class adj prima classe f.

first-hand adj diretto.

first name n nome m.

first rate adj di prim'ordine.

fiscal adj fiscale.

fish n pesce m; * vi pescare.

fishbone n lisca f.

fisherman n pescatore m.

fish farm n allevamento m di pesce.

fishing n pesca f.

fishing line n lenza f.

fishing rod n canna f da pesca.

fishing tackle n attrezzatura f da pesca.

fishmonger n pescivendolo m.

fishy adj sospetto.

fissure n fessura f.

fist n pugno m.

fit n attacco m; accesso m; * adj adatto; in forma; * vt andare bene a; **to ~ out** equipaggiare; * vi **to ~ in** integrarsi.

fitment n accessorio m.

fitness n idoneità f; forma f.

fitted carpet n moquette f.

fitted kitchen n cucina f componibile.

fitter n installatore m.

fitting n prova f; * adj opportuno. **~s** *npl* accessori *mpl*.

five *adj*, *n* cinque *m*.

fiver *n* (*fam*) biglietto *m* da cinque sterline.

fix *vt* fissare; riparare; sistemare; * *n* guaio *m*.

fixation *n* fissazione *f*.

fixative *n* fissativo *m*.

fixed *adj* fisso.

fixtures *npl* impianti *mpl*.

fizz *n* effervescenza *f*; * *vi* frizzare.

fizzy *adj* effervescente.

fjord *n* fiordo *m*.

flabbergasted *adj* sbalordito.

flabby *adj* flaccido.

flaccid *adj* flaccido.

flag *n* bandiera *f*; * *vi* stancarsi.

flagpole *n* pennone *m*.

flagrant *adj* flagrante.

flagship *n* nave *f* ammiraglia.

flail *vt* agitare.

flair *n* disposizione *f* naturale.

flak *n* fuoco *m* contraereo.

flake *n* scaglia *f*; * *vi* scrostarsi.

flaky *adj* scrostato.

flamboyant *adj* stravagante.

flame *n* fiamma *f*; * *vi* divampare.

flamingo *n* fenicottero *m*.

flammable *adj* infiammabile.

flank *n* fianco *m*; * *vt* fiancheggiare.

flannel *n* flanella *f*.

flap *n* linguetta *f*; ribalta *f*; panico *m*; * *vt*, *vi* sbattere.

flare *vi* sfolgorare; * *n* chiarore *m*.

flared *adj* svasato.

flash *n* lampo *m*; flash *m*; * *vi* lampeggiare.

flash cube *n* flash *m*.

flashy *adj* vistoso.

flask *n* fiaschetta *f*; termos *m*.

flat *adj* piatto; sgonfio; stonato; categorico; bemolle; * *n* appartamento *m*; (*auto*) gomma *f* a terra.

flatness *n* monotonia *f*.

flatten *vt* spianare.

flatter *vt* lusingare.

flattering *adj* lusinghiero.

flattery *n* lusinghe *fpl*.

flatulence *n* flatulenza *f*.

flaunt *vt* sfoggiare.

flautist *n* flautista *m/f*.

flavour *n* gusto *m*; sapore *m*.

flavourless *adj* insipido.

flaw *n* difetto *m*.

flawless *adj* perfetto.

flax *n* lino *m*.

flea *n* pulce *f*.

fleck *n* macchiolina *f*.

fledgling *n* uccellino *m*.

flee *vt*, *vi* fuggire.

fleece *n* vello *m*; * *vt* pelare.

fleet *n* flotta *f*.

fleeting *adj* passeggero.

flesh *n* carne *f*.

flesh wound *n* ferita *f* superficiale.

fleshy *adj* carnoso.

flex *n* filo *m*; * *vt* stirare.

flexibility *n* flessibilità *f*.

flexible *adj* flessibile.

flick *n* colpetto *m*; * *vt* dare un colpetto.

flicker *vi* tremolare; * *n* tremolio *m*.

flier *n* aviatore *m*.

flight *n* volo *m*; rampa *f*; fuga *f*.

flight deck *n* cabina *f* di pilotaggio.

flighty *adj* frivolo.

flimsy *adj* leggero.

flinch *vi* trasalire.

fling *vt* lanciare.

flint *n* silice *f*.

flip *vi*; **to ~ through** sfogliare; * *n* colpetto *m*.

flippant *adj* irriverente.

flipper *n* pinna *f*.

flirt *n* civetta *f*.

flirtation *n* flirt *m*.

flit vi svolazzare.

float vt galleggiare; * n galleggiante m.

flock n gregge m; * vi ammassarsi.

flog vt frustare.

flogging n fustigazione f.

flood n inondazione f; * vt inondare; * vi straripare.

floodlight n riflettore m.

floor n pavimento m; piano m; * vt pavimentare; sconcertare.

floorboard n asse f di pavimento.

floor show n spettacolo m.

flop n fiasco m.

floppy adj floscio.

flora n flora f.

floral adj floreale.

florid adj florido.

florist n fioraio m.

flotilla n flottiglia f.

flounder n passera f; * vi impappinarsi; dibattersi.

flour n farina f.

flourish vt brandire; * vi prosperare; * n svolazzo m; ostentazione f.

flourishing adj fiorente.

flout vt contravvenire.

flow vi fluire; * n corrente f; flusso m.

flow chart n organigramma m.

flower n fiore m; * vi fiorire.

flowerbed n aiuola f.

flowerpot n vaso m da fiori.

flowery adj a fiori.

fluctuate vi fluttuare.

fluctuation n fluttuazione f.

flue n canna f fumaria.

fluency n scioltezza f.

fluent adj scorrevole; corrente.

fluff n peluria f; * adj ~y di peluche.

fluid adj, n fluido m.

fluidity n fluidità f.

fluke n colpo m di fortuna.

fluorescent adj fluorescente.

fluoride n fluoruro m.

flurry n agitazione f; raffica f.

flush vi arrossire; * vt tirare l'acqua; * n sciacquone m; rossore m; * adj ~ with a livello di.

fluster vt innervosire; * n stato di agitazione f.

flustered adj agitato.

flute n flauto m.

flutter vt battere; * vi svolazzare; * n battito m.

flux n cambiamento m continuo.

fly vi volare; * n mosca f.

flying adj volante; * n volo m; aviazione f.

flying saucer n disco m volante.

flypast n parata f aerea.

flysheet n soprattetto m.

foal n puledro m.

foam n schiuma f; * vi schiumeggiare.

foam rubber n gommapiuma f.

foamy adj spumoso.

focal adj focale.

focus n fuoco m.

fodder n foraggio m.

foe n nemico m.

foetal adj fetale.

feotus n feto m.

fog n nebbia f.

foggy adj nebbioso.

fog lamp n faro m antinebbia.

foible n debole m.

foil vt frustrare; * n carta f stagnola; fioretto m.

fold n ovile m; piega f; * vt piegare; * vi piegarsi.

folder n cartella f.

folding adj pieghevole.

foliage n fogliame m.

folio n foglio m.

folk n gente f.

folklore n folklore m.

folk song n canzone m folk.

follow vt seguire; to ~ up esaminare a fondo.

follower n seguace m/f.

following adj seguente; * n seguito m.

folly n pazzia f.

foment vt fomentare.

fond adj affezionato; grande.

fondent n fondente m.

fondle vt accarezzare.

fondness n predilezione f; affetto m.

font n fonte f battesimale.

food n cibo m.

food poisoning n intossicazione f alimentare.

foodstuffs npl generi mpl alimentari.

fool n sciocco m; buffone m; * vt ingannare.

foolhardy adj temerario.

foolish adj insensato.

foolproof adj infallibile.

foolscap n carta f protocollo.

foot n piede m; **to put one's ~ down** imporsi.

footage n metraggio m.

football n calcio m.

footballer n calciatore m.

footbridge n passerella f.

foothill n collina f.

foothold n punto m d'appoggio.

footing n punto m d'appoggio.

footlights npl luci fpl della ribalta.

footman n lacchè m.

footnote n postilla f.

footpath n sentiero m.

footprint n orma f.

footstep n passo m.

footwear n calzatura f.

for prep per; a favore di; da; **as ~ me** quanto a me; **what for?** perché? * conj poiché.

forage n foraggio m; * vi cercare.

foray n incursione f.

forbearance n pazienza f.

forbid vt proibire.

forbidding adj minaccioso.

force n forza f; **~s** le forze f armate; * vt forzare.

forced adj forzato.

forceful adj forte.

forceps n forcipe m.

forcible adj convincente.

ford n guado m; * vt guadare.

fore n prua f; davanti m; * adj anteriore.

forearm n avambraccio m.

foreboding n presentimento m.

forecast vt prevedere; * n previsione f.

forecourt n piazzale m.

forefathers npl progenitori mpl.

forefinger n indice n.

forefront n avanguardia f.

foregoing adj precedente.

foregone conclusion n risultato m scontato.

foreground n primo m piano.

forehead n fronte f.

foreign adj straniero; estero; estraneo.

foreigner n straniero m.

foreign exchange n valuta f estera.

foreleg n zampa f anteriore.

foreman n caposquadra m, caporeparto m.

foremost adj più importante.

forename n nome m.

forenoon n mattina f.

forensic medicine n medicina f legale.

forerunner n precursore m.

foresee vt prevedere.

foreseeable adj prevedibile.

foreshadow vt presagire.

foresight n previdenza f.

foreskin n prepuzio m.

forest n foresta f.

forestall vt anticipare.

forester n guardia f forestale.

forestry n silvicoltura f.

foretaste n pregustamento m.

foretell vt predire.

forethought n previdenza f.

forever *adv* eternamente, per sempre.

forewarn *vt* preavvertire.

foreword *n* prefazione *f*.

forfeit *n* penitenza *f*; * *vt* perdere.

forge *n* fornace *f*; * *vt* forgiare; contraffare.

forger *n* contraffattore *m*.

forgery *n* contraffazione *f*.

forget *vt* dimenticare.

forgetful *adj* distratto.

forgetfulness *n* smemoratezza *f*.

forget-me-not *n* (*bot*) nontiscordardimé *m*.

forgive *vt* perdonare.

forgiveness *n* perdono *m*.

forgo *vt* rinunciare a.

fork *n* forchetta *f*; biforcazione *f*; * *vi* biforcarsi; * *vt* **to ~ out** sborsare.

forked *adj* biforcuto.

fork-lift truck *n* carello *m* elevatore.

forlorn *adj* sconsolato.

form *n* forma *f*; modulo *m*; banco *m*; classe *f*; * *vt* formare.

formal *adj* formale.

formality *n* formalità *f*.

format *n* formato *m*; * *vt* formattare.

formation *n* formazione *f*.

formative *adj* formativo.

former *adj* precedente; * *pron* **the ~** il primo.

formidable *adj* formidabile.

formula *n* formula *f*.

formulate *vt* formulare.

forsake *vt* abbandonare.

fort *n* forte *m*.

forte *n* forte *m*.

forthcoming *adj* prossimo, imminente.

forthright *adj* schietto.

forthwith *adv* subito.

fortieth *adj*, *n* quarantesimo *m*.

fortification *n* fortificazione *f*.

fortify *vt* fortificare; rafforzare.

fortitude *n* forza *f* d'animo.

fortnight *n* quindici giorni *mpl*.

fortress *n* fortezza *f*.

fortuitous *adj* fortuito.

fortunate *adj* fortunato.

fortune *n* fortuna *f*.

fortune-teller *n* chiromante *m/f*.

forty *adj*, *n* quaranta *m*.

forum *n* foro *m*.

forward *adj* in avanti; precoce; **~s** *adv* avanti * *n* attaccante *m*; * *vt* inoltrare.

forwardness *n* sfacciataggine *f*.

fossil *adj n* fossile *m*.

foster *vt* allevare; nutrire.

foster parent *n* genitore *m* affidatario.

foul *adj* disgustoso; * *n* fallo *m*; * *vt* impestare; sporcare.

foul play *n* gioco *m* scorretto; assassinio *m*.

found *vt* fondare.

foundation *n* fondazione *f*.

founder *n* fondatore *m*; * *vi* affondare.

foundling *n* trovatello *m*.

foundry *n* fonderia *f*.

fount *n* sorgente *f*.

fountain *n* fontana *f*.

four *adj*, *n* quattro *m*.

fourfold *adj* quadruplo.

four-letter word *n* parolaccia *f*.

four-poster (bed) letto *m* a baldacchino.

foursome *n* partita *f* a quattro.

fourteen *adj*, *n* quattordici *m*.

fourteenth *adj*, *n* quattordicesimo *m*.

fourth *adj*, *n* quarto *m*.

fowl *n* pollame *m*.

fox *n* volpe *f*; * *vt* lasciare perplesso.

foxglove *n* digitale *f*.

foyer *n* foyer *m*.

fracas n rissa f.
fraction n frazione f.
fracture n frattura f.
fragile adj fragile.
fragility n fragilità f.
fragment n frammento m.
fragmentary adj frammentario.
fragrance n fragranza f.
fragrant adj fragrante.
frail adj debole.
frailty n debolezza f.
frame n corporatura f; montatura f; telaio m; cornicia f; * vt incorniciare.
frame of mind n umore m.
framework n struttura f.
franc n franco m.
franchise n concessione f; franchigia f.
frank adj franco; * vt affrancare.
frankness n franchezza f.
frantic adj frenetico.
fraternal adj fraterno.
fraternity n fraternità f.
fraternize vi fraternizzare.
fratricide adj, n fratricida m/f.
fraud n truffa f.
fraudulent adj fraudolento.
fraught adj teso.
fray n zuffa f; * vi consumarsi.
freak n eccentrico m; capriccio m; * adj anormale.
freckle n lentiggine f.
freckled adj lentigginoso.
free adj libero; gratuito; * vt liberare.
freedom n libertà f.
free-for-all n parapiglia f generale.
freehold n proprietà f assoluta.
freelance n collaboratore m esterno.
freely adv liberamente.
freemason n massone m.
freemasonry n massoneria f.
freepost n affrancatura f a ca-

rica del destinatario.
free-range adj ruspante.
fresia n fresia f.
free trade n liberoscambismo m.
freewheel vi andare a ruota libera, andare in folle.
free will n spontanea volontà f.
freeze vt gelare, congelare, surgelare; * vi gelare, congelarsi; * n gelata f.
freeze-dried adj liofilizzato.
freezer n congelatore m.
freezing adj gelido.
freezing point n punto m di congelamento.
freight n nolo m.
freighter n piroscafo m da carico.
French bean n fagiolino m.
French fries npl patatine fpl fritte.
French window n porta f finestra.
frenzied adj forsennato, frenetico.
frenzy n frenesia f.
frequency n frequenza f.
frequent adj frequente; * vt frequentare.
fresco n affresco m.
fresh adj fresco; sfacciato; ~ **water** acqua dolce; * adv appena.
freshen vt, vi rinfrescare.
fresher n matricola f.
freshly adv appena.
freshness f freschezza f.
fret vi preoccuparsi.
friar n frate m.
friction n frizione f.
Friday n venerdì m; **Good ~** Venerdì m Santo.
fridge n frigo m.
fried adj fritto.
friend n amico m; **Society of ~s** Quaccheri mpl.
friendliness n cordialità f.

friendly *adj* amichevole.
friendship *n* amicizia *f*.
frieze *n* fregio *m*.
frigate *n* (*mar*) fregata *f*.
fright *n* spavento *m*.
frighten *vt* spaventare.
frightened *adj* spaventato, impaurito.
frightening *adj* spaventoso.
frightful *adj* terribile.
frigid *adj* frigido.
fringe *n* frangia *f*.
fringe benefits *npl* vantaggi *mpl*.
frisk *vt* perquisire.
frisky *adj* vispo.
fritter *n* frittella *f*; * *vt* sprecare.
frivolity *n* frivolezza *f*.
frivolous *adj* frivolo.
frizzy *adj* crespo.
fro *adv*: **to go to and ~ between** fare la spola tra.
frock *n* vestito *m*; tonaca *f*.
frog *n* rana *f*.
frolic *vi* sgambettare.
frolicsome *adj* giocoso.
from *prep* da; per.
frond *n* fronda *f*.
front *n* davanti *m*; fronte *m*; lungomare *m*; *adj* davanti.
frontal *adj* frontale.
front door *n* porta *f* d'ingresso.
frontier *n* frontiera *f*, confine *m*.
front page *n* prima pagina *f*.
front-wheel drive *n* trasmissione *f* anteriore.
frost *n* brina *f*, gelo *m*.
frostbite *n* congelamento *m*.
frostbitten *adj* congelato.
frosted glass *n* vetro *m* smerigliato.
frosty *adj* gelido; glaciale.
froth *n* schiuma *f*; * *vi* schiumare.
frothy *adj* schiumoso.
frown *vi* aggrottare le sopracciglia; * *n* cipiglio *m*.

frozen *adj* congelato, surgelato.
frugal *adj* frugale.
fruit *n* frutta *f*; frutto *m*.
fruiterer *n* fruttivendolo *m*.
fruitful *adj* fruttifero; fruttuoso.
fruition *vi*: **to come to ~** realizzarsi.
fruit juice *n* succo *m* di frutta.
fruitless *adj* vano.
fruit salad *n* macedonia *f*.
fruit tree *n* albero *m* da frutto.
frustrate *vt* frustrare.
frustated *adj* frustrato.
frustration *n* frustrazione *f*.
fry *vt* friggere.
frying pan *n* padella *f*.
fuchsia *n* fucsia *f*.
fuck *vt* fottere.
fudge *n* caramella *f* fondente.
fuel *n* combustibile *m*.
fuel tank *n* serbatoio *m* del carburante.
fugitive *adj, n* fuggitivo *m*.
fugue *n* (*mus*) fuga *f*.
fulcrum *n* fulcro *m*.
fulfil *vt* compiere.
fulfilment *n* compimento *m*; soddisfazione *f*.
full *adj* pieno.
full-length *adj* lungo; (*film*) lungometraggio.
full moon *n* luna *f* piena.
fullness *n* abbondanza *f*; ampiezza *f*.
full-scale *adj* su vasta scala.
full-time *adj* tempo pieno.
fully *adv* completamente.
fulsome *adj* insincero.
fumble *vi* brancolare; andare a tentoni.
fume *n* esalazione *f*; * *vi* emettere fumo (o vapore); essere arrabbiatissimo.
fumigate *vt* suffumicare.
fun *n* divertimento *m*.
function *n* funzione *f*.

functional *adj* funzionale.
fund *n* fondo *m*; * *vt* finanziare.
fundamental *adj* fondamentale.
funeral *n* funerale *m*.
funereal *adj* funereo.
fun fair *n* luna park
fungus *n* muffa *f*.
funnel *n* imbuto *m*.
funny *adj* buffo.
fur *n* pelo *m*.
fur coat *n* pelliccia *f*.
furious *adj* furioso.
furlong *n* 201 metri.
furlough *n* (*mil*) congedo *m*.
furnace *n* fornace *f*.
furnish *vt* arredare; fornire.
furnishings *npl* mobili *mpl*
furniture *n* mobili *mpl*.
furore *n* scalpore *m*.
furrier *n* pellicciaio *m*.
furrow *n* solco *m*; * *vt* solcare.

furry *adj* peloso.
further *adv* più avanti; oltre; ~ **to** con riferimento a; * *adj* ulteriore; * *vt* favorire.
further education *n* istruzione *f* superiore.
furthermore *adv* inoltre.
furthest *adv*, *adj* più lontano.
furtive *adj* furtivo.
fury *n* furia *f*.
fuse *n* fusibile *m*; * *vt* fondere.
fuse box *n* scatola *f* dei fusibili.
fuselage *n* fusoliera *f*.
fusion *n* fusione *f*.
fuss *adj* agitazione *f*; storie *fpl*.
fussy *adj* pignolo; schizzinoso.
futile *adj* futile.
futility *n* futilità *f*.
future *adj*, *n* futuro *m*.
fuzz *n* peluria *f*; (*fam*) polizia *f*.
fuzzy *adj* crespo; sfocato.

G

gab *n*: **to have the gift of the** ~ avere la lingua sciolta.
gabardine *n* gabardine *m*.
gabble *vt* borbottare.
gable *n* frontone *m*.
gadget *n* aggeggio *m*.
gaffe *n* gaffe *f*.
gag *n* bavaglio *m*; gag *f*; * *vt* imbavagliare.
gaggle *n* branco *m*.
gaiety *n* allegria *f*.
gaily *adv* allegramente.
gain *n* aumento *m*; guadagno *m*; * *vt* ottenere; guadagnare; aumentare.
gainful *adj* remunerativo.
gait *n* andatura *f*.
gala *n* festa *f*; gala *m*.
galaxy *n* galassia *f*.

gale *n* bufera *f*.
gall *n* bile *f*.
gallant *adj* gallante.
gall bladder *n* cistifellea *f*.
gallery *n* galleria *f*; tribuna *f*; museo *m*.
galley *n* galea *f*.
gallon *n* gallone *m*.
gallop *n* galoppo *m*; * *vi* galoppare.
gallows *npl* patibolo *m*.
gallstone *n* calcolo *m* biliare.
galore *adv* a profusione.
galvanize *vt* galvanizzare.
gambit *n* gambetto *m*.
gamble *vt*, *vi* giocare d'azzardo; * *n* azzardo *m*.
gambler *n* giocatore *m* d'azzardo.

gambling n gioco m d'azzardo.

game n gioco m; partita f; selvaggina f.

gamekeeper n guardacaccia m.

gammon n prosciutto m affumicato.

gamut n (mus) gamma f.

gander n maschio dell'oca.

gang n banda f.

gangrene n cancrena f.

gangster n gangster m.

gangway n passerella f.

gap n spazio m; vuoto m; intervallo m.

gape vi spalancarsi.

gaping adj a bocca aperta; aperto.

garage n autorimessa f, garage m; officina f.

garbled adj ingarbugliato.

garden n giardino m.

gardener n giardiniere m.

gardening n giardinaggio m.

gargle vi fare i gargarismi; * n gargarismo m; collutorio m.

gargoyle n gargolla f.

garish adj sgargiante.

garland n ghirlanda f.

garlic n aglio m.

garment n indumento m.

garnish vt guarnire; * n decorazione f.

garret n soffitta f.

garrison n (mil) guarnigione f.

garrulous adj loquace.

garter n giarrettiera f.

gas n gas m; * vt asfissiare col gas.

gas cylinder n bombola f.

gaseous adj gassoso.

gas fire n stufa f a gas.

gash n squarcio m; * vt squarciare.

gasket n guarnizione f.

gasp vi ansare; * n anelito m.

gas mask n maschera f antigas.

gas meter n contattore m del gas.

gas ring n fornello m a gas.

gassy adj gassoso.

gastric adj gastrico.

gastronomic adj gastronomico.

gasworks n impianto m di produzione del gas.

gate n cancello m.

gateway n porta f.

gate-crasher n intruso m.

gather vt radunare; raccogliere; dedurre.

gathering n raduno m.

gauche adj goffo.

gaudy adj vistoso.

gauge n calibro m; * vt misurare.

gaunt adj emaciato.

gauntlet n guanto m.

gauze n garza f.

gay adj allegro; omosessuale.

gaze vi fissare; * n sguardo m.

gazelle n gazzella f.

gazette n gazzetta f.

gear n cambio m, marcia f; attrezzatura f.

gearbox n scatola f del cambio.

gear lever n leva f del cambio.

gear wheel n ruota f dentata.

gel n gel m.

gelatine n gelatina f.

gelignite n gelatina f esplosiva.

gem n gemma f.

Gemini n Gemelli mpl.

gender n genere m.

gene n gene m.

genealogical adj genealogico.

genealogy n genealogia f.

general adj generale; * adv in ~ generalmente; * n generale m.

general election n elezioni fpl legislative.

generality n generalità f.

generalization n generalizzazione f.

generalize vi generalizzare.

generate vt generare.

generation n produzione f; generazione f.

generator n generatore m.
generic adj generico.
generosity n generosità f.
generous adj generoso.
genetics npl genetica f.
genial adj cordiale.
genitals npl genitali mpl.
genitive n genitivo m.
genius n genio m.
genteel adj snob.
gentile n gentile m.
gentle adj dolce.
gentleman n signore m; gentiluomo m.
gentleness n tenerezza f.
gently adv dolcemente.
gentry n piccola nobiltà f.
gents n toilette per uomini.
genuflect vi genuflettersi.
genuine adj genuino.
genus n genere m.
geographer n geografo m.
geographical adj geografico.
geography n geografia f.
geological adj geologico.
geologist n geologo m.
geology n geologia f.
geometric(al) adj geometrico.
geometry n geometria f.
geranium n (bot) geranio m.
geriatric adj geriatrico.
germ n (med) microbo m.
germinate vi germinare.
gestation n gestazione f.
gesticulate vi gesticolare.
gesture n gesto m.
get vt ottenere; ricevere; prendere; portare; afferrare; * vi arrivare a; diventare; cominciare a; farsi; **to ~ the better of** prevalere su qualcuno.
geyser n (geog) geyser m; scaldabagno m.
ghastly adj orrendo.
gherkin n cetriolino m.
ghost n fantasma m.
giant n gigante m.
gibberish n parole fpl incom-

prensibili.
gibbon n gibbone m.
gibe vi lanciare frecciate; * n frecciata f.
giblets npl frattaglie fpl.
giddiness n vertigine f.
giddy adj vertiginoso.
gift n dono m; regalo m.
gifted adj dotato.
gift voucher n buono m premio.
gigantic adj gigantesco.
giggle vi ridacchiare; * n risolino m.
gild vt dorare.
gilding, gilt n doratura f.
gill n branchia f; 0,142 litri.
gilt-edged adj di massima sicurezza.
gimmick n trovata f.
gin n gin m.
ginger n zenzero m; rossiccio m.
giraffe n giraffa f.
girder n trave f.
girdle n busto m.
girl n ragazza f.
girlfriend n amica f.
girlish adj di ragazza.
giro n postagiro m.
girth n circonferenza f.
gist n succo m.
give vt dare; regalare; attribuire; dedicare; * vi dare; donare; cedere; **to ~ away** rivelare; **to ~ back** restituire; **to ~ in** cedere; **to ~ off** sprigionare; **to ~ out** distribuire; **to ~ up** rinunciare.
gizzard n ventriglio m.
glacial adj glaciale.
glacier n ghiacciaio m.
glad adj contento; lieto; **I am ~ to see** mi fa molto piacere.
gladden vt rallegrare.
gladiator n gladiatore m.
glamorous adj affascinante; seducente.
glamour n fascino m.

glance n occhiata f; * vi dare un' occhiata a.

glancing adj di striscio.

gland n ghiandola f.

glare n bagliore m; * vi sfolgorare; **to ~ at** fulminare con lo sguardo.

glaring adj accecante; palese.

glass n vetro m; bicchiere m; calice m; **~es** npl occhiali mpl.

glassware n cristalleria f.

glassy adj vitreo.

glaze n smalto m.

glazier n vetraio m.

gleam n lucichio m; * vi luccicare.

gleaming adj lucente.

glean vt racimolare.

glee n gioia f.

glen n vallone m.

glib adj disinvolto.

glide vi planare; * n planata f.

glider n aliante m.

gliding n volo m con l'aliante.

glimmer n barlume m; * vi baluginare.

glimpse n sguardo passeggero; * vt intravedere.

glint vi scintillare; * n scintillio m.

glisten, glitter vi luccicare.

gloat vi gongolare.

global adj globale.

globe n globo m; mappamondo m.

gloom, gloominess n buio m.

gloomy adj cupo; deprimente.

glorification n glorificazione f.

glorify vt glorificare.

glorious adj glorioso.

glory n gloria f.

gloss n glossa f; lucentezza f; * vt chiosare; **to ~ over** mascherare.

glossary n glossario m.

glossy adj lucido.

glove n guanto m.

glove compartment n vano m portaoggetti.

glow vi ardere; rosseggiare; * n incandescenza f.

glower vi guardare con astio.

glucose n glucosio m.

glue n colla f; * vt incollare.

gluey adj colloso.

glum adj cupo.

glut n sovrabbondanza f.

glutinous adj appiccicoso.

glutton n ghiottone m.

gluttony n ghiottoneria f.

glycerine n glicerina f.

gnarled adj nodoso.

gnash vt digrignare.

gnat n zanzara f.

gnaw vt rosicchiare.

gnome n gnomo m.

gnu n gnu m.

go vi andare; andarsene; arrivare; **to ~ ahead** tirare avanti; **to ~ back** ritornare; **to ~ by** passare; **to ~ for** avventarsi; **to ~ in** entrare; **to ~ off** guastarsi; **to ~ on** continuare; **to ~ out** uscire; **to ~ up** salire; * n dinamismo m; tentativo m;

goad vt spronare.

go-ahead adj intraprendente; * n benestare m.

goal n goal m; scopo m.

goalkeeper n portiere m.

goalpost n palo m.

goat n capra f.

goatherd n capraio m.

gobble vt trangugiare.

go-between n intermediario m.

goblet n calice m.

goblin n folletto m.

God n Dio m.

godchild n figlioccio m.

goddaughter n figlioccia f.

goddess n dea f.

godfather n padrino m.

godforsaken adj sperduto.

godhead n divinità f.

godless adj empio.

godlike *adj* divino.

godliness *n* santità *f*.

godly *adj* pio.

godmother *n* madrina *f*.

godsend *n* dono del cielo; manna *f*.

godson *n* figlioccio *m*.

goggle *vi* sbarrare gli occhi.

goggles *npl* occhiali *mpl*.

going *n* andatura *f*; * *adj* ben avviato; corrente.

gold *n* oro *m*.

golden *adj* d'oro; ~ **rule** *n* regola *f* principale.

goldfish *n* pesce *m* rosso.

goldsmith *n* orefice *m*.

golf *n* golf *m*.

golf club *n* mazza *f* da golf; circolo *m* di golf.

golf course *n* campo *m* di golf.

golfer *n* giocatore *m* di golf.

gondola *n* gondola *f*.

gondolier *n* gondoliere *m*.

gong *n* gong *m*.

gonorrhoea *n* gonorrea *f*.

good *adj* buono; bello; bravo; gentile; * *n* bene *m*; ~**s** *npl* merci *fpl*.

goodbye! *excl* arrivederci! * *n* addio *m*.

goodies *npl* chicche *fpl*.

good-looking *adj* bello, piacente.

good-natured *adj* affabile.

goodness *n* bontà *f*.

goodwill *n* buona *f* volontà; avviamento *m*.

goose *n* oca *f*.

gooseberry *n* uva *f* spina.

goosepimples *npl* pelle *f* d'oca.

gore *n* spicchio *m*; * *vt* incornare.

gorge *n* (*geog*) gola *f*; * *vt* rimpinzarsi.

gorgeous *adj* sontuoso, splendido.

gorilla *n* gorilla *m*.

gormless *adj* tonto.

gorse *n* ginestra *f* spinosa.

gory *adj* sanguinoso.

goshawk *n* astore *m*.

gospel *n* vangelo *m*.

gossamer *n* mussolina *f*.

gossip *n* pettegolezzi *mpl*; pettegolo *m*; * *vi* chiacchierare.

gothic *adj* gotico.

gouge *vt* scavare.

goulash *n* gulasch *m*.

gourd *n* zucca *f*.

gourmet *n* buongustaio *m*.

gout *n* gotta *f*.

govern *vt* governare.

governess *n* governante *f*.

government *n* governo *m*.

governor *n* governatore *m*.

gown *n* abito *m*; toga *f*.

grab *vt* afferrare.

grace *n* grazia *f*; garbo *m*; proroga *f*; **to say** ~ dire il benedicite; * *vt* onorare.

graceful *adj* aggraziato, garbato.

gracious *adj* cortese; misericordioso.

gradation *n* gradazione *f*.

grade *n* categoria *f*; voto *m*; grado *m*; * *vt* classificare; graduare.

gradient *n* gradiente *m*.

gradual *adj* graduale.

graduate *vi* laurearsi; * *n* laureato *m*.

graduation *n* consegna delle lauree.

graffiti *n* graffiti *mpl*.

graft *n* innesto *m*; duro lavoro *m*; * *vt* innestare.

grain *n* cereali *mpl*; granello *m*; grana *f*.

gram *n* grammo *m*.

grammar *n* grammatica *f*.

grammatical *adj* grammaticale.

gramophone *n* grammofono *m*.

granary *n* granaio *m*.

grand *adj* magnifico; alto locato; eccezionale.

grandchild n nipote m/f.

granddad n nonno m.

granddaughter n nipotina f.

grandeur n grandiosità f.

grandfather n nonno m.

grandiose adj grandioso.

grandma n nonna f.

grandmother n nonna f.

grandparents npl nonni mpl.

grand piano n pianoforte m a coda.

grandson n nipotino m.

grandstand n tribuna f coperta.

granite n granito m.

granny n nonna f.

grant vt accordare; ammettere; **to take for ~ed** dare per scontato; * n sovvenzione f; borsa f di studio.

granulate vt granulare.

granule n granello m.

grape n chicco m d'uva; **bunch of ~s** grappolo m d'uva.

grapefruit n pompelmo m.

grapevine n vite f.

graph n grafico m.

graphic(al) adj grafico.

graphics npl grafica f.

grasp vt afferrare; * presa f; padronanza f.

grasping adj avido.

grass n erba f.

grasshopper n cavalletta f.

grassland n prateria f.

grass-roots npl base f.

grass snake n biscia f.

grassy adj erboso.

grate n grata f; * vt grattare; * vi cigolare.

grateful adj grato.

gratefulness n riconoscenza f.

gratification n soddisfazione f.

gratify vt soddisfare.

gratifying adj soddisfacente.

grating n grata f; * adj stridulo.

gratis adv gratis.

gratitude n gratitudine f.

gratuitous adj gratuito.

gratuity n mancia f.

grave n tomba f; * adj grave.

grave digger n becchino m.

gravel n ghiaia f.

gravestone n lapide f.

graveyard n cimitero m.

gravitate vi gravitare.

gravitation n gravitazione f.

gravity n gravità f.

gravy n sugo m dell'arrosto.

graze vi pascolare; * vt scorticare; * n scorticatura f.

grease n grasso m, unto m; * vt ungere, lubrificare.

greaseproof adj: **~ paper** carta f oleata.

greasy adj untuoso, unto.

great adj grande; meraviglioso; eminente.

greatness n grandezza f.

greed n avidità f.

greedy adj avido; goloso.

Greek n greco m.

green adj, n verde m; **~s** npl verdura f.

green belt n zona f verde.

greenery n verde m.

greengrocer n fruttivendolo m.

greenhouse n serra f.

greenish adj verdastro.

greet vt salutare.

greeting n saluto m.

greetings card n cartolina f d'auguri.

grenade n granata f.

grenadier n granatiere m.

grey adj, n grigio m.

greyhound n levriero m.

grid n grata f; rete f.

gridiron n graticolo m.

grief n dolore m.

grievance n lagnanza f.

grieve vt addolorare.

grievous adj penoso.

griffin n grifone m.

grill n griglia f; * vt cuocere alla griglia.

grille n inferriata f.

grim adj torvo; macabro.

grimace n smorfia f.

grime n sudiciume m.

grimy adj sudicio.

grin n largo sorriso m; * vi fare un largo sorriso.

grind vt macinare; * n trantran m.

grinder n macinino m.

grip n presa f; borsone m; * vt stringere.

gripe n colica f.

gripping adj appassionante.

grisly adj raccapricciante.

gristle n cartilagine f.

gristly adj cartilaginoso.

grit n pietrisco m.

grizzle vi piagnucolare.

groan vi gemere; * n gemito m.

grocer n negoziante m/f di alimentari.

groceries npl spesa f.

grocery n alimentari m.

groggy adj intontito.

groin n inguine m.

groom n palafreniere m; sposo m; * vt governare; aver cura di.

groove n solco m.

grope vi cercare a tastoni.

gross adj obeso; grossolano; lordo; * n grossa f.

grotesque adj grottesco.

grotto n grotta f.

ground n terra f, terreno m; campo m; motivo m; ~s fondi mpl; * vi incagliarsi.

ground floor n pian m terreno.

grounding n fondamento m; basi fpl.

groundless adj infondato.

groundsheet n telone m impermeabile.

groundwork n lavoro m preparatorio.

group n gruppo m; complesso m; * vt raggruppare.

grouse n urogallo m; mugugno m; * vi brontolare.

grove n boschetto m.

grovel vi strisciare.

grow vi crescere; aumentare; diventare; **to ~ up** diventare grande; * vt coltivare; aumentare.

grower n coltivatore m.

growing adj crescente; * n coltura f.

growl vi ringhiare; * n ringhio m.

grown-up n adulto m.

growth n crescita f; tumore m.

grub n larva f; (fam) cibo m.

grubby adj sudicio.

grudge n rancore m; * vt invidiare; dare a malincuore.

grudgingly adv malvolentieri.

gruelling adj estenuante.

gruesome adj agghiacciante.

gruff adj burbero.

grumble vi brontolare; * n brontolio m.

grumpy adj scorbutico.

grunt vi grugnire; * n grugnito m.

G-string n tanga m.

guarantee n garanzia f; * vt garantire.

guard n guardia f; protezione f; * vt fare la guardia a.

guarded adj circospetto.

guardroom n (mil) corpo m di guardia.

guardian n tutore m.

guardianship n tutela f.

guerrilla n guerrigliero m.

guerrilla warfare n guerriglia f.

guess vt, vi indovinare; supporre; * n supposizione f.

guesswork n congettura f.

guest n ospite m/f, invitato m.

guest room n camera f degli ospiti.

guesthouse n pensione f familiare.

guffaw n risata f fragorosa.

guidance n guida f; consigli
mpl.

guida vt guidare; * n guida f;
manuale m.

guide dog n cane m per ciechi.

guidelines npl direttive fpl.

guidebook n guida f.

guild n corporazione f.

guile n astuzia f.

guillotine n ghigliottina f; * vt
ghigliottinare.

guilt n colpa f, colpevolezza f.

guiltless adj senza colpa.

guilty adj colpevole.

guinea pig n porcellino m d'India; cavia f.

guise n sembianza f.

guitar n chitarra f.

guitarist n chitarrista m/f.

gulf n golfo m; abisso m.

gull n gabbiano m.

gullet n gola f.

gullibility n credulità f.

gullible adj credulone.

gully n burrone m.

gulp n boccata f; * vt inghiottire.

gum n gengiva f; colla f; * vt incollare.

gum tree n eucalipto m.

gun n fucile m, pistola f, rivoltella f.

gunboat n cannoniera f.

gun carriage n affusto m.

gunfire n colpi mpl d'arma da
fuoco.

gunman n uomo m armato.

gunner n artigliere m.

gunpoint n; **at ~** sotto la minaccia delle armi.

gunpowder n polvere f da sparo.

gunshot n sparo m.

gunsmith n armaiolo m.

gurgle n gorgoglio m; * vt gorgogliare.

guru n guru m.

gush vi sgorgare; * n ondata f.

gushing adj sgorgante; espansivo.

gusset n gherone m.

gust n folata f, raffica f.

gusto n gusto m.

gusty adj ventoso.

gut n intestino m; budello m; **~s**
npl budella f; * vt sventrare.

gutter n grondaia f, cunetta f.

guttural adj gutturale.

guy n tizio m; tirante m.

guzzle vt ingozzare.

gym(nasium) n palestra f.

gymnast n ginnasta m/f.

gymnastic adj ginnastico; * n
~s ginnastica f.

gynaecologist n ginecologo m.

gypsy n zingaro m.

gyrate vi roteare.

H

haberdasher n merciaio f.

haberdashery n merceria f.

habit n abitudine f; tonaca f.

habitable adj abitabile.

habitat n habitat m.

habitation n abitazione f.

habitual adj abituale.

hack n fendente m; scribacchino m; * vt tagliare.

hackneyed adj trito.

hacksaw n seghetto m per me-
talli.

haddock n eglefino m.

haematology n ematologia f.

haemoglobin n emoglobina f.

haemophilia n emofilia f.

haemorrhage n emorragia f.

haemorrhoids npl emorroidi fpl.

hag n befana f.

haggard adj tirato.

haggle vi contrattare.

hail n grandine f; * vi grandinare; * vt acclamare.

hailstone n chicco m di grandine.

hair n capelli mpl; chioma f; pelo m.

hairbrush n spazzola f per capelli.

haircut n taglio m dei capelli.

hairdo n pettinatura f.

hairdresser n parrucchiere m.

hair-dryer n asciugacapelli m, fon m.

hairless adj senza peli.

hairnet n reticella f.

hairpin n forcina f.

hairpin bend n tornante m.

hair remover n depilatore m.

hairspray n lacca f.

hairstyle n acconciatura f.

hairy adj peloso.

hake n nasello m.

halcyon adj sereno.

half n metà f; * adj metà, mezzo.

half-caste n meticcio m.

half-hearted adj svogliato.

half-hour n mezz'ora f.

half-moon n mezzaluna f.

half-price adj, adv a metà prezzo.

half-time n intervallo m.

halfway adv a metà strada.

half-yearly adj semestrale.

halibut n ippoglosso m.

halitosis n alitosi f.

hall n entrata f; salone m; villa f.

hallmark n marchio m.

hallow vt consacrare.

hallucination n allucinazione f.

halo n aureola f.

halt vt fermare; * vi fermarsi; * n fermata f; sosta f.

halting adj esitante.

halve vt dimezzare.

ham n prosciutto m; radioamatore m.

humburger n hamburger m.

hamlet n paesino m.

hammer n martello m; * vt martellare.

hammock n amaca f.

hamper n cesto m; * vt ostacolare.

hamster n criceto m.

hamstring n tendine m del ginocchio.

hand n mano f; **at ~** a portata di mano; * vt passare; consegnare.

handbag n borsa f.

handbook n manuale m.

handbrake n freno m a mano.

handcuffs npl manette fpl.

handful n manciata f.

handicap n menomazione; handicap m.

handicapped adj andicappato.

handicraft n artigianato m.

handiwork n lavorazione f a mano.

handkerchief n fazzoletto m.

handle n manico m; * vt maneggiare; trattare.

handlebars npl manubrio m.

handrail n corrimano m.

handshake n stretto m di mano.

handsome adj bello; considerevole.

handwriting n scrittura f.

handy adj sottomano; comodo.

handyman n tuttofare m.

hang vt appendere; impiccare; * vi pendere.

hangar n aviorimessa f.

hanger n gruccia f.

hanger-on n parassita m/f.
hang-gliding n deltaplano m.
hangman n boia m.
hangover n postumi mpl di una sbornia.
hang-up n complesso m.
hanker vi avere molto desiderio di.
haphazard adj casuale.
hapless adj sfortunato.
happen vi succedere; capitare; accadere.
happening n avvenimento m.
happily adv tranquillamente.
happiness n felicità f.
happy adj contento, felice.
happy-go-lucky adj spensierato.
harangue n aringa f; * vt aringare.
harass vt assillare.
harbinger n foriero m.
harbour n porto m; * vt covare.
hard adj duro; rigido; forte; difficile; ~ **of hearing** duro d'orecchio.
hardboard n faesite f.
hard-boiled adj sodo.
harden vt indurire.
hard-headed adj pratico.
hard-hearted adj duro (di cuore)
hardiness n resistenza f.
hardly adv appena.
hardness n durezza f.
hardship n privazioni fpl.
hard-up adj al verde.
hardware n ferramenta fpl.
hardwearing adj resistente.
hardy adj robusto.
hare n lepre f.
hare-brained adj insensato.
hare-lip n labbro n leporino.
harem n harem m.
haricot n fagiolo m bianco.
harlequin n arlecchino m.
harm n male m; danno m; * vt nuocere a; danneggiare.

harmful adj nocivo.
harmless adj innocuo.
harmonic adj armonico.
harmonica n armonica f.
harmonious adj armonioso.
harmonize vt, vi armonizzare.
harmony n armonia f.
harness n bardatura f; briglie fpl; * vt bardare.
harp n arpa f.
harpist n arpista m/f.
harpoon n arpione m.
harpsichord n clavicembalo m.
harrow n erpice m.
harrowing adj straziante.
harry vt assillare.
harsh adj severo.
harshness n severità f.
harvest n raccolto m; * vt fare il raccolto di.
harvester n (combine) mietitrice f.
hash n pasticcio m.
hashish n hascisc m.
hassock n inginocchiatoio m.
haste n fretta f; **to make** ~ affrettarsi.
hasten vt accelerare.
hastily adv in fretta e furia.
hasty adj affrettato.
hat n cappello m.
hatch vt elaborare; * vi schiudersi; * n boccaporto m.
hatchback n (auto) macchina f a tre/cinque porte.
hatchet n accetta f.
hate n odio m; * vt odiare.
hateful adj odioso.
hatred n odio m.
hatter n cappellaio m.
hat-trick n vincere per tre volte consecutive.
haughty adj superbo.
haul vt trascinare; * n tragitto m; retata f.
haulage n autotrasporto m.
haulier n autotrasportatore m.

haunch n coscia f.

haunt vt frequentare; abitare;
* n covo m.

haunted adj abitato dai fantasmi.

have vt avere; possedere; fare;
tenere.

haven n rifugio m.

haversack n zaino m.

havoc n danni mpl.

hawk n falco m; * vt vendere
per strada.

hawthorn n biancospino m.

hay n fieno m.

hay fever n raffreddore m da
fieno.

hayloft n fienile m.

haystack n pagliaio m.

hazard n rischio m; * vt rischiare.

hazardous adj rischioso.

haze n foschia f.

hazel n nocciolo m; * adj nocciola.

hazelnut n nocciola f.

hazy adj sfocato.

he pron egli, lui.

head n testa f; capo m; * vt essere in testa a.

headache n mal f di testa; gratt-
tacapo m.

headdress n copricapo m.

headland n capo m.

headlight n fanale m.

headlong adv a capofitto.

headmaster n preside m.

head office n sede f

headphones n cuffia f.

headquarters npl quartier m
generale.

headroom n altezza f.

headstrong adj testardo.

headwaiter n capocameriere
m.

headway n progresso m; **to
make ~** fare progresso.

heady adj inebriante.

heal vt guarire.

health n salute f.

healthy adj sano.

heap n mucchio m; * vt ammucchiare.

hear vt, vi sentire.

hearing n udito m.

hearing aid n apparecchio m
acustico.

hearsay n diceria f.

hearse n carro m funebre.

heart n cuore m; **by ~** a memoria.

heart attack n infarto m.

heartbreak n immenso dolore
m.

heartburn n bruciore m di stomaco.

heart failure n arresto m cardiaco.

heartfelt adj sincero.

hearth n focolare m.

heartily adv di gusto, di cuore.

heartiness n giovialità f.

heartless adj spietato.

hearty adj gioviale.

heat n calore m; * vt scaldare.

heater n stufa f.

heath n brughiera f.

heathen n pagano m.

heather n erica f.

heating n riscaldamento m.

heat-resistant adj termoresistente.

heatwave n ondata f di caldo.

heave vt strascinare a fatica;
* n sforzo m.

heaven n cielo m, paradiso m.

heavenly adj celeste; divino.

heavily adv pesantemente.

heavy adj pesante; intenso; opprimente.

Hebrew adj ebreo, ebraico; * n
ebreo m, ebraico m.

heckle vt fare azione di disturbo.

hectic adj movimentato.

hedge n siepe f; * vi premunirsi; tergiversare.

hedgehog *n* riccio *m*.
hedonism *n* edonismo *m*.
heed *vt* badare a; * *n* attenzione *f*.
heedless *adj* non curante.
heel *n* calcagno *m*; tacco *m*.
hefty *adj* pesante.
heifer *n* giovenca *f*.
height *n* altezza *f*.
heighten *vt* alzare; aumentare; * *vi* aumentare.
heinous *adj* atroce.
heir, heiress *n* erede *m/f*.
heirloom *n* ricordo *m* di famiglia.
helicopter *n* elicottero *m*.
helium *n* elio *m*.
hell *n* inferno *m*.
hellish *adj* infernale.
helm *n* timone *m*.
helmet *n* casco *m*.
help *vt* aiutare; assistere; soccorrere; * *n* aiuto *m*; aiutante *m/f*; soccorso *m*; assistenza *f*.
helper *n* assistente *m/f*.
helpful *adj* utile.
helping *n* porzione *f*.
helpless *adj* incapace.
helter-skelter *n* scivolo *m* a spirale.
hem *n* orlo *m*.
he-man *n* fusto *m*.
hemisphere *n* emisfero *m*.
hemlock *n* cicuta *f*.
hemp *n* canapa *f* indiana.
hen *n* gallina *f*.
henceforth *adv* d'ora innanzi.
henchman *n* accolito *m*.
hen-house *n* pollaio *m*.
hapatitis *n* epatite *f*.
her *pron* la, lei.
herald *n* araldo *m*; * *vt* preannunciare.
heraldry *n* araldica *f*.
herb *n* erba *f* aromatica.
herbaceous *adj* erbaceo.
herbalist *n* erborista *m/f*.
herbivorous *adj*, *n* erbivoro *m*.

herd *n* mandria *f*; gregge *m*.
here *adv* qui, qua.
hereabouts *adv* da queste parti.
hereafter *adv* da qui in avanti.
hereby *adv* con questo.
hereditary *adj* ereditario.
heredity *n* eredità *f*.
heresy *n* eresia *f*.
heretic *adj*, *n* eretico *m*.
herewith *adv* con la presente.
heritage *n* eredità *f*; patrimonio *m*.
hermetic *adj* ermetico.
hermit *n* eremita *m*.
hermitage *n* eremitaggio *m*.
hernia *n* ernia *f*.
hero *n* eroe *m*.
heroic *adj* eroico.
heroin *n* eroina *f*.
heroine *n* eroina *f*.
heroism *adj* eroismo.
heron *n* airone *m*.
herring *n* aringa *f*.
hers *pron* suo, di lei.
herself *pron* se stessa, lei stessa.
hesitant *adj* esitante.
hesitate *vi* esitare.
hesitation *n* esitazione *f*.
heterogeneous *adj* eterogeneo.
heterosexual *adj*, *n* eterosessuale *m/f*.
hew *vt* tagliare.
hexagon *n* esagono *m*.
hexagonal *adj* esagonale.
heyday *n* tempi *mpl* d'oro.
hi *exclam* ciao!
hiatus *n* lacuna *f*.
hibernate *vi* cadere in letargo.
hiccup *n* singhiozzo *m*; * *vi* avere il singhiozzo.
hidden *adj* nascosto.
hide *vt* nascondere; * *n* cuoio *m*.
hideaway *n* nascondiglio *m*.
hideous *adj* orribile.
hiding *n* botte *fpl*.
hierarchy *n* gerarchia *f*.

hieroglyphic *adj* geroglifico *m*; ~s *npl* geroglifici *mpl*.

hi-fi *n* stereo *m*; * *adj* hi-fi.

higgledy-piggledy *adj* alla rinfusa.

high *adj* alto.

highchair *n* seggiolone *m*.

high-handed *adj* prepotente.

highlands *npl* zona *f* montuosa.

highlight *n* clou *m*.

highly *adv* estremamente.

highly strung *adj* ipersensibile.

highness *n* altezza *f*.

high tide *n* alta marea *f*.

hijack *n* dirottamento *m*; * *vt* dirottare.

hijacker *n* dirottatore *m*.

hike *n* escursione *f* a piedi.

hilarious *adj* spassosissimo.

hilarity *n* ilarità *f*.

hill *n* collina *f*, colle *m*.

hillock *n* poggio *m*.

hillside *n* pendio *m*.

hilly *adj* collinoso.

hilt *n* impugnatura *f*.

him *pron* lo, lui.

himself *pron* lui stesso.

hind *adj* posteriore; * *n* cerva *f*.

hinder *vt* impedire.

hindrance *n* intralcio *m*.

hindquarters *npl* posteriore *m*.

hindsight *n* giudizio *m* retrospettivo.

hinge *n* cardine *m*, cerniera *f*.

hint *n* allusione *f*; * *vt* alludere.

hip *n* anca *f*.

hippopotamus *n* ippopotamo *m*.

hire *vt* noleggiare; * *n* noleggio *m*.

his *pron* suo, di lui.

hiss *vt* sibilare; * *n* sibilo *m*.

historian *n* storico *m*.

historic(al) *adj* storico.

history *n* storia *f*.

histrionic *adj* istrionico.

hit *vt* colpire; picchiare; sbattere; raggiungere; * *n* colpo *m*; successo *m*.

hitch *vt* **to ~ up** attaccare; tirare su; * *n* intoppo *m*.

hitch-hike *vi* fare l'autostop.

hitherto *adv* fino a ora.

hive *n* alveare *m*.

hoard *n* gruzzolo *m*; * *vt* accumulare.

hoar-frost *n* brina *f*.

hoarse *adj* rauco.

hoax *n* scherzo *m*; * *vt* ingannare.

hobble *vi* zoppicare.

hobby *n* hobby *m*, passatempo *m*.

hobbyhorse *n* chiodo fisso.

hobnob *vi* mescolarsi.

hockey *n* hockey *m*.

hocus-pocus *n* trucco *m*.

hoe *n* zappa *f*; * *vt* zappare.

hog *n* porco *m*; * *vt* accaparrarsi.

hoipoloi *n* gentaglia *f*.

hoist *vt* issare; * *n* montacarichi *m*.

hold *vt* tenere; mantenere; **to ~ up** ritardare; (bank) assaltare; * *n* presa *f*; stiva *f*;

hoder *n* possessore *m*; contenitore *m*.

holding *n* podere *m*; ~s azioni *fpl*.

holdup *n* rapina *f*; intoppo *m*.

hole *n* buca *f*, buco *m*, falla *f*; tana *f*; * *vt* bucare.

holiday *n* vacanza *f*.

holidaymaker *n* villeggiante *m*.

holiness *n* santità *f*.

hollow *adj* cavo; falso; * *n* cavità; * *vt* scavare.

holly *n* agrifoglio *m*.

hollyhock *n* malvone *m*.

holocaust *n* olocausto *m*.

holster n fondina f.
holy adj santo, religioso.
Holy Ghost n Spirito m Santo.
homage n omaggio m.
home n casa f; patria f; habitat m; istituto m.
homeland n patria f.
homely adj semplice, familiare.
homeless adj senza tetto.
home-made adj fatto in casa.
homesick n nostalgia f (di casa).
homeward adj verso casa.
homework n compito m.
homicidal adj omicida.
homicide n omicidio m.
homily n omelia f.
homing adj autocercante.
homoeopath adj, n omeopatico m.
homoeopathic adj omeopatico,
homoeopathy n omeopatia f.
homogeneity n omogeneità f.
homogeneous adj omogeneo.
homonym s omonimo m.
homosexual adj, n omosessuale m/f.
honest adj onesto.
honesty n onestà f.
honey n miele m.
honeycomb n nido m d'api.
honeymoon n luna f di miele.
honeysuckle n (bot) caprifoglio m.
honorary adj onorario.
honour n onore m; * vt onorare.
honourable adj onorevole.
hood n cappuccio m.
hoodlum n teppista m/f.
hoodwink vt imbrogliare.
hoof n zoccolo m.
hook n gancio m; by ~ or by crook di riffa o di raffa; * vt agganciare.
hooked adj (naso) aquilino; fanatico.
hooligan n teppista m/f.
hoop n cerchio m.

hooter n serena f; clacson m.
hop n saltello m; (bot) luppolo; * vi saltellare; ~ it! smamma!
hope n speranza f; * vi sperare.
hopeful adj fiducioso.
hopeless adj impossibile; incorreggibile; disperato.
horde n orda f.
horizon n orizzonte m.
horizontal adj orizzontale.
hormone n ormone m.
horn n corno m; clacson m.
hornet n calabrone m.
horny adj incallito.
horoscope n oroscopo m.
horrendous adj orrendo.
horrible adj orribile.
horrid adj odioso.
horrific adj spaventoso.
horrify vt fare inorridire.
horror n orrore m.
horror film n film m dell'orrore.
hors d'oeuvres npl antipasto m.
horse n cavallo m.
horseback adv: on ~ a cavallo.
horse chestnut n ippocastano m.
horsefly n tafano m.
horseman n cavaliere m.
horsmanship n equitazione f.
horsepower n cavallo m.
horse racing n corse fpl di cavalli.
horseradish n raffano m.
horseshoe n ferro m di cavallo.
horsewoman n ammazzone f.
horticulture n orticoltura f.
horticulturist n orticoltore m.
hosepipe n tubo m di gomma.
hosiery n calze fpl.
hospice n ospizio m.
hospitable adj ospitale.
hospital n ospedale m.
hospitality n ospitalità f.
host n ospite m; presentatore m;

moltitudine *f*; (*relig*) ostia *f*.
hostage *n* ostaggio *m*.
hostel *n* ostello *m*.
hostess *n* hostess *f*.
hostile *adj* ostile.
hostility *n* ostilità *f*.
hot *adj* caldo; piccante; focoso.
hotbed *n* (*fig*) focolaio *m*.
hot dog *n* hot dog *m*.
hotel *n* albergo *m*.
hotelier *n* albergatore *m*.
hot-headed *adj* impetuoso.
hot-house *n* serra *f*.
hotline *n* telefono *m* rosso.
hotplate *n* piastra *f*, scaldavivande *m*.
hotly *adv* accanitamente.
hound *n* segugio *m*; * *vt* perseguitare.
hour *n* ora *f*.
hour-glass *n* clessidra *f*.
hourly *adv* ogni ora.
house *n* casa *f*; (*polit*) camera *f*;
* *vt* sistemare, alloggiare.
houseboat *n* house boat *f*.
housebreaker *n* scassinatore
m.
household *n* casa *f*; famiglia *f*.
householder *n* capo famiglia
m/f.
housekeeper *n* governante *f*.
housekeeping *n* amministrazione *f* della casa.
house warming *n* festa *f* per
inaugurare la casa.
housewife *n* casalinga *f*.
housework *n* faccende *fpl*.
housing *n* alloggiamento *m*;
incastellatura *f*.
housing estate *n* quartiere *m*
residenziale.
hovel *n* tugurio *m*.
hover *vi* librarsi.
how *adv* come; ~ **do you do!**
piacere.
however *adv* comunque, tuttavia.
howl *vi* ululare; urlare; pian-

gere; * *n* ululato *m*.
hub *n* mozzo *m*; (*fig*) fulcro *m*.
hubbub *n* baccano *m*.
hubcap *n* coprimozzo *m*.
hue *n* tinta *f*.
huff *n*: **in a ~** imbronciato.
hug *vt* abbracciare; * *n* abbraccio *m*.
huge *adj* enorme.
hulk *n* nave *f* in disarmo; bestione.
hull *n* scafo *m*.
hullo *excl* ciao!; pronto.
hum *vi* ronzare; * *vt* canticchiare * *n* ronzio *m*.
human *adj* umano; * *n* essere
m umano.
humane *adj* umanitario.
humanist *n* umanista *m/f*.
humanitarian *adj* umanitario.
humanity *n* umanità *f*.
humanly *adv* umanamente.
humble *adj* umile; * *vt* umiliare.
humbly *adv* umilmente.
humbug *n* sciocchezze *fpl*.
humdrum *adj* monotono.
humid *adj* umido.
humidity *n* umidità *f*.
humiliate *vt* umiliare.
humiliation *n* umiliazione *f*.
humility *n* umiltà *f*.
humming-bird colibrì *m*.
humorist *n* umorista *m/f*.
humorous *adj* spiritoso.
humour *n* umorismo *m*; umore
m; * *vt* accontentare.
hump *n* gobba *f*.
hunch *n* impressione *f*; **~back**
gobbo *m*; * *adj* **~backed** gobbo.
hundred *adj*, *n* cento *m*.
hundredth *adj*, *n* centesimo *m*.
hundredweight *n* 50,8 kg.
hunger *n* fame *f*; * *vi* **to ~ after** desiderare moltissimo.
hunger strike *n* sciopero *m* della fame.

303

hungrily *adv* avidamente.
hungry *adj* affamato; **to be ~** aver fame.
hunt *vi* cacciare; cercare; * *n* caccia *f*; ricerca *f*.
hunter *n* cacciatore *m*.
hunting *n* caccia *f*.
huntsman *n* cacciatore *m*.
hurdle *n* ostacolo *m*.
hurl *vt* scagliare.
hurricane *n* uragano *m*.
hurried *adj* frettoloso.
hurry *vi* affrettarsi, fare in fretta; * *n* fretta *f*.
hurt *vt* ferire; danneggiare; far male; * *n* ferita *f*, lesione *f*.
hurtful *adj* ingiurioso.
husband *n* marito *m*.
hush *n* silenzio *m*; * *vt* quietare.
husk *n* guscio *m*; pula *f*.
husky *adj* rauco; cane *m* eschimese.
hustings *npl* comizi *mpl* elettorali.
hustle *vt* spingere; fare fretta a; * *n* trambusto *m*.
hut *n* baracca *f*.
hutch *n* gabbia *f*.
hyacinth *n* giacinto *m*.
hybrid *adj*, *n* ibrido *m*.
hydrangea *n* ortensia *f*.
hydrant *n* idrante *m*.

hydraulic *adj* idraulico; **~s** *npl* idraulica *f*.
hydroelectric *adj* idroelettrico.
hydrofoil *n* aliscafo *m*.
hydrogen *n* idrogeno *m*.
hydrophobia *n* idrofobia *f*.
hyena *n* iena *f*.
hygiene *n* igiene *f*.
hygienic *adj* igienico.
hymn *n* inno *m*.
hyperbole *n* iperbole *f*.
hypermarket *n* ipermercato *m*.
hypertension *n* ipertensione *f*.
hyphen *n* (*gr*) trattino *m*.
hypnosis *n* ipnosi *f*.
hypnotic *adj* ipnotico.
hypnotism *n* ipnotismo *m*.
hypochondria *n* ipocondria *f*.
hypochondriac *n* ipocondriaco *m*.
hypocrisy *n* ipocrisia *f*.
hypocrite *n* ipocrita *m/f*.
hypocritical *adj* ipocrita.
hypodermic *adj* ipodermico.
hypothesis *n* ipotesi *f*.
hypothetical *adj* ipotetico.
hysterectomy *n* isterectomia *f*.
hysteria *n* isterismo *m*.
hysterical *adj* isterico.
hysterics *npl* crisi *f* isterica.

I

I *pron* io
ice *n* ghiaccio *m*; gelato *m*; * *vt* glassare.
ice-axe *n* piccozza *f*.
iceberg *n* iceberg *m*.
ice-bound *adj* bloccato dal ghiaccio.
ice cream *n* gelato *m*.
ice rink *n* pista *f* di pattinaggio.
ice-skating *n* pattinaggio *m* sul ghiaccio.

icicle *n* ghiacciolo *m*.
icing *n* glassa *f*.
icon *n* icona *f*.
iconoclast *adj*, *n* iconoclasta *f*.
icy *adj* ghiacciato.
idea *n* idea *f*.
ideal *adj*, *n* ideale *m*.
idealist *n* idealista *m/f*.
identical *adj* identico.
identification *n* identificazione *f*.

identify vt identificare.

identity n identità f.

ideology n ideologia f.

idiom n frase f idiomatica.

idiomatic adj idiomatico.

idiosyncrasy n peculiarità f.

idiot n idiota m/f.

idiotic adj stupido.

idle adj pigro; inattivo; infondato.

idleness n pigrizia f.

idol n idolo m.

idolatry n idolatria f.

idolize vt idolatrare.

idyll n idillio m.

idyllic adj idillico.

i.e. adv cioè

if conj se, qualora.

igloo n igloo m.

ignite vt accendere.

ignition n iniezione f; accensione f.

ignition key n chiave f dell'accensione.

ignoble adj ignobile.

ignominious adj ignominioso.

ignominy n ignominia f.

ignoramus n ignorante m/f.

ignorance n ignoranza f.

ignorant adj ignorante.

ignore vt ignorare; fingere di non vedere.

ill adj malato; indisposto; cattivo; * ~s npl (fig) mali mpl.

ill-advised adj imprudente.

ill-bred adj maleducato.

illegal adj illegale.

illegality n illegalità f.

illegibile adj illeggibile.

illegitimacy n illegittimità f.

illegitimate adj illegittimo.

ill-fated adj infausto.

ill feeling n rancore m.

illicit adj illecito.

illiterate adj, n analfabeta m/f.

illness n malattia f.

illogical adj illogico.

ill-timed adj inopportuno.

ill-treat vt maltrattare.

illuminate vt illuminare.

illumination n illuminazione f.

illusion n illusione f.

illusory adj illusorio.

illustrate vt illustrare.

illustration n illustrazione f.

illustrative adj illustrativo.

illustrious adj illustre.

ill-will n malevolenza f.

image n immagine f.

imagery n linguaggio m figurato.

imaginable adj immaginabile.

imaginary adj immaginario.

imagination n immaginazione f.

imaginative adj ricco di immaginazione.

imagine vt immaginare.

imbalance n squilibrio m.

imbecile adj imbecille.

imbibe vt bere.

imbue vt imbevere.

imitate vt imitare.

imitation n imitazione f.

imitative adj imitativo.

immaculate adj impeccabile.

immaterial adj irrilevante.

immature adj immaturo.

immeasurable adj incommensurabile.

immediate adj immediato.

immense adj immenso.

immensity n enormità f.

immerse vt immergere.

immersion n immersione f.

immigrant n immigrato m.

immigration n immigrazione f.

imminent adj imminente.

immobile adj immobile.

immobility n immobilità f.

immoderate adj smoderato.

immodest adj impudico.

immoral adj immorale.

immorality n immoralità f.

immortal adj immortale.

immortality n immortalità f.

immortalize *vt* immortalare.
immune *adj* immune.
immunity *n* immunità *f*.
immunize *vt* immunizzare.
immutable *adj* immutabile.
imp *n* diavoletto *m*.
impact *n* impatto *m*.
impair *vt* danneggiare.
impale *vt* trafiggere.
impalpable *adj* impalpabile.
impart *vt* comunicare.
impartial *adj* imparziale.
impartiality *n* imparzialità *f*.
impassable *adj* intransitabile.
impasse *n* impasse *f*.
impassive *adj* impassibile.
impatience *n* impazienza *f*.
impatient *adj* impaziente.
impeach *vt* mettere sotto accusa.
impeccable *adj* impeccabile.
impecunious *adj* bisognoso.
impede *vt* ostacolare.
impediment *n* impedimento *m*.
impel *vt* costringere.
impending *adj* incombente.
impenetrable *adj* impenetrabile.
imperative *adj* tassativo; (*gr*)
imperativo.
imperceptible *adj* impercettibile.
imperfect *adj* difettoso; imperfetto.
imperfection *n* imperfezione *f*.
imperial *adj* imperiale.
imperialism *n* imperialismo *m*.
imperious *adj* imperioso.
impermeable *adj* impermeabile.
impersonal *adj* impersonale.
impersonate *vt* imitare.
impertinence *n* impertinenza
f.
impertinent *adj* impertinente.
imperturbable *adj* imperturbabile.
impervious *adj* impervio.

impetuosity *n* impetuosità *f*.
impetuous *adj* impetuoso.
impetus *n* spinta *f*.
impiety *n* empietà *f*.
impinge (on) *vi* urtare; ledere.
impious *adj* empio.
implacable *adj* implacabile.
implant *vt* innestare.
implement *n* utensile *m*; * *vt*
attuare.
implicate *vt* implicare.
implication *n* implicazione *f*.
implicit *adj* implicito.
implore *vt* implorare.
imply *vt* implicare.
impolite *adj* scortese.
impoliteness *n* scortesia *f*.
import *vt* importare; * *n* importazione *f*.
importance *n* importanza *f*.
important *adj* importante.
importation *n* importazione *f*.
importer *n* importatore *m*.
importunate *adj* importuno.
importune *vt* importunare.
impose *vt* imporre.
imposing *adj* imponente.
imposition *n* imposizione *f*.
impossibility *n* impossibilità *f*.
impossible *adj* impossibile.
impostor *n* impostore *m*.
impotence *n* impotenza *f*.
impotent *adj* impotente.
impound *vt* sequestrare.
impoverish *vt* impoverire.
impoverished *adj* impoverito.
impracticable *adj* impraticabile.
impractical *adj* privo di senso
pratico.
imprecation *n* imprecazione *f*
imprecise *adj* impreciso.
impregnable *adj* inattaccabile.
impregnate *vt* impregnare.
impregnation *n* impregnazione
f.
impress *vt* colpire, fare impressione a.

impression *n* impressione *f*.

impressionable *adj* impressionabile.

impressive *adj* imponente, che colpisce.

imprint *n* sigla editoriale; * *vt* imprimere.

imprison *vt* imprigionare.

imprisonment *n* reclusione *f*; **life ~** ergastolo *m*.

improbability *n* improbabilità *f*.

improbable *adj* improbabile.

impromptu *adj* improvvisato.

improper *adj* scorretto.

impropriety *n* scorrettezza *f*.

improve *vt*, *vi* migliorare.

improvement *n* miglioramento *m*.

improvident *adj* imprevidente.

improvise *vt*, *vi* improvvisare.

imprudence *n* imprudenza *f*.

imprudent *adj* imprudente.

impudence *n* sfrontatezza *f*.

impudent *adj* sfrontato.

impugn *vt* impugnare.

impulse *n* impulso *m*.

impulsive *adj* impulsivo.

impunity *n*: **with ~** impunemente.

impure *adj* impuro.

impurity *n* impurità *f*.

in *prep* in; a.

inability *n* inabilità *f*.

inaccessible *adj* inaccessibile.

inaccuracy *n* inesattezza *f*.

inaccurate *adj* inesatto.

inaction *n* inazione *f*.

inactive *adj* inattivo.

inactivity *n* inattività *f*.

inadequate *adj* inadeguato.

inadmissible *adj* inammissibile.

inadvertent *adj* involontario.

inadvisable *adj* sconsigliabile.

inane *adj* sciocco.

inanimate *adj* inanimato.

inapplicable *adj* inapplicabile.

inappropriate *adj* fuori luogo, inadatto.

inarticulate *adj* incapace di esprimersi.

inasmuch (as) *conj* poiché.

inattentive *adj* disattento.

inaudible *adj* non udibile.

inaugural *adj* inaugurale.

inaugurate *vt* inaugurare.

inauguration *n* inaugurazione *f*.

inauspicious *adj* infausto.

in-between *adj* intermedio.

inborn, inbred *adj* innato, congenito.

incalculable *adj* incalcolabile.

incandescent *adj* incandescente.

incantation *n* incantesimo *m*.

incapable *adj* incapace.

incapacitate *vt* rendere incapace.

incapacity *n* incapacità *f*.

incarcerate *vt* imprigionare.

incarnate *adj* incarnato.

incarnation *n* incarnazione *f*.

incautious *adj* incauto.

incendiary *adj* incendiario; **~ bomb** bomba *f* incendiaria.

incense *n* incenso *m*; * *vt* rendere furibondo.

incentive *n* incentivo *m*.

inception *n* principio *m*.

incessant *adj* incessante.

incest *n* incesto *m*.

incestuous *adj* incestuoso.

inch *n* pollice *m*; **~ by ~** a poco a poco.

incidence *n* incidenza *f*.

incident *n* avvenimento *m*; episodio *m*.

incidental *adj* secondario; fortuito.

incinerator *n* inceneritore *m*.

incipient *adj* incipiente.

incise *vt* incidere.

incision *n* incisione *f*.

incisive *adj* incisivo.

incisor *n* incisivo *m*.

incite *vt* incitare.

inclement *adj* inclemente.

inclination *n* tendenza *f*; inclinazione *f*; voglia *f*.

incline *vi* tendere a; * *n* pendenza *f*.

include *vt* includere.

including *adj* incluso.

inclusion *n* inclusione *f*.

inclusive *adj* incluso.

incognito *adj* in incognito.

incoherence *n* incoerenza *f*.

incoherent *adj* incoerente.

income *n* reddito *m*.

income tax *n* imposta *f* sul reddito.

incoming *adj* subentrante; in arrivo; montante.

incomparable *adj* incomparabile.

incompatibility *n* incompatibilità *f*.

incompatible *adj* incompatibile.

incompetence *n* incompetenza *f*.

incompetente *adj* incompetente.

incomplete *adj* incompleto.

incomprehensible *adj* incomprensibile.

inconceivable *adj* inimmaginabile.

inconclusive *adj* inconcludente.

incongruous *adj* incongruo.

inconsequential *adj* insignificante.

inconsiderate *adj* irriguardoso.

inconsistency *n* incoerenza *f*.

inconsistent *adj* contraddittorio.

inconsolable *adj* inconsolabile.

inconspicuous *adj* poco appariscente.

incontinence *n* incontinenza *f*.

incontinent *adj* incontinente.

incontrovertible *adj* incontrovertibile.

inconvenience *n* scomodità *f*; * *vt* incomodare.

inconvenient *adj* scomodo.

incorporate *vt* incorporare.

incorporation *n* incorporazione *f*.

incorrect *adj* scorretto.

incorrigible *adj* incorreggibile.

incorruptible *adj* incorruttibile.

increase *vt*, *vi* aumentare; * *n* aumento *m*.

increasing *adj* crescente.

incredible *adj* incredibile.

incredulity *n* incredulità *f*.

incredulous *adj* incredulo.

increment *n* incremento *m*.

incriminate *vt* incriminare.

incubate *vt* covare.

incubator *n* incubatrice *f*.

inculcate *vt* inculcare.

incur *vt* contrarre.

incurable *adj* incurabile.

incursion *n* incursione *f*.

indebted *adj* obbligato.

indecency *n* indecenza *f*.

indecent *adj* indecente.

indecision *n* indecisione *f*.

indecisive *adj* indeciso.

indeed *adv* infatti.

indefatigable *adj* infaticabile.

indefinable *adj* indefinibile.

indefinite *adj* indefinito.

indelible *adj* indelebile.

indelicate *adj* indelicato.

indemnify *vt* indennizzare.

indemnity *n* indennizzo *m*.

indent *vt* rientrare dal margine.

independence *n* indipendenza *f*

independent *adj* indipendente.

indescribable *adj* indescrivibile.

indestructable *adj* indistruttibile.

indeterminate *adj* indeterminato.
index *n* indice *m*.
index card *n* scheda *f*.
index finger *n* indice *m*.
indicate *vt* indicare; * *vi* mettere la freccia.
indication *n* indicazione *f*.
indicative *adj* indicativo.
indicator *n* segno *m*; freccia *f*; rivelatore *m*.
indict *vt* imputare.
indictment *n* imputazione *f*.
indifference *n* indifferenza *f*.
indifferent *adj* indifferente.
indigenous *adj* indigeno.
indigestion *n* indigestione *f*.
indignant *adj* indignato.
indignation *n* indignazione *f*.
indignity *n* umiliazione *f*.
indigo *adj, n* indaco *m*.
indirect *adj* indiretto.
indiscreet *adj* indiscreto.
indiscretion *n* indiscrezione *f*.
indiscriminate *adj* indiscriminato.
indispensable *adj* indispensabile.
indisposed *adj* indisposto.
indisposition *n* indisposizione *f*.
indisputable *adj* incontrovertibile.
indistinct *adj* indistinto.
indistinguishable *adj* indistinguibile.
individual *adj* individuale; * *n* individuo *m*.
individuality *n* individualità *f*.
indivisible *adj* indivisibile.
indoctrinate *vt* indottrinare.
indoctrination *n* indottrinamento *m*.
indolence *n* indolenza *f*.
indolent *adj* indolente.
indomitable *adj* indomabile.
indoors *adv* all'interno.
indubitable *adj* indubitabile.

induce *vt* persuadere.
inducement *n* incentivo *m*.
induction *n* induzione *f*.
indulge *vt* accontentare; viziare.
indulgence *n* indulgenza *f*.
indulgent *adj* indulgente.
industrial *adj* industriale.
industrial estate *n* zona *f* industriale.
industrialist *n* industriale *m/f*.
industrialize *vt* industrializzare.
industrious *adj* diligente.
industry *n* industria *f*.
inebriated *adj* ubriaco.
inedible *adj* immangiabile.
ineffable *adj* ineffabile.
ineffective, ineffectual *adj* inefficace.
inefficiency *n* inefficienza *f*.
inefficient *adj* inefficiente.
ineligible *adj* ineligibile.
inept *adj* inetto.
ineptitude *n* inettitudine *f*.
inequality *n* ineguaglianza *f*.
inequitable *adj* iniquo.
inert *adj* inerte.
inertia *n* inerzia *f*.
inescapable *adj* inevitabile.
inestimable *adj* inestimabile.
inevitable *adj* inevitabile.
inexcusable *adj* imperdonabile.
inexhuastible *adj* inesauribile.
inexorable *adj* inesorabile.
inexpensive *adj* economico.
inexperience *n* inesperienza *f*.
inexperienced *adj* inesperto.
inexplicable *adj* inspiegabile.
inexpressible *adj* inesprimibile.
inextricable *adj* inestricabile.
infallibility *n* infallibilità *f*.
infallible *adj* infallibile.
infamous *adj* infame.
infamy *n* infamia *f*.
infancy *n* infanzia *f*.

infant n bambino m.
infanticide n infanticidio m.
infantile adj infantile.
infantry n fanteria f.
infatuated adj infatuato.
infatuation n infatuazione f.
infect vt infettare.
infection n infezione f.
infectious adj infettivo.
infer vt dedurre.
inference n deduzione f.
inferior adj inferiore.
inferiority n inferiorità f.
infernal adj infernale.
inferno n inferno m.
infest vt infestare.
infidel adj, n infedele m.
infidelity n infedeltà f.
infiltrate vi infiltrarsi.
infinite adj infinito.
infinitive n (gr) infinito m; * adj
  infinitivo.
infinity n infinità f.
infirm adj infermo.
infirmary n infermeria f.
inflame vt infiammare.
inflammation n infiammazione
  f.
inflammatory adj incendiario.
inflatable adj gonfiabile.
inflate vt gonfiare.
inflation n inflazione f.
inflection n inflessione f.
inflexibility n inflessibilità f.
inflexible adj inflessibile.
inflict vt infliggere.
influence n influenza f; * vt influenzare.
influential adj influente.
influenza n influenza f.
influx n afflusso m.
inform vt informare.
informal adj informale.
informality n mancanza di formalità f.
informant n informatore m.
information n informazioni
  fpl.

infraction n infrazione f.
infra-red adj infrarosso.
infrastructure n infrastruttura f.
infrequent adj infrequente.
infringe vt infrangere.
infringement n violazione f.
infuriate vt rendere furioso.
infuse vt (fig) infondere; lasciare in infusione.
infusion n infusione f.
ingenious adj ingegnoso.
ingenuity adj ingegnosità f.
ingenuous adj ingenuo.
inglorious adj inglorioso.
ingot n lingotto m.
ingrained adj incancrenito.
ingratiate vi ingraziarsi.
ingratitude n ingratitudine f.
ingredient n ingrediente m.
inhabit vt abitare.
inhabitable adj abitabile.
inhabitant n abitante m/f.
inhale vt inalare.
inherent adj intrinseco.
inherit vt ereditare.
inheritance n eredità f.
inhibit vt inibire.
inhibited adj inibito.
inhibition n inibizione f.
inhospitable adj inospitale.
inhuman adj inumano.
inhumanity n inumanità f.
inimical adj ostile.
inimitable adj inimitabile.
iniquitous adj iniquo.
iniquity n iniquità f.
initial adj, n iniziale f.
initially adv all'inizio.
initiate vt iniziare.
initiation n iniziazione f.
initiative n iniziativa f.
inject vt iniettare.
injection n iniezione f.
injudicious adj imprudente.
injunction n ingiunzione f.
injure vt ferire.
injury n ferita f.

injustice n ingiustizia f.
ink n inchiostro m.
inkling n mezza idea f.
inlaid adj intarsiato.
inland adj interno; * adv nell'entroterra.
in-law n parente m acquisito.
inlay vt intarsiare.
inlet n insenatura f.
inmate n detenuto m.
inmost adj più intimo.
inn n locanda f.
innate adj innato.
inner adj interiore.
innermost adj più intimo.
inner tube n camera f d'aria.
innkeeper n locandiere m.
innocence n innocenza f.
innocent adj innocente.
innocuous adj innocuo.
innovate vi fare innovazioni.
innovation n innovazione f.
innuendo n insinuazione f.
innumerable adj innumerevole.
inoculate vt inoculare.
inoculation n inoculazione f.
inoffensive adj inoffensivo.
inopportune adj inopportuno.
inordinate adj eccessivo.
inorganic adj inorganico.
inpatient n ricoverato m.
input n alimentazione f; input m.
inquest n inchiesta f.
inquire vi indagare; informarsi; **to ~ after** richiedere di.
inquiry n domanda f; inchiesta f.
inquisition n inquisizione f.
inquisitive adj curioso.
inroad n incursione f.
insane adj pazzo, folle.
insanity n follia f; infermità f mentale.
insatiable adj insaziabile.
inscribe vt incidere.
inscription n iscrizione f; dedica f.

inscrutable adj imperscrutabile.
insect n insetto m.
insecticide n insetticida m.
insecure adj malsicuro.
insecurity n insicurezza f.
insemination n inseminazione f.
insensible adj privo di conoscenza.
insensitive adj insensibile.
inseparable adj inseparabile.
insert vt inserire; * n inserto m.
insertion n inserzione f.
inshore adj costiero.
inside n interno m; * adv, prep dentro.
inside out adv alla rovescia.
insidious adj insidioso.
insight n perspicacia f.
insignia n insegne fpl.
insignificant adj insignificante.
insincere adj insincero.
insincerity n insincerità f.
insinuate vt insinuare.
insinuation n insinuazione f.
insipid adj insipido.
insist vt, vi insistere.
insistence n insistenza f.
insistent adj insistente.
insole n soletta f.
insolence n insolenza f.
insolent adj insolente.
insoluble adj insolubile.
insolvency n insolvenza f.
insolvent adj insolvente.
insomnia n insonnia f.
insomuch adv a tal punto che.
inspect vt controllare.
inspection n controllo m; ispezione f.
inspector n ispettore m, controllore m.
inspiration n ispirazione f.
inspire vt ispirare.
instability n instabilità f.
instal vt installare.

installation *n* installazione *f*.
instalment *n* rata *f*; puntata *f*.
instance *n* esempio *m*.
instant *adj* immediato; solubile; * *n* istante *m*.
instantaneous *adj* istantaneo.
instead *adv* invece.
instep *n* collo *m*.
instigate *vt* istigare.
instigation *n* istigazione *f*.
instil *vt* instillare.
instinct *n* istinto *m*.
instinctive *adj* istintivo.
institute *vt* istituire; * *n* istituto *m*.
institution *n* istituzione *f*.
instruct *vt* istruire.
instruction *n* istruzione *f*.
instructive *adj* istruttivo.
instructor *n* istruttore *m*.
instrument *n* strumento *m*.
instrumental *adj* strumentale.
insubordinate *adj* insubordinato.
insubordination *n* insubordinazione *f*.
insufferable *adj* insopportabile.
insufficiency *n* insufficienza *f*.
insufficient *adj* insufficiente.
insular *adj* insulare.
insulate *vt* isolare.
insulating tape *n* nastro *m* isolante.
insulation *n* isolamento *m*.
insulin *n* insulina *f*.
insult *vt* insultare; * *n* insulto *m*.
insulting *adj* insultante.
insuperable *adj* insuperabile.
insurance *n* assicurazione *f*.
insurance policy *n* polizza *f* d'assicurazione.
insure *vt* assicurare.
insurer *n* assicuratore *m*.
insurgent *adj* ribelle; * *n* insorto *m*.
insurmountable *adj* insormontabile.
insurrection *n* insurrezione *f*.

intact *adj* intatto.
intake *n* immissione *f*.
integral *adj* integrante.
integrate *vt* integrare.
integration *n* integrazione *f*.
integrity *n* integrità *f*.
intellect *n* intelletto *m*.
intellectual *adj*, *n* intellettuale *m/f*.
intelligence *n* intelligenza *f*.
intelligent *adj* intelligente.
intelligentsia *n* intellighenzia *f*.
intelligible *adj* intelligibile.
intemperate *adj* rigido.
intend *vt* avere intenzione, intendere; destinare.
intense *adj* intenso.
intensify *vt* intensificare.
intensity *n* intensità *f*.
intensive *adj* intensivo.
intensive care unit *n* centro *m* di rianimazione.
intent *adj* assorto, intento; * *n* intenzione *f*, intento *m*.
intention *n* intenzione *f*.
intentional *adj* intenzionale.
inter *vt* seppellire.
interaction *n* interazione *f*.
intercede *vi* intercedere.
intercept *vt* intercettare.
intercession *n* intercessione *f*.
interchange *n* scambio *m*.
intercom *n* interfono *m*.
intercourse *n* rapporti *mpl*.
interest *vt* interessare; * *n* interesse *m*.
interesting *adj* interessante.
interest rate *n* tasso *m* d'interesse.
interfere *vi* interferire; intromettersi.
interference *n* interferenza *f*; intromissione *f*.
interim *adj* provvisorio.
interior *adj*, *n* interno *m*.
interior designer *n* arredatore *m*.

interjection *n* (*gr*) interiezione *f*.

interlock *vi* intrecciarsi.

interloper *n* intruso *m*.

interlude *n* intervallo *m*.

intermediary *n* intermediario *m*.

intermediate *adj* intermedio.

interment *n* seppellimento *m*.

interminable *adj* interminabile.

intermingle *vt* frammischiare.

intermission *n* interruzione *f*.

intermittent *adj* intermittente.

internal *adj* interno.

international *adj* internazionale.

interplay *n* interazione *f*.

interpose *vt* interporre.

interpret *vt* interpretare.

interpretation *n* interpretazione *f*.

interpreter *n* interprete *m/f*.

interregnum *n* interregno *m*.

interrelated *adj* correlato.

interrogate *vt* interrogare.

interrogation *n* interrogatorio *m*.

interrogative *adj* interrogativo.

interrupt *vt, vi* interrompere.

interruption *n* interruzione *f*.

intersect *vt* intersecare.

intersection *n* intersezione *f*.

intersperse *vt* inframmezzare.

intertwine *vt* intrecciare.

interval *n* intervallo *m*.

intervene *vi* sopraggiungere; intervenire.

intervention *n* intervento *m*.

interview *n* colloquio *m*, intervista *f*.

interviewer *n* intervistatore *m*.

intestate *adj* intestato.

intestinal *adj* intestinale.

intestine *n* intestino *m*.

intimacy *n* intimità *f*.

intimate *adj* intimo; * *vt* fare capire.

intimidate *vt* intimidire.

into *prep* in, dentro.

intolerable *adj* intollerabile.

intolerance *n* intolleranza *f*.

intolerant *adj* intollerante.

intonation *n* intonazione *f*.

intoxicate *vt* inebriare.

intoxication *n* ebbrezza *f*.

intractable *adj* intrattabile.

intransigence *n* intransigenza *f*.

intransitive *adj* (*gr*) intransitivo.

intravenous *adj* endovenoso.

intrepid *adj* intrepido.

intricacy *n* complessità *f*.

intricate *adj* intricato.

intrigue *n* intrigo *m*; tresca *f*; * *vt* incuriosire.

intriguing *adj* affascinante.

intrinsic *adj* intrinseco.

introduce *vt* introdurre; presentare.

introduction *n* introduzione *f*; presentazione *f*.

introductory *adj* introduttivo.

introspection *n* introspezione *f*.

introvert *n* introverso *m*.

intrude *vi* intromettersi.

intruder *n* intruso *m*.

intrusion *n* intrusione *f*.

intuition *n* intuito *m*.

intuitive *adj* intuitivo.

inundate *vt* inondare.

inundation *n* inondazione *f*.

inure *vt* assuefare.

invade *vt* invadere.

invader *n* invasore *m*.

invalid *adj*, invalido; nullo; * *n* invalido *m*.

invalidate *vt* annullare.

invaluable *adj* inestimabile.

invariable *adj* invariabile.

invasion *n* invasione *f*.

invective *n* invettiva *f*.

inveigle vt persuadere (con lusinghe).

invent vt inventare.

invention n invenzione f.

inventive adj inventivo.

inventor n inventore m.

inventory n inventario m.

inverse adj inverso.

inversion n inversione f.

invert vt capovolgere.

invertebrate adj invertebrato.

invest vt investire.

investigate vt indagare.

investigation n indagine f.

investigator n investigatore m.

investment n investimento m.

inveterate adj inveterato.

invidious adj ingiurioso.

invigilate vt sorvegliare.

invigorating adj tonificante.

invincible adj invincibile.

inviolable adj inviolabile.

invisible adj invisibile.

invitation n invito m.

invite vt invitare; sollecitare.

inviting adj invitante.

invoice n fattura f; * vt fatturare.

invoke vt invocare.

involuntary adj involontario.

involve vt coinvolgere.

involved adj complicato.

involvement n partecipazione f; complessità f.

invulnerable adj invulnerabile.

inward adj interiore.

iodine n iodio m.

I.O.U. (I owe you) n pagherò m.

irascible adj irascibile.

irate adj irato.

iris n iride f; (bot) iris f.

irksome adj seccante.

iron n ferro m; * vt, vi stirare.

ironic adj ironico.

ironing n roba f da stirare.

ironing board n asse f da stiro.

iron ore n minerale m di ferro.

ironworks n ferriera f.

irony n ironia f.

irradiate vt irradiare.

irrational adj irragionevole.

irreconcilable adj irreconciliabile.

irregular adj irregolare.

irregularity n irregolarità f.

irrelevant adj non pertinente.

irreligious adj irreligioso.

irreparable adj irreparabile.

irreplaceable adj insostituibile.

irrepressible adj irrefrenabile.

irreproachable adj irreprensibile.

irresistible adj irresistibile.

irresolute adj irresoluto.

irresponsible adj irresponsabile.

irretrievable adj irrecuperabile.

irreverence n irriverenza f.

irreverent adj irriverente.

irrigate vt irrigare.

irrigation n irrigazione f.

irritable adj irritabile.

irritant n sostanza f irritante.

irritate vt irritare.

irritating adj irritante.

irritation n irritazione f.

Islam n Islam m.

island n isola f.

islander n isolano m.

isle n isola f.

isolate vt isolare.

isolation n isolamento m.

issue n questione f; emissione f; rilascio m; numero m; prole f; * vt rilasciare; pubblicare; emettere.

isthmus n istmo m.

it pron esso.

italic n corsivo m.

itch n prurito m; * vi prudere.

item n voce f, articolo m.

itemize vt specificare uno per

uno.

itinerant *adj* ambulante.

itinerary *n* itinerario *m*.

its *pron* suo.

itself *pron* si, se stesso.

ivory *adj*, *n* avorio *m*.

ivy *n* edera *f*.

J

jab *n* colpo *m* di punta; * *vt* conficcare.

jabber *n* chiacchierio *m*; * *vi* chiacchierare.

jack *n* cric *m*; fante *m*.

jackal *n* sciacallo *m*.

jackdaw *n* taccola *f*.

jacket *n* giacca *f*.

jack-knife *n* coltello *m* a serramanico.

jackpot *n* il primo premio *m*.

jade *n* giada *f*.

jaded *adj* sfibrato.

jagged *adj* seghettato.

jaguar *n* giaguaro *m*.

jail *n* carcere *m*, prigione *f*.

jailbird *n* carcerato *m*.

jailer *n* carceriere *m*.

jam *n* marmellata *f*; ingorgo *m*; pasticcio *m*; * *vt* bloccare; ficcare; * *vi* incepparsi.

jangle *vi* produrre un rumore metallico.

janitor *n* portinaio *m*; bidello *m*.

January *n* gennaio *m*.

jar *vi* urtare; stonare; * *n* barattolo *m*.

jargon *n* gergo *m*.

jasmine *n* gelsomino *m*.

jaundice *n* itterizia *f*.

jaunt *n* gita *f*.

jaunty *adj* spigliato.

javelin *n* giavellotto *m*.

jaw *n* mascella *f*.

jay *n* ghiandaia *f*.

jazz *n* jazz *m*

jealous *adj* geloso.

jealousy *n* gelosia *f*.

jeans *npl* jeans *mpl*

jeep *n* jeep *f*.

jeer *vi* fischiare; * *n* fischi *mpl*.

jelly *n* gelatina *f*.

jelly-fish *n* medusa *f*.

jeopardize *vt* mettere in pericolo.

jerk *n* sobbalzo *m*; tonto *m*; * *vi* muoversi a scatti.

jerky *adj* a scatti.

jersey *n* maglia *f*.

jest *n* scherzo *m*; * *vt* scherzare.

jester *n* buffone *m*.

Jesuit *n* gesuita *f*.

Jesus *n* Gesù *m*.

jet *n* (*min*) giaietto *m*; getto *m*; jet *m*.

jet engine *n* motore *m* a reazione.

jettison *vt* alleggerirsi di.

jetty *n* molo *m*.

Jew *n* ebreo *m*.

jewel *n* gioiello *m*.

jeweller *n* gioielliere *m*.

jewellery *n* gioielli *mpl*.

Jewess *n* ebrea *f*.

jewish *adj* ebreo.

jib *n* (*mar*) braccio *m*.

jig *n* giga *f*.

jigsaw *n* puzzle *m*.

jilt *vt* piantare.

jinx *n* iettatore *m*.

job *n* lavoro *m*; compito *m*; impiego *m*.

jobless *adj* disoccupato.

jockey *n* fantino *m*.

jocular *adj* gioviale.

jog *vi* fare footing.

jogging *n* footing *m*.

join vt unire, collegare; * vi unirsi a; confluire; * n giuntura f.

joiner n falegname m.

joinery n falegnameria f.

joint n articolazione f; pezzo m di carne; spinello m; * adj comune.

jointly adv in comune.

joint-stock company n società f per azioni.

joke n battuta f; scherzo m; * vi scherzare.

joker n burlone m; (cards) jolly m.

jolly adj allegro.

jolt vt sobbalzare; * n scossa f.

jostle vt sballottare.

journal n periodico m.

journalism n giornalismo m.

journalist n giornalista m/f.

journey n viaggio m.

jovial adj gioviale.

joy n gioia f.

joyful, joyous adj lieto.

joystick n barra f di comando.

jubilant adj esultante.

jubilation n esultanza f.

jubilee n giubileo m.

judge n giudice m; * vt giudicare.

judgement n giudizio m.

judicial adj giudiziario.

judiciary n magistratura f.

judicious adj giudizioso.

judo n judo m.

jug n brocca f.

juggle vi fare giochi di destrezza.

juggler n giocoliere m.

juice n succo m.

juicy adj succoso.

juke-box n juke-box m.

July n luglio m.

jumble vt mescolare; * n accozzaglia f.

jump vt, vi saltare; * n salto m.

jumper n saltatore m; maglione m.

jumpy adj nervoso.

junction n incrocio m.

juncture n congiuntura f.

June n giugno m.

jungle n giungla f.

junior adj più giovane.

juniper n (bot) ginepro m.

junk n giunca f; cianfrusaglie fpl.

junky n drogato m.

junta n giunta f.

jurisdiction n giurisdizione f.

jurisprudence n giurisprudenza f.

juror n giurato m.

jury n giuria f.

just adj giusto; * adv proprio; appena; soltanto; ~ **as** altrettanto; ~ **now** attualmente.

justice n giustizia f.

justifiable adj giustificabile.

justification n giustificazione f.

justify vt giustificare.

jut vi; **to ~ out** sporgere.

jute n iuta f.

juvenile adj giovanile; minorile; * n minorenne m/f.

juxtaposition n giustapposizione f.

K

kaleidoscope n caleidoscopio m.

kangaroo n canguro m.

karate n karatè m.

kebab n spiedino m.

keel n (mar) chiglia f; * vi crollare.

keen adj entusiasta; tagliente; acuto.

keenness *n* entusiasmo *m*
keep *vt* tenere; mantenere; trattenere; osservare; * *n* vito e alloggio; torrione *m*.
keeper *n* guardiano *m*.
keepsake *n* ricordo *m*.
keg *n* barile *m*.
kennel *n* canile *m*.
kernel *n* gheriglio *m*.
kerosene *n* cherosene *m*.
ketchup *n* ketchup *m*.
kettle *n* bollitore *m*.
key *n* chiave *f*; (*mus*) tasto *m*.
keyboard *n* tastiera *f*.
keyhole *n* buco *m* della serratura.
keynote *n* nota *f* di chiave.
key-ring *n* portachiavi *m*.
keystone *n* chiave *f* di volta.
khaki *n* cachi *m*.
kick *vt* dare un calcio; * *n* calcio *m*.
kid *n* capretto *m*; ragazzino *m*; * *vt* scherzare.
kidnap *vt* rapire.
kidnapper *n* rapitore *m*.
kidnapping *n* sequestro *m* di persona.
kidney *n* rene *m*; (*cul*) rognone *m*.
kill *vt* uccidere, ammazzare.
killer *n* assassino *m*.
killing *adj* mortale; * *n* uccisione; * *vi* fare un bel colpo.
kill-joy *n* guastafeste *m/f*.
kiln *n* fornace *f*.
kilo *n* chilo *m*.
kilogramme *n* chilogrammo *m*.
kilometre *n* chilometro *m*.
kilt *n* kilt *m*.
kin *n* parenti *mpl*; **next of ~** parente più stretto.
kind *adj* gentile; * *n* genere *m*.
kindergarten *n* asilo *m*.
kind-hearted *adj* buono.
kindle *vt, vi* accendere.
kindness *n* gentilezza *f*.
kindred *adj* imparentato.
kinetic *adj* cinetico.

king *n* re *m*.
kingdom *n* regno *m*.
kingfisher *n* martin pescatore *m*.
kinky *adj* bizzarro.
kiosk *n* chiosco *m*.
kiss *n* bacio *m*; * *vt* baciare.
kit *n* equipaggiamento *m*.
kitchen *n* cucina *f*.
kitchen garden *n* orto *m*.
kite *n* aquilone *m*.
kitten *n* gattino *m*.
kleptomania *n* cleptomania *f*.
knack *n* abilità *f*.
knapsack *n* zaino *m*.
knave *n* furfante *m*; fante *m*.
knead *vt* impastare.
knee *n* ginocchio *m*.
knee-cap *n* rotula *f*.
kneel *vi* inginocchiarsi.
knell *n* rintocco *m* funebre.
knickers *npl* mutande *fpl*.
knife *n* coltello *m*.
knight *n* cavaliere *m*; (chess) cavallo *m*.
knit *vt* lavorare a maglia; aggrottare; **to ~ one's brow** aggrottare le sopracciglia.
knitting needle *n* ferro *m* da calza.
knitwear *n* maglieria *f*.
knob *n* pomo *m*; manopola *f*.
knock *vt, vi* bussare; colpire; **to ~ down** demolire; * *n* colpo *m*.
knocker *n* battente *m*.
knock-out *n* K.O. *m*.
knoll *n* monticello *m*.
knot *n* nodo *m*; * *vt* annodare.
knotty *adj* nodoso.
know *vt, vi* sapere; conoscere; riconoscere.
know-all *n* sapientone *m*.
knowing *adj* scaltro; * *adv* **~ly** consciamente.
knowledge *n* conoscenza *f*; sapere *m*.
knowledgeable *adj* informato.
knuckle *n* nocca *f*.
kudos *n* gloria *f*.

L

label *n* etichetta *f*.
laboratory *n* laboratorio *m*.
laborious *adj* faticoso.
labour *n* lavoro *m*; mano d'opera *f*; * *adj* (*pol*) laburista; **to be in** ~ avere le doglie; * *vt* faticare.
labourer *n* manovale *m*.
labyrinth *n* labirinto *m*.
lace *n* pizzo *m*; laccio *m*; * *vt* allacciare.
lacerate *vt* lacerare.
lack *vt*, *vi* mancare; * *n* mancanza *f*.
lackadaisical *adj* languido.
lackey *n* lacchè *m*.
laconic *adj* laconico.
lacquer *n* lacca *f*.
lad *n* ragazzo *m*.
ladder *n* scala *f*; * *vt* smagliare.
ladle *n* mestolo *m*.
lady *n* signora *f*.
ladybird *n* coccinella *f*.
ladykiller *n* dongiovanni *m*.
ladylike *adj* da signora.
lag *vi* restare indietro; * *vt* rivestire (con materiale isolante); * *n* **time** ~ lasso di tempo *m*.
lager *n* birra *f* bionda.
lagoon *n* laguna *f*.
laid-back *adj* rilassato.
lair *n* tana *f*.
laity *n* laici *mpl*.
lake *n* lago *m*.
lamb *n* agnello *m*.
lambswool *n* lamb's wool *m*.
lame *adj* zoppo.
lamé *n* lamé *m*.
lament *vt* lamentare; * *n* lamento *m*.
lamentable *adj* penoso.
laminated *adj* laminato.
lamp *n* lampada *f*.

lampoon *n* satira *f*.
lampshade *n* paralume *m*.
lance *n* lancia *f*; * *vt* incidere.
lancet *n* bisturi *m*.
land *n* terra *f*, terreno *m*; paese *m*; * *vt* atterrare; sbarcare.
land forces *n* forze *fpl* terrestri.
landing *n* pianerottolo *m*; atterraggio *m*; sbarco *m*.
landing strip *n* pista *f* d'atterraggio.
landlady *n* proprietaria *f*.
landlord *n* proprietario *m*.
landlubber *n* terraiolo *m*.
landmark *n* punto *m* di riferimento.
landowner *n* proprietario *m* terriero.
landscape *n* paesaggio *m*.
landslide *n* frana *f*.
lane *n* stradina *f*.
language *n* linguaggio *m*, lingua *f*.
languid *adj* languido.
languish *vi* languire.
lanky *adj* spilungone.
lantern *n* lanterna *f*.
lap *n* grembo *m*; giro *m*; * *vt* lambire; * *vi* lappare.
lapdog *n* cagnolino *m* di lusso.
lapel *n* risvolto *m*.
lapse *n* svista *f*; intervallo *m*; * *vi* scadere; sgarrare.
larceny *n* furto *m*.
larch *n* larice *m*.
lard *n* lardo *m*.
larder *n* dispensa *f*.
large *adj* grande; **at** ~ in libertà; * *adv* ~**ly** in gran parte.
large-scale *adj* in grande scala.
largesse *n* liberalità *f*.
lark *n* allodola *f*; scherzo *m*.
larva *n* larva *f*.

laryngitis *n* laringite *f*.

larynx *n* laringe *f*.

lascivious *adj* lascivo.

laser *n* laser *m*.

lash *n* ciglio *m*; frustata *f*; * *vt* frustare; legare.

lasso *n* lasso *m*.

last *adj* ultimo; scorso; * *adv* at ~ finalmente; ~ly in fine; * *vi* durare.

last-ditch *adj* ultimo.

lasting *adj* duraturo.

last minute *adj* dell'ultimo momento.

latch *n* chiavistello *m*.

late *adj* in ritardo, tardi; defunto; * *adv* ~ly ultimamente.

latecomer *n* ritardatario *n*

latent *adj* latente.

lateral *adj* laterale.

lathe *n* tornio *m*.

lather *n* schiuma *f*.

latitude *n* latitudine *f*.

latter *adj* ultimo; ~ly negli ultimi tempi.

lattice *n* reticolato *m*.

laudable *adj* lodevole.

laugh *vi* ridere; * *vt* **to ~ at** ridere di; * *n* risata *f*.

laughable *adj* ridicolo.

laughing stock *n* zimbello *m*.

laughter *n* risata *f*.

launch *vt* varare; * *n* varo; motolancia *f*.

launching *n* varo *m*.

launching pad *n* rampa *f* di lancio.

launder *vt* lavare.

laundrette *n* lavanderia *f* (automatica).

laundry *n* lavanderia *f*; biancheria *f*.

laurel *n* alloro *m*.

lava *n* lava *f*.

lavatory *n* gabinetto *m*.

lavender *n* (*bot*) lavanda *f*.

lavish *adj* sontuoso; * *vt* colmare di.

law *n* legge *f*.

law-abiding *adj* rispettoso delle leggi.

law and order *n* ordine *m* pubblico.

law court *n* tribunale *m*.

lawful *adj* legale.

lawless *adj* senza legge.

lawn *n* prato *m*.

lawnmower *n* tagliaerba *m*.

law suit *n* causa *f*.

lawyer *n* avvocato *m*.

lax *adj* permissivo.

laxative *n* lassativo *m*.

laxity *n* permissività *f*.

lay *vt* porre; posare; stendere; apparecchiare; * *adj* laico.

layabout *n* fannullone *m*.

layer *n* strato *m*.

layette *n* corredino *m*.

layman *n* laico *m*.

layout *n* disposizione *f*; impostazione *f*.

laze *vi* oziare.

laziness *n* pigrizia *f*.

lazy *adj* pigro.

lead *n* piombo *m*; indizio *m*; ruolo principale; guinzaglio *m*; filo *m*; * *vt* condurre, guidare; **to be in the ~** essere in testa; * *vi* andare avanti.

leader *n* capo *m*; leader *m*; guida *f*.

leadership *n* direzione *f*.

leading *adj* in testa; preminente; ~ **question** *n* domanda *f* tendenziosa.

leaf *n* (*bot*) foglia *f*; foglio *m*.

leaflet *n* volantino *m*.

leafy *adj* frondoso.

league *n* lega *f*; campionato *m*.

leak *n* perdita *f*; * *vt* perdere; divulgare; * *vi* perdere. **lean** *vi* pendere; appoggiarsi; * *vt* appoggiare; * *adj* magro.

leap *vi* saltare; balzare; * *n* salto *m*; balzare.

leapfrog *n* cavallina *f*.

leap year *n* anno *m* bisestile.
learn *vt* imparare.
learned *adj* colto.
learner *n* principiante *m/f*.
learning *n* cultura *f*.
lease *n* contratto *m* di affitto;
  * *vt* affittare.
leasehold *n* proprietà *f* in affitto.
leash *n* guinzaglio *m*.
least *adj, n* minimo *m*; * *adv*
  meno; **at ~** almeno; **not in the**
  ~ niente affatto.
leather *n* pelle *f*, cuoio *m*.
leave *n* autorizzazione *f*, permesso *m*; licenza *f*; * *vt* lasciare; restare; * *vi* partire.
leaven *vt* far lievitare.
leavings *npl* avanzi *mpl*.
lecherous *adj* lascivo.
lecture *n* conferenza *f*; * *vi* tenere una conferenza.
lecturer *n* docente *m* universitario.
ledge *n* sporgenza *f*; cengia *f*.
ledger *n* libro *m* mastro.
lee *adj* (*mar*) sottovento.
leech *n* sanguisuga *f*.
leek *n* (*bot*) porro *m*.
leer *vt* guardare con occhi vogliosi; * *n* espressione *f* libidinosa.
lees *npl* sedimento *m*.
leeward *adj* sottovento.
leeway *n* deriva *f*.
left *adj* sinistro; **on the ~** a sinistra.
left-handed *adj* mancino.
leftovers *npl* avanzi *mpl*.
leg *n* gamba *f*; coscia *f*; tappa *f*.
legacy *n* eredità *f*.
legal *adj* legale; * *adv* **~ly** legalmente.
legality *n* legalità *f*.
legalize *vt* legalizzare.
legal tender *n* moneta *f* a corso legale.
legate *n* nunzio *m* apostolico.

legation *n* legazione *f*.
legend *n* leggenda *f*.
legendary *adj* leggendario.
legible *adj* leggibile.
legion *n* legione *f*.
legislate *vt* legiferare.
legislation *n* legislazione *f*.
legislative *adj* legislativo.
legislator *n* legislatore *m*.
legislature *n* corpo *m* legislativo.
legitimacy *n* legittimità *f*.
legitimate *adj* legittimo; * *vt*
  legittimare.
leisure *n* svago *m*, tempo *m*
  libero; **~ly** *adj* tranquillo.
lemon *n* limone *m*.
lemonade *n* limonata *f*.
lemon tea *n* te *m* al limone.
lemon tree *n* albero *m* di
  limone.
lend *vt* prestare.
length *n* lunghezza *f*; durata; **at**
  ~ esaurientemente.
lengthen *vt* allungare.
lengthways *adv* per la lunghezza.
lengthy *adj* lungo.
lenient *adj* indulgente.
lens *n* lente *f*, obiettivo *m*.
Lent *n* quaresima *f*.
lentil *n* lenticchia *f*.
leopard *n* leopardo *m*.
leotard *n* body *m*.
leper *n* lebbroso *m*.
leprosy *n* lebbra *f*.
lesbian *adj* lesbico; * *n* lesbica
  f.
less *adj, pron* meno; * *adv*
  meno; * *prep* meno.
lessen *vt, vi* diminuire.
lesser *adj* minore.
lesson *n* lezione *f*.
lest *conj* nel timore che.
let *vt* lasciare; affittare.
lethal *adj* letale.
lethargic *adj* letargico.
lethargy *n* indolenza *f*.

letter *n* lettera *f*.

lettering *n* iscrizione *f*.

letter of credit *n* lettera *f* di credito.

lettuce *n* lattuga *f*.

leukaemia *n* leucemia *f*.

level *adj* piano, piatto, alla pari; * *n* livello *m*; * *vt* livellare, spianare.

level-headed *adj* equilibrato.

lever *n* leva *f*.

leverage *n* forza *f*.

levity *n* frivolezza *f*.

levy *n* imposta *f*; * *vt* imporre.

lewd *adj* osceno.

lexicon *n* lessico *m*.

liability *n* responsabilità *f*.

liable *adj* responsabile; soggetto; * *adv* probabile.

liaise *vi* mantenere i contatti con.

liaison *n* coordinamento *m*.

liar *n* bugiardo *m*.

libel *n* diffamazione *f*; * *vt* diffamare.

libellous *adj* diffamatorio.

liberal *adj* liberale.

liberality *n* liberalità *f*.

liberate *vt* liberare.

liberation *n* liberazione *f*.

libertine *n* libertino *m*.

liberty *n* libertà *f*.

libido *n* libido *f*.

Libra *n* Bilancia *f*.

librarian *n* bibliotecario *m*.

library *n* biblioteca *f*.

libretto *n* libretto *m*.

licence *n* autorizzazione *f*; cannone *m*; patente *f*.

licentious *adj* licenzioso.

lichen *n* (*bot*) lichene *m*.

lick *vt* leccare; * *n* leccata *f*.

lid *n* coperchio *m*.

lie *n* menzogna *f*; * *vi* mentire; sdraiarsi.

lieu *n*: **in ~ of** invece di.

lieutenant *n* tenente *m*.

life *n* vita *f*.

lifeboat *n* lancia *f* di salvataggio.

life-guard *n* bagnino *m*.

life jacket *n* giubbotto *m* di salvataggio.

lifeless *adj* privo di vita.

lifelike *adj* realistico.

lifeline *n* sagola *f* di salvataggio.

life sentence *n* ergastolo *m*.

life-sized *adj* in grandezza naturale.

lifespan *n* durata *f* della vita.

lift *vt* sollevare; revocare; * *n* ascensore *m*; montacarichi *mpl*; passaggio *m*.

ligament *n* legamento *m*.

light *n* luce *f*; * *adj* chiaro; leggero; * *vt* accendere; illuminare.

light bulb *n* lampadina *f*.

lighten *vi* alleggerire.

lighter *n* accendino *m*.

light-headed *adj* stordito.

lighthearted *adj* spensierato.

lighthouse *n* faro *m*.

lighting *n* illuminazione *f*.

lightly *adv* leggermente.

lightning *n* fulmine *m*.

lightning conductor *n* parafulmine *m*.

lightweight *adj* leggero; * *n* peso *n* leggero.

light year *n* anno *m* luce.

ligneous *adj* ligneo.

like *adj* simile; * *prep* come; * *vt* piacere; **I ~ coffee** il caffè mi piace; **he ~s chocolates** gli piacciono i cioccolatini; **which do you ~ best?** quale preferisci?

likeable *adj* simpatico.

likelihood *n* probabilità *f*.

likely *adj* probabile.

liken *vt* paragonare.

likeness *n* somiglianza *f*.

likewise *adv* altrettanto.

liking *n* simpatia *f*.

lilac n lilla m.

lily n giglio m; ~ of the valley n mughetto m.

limb n arto m.

limber adj flessibile.

lime n calce f; tiglio m; laim f, limetta f.

limestone n calcare m.

limit n limite m; * vt limitare.

limitation n limitazione f.

limitless adj illimitato.

limousine n limousine f.

limp vi zoppicare; * n zoppicamento m; * adj floscio, molle.

limpet n patella f.

limpid adj limpido.

line n linea f; tratto m; ruga f; lenza f; fila f; riga f; * vt foderare.

lineage n stirpe f.

linear adj lineare.

lined adj rigato; foderato.

linen n lino m.

liner n transatlantico m.

linesman n guardalinee m.

linger vi indugiare.

lingerie n biancheria f intima.

lingering adj persistente.

linguist n linguista m/f.

linguistic adj linguistico.

linguistics n linguistica f.

liniment n linimento m.

lining n fodera f.

link n legame m; anello m; * vt collegare.

linnet n fanello m.

linoleum n linoleum m.

linseed n: ~ oil semi di lino.

lint n garza f.

lintel n architrave f.

lion n leone m.

lioness n leonessa f.

lip n labbro m.

lip read vt, vi capire dal movimento delle labbra.

lip salve n burro m di cacao.

lipstick n rossetto m.

liqueur n liquore m.

liquid adj, n liquido m.

liquidate vt liquidare.

liquidation n liquidazione f.

liquidize vt passare al frullatore.

liquidizer n frullatore m.

liquor n bevande fpl alcoliche.

liquorice n liquirizia f.

lisp vi essere bleso; * n pronuncia f blesa.

list n lista f, elenco m; * vt elencare.

listen vi ascoltare.

listless adj apatico.

litany n litania f.

literal adj letterale.

literary adj letterario.

literate adj che sa leggere e scrivere.

literature n letteratura f.

lithe adj agile.

lithograph, lithography n litografia f.

litigation n causa f (giudiziaria).

litigious adj litigioso.

litre n litro m.

litter n rifiuti mpl; (zool) cucciolata f.

little adj piccolo; * pron poco; * adv ~ by ~ gradualmente; * n poco m.

liturgy n liturgia f.

live vi vivere, abitare; to ~ on vivere di; to ~ up to essere all'altezza di; * adj vivo; inesploso.

livelihood n sostentamento m.

liveliness n vivacità f.

lively adj vivace.

liven up vt ravvivare.

liver n fegato m.

livery n livrea f.

livestock n bestiame m.

livid adj furibondo; livido.

living adj vivente, vita.

living room n soggiorno m.

lizard n lucertola f.

load *vt* caricare; * *n* carico *m*.

loaded *adj* carico.

loaf *n* pane *m*; **meat** ~ polpettone *m*.

loafer *n* bighellone *m*.

loam *n* terriccio *m*.

loan *n* prestito *m*; * *vt* prestare.

loathe *vt* detestare.

loathing *n* ribrezzo *m*.

loathsome *adj* ripugnante.

lobby *n* atrio *m*; gruppo *m* di pressione.

lobe *n* lobo *m*.

lobster *n* aragosta *f*.

local *adj* locale.

local anaesthetic *n* anestesia *f* locale.

local government *n* amministrazione *f* locale.

locality *n* località *f*.

localize *vt* localizzare.

locally *adv* nelle vicinanze.

locate *vt* collocare.

location *n* posizione *f*.

loch *n* (*Scot*) lago *m*.

lock *n* serratura *f*; chiusa *f*; sterzo *m*; (hair) ciocca *f*; * *vt* chiudere a chiave.

locker *n* armadietto *m*.

locket *n* medaglione *m*.

lockout *n* serrata *f*.

locksmith *n* fabbro *m*.

lock-up *n* prigione *f*.

locomotive *n* locomotiva *f*.

locust *n* locusta *f*.

lodge *n* portineria *f*; loggia *f*; * *vi* alloggiare.

lodger *n* pensionante *m/f*.

loft *n* soffitta *f*.

lofty *adj* altezzoso.

log *n* tronco *m*.

logbook *n* (*mar*) giornale *m* di bordo; libretto *m* di circolazione.

logic *n* logica *f*.

logical *adj* logico.

logo *n* logo *m*.

loin *n* fianchi *mpl*; (*cul*) lombata *f*.

loiter *vi* bighellonare.

loll *vi* ciondolare.

lollipop *n* lecca lecca *m*.

loneliness *n* solitudine *f*.

lonely *adj* solitario.

long *adj* lungo; * *vi* desiderare.

long-distance *n*: ~ **call** interurbano *m*.

longevity *n* longevità *f*.

longing *n* desiderio *m*.

longitude *n* longitudine *f*.

long-range *adj* a lungo raggio.

long-term *adj* a lungo termine.

long wave *adj* a onda *f* lunga.

long-winded *adj* prolisso.

look *vt* guardare; * *vi* guardare; sembrare; assomigliare; **to** ~ **after** occuparsi di; **to** ~ **for** cercare; **to** ~ **forward to** non vedere l'ora di fare qc; * *n* occhiata *f*; aria *f*; aspetto *m*.

looking glass *n* specchio *m*.

look-out *n* (mil) sentinella *f*.

loom *n* telaio *m*; * *vi* apparire indistintamente.

loop *n* cappio *m*.

loophole *n* scappatoia *f*.

loose *adj* allentato; sciolto; staccato; dissoluto.

loosen *vt* allentare.

loot *vt* saccheggiare; * *n* bottino *m*.

lop *vt* tagliare.

lop-sided *adj* sbilenco.

loquacious *adj* loquace.

loquacity *n* loquacità *f*.

lord *n* signore *m*.

lore *n* tradizioni *fpl*.

lorry *n* camion *m*.

lose *vt*, *vi* perdere.

loser *n* perdente *m*.

loss *n* perdita *f*; **to be at a** ~ non saper come fare.

lost property office *n* ufficio *m* oggetti smarriti.

lot *n* destino *m*, sorte *f*; partita

f; lotto *m*; molto *m*.

lotion *n* lozione *f*.

lottery *n* lotteria *f*.

loud *adj* forte.

loudspeaker *n* altoparlante *m*.

lounge *n* salone *m*, sala *f* d'attesa.

louse *n* pidocchio *m*.

lousy *adj* schifoso; pessimo.

lout *n* zotico *m*.

lovable *adj* adorabile.

love *n* amore *m*; **to fall in ~** innamorarsi; * *vt* amare, voler bene a.

love letter *n* lettera *f* d'amore.

love life *n* vita *f* sentimentale.

lovely *adj* bello.

lover *n* amante *m/f*.

love-sick *adj* malato d'amore.

loving *adj* affettuoso.

low *adj* basso; scadente; malfamato; * *n* depressione *f*; * *vi* muggire.

low-cut *adj* scolato.

lower *adj* inferiore; * *vt* calare; ridurre.

lowland *n* bassopiano *m*.

lowly *adj* umile.

loyal *adj* leale.

loyalty *n* lealtà *f*.

lozenge *n* pastiglia *f*; (*geom*) losanga *f*.

lubricant *n* lubrificante *m*.

lubricate *vt* lubrificare.

lucid *adj* lucido.

luck *n* fortuna *f*.

luckily *adv* fortunatamente.

luckless *adj* sventurato.

lucky *adj* fortunato.

lucrative *adj* lucrativo.

ludicrous *adj* ridicolo.

lug *vt* trascinare.

luggage *n* bagagli *mpl*.

lugubrious *adj* lugubre.

lukewarm *adj* tiepido.

lull *vt* calmare; * *n* tregua *f*.

lullaby *n* ninnananna *f*.

lumbago *n* lombaggine *f*.

lumberjack *n* taglialegna *m*.

luminous *adj* luminoso.

lump *n* zolletta *f*; grumo *m*; nodulo *m*; * *vi* **to ~ together** mettere insieme.

lump sum *n* pagamento *m* unico.

lunacy *n* pazzia *f*.

lunar *adj* lunare.

lunatic *adj*, *n* matto *m*, pazzo *m*.

lunch, luncheon *n* pranzo *m*, (seconda) colazione *f*.

lung *n* polmone *m*.

lurch *n* sobbalzo *m*; * *vt* sobbalzare.

lure *n* richiamo; * *vt* attirare (con l'inganno).

lurid *adj* orrendo; fiammeggiante.

lurk *vi* girare furtivamente.

luscious *adj* appetitoso.

lush *adj* lussureggiante.

lust *n* libidine *f*; * *vi* desiderare.

lustre *n* lustro *m*.

lustful *adj* libidinoso.

lusty *adj* vigoroso.

lute *n* liuto *m*.

luxuriant *adj* lussureggiante.

luxurious *adj* lussuoso.

luxury *n* lusso *m*.

lying *adj* bugiardo.

lymph *n* linfa *f*.

lynch *vt* linciare.

lynx *n* lince *f*.

lyrical *adj* lirico.

lyrics *npl* parole *fpl*.

M

macaroni n maccheroni mpl.
macaroon n amaretto m.
mace n mazza f; macis m/f.
macerate vt macerare.
machination n macchinazione f.
machine n macchina f.
machine gun n mitragliatrice f.
machinery n macchinari mpl.
mackerel n sgombro m.
mackintosh n impermeabile m.
mad adj pazzo.
madam n signora f.
madden vt far impazzire.
madder n (bot) robbia f.
madhouse n manicomio m.
madly adv follemente.
madman n folle m.
madness n follia f.
maestro n maestro m.
magazine n rivista f; caricatore m.
maggot n baco m.
magic n magia f; * adj magico.
magician n mago m.
magistrate n magistrato m.
magnanimity n magnanimità f.
magnanimous adj magnanimo.
magnate n magnate m.
magnesia n magnesia f.
magnesium n magnesio m.
magnet n calamita f.
magnetic adj magnetico.
magnetism n magnetismo.
magnificence n magnificenza f.
magnificent adj magnifico.
magnify vt ingrandire.
magnifying glass n lente f d'ingrandimento.

magnitude n vastità f.
magpie n gazza f.
mahogany n mogano m.
maid n cameriera f.
maiden n fanciulla f; * adj inaugurale.
maiden name n nome m da ragazza.
mail n posta f; * vt spedire (per posta).
mailing list n indirizzario m.
mail-order n vendita f per corrispondenza.
mail train treno m postale.
maim vt storpiare.
main adj principale; * n conduttura f principale.
mainland n continente m.
main-line n (rail) linea f principale.
mainly adv principalmente.
main road n strada f principale.
mainstay n sostegno m.
maintain vt mantenere.
maintenance n mantenimento m; manutenzione f.
maize n granturco m.
majestic adj maestoso.
majesty n maestà f.
major adj maggiore; * n (mil) maggiore m.
majority n maggioranza f.
make vt fare; fabbricare; to ~ for essere diretto a; to ~ up inventare; to ~ up for rimediare; * n marca f.
make-believe n finzione f.
makeshift adj improvvisato.
make-up n trucco m; composizione f.
maladjusted adj disadattato.
malady n malattia f.
malaise n malessere m.

malaria n malaria f.

malcontent adj, n malcontento m.

male adj maschile; * n maschio m.

malevolent adj malevolo.

malfunction n cattivo funzionamento m.

malice n malizia f.

malicious adj cattivo.

malign adj malefico; * vt calunniare.

malignant adj maligno.

mall n viale m.

malleable adj malleabile.

mallet n mazzuolo m.

mallow n (bot) malva f.

malnutrition n denutrizione f.

malpractice n negligenza f.

malt n malto m.

maltreat vt maltrattare.

mammal n mammifero m.

mammoth n mammut m; * adj colossale.

man n uomo m; * vt (mil) fornire di uomini.

manacle n manetta f.

manage vt gestire

manageable adj maneggevole.

management n gestione f.

manager n gestore m, manager m.

manageress n direttrice f.

managerial adj dirigente.

managing director n amministratore m delegato.

mandarin n mandarino m.

mandate n mandato m.

mandatory adj obbligatorio.

mandolin n mandolino m.

mane n criniera f.

manful adj valoroso.

manganese n manganese m.

manger n mangiatoia f.

mangle n strizzatoio m; * vt stritolare.

mango n mango m.

mangy adj rognoso.

manhandle vt malmenare.

manhood n virilità f.

man-hour n ora f di lavoro.

mania n mania f.

maniac n maniaco m.

manic adj maniaco.

manicure n manicure f.

manifest adj palese; * vt manifestare.

manifestation n manifestazione f.

manifesto n manifesto m.

manipulate vt manipolare.

manipulation n manipolazione f.

mankind n umanità f.

manliness n virilità f.

manly adj virile.

man-made adj artificiale.

manner n maniera f; ~s educazione f.

manoeuvrable adj maneggevole.

manoeuvre n manovra f; * vt, vi manovrare.

manor n maniero m.

manpower n manodopera f.

mansion n palazzo m.

manslaughter n omicidio m colposo.

mantelpiece n mensola f del caminetto.

manual adj, n manuale m.

manufacture n fabbricazione f; * vt fabbricare.

manufacturer n fabbricante m.

manure n concime m; * vt concimare.

manuscript n manoscritto m.

many adj molti, tanti; ~ a time più volte; how ~? quanti?; as ~ as tanti quanti.

map n carta f, pianta f; * vt tracciare una mappa.

maple n acero m.

mar vt sciupare.

marathon n maratona f.

marauder n saccheggiatore m.

marble n marmo m; bilia f; * adj di marmo.

March n marzo m.

march n marcia f; * vi marciare.

marchpast n sfilata f.

mare n giumenta f.

margarine n margarina f.

margin n margine m.

marginal adj marginale.

marigold n calendola f.

marijuana n marijuana f.

marina n marina f.

marinade n marinata f.

marinate vt marinare.

marine adj marino; * n marina f.

mariner n marinaio m.

marital adj coniugale.

maritime adj marittimo.

marjoram n maggiorana f.

mark n segno m; voto m; marco m; * vt macchiare; segnare; correggere.

marker n marcatore m.

market n mercato m.

marketable adj vendibile.

marketing n marketing m.

marketplace n mercato m.

market research n ricerca f di mercato.

marksman n tiratore m scelto.

marmalade n marmellata f d'arance.

maroon adj bordeaux; ~ed abbandonato, isolato.

marquee n grande tenda f.

marriage n matrimonio m.

marriage certificate n certificato m di matrimonio.

married adj sposato, coniugato.

marrow n midollo m; (bot) zucca f.

marry vt sposare; * vi sposarsi.

marsh n palude f.

marshal n maresciallo m; * vt schierare.

marshy adj paludoso.

marsupial adj, n marsupiale m.

marten n martora f.

martial adj marziale; ~ law stato d'assedio.

martin n balestruccio m.

martyr n martire m.

martyrdom n martirio m.

marvel n meraviglia f; * vi stupirsi.

marvellous adj meraviglioso.

marzipan n marzapane m.

mascara n mascara m.

mascot n portafortuna m.

masculine adj, n maschile m.

mash n pastone m; purè m; * vt schiacciare.

mask n maschera f; * vt mascherare.

masochist n masochista m/f.

mason n muratore m; massone m.

masonry n muratura f; massoneria f.

masquerade n mascherata f.

mass n messa f; massa f; * vt adunare; * vi adunarsi.

massacre n massacro m; * vt massacrare.

message n massaggio m; * vt massaggiare.

masseur n massaggiatore m.

masseuse n massaggiatrice f.

massive adj massiccio.

mass media n mass media mpl.

mast n albero m.

master n padrone m; insegnante m; * vt dominare; (fig) impadronirsi.

masterly adj magistrale.

mastermind n cervello m.

masterpiece n capolavoro m.

mastery n padronanza f.

masticate vt masticare.

mastiff n mastino m (inglese).

masturbate vi masturbarsi.

masturbation n masturbazione f.

mat *n* tappetino *m*, zerbino *m*.

match *n* fiammifero *m*; partita *f*, incontro *m*; pari *m/f*, uguale *m/f*; * *vt* uguagliare; * *vi* intonarsi; corrispondere.

matchbox *n* scatola *f* per fiammiferi..

matchless *adj* impareggiabile.

matchmaker *n* sensale *m/f* di matrimoni.

mate *n* compagno *m*; * *vt* accoppiare; * *vi* accoppiarsi.

material *adj* materiale; * *n* stoffa *f*, tessuto *m*; materiale *m*.

materialism *n* materialismo *m*.

maternal *adj* materno.

maternity *n* maternità *f*.

mathematical *adj* matematico.

mathematician *n* matematico *m*.

mathematics *npl* matematica *f*.

maths *npl* matematica *f*.

matinée *n* matinée *f*.

mating *n* accoppiamento *m*.

matins *npl* mattutino *m*.

matriculate *vi* immatricolarsi.

matriculation *n* immatricolazione *f*.

matrimonial *adj* coniugale.

matt *adj* opaco.

matted *adj* infeltrito.

matter *n* materia *f*; faccenda *f*; **what is the ~?** cosa c'è?; **a ~ of fact** per la verità; * *vi* importare.

mattress *n* materasso *m*.

mature *adj* maturo; * *vi* maturarsi.

maturity *n* maturità *f*.

maul *vt* sbranare.

mausoleum *n* mausoleo *m*.

mauve *adj* malva.

maxim *n* massima *f*.

maximize *vt* massimizzare.

maximum *adj*, *n* massimo *m*.

May *n* maggio *m*; **~ Day** il primo maggio *m*; **mayday** S.O.S. *m*.

maybe *adv* forse, può darsi.

mayonnaise *n* maionese *f*.

mayor *n* sindaco *m*.

mayoress *n* sindaca *f*.

maze *n* laberinto *m*.

me *pron* mi, me.

meadow *n* prato *m*.

meagre *adj* magro.

meal *n* farina *f*; pasto *m*.

mean *adj* avaro; meschino; medio; * *n* mezzo *m*; **~s** mezzi *mpl*; **in the ~time, meanwhile** nel frattempo; * *vt* significare; intendere.

meander *vi* serpeggiare.

meaning *n* significato *m*.

meaningful *adj* significativo.

meaningless *adj* senza senso.

meanness *n* avarizia *f*.

measles *n* morbillo *m*.

measure *n* misura *f*; provvedimento *m*; * *vt* misurare.

measurement *n* misurazione *f*, misura *f*.

meat *n* carne *f*.

meatball *n* polpetta *f* di carne.

meaty *adj* di carne.

mechanic *n* meccanico *m*.

mechanical *adj* meccanico.

mechanics *npl* meccanica *f*.

mechanism *n* meccanismo *m*.

mechanize *vt* meccanizzare.

medal *n* medaglia *f*.

medallion *n* medaglione *m*.

meddle *vi* immischiarsi.

meddler *n* impiccione *m*.

media *npl* media *mpl*.

mediate *vi* mediare.

mediation *n* mediazione *f*.

mediator *n* mediatore *m*.

medical *adj* medico; * *n* visita *f* medica.

medicate *vt* medicare.

medicated *adj* medicato.

medicinal *adj* medicinale.

medicine *n* medicina *f*.

medieval *adj* medievale.

mediocre *adj* mediocre.

mediocrity n mediocrità f.

meditate vi meditare.

meditation n meditazione f.

meditative adj meditativo.

Mediterranean adj mediterraneo; * n Mediterraneo m.

medium n mezzo; * adj medio.

medium wave n onde fpl medie.

medley n pot-pourri m.

meek adj mite.

meet vt incontrare; soddisfare; **they met with an accident** hanno avuto un incidente.

meeting n incontro m; riunione f; raduno m.

megalomaniac n megalomane m/f.

megaphone n megafono m.

melancholy n malinconia f; * adj malinconico.

mellow adj maturo; addolcito; * vt maturare; * vi addolcirsi.

melodious adj melodioso.

melodrama n melodramma f.

melody n melodia f.

melon n melone m.

melt vt fondere, sciogliere.

melting point n punto m di fusione.

member n membro m; socio m.

membership n iscrizione f.

membrane n membrana f.

memento n ricordo m.

memo n promemoria m.

memoir n saggio m monografico.

memorable adj memorabile.

memorandum n memorandum m.

memorial n monumento m; * adj commemorativo.

memorize vt imparare a memoria.

memory n memoria f; ricordo m.

menace n minaccia f; * vt minacciare.

menacing adj minaccioso.

menagerie n serraglio m.

mend vt aggiustare, accomodare.

mending n rammendo m.

menial adj servile.

meningitis n meningite f.

menopause n menopausa f.

menstruation n mestruazione f.

mental adj mentale.

mentality n mentalità f.

mentally adv mentalmente.

mention n menzione f; * vt accennare a.

mentor n mentore m.

menu n menu m.

mercantile adj mercantile.

mercenary adj, n mercenario m.

merchandise n merce f.

merchant n commerciante m/f.

merchant navy n marina f mercantile.

merciful adj misericordioso.

merciless adj spietato.

mercury n mercurio m.

mercy n misericordia f.

mere adj puro; ~ly semplicemente.

merge vi fondersi, confluire.

merger n fusione f.

meridian adj, n meridiano m.

meringue n meringa f.

merit n merito m; * vt meritare.

meritocracy n meritocrazia f.

meritorious adj meritorio.

mermaid n sirena f.

merrily adv gaiamente.

merriment n allegria f.

merry adj allegro; brillo.

merry-go-round n giostra f.

mesh n maglia f.

mesmerize vt ipnotizzare.

mess n disordine m; pasticcio m; * vt **to ~ up** scompigliare.

message n messaggio m.

messenger *n* messaggero *m*.
metabolism *n* metabolismo *m*.
metal *n* metallo *m*.
metallic *adj* metallico.
metallurgy *n* metallurgia *f*.
metamorphosis *n* metamorfosi *f*.
metaphor *n* metafora *f*.
metaphoric(al) *adj* metaforico.
metaphysical *adj* metafisico.
metaphysics *n* metafisica *f*.
mete (out) *vi* ripartire.
meteor *n* meteora *f*.
meteorite *n* meteorite *m*.
meteorological *adj* meteorologico.
meteorology *n* meteorologia *f*.
meter *n* contattore *m*.
methane *n* metano *m*.
method *n* metodo *m*.
methodical *adj* metodico.
methylated spirits *npl* alcol *m* denaturato.
metric *adj* metrico.
metropolis *n* metropoli *f*.
metropolitan *adj* metropolitano.
mettle *n* fegato *m*.
mew *n* miagolio *m*; * *vi* miagolare.
mezzanine *n* mezzanino *m*.
microbe *n* microbo *m*.
microchip *n* chip *m*.
microphone *n* microfono *m*.
microscope *n* microscopio *m*.
microscopic *adj* microscopico.
microwave *n* microonda *f*.
mid *adj* metà.
mid-day *n* mezzogiorno *m*.
middle *adj* centrale; * *n* mezzo *m*, centro *m*.
middle name *n* secondo nome *m*.
middleweight *n* peso *m* medio.
middling *adj* medio; mediocre.
midge *n* moscerino *m*.
midget *n* nano *m*.
midnight *n* mezzanotte *m*.

midriff *n* diaframma *m*.
midst *prep* in mezzo a.
midsummer *n* piena estate *f*.
midway *adv* a metà strada.
midwife *n* ostetrica *f*.
midwifery *n* ostetricia *f*.
midwinter *n* pieno inverno *m*.
might *n* forza *f*.
mighty *adj* possente.
migraine *n* emicrania *f*.
migrate *vi* migrare.
migration *n* migrazione *f*.
migratory *adj* migratore.
mild *adj* mite.
mildew *n* muffa *f*.
mile *n* miglio *m*.
mileage *n* chilometraggio *m*.
milometer *n* contachilometri *m*.
milestone *n* pietra *f* miliare.
milieu *n* ambiente *m* sociale.
militant *adj* militante *m/f*.
military *adj* militare; * *n* esercito *m*.
militate *vi* militare.
militia *n* milizia *f*.
milk *n* latte *m*.
milkshake *n* frappé *m*.
milky *adj* latteo; **M~ Way** *n* Via Lattea *f*.
mill *n* mulino *m*; fabbrica *f*; * *vt* macinare.
millennium *n* millennio *m*.
miller *n* mugnaio *m*.
millet *n* (*bot*) miglio *m*.
milligramme *n* milligrammo *m*.
millilitre *n* millilitro *m*.
millimetre *n* millimetro *m*.
milliner *n* modista *f*.
million *n* milione *m*.
millionaire *n* milionario *m*.
millionth *adj*, *n* milionesimo *m*.
millipede *n* millepiedi *m*.
millstone *n* macina *f*.
mime *n* mimmo *m*; * *vt*, *vi* mimare.
mimic *n* imitatore; * *vt* imitare.

mimicry n imitazione f.

mince vt tritare; * n carne f macinata.

mincer n tritacarne m.

mind n mente f; * vt badare a; * vi preoccuparsi.

minded adj: **open ~** di mente aperta.

mindful adj consapevole.

mindless adj insensato.

mine pron mio; * n miniera f; mina f; * vt estrarre, minare.

minefield n campo m minato.

miner n minatore m.

mineral adj, n minerale m.

mineralogy n mineralogia f.

mineral water n acqua f minerale.

minesweeper n dragamine m.

mingle vt mescolare.

miniature n miniatura f.

minimal adj minimo.

minimize vt minimizzare.

minimum n minima f.

mining n estrazione f mineraria.

minion n servo m favorito.

minister n ministro m; * vi assistere.

ministerial adj ministeriale.

ministry n ministero m.

mink n visone m.

minnow n pesciolino m d'acqua dolce.

minor adj minore; * n minorenne m/f.

minority n minoranza f.

minstrel n menestrello m.

mint n (bot) menta; zecca f; * vt coniare.

minuet n minuetto m.

minus adv meno.

minute n minuto m; **~s** verbale.

minute adj minuscolo.

miracle n miracolo m.

miraculous adj miracoloso.

mirage n miraggio m.

mire n melma f.

mirror n specchio m; * vt riflettere.

mirth n ilarità f.

misadventure n disavventura f.

misanthropist n misantropo m.

misapprehension n equivoco m.

misbehave vi comportarsi male.

misbehaviour n cattiva condotta f.

miscalculate vt calcolare male.

miscarriage n aborto m spontaneo; **~ of justice** errore giudiziario.

miscarry vi abortire.

miscellaneous adj vario.

miscellany n miscellanea f.

mischief n birichinata f; cattiveria f.

mischievous adj birichino; malizioso.

misconception n idea f sbagliata.

misconduct n cattiva condotta f.

misconstrue vt fraintendere.

miscreant adj scellerato.

misdeed n misfatto m.

misdemeanour n trasgressione f.

misdirect vt indirizzare male.

miser n avaro m.

miserable adj infelice.

miserly adj taccagno.

misery n tristezza f, miseria f.

misfit n disadattato m.

misfortune n disgrazia f.

misgiving n apprensione f.

misguided adj malaccorto.

mishandle vt bistrattare.

mishap n incidente m.

misinform vt informare male.

misinterpret vt interpretare male.

misjudge vt calcolare male.

mislay *vt* smarrire.

mislead *vt* trarre in inganno.

mismanage *vt* amministrare male.

mismanagement *n* cattiva amministrazione *f*.

misnomer *n* termine *m* improprio.

misogynist *n* misogino *m*.

misplace *vt* smarrire.

misprint *n* errore *m* di stampa.

Miss *n* signorina *f*.

miss *vt* perdere; mancare; evitare; * *n* colpo *m* mancato.

missal *n* messale *m*.

misshapen *adj* deforme.

missile *n* missile *m*.

missing *adj* mancante.

mission *n* missione *f*.

missionary *n* missionario *m*.

misspent *adj* sprecato.

mist *n* foschia *f*; * *vi* **to ~ up** appannarsi.

mistake *vt* sbagliare; * *vi* sbagliarsi; * *n* errore *m*, sbaglio *m*.

Mister *n* signore *m*.

mistletoe *n* vischio *m*.

mistreat *vt* maltrattare.

mistress *n* amante *f*; padrona *f*.

mistrust *vt* diffidare di; * *n* diffidenza *f*.

mistrustful *adj* diffidente.

misty *adj* brumoso.

misunderstand *vt* fraintendere.

misunderstanding *n* malinteso *m*.

misuse *vt* abusare di; * *n* abuso *m*.

mite *n* acaro *m*.

mitigate *vt* mitigare.

mitigation *n* mitigazione *f*.

mitre *n* mitra *f*.

mitten *n* muffola *f*.

mix *vt* mescolare; * *n* mescolanza *f*.

mixed *adj* assortito; misto.

mixed-up *adj* confuso.

mixer *n* frullatore *m*; betoniera *f*.

mixture *n* mistura *f*; miscela *f*.

mix-up *n* malinteso *m*.

moan *n* gemito *m*; * *vi* gemere.

moat *n* fossato *m*.

mob *n* folla *f*.

mobile *adj* mobile.

mobile home *n* casa *f* viaggiante.

mobility *n* mobilità *f*.

mobilize *vt* (*mil*) mobilitare.

moccasin *n* mocassino *m*.

mock *vi* beffarsi; * *n* finto *m*.

mockery *n* scherno *m*.

mocking *n* beffardo *m*.

mock-up *n* modello *m*.

mode *n* modo *m*.

model *n* modello *m*; indossatore *m*; * *vt* modellare; indossare; * *vi* posare.

moderate *adj*, *n* moderato *m*; * *vi* attenuarsi.

moderation *n* moderazione *f*.

modern *adj* moderno.

modernization *n* modernizzazione *f*.

modernize *vt* modernizzare.

modest *adj* modesto.

modesty *n* modestia *f*.

modicum *n* piccola quantità *f*.

modification *n* modifica *f*.

modify *vt* modificare.

modulate *vt* modulare.

modulation *n* (*mus*) modulazione *f*.

module *n* modulo *m*.

mohair *n* mohair *m*.

moist *adj* umido.

moisten *vt* inumidire.

moisture *n* umidità *f*.

molar *n* molare *m*.

molasses *npl* melassa *f*.

mole *n* neo *m*; talpa *f*.

molecule n molecola f.

molest vt molestare.

mollify vt pacificare.

mollusc n mollusco m.

mollycoddle vt coccolare.

molten adj fuso.

moment n momento m.

momentary adj momentaneo.

momentous adj importante.

momentum n momento m.

monarch n monarca m.

monarchy n monarchia f.

monastery n monastero m.

monastic adj monastico.

Monday n lunedì m.

monetary adj monetario.

money n denaro m, soldi mpl.

money order n vaglia m postale.

mongol n mongoloide m/f.

mongrel n bastardo m.

monitor n monitor m.

monk n monaco m.

monkey n scimmia f.

monochrome adj monocromatico.

monocle n monocolo m.

monologue n monologo m.

monopolize vt monopolizzare.

monopoly n monopolio m.

monosyllable n monosillabo m.

monotonous adj monotono.

monotony n monotonia f.

monoxide n monossido m.

monsoon n monsone m.

monster n mostro m; * adj gigantesco.

monstrosity n mostruosità f.

monstrous adj colossale; mostruoso.

montage n fotomontaggio m.

month n mese m.

monthly adj mensile.

monument n monumento m.

monumental adj monumentale.

moo vi muggire; * n muggito m.

mood n (gr) modo m; umore m.

moody adj lunatico.

moon n luna f.

moonbeam n raggio m di luna.

moonlight n chiaro m di luna.

moor n brughiera f; * vt ormeggiare.

moorland n brughiera f.

moose n alce m.

mop n scopa f di filacce; * vt passare lo straccio.

mope vi essere avvilito.

moped n ciclomotore m.

moral adj morale; * npl ~s principi morali.

morale n morale m.

moralist n moralista m/f.

morality n moralità f.

moralize vi moraleggiare.

morass n pantano m.

morbid adj morboso.

more adj più, ancora, altro; **once ~** un'altra volta; * adv ~ **and ~** sempre di più.

moreover adv inoltre.

morgue n orbitorio m.

morning n mattina f; **good ~** buon giorno.

moron n idiota m/f.

morose adj imbronciato.

morphine n morfina f.

Morse Code n alfabeto m Morse.

morsel n boccone m.

mortal adj, n mortale m.

mortality n mortalità f.

mortar n mortaio m.

mortgage n ipoteca f; * vt ipotecare.

mortification n mortificazione f.

mortify vt mortificare.

mortuary n orbitorio m.

mosaic n mosaico m.

mosque n moschea f.

mosquito n zanzara f.

moss n muschio m.

mossy adj muscoso.

most adj più; * pron quasi tutto.

motel n motel m.

moth n tarma f.

mothball n pallina f di naftalina.

mother n madre f.

motherhood n maternità f.

mother-in-law n suocera f.

motherly adj materno.

mother-of-pearl n madreperla f.

mother-to-be n futuro mamma f.

mother tongue n lingua f madre.

motif n motivo m.

motion n moto m, movimento m; cenno m.

motionless adj immobile.

motion picture n film m.

motivate vt motivare.

motivation n motivazione f.

motive n motivo m.

motley adj variopinto.

motor n motore m.

motorbike n moto f.

motorboat n motoscafo f.

motorcycle n motocicletta f.

motorist n automobilista m/f.

motorway n autostrada f.

mottled adj variopinto.

motto n motto m.

mould n muffa f; stampo m; * vt plasmare.

moulding n modanatura f.

mouldy adj ammuffito.

moult vt fare la muta.

mound n mucchio m.

mount n monte m; piedistallo m; * vt montare a; salire.

mountain n montagna f.

mountaineer n alpinista m/f.

mountaineering n alpinismo m.

mountainous adj montagnoso.

mourn vt, vi piangere.

mourner n chi piange la morte di qualcuno.

mournful adj lugubre.

mourning n lutto m.

mouse n topo m.

mousse n mousse f.

moustache n baffi mpl.

mouth n bocca f.

mouthful n boccone m.

mouth organ n armonica f.

mouthpiece n bocchino m; portavoce m/f.

mouthwash n colluttorio m.

mouthwatering adj che fa venire l'acquolina in bocca.

moveable adj movibile.

move * vt spostare, muovere; commuovere; * vi traslocare; * n mossa f, movimento m, trasloco m.

movement n movimento m.

movie n film m.

movie camera n cinepresa f.

moving adj mobile; commovente.

mow vt falciare.

mower n falciatrice f.

Mrs n signora f.

much adj, pron, adv molto.

muck n letame m.

mucous adj mucoso.

mucus n muco m.

mud n fango m.

muddle n confusione f.

muddy adj fangoso.

mudguard n parafango m.

muff n manicotto m.

muffle vt imbacuccare.

mug n tazzone m; boccale m; * vt aggredire.

mugger n rapinatore m.

muggy adj afoso.

mulberry n mora di gelso; ~ **tree** gelso m.

mule n mulo m.

mull vt scaldare con aromi; rimuginare.

multifarious adj svariato.

multiple adj, n multiplo m.

multiplication n moltiplicazione f; ~ **table** tavola f pitagorica.

multiply *vt* moltiplicare.
multitude *n* moltitudine *f*.
mumble *vt, vi* borbottare.
mummy *n* mummia *f*; mamma *f*.
mumps *npl* orecchioni *mpl*.
munch *vt* sgranocchiare.
mundane *adj* banale.
municipal *adj* municipale.
municipality *n* comune *m*.
munificence *n* munificenza *f*.
munitions *npl* munizioni *fpl*.
mural *n* pittura *f* murale; * *adj* murale.
murder *n* omicidio *m*, assassinio *m*; * *vt* assassinare.
murderer *n* assassino *m*.
murderess *n* assassina *f*.
murderous *adj* micidiale.
murky *adj* torbido.
murmur *n* mormorio *m*; * *vt, vi* mormorare.
muscle *n* muscolo *m*.
muscular *adj* muscolare.
muse *vt* sognare; * *n* musa *f*.
museum *n* museo *m*.
mush *n* pappa *f*.
mushroom *n* fungo *m*; * *vi* svilupparsi rapidamente.
music *n* musica *f*.
musical *adj* musicale.
musician *n* musicista *m/f*.
musk *n* muschio *m*.
muslin *n* mussola *f*.
mussel *n* cozza *f*.

must *mod aux vb* dovere; * *n* necessità *f*.
mustard *n* senape *f*.
muster *vt* radunare; * *n* appello *m*.
musty *adj* stantio.
mutant *adj, n* mutante *m*.
mutate *vt, vi* cambiare, mutare.
mute *adj* muto.
muted *adj* attutito.
mutilate *vt* mutilare.
mutilation *n* mutilazione *f*.
mutiny *n* ammutinamento *m*; * *vi* ammutinarsi.
mutter *vt, vi* borbottare; * *n* borbottio *m*.
mutton *n* montone *m*.
mutual *adj* reciproco.
muzzle *n* muso *m*; museruola *f*.
my *pron* mio.
myopic *adj* miope.
myriad *n* miriade *f*.
myrrh *n* mirra *f*.
myrtle *n* mirto *m*.
myself *pron* io stesso, me stesso.
mysterious *adj* misterioso.
mystery *n* mistero *m*.
mystic *n* mistico *m*.
mystical *adj* mistico.
mystify *vt* lasciare perplesso.
mystique *n* fascino *m*.
myth *n* mito *m*.
mythology *n* mitologia *f*.

N

nab *vt* acciuffare.
nag *n* ronzino *m*; brontolone *m*; * *vt* assillare.
nagging *adj* brontolone; insistente; * *n* brontolii *mpl*.
nail *n* unghia *f*; chiodo *m*; * *vt* inchiodare.
nailbrush *n* spazzolino *m* da

unghie.
nailfile *n* limetta *f*.
nail varnish *n* smalto per unghie.
naïve *adj* ingenuo.
naked *adj* nudo.
name *n* nome *m*; * *vt* chiamare; nominare; stabilire.

nameless *adj* ignoto.

namely *adv* cioè.

namesake *n* omonimo *m*.

nanny *n* bambinaia *f*.

nap *n* pisolino *m*; pelo *m*; * *vi* schiacciare un pisolino.

napalm *n* napalm *m*.

nape *n* nuca *f*.

napkin *n* tovagliolo *m*.

narcissus *n* (bot) narciso *m*.

narcotic *adj, n* narcotico *m*.

narked *adj* scocciato.

narrate *vt* narrare.

narration *n* narrazione *f*.

narrative *adj* narrativo; * *n* narrazione *f*.

narrow *adj* stretto; * *vt* restringere; * *vi* stringersi.

narrow-minded *adj* meschino; **~ness** meschinità *f*.

nasal *adj* nasale.

nasturtium *n* nasturzio *m*.

nasty *adj* cattivo, sgradevole, maligno.

nation *n* nazione *f*.

national *adj* nazionale; * *n* cittadino *m*.

nationalism *n* nazionalismo *m*.

nationalist *adj, n* nazionalista *m/f*.

nationality *n* nazionalità *f*.

nationalize *vt* nazionalizzare.

nationwide *adj* a livello nazionale.

native *adj* natale; indigeno * *n* nativo *m*; indigeno *m*.

native language *n* madre lingua *f*.

Nativity *n* Natività *f*.

natural *adj* naturale.

naturalist *n* naturalista *m/f*.

naturalize *vt* naturalizzare.

nature *n* natura *f*.

naught *n* (*poet*) nulla *m*.

naughty *adj* disubbidiente; spinto.

nausea *n* nausea *f*.

nauseate *vt* nauseare.

nauseous *adj* nauseabondo.

nautical *adj* nautico.

naval *adj* navale.

nave *n* navata *f*.

navel *n* ombelico *m*.

navigate *vt, vi* navigare.

navigation *n* navigazione *f*.

navy *n* marina *f*.

Nazi *adj, n* nazista *m/f*.

near *prep, adj, adv* vicino; * *vi* avvicinarsi a.

nearby *adj, adv* vicino.

nearly *adv* quasi.

near-sighted *adj* miope.

neat *adj* ordinato.

nebulous *adj* nebuloso.

necessarily *adv* necessariamente.

necessary *adj* necessario.

necessitate *vt* rendere necessario.

necessity *n* necessità *f*.

neck *n* collo *m*.

necklace *n* collana *f*.

nectar *n* nettare *m*.

née *adj* nata; **~ Brown** nata Brown.

need *n* bisogno *m*; * *vt* aver bisogno di.

needle *n* ago *m*; * *vt* punzecchiare.

needless *adj* inutile.

needlework *n* cucito *m*.

needy *adj* bisognoso.

negation *n* negazione *f*.

negative *adj* negativo; * *n* (*gr*) negazione *f*; (*phot*) negativa *f*.

neglect *vt* trascurare.

negligee *n* négligé *m*.

negligence *n* negligenza *f*.

negligent *adj* negligente.

negligibile *adj* trascurabile.

negotiate *vt* trattare; superare.

negotiation *n* trattativa *f*.

Negress *n* negra *f*.

Negro *adj, n* negro *m*.

neigh *vi* nitrire; * *n* nitrito *m*.

neighbour *n* vicino *m*.

neighbourhood n vicinato m.
neighbouring adj confinante.
neighbourly adv da buon vicino.
neither adv, pron, adj né; * conj nemmeno, neanche, neppure.
neon n neon m.
neon sign n insegna f al neon.
nephew n nipote m.
nepotism n nepotismo m.
nerve n nervo m.
nerve-racking adj snervante.
nervous adj nervoso, ansioso.
nervous breakdown n esaurimento m nervoso.
nest n nido m; * vi nidificare.
nest egg n (fig) gruzzolo m.
nestle vi accoccolarsi.
net n rete f; * adj netto.
netball n specie di pallacanestro.
netting n rete f metallica.
nettle n ortica f.
network n rete f.
neurosis n nevrosi f.
neurotic adj, n nevrotico m.
neuter adj (gr) neutro; * vt castrare.
neutral adj neutrale; neutro; * n folle f.
neutrality n neutralità f.
neutralize vt neutralizzare.
neutron n neutrone m.
neutron bomb bomba f al neutrone.
never adv mai; ~ mind non fa niente.
never-ending adj interminabile.
nevertheless adv ciò nonostante.
new adj nuovo.
newborn adj neonato.
newcomer n nuovo arrivato m.
new-fangled adj stramoderno.
news npl notizie fpl; notiziario m, telegiornale m; giornale radio m.

news agency n agenzia f stampa.
newsagent n giornalaio m.
newscaster n annunciatore m.
news flash n flash m.
newsletter n bollettino m.
newsreel n cinegiornale m.
New Year n Anno m Nuovo; ~'s Day capodanno; ~'s Eve la notte di San Silvestro.
newt n tritone m.
next adj prossimo, successivo; * adv dopo; * n prossimo m; * prep accanto a.
nib n pennino m.
nibble vt rosicchiare.
nice adj simpatico, piacevole, gentile, bello.
nice-looking adj bello.
niche n nicchia f.
nick n taglietto m; * vt (sl) fregare; in the ~ of time appena in tempo.
nickel n nichel m.
nickname n soprannome m; * vt soprannominare.
nicotine n nicotina f.
niece n nipote f.
niggling adj persistente; pignolo; insignificante.
night n notte f; by ~ di notte; good ~ buona notte.
nightclub n night m.
nightfall n crepuscolo m.
nightingale n usignolo m.
nightly adv ogni notte; * adj di ogni notte.
nightmare n incubo m.
night school n scuola f serale.
nightshade n: deadly ~ belladonna f.
night shift n turno m di notte.
night-time n notte f.
nihilist n nichilista m/f.
nil n nulla m, zero m.
nimble adj agile.
nine adj, n nove m.
nineteen adj, n diciannove.

nineteenth *adj, n* diciannovesimo *m*.

ninetieth *adj, n* novantesimo *m*.

ninth *adj, n* nono *m*.

nip *vt* pizzicare; * *n* pizzico *m*; bicchierino *m*.

nipple *n* capezzolo *m*.

nippy *adj* pungente.

nit *n* lendine *m*; scemo *m*.

nitrogen *n* azoto *m*.

no *adv* no; * *adj* nessuno.

nobility *n* nobiltà *f*.

noble *adj, n* nobile *m*.

nobleman *n* nobiluomo *m*.

nobody *n* nullità *f*; * *pron* nessuno.

nocturnal *adj* notturno.

nod *n* cenno *m* del capo; * *vi* fare un cenno col capo.

noise *n* rumore *m*; fracasso *m*.

noisily *adv* rumorosamente.

noisy *adj* rumoroso.

nomad *n* nomade *m/f*.

nom de plume *n* pseudonimo *m*.

nominal *adj* nominale.

nominate *vt* nominare.

nomination *n* nomina *f*.

nominative (*gr*) *adj, n* nominativo *m*.

nominee *n* candidato *m*.

non-alcoholic *adj* analcolico.

non-aligned *adj* non allineato.

nonchalant *adj* disinvolto.

non-committal *adj* evasivo.

nonconformist *adj, n* anticonformista *m/f*.

nondescript *adj* indefinito.

none *pron* nessuno, niente.

nonentity *n* nullità *f*.

nontheless *adv* nondimeno.

non-existent *adj* inesistente.

non-plus *vt* sconcertare.

nonsense *n* sciocchezze *fpl*.

nonsensical *adj* sciocco.

non-stick *adj* antiaderente.

non-stop *adj* diretto; continuo.

noodles *npl* tagliatelle *fpl*.

nook *n* angolino *m*.

noon *n* mezzogiorno *m*.

noose *n* cappio *m*.

nor *conj* né.

norm *n* norma *f*.

normal *adj* normale.

north *n* nord *m*, settentrione *m*; * *adj* nord.

North America *n* America *f* del nord.

north-east *n* nordest *m*.

northerly *adj* del nord; verso nord.

northern *adj* settentrionale, del nord.

north pole *n* polo *m* nord.

northwards *adv* verso nord.

north-west *n* nordovest *m*.

nose *n* naso *m*.

nosebleed *n* emorragia *f* nasale.

nosedive *n* picchiata *f*.

nos(e)y *adj* curioso.

nostalgia *n* nostalgia *f*.

nostril *n* narice *f*.

not *adv* non.

notable *adj* notevole.

notably *adv* notevolmente.

notary *n* notaio *m*.

notation *n* notazione *f*.

notch *n* tacca *f*; * *vt* intaccare.

note *n* nota *f*; biglietto *m*; * *vt* notare.

notebook *n* taccuino *m*.

noted *adj* famoso.

notepad *n* bloc-notes *m*.

notepaper *n* carta *f* da lettere.

nothing *n* niente; * *adv* per niente; **think ~ of it!** s'immagini!

notice *n* avviso *m*; preavviso *m*; recensione *f*; * *vt* accorgersi di.

noticeable *adj* percettibile.

notification *n* notifica *f*.

notify *vt* notificare.

notion *n* idea *f*; nozione *f*.

notoriety *n* notorietà *f*.

notorious adj famigerato.

notwithstanding conj benché;
 * adv ciononostante; * prep
 nonostante.

nougat n torrone m.

nought n zero m.

noun n (gr) sostantivo m.

nourish vt nutrire.

nourishing adj nutriente.

nourishment n nutrimento m.

novel n romanzo; * adj originale.

novelist n romanziere m.

novelty n novità f.

November n novembre m.

novice n novizio m.

now adv adesso, ora; * conj
 adesso che, ora che; ~ **and
 then** ogni tanto.

nowadays adv oggigiorno.

nowhere adv in nessun posto.

noxious adj nocivo.

nozzle n bocchetta f.

nuance n sfumatura f.

nuclear adj nucleare.

nucleus adj nucleo.

nude adj, n nudo m.

nudge n gomitata f.

nudist adj, n nudista m/f.

nudity n nudità f.

nuisance n seccatura f.

null adj nullo.

nullify vt annullare.

numb adj intorpidito; * vt intorpidire.

number n numero m; * vt numerare; contare.

numbness n intorpidimento m.

numeral n numerale m.

numerical adj numerico.

numerous adj numeroso.

nun n suora f.

nuptual adj nuziale.

nurse n infermiere m.

nursery n camera f dei bambini; vivaio m.

nursery rhyme n filastrocca f.

nursery school n asilo m infantile.

nursing home n clinica f.

nurture vt nutrire.

nut n noce (walnut), mandorla
 (almond), nocciola (hazelnut);
 (mech) dado; (sl) matto m;
 * adj (sl) svitato.

nutcrackers npl schiaccianoci
 m.

nutmeg n noce f moscata.

nutritious adj nutriente.

nut shell n guscio m di noce.

nylon n nailon m.

nymphomaniac n ninfomane f.

O

oaf n zoticone m

oak n quercia f.

oar n remo m.

oasis n oasi f.

oat n avena f.

oath n giuramento m.

oatmeal n farina f d'avena.

oats npl avena f.

obedience n ubbidienza f.

obedient adj ubbidiente.

obese adj obeso.

obesity n obesità f.

obey vt ubbidire.

obituary n necrologio m.

object n oggetto m; * vt obbiet-
 tare.

objection n obbiezione f.

objectionable adj antipatico.

objective n obiettivo m.

obligation n obbligo m.

obligatory adj obbligatorio.

oblige vt obbligare.

obliging adj gentile.

oblique adj obliquo.

obliterate *vt* cancellare.

oblivion *n* oblio *m*.

oblivious *adj* ignaro.

oblong *adj* oblungo; * *n* rettangolo *m*.

obnoxious *adj* detestabile.

oboe *n* oboe *m*.

obscene *adj* osceno.

obscenity *n* oscenità *f*.

obscure *adj* oscuro; * *vt* oscurare.

obscurity *n* anonimato *m*.

observance *n* osservanza *f*.

observant *adj* attento.

observation *n* osservazione *f*.

observatory *n* osservatorio *m*.

observe *vt* osservare.

observer *n* osservatore *m*.

obsess *vt* ossessionare.

obsessive *adj* ossessivo.

obsolete *adj* obsoleto.

obstacle *n* ostacolo *m*.

obstinate *adj* ostinato.

obstreperous *adj* turbulento.

obstruct *vt* ostruire.

obstruction *n* ostruzione *f*.

obtain *vt* ottenere.

obtainable *adj* ottenibile.

obtrusive *adj* invadente.

obtuse *adj* ottuso.

obvious *adj* ovvio.

occasion *n* occasione *f*; * *vt* causare.

occasional *adj* occasionale.

occupant, occupier *n* inquilino *m*, titolare *m*.

occupation *n* mestiere *m*; occupazione *f*.

occupy *vt* occupare.

occur *vi* accadere.

occurrence *n* evento *m*.

ocean *n* oceano *m*.

ocean-going *adj* d'alto mare.

oceanic *adj* oceanico.

ochre *n* ocra *f*.

octagon *n* ottagono *m*.

octane *n* ottano *m*.

octave *n* ottava *f*.

October *n* ottobre *m*.

octupus *n* piovra *f*.

oculist *n* oculista *m/f*.

odd *adj* strano; dispari; scompagnato.

oddity *n* bizzarria *f*.

odd jobs *npl* lavoretti *mpl*.

odds *npl* probabilità *f*.

ode *n* ode *f*.

odious *adj* odioso.

odour *n* odore *m*.

odourless *adj* inodore.

odyssey *n* odissea *f*.

oesophagus *n* esofago *m*.

oestrogen *n* estrogeno *m*.

of *prep* di.

off *adv* distante; * *adj* spento; andato a male; * *prep* da.

offal *n* frataglie *fpl*.

offence *n* infrazione *f*; offesa *f*.

offend *vt* offendere.

offender *n* trasgressore *m*.

offensive *adj* offensivo.

offer *n* offerta *f*; * *vt* offrire.

offering *n* offerta *f*.

offhand *adj* brusco.

office *n* ufficio *m*.

office block *n* palazzo *m* per uffici.

office hours *npl* orario *m* d'ufficio.

officer *n* ufficiale *m*.

office worker *n* impiegato *m*.

official *adj* ufficiale; * *n* funzionario *m*.

officiate *vi* ufficiare.

officious *adj* invadente.

off-key *adj* stonato.

off-peak *adj* tariffa ridotta.

off-season *adj* bassa stagione.

offset *n* offset *m*; * *vt* bilanciare.

offshoot *n* germoglio *m*.

offshore *adj* al largo.

offside *adj* in fuorigioco.

offspring *n* prole *f*.

offstage *adj* dietro le quinte.

often *adv* spesso, di frequente.

ogle *vt* occhieggiare.

ogre *n* orco *m*.

oil *n* olio *m*; petrolio *m*; * *vt* oleare.

oilcan *n* oleatore *m*.

oilfield *n* giacimento *m* petrolifero.

oil painting *n* quadro *m* a olio.

oil rig *n* impianto *m* di trivellazione per pozzi petroliferi.

oil tanker *n* petroliera *f*.

oil well *n* pozzo *m* petrolifero.

oily *adj* oleoso.

ointment *n* unguento *m*.

O.K., okay *excl* O.K., va bene; * *vt* approvare.

old *adj* vecchio, anziano; precedente.

old age *n* vecchiaia *f*.

old-fashioned *adj* antiquato.

oleander *n* oleandro *m*.

olive *n* oliva *f*; ~ **tree** *n* ulivo *m*.

olive oil *n* olio *m* d'oliva.

omelet(te) *n* frittata *f*.

omen *n* auspicio *m*.

ominous *adj* infausto.

omission *n* omissione *f*.

omit *vt* omettere.

omnipotent *adj* onnipotente.

omnivorous *adj* onnivoro.

on *prep* su, a, sopra; * *adj* acceso.

once *adv* una volta; **at ~** subito; **all at ~** improvisamente; **~ more** ancora una volta.

oncoming *adj* che si avvicina in senso contrario.

one *adj* uno, unico, stesso; * *n* uno *m*.

one-man *adj* individuale.

onerous *adj* gravoso.

oneself *pron* se stesso.

one-sided *adj* unilaterale.

one-to-one *adj* univoco.

one way *adj* a senso unico.

ongoing *adj* in corso.

onion *n* cipolla *f*.

onlooker *n* spettatore *m*.

only *adj* solo; * *adv* solo, solamen-te.

onrush *adj* afflusso.

onset *n* inizio *m*.

onslaught *n* attacco *m*.

onus *n* gravame *m*.

onwards *adj* in avanti.

ooze *vi* trasudare; * *n* melma *f*.

opal *n* opale *m/f*

opaque *adj* opaco.

open *adj* aperto; * *vt* aprire; **to be ~ with sb** essere franco.

opening *n* apertura *f*; inaugurazione *f*; breccia *f*.

open-minded *adj* aperto.

openness *n* franchezza *f*.

opera *n* opera *f*.

opera house *n* teatro *m* lirico.

operate *vt* azionare; * *vi* funzionare; operare.

operatic *adj* lirico.

operation *n* operazione *f*; intervento *m*.

operational *adj* operativo.

operative *adj* operante.

operator *n* centralinista *m/f*.

ophthalmic *adj* oftalmico.

opine *vt* ritenere.

opinion *n* opinione *f*, parere *m*.

opinionated *adj* dogmatico.

opinion poll *n* sondaggio *m* di opinione.

opium *n* oppio *m*.

opponent *n* avversario *m*.

opportune *adj* opportuno.

opportunist *n* opportunista *m/ f*.

opportunity *n* occasione *f*.

oppose *vt* opporsi a.

opposing *adj* avversario.

opposite *adv* di fronte; * *n* contrario *m*.

opposition *n* opposizione *f*.

oppress *vt* opprimere.

oppression *n* oppressione *f*.

oppressive *adj* oppressivo.

oppressor *n* oppressore *m*.

opt *vi* optare.

optic(al) *adj* ottico; * *npl* ~s ottica *f*.

optician *n* ottico *m*.

optimist *n* ottimista *m/f*.

optimistic *adj* ottimistico.

optimum *adj* ottimale.

option *n* scelta *f*, opzione *f*.

optional *adj* facoltativo.

opulent *adj* opulento.

or *conj* o.

oracle *n* oracolo *m*.

oral *adj*, *n* orale *m*; ~**ly** *adv* oralmente.

orange *n* arancia *f*; ~ **tree** *n* arancio *m*; (colour) arancio *m*.

orangeade *n* aranciata *f*.

oration *n* orazione *f*.

orator *n* oratore *m*.

orbit *n* orbita *f*; * *vt* orbitare.

orchard *n* frutteto *m*.

orchestra *n* orchestra *f*.

orchestral *adj* orchestrale.

orchid *n* orchidea *f*.

ordain *vt* ordinare.

ordeal *n* prova *f* ardua.

order *n* ordine *m*, comando *m*, ordinazione *f*; * *vt*, *vi* ordinare.

order form *n* ordine *m*.

orderly *adj* ordinato; * *n* inserviente *m*.

ordinance *n* ordinanza *f*.

ordinarily *adv* normalmente.

ordinary *adj* abituale, comune; ordinario.

ordination *n* ordinazione *f*.

ordnance *n* artiglieria *f*.

ore *n* minerale *m* grezzo.

oregano *n* origano *m*.

organ *n* organo *m*.

organic(al) *adj* organico.

organism *n* organismo *m*.

organist *n* organista *m/f*.

organization *n* organizzazione *f*.

organize *vt* organizzare.

orgasm *n* orgasmo *m*.

orgy *n* orgia *f*.

oriental *adj* orientale.

orientate *vt* orientare.

orifice *n* orifizio *m*.

origin *n* origine *f*.

original *adj*, *n* originale *m*.

originality *n* originalità *f*.

originate *vi* avere origine.

ornament *n* ornamento *m*; * *vt* ornare.

ornamental *adj* ornamentale.

ornate *adj* ornato.

orphan *adj*, *n* orfano *m*.

orphanage *n* orfanotrofio *m*.

orthodox *adj* ortodosso.

orthodoxy *n* ortodossia *f*.

orthography *n* ortografia *f*.

orthopaedic *adj* ortopedico; * *n* ~**s** ortopedia *f*.

oscillate *vi* oscillare.

osprey *n* falco *m* pescatore.

ossify *vi* ossificarsi.

ostensibly *adv* apparentemente.

ostentatious *adj* pretenzioso.

osteopathy *n* osteopatia *f*.

ostracize *vt* ostracizzare.

ostrich *n* struzzo *m*.

other *adj*, *pron* altro; * *adv* ~ **than** diversamente.

otherwise *adv* diversamente, altrimenti.

otter *n* lontra *f*.

ouch! *excl* ahi!

ought *vb aux* dovere.

ounce *n* oncia *f*.

our *adj* nostro.

ourselves *pron* noi stessi.

oust *vt* scacciare.

out *adv* fuori; * *prep* fuori, per, da, senza.

outback *n* entroterra *m*.

outboard *n* fuoribordo *m*.

outbreak *n* scoppio *m*.

outburst *n* scoppio *m*.

outcast *n* emarginato *m*.

outcome *n* esito *m*.

outcry *n* protesta *f*.

outdated *adj* sorpassato.

outdo *vt* superare.

outdoor *adj* all'aperto; **~s** *adv* all'aperto.

outer *adj* esterno.

outer space *n* spazio *m* cosmico.

outfit *n* costume *m*; organizzazione *f*.

outgoing *adj* uscente.

outgrow *vt* diventare troppo grande per.

outhouse *n* costruzione *f* annessa.

outing *n* escursione *f*.

outlandish *n* stravagante.

outlaw *n* fuorilegge *m*; * *vt* bandire.

outlay *n* spesa *f*.

outlet *n* scarico *m*; punto *m* vendita.

outline *n* contorno *m*; * *vt* riassumere.

outlive *vt* sopravvivere a.

outlook *n* veduta *f*.

outlying *adj* periferico.

outmoded *adj* sorpassato.

outnumber *vt* superare numericamente.

out-of-date *adj* scaduto; fuori moda.

outpatient *n* paziente *m* esterno.

outpost *n* avamposto *m*.

output *n* produzione *f*; rendimento *m*.

outrage *n* atrocità *f*; sdegno *m*; * *vt* oltraggiare.

outrageous *adj* scandaloso.

outright *adv* nettamente; * *adj* netto; schietto.

outrun *vt* superare.

outset *n* inizio *m*.

outshine *vt* eclissare.

outside *n* esterno *m*; * *adj* esterno; * *adv* fuori, * *prep* fuori di.

outsider *n* estraneo *m*.

outsize *n* taglia forte.

outskirts *npl* periferia *f*.

outspoken *adj* franco.

outstanding *adj* eccezionale; insolito.

outstretched *adj* disteso.

outstrip *vt* sorpassare.

outward *adj* esterno; apparente.

outweigh *vt* avere più importanza di.

outwit *vt* essere più furbo di.

oval *adj*, *n* ovale *m*.

ovary *n* ovaia *f*.

oven *n* forno *m*.

ovenproof *adj* pirofilo.

over *prep* su, sopra; * *adj* finito; **~ again** da capo; **~ and ~** mille volte.

overall *adj* generale; **~s** *npl* tuta *f*.

overawe *vt* intimidire.

overbalance *vt* sbilanciarsi.

overbearing *adj* prepotente.

overboard *adv* fuori bordo.

overcast *adj* coperto.

overcharge *vt* far pagare troppo.

overcoat *n* soprabito *m*.

overcome *vt* sopraffare.

overconfident *adj* presuntuoso.

overcrowded *adj* sovraffollato.

overdo *vt* esagerare.

overdose *n* overdose *f*.

overdraft *n* conto *m* scoperto.

overdue *adj* scaduto.

overestimate *vt* sopravvalutare.

overflow *vt*, *vi* traboccare; * *n* troppopieno *m*.

overgrown *adj* coperto di vegetazione.

overgrowth *n* vegetazione *f* densa.

overhang *vi* sporgere.

overhanging *adj* sporgente.

overhaul *vt* revisionare; * *n* revisione *f*.

overhead *adv* in alto; * *adj* soppraelevato.

overhear *vt* sentire per caso.

overjoyed *adj* felicissimo.

overkill *n* strafare *m*.

overland *adj, adv* per (via) di terra.

overlap *n* sovrapposizione *f*; * *vi* sovrapporsi.

overleaf *adv* a tergo.

overload *vt* sovraccaricare.

overlook *vt* dare su; chiudere un occhio su; trascurare.

overnight *adv* di notte.

overpass *n* cavalcavia *m*.

overpower *vt* sopraffare.

overpowering *adj* soffocante.

overrate *vt* sopravvalutare.

override *vt* non tenere conto di.

overriding *adj* preponderante.

overrule *vt* prevalere su.

overrun *vt* invadere; * *vi* protrarsi.

overseas *adv* all'estero; * *adj* estero.

oversee *vt* sorvegliare.

overseer *n* sorvegliante *m*.

overshadow *vt* eclissare.

overshoot *vt* andare oltre.

oversight *n* svista *f*.

oversleep *vi* svegliarsi troppo tardi.

overspill *n* eccedenza *f* di popolazione.

overstate *vt* esagerare.

overstep *vt* oltrepassare.

overt *adj* evidente.

overtake *vt* superare.

overthrow *vt* rovesciare; * *n* rovesciamento *m*.

overtime *n* straordinario *m*.

overtone *n* sfumatura *f*.

overture *n* (*mus*) ouverture *f*.

overturn *vt* capovolgere.

overweight *n* eccedenza *f* di peso.

overwhelm *vt* sopraffare, sommergere.

overwhelming *adj* schiacciante.

overwork *vi* lavorare troppo; * *n* lavoro *m* eccessivo.

owe *vt* dovere.

owing *adj* da pagare; * *prep* ~ **to** a causa di.

owl *n* civetta *f*, gufo *m*.

own *adj* proprio; * *vt* possedere; * *vi* **to** ~ **up** ammettere.

owner *n* proprietario *m*.

ownership *n* proprietà *f*.

ox *n* bue *m*; **~en** *npl* buoi *mpl*.

oxidize *vt* ossidare.

oxygen *n* ossigeno *m*.

oyster *n* ostrica *f*.

ozone *n* ozono *m*.

P

pa *n* (*fam*) babbo *m*.

pace *n* passo *m*; * *vi* camminare su e giù.

pacemaker *n* pace-maker *m*.

pacific *adj* pacifico; * *n* pacifico *m*.

pacification *n* pacificazione *f*.

pacifism *n* pacifismo *m*.

pacifist *n* pacifista *m/f*.

pacify *vt* calmare, placare.

pack *n* pacco *m*; branco *m*; * *vt* imballare; stipare di; * *vi* fare le valigie.

package *n* pacchetto *m*; * *vt* confezionare.

package holiday *n* vacanza *f* organizzata.

packet *n* pacchetto *m*.

packing *n* imballaggio *m*.

pact *n* patto *m*.

pad n cuscinetto m; blocchetto m; rampa f di lancio; (sl) casa f; * vt imbottire.

padding n imbottitura f.

paddle vi sguazzare; * n pala f.

paddle steamer n battello m a ruote.

paddock n recinto m.

paddy risaia f.

padlock n lucchetto m.

pagan adj, n pagano m.

page n paggio m; pagina f.

pageant n corteo m in maschera.

pageantry n sfarzo m.

pail n secchio m.

pain n dolore m; * vt addolorare.

pained adj addolorato.

painful adj doloroso.

painkiller n antidolorifico m.

painless adj indolore.

painstaking adj coscienzioso.

paint n tinta f; vernice; * vt dipingere; verniciare.

paintbrush n pennello m.

painter n pittore m; imbianchino m.

painting n quadro m; pittura f.

paintwork n vernice f.

pair n paio m, copia f.

pal n (fam) amico m.

palatable adj gradevole al palato.

palate n palato m.

palatial adj sontuoso.

palaver n trambusto m.

pale adj pallido.

palette n tavolozza f.

pall n drappo m funebre; * vi diventare noioso.

pallet n paletta f.

palliative adj, n palliativo m.

pallid adj pallido.

pallor n pallore m.

palm n palma f.

palmist n chiromante m/f.

Palm Sunday n domenica delle Palme.

palpable adj palpabile.

palpitation n palpitazione f.

paltry adj irrisorio.

pamper vt viziare.

pamphlet n opuscolo m.

pan n pentola f.

panacea n panacea f.

panache n stile m.

pancake n frittella f.

pancreas n pancreas m.

panda n panda m.

pandemonium n pandemonio m.

pane n vetro m.

panel n pannello m; giuria f.

panelling n rivestimento m di pannelli.

pang n dolore m acuto.

panic adj, n panico m.

panicky adj allarmista.

panic-stricken adj in preda al panico.

panorama n panorama m.

pansy n (bot) pensée f.

pant vi ansimare.

panther n pantera f.

panties npl mutandine fpl.

pantihose n collant m.

pantry n dispensa f.

pants npl mutande fpl, slip m.

papacy n papato m.

papal adj papale.

paper n carta f; relazione f; giornale m; ~s pl documenti mpl; * vt tappezzare.

paperback n tascabile m.

paper clip n fermaglio m.

paperweight n fermacarte m.

paperwork n lavoro m d'ufficio.

paprika n paprica f.

par n parità f; **above ~** sopra la media.

parable n parabola f.

parachute n paracaduta m.

parade n sfilata f, parata f.

paradise n paradiso m.

paradox n paradosso m.

paradoxical adj paradossale.

parafin n kerosene m.

paragon n modello m perfetto.

paragraph n paragrafo m.

parallel adj parallelo; * n parallela f.

paralysis n paralisi f.

paralytic(al) adj paralitico.

paralyze vt paralizzare.

paramount adj sommo.

paranoid adj paranoico.

parapet n parapetto m.

paraphernalia n armamentario m.

parasite n parassita m.

parasol n parasole m.

paratrooper n paracadutista m.

parcel n pacco m; * vt impacchettare.

parch vt inaridire.

parched adj riarso.

parchment n pergamena f.

pardon n perdone m; * vt perdonare.

parent n genitore m/f.

parentage n natali mpl.

parental adj dei genitori.

parenthesis n parentesi fpl.

parish n parrocchia f.

parishioner n parrocchiano m.

parity n parità f.

park n parco m; * vt, vi parcheggiare.

parking n parcheggiare m.

parking meter n parchimetro m.

parking ticket n multa f per sosta vietata.

parlance n gergo m.

parliament n parlamento m.

parliamentary adj parlamentare.

parlour n salotto m.

Parmesan n parmigiano m.

parody n parodia f; * vt parodiare.

parole n libertà f provvisoria.

parricide n parricida m/f; n parricidio m.

parrot n pappagallo m.

parsley n prezzemolo m.

parsnip n pastinaca f.

parson n pastore m.

part n parte f; * vt separare; * vi lasciarsi; **to ~ with** disfarsi di.

partial adj parziale.

participant n partecipante m/f.

participate vi partecipare.

participation n partecipazione f.

participle n (gr) participio m.

particle n particella f.

particular adj particolare; pignolo; * n particolare m.

parting n separazione f; riga f; * adj d'addio.

partisan adj, n partigiano m.

partition n parete f divisoria.

partner n partner m/f, socio m.

partnership n associazione f.

partridge n pernice f.

party n partito m; festa f.

pass vt passare; sorpassare; superare; approvare; * vi passare; accadere; **to ~ away** mancare; * n passo m; lasciapassare m; sufficienza f; **to make a ~ at** fare delle avances a.

passable adj passabile.

passage n passaggio m.

passbook n libretto m di risparmio.

passenger n passeggero m.

passer-by n passante m.

passing adj passeggero.

passion n passione f.

passionate adj appassionato.

passion flower n passiflora f.

passive adj, n passivo m.

passkey n passe-partout m.

Passover n Pasqua f ebraica.

passport n passaporto m.

password n parola f d'ordine.

past adj passato; * n passato m; * prep davanti; oltre; passato.

pasta *n* pasta *f*.

paste *n* pasta *f*, impasto *m*; * *vt* appiccicare.

pastel *adj*, *n* pastello *m*.

parteurized *adj* pastorizzato.

pastime *n* passatempo *m*.

pastor *n* pastore *m*.

pastoral *adj* pastorale.

pastry *n* pasta *f*.

pasture *n* pascolo *m*.

pasty *adj* smorto.

pat *vi* dare dei colpetti leggeri; * *n* colpetto *m*.

patch *n* toppa *f*; * *vt* rattoppare; **to ~ up** appianare.

patchwork *n* patchwork *m*.

pâté *n* pâté *m*.

patent *adj* palese; brevettato; * *n* brevetto *m*; * *vt* brevettare.

patent leather *n* pelle *f* lucida.

paternal *adj* paterno.

paternity *n* paternità *f*.

path *n* sentiero *m*.

pathetic *adj* patetico.

pathological *adj* patologico.

pathology *n* patologia *f*.

pathos *n* pathos *m*.

pathway *n* sentiero *m*.

patience *n* pazienza *f*.

patient *adj*, *n* paziente *m*.

patio *n* terrazza *f*.

patriarch *adj* patriarca.

patrio *n* patriota *m/f*.

patriotic *adj* patriottico.

patriotism *n* patriottismo *m*.

patrol *n* pattuglia *f*; * *vt* perlustrare.

patrol car *n* auto *f* della polizia.

patron *n* mecenate *m/f*; patrono *m*.

patronage *n* patrocinio *m*.

patronize *vt* trattare con condiscendenza; frequentare.

patter *n* parlantina *f*; * *vi* picchiettare.

pattern *n* disegno *m*, modello *m*.

paunch *n* pancia *f*.

pauper *n* indigente *m/f*.

pause *n* pausa *f*; * *vi* fare una pausa.

pave *vt* lastricare.

pavement *n* marciapiede *m*.

pavilion *n* padiglione *m*.

paving stone *n* lastra *f* di pavimentazione *f*.

paw *n* zampa *f*; * *vt* scalpitare, dare una zampata.

pawn *n* pedone *m*; (*fig*) pedina *f*; * *vt* impegnare.

pawn broker *n* prestatore *m* su pegno.

pawnshop *n* monte *m* di pietà.

pay *vt*, *vi* pagare; **to ~ back** rimborsare; **to ~ off** saldare; * *n* paga *f*.

payable *adj* pagabile.

pay day *n* giorno *m* di paga.

payee *n* beneficiario *m*.

payment *n* pagamento *m*.

pay-phone *n* telefono *m* pubblico.

payroll *n* lista *f* del personale.

pea *n* pisello *m*.

peace *n* pace *f*.

peaceful *adj* pacifico.

peach *n* pesca *f*; **~ tree** pesco *m*.

peacock *n* pavone *m*.

peak *n* cima *f*.

peak hours *npl* ore; *fpl* di punta.

peal *n* scampanio *m*.

peanut *n* arachide *f*.

pear *n* pera *f*; **~ tree** *n* pero *m*.

pearl *n* perla *f*.

peasant *n* contadino *m*.

peat *n* torba *f*.

pebble *n* ciottolo *m*.

peck *n* beccata *f*; bacetto *m*; * *vt* beccare.

pecking order *n* ordine *m* gerarchico.

peculiar *adj* strano.

peculiarity *n* peculiarità *f*.

pedagogic(al) *adj* pedagogico.
pedal *n* pedale *m*; * *vi* pedalare.
pedant *n* pedante *m/f*.
pedantic *adj* pedante.
peddle *vt* spacciare.
pederast *n* pederasta *m*.
pedestal *n* piedistallo *m*.
pedestrian *n* pedone *m*; * *adj* mediocre.
pediatrician *n* pediatra *m/f*.
pediatrics *n* pediatria *f*.
pedicure *n* pedicure *f*.
pedigree *n* pedigree *m*.
pedlar *n* spacciatore *m*.
pee *vi* (fam) pisciare.
peek *vi* sbirciare.
peel *vt* sbucciare; * *vi* spellarsi; * *n* buccia *f*.
peeler *n* sbucciapatate *m*.
peep *vi* squittire; spiare.
peephole *n* spioncino *m*.
peer *n* pari *m/f*; * *vi* scrutare.
peerless *adj* impareggiabile.
peeved *adj* stizzito.
peevish *adj* stizzoso.
peg *n* molletta *f*; picchetto *m*; * *vt* fissare.
pejorative *adj* peggiorativo.
pelican *n* pellicano *m*.
pellet *n* pallottola *f*.
pelt *vt* tempestare; lapidare; * *vi* (fam) it was ~ing with rain pioveva a dirotto; * *n* pelle *f* greggia.
pelvis *n* bacino *m*.
pen *n* penna *f*; recinto *m*; * *vt* scrivere; rinchiudere.
penal *adj* penale.
penalty *n* pena *f*.
penance *n* penitenza *f*.
penchant *n* debole *m*.
pencil *n* matita *f*, lapis *m*.
pencil case *n* astuccio *m* per matite.
pendant *n* pendaglio *m*.
pending *adj* in sospeso.
pendulum *n* pendolo *m*.
penetrate *vt*, *vi* penetrare.

pen friend *n* corrispondente *m/f*.
penguin *n* pinguino *m*.
penicillin *n* penicillina *f*.
peninsula *n* penisola *f*.
penis *n* pene *m*.
penitence *n* penitenza *f*.
penitent *adj*, *n* pentito *m*.
penitentiary *n* penitenziario *m*.
penknife *n* temperino *m*.
pennant *n* fiamma *f*.
penniless *adj* senza un soldo.
penny *n* penny *m*.
pension *n* pensione *f*.
pensive *adj* pensoso.
pentagon *n* pentagono *m*.
Pentecost *n* Pentecoste *f*.
penthouse *n* attico *m*.
pent-up *adj* represso.
penultimate *adj* penultimo.
penury *n* indigenza *f*.
peony *n* peonea *f*.
people *n* gente *f*, popolo *m*, persone *fpl*; * *vt* popolare.
pep *n* dinamismo *m*; * *vt* to ~ up animare.
pepper *n* pepe *m* peperone *m*; * *vt* pepare.
peppermint *n* menta *f* peperita.
per *prep* per.
per annum *adv* all'anno.
per capita *adj*, *adv* pro capite.
perceive *vt* percepire.
percentage *n* percentuale *f*.
perception *n* percezione *f*.
perch *n* pesce *m* persico; posatoio *m*; * *vi* appollaiarsi.
percolate *vt*, *vi* filtrare.
percolator *n* caffettiera *f* a filtro.
percussion *n* percussione *f*.
peremptory *adj* perentorio.
perennial *adj* perenne.
perfect *adj* perfetto; * *vt* perfezionare.
perfection *n* perfezione *f*.
perfidious *adj* perfido.

perforate vt perforare.
perforation n perforazione f.
perform vt svolgere; rappresentare; eseguire; * vi esibirsi.
performance n rappresentazione f; interpretazione f; rendimento m.
performer n artista m/f.
perfume n profumo m; * vt profumare.
perfunctory adj superficiale.
perhaps adv forse.
peril n pericolo m.
perilous adj pericoloso.
perimeter n perimetro m.
period n periodo m; ora f; punto m; mestruazioni fpl.
periodic(al) adj periodico.
periodical n periodico m.
peripheral adj periferico.
periphery n periferia f.
periscope n periscopio m.
perish vi perire.
perishable adj deperibile.
peritonitis n peritonite f.
perjure vt spergiurare.
perjury n spergiuro m.
perk n vantaggio m.
perky adj allegro.
perm n permanente f.
permanent adj permanente.
permeate vt permeare; * vi filtrare, pervadere.
permissible adj ammissibile.
permission n permesso m.
permissive adj permissivo.
permit vt, vi permettere; * n autorizzazione f.
permutation n permutazione f.
perpendicular adj, n perpendicolare f.
perpetrate vt perpetrare.
perpetual adj perpetuo.
perpetuate vt perpetuare.
perplex vt lasciare perplesso.
persecute vt perseguitare.
persecution n persecuzione f.

perseverance n perseveranza f.
persevere vi perseverare.
persimmon n cachi m.
persist vi persistere.
persistence n perseveranza f.
persistent adj persistente.
person n persona f.
personable adj prestante.
personage n personaggio m.
personal adj personale.
personal assistant n segretaria f personale.
personal column n annunci mpl personali.
personal computer n personal computer m.
personality n personalità f.
personification n personificazione f.
personify vt personificare.
personnel n personale m.
perspective n prospettiva f.
perspiration n traspirazione f.
perspire vi traspirare.
persuade vt persuadere.
persuasion n persuasione f.
persuasive adj persuasivo.
pert adj impertinente.
pertain vi to ~ to riferirsi a; ~ing to relativo a.
pertinent adj pertinente.
perturb vt turbare.
perusal n lettura f.
peruse vt leggere.
pervade vt pervadere.
perverse adj perverso.
pervert n pervertito m; * vt pervertire.
pessimist n pessimista m/f.
pest n insetto m nocivo; peste f.
pester vt tormentare.
pet n animale m domestico; beniamino m; * vt accarezzare.
petal n petalo m.
petite adj minuta.
petition n petizione f; * vt presentare una petizione a.

petrified *adj* impietrito.
petrol *n* benzina *f*.
petroleum *n* petrolio *m*.
petticoat *n* sottoveste *f*.
pettiness *n* meschinità *f*.
petty *adj* insignificante.
petty cash *n* fondo *m* per piccole spese.
petty officer *n* sottufficiale *m* di marina.
petulant *adj* irritabile.
pew *n* banco *m*.
pewter *n* peltro *m*.
phalic *adj* fallico.
phantom *adj*, *n* fantasma *m*.
Pharaoh *n* faraone *m*.
pharmaceutic(al) *adj* farmaceutico.
pharmacist *n* farmacista *m/f*.
pharmacy *n* farmacia *f*.
phase *n* fase *f*.
pheasant *n* fagiano *m*.
phonomenal *adj* fenomenale.
phenomenon *n* fenomeno *m*.
phial *n* fiala *f*.
philanderer *n* donnaiolo *m*.
philanthropic *adj* filantropico.
philanthropist *n* filantropo *m*.
philanthropy *n* filantropia *f*.
philately *n* filatelia *f*.
philharmonic *adj* filarmonico.
philologist *n* filologo *m*.
philology *n* filologia *f*.
philosopher *n* filosofo *m*.
philosophic(al) *adj* filosofico.
philosophize *vi* filosofare.
philosophy *n* filosofia *f*.
phlegm *n* flemma *f*.
phlegmatic(al) *adj* flemmatico.
phobia *n* fobia *f*.
phoenix *n* fenice *f*.
phone *n* telefono *m*; * *vt* telefonare; * *vt* **to ~ back** richiamare.
phone book *n* elenco *m* telefonico.
phone box, phone booth *n*

cabina *f* telefonica.
phone call *n* telefonata *f*.
phoneme (*ling*) *n* fonema *m*.
phonetic *adj* fonetico; **~s** *n* fonetica *f*.
phoney *adj* falso.
phosphate *n* fosfato *m*.
phosphorescent *adj* fosforescente.
phosphorus *n* fosforo *m*.
photocopier *n* fotocopiatrice *f*.
photocopy *n* fotocopia *f*; * *vt* fotocopiare.
photogenic *adj* fotogenico.
photograph *n* fotografia *f*; * *vt* fotografare.
photographer *n* fotografo *m*.
photographic *adj* fotografico.
photography *n* fotografia *f*.
photosynthesis *n* fotosintesi *f*.
phrase *n* frase *f*; * *vt* esprimere.
phrase book *n* frasario *m*.
physical *adj* fisico.
physical education *n* educazione *f* fisica.
physician *n* medico *m*.
physicist *n* fisico *m*.
physics *n* fisica *f*.
physiological *adj* fisiologico.
physiologist *n* fisiologo *m*.
physiology *n* fisiologia *f*.
physiotherapy *n* fisioterapia *f*.
physique *n* fisico *m*.
pianist *n* pianista *m/f*.
piano *n* pianoforte *m*.
piccolo *n* ottavino *m*.
pick *n* piccone *m*; scelta *f*; * *vt* scegliere; cogliere; **to ~ on** prendersela con; **to ~ out** individuare; **to ~ up** raccogliere; rimorchiare; passare a prendere.
pickaxe *n* piccone *m*.
picket *n* picchetto *m*; * *vt*, *vi* picchettare.
pickle *n* pasticcio *m*; **~s** sottaceti *mpl*; * *vt* mettere sottaceto.
pickpocket *n* borsaiolo *m*.

pickup n pickup m; (auto) camioncino m.

picnic n picnic m.

pictorial adj illustrato.

picture n quadro m; fotografia f; disegno m; * vt immaginare.

picture book n libro m illustrato.

picturesque adj pittoresco.

pie n torta f; pasticcio m.

piece n pezzo m.

piecemeal adv poco alla volta; * adj frammentario.

piecework n lavoro m a cottimo.

pier n pontile m.

pierce vt forare.

piercing adj lacerante.

piety n pietà f.

pig n maiale m, porco m; (fam) stronzo m.

pigeon n piccione m.

pigeonhole n casella f.

piggy bank n salvadanaio m.

pig-headed adj cocciuto.

pigsty n porcile m.

pigtail n treccina f.

pike n lucio m.

pilchard n sardina f.

pile n mucchio m; pila f; ~s emorroidi fpl. * vt impilare; ammucchiare.

pile-up n tamponamento m a catena.

pilfer vt rubacchiare.

pilgrim n pellegrino m.

pilgrimage n pellegrinaggio m.

pill n pillola f.

pillage vt saccheggiare.

pillar n pilastro m, colonna f.

pillion n sellino m posteriore.

pillow n guanciale m.

pillow case n federa f.

pilot n pilota m/f; * vt pilotare.

pilot light n fiammella f di sicurezza.

pimento n pepe m garofanato.

pimp n magnaccia m.

pimple n foruncolo m.

pin n spillo m; ~s and needles n formicolio m; * vt attaccare con uno spillo.

pinafore n grembiule m.

pinball n flipper m.

pincers n pinze fpl.

pinch vt pizzicare; fregare; * n pizzicotto m; pizzico m.

pincushion n puntaspilli m.

pine (bot) n pino m; * vi languire.

pineapple n ananas m.

ping n tintinnio m.

ping-pong n ping-pong m.

pinion n pignone m.

pink n rosa m.

pinnacle n pinnacolo m.

pinpoint vt localizzare con esattezza.

pinstripe n gessato m.

pint n pinta f.

pioneer n pioniere m.

pious adj pio.

pip n seme m.

pipe n tubo m; pipa f; ~s cornamusa m.

pipe cleaner n scovolino m.

pipe dream n sogno m impossibile.

pipeline n conduttura f.

piper n suonatore m di cornamusa.

piping n tubature fpl.

piquant adj piccante; stimolante.

pique n ripicca f.

piracy n pirateria f.

pirate n pirata m.

pirouette n piroetta f.

Pisces n Pesci mpl.

piss vi (fam) pisciare.

pissed adj ubriaco.

pistachio n pistacchio m.

pistol n pistola f.

piston n stantuffo m.

pit n buca f; cava f.

pitch n pece f; campo m; intonazione *f*; * *vt* lanciare; piantare.

pitchblack *adj* buio pesto.

pitcher *n* brocca *f*.

pitchfork *n* forcone *m*.

pitfall *n* tranello *m*.

pithy *adj* arguto; vigoroso.

pitiable *adj* pietoso.

pitiful *adj* pietoso.

pittless *adj* spietato.

pittance *n* miseria *f*.

pity *n* compassione *f*; peccato *m*; * *vt* compatire.

pivot *n* perno *m*.

pixie *n* folletto *m*.

pizza *n* pizza *f*.

placard *n* cartello *m*.

placate *vt* placare.

place *n* luogo *m*, posto *m*; * *vt* posare, mettere; situare; piazzare.

placebo *n* placebo *m*.

placenta *n* placenta *f*.

placid *adj* placido.

plagiarism *n* plagio *m*.

plague *n* peste *f*; * *vt* tormentare.

plaice *n* passera *f* di mare.

plaid *n* tessuto *m* scozzese.

plain *adj* evidente; semplice; in tinta unita; * *n* pianura *f*.

plain clothes *adj* in borghese.

plaintiff *n* attore *m*.

plait *n* treccia *f*; * *vt* intrecciare.

plan *n* piano *m*; * *vt* pianificare; organizzare.

plane *n* (*bot*) platano *m*; pialla *f*, * *adj* piano; * *vt* piallare; * *vi* planare.

planet *n* pianeta *m*.

planetarium *n* planetario *m*.

plank *n* tavola *f*.

plankton *n* plancton *m*.

planner *n* pianificatore *m*.

planning *n* pianificazione *f*.

plant *n* pianta *f*; impianto *m*; stabilimento *m*; * *vt* piantare.

plantation *n* piantagione *f*.

plaque *n* placca *f*.

plasma *n* plasma *m*.

plaster *n* intonaco *m*; gesso *m*; cerotto *m*; * *vt* intonacare.

plastered *adj* (fam) ubriaco.

plasterer *n* intonacatore *m*.

plastic *adj* plastico; * *n* plastica.

plastic surgery *n* chirurgia *f* plastica.

plate *n* piatto *m*; targa *f*; piastra *f*; * *vt* placcare.

plateau *n* altopiano *m*.

plate glass *n* vetro *m* piano.

platform *n* piattaforma *f*; binario *m*.

platinum *n* platino *m*.

platitude *n* banalità *f*.

platonic *adj* platonico.

platoon *n* plotone *m*.

platter *n* piatto *m* da portata.

plausible *adj* plausibile.

play *n* gioco *m*; commedia *f*; * *vt* giocare; suonare; interpretare; * *vi* giocare; suonare; **to ~ down** minimizzare.

playboy *n* playboy *m*.

player *n* giocatore *m*; suonatore *m*.

playful *adj* giocherellone.

playground *n* cortile *m* per la ricreazione.

play group *n* asilo *m* infantile.

play-off *n* partita *f* di spareggio.

playpen *n* box *m*.

playwright *n* drammaturgo *m*.

plea *n* supplica *f*.

plead *vt* difendere; * *vi* implorare.

pleasant *adj* piacevole.

please *vi* piacere; * *vt* accontentare; * *excl* per piacere.

pleased *adj* contento, lieto.

pleasing *adj* piacevole.

pleasure *n* piacere *m*.

pleat *n* piega; * *vt* pieghettare.

plebeian adj, n plebeo m.

pledge n pegno m; * vt impegnare.

plenary adj plenario.

plentiful adj abbondante.

plenty n abbondanza f.

plethora n pletora f.

pleurisy n pleurite f.

pliable, pliant adj malleabile.

pliers npl pinze fpl.

plight n situazione f (critica).

plinth n plinto m.

plod vi sgobbare; arrancare.

plonk n vino m ordinario.

plot n appezzamento m; complotto m; trama f; * vt tracciare; * vi complottare.

plough n aratro m; * vt arare; **to ~ back** reinvestire; * vi arare.

ploy n stratagemma m.

pluck vt cogliere; pizzicare; spennare; * n coraggio m.

plucky adj coraggioso.

plug n tappo m; spina f; * vt tappare.

plughole n scarico m.

plum n prugna f (tree) prugno m, susina f (tree) susino m.

plumage n piumaggio m.

plumb n piombo m; * vt scandagliare.

plumber n idraulico m.

plume n piuma f.

plump adj paffuto.

plunder n saccheggio m; bottino m; * vt saccheggiare.

plunge vt immergere; conficcare; * vi tuffarsi; precipitare; * n tuffo m.

plunger n sturalavandini m.

pluperfect n (gr) piuccheperfetto m.

plural adj, n plurale m.

plurality n pluralità f.

plus n vantaggio m; più m; * prep più; * adj positivo.

plush n felpa f; * adj sontuoso.

plutonium n plutonio m.

ply vt maneggiare; esercitare; incalzare; * vi fare la spola tra; * n strato m; velo m.

plywood n compensato m.

pneumatic adj pneumatico.

pneumatic drill n martello pneumatico.

pneumonia n polmonite f.

poach vi cacciare di frodo; * vt cuocere in bianco.

poached egg n uovo m in camicia.

poacher n bracconiere m.

poaching n bracconaggio m.

pocket n tasca f; * vt intascare.

pocket money n paga f settimanale.

pod n baccello m.

podgy adj grassottello.

podium n podio m.

poem n poesia f.

poet n poeta m.

poetess n poetessa f.

poetic adj poetico.

poetry n poesia f.

poignant adj struggente.

point n punto m; virgola f; punta f; scopo m; **~ of view** punto m di vista; * vt puntare; indicare.

point-blank adv a bruciapelo.

pointed adj appuntito.

pointer n lancetta f; pointer m; indizio m.

pointless adj inutile.

poise n portamento m.

poison n veleno m; * vt avvelenare.

poisoning n avvelenamento m.

poisonous adj velenoso.

poke vt dare un colpetto a; * n colpetto m.

poker n attizzatoio m; poker m.

poker-faced adj dalla faccia impassibile.

poky adj angusto.

polar adj polare.

polarity n polarità f.

polarize vt polarizzare.

pole n palo m; asta f; polo m.

pole vault n salto con l'asta.

polemic n polemica f.

police n polizia f; * vt presidiare.

policeman n poliziotto m.

police station n posto m di polizia.

policewoman n donna f poliziotto.

policy n politica f; polizza f.

polio n polio f.

polish vt lucidare; lustrare; **to ~ off** sbrigare; * n lucido m, cera f; lucidata f; raffinatezza f.

polished adj lucidato; raffinato.

polite adj educato.

politeness n educazione f.

politic adj accorto.

political adj politico.

politician n politico m.

politics npl politica f.

polka n polca f; **~ dot** n pois m.

poll n votazione f; sondaggio m.

pollen n polline m.

pollute vt inquinare.

pollution n inquinamento m.

polo n polo m.

polyandry n poliandria f.

polyester n poliestere m.

polyethylene n polietilene m.

polygamy n poligamia f.

polyglot n poliglotta m/f.

polygon n poligono m.

polyp n polipo m.

polystyrene n polistirolo m.

polytechnic adj, n politecnico m.

polythene n politene m.

pomegranate n melagrana f.

pomp n fasto m.

pompom n pompon m.

pompous adj pomposo.

pond n laghetto m.

ponder vt ponderare.

ponderous adj pesante.

pontiff n pontefice m.

pontoon n pontone m; ventuno m.

pony n pony m.

ponytail n coda f di cavallo.

poodle n barboncino m.

poof n (fam) finocchio m.

pool n pozza f; piscina f; cassa f comune; riserva f; biliardo m; * vt mettere insieme.

poor adj povero; misero; **the ~** i poveri mpl.

poorly adj indisposto.

pop n schiocco m; bevanda f gassata; * adj pop; * vt fare scoppiare; **to ~ in** fare un salto.

pop music n musica f pop.

popcorn n pop-corn m.

Pope n papa m.

poplar n pioppo m.

popper n bottone m automatico.

poppet n tesoro m.

poppy n papavero m.

populace n popolo m.

popular adj popolare; benvoluto.

popularity n popolarità f.

popularize vt rendere popolare, diffondere.

populate vt popolare.

population n popolazione f.

populous adj popoloso.

porcelain n porcellana f.

porch n veranda f.

porcupine n porcospino m.

pore n poro m.

pork n maiale m.

pornography n pornografia f.

porous adj poroso.

porpoise n focena f.

porridge n porridge m.

port n porto m; (mar) babordo m.

portable adj portatile.

portal n portale m.

porter n portinaio m; facchino m.

portfolio n portafoglio m; cartella f.

porthole n oblò m.

portico n portico m.

portion n porzione f.

portly adj corpulento.

portrait n ritratto m.

portray vt ritrarre.

pose n posa f; * vi posare; * vt porre.

posh adj elegante, sontuoso.

position n posizione f; impiego m; * vt sistemare.

positive adj positivo.

posse n squadra f d'armati.

possess vt possedere.

possession n possesso m.

possessive adj possessivo.

possibility n possibilità f.

possibile adj possibile.

post n palo m; posta f; posto m; * vt spedire per posta; affiggere.

postage n affrancatura f.

postage stamp n francobollo m.

postal adj postale.

post box n cassetta f delle lettere.

postcard n cartolina f.

postcode n codice m di avviamento postale.

postdate vt postdatare.

poster n manifesto m, poster m.

posterior n deretano m, posteriore m.

posterity n posterità f.

postgraduate adj di specializzazione (dopo la laurea).

posthumous adj postumo.

postman n postino m.

postmark n timbro m postale.

post-mortem n autopsia f.

post office n ufficio m postale.

postpone vt rimandare.

postscript n poscritto m.

postulate vt postulare.

posture n portamento m.

posy n mazzolino m.

pot n pentola f; vasetto m; erba f; * vt invasare.

potasium n potassio m.

potato n patata f.

potbellied adj panciuto.

potent adj potente.

potential adj, n potenziale m.

pothole n cavità f; buca f.

potion n pozione f.

potted adj conservato (in vaso); condensato.

potter n vasaio m.

pottery n ceramica f.

potty adj (fam) vasino.

pouch n borsa f marsupio.

poultice n impiastro m.

poultry n pollame m.

pounce n balzo m; * vt balzare.

pound n libra f; (lira) sterlina; canile municipale; deposito auto; * vt picchiare, pestare.

pour vt versare; * vi to ~ with rain piovere a dirotto.

pout vi fare il broncio; * n broncio m.

poverty n miseria f; povertà f.

powder n polvere f; * vt ridurre in polvere; * vi incipriarsi.

powder compact n portacipria m.

powdered milk n latte m in polvere.

powder puff n piumino m della cipria.

powdery adj farinoso.

power n forza f, potenza f; capacità f; potere m; * vt azionare.

powerful adj potente; possente.

powerless adj impotente.

power station n centrale f elettrica.

practicable adj praticabile.

practical adj pratico.

practicality n senso m pratico.
practical joke n beffa f.
practice n abitudine f; esercizio m; pratica f; **doctor's ~** studio.
practise vi esercitarsi a; praticare.
practitioner n professionista m/f.
pragmatic adj pragmatico.
prairie n prateria f.
praise n elogio m; * vt lodare.
praiseworthy adj lodevole.
prance vi caracollare; pavoneggiarsi.
prank n burla f.
prattle vt blaterare.
prawn n gambero m.
pray vi pregare.
prayer n preghiera f.
preach vt, vi predicare.
preacher n predicatore m.
preamble n preambolo m.
precarious adj precario.
precaution n precauzione f.
precautionary n precauzionale.
precede vt precedere.
precedence n precedenza f.
precedent n precedente m.
preceding adj precedente.
precinct n circoscrizione f.
precious adj prezioso.
precipice n precipizio m.
precipitate vt accelerare; * adj precipitoso.
precise adj preciso.
precision n precisione f.
preclude vt precludere.
precocious adj precoce.
preconceived adj preconcetto.
preconception n preconcetto m.
precondition n condizione f indispensabile.
precursor n precursore m.
predator n predatore m.
predecessor n predecessore m.

predestination n predestinazione f.
predict vt predire.
predictable adj prevedibile.
prediction n predizione f.
predilection n predilezione f.
predominance n predominanza f.
predominant adj predominante.
predominate vt predominare.
preeminent adj eccezionale.
preen vt agghindarsi.
prefab n casetta f prefabbricata.
preface n prefazione f.
prefer vt preferire.
preferable adj preferibile.
preferably adv di preferenza.
preference n preferenza f.
preferential adj preferenziale.
prefix n prefisso m.
pregnancy n gravidanza f.
pregnant adj in cinta, gravida f.
prehistoric adj preistorico.
prejudice n pregiudizio m; * vt pregiudicare.
prejudiced adj essere prevenuto.
prejudicial adj pregiudizievole.
preliminary adj preliminare.
prelude n preludio m.
premarital adj prematrimoniale.
premature adj prematuro.
premeditate vt premeditare.
premeditate n premeditazione f.
premier n premier m.
premiere n prima f.
premise n premessa f.
premises npl locali mpl.
premium n premio m.
premonition n presentimento m.

preoccupy *vt* preoccupare.

prepaid *adj* pagato in anticipo; affrancato.

preparation *n* preparazione *f*.

preparatory *adj* preparatorio.

prepare *vt* preparare.

preponderance *n* preponderanza *f*.

preposition *n* preposizione *f*.

preposterous *adj* assurdo.

prerequisite *n* presupposto *m* necessario.

prerogative *n* prerogativa *f*.

prescribe *vi* prescrivere.

prescription *n* ricetta *f*.

presence *n* presenza *f*.

present *n* presente *m*; * *adj* presente; attuale; * *vt* presentare.

presentable *adj* presentabile.

presentation *n* presentazione *f*.

presenter *n* presentatore *m*.

presentiment *n* presentimento *m*.

preservation *n* conservazione *f*.

preservative *n* conservante *m*.

preserve *vt* conservare; * *n* conserva *f*.

preside *vi* presiedere.

presidency *n* presidenza *f*.

president *n* presidente *m*.

presidential *adj* presidenziale.

press *vt, vi* premere; stirare; * *n* pressa *f*; torchio *m*; stampa *f*.

press agent *n* agente *m* pubblicitario.

press conference *n* conferenza *f* stampa.

pressing *adj* pressante.

pressure *n* pressione *f*.

pressure cooker *n* pentola *f* a pressione.

pressure group *n* gruppo *m* di pressione.

pressurize *vt* pressurizzare.

prestige *n* prestigio *m*.

presumable *adj* probabile.

presume *vt* supporre.

presumption *n* presunzione *f*.

presumptuous *adj* presuntuoso.

presuppose *vt* presupporre.

pretence *n* pretesa *f*.

pretend *vi* fingere.

pretender *n* pretendente *m/f*.

pretentious *adj* pretenzioso.

preterite *n* passato *m*.

pretext *n* pretesto *m*.

pretty *adj* grazioso; * *adv* piuttosto.

prevail *vi* prevalere.

prevailing *adj* attuale.

prevalent *adj* diffuso.

prevaricate *vt* tergiversare.

prevent *vt* prevenire.

prevention *n* prevenzione *f*.

preventive *adj* preventivo.

preview *n* anteprima *f*.

previous *adj* precedente.

pre-war *adj* dell'anteguerra.

prey *n* preda *f*.

price *n* prezzo *m*.

priceless *adj* di valore inestimabile.

price list *n* listino *m* prezzi.

prick *vt* bucare; pungere; * *n* puntura *f*; (*fam*) cazzo *m*.

prickle *n* spina *f*.

prickly *adj* spinoso.

pride *n* orgoglio *m*; branco *m*.

priest *n* prete *m*.

priestess *n* sacerdotessa *f*.

priesthood *n* sacerdozio *m*.

priestly *adj* sacerdotale.

prig *n* borioso *m*.

prim *adj* per benino.

primacy *n* (*relig*) primazia *f*.

primarily *adj* essenzialmente.

primary *adj* principale.

primate *n* primate *m*.

prime *n* apice *m*; * *adj* principale; * *vt* preparare.

Prime Minister *n* Primo Ministro *m*.

primeval *adj* primordiale.

primitive *adj* primitivo.

primrose *n* (*bot*) primula *f*.

prince *n* principe *m*.

princess *n* principessa *f*.

principal *adj* principale; * *n* preside *m*.

principality *n* principato *m*.

principle *n* principio *m*.

print *vt* stampare; * *n* impronta *f*; stampato *m*; stampa *f*; out of ~ esaurito.

printed matter *n* stampe fpl.

printer *n* tipografo *m*; stampante *f*.

printing *n* stampa *f*; stampatello *m*.

prior *adj* precedente; * *n* priore *m*.

priority *n* priorità *f*.

priory *n* prioria *f*.

prise *vt* aprire facendo leva.

prism *n* prisma *m*.

prison *n* prigione *f*.

prisoner *n* prigioniero *m*.

pristine *adj* immacolato.

privacy *n* privacy *f*.

private *adj* privato; confidenziale; * *n* soldato *m* semplice.

private detective *n* detective *m* privato.

privet *n* ligustro *m*.

privilege *n* privilegio *m*.

prize *n* premio *m*; * *vt* valutare.

prize-giving *n* premiazione *f*.

prizewinner *n* premiato *m*.

pro *adj* professionista

probability *n* probabilità *f*.

probable *adj* probabile.

probation *n* periodo *m* di prova; libertà *f* condizionale.

probe *n* sonda *f*; * *vt* sondare.

problem *n* problema *m*.

problematical *adj* problematico.

procedure *n* procedura *f*.

proceed *vi* procedere; ~s *npl* ricavato *m*.

proceedings *n* provvedimenti mpl.

process *n* processo *m*, procedimento *m*; *vt* trattare.

procession *n* processione *f*.

proclaim *vt* proclamare.

proclamation *n* proclama *m*.

procrastinate *vt* procrastinare.

procreation *n* procreazione *f*.

procure *vt* procurare.

procurement *n* approvvigionamento *m*.

prod *vi* essere di stimolo a; * *n* colpetto *m*.

prodigal *adj* prodigo.

prodigious *adj* prodigioso.

prodigy *n* prodigio *m*.

produce *vt* produrre; * *n* prodotto *m*.

producer *n* produttore *m*; regista *m/f*.

product *n* prodotto *m*.

production *n* produzione *f*.

production line *n* catena *f* di montaggio.

productive *adj* produttivo.

productivity *n* produttività *f*.

profane *adj* profano.

profess *vt* professare.

profession *n* professione *f*.

professional *adj* professionale; * *n* professionista *m/f*.

professor *n* professore *m*.

proffer *vt* profferire.

proficiency *n* competenza *f*.

proficient *adj* competente.

profile *n* profilo *m*.

profit *n* profitto *m*; * *vi* approfittare.

profitability *n* redditività *f*.

profitable *adj* redditizio.

profiteer *vt* specolare; * *n* speculatore *m*.

profound *adj* profondo.

profuse *adj* copioso.

profusion *n* profusione *f*.

prognosis *n* prognosi *f*.

programme n programma m.

programmer n programmatore m.

programming n programmazione f.

progress n progresso m; * vi procedere.

progression n progressione f.

progressive adj progressivo.

prohibit vt proibire; vietare.

prohibition n proibizione f.

project vt proiettare; * n progetto m.

projectile n proiettile m.

projection n proiezione f.

projector n proiettore m.

prolapse n prolasso m.

proletarian adj, n proletario m.

proletariat n proletariato m.

prolific adj prolifico.

prologue n prologo m.

prolix adj prolisso.

prolong vt prolungare.

prom n (fam) lungomare m;

promenade n passeggiata f.

prominence n prominenza f.

prominent adj prominente.

promiscuous adj promiscuo.

promise n promessa f; * vt promettere.

promising adj promettente.

promontory n promontorio m.

promote vt promuovere.

promoter n promotore m.

promotion n promozione f.

prompt adj tempestivo; * vt suggerire.

prompter n suggeritore m.

prone adj a faccia in giù; soggetto a.

prong n rebbio m.

pronoun n pronome m.

pronounce vt pronunciare.

pronounced adj netto.

pronouncement n dichiarazione f.

pronunciation n pronuncia f.

proof n prova f; bozza f.

prop vt appoggiare; * n sostegno m.

propaganda n propaganda f.

propel vt spingere.

propeller n elica f.

propensity n propensione f.

proper adj appropriato; giusto; decente.

property n proprietà f.

prophecy n profezia f.

prophesy vt profetizzare.

prophet n profeta m.

prophetic adj profetico.

proportion n proporzione f.

proportional adj proporzionale.

proportionate adj proporzionato.

proposal n proposta f.

propose vt proporre.

proposition n proposizione f.

proprietor n proprietario m.

propriety n decoro m.

propulsion n propulsione f.

prosaic adj prosaico.

prose n prosa f.

prosecute vt proseguire; * vi ricorrere in giudizio.

prosecution n azione f giudiziaria.

prosecutor n procuratore m.

prospect n prospettiva f; * vt esplorare.

prospective adj futuro.

prospector n prospettore m.

prospectus n prospetto m.

prosper vi prosperare.

prosperity n prosperità f.

prosperous adj prospero.

prostitute n prostituta f.

prostitution n prostituzione f.

prostrate adj prostrato.

protagonist n protagonista m/f.

protect vt proteggere.

protection n protezione f.

protective adj protettivo.

protector n protettore m.
protégé n protetto m.
protein n proteina f.
protest vt, vi protestare; * n protesta f.
Protestant n protestante m.
protester n contestatore m.
protocol n protocollo m.
prototype n prototipo m.
protracted adj protratto.
protrude vi sporgere.
proud adj orgoglioso.
prove vt dimostrare, provare; vi rivelarsi.
proverb n proverbio m.
proverbial adj proverbiale.
provide vt fornire; **to ~ for** provvedere a.
provided conj:~ **that** a patto che.
providence n provvidenza f.
province n provincia f.
provincial adj provinciale.
provision n fornitura f.
provisional adj provvisorio.
proviso n clausola f.
provocation n provocazione f.
provocative adj provocatorio.
provoke vi provocare.
prow n (mar) prua f.
prowess n prodezza f.
prowl vi aggirarsi.
prowler n chi si aggira furtivamente.
proximity n vicinanza f.
proxy n procura f.
prudence n prudenza f.
prudent adj prudente.
prudish adj puritano.
prune vt potare; * prugna.
prurient adj libidinoso.
prussic acid n acido m prussico.
pry vi curiosare; * vt sollevare con una leva.
psalm n salmo m.
pseudonym n pseudonimo m.
psyche n psiche f.

psychiatric adj psichiatrico.
psychiatrist n psichiatra m/f.
psychiatry n psichiatria f.
psychic adj psichico.
psychoanalysis n psicanalisi f.
psychoanalyst n psicanalista m/f.
psychological adj psicologico.
psychologist n psicologo m.
psychology n psicologia f.
psychopath n psicopatico m.
pshychosomatic adj psicosomatico.
pub n pub m.
puberty n pubertà f.
pubic adj pubico.
public adj, n pubblico m.
public address system n impianto di amplificazione m.
publican n gestore di un pub m.
publication n pubblicazione f.
publicity n pubblicità f.
publicize vt reclamizzare.
public school n scuola f superiore privata.
publish vt pubblicare.
publisher n editore m.
publishing n editoria f.
pucker vt increspare.
pudding n dolce m; budino m; dessert m.
puddle n pozzanghera f.
peurile adj puerile.
puff n soffio m; * vi ansimare, soffiare.
puff pastry n pasta f sfoglia.
puffin n pulcinella f di mare.
puffy adj gonfio.
pug n carlino m.
puke vt, vi vomitare.
pull vi tirare; **to ~ down** demolire; **to ~ in/up** fermarsi; **to ~ off** portare a termine; **to ~ through** cavarsela; * tirata f; attrazione f.
pulley n puleggia f.
pullover n pullover m.

pulp n pasta (di legno) f; polpa f.

pulpit n pulpito m.

pulsate vi pulsare.

pulse n polso m.

pulverize vt polverizzare.

puma n puma m.

pumice n pomice f.

pummel vt prendere a pugni.

pump n pompa f; * vt pompare.

pumpkin n zucca f.

pun n gioco m di parole.

punch n pugno m; perforatrice f; punzonatrice f; * vt dare un pugno; forare.

punctual adj puntuale.

punctuate vt punteggiare.

punctuation n punteggiatura f.

pundit n esperto m.

pungent adj pungente.

punish vt punire.

punishment n punizione f.

punk n punk m.

punt n barchino m.

puny adj gracile; striminzito.

pup n cucciolo m.

pupil n allievo m; pupila f.

puppet n burattino m.

puppy n cagnolino m.

purchase vt acquistare; * n acquisto m; presa f.

purchaser n acquirente m/f.

pure adj puro.

purée n purè m.

purge n purga f; * vt purgare.

purification n depurazione f.

purify vt depurare.

purist n purista m/f.

puritan adj, n puritano m.

purity n purezza f.

purl n rovescio m.

purple adj, n viola m.

purport vt voler sembrare; * n

significato m.

purpose n scopo m; **on ~** apposta.

purposeful adj risoluto.

purr vi fare le fusa.

purse n borsellino m; portamonete m.

purser n commissario m di bordo.

pursue vt inseguire; proseguire.

pursuit n inseguimento m; attività f.

purveyor n fornitore m.

pus n pus m.

push vt spingere; **to ~ aside** scartare; **to ~ off** smammare; * vi **to ~ on** perseverare; * n spinta f.

pusher n spiacciatore m.

pussy n (fam) micio m.

pussy willow n (bot) salicone m.

put vt mettere, posare; esprimere; **to ~ away** mettere via; **to ~ down** sopprimere; **to ~ forward** proporre; **to ~ off** rimandare; disanimare; schifare; estinguere, spegnere; **to ~ on** affettare; accendere; organizzare; **to ~ out** spegnere; costruire; contrariare; **to ~ up** alzare; ospitare; fornire, provvedere.

putrid adj putrido.

putt n putting m.

putty n stucco m.

puzzle n rompicapo m, rebus m, puzzle m.

puzzling adj sconcertante.

pylon n pilone m.

pyramid n piramide f.

pyromaniac n piromane m/f.

python n pitone m.

Q

quack *vi* fare qua qua; * *n* qua qua *m*; (*fam*) ciarlatano *m*.

quadrangle *n* quadrangolo *m*; cortile *m*.

quadrant *n* quadrante *m*.

quadrilateral *adj* quadrilatero.

quadruped *n* quadrupede *m*.

quadruple *adj* quadruplo.

quadruplet *n* uno di quattro gemelli.

quagmire *n* pantano *m*.

quail *n* quaglia *f*.

quaint *adj* pittoresco; singolare.

quake *vi* tremare.

Quaker *n* quacchero *m*.

qualification *n* qualifica *f*; riserva *f*.

qualified *adj* qualificato; condizionato.

qualify *vt* qualificare.

quality *n* qualità *f*.

qualm *n* scrupolo *m*.

quandary *n* perplessità *f*.

quantitative *adj* quantitativo.

quantity *n* quantità *f*.

quarantine *n* quarantena *f*.

quarrel *n* litigio *m*; * *vi* litigare.

quarrelsome *adj* litigioso.

quarry *n* preda *f*; cava *f*.

quarter *n* quarto *m*; ~ **of an hour** un quarto d'ora; quartiere *m*; * *vt* dividere in quattro.

quarterly *adj* trimestrale.

quartermaster *n* furiere *m*.

quartet *n* (*mus*) quartetto *m*.

quartz *n* (*min*) quarzo *m*.

quash *vt* stroncare; respingere.

quay *n* molo *m*.

queasy *adj* nauseato.

queen *n* regina *f*.

queer *adj* strano; (*fam*) omosessuale; * *n* (*fam*) *m* finocchio *m*.

quell *vt* reprimere.

quench *vt* estinguere, appagare.

query *n* domanda *f*; * *vt* contestare.

quest *n* ricerca *f*.

question *n* domanda *f*; questione *f*; * *vt* interrogare.

questionable *adj* discutibile.

questioner *n* interrogante *m/f*.

question mark *n* punto *m* interrogativo.

questionnaire *n* questionario *m*.

queue *n* coda *f*.

quibble *vi* cavillare; * *n* cavillo *m*.

quick *adj* veloce; * *n* vivo *m*.

quicken *vt* affrettare.

quicksand *n* sabbie *fpl* mobili.

quicksilver *n* mercurio *m*.

quick-witted *adj* sveglio.

quid *n* sterlina *f*.

quiet *adj* silenzioso, tranquillo; * *n* silenzio *m*.

quieten *vt* placare.

quill *n* (*ornith*) penna *f*.

quilt *n* trapunta *f*.

quince *n* cotogna *f*; (tree) cotogno *m*.

quinine *n* chinino *f*.

quintet *n* (*mus*) quintetto *m*.

quintuplet *n* uno di cinque gemelli.

quip *n* battuta *f*; * *vi* motteggiare

quirk *n* bizzarria *f*.

quit *vt* lasciare; smettere; * *vi* dimettersi.

quite adv proprio, piuttosto.

quits *adj* pari.

quiver *vi* tremare; * *n* faretra *f*.

quixotic *adj* donchisciottesco.
quiz *n* quiz *m*; * *vt* interrogare.
quizzical *adj* canzonatorio; interrogativo.
quorum *n* quorum *m*.
quota *n* quota *f*.

quotation *n* citazione *f*; preventivo *m*.
quotation marks *npl* virgolette *fpl*.
quote *vt* citare; indicare.
quotient *n* quoziente *m*.

R

rabbi *n* rabbino *m*.
rabbit *n* coniglio *m*.
rabbit hutch *n* conigliera *f*.
rabble *n* canaglia *f*.
rabid *adj* idrofobo.
rabies *n* rabbia *f*.
raccoon *n* procione *m*.
race *n* corsa *f*; razza *f*; * *vt* gareggiare contro; * *vi* correre.
racer *n* corridore *m*.
racial *adj* razziale.
racialist *n* razzista *m/f*.
racing *n* corsa *f*.
racism *n* razzismo *m*.
rack *n* rastrelliera *f*; * *vi* scervellarsi.
racket *n* racchetta *f*; fracasso *m*; racket *m*.
racy *adj* spigliato.
radar *n* radar *m*.
radial *adj* radiale.
radiance *n* splendore *m*.
radiant *adj* radiante.
radiate *vt* irraggiare.
radiation *n* radiazione *f*.
radiator *n* radiatore *m*; termosifone *m*.
radical *adj, n* radicale *m*.
radio *n* radio *f*.
radioactive *adj* radioattivo.
radioactivity *n* radioattività *f*.
radiographer *n* radiologo *m*.
radiography *n* radiografia *f*.
radish *n* ravanello *m*.
radium *n* radio *m*.
radius *n* raggio *m*.

raffia *n* rafia *f*.
raffle *n* riffa; * *vt* mettere in palio.
raft *n* zattera *f*.
rafter *n* puntone *m*.
rag *n* straccio *m*, cencio *m*.
rage *n* colera *f*, furia *f*; * *vi* infuriarsi.
ragged *adj* stracciato.
raging *adj* furioso.
raid *n* irruzione *f*; rapina *f*; * *vt* fare irruzione in; saccheggiare.
raider *n* rapinatore *m*.
rail *n* sbarra *f*; corrimano *m*; rotaia *f*; * *vi* to ~ against inveire.
railings *npl* cancellata *f*.
railway *n* ferrovia *f*.
railwayman *n* ferroviere *m*.
rain *n* pioggia *f*; * *vi* piovere.
rainbow *n* arcobaleno *m*.
raincoat *n* impermeabile *m*.
rain fall *n* precipitazione *f*.
rain water *n* acqua *f* piovana.
rainy *adj* piovoso.
raise *vt* sollevare; erigere; alzare; * *n* aumento *m*.
raisin *n* uvetta *f*.
rake *n* rastrello *m*; libertino *m*; * *vt* rastrellare.
rakish *adj* dissoluto.
rally *n* raduno *m*; rally *m*; * *vi* radunare; riunire.
ram *n* montone *m*, ariete; * *vt* speronare; ficcare.

ramble n escursione f; * vi fare escursione; divagare.

rambler n escursionista m/f.

ramification n ramificazione f.

ramify vi ramificare.

ramp n rampa f.

rampage vi scatenarsi.

rampant adj rampante.

rampart n bastione m.

ramrod n calcatoio m.

ramshackle adj sgangherato.

ranch n ranch m.

rancid adj rancido.

rancour n rancore m.

random adj a caso.

range n portata f; autonomia f; gamma f; catena f; * vi variare, estendersi.

ranger n; (forest) ~ guardia f forestale.

rank adj puzzolente, rancido; * n grado; posteggio m; * vt ritenere.

rankle vi bruciare.

ransack vt rovistare.

ransom n riscatto m; * vt riscattare.

rant vi tuonare.

rap vt bussare a; * n bussata f.

rapacious adj rapace.

rape n stupro m; * vt violentare, stuprare.

rapid adj rapido; ~s npl rapida f.

rapidity n rapidità f.

rapier n spadino m.

rapist n violentatore m, stupratore m.

rapport n rapporto m.

rapt adj rapito.

rapture n estasi f.

rapturous adj estasiato.

rare adj raro; al sangue.

rarity n rarità f.

rascal n mascalzone m.

rash adj avventato; * n sfogo, orticaria f.

rasher n fettina f (di pancetta).

rasp n raspa f; stridio m; * vt raspare; vi gracchiare.

raspberry n lampone m; ~ bush lampone m.

rat n ratto m.

ratchet n dente m di arresto.

rate n tasso m; tariffa f; * vt valutare.

rather adv piuttosto.

ratification n ratifica f.

ratify vt ratificare.

rating n valutazione f.

ratio n rapporto m.

ration n razione f; * vt razionare.

rational adj ragionevole; razionale.

rationality n razionalità f.

rationalize vt razionalizzare.

rattan n canna f d'India.

rattle vt innervosire; acciottolare; * vi sferragliare; blaterare; * n rumore m secco; acciottolio m; raganella f; rantolo m; sonaglio m.

rattlesnake n crotalo m.

ratty adj incavolato.

raucous adj rauco.

ravage vt devastare; * n devastazione f.

rave vi farneticare.

raven n corvo m.

ravenous adj famelico.

ravine n burrone m.

ravish vt estasiare; violentare.

ravishing adj incantevole.

raw adj crudo, greggio; gelido.

raw deal n bidonata f.

ray n raggio m; razza f.

raze vt ~ to the ground radere al suolo.

razor n rasoio m.

re prep (comm) oggetto.

reach vt raggiungere; * vi estendersi; * n portata f; tratto m.

react vi reagire.

reaction n reazione f.

reactionary n reazionario m.

reactor n reattore m.

read vt leggere; * vi studiare.

readable adj leggibile.

reader n lettore m; antologia f.

readily adv prontamente.

readiness n prontezza f,

reading n lettura f.

reading room n sala f di lettura.

readjust vt regolare; * vi riadattarsi.

ready adj pronto.

real adj vero, reale; ~ly adv davvero.

realism n realismo m.

realist n realista m/f.

realistic adj realistico.

reality n realtà f.

realization n realizzazione f.

realize vi rendersi conto di; * vt realizzare.

realm n regno m.

ream n risma f.

reap vt mietere.

reaper n mietitore m.

reappear vi ricomparire.

rear n parte f posteriore; * adj posteriore; * vt allevare; * vi impennarsi.

rearmament n riarmo m.

rear-view mirror n retrovisore m.

reason n ragione f, motivo m; * vi ragionare.

reasonable adj ragionevole.

reasonably adj abbastanza.

reasoning n ragionamento m.

reassure vt rassicurare.

rebate n rimborso m.

rebel adj, n ribelle m/f; * vi ribellarsi.

rebellion n ribellione f.

rebellious adj ribelle.

rebound vi rimbalzare.

rebuff n rifiuto m; * vt rifiutare.

rebuild vt ricostruire.

rebuke vt rimproverare; * n

rimprovero m.

rebut vt confutare.

recalcitrant adj recalcitrante.

recall vt richiamare; ricordare; * n richiamo m.

recant vt abiurare.

recantation n ritrattazione f.

recapitulate vt, vi ricapitolare.

recapture vt riprendere.

recede vi ritrarsi.

receipt n ricevuta f.

receive vt ricevere.

receiver n ricevitore m.

recent adj recente.

receptacle n recipiente m.

reception n ricevimento m; reception f; accettazione f.

recess n rientranza f; intervallo m.

recession n recessione f.

recharge vt ricaricare.

recipe n ricetta f.

recipient n destinatario m.

reciprocal adj reciproco.

reciprocate vt, vi contraccambiare.

recital n concerto m; recita f.

recite vt, vi recitare.

reckless adj spericolato.

reckon vt calcolare; credere.

reckoning n calcoli mpl.

reclaim vt bonificare; ricuperare.

recline vi essere sdraiato.

reclining adj ribaltabile.

recluse n recluso m.

recognition n riconoscimento m.

recognize vt riconoscere.

recoil vi indietreggiare.

recollect vt rammentare.

recollection n ricordo m.

recommend vt raccomandare; consigliare.

recommendation n raccomandazione f.

recompense n ricompensa f; * vt ricompensare.

reconcilable *adj* conciliabile.
reconcile *vt* riconciliare.
reconciliation *n* riconciliazione *f*.
recondite *adj* astruso.
reconnoitre *vt*, *vi* fare una ricognizione.
reconsider *vt* riconsiderare.
reconstruct *vt* ricostruire.
record *vt* annotare; registrare; * *n* registro *m*; precedenti penali *mpl*; record *m*; disco *m*; ~s annali *mpl*; archivi *mpl*.
recorder *n* registratore *m*; (*mus*) flauto *m*.
recount *vt* raccontare.
recourse *n* ricorso *m*.
recover *vt* ricuperare; ricoprire; * *vi* riprendersi.
recovery *n* ricupero *m*; ripresa *f*.
recreation *n* ricreazione *f*.
recriminate *vi* recriminare.
recrimination *n* recriminazione *f*.
recruit *vt* reclutare; * *n* recluta *f*.
recruitment *n* reclutamento.
rectangle *n* rettangolo *m*.
rectangular *adj* rettangolare.
rectification *n* rettifica *f*.
rectify *vt* rettificare.
rectilinear *adj* rettilineo.
rectitude *n* rettitudine *m*.
rector *n* rettore *m*.
rectum *n* retto *m*.
recumbent *adj* disteso.
recuperate *vi* ristabilirsi.
recuperation *n* convalescenza *f*.
recur *vi* ripetersi.
recurrence *n* ricorrenza *f*.
recurrent *adj* ricorrente.
red *adj*, *n* rosso *m*.
redden *vt* arrossare; * *vi* arrossire.
reddish *adj* rossiccio.
redeem *vt* redimere.

redeemable *adj* ammortizzabile.
Redeemer *n* Redentore *m*.
redemption *n* redenzione *f*.
redhanded *adj* in flagrante.
redhot *adj* rovente.
red-letter day *n* giorno *m* memorabile.
redness *n* rossore *m*.
redolent *adj* profumato.
redouble *vt* raddoppiare.
redress *vt* riparare; * *n* riparazione *f*.
redskin *n* pellerossa *m/f*.
red tape *n* (*fig*) burocrazia *f*.
reduce *vt* ridurre; * *vi* diminuire.
reduction *n* riduzione *f*.
redundancy *n* ridondanza *f*; licenziamento *m*.
redundant *adj* ridondante; licenziato.
reed *n* canna *f*.
reedy *adj* acuto.
reef *n* scogliera *f*.
reek *n* puzzo *m*; * *vi* puzzare.
reel *n* mulinello *m*; bobina *f*; * *vi* barcollare.
re-election *n* rielezione *f*.
re-entry *n* rientro *m*.
re-establish *vt* ristabilire.
refectory *n* refettorio *m*.
refer *vi* riferirsi a; consultare; * *vt* rimandare.
referee *n* arbitro *m*.
reference *n* riferimento *m*.
referendum *n* referendum *m*.
refill *n* ricambio; * *vt* riempire.
refine *vt* raffinare.
refinement *n* raffinatezza *f*.
refinery *n* raffineria *f*.
refit *vt* raddobbare; * raddobbo *m*.
reflating *vt* rilanciare.
reflect *vt*, *vi* riflettere; * *vt* rispecchiare.
reflection *n* riflessione *f*; riflesso *m*.

reflector n catarifrangente m.

reflex adj, n riflesso m.

reflexive adj riflessivo.

reform vt riformare; * n riforma f.

Reformation n Riforma f.

reformer n riformatore m.

reformist n riformista m/f.

refract vt rifrangere.

refraction n rifrazione f.

refrain vi astenersi; * n ritornello m;

refresh vt rinfrescare.

refreshment n ristoro m.

refrigerate vt refrigerare.

refrigerator n frigorifero m.

refuel vi rifornirsi di carburante.

refuge n riparo m, rifugio m.

refugee n profugo m.

refund vt rimborsare; * n rimborso m.

refurbish vt rinnovare.

refusal n rifiuto m.

refuse vt rifiutare; * n rifiuti mpl.

refute vt confutare.

regain vt riguadagnare.

regal adj regale.

regale vt intrattenere.

regalia n insegne fpl reali.

regard vt considerare; riguardare; * n riguardo m.

regarding prep riguardo a.

regardless adv senza riguardo.

regatta n regata f.

regency n reggenza f.

regenerate vt rigenerare; * adj rigenerato.

regeneration n rigenerazione f.

regent n reggente m/f.

régime n regime m.

regiment n reggimento m.

region n regione f.

regional adj regionale.

register n registro m; * vt registrare; immatricolare; * vi

iscriversi; **~ed letter** n raccomandata f.

registrar n ufficiale m di stato civile.

registration n registrazione f.

registry n; **~ office** anagrafe f.

regress vi regredire.

regression n regresso m.

regressive adj regressivo.

regret n rimpianto m; rammarico m; * vt rimpiangere; dispiacersi di.

regrettable adj deplorevole.

regular adj regolare; fedele.

regularity n regolarità f.

regulate vt regolare.

regulation n regolamento m.

regulator n regolatore m.

rehabilitate vt riabilitare.

rehabilitation n riabilitazione f.

rehearsal n prova f.

rehearse vt provare.

reign n regno m; * vi regnare.

reimburse vt rimborsare.

reimbursement n rimborso m.

rein n redine f.

reincarnation n reincarnazione f.

reindeer n renna f.

reinforce vt rinforzare.

reinstate vt reintegrare.

reinsure vt riassicurare.

reissue n ristampa f.

reiterate vt reiterare.

reiteration n reiterazione f.

reject vt scartare; * n scarto m.

rejection n rigetto m;

rejoice vi rallegrarsi.

rejoicings npl festeggiamenti mpl.

rejuvenate vt ringiovanire.

relapse vi ricadere; * n ricaduta f.

relate vt collegare; raccontare.

related adj affine; imparentato.

relation n relazione f; rapporto *m*; parente *m/f*.

relationship *n* nesso *m*; relazione *f*; legami *mpl* di parentela.

relative *adj* relativo; **~ly** *adv* abbastanza; * *n* parente *m/f*.

relax *vt* rilassare.

relaxation *n* relax *m*.

relay *n* ricambio *m*; relé *m*; * *vt* ritrasmettere; passare.

release *vt* rilasciare; mollare; emettere; * *n* rilascio *m*; emissione *f*; uscita *f*.

relegate *vt* relegare.

relegation *n* relegazione *f*.

relent *vi* cedere.

relentless *adj* implacabile.

relevance *n* pertinenza *f*.

relevant *adj* pertinente.

reliable *adj* affidabile.

reliance *n* dipendenza *f*.

relic *n* reliquia *f*.

relief *n* sollievo *m*; rilievo *m*.

relieve *vt* alleviare.

religion *n* religione *f*.

religious *adj* religioso.

relinquish *vt* rinunciare a.

relish *n* gusto *m*; condimento *m*; * *vt* gustare.

reluctance *n* riluttanza *f*.

reluctant *adj* restio.

rely *vi* contare su.

remain *vi* rimanere.

remainder *n* resto *m*; avanzo *m*.

remains *npl* resti *mpl*; avanzi *mpl*.

remand *vt* rimandare in carcere; * *n* detenzione *f* preventiva.

remark *n* osservazione *f*; * *vt* osservare.

remarkable *adj* notevole.

remarry *vi* risposarsi.

remedial *adj* correttivo.

remedy *n* rimedio *m*; * *vt* rimediare.

remember *vt* ricordare.

remembrance *n* ricordo *m*.

remind *n* ricordare.

reminder *n* sollecito *m*.

reminiscence *n* reminiscenza *f*.

remiss *adj* negligente.

remission *n* remissione *f*.

remit *vt* rimettere.

remittance *n* rimessa *f*.

remnant *n* scampolo *m*; resto *m*.

remodel *vt* rimodellare.

remonstrate *vi* protestare.

remorse *n* rimorso *m*.

remorseless *adj* spietato.

remote *adj* remoto; vago.

remote control *n* telecomando *m*.

removable *adj* asportabile.

removal *n* trasloco *m*; eliminazione *f*; rimozione *f*.

remove *vt* togliere; rimuovere; eliminare; asportare.

remunerate *vt* rimunerare.

remuneration *n* rimunerazione *f*.

Renaissance *n* Rinascimento *m*.

renal *adj* renale.

render *vt* rendere; interpretare.

rendezvous *n* appuntamento *m*; * *vi* ritrovarsi.

renegade *n* rinnegato *m*.

renew *vt* rinnovare.

renewal *n* rinnovo *m*.

rennet *n* caglio *m*.

renounce *vt* rinunciare.

renovate *vt* rinnovare.

renovation *n* restauro *m*.

renown *n* rinomanza *f*.

renowned *adj* rinomato.

rent *n* affitto *m*, pigione *m*; * *vt* affittare.

rental *n* nolo *m*.

renunciation *n* rinuncia *f*.

reopen *vt* riaprire.

reorganization *n* riorganizzazione *f*.

reorganize *vt* riorganizzare.

repair *vt* aggiustare, riparare; * *n* riparazione *f*.

reparable *adj* riparabile.

reparation *n* riparazione *f*.

repartee *n* conversazione *f* brillante.

repatriate *vt* rimpatriare.

repay *vt* restituire; ricambiare.

repayment *n* rimborso *m*.

repeal *vt* abrogare; * *n* abrogazione *f*.

repeat *vt* ripetere; * *n* replica *f*.

repeatedly *adv* ripetutamente.

repel *vt* respingere.

repent *vi* pentirsi.

repentance *n* pentimento *m*.

repentant *adj* pentito.

repercussions *npl* ripercussione *fpl*.

repertoire, repertory *n* repertorio *m*.

repetition *n* ripetizione *f*.

replace *vt* rimpiazzare; sostituire.

replacement *n* sostituto *m*.

replenish *vt* rifornire.

replete *adj* sazio.

replica *n* replica *f*.

reply *n* risposta *f*; * *vt*, *vi* rispondere.

report *vt* riportare; denunciare; * *n* rapporto *m*; pagella *f*; reportage *m*.

reporter *n* cronista *m/f*.

repose *vi* riposare; * *n* riposo *m*.

repository *n* deposito *m*.

repossess *vt* ricuperare.

reprehend *vt* rimproverare.

reprehensibile *adj* riprovevole.

represent *vt* rappresentare.

representation *n* rappresentazione *f*.

representative *adj* rappresentativo; * *n* rappresentante *m*.

repress *vt* reprimere.

repression *n* repressione *f*.

repressive *adj* repressivo.

reprieve *vt* concedere una proroga; * *n* proroga *f*.

reprimand *vt* rimproverare; * *n* rimprovero *m*.

reprint *n* ristampa *f*.

reprisals *npl* rappresaglie *fpl*.

reproach *n* rimprovero; * *vt* rimproverare.

reproachful *adj* di rimprovero.

reproduce *vt* riprodurre.

reproduction *n* riproduzione *f*.

reptile *n* rettile *m*.

republic *n* repubblica *f*.

republican *n* repubblicano *m*.

repudiate *vt* ripudiare.

repugnance *n* ripugnanza *f*.

repugnant *adj* ripugnante.

repulse *vt* respingere.

repulsion *n* repulsione *f*.

repulsive *adj* ripugnante.

reputable *adj* stimabile; attendibile.

reputation *n* reputazione *f*.

repute *vt* ritenere; * *n* reputazione *f*.

request *n* richiesta *f*; * *vt* richiedere.

require *vt* richiedere.

requirement *n* esigenza *f*.

requisite *adj*, *n* occorrente *m*.

requisition *n* requisizione *f*; * *vt* requisire.

requite *vt* contraccambiare.

rescind *vt* rescindere.

rescue *vt* salvare; * *n* salvataggio *m*.

research *vi* fare ricerca; * *n* ricerca *f*.

resemblance *n* somiglianza *f*.

resemble *vt* somigliare.

resent *vt* risentirsi per.

resentful *adj* pieno di risentimento.

resentment *n* risentimento *m*.

reservation *n* prenotazione *f*; riserva *f*.

reserve vt prenotare; riservare; * n riserva f; riservo m.

reservoir n bacino m idrico.

reside vi risiedere.

residence n residenza f.

resident adj, n residente m/f.

residual adj residuo.

residue n residuo m.

resign vi dimettersi.

resignation n dimissioni fpl.

resigned adj rassegnato.

resilient adj elastico.

resin n resina f.

resinous adj resinoso.

resist vt, vi resistere.

resistance n resistenza f.

resolute adj risoluto.

resolution n determinazione f; risoluzione f; definizione f.

resolve vt decidere; risolvere; * n risolutezza f.

resonance n risonanza f.

resonant adj risonante.

resort vi fare ricorso a; * n ricorso m; località f di villeggiatura.

resound vi risonare.

resounding adj clamoroso.

resource n risorsa f.

respect n rispetto m; **in some ~s** sotto certi aspetti; * vt rispettare.

respectability n rispettabilità f.

respectable adj rispettabile.

respectful adj rispettoso.

respecting prep riguardante.

respective adj rispettivo.

respirator n respiratore m.

respiration n respirazione f.

respiratory adj respiratorio.

respite n tregua f; * vt dare respiro a.

resplendent adj risplendente.

respond vi rispondere.

respondent n (law) convenuto m.

response n risposta f.

responsibility n responsabilità f.

responsibile adj responsabile.

responsive adj che reagisce bene.

rest n riposo m; pausa f; appoggio m; resto m; * vt riposare; * vi riposarsi; poggiare.

restaurant n ristorante m.

restful adj riposante.

restitution n restituzione f.

restive adj irrequieto.

restless adj irrequieto.

restoration n restauro m; **the R~** la Restaurazione f.

restore vt restaurare; restituire.

restrain vt trattenere.

restraint n restrizione f.

restrict vt limitare.

restriction n restrizione f.

restrictive adj restrittivo.

result vi avere come risultato; * n risultato m.

resume vt, vi riprendere.

résumé n riassunto m.

resumption n ripresa f.

resurrection n risurrezione f.

resuscitate vt risuscitare.

retail vt vendere al dettaglio; * adj al dettaglio.

retailer n dettagliante m/f.

retain vt tenere; conservare.

retainer n onorario m.

retake vt riprendere.

retaliate vi vendicarsi.

retaliation n rappresaglie fpl.

retarded adj ritardato.

retch vi avere conati di vomito.

retention n ritenzione f.

retentive adj ritentivo.

reticence n reticenza f.

retina n retina f.

retinue n seguito m.

retire vt mandare in pensione; * vi ritirarsi, andare in pensione.

retired adj pensionato.

retirement *n* ritiro *m*; l'andare in pensione.

retort *vt* ribattere; * *n* risposta *f*; storta *f*.

retouch *vt* ritoccare.

retrace *vt* ripercorrere.

retract *vt* ritrattare; ritirare.

retrain *vt, vi* riqualificare.

retraining *n* riqualificazione *f*.

retreat *n* rifugio *m*; * *vi* ritirarsi.

retribution *n* retribuzione *f*.

retrieval *n* ricupero *m*.

retrieve *vt* ricuperare; (*comp*) richiamare.

retriever *n* cane *m* da riporto.

retrograde *adj* retrogrado.

retrospect; in ~ ripensandoci.

retrospective *adj* retrospettivo; * *n* retrospettiva *f*.

return *vt* restituire; * *vi* tornare; * *n* ritorno *m*; resa *f*; guadagno *m*; (ticket) andata e ritorno.

reunion *n* riunione *f*.

reunite *vt* riunire; * *vi* riunirsi.

revalue *vt* rivalutare.

revamp *vt* modernizzare.

reveal *vt* rivelare.

revel *vt* far baldoria.

revelation *n* rivelazione *f*.

revelry *n* baldoria *f*.

revenge *vt* vendicare; * *n* vendetta *f*.

revengeful *adj* vendicativo.

revenue *n* reddito *m*.

reverberate *vi* rimbombare.

reverberation *n* rimbombo *m*.

revere *vt* venerare.

reverence *n* venerazione *f*.

Reverend *n* reverendo *m*.

reverent, reverential *adj* reverente.

revery *n* fantasticheria *f*.

reversal *n* inversione *f*.

reverse *vt* invertire; * *vi* fare marcia indietro; * *n* opposto *m*; rovescio *m*; retromarcia *f*; * *adj* inverso; marcia indietro.

reversible *adj* double-face.

revert *vi* ritornare.

review *vt* fare una revisione di; recensire; * *n* revisione *f*; rivista *f*.

reviewer *n* recensore *m*.

revile *vt* oltraggiare, insultare.

revise *vt* ripassare; rivedere.

revision *n* ripasso *m*; revisione *f*.

revival *n* risveglio *m*; ripristino *m*.

revive *vt* rianimare.

revoke *vt* abrogare.

revolt *vi* ribellarsi; * *vt* rivoltare; * *n* rivolta *f*.

revolting *adj* rivoltante.

revolution *n* rivoluzione *f*.

revolutionary *adj, n* rivoluzionario *m*.

revolve *vt, vi* girare.

revolver *n* rivoltella *f*.

revolving *adj* girevole.

revue *n* revista *f*.

revulsion *n* ripugnanza *f*.

reward *vt* premiare; * *n* ricompensa *f*.

rhapsody *n* rapsodia *f*.

rhetoric *n* retorica *f*.

rhetorical *adj* retorico.

rheumatic *adj* reumatico.

rheumatism *n* reumatismo *m*.

rhinoceros *n* rinoceronte *m*.

rhododendron *n* rododendro *m*.

rhombus *n* rombo *m*.

rhubarb *n* rabarbaro *m*.

rhyme *n* rima *f*; * *vi* fare rima con.

rhythm *n* ritmo *m*.

rhythmical *adj* ritmico.

rib *n* costola *f*.

ribald *adj* sguaiato.

ribbon *n* nastro *m*.

rice *n* riso *m*.

rich *adj* ricco.

riches npl ricchezze fpl.
richness n ricchezza f.
rickets n rachitismo m.
rickety adj traballante.
rickshaw n risciò m.
ricochet vi rimbalzare.
rid vt sbarazzare.
riddance n liberazione; * excl good ~! che liberazione!.
riddle n indovinello m; setaccio m; * vt crivellare.
ride vi cavalcare; andare; * n cavalcata f; giro m.
rider n cavallerizzo m; clausola f addizionale.
ridge n cresta f; crinale m.
ridicule n ridicolo m; * vt mettere in ridicolo.
ridiculous adj ridicolo.
riding n equitazione f.
riding school n scuola f di equitazione.
rife adj diffuso; imperversare.
riffraff n gentaglia f.
rifle vt svaligiare; * vi frugare; * n fucile m; carabina f.
rifleman n bersagliere m.
rift n spaccatura f.
rig vt truccare; * n impianto m di trivellazione.
rigging n (mar) cordame m.
right adj giusto, retto; adatto; destro; diritto; corretto; * adv completamente; bene; giustamente; * n diritto m; destra f; * vt raddrizzare; correggere; **to be ~** avere ragione.
righteous adj virtuoso.
righteousness n rettitudine f.
rightful adj legittimo.
rigid adj rigido.
rigidity n rigidezza f.
rigmarole n trafila f.
rigorous adj rigoroso.
rigour n rigore m.
rim n orlo m.
rind n buccia f; cotenna f.
ring n anello m; cerchio m; ring m; squillo m; scampanellata f; * vt accerchiare; suonare; * vi telefonare; suonare; risuonare.
ringleader n capobanda m.
ringlet n boccolo m.
ringworm n tricofizia f.
rink n pista f di pattinaggio.
rinse vt sciacquare; * n sciacquatura f.
riot n disordini mpl; sommossa f; * vi tumultuare.
rioter n rivoltoso m.
riotous adj chiassoso.
rip vt strappare; * n strappo m; **to let ~** scatenarsi.
ripe adj maturo, stagionato.
ripen vt, vi maturare.
rip off vt pelare.
ripple vi increspare; * n increspatura f.
rise vi alzarsi; sorgere; lievitare; aumentare; * n sorgere m; ascesa f; aumento m; salita f.
rising n sommossa f; * adj crescente; montante.
risk n rischio m; * vt rischiare.
risky adj rischioso.
risqué adj spinto.
rissole n polpetta f.
rite n rito m.
ritual adj, n rituale m.
rival adj, n rivale m; * vt rivaleggiare.
rivalry n rivalità f.
river n fiume m.
rivet n ribattino m; * vt rivettare.
rivulet n ruscelletto m.
roach n (**cock~**) blatta f; leucisco m rosso.
road n strada f, via f.
roadsign n cartello m stradale.
roadworks npl lavori mpl stradali.
roam vi gironzolare.

roan n roano m.

roar vi ruggire; * n ruggito m.

roaring adj strepitoso.

roast vt arrostire; torrefare; * n arrosto m.

roast beef n rosbif m.

rob vt derubare.

robber n rapinatore m.

robbery n rapina f.

robe n tunica f; accappatoio m.

robin pettirosso m.

robot n robot m.

robust adj robusto.

rock n roccia f; (mus) rock m; * vt cullare; * vi dondolare; oscillare.

rocket n razzo m

rocking chair n sedia f a dondolo.

rock salt n salgemma m.

rocky adj roccioso; vacillante.

rod n bacchetta f; bastone m.

rodent n roditore m.

roe n uova fpl di pese.

roebuck n capriolo m maschio.

rogue n mascalzone m.

roguish adj malizioso.

role n ruolo m;

roll vt, vi rotolare; * n rotolo m; rullino m; panino m; lista f.

roller n rullo m; rotella f; bigodino m.

roller skate n patino m a rotelle.

rolling pin n matterello m.

Roman Catholic adj, n cattolico m.

romance n storia f d'amore.

romantic adj romantico.

romp vi giocare chiassosamente; * n gioco m chiassoso.

rompers npl tutina f.

roof n tetto m; * vt mettere il tetto.

rook n corvo m; (chess) torre f.

room n stanza f; spazio m; posto m.

roomy adj spazioso.

roost n posatoio m; * vi appollaiarsi.

rooster n gallo m.

root n radice f; * vt far radicare; * vi attecchire; **to ~ out** eradicare.

rooted adj inchiodato.

rope n fune f; corda f; * vt legare.

ropey adj scadente.

rosary n rosario m.

rose n rosa f; rosone m di stucco; (watering can) cipolla f.

rosebed n rosaio m.

rosebud n bocciolo m di rosa.

rosemary n rosmarino m.

rosette n coccarda f.

rosé wine n vino m rosato.

rosewood n palissandro m.

rostrum n podio m.

rosy adj roseo.

rot vi marcire; * n marciume m.

rotate vi rotare.

rotation n rotazione f.

rote n; **by ~** a memoria.

rotten adj marcio; schifoso.

rotund adj grassoccio.

rouble n rublo m.

rouge n belletto m.

rough adj ruvido, rozzo; rauco; approssimativo; burrascoso.

rough-and-ready adj rudimentale.

rough-and-tumble n zuffa f.

roughen vt irruvidire.

roughly adv brutalmente; grossolanamente.

roughness n ruvidità f.

roulette n roulette f.

round adj rotondo; * n cerchio m; giro m; round m; * prep intorno a; * vt arrotondare.

roundabout adj indiretto; * n giostra f; rotatoria f.

roundup n retata f.

rouse vt svegliare; scuotere.

rousing adj trascinante.

rout n disfatta f; * vt sbaragliare.

route n itinerario m, percorso m; rotta f.

routine n routine f, tran tran m; * adj comune, abituale.

rove vi vagare.

rover n giramondo m/f.

roving adj vagabondo.

row n baccano m; lite f; * vi litigare.

row n fila f; * vt remare.

rowdy adj turbolento.

rower n rematore m.

royal adj reale.

royalist n realista f.

royalty n reali mpl; royalty m.

rub vt strofinare, sfregare; * n strofinamento m.

rubber n gomma f; cauccciù m.

rubber-band n elastico m.

rubbish n spazzatura f, immondizie fpl.

rubble n macerie fpl.

rubic n rubrica f.

ruby adj, n rubino m.

rucksack n zaino m.

rudder n timone m.

ruddy adj rubicondo.

rude adj indecente, brusco, villano.

rudeness n maleducazione f.

rudiment n rudimento m.

rue vt pentirsi di; (bot) ruta f.

rueful adj mesto.

ruffian adj manigoldo.

ruffle vt arruffare.

rug n tappeto m; plaid m.

rugby n rugby m.

rugged adj accidentato; frastagliato; marcato.

ruin n rudere m, rovina f; * vt rovinare.

ruinous adj disastroso.

rule n regola f; regolamento m; * vt governare; decretare; rigare; * vi regnare.

ruler n sovrano m; righello m.

rum n rum m; * adj strambo.

rumble vi brontolare; * vt scoprire; * n rombo m.

ruminate vt ruminare.

rummage vt rovistare, frugare.

rumour n voce f.

rump n groppa f.

rumpus n putiferio m.

run vt correre; dirigere; gestire; organizzare; * vi correre; funzionare; scorrere; collare; * n corsa f; giro m; tragitto m; serie f; recinto m; smagliatura f.

runaway adj, n fuggitivo m.

rung n piolo m; traversa f.

runner n corridore m; guida f.

running adj corrente; * n gestione f.

runny adj sciolto.

run-of-the-mill adj banale.

runway n pista f.

rupture n rottura f; * vt rompere.

rural adj rurale.

ruse n astuzia f.

rush n giunco m; ressa f; premura f; fretta f; * vt fare fretta a; * vi precipitarsi.

rusk n fetta f biscottata.

russet adj marrone rossiccio.

rust n ruggine f; * vt, vi arrugginire.

rustic adj rustico; * n contadino m.

rustle vi frusciare; * n fruscio m.

rusty adj rugginoso.

rut n solco m.

ruthless adj spietato.

rye n segale f.

S

Sabbath *n* domenica *f*.

sable *n* zibellino *m*.

sabotage *n* sabotaggio *m*; * *vt* sabotare.

saccharin *n* saccarina *f*.

sachet *n* bustina *f*.

sack *n* sacco *m*; saccheggio *m*; * *vt* licenziare; saccheggiare.

sacrament *n* sacramento *m*.

sacred *adj* sacro.

sacrifice *n* sacrificio *m*; * *vt* sacrificare.

sacrificial *adj* sacrificale.

sacrilege *n* sacrilegio *m*.

sacrilegious *adj* sacrilego.

sacrosanct *adj* sacrosanto.

sad *adj* triste; deplorevole.

sadden *vt* rattristare.

saddle *n* sella *f*; * *vt* sellare.

saddler *n* sellaio *m*.

sadism *n* sadismo *m*.

sadist *n* sadico *m*.

sadistic *adj* sadico.

sadness *n* tristezza *f*.

safari *n* safari *m*.

safe *adj* salvo; sicuro; ~ **and sound** sano e salvo; * *n* cassaforte *f*.

safe-conduct *n* salvacondotto *m*.

safeguard *n* salvaguardia *f*; * *vt* salvaguardare.

safety *n* sicurezza *f*.

safety belt *n* cintura *f* di sicurezza.

safety pin *n* spilla *f* da balia.

saffron *n* zafferano *m*.

sag *vi* incurvarsi.

saga *n* saga *f*.

sage *n* (*bot*) salvia *f*; saggio *m*; ; * *n* saggio *m*.

Sagittarius *n* Sagittario *m*.

sago *n* (*bot*) sagù *m*.

sail *n* vela *f*; pala *f*; * *vt* con-

durre; * *vi* salpare, navigare.

sailing *n* vela *f*.

sailor *n* marinaio *m*.

saint *n* santa *f*.

saintly *adj* santo.

sake *n*: **for God's** ~ per amor di Dio.

salad *n* insalata *f*.

salad bowl *n* insalatiera *f*.

salad dressing *n* condimento *m* per insalata.

salamander *n* salamandra *f*.

salami *n* salame *m*.

salary *n* stipendio *m*.

sale *n* vendita *f*; svendita *f*.

saleable *adj* vendibile.

salesman *n* commesso *m*.

saleswoman *n* commessa *f*.

salient *adj* saliente.

saline *adj* salino.

saliva *n* saliva *f*.

salivate *vi* salivare.

sallow *adj* giallastro.

sally *n* battuta *f*.

salmon *n* salmone *m*.

salmon trout *n* trota *f* salmonata.

salon *n* salone *m*.

saloon *n* salone *m*; saloon *m*.

salt *n* sale *m*; * *vt* salare.

salt cellar *n* saliera *f*.

saltpeter *n* salnitro *m*.

saltworks *npl* salina *f*.

salty *adj* salato.

salubrious *adj* salubre.

salutary *adj* salutare.

salute *vt* salutare; * *n* saluto *m*.

salvage *vt* ricuperare; * *n* salvataggio *m*.

salvation *n* salvezza *f*.

salve *n* unguento *m*; * *vt* placare.

salver *n* vassoio *m*.

salvo *n* salva *f*.

same *adj, pron* stesso.

sameness *n* monotonia *f*.

sample *n* campione *m*; * *vt* assaggiare.

sampler *n* saggio *m* di ricamo.

sanatorium *n* convalescenziario *m*.

sanctify *vt* santificare.

sanctimonious *adj* moraleggiante.

sanction *n* sanzione *f*; * *vt* sancire.

sanctity *n* santità *f*.

sanctuary *n* santuario *m*.

sand *n* sabbia *f*; * *vt* cartavetrare; cospargere di sabbia.

sandal *n* sandalo *m*.

sandbag *n* sacco *m* di sabbia.

sandblast *vt* sabbiare.

sandpaper *n* carta *f* vetrata.

sandpit *n* buca *f* di sabbia.

sandstone *n* arenaria *f*.

sandwich *n* tramezzino *m*, sandwich *m*.

sandy *adj* sabbioso.

sane *adj* sano di mente.

sangfroid *n* sangue *m* freddo.

sanguine *adj* ottimista.

sanitary towel *n* assorbente *m*.

sanity *n* sanità *f* mentale.

sap *n* linfa *f*; * *vt* fiaccare.

sapling *n* alberello *m*.

sapphire *n* zaffiro *m*.

sarcasm *n* sarcasmo *m*.

sarcastic *adj* sarcastico.

sarcophagus *n* sarcofago *m*.

sardine *n* sardina *f*.

sardonic *adj* sardonico.

sash *n* fusciacca *f*; telaio *m*; ~ **window** *n* finestra *f* a saliscendi.

Satan *n* Satana *m*.

satanic(al) *adj* satanico.

satchel *n* cartella *f*.

satellite *n* satellite *m*.

satiate *vt* saziare.

satin *n* raso *m*.

satire *n* satira *f*.

satiric(al) *adj* satirico.

satirist *n* scrittore (etc) *m* satirico.

satirize *vt* satireggiare.

satisfaction *n* soddisfazione *f*.

satisfactory *adj* soddisfacente.

satisfy *vt* soddisfare.

saturate *vt* saturare.

Saturday *n* sabato *m*.

satyr *n* satiro *m*.

sauce *n* salsa *f*.

saucepan *n* pentola *f*.

saucer *n* piattino *m*.

saucy *adj* provocante.

saunter *vi* andare a zonzo.

sausage *n* salsiccia *f*; salame *m*.

savage *adj, n* selvaggio *m*; * *vt* sbranare.

savagery *n* ferocia *f*.

savannah *n* savana *f*.

save *vt* salvare; risparmiare; parare; * *n* parata *f*; * *prep* salvo.

saveloy *n* cervellata *f*.

saver *n* risparmiatore *m*.

saving *n* risparmio *m*; ~s risparmi *mpl*.

savings account *n* libretto *m* di risparmio.

savings bank *n* cassa *f* di risparmio.

Saviour *n* salvatore *n*.

savour *n* sapore *m*; * *vt* assaporare.

savoury *adj* salato; *n* piatto *m* salato.

saw *n* sega *f*; * *vt* segare.

sawdust *n* segatura *f*.

sawmill *n* segheria *f*.

saxophone *n* sassofono *m*.

say *vt, vi* dire; indicare.

saying *n* detto *m*.

scab *n* crosta *f*; crumiro *m*.

scabbard *n* fodero *m*.

scaffold *n* patibolo *m*.

sfaffolding *n* impalcatura *f*.

scald *n* scottatura; * *vt* scottare.

scale n scaglia f; squama f; scala f; * vt squamare; scalare.

scales n bilancia f.

scallop n (zool) pettine m; smerlo m; * vt smerlare.

scalp n cuoio m capelluto; * vt scotennare.

scalpel n bisturi m.

scamp n peste f.

scamper vi sgambettare.

scampi npl gamberoni mpl.

scan vt scrutare, scandagliare; * vi scandire; * n ecografia f.

scandal n scandalo m.

scandalize vt scandagliare.

scandalous adj scandaloso.

scant adj scarso.

scanty adj scarso, succinto.

scapegoat n capro m espiatorio.

scar n cicatrice f; * vt sfregiare; * vi cicatrizzarsi.

scarce adj scarso; ~ly adv appena.

scarcity n scarsità f.

scare vt spaventare; impaurire; * n spavento m.

scarecrow n spaventapasseri m.

scaremonger n allarmista m/f.

scarf n sciarpa f, foulard m.

scarlet adj, n scarlatto m.

scarlet fever n scarlattina f.

scarp n scarpata f.

scathing adj sprezzante.

scatter vt sparpagliare; * vi disperdersi.

scatterbrain n scervellato m.

scavenger n animale m necrofago.

scenario n copione m.

scene n scena f; luogo m.

scenery n paesaggio m.

scenic adj pittoresco.

scent n profumo m; pista f; * vt profumare; fiutare.

scentless adj inodoro.

sceptic n scettico; ~al adj scettico.

scepticism n scetticismo m.

sceptre n scettro m.

schedule n programma m; orario m; tabella f.

scheduled flight n volo m di linea.

schematic adj schematico.

scheme n piano m; * vi tramare.

schemer n intrigante m/f.

scheming adj intrigante.

schism n scisma m.

schizophrenia n schizofrenia f.

scholar n studioso m.

scholarly adj dotto.

scholarship n erudizione f, borsa f di studio.

scholastic adj scolastico.

school n scuola f; facoltà f; banco m; * vt addestrare.

schoolboy n scolaro m.

schoolgirl n scolara f.

schooling n istruzione f.

schoolmaster n maestro m, insegnante m.

schoolmistress n maestra f, insegnante f.

schoolteacher n maestro m, insegnante m/f.

schooner n schooner m.

sciatica n sciatica f.

science n scienza f.

science fiction n fantascienza f.

scientific adj scientifico.

scientist n scienziato m.

scimitar n scimitarra f.

scintillating adj scintillante.

scissors npl forbice fpl.

sclerosis n sclerosi f.

scoff vi ridere; * vt papparsi.

scold vt sgridare.

scoop n paletta f; mestolo m; colpo m giornalistico; * vt accaparrarsi.

scooter *n* monopattino *m*; scooter *m*.

scope *n* possibilità *fpl*, ambito *m*, capacità *f*.

scorch *vt* bruciacchiare; * *n* bruciacchiatura *f*.

score *n* punteggio *m*; motivo *m*; scalfittura *f*; (*mus*) partitura *f*; * *vt* segnare; incidere; (*mus*) orchestrare.

scoreboard *n* tabellone *m*.

scorn *vt* disprezzare; * *n* disprezzo *m*.

scornful *adj* sprezzante.

Scorpio *n* Scorpione *m*.

scorpion *n* scorpione *m*.

scotch *vt* stroncare.

scoundrel *n* farabutto *m*.

scour *vt* sfregare; *vi* setacciare.

scourge *n* flagello *m*.

scout *n* ricognitore *m*; * *vi* andare alla ricerca di.

scowl *n* sguardo torvo; * *vi* accigliarsi.

scraggy *adj* scheletrico.

scramble *vi* inerpicarsi; * *vt* (*culin*) strapazzare; ingarbugliare; * *n* parapiglia *f*; gara *f* di motocross.

scrap *n* pezzetto *m*; briciolo *m*; ferraglia *f*; baruffa *f*; * *vt* demolire.

scrape * *vt* scorticare; raschiare; * *vi* grattare; * *n* raschiatura *f*; guaio *m*.

scraper *n* raschietto *m*.

scratch *vt* graffiare; grattare; cancellare; * *n* graffio *m*.

scrawl *vt* scribacchiare; * *n* graffia *n* illeggibile.

scream *vt*, *vi* urlare; * *n* urlo *m*, strillo *m*.

screech *vi* strillare, stridere; * *n* strido *m*.

screen *n* paravento *m*; schermo *m*; * *vt* nascondere; proiettare; (*fig*) vagliare.

screenplay *n* sceneggiatura *f*.

screw *n* vite *f*; elica *f*; (*sl*) secondino *m* * *vt* avvitare; spiegazzare.

screwdriver *n* cacciavite *m*.

scribble *vi* scarabocchiare; * *n* scarabocchio *m*.

scribe *n* scriba *m*.

scrimmage *n* tafferuglio *m*.

script *n* copione *m*, scrittura *f*.

Scripture *n* Sacre Scritture *fpl*.

scroll *n* rotolo *m* di pergamena.

scrotum *n* scroto *m*.

scrounge *vt*, *vi* scroccare.

scrounger *n* scroccone *m/f*.

scrub *vt* strofinare; cancellare; * *n* boscaglia *f*; strofinata *f*.

scruffy *adj* trasandato.

scrum *n* (*sport*) mischia *f*.

scrumptious *adj* delizioso.

scruple *n* scrupolo *m*.

scrupulous *adj* scrupoloso.

scrutinize *vt* scrutare.

scrutiny *n* scrutinio *m*.

scuffle *n* tafferuglio *m*; * *vi* azzuffarsi.

scull *vt* remare.

scullery *n* retrocucina *m*.

sculpt *vt*, *vi* scolpire.

sculptor *n* scultore *m*.

sculpture *n* scultura *f*.

scum *n* (*fig*) feccia *f*.

scurrilous *adj* scurrile.

scurvy *n* scorbuto *m*.

scuttle *n* secchio *m*; * *vt* autoaffondare; * *vi* sgattaiolare via.

scythe *n* falce *f*; * *vt* falciare.

sea *n* mare *m*.

sea breeze *n* brezza *f* marina.

seafood *n* frutti *mpl* di mare.

sea front *n* lungomare *m*.

seagull *n* gabbiano *m*.

sea horse *n* cavalluccio *m* marino.

seal *n* foca *f*; sigillo *m*; * *vt* sigillare.

sealing wax *n* ceralacca *f*.

seam *n* cucitura *f*; vena *f*.

seaman *n* marinaio *m*.

seamanship *n* tecnica *f* di navigazione.

seamstress *n* sarta *f*.

seamy *adj* malfamato.

sea plane *n* idrovolante *m*.

seaport *n* porto *m* di mare.

sear *vt* cauterizzare.

search *vt* perquisire; perlustrare; * *vi* cercare; * *n* ricerca *f*; perquisizione *f*.

searchlight *n* riflettore *m*.

seashore *n* riva *f* del mare.

seasick *vt* avere il mal di mare.

seasickness *n* mal di mare.

seaside *n* spiaggia *f*.

season *n* stagione *f*; * *vt* stagionare; condire.

seasonable *adj* di stagione.

seasoning *n* condimento *m*.

season ticket *n* abbonamento *m*.

seat *n* sedia *f*; posto *m*; sedile *m*; sellino *m*; seggio *m*; sede *f*; * *vt* far sedere.

seat belt *n* cintura *f* di sicurezza.

seaweed *n* alghe *fpl*.

seaworthy *adj* in condizione di navigare.

secateurs *n* forbici *fpl* per potare.

secede *vi* ritirarsi.

secession *n* secessione *f*.

secluded *adj* appartato.

seclusion *n* isolamento *m*.

second *adj* secondo; * *n* secondo *m*; * *vt* appoggiare; distaccare.

secondary *adj* secondario.

secondary school *n* scuola *f* secondaria.

secondhand *adj* di seconda mano.

secondment *n* distaccamento *m*.

secrecy *n* segretezza *f*.

secret *adj*, *n* segreto *m*.

secretariat *n* segretariato *m*.

secretary *n* segretario *m*.

secrete *vt* secernere; nascondere.

secretion *n* secrezione *f*.

secretive *adj* riservato.

sect *n* setta *f*.

sectarian *n* settario *m*.

section *n* sezione *f*, tratto *m*.

sector *n* settore *m*.

secular *adj* laico; secolare.

secure *adj* sicuro; * *vt* assicurare; garantire.

security *n* sicurezza *f*.

sedate *adj* pacato.

sedative *adj*, *n* calmante *m*.

sedentary *adj* sedentario.

sediment *n* sedimento *m*, fondo *m*.

sedition *n* sedizione *f*.

seditious *adj* sedizioso.

seduce *vt* sedurre.

seducer *n* seduttore *m*.

seduction *n* seduzione *f*.

seductive *adj* seducente.

sedulous *adj* assiduo.

see *vt* vedere; capire; accompagnare; * *n* sede *f* vescovile.

seed *n* seme *m*; * *vt* seminare.

seedling *n* piantina *m*.

seedy *adj* squallido.

seeing conj: ~ **that** visto che.

seek *vt* cercare.

seem *vi* sembrare, parere.

seeming *n* apparente; **~ly** *adj* a quanto pare.

seemly *adj* decoroso.

seep *vi* filtrare.

seer *n* veggente *m/f*.

seesaw *n* altalena *f*; * *vi* oscillare.

seethe *vi* bollire.

see-through *adj* trasparente.

segment *n* segmento *m*; spicchio *m*.

segregate *vt* segregare.

segregation *n* segregazione *f*.

seize *vt* afferrare; cogliere.

seizure *n* attacco *m*; confisca *f*.

seldom *adj* raramente.

select *vt* selezionare, scegliere; * *adj* scelto; esclusivo.

selection *n* scelta *f*, selezione *f*.

self *n* io *m*, se *m* stesso.

self-centred *adj* egocentrico.

self-confident *adj* sicuro di sé.

self-conscious *adj* impacciato.

self-contained *adj* indipendente.

self-control *n* autocontrollo *m*.

self-defeating *adj* futile.

self-defence *n* autodifesa *f*.

self-denial *n* astinenza *f*.

self-discipline *n* autodisciplina *f*.

self-employed *adj* che lavoro in proprio.

self-esteem *n* amor *m* proprio.

self-evident *adj* lampante.

self-governing *adj* autonomo.

self-interest *n* interesse *m* personale.

selfish *adj* egoista.

selfishness *n* egoismo *m*.

selfless *adj* altruista.

self-pity *n* autocommiserazione *f*.

self-portrait *n* autoritratto *m*.

self-possessed *adj* composto.

self-respect *n* rispetto *m* di sé.

self-righteous *adj* compiaciuto.

self-sacrifice *n* abnegazione *f*.

selfsame *adj* stesso.

self-satisfied *adj* soddisfatto di sé.

self-service *adj* self-service.

self-styled *adj* sedicente.

self-sufficient *adj* autosufficiente.

self-taught *adj* autodidatta.

self-willed *adj* ostinato.

sell *vt* vendere.

seller *n* venditore *m*.

sell-off *vt* liquidare.

sellotape *n* scotch *m*.

sell-out *n* capitolazione *f*.

semantics *npl* semantica *f*.

semblance *n* apparenza *f*.

semen *n* sperma *m*.

semicircle *n* semicerchio *m*.

semicircular *adj* semicircolare.

semicolon *n* punto e virgola *m*.

semiconductor *n* semiconduttore *m*.

semifinal *n* semifinale *f*.

seminal *adj* fondamentale.

seminar *n* seminario *m*.

seminary *n* seminario *m*.

semiprecious *adj* semiprezioso.

semolina *n* semolino *m*.

senate *n* senato *m*.

senator *n* senatore *m*.

send *vt* mandare, inviare; spedire.

sender *n* mittente *m/f*.

senile *adj* senile.

senility *n* senilità *f*.

senior *adj* maggiore, superiore.

seniority *n* anzianità *f*.

senna *n* (*bot*) senna *f*.

sensation *n* sensazione *f*, scalpore *m*.

sense *n* senso *m*; ragione *f*; senno *m*; * *vt* intuire, avvertire.

senseless *adj* insensato; privo di sensi.

sensibility *n* suscettibilità *f*.

sensible *adj* assennato; pratico.

sensitive *adj* sensibile.

sensitivity *n* sensibilità *f*.

sensual *adj* sensuale.

sensuality *n* sensualità *f*.

sensuous *adj* voluttuoso.

sensuality *n* sensualità *f*.

sentence *n* frase *f*; sentenza *f*; * *vt* condannare.

sententious *adj* sentenzioso.

sentiment *n* sentimento *m*.

sentimental *adj* sentimentale.

sentinel, sentry *n* sentinella *f*.

sentry box garitta *f*.

separable *adj* separabile.

separate *vt* separare; * *adj* separato; **~ly** *adv* separatamente.

separation *n* separazione *f*.

September *n* settembre *m*.

septic *adj* settico.

septicaemia *n* setticemia *f*.

supulchre *n* sepolcro *m*.

sequel *n* seguito *m*.

sequence *n* successione *f*, sequenza *f*.

sequin *n* lustrino *m*.

sequester *vt* segregare.

sequestrate *vt* sequestrare.

seraglio *n* serraglio *m*.

serenade *n* serenata *f*; * *vt* fare la serenata a.

serene *adj* sereno.

serenity *n* serenità *f*.

serge *n* serge *f*.

sergeant *n* sergente *m*.

serial *n* opera *f* a puntate.

series *n* serie *f*.

serious *adj* serio; grave.

sermon *n* sermone *m*.

serpent *n* serpente *m*.

serpentine *n* serpentina *f*.

serrated *adj* seghettato.

serum *n* siero *m*.

servant *n* domestico *m*.

serve *vt*, *vi* servire; * *vt* **to ~ a warrant** notificare.

service *n* servizio *m*; funzione *f*; revisione; * *vt* revisionare.

service station *n* stazione *f* di servizio.

serviceable *adj* pratico.

serviette *n* tovagliolo *m*.

servile *adj* servile.

session *n* seduta *f*; anno *m*.

set *vt* porre; regolare; stabilire; assegnare; * *vi* tramontare; saldarsi; indurirsi; * *n* serie *f*, raccolta *f*, batteria *f*; set *m*; apparecchio *m*; * *adj* fisso; obbligatorio; stabilito; deciso.

settee *n* divano *m*.

setter *n* setter *m*.

setting *n* ambiente *m*, posizione *f*.

settle *vt* sistemare; definire; saldare; appianare; colonizzare; * *vi* depositarsi; insediarsi; concordare.

settlement *n* regolamento *m*; accordo *m*; insediamento *m*.

settler *n* colono *m*.

set-to *n* zuffa *f*.

seven *adj*, *n* sette *m*.

seventeen *adj*, *n* diciasette *m*.

seventeenth *adj*, *n* diciassettesimo *m*.

seventh *adj*, *n* settimo *m*.

seventieth *adj*, *n* settantesimo *m*.

seventy *adj*, *n* settanta *m*.

sever *vt* tagliare, troncare.

several *adj* parecchi.

severance *n* rottura *f*.

severe *adj* severo.

severity *n* severità *f*.

sew *vt*, *vi* cucire.

sewage *n* acque *fpl* di fogna.

sewer *n* fogna *f*.

sewing machine *n* macchina *f* da cucire.

sex *n* sesso *m*; rapporti *mpl* sessuali.

sexism *n* sessismo *m*.

sexist *adj* sessista.

sextant *n* sestante *m*.

sextet *n* sestetto *m*.

sexton *n* sagrestano *m*.

sexual *adj* sessuale.

sexuality *n* sessualità *f*.

sexy *adj* sexy.

shabbiness *n* trasandatezza *f*.

shabby *adj* malandato.

shack *n* baracca *f*.

shackle *vt* ammanettare; * *npl* **~s** pastoie *fpl*.

shade *n* ombra *f*; paralume *m*; tonalità *f*; * *vt* riparare.

shadow *n* ombra *f*; * *vt* pedinare.

shadowy *adj* vago.

shady adj ombroso.

shaft n asta f, albero m.

shaggy adj ispido.

shake vt scuotere; * vi tremare; **to ~ hands** dare la mano; * n scossa f.

shaking n scrollata f.

shaky adj traballante, vacillante.

shallot n scalogno m.

shallow adj poco profondo.

sham vt, vi fingere; * n messa in scena; impostore m; * adj simulato.

shambles npl macello m.

shame n vergogna f; peccato m; * vt disonorare; far vergognare.

shamefaced adj vergognoso.

shameful adj vergognoso.

shameless adj spudorato.

shammy n pelle f di camoscio.

shampoo n shampoo m.

shamrock n trifoglio m.

shank n stinco m; gambo m.

shanty n canzone f marinaresca; baracca f.

shanty town n bidonville f

shape vt formare; * n forma f.

shapeless adj informe.

shapely adj ben fatto.

share n parte f; azione f; * vt dividere; condividere.

shareholder n azionista m/f.

share-out n spartizione f.

shark n squalo m, pesce m cane.

sharp adj affilato, aguzzo; brusco; nitido; acuto; in diesis.

sharpen vt affilare, temperare.

sharpener n temperamatite m.

sharply adv bruscamente.

sharp-tempered adj irascibile.

shatter vt frantumare.

shattered adj sconvolto; distrutto.

shatter-proof adj infrangibile.

shave vt radere; * vi radersi.

shaver n rasoio m elettrico.

shaving n (wood) truciolo m.

shaving brush n pennello m da barba.

shawl n scialle m.

she pron ella, lei.

sheaf n covone m; fascio m.

shear vt tosare; * npl ~s cesoie fpl.

sheath n guaina f; preservativo m.

shed vt perdere; versare; emanare; * n capanno m.

sheen n lucentezza f.

sheep n pecora f.

sheepfold n ovile m.

sheep dog n cane m pastore.

sheepish adj imbarazzato.

sheepskin n pelle f di montone, shearling m.

sheer adj puro, trasparente; a picco.

sheet n lenzuolo m; foglio m.

sheet lightning n lampeggio m diffuso.

sheik n sceicco m.

shelf n ripiano m.

shell n conchiglia f; guscio m; struttura f; * vt sgranare; bombardare.

shellfish n crostaceo m.

shelter n riparo m; rifugio m; * vt riparare.

shelve vt accantonare.

shelving n scaffalature fpl.

shepherd n pastore m.

sherbet n sorbetto m.

sheriff n sceriffo m.

sherry n sherry m.

shield n scudo m; * vt proteggere.

shift vt spostare; trasferire; * n cambiamento m; turno m:

shifty adj losco.

shilling n scellino m.

shimmer vi luccicare.

shin n stinco m.

shinbone n tibia f.

shine vt lustrare; * vi brillare;

* *n* lucentezza *f*.

shingle *n* ciottoli *mpl*; **~s** *npl* herpes zoster *m*.

shining *adj* lucente.

shiny *adj* lucido.

ship *n* nave *f*; * *vt* imbarcare; spedire.

shipment *n* carico *m*.

shipowner *n* armatore *m*.

shipper *n* spedizioniere *m*.

shipping *n* navigazione *f*.

shipwreck *n* naufragio *m*.

shipyard *n* cantiere *m* navale.

shire *n* contea *f*.

shirk *vt* scansare.

shirker *n* scansafatiche *m/f*.

shirt *n* camicia *f*.

shit *n* (*vulg*) merda *f*.

shiver *n* brivido *m*; * *vi* rabbrividire.

shoal *n* banco *m*.

shock *n* scossa *f*; shock; * *vt* scioccare; * *vi* scandalizzare.

shock absorber *n* ammortizzatore *m*.

shocking *adj* scandaloso.

shoddy *adj* scadente.

shoe *n* scarpa *f*; **horse ~** ferro di cavallo; * *vt* ferrare.

shoehorn *n* calzante *m*.

shoelace *n* laccio *m*, stringa *f*.

shoemaker *n* calzolaio *m*.

shoeshop *n* calzoleria *f*.

shoestring *n* (*fam*) quattro soldi *m*.

shoot *vt* sparare; fucilare; lanciare; (film) girare; * *vi* sparare; * *n* germoglio *m*; partita *f* di caccia.

shooting *n* sparatoria *f*; fucilazione *f*; * *adj* lancinante.

shop *n* negozio *m*; officina *f*; * *vi* fare la spesa; * *vt* tradire.

shoplift *vi* taccheggiare.

shoplifter *n* taccheggiatore *m*.

shopping *n* spesa *f*.

shopping centre *n* centro *m* commerciale.

shore *n* sponda *f*.

short *adj* basso; corto; breve; **~ly** *adv* tra poco.

shortage *n* carenza *f*.

short-circuit *n* corto circuito *m*.

shortcoming *n* difetto *m*.

shorten *vt* accorciare.

shorthand *n* stenografia *f*.

shorts *npl* calzoncini *mpl*.

short-sighted *adj* miope.

short-sightedness *n* miopia *f*.

shortwave *adj* a onde corte.

shot *n* sparo *m*; tiratore *m*; iniezione *f*; foto *f*.

shotgun *n* fucile *f* da caccia.

shoulder *n* spalla *f*; * *vt* accollarsi.

shout *vt*, *vi* gridare; * *n* grido *m*.

shouting *n* grida *fpl*.

shove *vt*, *vi* spingere; * *n* spintone *m*.

shovel *n* pala *f*; * *vt* spalare.

show * *vt* mostrare; esporre; presentare; segnare; * *vt* vedersi; * *n* manifestazione *f*, esposizione *f*; spettacolo *m*; fiera *f*; figura *f*:

show business *n* mondo *m* dello spettacolo.

showcase *n* vetrina *f*.

shower *n* acquazzone *m*; doccia *f*; * *vt* coprire; * *vi* fare la doccia.

show-off *n* esibizionista *m/f*.

showroom *n* show-room *m*.

showy *adj* vistoso.

shred *n* brandello *m*; briciolo *m*; * *vt* stracciare; trinciare.

shrew *n* toporagno *m*; bisbetica *f*.

shrewd *adj* accorto.

shrewdness *n* accortezza *f*.

shriek * *vi* strillare; * *n* strillo *m*.

shrill *adj*.stridulo.

shrimp *n* gamberetto *m*.

shrine n santuario m.

shrink vi restringersi.

shrivel vi rinsecchirsi.

shroud n sudario m; * vt avvolgere.

Shrove Tuesday n martedì m grasso.

shrub n cespuglio m.

shrug n alzata f di spalle.

shudder vi rabbrividire; vibrare; * n brivido m; vibrazione f.

shuffle vt strascicare; mescolare; * n passo m strascicato; mescolata f.

shun vt evitare.

shunt vt (rail) smistare.

shut vt chiudere; * vi chiudersi.

shutter n persiana f; saracinesca f; otturatore m.

shuttle n spola f; navetta f; * vi fare la spola.

shuttlecock n volano m.

shy adj timido.

shyness n timidezza f.

sibling n fratello m, sorella f.

sick adj malato; macabro; * vi vomitare.

sick bay n infermeria f.

sicken vt nauseare; * vi ammalarsi.

sickle n falce f.

sickly adj malaticcio; stucchevole.

sickness n malattia f.

side n fianco m, lato m; faccia f; ciglio m; parte f; squadra f; * adj laterale; * vi parteggiare per.

sideboard n credenza f.

sidelight n luce f di posizione.

sidelong adj di traverso.

side-step vt illudere.

side-track vt sviare.

sideways adj laterale.

siding n (rail) binario m di raccordo.

sidle vi procedere furtivamente.

siege n assedio m.

sieve n setaccio; * vt setacciare.

sift vt setacciare.

sigh vi sospirare; * n sospiro m.

sight n vista f; spettacolo m; mirino m; ~s attrazioni fpl turistiche.

sightseeing n turismo m.

sign n segno m; gesto m; indizio m; segnale m; * vt, vi firmare.

signal n segnale m; * vt, vi segnalare.

signalman n deviatore m.

signatory n firmatario m.

signature n firma f; (mus) segnatura f.

significance n significato m.

significant adj significativo.

signify vt significare.

signpost n indicazione f stradale.

silence n silenzio m; * vt fare tacere.

silencer n silenziatore m.

silent adj silenzioso.

silhouette n sagoma f.

silicon chip n chip m.

silk n seta f.

silkscreen printing n serigrafia f.

silkworm n bacco m da seta.

silky adj vellutato.

sill n davanzale m.

silly adj sciocco.

silo n silo m.

silt n limo m.

silver n argento m; argenteria f.

silversmith n argentiere m.

silvery adj argentato.

similar adj simile.

similarity n somiglianza f.

simile n similitudine f.

simmer vi sobbollire; **to ~ down** calmarsi.

simper vi sorridere in modo sciocco; * n sorrisetto m sciocco.

simple *adj* semplice; ingenuo.
simpleton *n* sempliciotto *m*.
simplicity *n* semplicità *f*.
simplification *n* semplificazione *f*.
simplify *vt* semplificare.
simply *adv* semplicemente.
simulate *vt* simulare.
simulation *n* simulazione *f*.
simultaneous *adj* simultaneo.
sin *n* peccato *m*; * *vi* peccare.
since *adv* da allora; * *prep* da; * *conj* siccome.
sincere *adj* sincero; **yours ~ly** *adv* distinti saluti.
sincerity *n* sincerità *f*.
sinecure *n* sinecura *f*.
sinew *n* tendine *m*.
sinewy *adj* muscoloso.
sinful *adj* peccaminoso.
sing *vt*, *vi* cantare.
singe *vt* bruciacchiare.
singer *n* cantante *m/f*.
singing *n* canto *m*.
single *adj* solo, unico, celibe, nubile; * *n* singolo *m*; di andata; * *vt* **to ~ out** scegliere.
singly *adv* a uno a uno.
singular *adj* singolare; strano.
singularity *n* singolarità *f*.
sinister *adj* sinistro.
sink *vi* affondare; cedere; abbassarsi; sommergersi; * *vt* scavare; * *n* lavello *m*, acquaio *m*.
sinking *n* naufragio *m*.
sinner *n* peccatore *m*.
sinuous *adj* sinuoso.
sinus *n* seno *m*.
sip *vt* sorseggiare; * *n* sorso *m*.
siphon *n* sifone *m*; * *vt* travasare.
sir *n* signore *m*.
sire *vt* generare.
siren *n* sirena *f*
sirloin *n* controfiletto *m*.
sister *n* sorella *f*; suora *f*.
sister-in-law *n* cognata *f*.

sisterly *adj* da sorella.
sit *vi* sedersi; riunirsi.
site *n* ubicazione *f*; * *vt* collocare.
sit-in *n* sit-in *m*.
sitting *n* seduta *f*.
sitting room *n* salotto *m*.
situated *adj* situato.
situation *n* posizione *f*, situazione *f*.
six *adj*, *n* sei *m*.
sixteen *adj*, *n* sedici *m*.
sixteenth *adj*, *n* sedicesimo *m*.
sixth *adj*, *n* sesto *m*.
sixtieth *adj*, *n* sessantesimo *m*.
sixty *adj*, *n* sessanta *m*.
size *n* dimensioni *fpl*; taglia *f*; misura *f*; numero *m*.
sizeable *adj* considerevole.
sizzle *vi* sfrigolare.
skate *n* razza *f*; patino *m*; * *vi* patinare.
skateboard *n* skateboard *m*.
skating *n* pattinaggio *m*.
skating rink *n* pista *f* di pattinaggio.
skein *n* matassa *f*.
skeleton *n* scheletro *m*.
skeleton key *n* passe-partout *m*.
sketch *n* schizzo *m*; abbozzo *m*; sketch *m*; * *vt* schizzare.
skewer *n* spiedo *m*.
ski *n* sci *m*; * *vi* sciare.
ski boot *n* scarpone *m* da sci.
skid *n* slittamento *m*; * *vi* slittare.
skier *n* sciatore *m*.
skiing *n* sci *m*.
skill *n* capacità *f*, abilità *f*, tecnica *f*.
skilled *adj* abile, specializzato.
skilful *adj* abile.
skim *vt* schiumare; scremare.
skimmed milk *n* latte *m* scremato.
skin *n* pelle *f*; buccia *f*; pellicola *f*; * *vt* spellare; sbucciare.

skin diving n immersione con autorespiratore.

skinned adj scoiato.

skinny adj mingherlino.

skip vi saltellare; * vt saltare; * n saltello m.

skipper n capitano m.

skirmish n scaramuccia f.

skirt n gonna f; * vt aggirare.

skirting board n battiscopa m.

skit n sketch m satirico.

skittish adj ombroso; vivace.

skittle n birillo m.

skive vi svignarsela.

skulk vi aggirarsi furtivamente.

skull n cranio m; teschio m.

skullcap n zucchetto m; papalina f.

skunk n moffetta f.

sky n cielo m.

sky blue n celeste m

sky lark n allodola f.

slylight n lucernario m.

skyscraper n grattacielo m.

slab n lastra f.

slack adj lento; negligente; stagnante.

slacken vt allentare; * vi allentarsi.

slacker n lavativo m.

slackness n negligenza f; mancanza f di tensione.

slag n scorie fpl.

slam vt, vi sbattere; * n colpo m; (cards) slam m.

slander vt calunniare; * n calunnia f.

slanderous adj calunnioso.

slang n slang m, gergo m.

slant vt inclinare; * vi pendere; * n pendenza f.

slanting adj inclinato.

slap n schiaffo m, ceffone m; * adv in pieno; * vt dare uno schiaffo.

slash vt tagliare, sfregiare; * n taglio m.

slat n stecca f.

slate n ardesia f; * vt criticare.

slaughter n macellazione f; massacro m; strage f; * vt macellare; massacrare; trucidare.

slaughterhouse n mattatoio m.

slave n schiavo m; * vi sgobbare.

slave driver n aguzzino m.

slaver vi sbavare.

slavery n schiavitù f.

slavish adj servile.

slay vt uccidere.

sleazy adj squallido.

sled, sledge, sleigh n slitta f.

sledgehammer n martello m da fabbro.

sleek adj lucente, liscio.

sleep vi dormire; * n sonno m.

sleeper n (rail) traversina f; cuccetta f.

sleepily adv con aria assonata.

sleepiness n sonnolenza f.

sleeping adj addormentato.

sleeping bag sacco m a pelo.

sleeping pill n sonnifero m.

sleepless adj insonne.

sleepwalking n sonnambulismo m.

sleep walker n sonnambulo m.

sleepy adj sonnolento, assonnato.

sleet n nevischio m.

sleeve n manica f.

sleight; n ~ of hand destrezza di mano.

slender adj snello; scarso.

slenderness n snellezza f.

sleuth n segugio m.

slice n fetta f; paletta f; * vt affettare.

slicer n affettatrice f.

slick n macchia f d'olio.

slide vi scivolare; * n scivolo m, scivolone m; frana f; diapositiva f.

sliding adj scorrevole.

slight adj minuto; * n affronto m; * vt snobbare.

slightly adv leggermente.

slim adj esile; insufficiente.

slime n melma f; bava f.

slimming adj dimagrante.

slimy adj viscido, melmoso.

sling n fionda f; fascia f; * vt scagliare.

slink vi svignarsela.

slip vi scivolare; sfuggire; sbagliarsi; * n smottamento m; scivolata f; sbaglio m; sottoveste f; federa f; foglietto m.

slipper n pantofola f.

slippery adj scivoloso, sdrucciolevole.

slipshod adj sciatto.

slipway n scalo m.

slit vt tagliare; * n fessura f, spacco m.

sliver n scheggia f.

slob n sciattone m.

slobber vi sbavare.

sloe n (bot) prugnola f.

slog n faticata f; * vi faticare.

slogan n slogan m.

slogger n sgobbone m.

sloop n scialuppa f.

slop vt traboccare.

slope n versante m, pendio m; * vi essere inclinato.

sloping adj inclinato.

sloppy adj trasandato; sdolcinato; brodoso.

slot n fessura f, scanalatura f.

sloth n accidia f.

slothful adj accidioso.

slouch vi camminare dinoccolato.

slovenly adj sciatto.

slow adj lento; ~ly adv piano; * vt, vi rallentare.

slowness n lentezza f.

slow-worm n orbettino m.

slug n lumaca f.

sluggish adj fiacco; lento.

sluice n chiusa f; * vt lavare.

slum n bassofondi mpl; catapecchia f.

slumber vi dormire; * n sonno m.

slump n crollo m, caduta f; * vi cadere, crollare.

slur vt articolare male; * n macchia f; affronto m; (mus) legatura f.

slush n poltiglia f.

slut n sgualdrina f.

sly adj astuto; scaltro.

slyness n astuzia f.

smack n schiaffo m; schiocco m; * vt sculacciare, schiaffeggiare.

small adj piccolo.

smallish adj piccolino.

smallness n piccolezza f.

smallpox n violo m.

smalltalk n conversazione f mondana.

smarmy adj (fam) untuoso.

smart adj elegante, chic; sveglio; svelto; * vi bruciare.

smart-aleck adj sapientone.

smartly adv elegantemente.

smartness n eleganza f; acutezza f.

smash vt rompere; frantumare; * n fracasso m; scontro m; successone m.

smashing adj meraviglioso.

smattering s infarinatura f.

smear n traccia f; (med) striscio m; * vt spalmare; sporcare; diffamare.

smell n olfatto m, fiuto m; odore; profumo m; puzzo m; * vt sentire odore di; * vi sapere; puzzare.

smelly adj puzzolente.

smelt vt fondere.

smile vi sorridere; * n sorriso m.

smirk vi sorridere compiaciuto; * n sorriso m compiaciuto.

smite vt colpire.

smith n fabbro m.

smithy n fucina f.

smock n blusa f.

smog n smog m.

smoke vt fumare; affumicare; * vi fumare; * n fumo m.

smoked adj affumicato.

smokeless adj senza fumo.

smoker n fumatore m.

smoking adj fumante, fumo; **no ~** vietato fumare.

smoky adj fumoso.

smooch vi sbaciucchiarsi.

smooth adj liscio; omogeneo; * vt lisciare, spianare.

smoothly adv liscio.

smoothness n levigatezza f.

smother vt soffocare.

smoulder vi covare sotto la cenere.

smudge vt imbrattare; * n macchia f.

smug adj compiaciuto.

smuggle vt contrabbandare.

smuggler n contrabbandiere m.

smuggling n contrabbando m.

smut n granellino m di fuliggine; sconcezze fpl.

smutty adj sporco; sconcio.

snack n spuntino m.

snack bar n tavola f calda.

snag n intoppo m.

snail n chiocciola f.

snake n serpente m.

snap vt rompere; schioccare; fotografare; **to ~ sb's head off** rispondere male a qualcuno; * n schiocco ; rubamazzo; * adj improvviso.

snapdragon n (bot) antirrino m.

snappy adj elegante; vivace.

snare n trappola f.

snarl n ringhio m; * vi ringhiare.

snarl-up n intasamento m.

snatch vt strappare; afferrare; cogliere; * n furto m, rapimento m; pezzo m.

sneak; vi fare la spia; **to ~ in** entrare di soppiatto; * n spione m.

sneaking adj segreto.

sneer vi sogghignare; * n sogghigno m.

sneeze vi starnutire; * n starnuto m.

snide adj maligno.

sniff vt annusare; sniffare.

snigger vi ridacchiare; * n risolino m.

snip vt tagliare; * n ritaglio m; affare m.

snipe n beccaccino m.

sniper n franco tiratore m.

snippet n frammento m.

snivel vi piagnucolare.

snivelling adj piagnoloso.

snob n snob m/f.

snobbish adj snob.

snobbery n snobismo m.

snooker n bigliardo m.

snoop vi curiosare.

snooper n ficcanaso m.

snooty adj altezzoso.

snooze n sonnellino m; * vi sonnecchiare.

snore vi russare.

snorkel n respiratore m a tubo.

snort vi sbuffare; * n sbuffata f.

snot n moccio m.

snotty adj moccioso.

snout n muso m.

snow n neve f; * vi nevicare.

snowball n palla f di neve.

snowdrop n (bot) bucaneve m.

snowman n pupazzo m di neve.

snowplow n spazzaneve m.

snowy adj nevoso.

snub vt snobbare; * n affronto m.

snub-nosed adj camuso.

snuff n tabacco m da fiuto.

snuffbox n tabacchiera f.

snug adj accogliente.

so *adv* così, in questo modo; * *conj* affinché.

soak *vt* inzuppare; mettere a mollo.

soap *n* sapone *m*; * *vt* insaponare.

soap box *n* palco *n* improvvisato.

soap opera *n* telenovella *f*.

soap powder *n* detersivo *m*.

soapsuds *npl* saponata *f*.

soapy *adj* insaponato.

soar *vi* librarsi.

sob *vi* singhiozzare; *n* singhiozzo *m*.

sober *adj* sobrio.

sobriety *n* sobrietà *f*.

so-called *adj* cosiddetto.

soccer *n* calcio *m*.

sociable *adj* socievole.

socialism *n* socialismo *m*.

socialist *n* socialista *m/f*.

social work *n* assistenza *f* sociale.

social worker *n* assistente *m/f* sociale.

society *n* società *f*, compagnia *f*.

sociological *adj* sociologico.

sociologist *n* sociologo *m*.

sociology *n* sociologia *f*.

sock *n* calzino *m*, calzettone *m*; pugno *m*; * *vt* picchiare.

socket *n* orbita *f*; presa *f*.

sod *n* zolla *f*; bastardo *m*.

soda *n* soda *f*; selz *m*.

sodden *adj* fradicio.

sodium *n* sodio *m*.

sofa *n* sofà *m*.

soft *adj* morbido, soffice; dolce; indulgente; ~ly *adv* silenziosamente.

soft drink *n* analcolico *m*.

soften *vt* ammorbidire.

softener *n* ammorbidente *m*.

soft-hearted *adj* dal cuore tenero.

softness *n* morbidezza *f*.

soft-pedal *vt* minimizzare.

soft-spoken *adj* dalla voce dolce.

software *n* software *m*.

soggy *adj* bagnato.

soil *vt* sporcare; infangare; * *n* terreno *m*.

solace *n* consolazione *f*.

solar *adj* solare.

solarium *n* solarium *m*.

solder *vt* saldare; * *n* lega *f* per saldatura.

soldier *n* soldato *m*; **to ~ on** perseverare.

sole *n* pianta *f* del piede; suola *f*; sogliola *f*; * *adj* unico; esclusivo; * *vt* risolare.

solecism *n* (*gr*) solecismo *m*.

solemn *adj* solenne.

solemnity *n* solennità *f*.

solemnize *vt* solennizzare.

solicit *vt* sollecitare.

solicitor *n* avvocato *m*.

solicitous *adj* ansioso.

solicitude *n* sollecitudine *m*.

solid *adj*, *n* solido *m*.

solidarity *n* solidarietà *f*.

solidify *vi* solidificare.

solidity *n* solidità *f*.

soliloquy *n* soliloquio *m*.

solitaire *n* solitario *m*.

solitary *adj* solitario.

solitude *n* solitudine *f*.

solo *n* (*mus*) assolo *m*.

soloist *n* solista *m/f*.

solstice *n* solstizio *m*.

soluble *adj* solubile.

solution *n* soluzione *f*.

solve *vt* risolvere.

solvency *n* solvenza *f*.

solvent *adj*, *n* solvente *m*.

sombre *adj* tetro.

some *adj* di, qualche, alcuno, certo; * *pron* alcuni, certi; * *adv* circa.

somebody *pron* qualcuno.

somehow *adv* in qualche modo.

somersault n capriola f; salto m mortale.

something pron qualcosa.

sometime adv un giorno.

sometimes adv qualche volta.

somewhat adv piuttosto, alquanto.

somewhere adv da qualche parte; circa.

somnambulism n sonnambulismo m.

somnambulist n sonnambulo m.

somnolence n sonnolenza f.

son n figlio m.

sonata n sonata f.

song n (mus) canzone f; canto m.

sonic adj sonico.

son-in-law n genero m.

sonnet n sonetto m.

sonorous adj sonoro.

soon adv presto; **as ~ as possible** appena possibile.

sooner adv prima; piuttosto.

soot n fuliggine f.

soothe vt calmare.

soothing adj calmante; rassicurante.

soothsayer n indovino m.

sop n (fig) concessione f atta a placare.

sophisticated adj sofisticato, raffinato.

sophistication n complessità f.

soporific adj soporifero.

soppy adj sciocco.

soprano n soprano m/f.

sorbet n sorbetto m.

sorcerer n stregone m.

sorceress n maga f.

sorcery n stregoneria f.

sordid adj meschino.

sore n piaga f; * adj indolenzito; doloroso.

sorrel n (bot) acetosa f.

sorrow n dolore m.

sorrowful adj addolorato.

sorry adj dispiacente; pietoso; * vi dispiacersi; * excl scusa, scusi.

sort n genere n, tipo m, specie f; * vt classificare; smistare; risolvere.

so-so adv così così.

soufflé n soufflé m.

sought-after adj richiesto.

soul n anima f.

sound adj sano; valido; profondo; * n suono m, rumore m; volume m; (geog) stretto m; * vt suonare; sondare; * vi suonare.

sound effect n effetto m sonoro.

sounding n scandaglio m.

soundness n sanità f; validità f.

soundproof adj isolato acusticamente.

soundtrack n colonna f sonora.

soup n minestra f, zuppa f.

sour adj acido, acre.

source n sorgente f.

sourness n acidità f.

souse vt mettere in salamoia.

south n sud m, meridione m; * adj sud, meridionale.

southerly, southern adj del sud.

southward(s) adv verso sud.

souvenir n souvenir m, ricordo m.

sovereign adj, n sovrano m.

sovereignty n sovranità f.

sou'wester n capello m incerato.

soviet adj sovietico.

sow n scrofa f.

sow vt seminare.

sowing n semina f.

soya n soia f.

spa n stazione f termale.

space n spazio m; * vt distanziare.

spacecraft n veicolo m spaziale.

spaceman/woman n astronauta m/f, cosmonauta m/f.

spacious adj spazioso.

spade n vanga f, paletta f; ~s picche.

spaghetti n spaghetti mpl.

span n spanna f; * vt attraversare; abbracciare.

spaniel n spaniel m.

spangle n lustrino m.

spank vt sculacciare.

spanner n chiave f fissa.

spar n albero m; * vi bisticciare.

spare vt risparmiare; prestare; * adj di riserva; in più; asciutto; * n pezzo m di ricambio; ~ time tempo libero; ~ wheel ruota di scorta.

sparing adj moderato; ~ly adv frugalmente.

spark n scintilla f; vi provocare

sparkle n scintillio m; vi scintillare.

spark(ing) plug n candela f.

sparkling adj frizzante.

sparrow n passero m.

sparrowhawk n sparviero m.

sparse adj rado; scarso.

spartan adj spartano.

spasm n spasmo m.

spasmodic adj spasmodico.

spastic adj, n spastico m.

spate n valanga f.

spatial adj spaziale.

spatter vt schizzare.

spatula n spatola f.

spawn n uova fpl; * vi deporre le uova.

speak vt dire; parlare; vi parlare.

speaker n interlocutore m; oratore m; altoparlante m.

spear n lancia f; * vt trafiggere.

special adj speciale; particolare.

specialist n specialista m/f;

* adj specializzato.

speciality n specialità f.

specialization n specializzazione f.

species n specie f.

specific adj specifico.

specifically adv esplicitamente.

specification n specificazione f.

specify vt specificare.

specimen n campione m.

specious adj specioso.

speck(le) n macchiolina f.

speckled adj screziato.

spectacle n spettacolo m; ~s npl occhiali mpl.

spectacular n colossal m.

spectator n spettatore m.

spectral adj spettrale.

spectre n spettro m.

speculate vi speculare.

speculative adj speculativo.

speech n parola f; parlata f; linguaggio m; discorso m.

speechless adj senza parola.

speed n velocità f, rapidità f; marcia f; * vi procedere velocemente; andare a velocità eccessiva.

speedboat n motoscafo m da corsa.

speeding n eccesso m di velocità f.

speed limit n limite m di velocità.

speedometer n tachimetro m.

speedway n circuito m di gara.

speedy adj veloce, rapido.

spell n incantesimo m; periodo m; * vt dire/scrivere lettera per lettera.

spelling n ortografia f.

spend vt spendere; trascorrere.

spending n spesa f.

spendthrift n spendaccione m.

spent adj usato; esaurito.

sperm n sperma m.

sperm whale n capodoglio m.

spew vt, vi vomitare.

sphere n sfera f.

spherical adj sferico.

sphinx n sfinge f.

spice n droga f; spezie fpl; * vt drogare.

spicy adj piccante.

spider n ragno m.

spider-web n ragnatela f.

spigot n tappo m.

spike n punta f; chiodo m; * vt infilzare; munire di chiodi.

spiky adj spinoso.

spill vt rovesciare, versare.

spin vt filare; prolungare; * vi girare * n giro m; effetto m; giretto m.

spinach n spinaci mpl.

spinal adj spinale.

spindle n fuso m.

sprin-drier n centrifuga f.

spine n spina f dorsale.

spine-chilling adj agghiacciante.

spineless adj smidollato.

spinet n (mus) spinetta f.

spinner n tessitore m.

spinning wheel n filatoio m.

spin-off n prodotto m secondario.

spinster n zitella f.

spiral adj, n spirale f.

spire n guglia f.

spirit n spirito m; coraggio m; ~s liquori mpl.

spirited adj energico, vivace.

spirit lamp n lampada f a spirito.

spiritual adj spirituale.

spiritualist n spiritista m/f.

spirituality n spiritualità f.

spit n spiedo m; sputo m; * vt, vi sputare.

spite n dispetto m; * conj **in ~ of** nonostante, malgrado; * vt fare dispetto a.

spiteful adj dispettoso, maligno.

spittle n sputo m.

splash vt, vi schizzare; * n tonfo m; spruzzo m.

spleen n milza f.

splendid adj splendido.

splendour n splendore m.

splice vt giuntare.

splint n stecca f.

splinter n scheggia f; vi scheggiarsi.

split n fessura f; spacco m; scissione f; * vt spaccare; dividere; * vi spaccarsi.

splutter vi sputacchiare.

spoil vt rovinare; * vi guastarsi; * n bottino m.

spoil sport n guastafeste m/f

spoilt adj viziato.

spoke n raggio m.

spokesman n portavoce m.

spokeswoman n portavoce f.

sponge n spugna f; pan di Spagna; * vt lavare con una spugna; scroccare.

sponger n scroccone m.

spongy adj spugnoso.

sponsor n promotore m; sponsor m/f; * vt promuovere; sponsorizzare.

sponsorship n promozione f, sponsorizzazione f.

spontaneity n spontaneità f.

spontaneous adj spontaneo.

spook n (fam) fantasma m.

spooky adj sinistro.

spool n bobina f.

spoon n cucchiaio m.

spoonful n cucchiaiata f.

sporadic adj sporadico.

sport n sport m; divertimento m; persona f di spirito.

sports car n automobile f sportiva.

sportsman n sportivo m.

sportswear n abbigliamento m sportivo.

sportswoman n sportiva f.

spot n macchia f; puntino m;

pois *m*; foruncolo *m*; posto *m*;
* *vt* macchiare; notare.
spotless *adj* pulitissimo.
spotlight *n* spot *m*, riflettore *m*.
spot-on *adj* esatto.
spotted *adj* a pois; macchiato.
spotty *adj* pieno di foruncoli.
spouse *n* sposo *m*, sposa *f*.
spout *n* becco *m*; * *vi* gettare;
(*fig*) declamare.
sprain *n* slogatura *f*; * *vt* slog-
arsi.
sprat *n* spratto *m*.
sprawl *vi* sdraiarsi/sedersi in
modo scomposto.
spray *n* getto *m*, spruzzo *m*;
spray *m*; mazzolino *m*; * *vt*
spruzzare.
spread *vt* spiegare; spalmare;
cospargere; propagare; * *n*
propagazione *f*; apertura *f*;
banchetto *m*.
spree *n* baldoria *f*.
sprig *n* ramoscello *m*.
sprightly *adj* vivace.
spring *vi* saltare; sorgere; * *n*
sorgente *f*; primavera *f*; salto
m; molla *f*.
springboard *n* trampolino *m*.
springtime *n* primavera *f*.
springy *adj* molleggiato.
sprinkle *vt* cospargere.
sprinkling *n* spruzzatina *f*.
sprint *n* sprint *m*.
sprout *n* germoglio *m*; cavolino
m; * *vi* germogliare.
spruce *n* abete *m*; * *adj* azzimato.
spry *adj* arzillo.
spud *n* (*fam*) patata *f*.
spur *n* sperone *m*, sprone *m*;
* *vt* spronare.
spurious *adj* falso.
spurn *vt* rispingere.
sputter *vi* scoppiettare.
spy *n* spia *f*; * *vt* scorgere; * *vi*
spiare.
spying *n* spionaggio *m*.

squabble *vi* bisticciarsi; * *n*
battibecco *m*.
squad *n* plotone *m*.
squadron *n* squadrone *m*.
squalid *adj* squallido.
squall *n* burrasca *f*; * *vi* strillare.
squalor *n* squallore *m*.
squander *vt* sperperare.
square *adj* quadrato; onesto;
* *n* quadrato *m*; quadro; piazza *f*; (*fam*) matusa *m*; * *vt* squadrare; * *vi* quadrare.
squarely *adv* direttamente.
squash *n* concentrato *m* di
frutta; calca *f*; squash *m*; * *vt*
schiacciare.
squat *vi* acquattarsi; * *adj*
tarchiato.
squatter *n* occupatore *m* abusivo.
squaw *n* squaw *f*.
squeak *vi* cigolare; squittire;
* *n* cigolio *m*, squittio *m*.
squeal *vi* strillare; * *n* strillo *m*.
squeamish *adj* nauseato.
squeeze *vt* premere; strizzare,
spremere; * *n* stretta *f*; strizzata *f*.
squib *n* petardo *m*.
squid *n* calamaro *m*.
squint *vi* essere strabico; * *n*
strabismo *m*.
squirm *vi* contorcersi.
squirrel *n* scoiatolo *m*.
squirt *vi* schizzare; * *vt* spruzzare; * *n* schizzo *m*.
stab *vt* pugnalare; * *n* coltellata *f*; fitta *f*.
stabbing *adj* lancinante.
stability *n* stabilità *f*.
stabilize *vt* stabilizzare.
stable *n* stalla *f*; scuderia *f*; ~s
maneggio *m*; * *adj* stabile.
stack *n* mucchio *m*; comignolo
m; * *vt* accatastare.
staff *n* personale *m*; bastone *m*;
pentagramma *m*.

stag n cervo m.

stage n palco m; stadio m; tappa f.

stagger vi barcollare; * vt sbalordire; scaglionare.

staggering adj sbalorditivo.

stagnant adj stagnante.

stagnate vi stagnare.

stagnation n ristagno m.

staid adj posato.

stain vt macchiare; tingere; * n macchia f; colorante m.

stainless adj inossidabile.

stair n scalino; ~s npl scale fpl.

staircase n scala f.

stake n palo m; puntata f; * vt (fig) rivendicare.

stalactite n stalattite f.

stalagmite n stalagmite f.

stale adj stantio; raffermo.

stalemate n stallo m.

stalk vt inseguire; * n gambo m, torsolo m.

stall n stalla f; bancarella f; stand m; ~s platea f; * vi andare in stallo; bloccarsi.

stallholder n bancarellista m/f.

stallion n stallone m.

stalwart adj prode.

stamen n stame m.

stamina n resistenza f.

stammer vt, vi balbettare; * n balbuzie f.

stamp vt pestare; affrancare; timbrare; * n francobollo m; timbro m.

stampede n fuga f precipitosa.

stance n posizione f.

stand vt mettere; reggere a; sopportare; offire; * vi stare in piedi; trovarsi; riposare; presentarsi; * n posizione f; stand m; leggio m; **to ~ up** alzarsi.

standard n insegna f; standard m; * adj standard, classico.

stand-in n controfigura f.

standing adj in piedi; permanente; * n rango m.

stand-offish adj freddo.

standstill n punto m morto.

staple n graffetta f; prodotto m principale; * adj base.

stapler n cucitrice f.

star n stella f; asterisco m; divo m.

starboard n tribordo m.

starch n amido m; * vt inamidare.

stardom n celebrità f.

stare vt fissare; * n sguardo m fisso.

starfish n stella f di mare.

stark adj austero.

starling n storno m.

starry adj stellato.

start vt cominciare; iniziare; avviare; * vi cominciare; partire; trasalire; * n sobbalzo m; inizio m; vantaggio m.

starter n starter m, motorino d'avviamento; antipasto m.

startle vt spaventare.

startling adj sorprendente.

starvation n inedia f.

starve vt far morire di fame; * vi morire di fame.

starving adj affamato.

state n stato m; condizione f; agitazione f; * vt affermare; indicare.

stateless adj apolide.

stately adj maestoso.

statement n dichiarazione f; deposizione f; estratto m conto.

statesman n statista m.

statesmanship n abilità f politica.

static adj statico; * n disturbo m.

station n stazione f; * vt stanziare; piazzare.

stationary adj fermo, stazionario.

stationer n cartolaio m.

stationery n cancelleria f.

statistical *adj* statistico.

statistics *npl* statistica *f*.

statuary *adj* statuario.

statue *n* statua *f*.

stature *n* statura *f*; *(fig)* levatura *f*.

status *n* stato *m*, status *m*.

statute *n* statuto *m*.

staunch *adj* convinto.

stave; *vi* to ~ off allontanare.

stay *n* soggiorno *m*, degenza *f*; sospensione *f* dell'esecuzione; * *vi* rimanere, restare, stare; alloggiare; * *vt* sospendere, fermare.

stead *n*: to stand in good ~ essere utile a qualcuno.

steadfast *adj* risoluto.

steadily *adv* saldamente.

steady *adj* fermo, saldo; costante; fisso; * *vt* tenere fermo; calmare.

steak *n* bistecca *f*.

steal *vt* rubare.

stealth *n*; by ~ furtivamente.

stealthy *adj* furtivo.

steam *n* vapore *m*; * *vt* cuocere a vapore; * *vi* fumare.

steamer *n* piroscafo *m*.

steamroller *n* rullo *m* compressore.

steel *n* acciaio *m*.

steelworks *n* acciaieria *f*.

steelyard *n* stadera *f*.

steep *adj* ripido; * *vt* immergere; impregnare.

steeple *n* campanile *m*.

steeplechase *n* steeplechase *m*.

steer *n* manzo *m*; * *vt* guidare; * *vi* sterzare.

steering wheel *n* volante *m*.

stem *n* stelo *m*; * *vt* arrestare.

stench *n* puzzo *m*.

stencil *n* matrice *f*.

stenographer *n* stenografo *m*.

stenography *n* stenografia *f*.

step *n* passo *m*; misura *f*; gradino *m*; * *vi* fare un passo.

stepbrother *n* fratellastro *m*.

stepdaughter *n* figliastra *f*.

stepfather *n* patrigno *m*.

stepmother *n* matrigna *f*.

stepsister *n* sorellastra *f*.

stepson *n* figliastro *m*.

stereo *n* stereo *m*, stereofonia *f*.

stereotype *n* stereotipo *m*.

sterile *adj* sterile.

sterility *n* sterilità *f*.

sterilize *vt* sterilizzare.

sterling *n* sterlina *f*; * *adj* genuino.

stern *adj* severo; * *n* *(mar)* poppa *f*.

sternum *n* sterno *m*.

stethoscope *n* stetoscopio *m*.

stevedore *n* scaricatore *m* di porto.

stew *vt* stufare; * *n* stufato *m*.

steward *n* steward *m*.

stewardess *n* hostess *f*.

stick *n* bastone *m*, bastoncino; asticella *f*; * *vt* incollare; conficcare; * *vi* appiccicarsi; bloccarsi; incepparsi; attenersi a; to ~ out sporgere.

sticker *n* adesivo *m*.

sticky *adj* appiccicoso.

stiff *adj* rigido, duro; indolenzito; difficile.

stiffen *vt* irrigidire; * *vi* irrigidirsi.

stiff neck *n* torcicollo *m*.

stiffness *n* rigidità *f*.

stifle *vt*, *vi* soffocare.

stifling *adj* soffocante.

stigma *n* stigma *m*.

stigmatize *vt* stigmatizzare.

stile *n* scaletta *f*.

stiletto *m* stiletto *m*.

still *adj* fermo, immobile; non gassato; * *n* alambicco; ~ life natura *f* morta; * *adv* ancora;

stillborn *adj* nato morto.

stillness *n* immobilità *f*.

stilt *n* trampolo *m*.

stimulant n stimolante m.

stimulate vt stimolare.

stimulation n stimolazione f.

stimulus n stimolo m.

sting vt pungere; pizzicare; * vi bruciare; * n pungiglione m, puntura f.

stingy adj spilorcio.

stink vi puzzare; * n puzzo m; (sl) putiferio m.

stinker n (sl) fetente m/f.

stint n dovere m.

stipulate vt stabilire.

stipulation n stipulazione f.

stir vt mescolare; agitare; risvegliare; * vi muoversi; * n scalpore m.

stirrup n staffa f.

stitch vt cucire; * n punto m; maglia f; fitta f al fianco.

stoat n ermellino m.

stock n provvista f, stock m; bestiame m; brodo m; stirpe f; ~s npl titoli mpl; * adj solito; * vt tenere; rifornire.

stockade n palizzata f.

stockbroker n agente m/f di cambio.

stock exchange n borsa f valori.

stockholder n azionista m/f.

stocking n calza f.

stockist n fornitore m.

stock market n mercato m azionario.

stock pile n scorta f.

stockroom n magazzino m.

stock taking n inventario m.

stoic n stoico m.

stoical adj stoico.

stoicism n stoicismo m.

stoke vt atticizzare.

stole n stola f.

stolid adj impassibile.

stomach n stomaco m, ventre f; * vt sopportare.

stone n pietra f; * vt lapidare.

stone-deaf adj sordo come una campana.

stony adj sassoso.

stool n sgabello m.

stoop vi chinarsi, abbassarsi.

stop vt arrestare, fermare; impedire; smettere; bloccare; * vi cessare, fermarsi; * n arresto m, pausa f; sosta f; fermata f; punto.

stopover n breve sosta f.

stoppage n sospensione f; trattenuta f; sciopero m.

stopper n tappo m.

stopwatch n cronometro m.

storage n immagazzinamento m.

store n provvista f; deposito m; grande magazzino m; * vt accumulare; immagazzinare.

storekeeper n negoziante m.

storey n piano m.

stork n cicogna f.

storm n tempesta f; temporale m; * vt prendere d'assalto; * vi infuriare.

stormy adj burrascoso.

story n storia f, trama f, racconto m; articolo m.

stout adj robusto.

stoutness n pinguedine f.

stove n stufa f.

stow vt (mar) stivare.

straggle vi estendersi disordinatamente.

straight adj diritto; liscio; onesto; semplice; eterosessuale; * adv diritto; direttamente.

straightaway adv subito.

straighten vt raddrizzare.

straightforward adj franco; chiaro.

strain vt tendere, tirare; slogare; affaticare; passare; * n tensione f; pressione f; sforzo m; (med) strappo m; (biol) razza f.

strainer n passino m.

strait n stretto m.

strait-jacket camicia f di forza.

strand n ciocca f.

strange adj sconosciuto; strano.

stranger n sconosciuto m, forestiero m.

strangle vt strangolare, strozzare.

strangler n strozzatore m.

strangulation n strangolamento m.

strap n cinturino m; spallina f; tracollo m; * vt legare, fasciare.

strapping adj ben piantato.

stratagem n stratagemma m.

strategic adj strategico.

strategy n strategia f.

stratum n strato m.

straw n paglia f; cannuccia f.

strawberry n fragola f.

stray vi smarrirsi; * adj randagio.

streak n striscia f; vena f; * vt striare; rigare.

stream n ruscello m; (fig) fiume; * vt grondare; * vi scorrere.

streamer n stella f filante.

street n strada f.

strength n forza f; resistenza f; gradazione f alcolica.

strengthen vt rinforzare; * vi consolidarsi.

strenuous adj energico; faticoso.

stress n sforzo m, stress m, tensione f; enfasi f; * vt mettere in rilievo.

stressed adj accentato.

stressful adj stressante.

stretch vt tendere, stendere; far bastare; * vi stiracchiarsi; esagerare; * n elasticità f; distesa f; tratto m.

stretcher n barella f.

strew vt spargere.

strict adj severo, rigido; stretto; ~**ly speaking** a rigor di termini.

strictness n severità f.

stride n passo m; * vt camminare a grandi passi.

strife n conflitto m.

strike vt colpire; sbattere contro; accendere; scoprire; * vi scioperare; rintoccare; * n sciopero m; scoperta f; attacco m.

striker n scioperante m/f.

striking adj che fa colpo.

string n spago m; filo m, corda f; * vt infilare; incordare.

stringent adj rigoroso; stringente.

stringy adj fibroso.

strip vt spogliare; sverniciare; smontare; * vi spogliarsi; * n striscia f; divisa f.

stripe n riga f.

stripper n spogliarellista m/f.

striptease n spogliarello m.

strive vi sforzarsi.

stroke * n colpo m; carezza f; rintocco m; * vt accarezzare.

stroll n passeggiatina f; * vi gironzolare.

strong adj forte; resistente; concentrato.

strongbox n cassaforte f.

stronghold n fortezza f.

strontium n stronzio m.

structure n struttura f; * vt strutture.

struggle vt, vi lottare; * n lotta f.

strum vt (mus) strimpellare.

strychnine n stricnina f.

strut vi pavoneggiarsi; * n supporto m.

stub n mozzicone m; matrice f.

stubble n stoppia f; barba f corta.

stubborn adj cocciuto.

stubbornness n testardaggine f.

stucco n stucco m.

stud n chiodo m; stallone m.

student n studente m.

stud horse n stallone m.

studio n studio m.

studio apartment n appartamento m monolocale.

studious adj studioso.

study n studio m; * vt, vi studiare.

stuff n roba f; * vt riempire; imbottire; farcire.

stuffing n imbottitura f; ripieno m.

stuffy adj mal ventilato m; antiquato.

stumble vi inciampare.

stumbling block n ostacolo m.

stump n troncone m; * vt sconcertare.

stun vt tramortire.

stunning adj splendido.

stunt n acrobazia f; * vt arrestare.

stunted adj striminzito.

stuntman n stunt-man m.

stupefy vt intontire; stupire.

stupendous adj stupendo.

stupid adj stupido.

stupidity n stupidità f.

stupor n intontimento m.

sturdiness n robustezza f.

sturdy adj robusto; solido.

sturgeon n storione m.

stutter n balbuzie fpl; * vt, vi balbettare.

sty n porcile m.

sty(e) n orzaiolo m.

style n stile m; classe f.

stylish adj elegante.

stylus n puntina f.

suave adj garbato.

subconscious adj subcosciente; * n subconscio m.

subcontract vt subappaltare.

subdivide vt suddividere.

subdue vt sottomettere; dominare; * adj ~d pacato, tenue.

subject adj assoggettato; soggetto a; * n suddito m; soggetto m; argomento m; materia f; * vt sottoporre.

subjection n sottomissione f.

subjective adj soggettivo.

subjugate vt soggiogare.

subjunctive adj, n congiuntivo m.

sublet vt, vi subaffittare.

sublimate vt sublimare.

sublime adj sublime.

subliminal adj subliminale.

submachine gun n mitragliatore m.

submarine n sommergibile m.

submerge vt sommergere.

submersion n sommersione f.

submission n sottomissione f.

submissive adj sottomesso.

submit vt presentare; * vi cedere a.

subnormal adj subnormale.

subordinate adj subalterno; (gr) subordinato; * n subalterno m; subordinato m; * vt subordinare.

subordination n subordinazione f.

subpoena n citazione f; * vt citare in giudizio.

subscribe vi abbonarsi; approvare.

subscriber n abbonato m.

subscription n abbonamento m.

subsequent adj successivo.

subservient adj remissivo.

subside vi decrescere; avvallarsi.

subsidence adj avvallamento.

subsidiary n sussidiario m; complimentare.

subsidize vt sovvenzionare.

subsidy n sovvenzione f.

subsist vi vivere di

subsistence n sopravvivenza f.

substance n sostanza f.

substantial adj sostanzioso; sostanziale; notevole.

substantiate vt comprovare.

substantive adj, n sostantivo m.

substitute *vt, vi* sostituire; * *n* sostituto *m*.

substitution *n* sostituzione *f*.

subterfuge *n* sotterfugio *m*.

subterranean *adj* sotterraneo.

subtitle *n* sottotitolo *m*.

subtle *adj* sottile.

subtlety *n* sottigliezza *f*.

subtly *adj* sottilmente.

subtract *vt* sottrarre.

subtraction *n* sottrazione *f*.

suburb *n* sobborgo *m*.

suburban *adj* suburbano.

suburbia *n* periferia *f*.

subversion *n* sovversione *f*.

subversive *adj, n* sovversivo *m*.

subvert *vt* sovvertire.

subway *n* sottopassaggio *m*.

succeed *vi* riuscire; * *vt* succedere.

succeeding *adj* successivo; futuro.

success *n* successo *m*; riuscita *f*.

successful *adj* riuscito; affermato.

succession *n* serie *f*; successione *f*.

successive *adj* consecutivo.

successor *n* successore *m*.

succinct *adj* succinto.

succulent *adj* succulento; * *n* pianta *f* grassa.

succumb *vi* soccombere.

such *adj* tale; **~ as** come; * *adv* talmente; così.

suck *vt, vi* succhiare.

sucker *n* ventosa *f*; citrullo *m*.

suckle *vt* allattare.

suction *n* aspirazione *f*.

sudden *adj* improvviso.

suds *npl* saponata *f*.

sue *vt* citare; * *vi* intentare causa.

suede *n* pelle *f* scamosciata.

suet *n* grasso *m* di rognone.

suffer *vt* soffrire; tollerare; * *vi* soffrire.

suffering *n* sofferenza *f*.

suffice *vt* bastare.

sufficient *adj* sufficiente.

suffocate *vt, vi* soffocare.

suffocation *n* soffocazione *f*.

suffrage *n* suffragio *m*.

suffragette *n* suffragetta *f*.

suffuse *vi* spandersi su.

sugar *n* zucchero *m*; * *vt* zuccherare.

sugar beet *n* barbabietola *f* da zucchero.

sugar cane *n* canna *f* da zucchero.

sugar lump *n* zolletta *f* di zucchero.

sugary *adj* zuccherato.

suggest *vt* suggerire.

suggestion *n* suggerimento *m*; punta *f*.

suggestive *adj* spinto.

suicidal *adj* suicida.

suicide *n* suicidio *m*; suicida *m/f*.

suit *n* completo *m*; tailleur *m*; causa *f*; colore *m*; * *vt* adattare; andare bene a; contentare.

suitable *adj* adatto, appropriato.

suitably *adv* adeguatamente.

suitcase *n* valigia *f*.

suite *n* suite *f*; appartamento *m*.

suitor *n* corteggiatore *m*.

sulk *vi* tenere il broncio.

sulky *adj* imbronciato.

sullen *adj* scontroso.

sulphate *adj* solfato.

sulphide *n* solfuro *m*.

sulphur *n* zolfo *m*.

sulphuric *adj* solforico.

sultan *n* sultano *m*.

sultana *n* uva *f* sultanina.

sultry *adj* afoso; passionale.

sum *n* somma *f*; **to ~ up** riassumere.

summary *n* riassunto *m*.

summer *n* estate *f*.

summerhouse *n* padiglione *m*.

summit n cima f, vetta f; vertice m.

summon vt convocare.

summons n mandato m di comparizione.

sumptuous adj sontuoso.

sun n sole m.

sunbathe vi prendere il sole.

sunburn n scottatura f.

sunburnt adj scottato.

Sunday n domenica f.

sundial n meridiana f.

sundown n tramonto m.

sundry adj diversi.

sunflower n girasole m.

sunglasses npl occhiali mpl da sole.

sunken adj infossato.

sunless adj senza sole.

sunlight n luce f del sole.

sunny adj assolato, soleggiato; radioso.

sunrise n alba f.

sun roof n tetto m apribile.

sunset n tramonto m.

sunshade n parasole m.

sunshine n luce f del sole.

sunstroke n insolazione f.

suntan n abbronzatura f, tintarella f.

suntan oil n olio m solare.

super adj (fam) fantastico.

superannuation n pensione f.

superb adj superbo.

supercilious adj altezzoso.

superficial adj superficiale.

superfluous adj superfluo.

superhuman adj sovrumano.

superintendent n soprintendente m/f.

superior adj, n superiore m/f.

superiority n superiorità f.

superlative adj, n superlativo m.

superman n superuomo m.

supermarket n supermercato m.

supernatural adj, n sopran- naturale m.

superpower n superpotenza f.

supersede vt soppiantare.

supersonic adj supersonico.

superstition n superstizione f.

superstitious adj superstizioso.

superstructure n sovrastruttura f.

supertanker n superpetroliera f.

supervene vi sopravvenire.

supervise vt sorvegliare.

supervision n sorveglianza f.

supervisor n sorvegliante m/f.

supine adj supino.

supper n cena f.

supplant vt soppiantare.

supple adj flessibile.

supplement n supplemento m; * vt integrare.

supplementary adj supplementare.

supplication n supplica f.

supplier n fornitore m.

supply vt fornire; * n fornitura f.

support vt sostenere; mantenere; appoggiare; * n sostegno m.

supporter n sostenitore m; tifoso m.

suppose vt supporre.

supposed adj presunto.

supposition n supposizione f.

suppository n supposta f.

suppress vt reprimere; sopprimere.

suppression n repressione f.

supremacy n supremazia f.

supreme adj supremo; sommo.

surcharge n sovrapprezzo m.

sure adj sicuro, certo; **be ~ to do something** mi raccomando.

surefire adj infallibile.

sureness n certezza f.

surety n caparra f.

surf n (mar) cavalloni mpl.
surface n superficie f; * vt asfaltare; * vi risalire in superficie.
surfboard n surf m.
surfeit n sovrabbondanza f.
surge n ondata f; * vi riversarsi.
surgeon n chirurgo m.
surgery n chirurgia f; ambulatorio m.
surgical adj chirurgico.
surly adj burbero.
surmise vt congetturare; * n congettura f.
surmount vt sormontare.
surmountable adj sormontabile.
surname n cognome m.
surpass vt superare.
surplice n cotta f.
surplus n surplus m; * adj di sovrappiù.
surprise vt sorprendere; * n sorpresa f.
surprising adj sorprendente.
surrealism n surrealismo m.
surrealistic adj surreale.
surrender vt rinunciare a; * vi arrendersi; * n resa f.
surreptitious adj furtivo.
surrogate adj, n surrogato m.
surround vt circondare; n borgo m.
survey vt guardare; esaminare; * n indagine f; perizia f; rilevamento m.
survive vt, vi sopravvivere.
survivor n superstite m/f.
susceptibility n suscettibilità f.
susceptible adj predisposto.
suspect vt sospettare; * adj sospetto; * n persona f sospetta.
suspend vt sospendere.
suspense n suspense m; incertezza f.
suspension n sospensione f.

suspension bridge n ponte m sospeso.
suspicion n sospetto m.
suspicious adj sospettoso.
sustain vt sostenere; subire.
sustenance n nutrimento m.
suture n sutura f.
swab n tampone m.
swagger vi pavoneggiarsi.
swallow n deglutizione; rondine f; * vt, vi inghiottire.
swamp n palude f; * vt inondare.
swampy adj paludoso.
swan n cigno m.
swap vt scambiare; * n scambio m.
swarm n sciame m; * vi sciamare.
swarthy adj di colorito scuro.
swastika n svastica f.
swat vt schiacciare.
swathe vt avvolgere.
sway vi ondeggiare; oscillare; * vt influenzare; * n ondeggiamento m; influenza f.
swear vt, vi giurare, vi bestemmiare.
swearword n parolaccia f.
sweat n sudore m; * vt, vi sudare.
sweater n maglione m.
sweatshirt n felpa f.
sweep vt, vi scopare; spazzare; * n scopata f; spazzacamino m; ampio gesto m.
sweeping adj generico, radicale.
sweepstake n lotteria f.
sweet adj dolce, carino; * n caramella f; dolce m.
sweetbreads npl animelle fpl.
sweeten vt zuccherare, addolcire.
sweetener n dolcificante m.
sweetheart n tesoro m.
sweetness n dolcezza f.
swell vi gonfiarsi; * n mare m

lungo; * *adj* eccezionale.
swelling *n* gonfiore *m*.
sweltering soffocante.
swerve *n* sterzata *f*; *vi* sterzare.
swift *adv* rapido; *n* rondone *m*.
swiftness *n* rapidità *f*.
swill *vt* risciacquare; tracannare; * *n* brodaglia *f*.
swim *vt*, *vi* nuotare; * *n* nuotata *f*.
swimming *n* nuoto *m*.
swimming pool *n* piscina *f*.
swimsuit *n* costume *m* da bagno.
swindle *vt* truffare; * *n* truffa *f*.
swindler *n* imbroglione *m*.
swine *n* suini *mpl*.
swing *vt* dondolare; brandire; influenzare; * *vi* dondolare; penzolare; * *n* oscillazione *f*; altalena *f*; ritmo *m*; swing *m*.
swingeing *adj* drastico.
swinging door *n* porta *f* a vento.
swirl *n* turbinio *m*.
switch *n* interruttore *m*; mutamento *m*; * *vt* cambiare; invertire; **to ~ off** spegnere; **to ~ on** accendere.
switchboard *n* centralino *m*.
swivel *vi* girarsi; * *n* perno *m*.
swoon *vi* svenire; * *n* svenimento *m*.
swoop *vi* scendere in picchiata; fare un incursione; * *n* picchiata *f*; incursione *f*.

sword *n* spada *f*.
swordfish *n* pesce *f* spada.
swordsman *n* spadaccino *m*.
sycamore *n* sicomoro *m*.
sycophant *n* leccapiedi *m/f*.
syllable *n* sillaba *f*.
syllabus *n* programma *m*.
syllogism *n* sillogismo *m*.
sylph *n* silfo *m*.
symbol *n* simbolo *m*.
symbolic *adj* simbolico.
symbolize *vt* simboleggiare.
symmetrical *adj* simmetrico.
symmetry *n* simmetria *f*.
sympathetic *adj* comprensivo.
sympathize *vi* compatire.
sympathy *n* comprensione *f*.
symphony *n* sinfonia *f*.
symposium *n* simposio *m*.
sumptom *n* sintomo *m*.
synagogue *n* sinagoga *f*.
synchronize *vt* sincronizzare.
syndicate *n* sindacato *m*.
syndrome *n* sindrome *f*.
synod *n* sinodo *m*.
synonym *n* sinonimo *m*.
synonymous *adj* sinonimo di.
synopsis *n* sinossi *f*.
syntax *n* sintassi *f*.
sythesis *n* sintesi *f*.
syphilis *n* sifilide *f*.
syringe *n* siringa *f*; * *vt* siringare.
system *n* sistema *m*
systematic *adj* sistematico.
systems analyst *n* analista *m/f* sistemi.

T

tab *n* linguetta *f*; laccetto *m*.
tabby *n* soriano *m*.
tabernacle *n* tabernacolo *m*.
table *n* tavolo *m*; tavola *f*; tabella *f*; **~ d'hôte** pasto a prezzo fisso; * *vt* presentare.

tablecloth *n* tovaglia *f*.
tablespoon *n* cucchiaio *m* da portata.
tablet *n* lapide *f*; compressa *f*;
table tennis *n* ping pong *m*.
taboo *n* tabù *m*.

tabulate *vt* mettere in colonna.

tabulator *n* tabulatore *m*.

tacit *adj* tacito.

taciturn *adj* taciturno.

tack *n* bulletta *f*; (*naut*) bordo *m*; (sewing) punto *m* d'imbastitura; * *vt* fissare con chiodi; imbastire; * *vi* bordeggiare.

tackle *n* paranco *m*; attrezzatura *f*; * *vt* affrontare.

tact *n* tatto *m*.

tactical *adj* tattico.

tactics npl tattica *f*.

tactless *adj* indelicato.

tadpole *n* girino *m*.

taffeta *n* taffettà *m*.

tag *n* etichetta *f*.

tail *n* coda *f*; * *vt* pedinare.

tailback *n* coda *f*.

tailgate *n* portellone *m* posteriore.

tailor *n* sarto *m*; * *vt* confezionare.

tailor-made *adj* fatto su misura.

tailwind *n* vento *m* in coda.

taint *vt* infangare; * *n* macchia *f*.

tainted *adj* contaminato.

take *vt* prendere; portare; accettare; contenere; sopportare; * *vi* attecchire; **to ~ after** assomigliare; **to ~ away** togliere; **to ~ back** ritirare; **to ~ down** smontare; demolire; **to ~ in** abbindolare; capire; **to ~ off** decollare; **to ~ on** addossarsi; assumere; **to ~ out** invitare; togliere; **to ~ to** prendere in simpatia; **to ~ up** occupare; cominciare; * *n* ripresa *f*.

takeaway *n* rosticceria *f*.

takeoff *n* decollo *m*; imitazione *f*.

takeover *n* assorbimento *m*.

takings npl introiti mpl.

talc, talcum powder *n* talco *m*.

talent *n* talento *m*.

talented *adj* di talento.

talisman *n* talismano *m*.

talk *vt*, *vi* parlare; * *n* conversazione *f*; conferenza *f*.

talkative *adj* loquace.

tall *adj* alto.

tally *vi* corrispondere a.

talon *n* artiglio *m*.

tambourine *n* tamburino *m*.

tame *adj* addomesticato; * *vt* addomesticare; domare.

tamper *vi* manomettere.

tampon *n* tampone *m*.

tan *vi* abbronzarsi; * *n* abbronzatura *f*.

tang *n* sapore *m* o odore *m* forte.

tangent *n* tangente *f*.

tangerine *n* mandarino *m*.

tangible *adj* tangibile.

tangle *vt* aggrovigliare; * *n* groviglio *m*.

tank *n* serbatoio *m*; cisterna *f*; carro armato *m*.

tanker *n* autocisterna *f*; nave *f* cisterna.

tanned *adj* abbronzato.

tantalize *vt* tormentare.

tantalizing *adj* allettante.

tantamount *vi* equivalere a;

tantrum *n* collera *f*.

tap *vt* intercettare; sfruttare; * *vi* bussare; * *n* rubinetto *m*; colpetto *m*.

tape *n* nastro *m*; fettuccia *f*; * *vt* registrare.

tape measure *n* metro *m*, nastro *m*.

taper *n* cerino *m*.

tape recorder *n* registratore *m*.

tapestry *n* arazzo *m*.

tapeworm *n* tenia *f*.

tar *n* catrame *m*.

tarantula *n* tarantola *f*.

target *n* bersaglio *m*; obiettivo *m*.

tariff *n* tariffa *f*.

tarmac *n* macadam *m* al catrame.

tarnish *vt* ossidare.

tarpaulin *n* telone *m* incerato.

tarragon *n* (*bot*) dragoncello *m*.

tart *adj* aspro; * *n* crostata *f*; (*fam*) sgualdrina.

tartan *n* tartan *m*.

tartar *n* tartaro *m*.

task *n* compito *m*.

tassle *n* tappa *f*.

taste *n* gusto *m*; sapore *m*; * *vt* assaggiare; assaporare.

tasteful *adj* di gusto.

tasteless *adj* di cattivo gusto; insipido.

tasty *adj* saporito.

tattoo *n* tatuaggio *m*; (*mil*) parata *f* militare; * *vt* tatuare.

tatty *adj* mal ridotto.

taunt *vt* prendere in giro; * *n* presa *f* in giro.

Taurus *n* Toro *m*.

taut *adj* teso.

tautological *adj* tautologico.

tautology *n* tautologia *f*.

tavern *n* taverna *f*.

tawdry *adj* pacchiano.

tax *n* tassa *f*; imposta *f*; * *vt* tassare; gravare.

taxable *adj* imponibile.

taxation *n* tassazione *f*.

tax collector *n* esattore *m* delle imposte.

tax-free *adj* esente da imposta.

taxi *n* taxi *m*; * *vi* rullare.

taxi driver *n* tassista *m/f*.

taxi rank *n* posteggio *m* di taxi.

tax payer *n* contribuente *m/f*.

tax relief *n* agevolazioni *fpl* fiscali

tax return *n* dichiarazione *f* dei redditi.

tea *n* tè *m*.

teach *vt*, *vi* insegnare.

teacher *n* insegnante *m/f*; maestro *m*; professore *m*.

teaching *n* insegnamento *m*.

teacup *n* tazza *f* da tè.

teak *n* tek *m*.

team *n* équipe *f*, squadra *f*.

teamwork *n* lavoro *m* d'équipe.

teapot *n* teiera *f*.

tear *vt* strappare; * *n* strappo *m*.

tear *n* lacrima *f*.

tearful *adj* in lacrime.

tear gas *n* gas *m* lacrimogeno.

tease *vt* stuzzicare; * *n* burlone *m*.

tea-service, tea-set *n* servizio *m* da tè.

teaspoon *n* cucchiaino *m*.

teat *n* tettarella *f*.

technical *adj* tecnico.

technicality *n* tecnicità *f*.

technician *n* tecnico *m*.

technique *n* tecnica *f*.

technological *adj* tecnologico.

technology *n* tecnologia *f*.

teddy (bear) *n* orsacchiotto *m*.

tedious *adj* noioso.

tedium *n* tedio *m*.

tee *n* tee *m*.

teem *vi* brulicare.

teenage *adj* adolescenziale; **~r** *n* adolescente *m/f*; teenager *m/f*.

teens *npl* età fra i 13 ed i 19 anni.

teeth *npl* denti *mpl*.

teethe *vi* mettere i denti.

teetotal *adj* astemio.

teetotaller *n* astemia *m/f*.

telecommunications *npl* telecomunicazioni *fpl*.

telegram *n* telegramma *m*.

telegraph *n* telegrafo *m*.

telegraphic *adj* telegrafico.

telepathy *n* telepatia *f*.

telephone *n* telefono *m*.

telephone call *n* telefonata *f*.

telephone directory *n* elenco *m* telefonico.

telephone number *n* numero *m* di telefono.

telephonist n telefonista m/f.

telescope n telescopio m.

televise vt trasmettere per televisione.

television n televisione f.

television set n televisore m.

telex n telex m.

tell vt dire; raccontare; indicare; distinguere; * vi parlare; sapere.

teller n cassiere m.

telling adj rivelatore.

telltale adj rivelatore; * n spione m.

temerity n audacia f.

temper vt moderare; * n indole f; temperamento m; collera f.

temperament n temperamento m.

temperamental adj capriccioso.

temperance adj astinenza dall'alcol.

temperate adj temperato.

temperature n temperatura f.

tempest n tempesta f.

tempestuous adj burrascoso.

template n sagoma f.

temple n tempio m; (anat) tempia f.

temporarily adv temporaneamente.

temporary adj provvisorio.

tempt vt tentare.

temptation n tentazione f.

tempting adj allettante.

ten adj, n dieci m.

tenable adj sostenibile.

tenacious adj tenace.

tenacity n tenacia f.

tenancy n contratto m d'affitto.

tenant n inquilino m.

tend vt tendere; curare.

tendency n tendenza f.

tender adj tenero; sensibile; * n tender m; offerta f; * vt presentare; offrire.

tenderness n tenerezza f.

tendon n tendine m.

tenement n casamento m.

tenet n principio m.

tennis n tennis m.

tennis court n campo m da tennis.

tennis player n tennista m/f.

tennis racket n racchetta f da tennis.

tenor n tenore m; * adj tenorile.

tense n (gr) tempo m; * adj teso; * vt tendere.

tension n tensione f.

tent n tenda f.

tentacle n tentacolo m.

tentative adj esitante.

tenth adj, n decimo m.

tenuous adj tenue.

tenure n possesso m.

tepid adj tiepido.

term n termine m; trimestre m; ~s npl condizioni fpl: * vt chiamare.

terminal adj incurabile; * n terminale m; capolinea m.

terminate vt, vi terminare.

termination n recisione f.

terminus n capolinea m.

termite n termite f.

terrace n terrazza f.

terrain n terreno m.

terrestrial adj terrestre.

terrible adj terribile.

terrier n terrier m.

terrific adj stupendo; enorme.

terrify vt terrificare.

territorial adj territoriale.

territory n territorio m.

terror n terrore m; peste f.

terrorism n terrorismo m.

terrorist n terrorista m/f.

terrorize vt terrorizzare.

terse adj conciso.

test n prova f; collaudo m; esame m; * vt controllare; collaudare; sperimentare.

testament n testamento m.

testicle n testicolo m.

testify *vi* testimoniare.
testimonial *n* referenze *fpl*.
testimony *n* testimonianza *f*.
test pilot *n* pilota *m* collaudatore.
test-tube *n* provetta *f*.
testy *adj* irritabile.
tetanus *n* tetano *m*.
tether *vt* legare; * *n* laccio *m*.
text *n* testo *m*.
textbook *n* libro *m* di testo.
textile *adj* tessile; ~s *npl* tessuti *mpl*.
textual *adj* testuale.
texture *n* consistenza *f*.
than *conj* che; di;
thank *vt* ringraziare.
thankful *adj* grato, riconoscente.
thankfulness *n* gratitudine *f*.
thankless *adj* ingrato.
thanks *npl* grazie *fpl*.
thanksgiving *n* ringraziamento *m*.
that *adj* quel; * *pron* ciò; * *dem pron* così; * *rel pron* che; * *conj* che; **so** ~ affinché.
thatch *n* copertura *f* di paglia.
thaw *n* disgelo *m*; * *vt* scongelare.
the *def art* il.
theatre *n* teatro *m*.
theatre-goer *n* habitué *m/f* del teatro.
theatrical *adj* teatrale.
theft *n* furto *m*.
their *poss adj* loro.
them *pron* gli; loro.
theme *n* tema *m*.
themselves *pron* si; se stessi.
then *adv* allora; poi; **now and** ~ ogni tanto.
theologic(al) *adj* teologico.
theologian *n* teologo *m*.
theology *n* teologia *f*.
theorem *n* teorema *f*.
theoretic(al) *adj* teoretico.
theorist *n* teorico *m*.

theorize *vt* teorizzare.
theory *n* teoria *f*.
therapeutic *adj* terapeutico; ~s *npl* terapeutica *f*.
therapist *n* terapista *m/f*.
therapy *n* terapia *f*.
there *adv* la, lì.
thereabout(s) *adv* nei pressi.
thereafter *adv* in seguito.
thereby *adv* con ciò.
therefore *adv* quindi.
thermal *adj* termale.
thermometer *n* termometro *m*.
thermostat *n* termostato *m*.
thesaurus *n* dizionario *m* dei sinonimi.
these *dem adj*, *dem pron* questi.
thesis *n* tesi *f*
they *pers pron* essi
thick *adj* grosso; spesso; ottuso.
thicken *vt* ispessire; * *vi* infittirsi.
thicket *n* boscaglia *f*.
thickness *n* spessore *m*.
thickset *adj* tozzo.
thickskinned *adj* coriaceo.
thief *n* ladro *m*.
thigh *n* coscia *f*.
thimble *n* ditale *m*.
thin *adj* sottile; magro; * *vt* diradarsi.
thing *n* cosa *f*; ~s *npl* roba *f*.
think *vi* pensare; credere; **to** ~ **over** riflettere su; **to** ~ **up** escogitare.
thinker *n* pensatore *m*.
thinking *adj* ragionevole; * *n* pensiero *m*.
third *adj*, *n* terzo *m*.
third-rate *adj* scadente.
thirst *n* sete *f*.
thirsty *adj* assetato.
thirteen *adj*, *n* tredici *m*.
thirteenth *adj*, *n* tredicesimo *m*.
thirtieth *adj*, *n* trentesimo *m*.

thirty *adj, n* trenta *m*.

this *dem adj, dem pron* questo.

thistle *n* cardo *m*.

thorax *n* torace *m*.

thorn *n* spina *f*.

thorny *adj* spinoso.

thorough *adj* minuzioso; approfondito.

thoroughbred *adj, n* purosangue *m/f*.

thoroughfare *n* strada *f* transitabile.

those *dem adj* quei; * *dem pron* quelli.

though *conj* benché; * *adv* tuttavia.

thought *n* pensiero *m*.

thoughtful *adj* pensieroso; gentile.

thoughtless *adj* sconsiderato.

thousand *adj, m* mille *m*.

thousandth *adj, n* millesimo *m*.

thrash *vt* percuotere.

thread *n* filo *m*; * *vt* infilare.

threadbare *adj* consumato.

threat *n* minaccia *f*.

threaten *vt* minacciare.

three *adj, n* tre *m*.

three-dimensional *adj* tridimensionale.

three-ply *adj* a tre capi.

thresh *vt* trebbiare.

threshold *n* soglia *f*.

thrift *n* parsimonia *f*.

thrifty *adj* parsimonioso.

thrill *vt* entusiasmare; * *vi* fremere; * *n* brivido; fremito *m*.

thriller *n* thriller *m*.

thrive *vi* prosperare.

thriving *adj* fiorente.

throat *n* gola *f*.

throb *vi* palpitare; pulsare; * *n* battito *m*.

thrombosis *n* trombosi *f*.

throne *n* trono *m*.

throng *n* moltitudine *f*; * *vt* affollare.

throttle *n* gas *m*; * *vt* strozzare.

through *prep* attraverso; per; * *adj* finito; di passaggio.

throughout *prep* in tutto; * *adv* dappertutto.

throw *vt* lanciare; gettare; **to ~ away** butar via; **to ~ off** sbarazzarsi di; **to ~ up** vomitare; * *n* lancio *m*.

throwaway *adj* monouso.

thrush *n* tordo *m*; (*med*) candida *f*.

thrust *vt* spingere con forza; * *n* spintone *m*.

thud *n* tonfo *m*.

thug *n* teppista *m/f*.

thumb *n* pollice *m*.

thump *n* colpo *m*; tonfo; * *vt, vi* picchiare.

thunder *n* tuono *m*; * *vi* tonare.

thunderbolt *n* fulmine *m*.

thunderclap *n* rombo *m* di tuono.

thunderstorm *n* temporale *m*.

thundery *adj* da temporale.

Thursday *n* giovedì *m*.

thus *adv* così; perciò.

thwart *vt* ostacolare.

thyme *n* (*bot*) timo *m*.

thyroid *n* tiroide *f*.

tiara *n* diadema *m*.

tic *n* tic *m*.

tick *n* tic tac *m*; segno *m*; zecca *f*; * *vt* spuntare; ticchettare; **to ~ over** andare al minimo.

ticket *n* biglietto *m*.

ticket collector *n* bigliettaio *m*.

ticket office *n* biglietteria *f*.

tickle *vt* fare il solletico a.

ticklish *adj* che soffre il solletico.

tidal *adj* (*mar*) di marea.

tidal wave *n* onda *f* anomala.

tiddly *adj* brillo.

tide *n* marea *f*; ondata *f*.

tidiness *n* ordine *m*.

tidy *adj* ordinato; * *vt* mettere in ordine.

tie *vt* legare; allacciare; * *vi* pareggiare; **to ~ up** (*mar*) ormeggiare; concludere; * *n* cravatta *f*; pareggio *m*.

tier *n* fila *f*.

tiff *n* battibecco *m*.

tiger *n* tigre *f*.

tight *adj* stretto; sbronzo.

tighten *vt* stringere.

tightfisted *adj* tirchio.

tightrope *n* corda *f* (da acrobata).

tights *n* collant *m*.

tigress *n* tigre femmina.

tile *n* tegola *f*; mattonella *f*; * *vt* piastrellare.

tiled *adj* a piastrelle.

till *vt* coltivare; * *n* cassa *f*.

tiller *n* barra *f*.

tilt *n* pendio *m*; * *vt* inclinare.

timber *n* legname *m*.

time *n* tempo *m*; momento *m*; periodo *m*; ora *f*; era *f*; volta *f*; ~ * *vt* programmare; cronometrare; **to have a good ~** divertirsi.

time bomb *n* bomba *f* a orologeria.

time lag *n* intervallo *m* di tempo.

timeless *adj* eterno.

timely *adj* opportuno.

timer *n* timer *m*.

time scale *n* scala *f* cronologica.

time zone *n* fuso *m* orario.

timetable *n* orario *m*.

timid *adj* timido.

timidity *n* timidezza *f*.

timing *n* tempismo *m*.

tin *n* stagno *m*; scattola *f*; * *vt* inscatolare.

tinfoil *n* carta *f* stagnola.

tinge *n* punta *f*.

tingle *vi* formicolare; * *n* formicolio *m*.

tingling *n* formicolio *m*.

tinker *vi* trastullarsi.

tinkle *vi* tintinnare.

tin opener *n* apriscatole *m*.

tinplate *n* latta *f*.

tinsel *n* fili *mpl* argentati.

tint *n* sfumatura *f*; * *vt* tingere.

tiny *adj* minuscolo.

tip *n* punta *f*; mancia *f*; suggerimento *m*; discarica; * *vt* dare la mancia a; pronosticare; rovesciare; * *vi* rovesciarsi.

tip-off *n* soffiata *f*.

tipsy *adj* brillo.

tiptoe *vi* camminare in punta dei piedi.

tirade *n* tirata *f*.

tire *vt* stancare.

tired *adj* stanco.

tiredness *n* stanchezza *f*.

tireless *adj* instancabile.

tiresome *adj* seccante.

tiring *adj* faticoso.

tissue *n* velina *f*; fazzolettino *m* di carta; (*anat*) tessuto *m*.

tissue paper *n* carta *f* velina.

tit *n* cincia *f*.

titbit *n* leccornia *f*.

titillate *vt* titillare.

title *n* titolo *m*.

title deed *n* atto *m* di proprietà.

title page *n* frontespizio *m*.

titter *vi* ridacchiare; * *n* risatina *f* stupida.

to *prep* a; secondo; per; da.

toad *n* rospo *m*.

toadstool *n* fungo *m* velenoso.

toast *vt* tostare; brindare; * *n* pane *m* tostato; brindisi *m*.

toaster *n* tostapane *m*.

tobacco *n* tabacco *m*.

tobacconist *n* tabaccaio *m*.

toboggan *n* slittino *m*.

today *adv*, *n* oggi *m*.

toddler *n* bambino *m* che fa i primi passi.

toddy *n* grog *m*, ponce *m*.

toe n dito m del piede.

toffee n caramella f mou.

together adv insieme.

toil vi faticare; * n fatica f.

toilet n gabinetto m, toilette f.

toilet bag n nécessaire m da toilette.

toilet bowl n vaso m del gabinetto.

toilet paper n carta f igienica.

toiletries npl articoli mpl da toilette.

token n buono m; segno m; * adj simbolico.

tolerable adj sopportabile.

tolerance n sopportazione f; tolleranza f.

tolerant adj tollerante.

tolerate vt tollerare.

toll n pedaggio m.

tomato n pomodoro m.

tomb n tomba f.

tomboy n maschiaccio m.

tombstone n pietra f tombale.

tome n tomo m.

tomcat n gatto m.

tomorrow adv, n domani m.

ton n tonnellata f.

tone tono m; * vi intonarsi; **to ~ down** attenuare.

tone-deaf adj che non ha orecchio.

tongs npl pinza f.

tongue n lingua f.

tongue-tied adj ammutolito.

tongue-twister n scioglilingua m.

tonic n (med) ricostituente m; acqua f tonica.

tonight adv stasera.

tonnage n tonnellaggio m.

tonsil n tonsilla f.

tonsillitis n tonsillite f.

tonsure n tonsura f.

too adv troppo, anche.

tool n arnese m, attrezzo m, strumento m.

tool box n cassetta f degli attrezzi.

toot vi suonare il clacson.

tooth n dente m.

toothache n mal m di denti.

toothbrush n spazzolino m da denti.

toothless adj sdentato.

toothpaste n dentifricio m.

toothpick n stuzzicadenti m.

top n cima f; superficie f; tappo m; trottola f; **big ~** tendone m; * adj ultimo; migliore; * vt sormontare; superare.

topaz n topazio m.

top hat n cilindro m.

topic n argomento m.

topless adj a seno scoperto.

top-level adj ad alto livello.

topmost adj il più alto.

topography n topografia f.

topple vi cadere; * vt rovesciare.

top-secret adj segretissimo.

topsy-turvy adv, adj sottosopra.

torch n torcia f, (fam) pila f.

torment vt tormentare; * n tormento m.

tornado n tornado m.

torpedo n siluro m.

torpid adj intorpidito.

torrent n torrente m.

torrential adj torrenziale.

torrid adj torrido.

torso n torso m.

tortoise n tartaruga f.

tortoiseshell n guscio m di tartaruga.

tortuous adj tortuoso.

torture n tortura f; * vt torturare.

toss vt lanciare; sballottare; disarcionare.

total adj totale; **~ly** adv completamente; * n totale m; * vt ammontare.

totalitarian adj totalitario.

totality n totalità f.
totter vi vacillare.
touch vt toccare; commuovere; uguagliare; **to ~ on** sfiorare; **to ~ up** ritoccare; * n tatto m; tocco m; pizzico m; contatto m.
touch-and-go adj incerto.
touchdown n atterraggio m.
touched adj commosso; tocco.
touching adj commovente.
touchy adj permaloso.
tough adj resistente; faticoso.
toughen vt rinforzare.
toupee n parrucchino m.
tour n giro m; tournée f; visita f; * vt fare un giro.
touring n turismo m.
tourism n turismo m.
tourist n turista m/f.
tourist office n ufficio m del turismo.
tournament n torneo m.
tow n rimorchio m; * vt rimorchiare.
toward(s) prep verso.
towel n asciugamano m.
towelling n spugna f.
towel rail n portasciugamano m.
tower n torre f.
towering adj imponente.
town n città f.
town clerk n segretario m comunale.
town hall n municipio m.
towrope n cavo m per rimorchio.
toxic adj tossico.
toxin n tossina f.
toy n giocattolo m; vi **to ~ with** giocherellare.
trace n traccia f; * vt tracciare; rintracciare.
trachea n trachea f.
track n orma f; sentiero m; pista f; binario m; * vt essere sulle tracce di.
tracksuit n tuta f da ginnastica.

tract n distesa f; trattatello m.
traction n trazione f.
tractor n trattore m.
trade n commercio m; industria f; mestiere f; * vt barattare; * vi commerciare.
trade fair n fiera f campionaria.
trademark n marchio m.
trade name n nome m depositato.
trader n commerciante m.
tradesman n fornitore m.
trade union n sindacato m.
trade unionism n sindacalismo m.
trade unionist n sindacalista m/f.
trading n commercio m; * adj commerciale.
tradition n tradizione f.
traditional adj tradizionale.
traffic n traffico m; * vi trafficare.
traffic jam n ingorgo m.
trafficker n trafficante m/f.
traffic lights npl semaforo m.
tragedy n tragedia f.
tragic adj tragico; **~ally** adv tragicamente.
tragicomedy n tragicommedia f.
trail vt trascinare; pedinare; * vi strisciare; * n scia f; orma f; sentiero m.
trailer n rimorchio m; prossimamente m.
train vt addestrare; allenare; * vi fare tirocinio; * n treno m; codazzo m; serie f.
trained adj diplomato; allenato.
trainee n apprendista m/f; tirocinante m/f.
trainer n allenatore m; **~s** npl scarpe fpl da ginnastica.
training n allenamento m; addestramento m.

trait *n* caratteristica *f*.
traitor *n* traditore *m*.
tram *n* tram *m*.
tramp *n* vagabondo *m*; * *vi* camminare pesantemente.
trample *vt* calpestare.
trance *n* trance *f*.
tranquil *adj* tranquillo.
tranquillizer *n* tranquillante *m*.
transact *vt* trattare.
transaction *n* operazione *f*.
transatlantic *adj* transatlantico.
transcend *vt* trascendere.
transcription *n* trascrizione *f*.
transfer *vt* trasferire; * *n* trasferimento *m*.
transferable *adj* trasferibile.
transfix *vt* trafiggere.
transform *vt* trasformare.
transformation *n* trasformazione *f*.
transformer *n* trasformatore *m*.
transfusion *n* trasfusione *f*.
transgress *vi* trasgredire.
transient *adj* transitorio.
transistor *n* transistor *m*.
transit *n* transito *m*.
transition *n* transizione *f*.
transitive *adj* transitivo.
translate *vt, vi* tradurre.
translation *n* traduzione *f*.
translator *n* traduttore *m*.
transmission *n* trasmissione *f*.
transmit *vt* trasmettere.
transmitter *n* emittente *f*.
transparency *n* trasparenza *f*; diapositiva *f*.
transparent *adj* trasparente.
transpire *vi* traspirare; succedere.
transplant *vt* trapiantare; * *n* trapianto *m*.
transport *vt* trasportare; * *n* trasporto *m*.
transportation *n* trasporto *m*.

transvestite *n* travestito *m*.
trap *n* trappola *f*; (*fam*) boccaccia *f*; calesse *m*; * *vt* intrappolare.
trap door *n* botola *f*.
trapeze *n* trapezio *m*.
trappings *npl* bardatura *f*.
trash *n* spazzatura *f*.
trashy *adj* di scarto.
trauma *n* trauma *m*.
traumatic *adj* traumatizzante.
travel *vi* viaggiare; * *n* viaggi *mpl*.
travel agency *n* agenzia *f* viaggi.
traveller *n* viaggiatore *m*.
traveller's cheque *n* assegno *m* turistico.
travelling *adj* intinerante; di viaggio.
travel sickness *n* mal *m* di macchina/d'aerea/di mare.
travesty *n* parodia *f*.
trawler *n* peschereccio *m*.
tray *n* vassoio *m*.
treacherous *adj* sleale.
treachery *n* slealtà *f*.
treacle *n* melassa *f*.
tread *vt* calpestare; * *vi* pestare; * *n* passo *m*; battistrada *m*.
treason *n* tradimento *m*.
treasure *n* tesoro *m*; *vt* stimare.
treasurer *n* tesoriere *m*.
treat *vt* trattare; considerare; offrire; curare; * *n* sorpresina *f*.
treatise *n* trattato *m*.
treatment *n* trattamento *m*.
treaty *n* trattato *m*.
treble *adj* triplo; alto; * *vt* triplicare.
treble clef *n* chiave *f* di sol.
tree *n* albero *m*.
trek *n* spedizione *f*.
trellis *n* graticcio *m*.
tremble *vi* tremare; * *n* tremito *m*.

trembling n tremito m.

tremendous adj enorme; tremendo.

tremor n scossa f.

trench n fosso m; trincia f; ~ **coat** n trench m.

trend n andamento m.

trepidation n trepidazione f.

trespass vt transitare abusivamente.

trestle n cavalletto m.

trial n processo m; prova f.

triangle n triangolo m.

triangular adj triangolare.

tribal adj tribale.

tribe n tribù f.

tribulation n tribolazione f.

tribunal n tribunale m.

tributary n affluente m.

tribute n tributo m.

trick n scherzo m; trucco m; inganno m; * vt ingannare.

trickery n astuzia f.

trickle vi gocciolare; * n rivolo m.

tricky adj difficile.

tricycle n triciclo m.

trifle n sciocchezza f; zuppa f inglese; * vi prendere alla leggera.

trifling adj insignificante.

trigger n grilletto m; * vt scatenare.

trigonometry n trigonometria f.

trill n trillo m; * vi trillare.

trilogy n trilogia f.

trim adj snello; * n spuntata f; * vt spuntare.

trimmings npl accessori mpl.

Trinity n Trinità f.

trinket n ninnolo m.

trio n trio m.

trip vi inciampare; * n viaggio m; gita f; trip m.

tripe n trippa f.

triple adj triplo.

triplets npl tre gemelli mpl.

triplicate adj triplice; * n in triplice copia.

tripod n treppiede m.

trite n trito.

triumph n trionfo m.

triumphal adj trionfale.

triumphant adj trionfante.

trivia n banalità fpl.

triviality n frivolezza f.

trolley n carello m.

trombone n trombone m.

troop n squadrone m; ~**s** npl truppe fpl.

trophy n trofeo m.

tropical adj tropicale.

trot n trotto m; * vi trottare.

trouble vt preoccupare; disturbare; * n problemi mpl; guai mpl.

troubled adj travagliato.

troublemaker n attaccabrighe m/f.

troubleshooter n esperto m.

troublesome adj fastidioso.

trough n mangiatoia f; cavo m.

troupe n troupe f.

trousers npl pantaloni mpl.

trout n trota f.

trowel n cazzuola f.

truant n: **to play** ~ marinare la scuola.

truce n tregua f.

truck n camion m.

truck driver n camionista m.

truculent adj bellicoso.

trudge vi trascinarsi.

true adj vero; sincero; fedele.

truelove n vero amore m.

truffle n tartufo m.

truly adv veramente.

trump n atout m.

trumpet n tromba f.

truncheon n manganello m.

trunk n tronco m; proboscide f; baule m.

truss n cinto m erniario; * vt legare stretto.

trust n fiducia f; (com) trust m; * vt fidarsi.

trusted *adj* fidato.

trustee *n* amministratore *m*.

trustful *adj* fiducioso.

trustworthy *adj* attendibile.

trusty *adj* fidato.

truth *n* verità *f*.

truthful *adj* veritiero.

try *vt* provare; cercare; verificare; processare; * *vi* provare; * *n* tentativo *m*; meta *f*;

trying *adj* duro.

tsar *n* zar *m*.

T-shirt *n* maglietta *f*.

tub *n* mastello *m*; vaschetta *f*.

tuba *n* tuba *f*.

tube *n* tubo *m*; metrò *m*.

tuberculosis *n* tubercolosi *f*.

tubing *n* tubazione *f*.

tuck *n* pinze *f*; * *vt* infilare.

Tuesday *n* martedì *m*.

tuft *n* ciuffo *m*.

tug *vt* dare uno strattone a; * *n* strattone *m*; rimorchiatore *m*.

tuition *n* lezioni *fpl*.

tulip *n* tulipano *m*.

tumble *vt* ruzzolare; * *n* capitombolo *m*.

tumble-down *adj* cadente.

tumbler *n* bicchiere *m*.

tummy *n* pancia *f*.

tumour *n* tumore *m*.

tumultuous *adj* tumultuoso.

tuna *n* tonno *m*.

tune *n* melodia *f*; * *vt, vi* accordare.

tuneful *adj* melodioso.

tuner *n* sintonizzatore *m*; accordatore *m*.

tunic *n* tunica *f*.

tuning fork *n* diapason *m*.

tunnel *n* galleria *f*; tunnel *m*.

turban *n* turbante *m*.

turbine *n* turbina *f*.

turbulence *n* turbolenza *f*.

turbulent *adj* turbolento.

tureen *n* zuppiera *f*.

turf *n* zolla *f* erbosa; **to ~ out** buttar fuori.

turgid *adj* ampolloso.

turkey *n* tacchino *m*.

turmeric *n* curcuma *f*.

turmoil *n* confusione *f*.

turn *vt* girare; voltare; trasformare; tornire; * *vi* girare; virare; **to ~ back** tornare in dietro; **to ~ down** abbassare; rifiutare; **to ~ in** consegnare; **to ~ off** spegnere; **to ~ on** accendere; **to ~ out** rivelarsi; **to ~ over** capovolgersi; voltare; **to ~ round** girarsi; **to ~ up** arrivare; alzare; * *n* giro *m*; curva *f*; crisi *f*; turno *m*; numero *m*.

turncoat *n* voltagabbana *m/f*.

turning *n* curva *f*.

turnip *n* rapa *f*.

turnover *n* giro *m* d'affari.

turnstile *n* cancelletto *m* girevole.

turntable *n* piatto *m*.

turpentine *n* trementina *f*.

turquoise *adj, n* turchese *m*.

turret *n* torretta *f*.

turtle *n* tartaruga *f* acquatica.

turtledove *n* tortora *f*.

tusk *n* zanna *f*.

tussle *n* baruffa *f*.

tutor *n* insegnante *m* privato.

twang *n* suono *m* acuto.

tweezers *npl* pinzette *fpl*.

twelfth *adj, n* dodicesimo *m*.

twelve *adj, n* dodici *m*.

twentieth *adj, n* ventesimo *m*.

twenty *adj, n* venti *m*.

twice *adv* due volte.

twig *n* ramoscello *m*.

twilight *n* crepuscolo *m*.

twin *adj, n* gemello *m*.

twine *vi* attorcigliarsi; * *n* cordicella *f*.

twinge *n* fitta *f*.

twinkel *vi* scintillare; * *n* scintillio.

twirl *vt* far roteare; * *vi* volteggiare; * *n* piroetta *f*.

twist *vt* attorcigliare; * *vi* slo-

garsi; attorcigliarsi; * *n* piega
f; sviluppo *m*; twist *m*.
twitch *vi* contrarsi; * *n* tic *m*.
twitter *vi* cinguettare; * *n* cinguettio *m*.
two *adj, n* due *m*.
two-door *adj* a due porte.
two-faced *adj* falso.
twofold *adj* doppio.
two-seater *adj* biposto.
twosome *n* coppia *f*.
tycoon *n* magnate *m*.
type *n* tipo *m*; carattere *m*; * *vt*
battere a macchina.
typeface *n* carattere *m* tipografico.

typescript *n* dattiloscritto *m*.
typewriter *n* macchina *f* da
scrivere.
typewritten *adj* dattiloscritto.
typhoid *n* tifoidea *f*.
typhoon *n* tifone *m*.
typhus *n* tifo *m*.
typical *adj* tipico.
typing *n* dattilografia *f*.
typist *n* dattilografo *m*.
typographer *n* tipografo *m*.
tyrannical *adj* tirannico.
tyranny *n* tirannia *f*.
tyrant *n* tiranno *m*.
tyre *n* gomma *f*.

U

ubiquitous *adj* onnipresente.
udder *n* mammella *f*.
ugh *excl* puah!
ugliness *n* bruttezza *f*.
ugly *adj* brutto.
ulcer *n* ulcera *f*.
ulterior *adj* ulteriore.
ultimate *adj* finale; supremo.
ultimatum *n* ultimatum *m*.
ultramarine *adj, n* oltremarino *m*.
ultrasound *n* ecografia *f*.
umbilical cord *n* cordone *m*
ombelicale.
umbrella *n* ombrello *m*.
umpire *n* arbitro *m*.
umpteen *adj* parecchi.
umpteenth *n* ennesimo *m*.
unable *adj* incapace.
unaccompanied *adj* non accompagnato.
unaccountable *adj* inesplicabile.
unaccustomed *adj* non abituato.
unacknowleged *adj* senza risposta.

unacquainted *adj* non al corrente; ignorare.
unadorned *adj* disadorno.
unadulterated *adj* puro.
unaffected *adj* naturale.
unaided *adj* senza aiuto.
unalterable *adj* inalterabile.
unaltered *adj* inalterato.
unambitious *adj* poco ambizioso.
unanimity *n* unanimità *f*.
unanimous *adj* unanime.
unanswerable *adj* irrefutabile.
unanswered *adj* senza risposta.
unapproachable *adj* inavvicinabile.
unarmed *adj* disarmato.
unashamed *adj* sfrontato.
unassuming *adj* modesto.
unattached *adj* staccato; libero.
unattainable *adj* irraggiungibile.
unattended *adj* incustodito.
unauthorized *adj* non auto-
rizzato.

unavailable *adj* non disponibile.

unavoidable *adj* inevitabile.

unaware *adj* ignaro.

unawares *adv* alla sprovvista.

unbalanced *adj* squilibrato.

unbearable *adj* insopportabile.

unbecoming *adj* indecoroso, sconveniente.

unbelievable *adj* incredibile.

unbend *vi* distendersi; * *vt* raddrizzare.

unbiased *adj* imparziale.

unblemished *adj* senza macchia.

unblock *vt* sbloccare.

unborn *adj* non ancora nato.

unbounded *adj* sconfinato.

unbreakable *adj* infrangibile.

unbroken *adj* intatto; ininterrotto; insuperato.

unbutton *vt* sbottonare.

uncalled-for *adj* fuori luogo.

uncanny *adj* sconcertante.

unceasing *adj* incessante.

unceremonious *adj* brusco.

uncertain *adj* incerto.

uncertainty *n* incertezza *f*.

unchallenged *adj* incontestato.

unchanged *adj* invariato.

unchanging *adj* immutabile.

uncharitable *adj* severo.

unchecked *adj* incontrollato.

unchristian *adj* poco cristiano.

uncivil *adj* incivile.

uncivilized *adj* selvaggio.

uncle *n* zio *m*.

uncombed *adj* spettinato.

uncomfortable *adj* scomodo.

uncomfortably *adv* in modo disagevole.

uncommon *adj* insolito.

uncompromising *adj* assoluto.

unconcerned *adj* tranquillo.

unconditional *adj* incondizionato.

unconfirmed *adj* non confermato.

unconnected *adj* sconnesso.

unconquerable *adj* invincibile.

unconscious *adj*, privo di sensi; inconscio; * *n* inconscio *m*

unconstrained *adj* disinvolto.

uncontrollable *adj* incontrollabile.

unconventional *adj* non convenzionale.

unconvincing *adj* non convincente.

uncooked *adj* crudo.

uncork *vt* stappare.

uncorrected *adj* non riveduto.

uncouple *vt* sganciare.

uncouth *adj* rozzo.

uncover *vt* scoprire.

unction *n* unzione *f*.

uncultivated *adj* incolto.

uncut *adj* non tagliato.

undamaged *adj* intatto.

undaunted *adj* imperterrito.

undecided *adj* indeciso.

undefeated *adj* imbattuto.

undefined *adj* indefinito.

undeniable *adj* innegabile.

under *prep* sotto; secondo; * *adv* sotto.

under-age *adj* minorenne.

undercarriage *n* carello *m* d'atterraggio.

undercharge *vt* far pagare di meno.

undercoat *n* prima *f* mano.

undercover *adj* clandestino.

undercurrent *n* vena *f* nascosta.

undercut *vt* vendere a minor prezzo di.

underdeveloped *adj* sottosviluppato.

underdog *n* perdente *m*.

underdone *adj* poco cotto.

underestimate *vt* sotto valutare.

underexposed *adj* sottoesposto.

underfed *adj* denutrito.
undergo *vt* subire.
undergraduate *n* studente *m* universitario.
underground *n* (rail) metropolitana *f*; controcultura *f*; * *adj* sotterraneo.
undergrowth *n* sottobosco *m*.
underhand *adj* equivoco.
underlie *vt* essere alla base di.
underline *vt* sottolineare.
undermine *vt* minare.
underneath *prep*, *adv* sotto.
undernourished *adj* denutrito.
underpaid *adj* mal pagato.
underpants *npl* slip *m*.
underpass *n* sottopassaggio *m*.
underplay *vt* minimizzare.
underprivileged *adj* svantaggiato.
underrate *vt* sottovalutare.
undersecretary *n* sottosegretario *m*.
underside *n* parte *f* di sotto.
undersigned *adj*, *n* sottoscritto *m*.
understand *vt* capire; credere; * *vi* capire.
understandable *adj* comprensibile.
understanding *n* comprensione *f*; intesa *f*; * *adj* comprensivo.
understate *vt* sminuire.
understatement *n* minimizzare *m*.
understudy *n* doppio *m*.
undertake *vt* assumersi.
undertaker *n* impresario *m* di pompe funebri.
undertaking *n* impresa *f*; assicurazione *f*.
undervalue *vt* sottovalutare.
underwater *adj* subacqueo; sottomarino.
underwear *n* biancheria *f* intima.

underweight *adj* sottopeso.
underworld *n* malavita *f*.
underwrite *vt* sottoscrivere.
underwriter *n* assicuratore *m*.
undeserved *adj* immeritato.
undeserving *adj* indegno.
undesirable *adj* sgradevole.
undetermined *adj* indeterminato.
undigested *adj* non digerito.
undiminished *adj* non diminuito.
undisciplined *adj* indisciplinato.
undisguised *adj* palese.
undismayed *adj* imperterrito.
undisputed *adj* incontrastato.
undisturbed *adj* imperturbato.
undivided *adj* completo.
undo *vt* disfare; slacciare.
undoing *n* rovina *f*.
undoubted *adj* indubbio.
undress *vi* spogliare.
undue *adj* esagerato.
undulating *adj* ondulato.
unduly *adv* eccessivamente.
undying *adj* imperituro.
unearth *vt* dissotterrare.
unearthly *adj* innaturale.
uneasy *adj* inquieto; precario.
uneconomic *adj* antieconomico.
uneducated *adj* incolto.
unemotional *adj* impassibile.
unemployed *adj*, *n* disoccupato *m*.
unemployment *n* disoccupazione *f*.
unending *adj* interminabile.
unendurable *adj* insopportabile.
unenviable *adj* poco invidiabile.
unequal *adj* disuguale.
unequalled *adj* insuperato.
unequivocal *adj* inequivocabile.
unerring *adj* infallibile.

uneven *adj* ineguale; accidentato.

unexpected *adj* inatteso.

unexplained *adj* inspiegato.

unexplored *adj* inesplorato.

unfailing *adj* immancabile.

unfair *adj* ingiusto.

unfaithful *adj* infedele.

unfaithfulness *n* infedeltà *f*.

unfaltering *adj* risoluto.

unfamiliar *adj* sconosciuto.

unfashionable *adj* fuori moda.

unfasten *vt* slacciare.

unfathomable *adj* insondabile.

unfavourable *adj* sfavorevole.

unfeeling *adj* insensibile.

unfinished *adj* incompiuto.

unfit *adj* inadatto.

unflagging *adj* instancabile.

unfold *vt* spiegare; * *vi* schiudersi.

unforeseeable *adj* imprevedibile.

unforeseen *adj* imprevisto.

unforgettable *adj* indimenticabile.

unforgiveable *adj* imperdonabile.

unfortunate *adj* sfortunato.

unfounded *adj* infondato.

unfriendly *adj* ostile.

unfruitful *adj* infruttuoso.

unfurnished *adj* non ammobiliato.

ungainly *adj* goffo.

ungovernable *adj* ingovernabile.

ungrateful *adj* ingrato.

unhappily *adv* sfortunatamente.

unhappiness *n* infelicità *f*.

unhappy *adj* infelice.

unharmed *adj* illeso.

unhealthy *adj* malsano; malaticcio.

unheard-of *adj* inaudito.

unheeding *adj* disattento.

unhinge *vi* scardinare.

unhook *vt* sganciare.

unhoped-for *adj* insperato.

unhurt *adj* sano e salvo.

unhygienic *adj* insalubre.

unicorn *n* unicorno *m*.

unification *n* unificazione *f*.

uniform *adj* uniforme; * *n* divisa *f*.

uniformity *n* uniformità *f*.

unify *vt* unire; unificare.

unilateral *adj* unilaterale.

unimaginable *adj* inimmaginabile.

unimpaired *adj* intatto.

unpeachable *adj* irreprensibile.

unimportant *adj* trascurabile.

uninformed *adj* non al corrente.

uninhabitable *adj* inabitabile.

uninhabited *adj* disabitato.

uninjured *adj* incolume.

unintelligible *adj* inintelligibile.

unintentional *adj* involontario.

uninterested *adj* indifferente.

uninteresting *adj* privo d'interesse.

uninterrupted *adj* ininterrotto.

uninvited *adj* non invitato.

union *n* unione *f*; sindacato *m*.

unionist *n* sindacalista *m*.

unionize *vt* sindacalizzare.

unique *adj* unico; ~ly *adv* eccezionalmente.

unison *n* unisono *m*.

unit *n* unità *f*; reparto *m*.

unite *vt* unire; unificare.

united *adj* unito.

unity *n* unità *f*; unione *f*.

universal *adj* universale.

universe *n* universo *m*.

university *n* università *f*.

unjust *adj* ingiusto.

unjustified *adj* ingiustificato.

unkempt *adj* scarmigliato.

unkind *adj* scortese; crudele.

unknowingly *adv* inconsapevolmente.

unknown *adj* sconosciuto, ignoto.

unlawful *adj* illecito.

unleash *vt* liberare.

unless *conj* a meno che.

unlicensed *adj* senza licenza.

unlike *adj* dissimile.

unlikely *adj* improbabile; inverosimile.

unlikelihood *n* improbabilità *f*.

unlimited *adj* illimitato.

unlined *adj* sfoderato.

unload *vt, vi* scaricare.

unlock *vt* aprire.

unloveable *adj* antipatico.

unluckily *adv* purtroppo.

unlucky *adj* sfortunato; disgraziato.

unmanageable *adj* intrattabile; poco maneggevole.

unmarried *adj* scapolo (man); nubile (woman).

unmask *vt* smascherare.

unmentionable *adj* innominabile.

unmerciful *adj* spietato.

unmerited *adj* immeritato.

unmindful *adj* dimentico.

unmistakable *adj* inconfondibile.

unmitigated *adj* assoluto.

unmotivated *adj* immotivato.

unmoved *adj* indifferente.

unnamed *adj* anonimo.

unnatural *adj* innaturale.

unnecessary *adj* non necessario.

unneighbourly *adj* non da buon vicino.

unnoticed *adj* inosservato.

unobserved *adj* inosservato.

unobtainable *adj* introvabile.

unobstrusive *adj* discreto.

unoccupied *adj* libero; vuoto.

unoffending *adj* inoffensivo.

unofficial *adj* ufficioso.

unorganized *adj* disorganizzato.

unorthodox *adj* eterodosso.

unpack *vt* disfare.

unpaid *adj* non retribuito.

unpalatable *adj* immangiabile.

unparalleled *adj* senza pari.

unpleasant *adj* spiacevole.

unpleasantness *n* sgradevolezza *f*.

unplug *vt* staccare.

unpolished *adj* non lucidato.

unpopular *adj* impopolare.

unpractised *adj* inesercitato.

unprecedented *adj* senza precedenti.

unpredictable *adj* imprevedibile.

unprejudiced *adj* obiettivo.

unprepared *adj* impreparato.

unproductive *adj* improduttivo.

unprofitable *adj* non redditizio.

unpronounceable *adj* impronunciabile.

unprotected *adj* indifeso.

unpublished *adj* inedito.

unpunished *adj* impunito.

unqualified *adj* non qualificato; incondizionato.

unquestionable *adj* indiscutibile.

unquestioned *adj* indiscusso.

unravel *vt* dipanare.

unreadable *adj* illeggibile.

unreal *adj* irreale.

unrealistic *adj* illusorio.

unreasonable *adj* irrazionale; irragionevole.

unrecognizable *adj* irriconoscibile.

unrefined *adj* greggio.

unrelated *adj* senza nesso; non imparentato.

unrelenting *adj* implacabile.

unreliable *adj* non attendibile.

unremitting *adj* incessante.
unrepeatable *adj* irrepetibile.
unrepentant *adj* impenitente.
unrepresentative *adj* atipico.
unreserved *adj* incondizionato.
unrest *n* agitazione *f*.
unrestrained *adj* sfrenato.
unripe *adj* acerbo.
unrivalled *adj* senza pari.
unroll *vt* srotolare.
unruly *adj* indisciplinato.
unsafe *adj* pericoloso.
unsaleable *adj* invendibile.
unsatisfactory *adj* poco soddisfacente; insufficiente.
unsatisfying *adj* insoddisfacente.
unsavoury *adj* poco raccomandabile.
unscathed *adj* indenne.
unscrew *vt* svitare.
unscrupulous *adj* senza scrupoli.
unseemly *adj* indecoroso.
unseen *adj* inosservato.
unselfish *adj* altruista.
unsettle *vt* scombussolare.
unsettled *adj* instabile.
unshakable *adj* irremovibile.
unshaken *adj* non scosso.
unshrinkable *adj* irrestringibile.
unsightly *adj* non bello a vedersi.
unskilful *adj* inesperto.
unskilled *adj* non specializzato.
unsociable *adj* poco socievole.
unsold *adj* invenduto.
unsound *adj* cagionevole.
unspeakable *adj* indicibile.
unstable *adj* instabile.
unsteady *adj* vacillante.
unstudied *adj* spontaneo.
unsuccessful *adj* non riuscito.
unsuitable *adj* inadatto; inopportuno.
unsure *adj* incerto.

unswerving *adj* ferreo.
unsympathetic *adj* non comprensivo.
untamed *adj* indomato.
untangle *vt* sbrogliare.
untapped *adj* non sfruttato.
untenable *adj* insostenibile.
unthinkable *adj* impensabile.
unthinking *adj* irriguardoso.
untidiness *n* disordine *m*.
untidy *adj* disordinato.
untie *vt* sciogliere.
until *prep* fino a; * *conj* finché.
untimely *adj* prematuro.
untiring *adj* infaticabile.
untold *adj* mai rivelato.
untouchable *n* paria *m*.
untouched *adj* incolume; non toccato.
untoward *adj* increscioso.
untranslatable *adj* intraducibile.
untried *adj* non messo alla prova.
untroubled *adj* calmo.
untrue *adj* falso.
untrustworthy *adj* indegno di fiducia.
untruth *n* falsità *f*.
unused *adj* inutilizzato.
unusual *adj* insolito.
unvaried *adj* monotono.
unveil *vt* svelare.
unwavering *adj* incrollabile.
unwelcome *adj* non gradito.
unwell *adj* indisposto.
unwieldy *adj* poco maneggevole.
unwilling *adj* riluttante; ~ly *adv* malvolentieri.
unwind *vt* srotolare; * *vi* distendersi.
unwise *adj* avventato.
unwitting *adj* involontario.
unworkable *adj* inattuabile.
unworthy *adj* indegno.
unwrap *vt* scartare.
unwritten *adj* tacito.

up *adv* su.
upbringing *n* educazione *f*.
update *vt* aggiornare.
upheaval *n* sconvolgimento *m*.
uphill *adj* in salita; faticoso.
uphold *vt* sostenere.
upholstery *n* tappezzeria *f*.
upkeep *n* manutenzione *f*.
uplift *vt* sollevare.
upper *adj* superiore; * *n* tomaia *f*.
upper-class *adj* dell'alta borghesia.
upper-hand *n* (fig) vantaggio *m*.
uppermost *adj* dominante.
upright *adj* ritto; retto; * *adv* diritto; * *n* montante *m*.
uprising *n* insurrezione *f*.
uproar *n* trambusto *m*.
uproarious *adj* fragoroso.
uproot *vt* sradicare.
upset *vt* rovesciare; turbare; scombussolare; * *n* contrattempo *m*; * *adj* turbato; scombussolato; offeso.
upshot *n* risultato *m*.
upside-down *adv* sottosopra; * *adj* capovolto.
upstairs *adv* di sopra; * *n* piano *m* di sopra.
upstanding *adj* aitante.
upstart *n* parvenu *m*.
uptight *adj* teso.
up-to-date *adj* aggiornato; attuale.
upturn *n* ripresa *f*.
upward *adj* verso l'alto; ~s *adv* verso l'alto; in su.

uranium *n* uranio *m*.
urban *adj* urbano.
urbane *adj* civile.
urchin *n* monello *m*.
urge *vt* insistere; **to ~ on** spronare; * *n* impulso *m*.
urgency *n* urgenza *f*.
urgent *adj* urgente; pressante.
urinal *n* vespasiano *m*.
urinate *vi* orinare.
urine *n* orina *f*.
urn *n* urna *f*.
us *pron* noi; ci.
usable *adj* utilizzabile.
usage *n* usanza *f*; uso *m*.
use *n* uso *m*; impiego *m*; * *vt* usare; adoperare.
used *adj* usato.
useful *adj* utile.
usefulness *n* utilità *f*.
useless *adj* inutile.
uselessness *n* inutilità *f*.
user-friendly *adj* di facile uso.
usher *n* usciere *m*.
usherette *n* maschera *f*.
usual *adj* solito; ~ly *adv* di solito
usurer *n* usuraio *m*.
usurp *vt* usurpare.
usury *n* usura *f*.
utensil *n* utensile *m*.
uterus *n* utero *m*.
utility *n* utilità *f*.
utilize *vt* utilizzare.
utmost *n* massimo *m*; estremo *m*; * *adj* totale.
utter *adj vt* pronunciare.
utterly *adv* completamente.

V

vacancy *n* vuoto *m*; stanza *f* libera.
vacant *adj* libero; vacuo.
vacate *vt* lasciare.
vacation *n* vacanza *f*.

vaccinate *vt* vaccinare.
vaccination *n* vaccinazione *f*.
vaccine *n* vaccino *m*.
vacillate *vt* vacillare.
vacuous *adj* vacuo.

vacuum n vuoto m.
vacuum flask n termos m.
vagabond n vagabondo m.
vagina n vagina f.
vagrant n vagabondo m.
vague adj vago.
vain adj vano; vanitoso.
valet n cameriere m personale.
valiant adj coraggioso.
valid adj valido.
validate vt convalidare.
validity n validità f.
valley n valle f.
valour n coraggio m.
valuable adj prezioso; ~s npl preziosi mpl.
valuation n valutazione f; stima f.
value n valore m; * vt valutare.
valued adj stimato.
valve n valvola f.
vampire n vampiro m.
van n furgone m.
vandal n vandalo m.
vandalism n vandalismo m.
vandalize vt vandalizzare.
vanguard n avanguardia f.
vanilla n vaniglia f.
vanish vi svanire.
vanity n vanità f.
vanquish vt sconfiggere.
vantage point n punto m d'osservazione.
vapid adj scipito.
vaporize vt vaporizzare.
vapour n vapore m.
variable adj variabile.
variance n discordanza f.
variant n variante f.
variation n variazione f.
varicose vein n vena f varicosa.
varied adj vario.
variety n varietà f.
various adj vario.
varnish n vernice f trasparente.
vary vt, vi variare.
vase n vaso m.

vasectomy n vasectomia f.
vaseline n vaselina f.
vast adj vasto.
VAT n IVA.
vat n tino m.
vault n volta f; * vt saltare con un balzo.
veal n vitello m.
veer vi virare.
vegetable n ortaggio m; ~s npl verdure fpl.
vegetable garden n orto m.
vegetarian adj, n vegetariano m.
vegetate vi vegetare.
vegetation n vegetazione f.
vehemence n veemenza f.
vehement adj veemente.
vehicle n veicolo m.
veil n velo m; * vt velare.
vein n vena f.
velocity n velocità f.
velvet n velluto m.
venal adj venale.
vendetta n vendetta f.
vending machine n distributore m automatico.
vendor n venditore m.
veneer n impiallacciatura f.
venerable adj venerabile.
venerate vt venerare.
veneration n venerazione f.
venereal adj venereo.
vengeance n vendetta f.
venial adj veniale.
venison n carne f di cervo.
venom n veleno m.
venomous adj velenoso.
vent n presa f d'aria; spacco m; * vt sfogare.
ventilate vt ventilare.
ventilation n ventilazione f.
ventilator n ventilatore m.
ventriloquist n ventriloquo m.
venture n impresa f; vt rischiare.
venue n luogo m d'incontro.
veranda(h) n veranda f.

verb *n* verbo *m*.
verbal *adj* verbale.
verbatim *adj*, *adv* parola per parola.
verbose *adj* verboso.
verdict *n* verdetto *m*.
verge *n* bordo *m*; orlo *m*.
verification *n* verifica *f*.
verify *vt* verificare.
veritable *adj* vero.
vermin *n* animali *mpl* nocivi.
vermouth *n* vermut *m*.
versatile *adj* versatile.
verse *n* verso *m*; poesia *f*.
versed *adj* pratico.
version *n* versione *f*.
versus *prep* contro.
vertebra *n* vertebra *f*.
vertebrate *adj*, *n* vertebrato *m*.
vertex *n* vertice *m*.
vertical *adj*, *n* verticale *f*.
vertigo *n* vertigine *f*.
verve *n* verve *f*.
very *adj* stesso; solo; * *adv* molto.
vessel *n* vascello *m*; recipiente *m*.
vest *n* canottiera *f*.
vestibule *n* atrio *m*.
vestige *n* vestigio *m*.
vestment *n* paramento *m*.
vestry *n* sagrestia *f*.
vet *vt* esaminare; * *n* veterinario *m*.
veteran *n* veterano *m*.
veterinary *adj* veterinario; * *n*
~ **surgeon** veterinario *m*.
veto *n* veto *m*; * *vt* porre il veto.
vex *vt* irritare.
vexed *adj* irritato.
via *prep* attraverso; via.
viable *adj* attuabile.
viaduct *n* viadotto *m*.
vial *n* fiala *f*.
vibrant *adj* vibrante.
vibrate *vi* vibrare.
vibration *n* vibrazione *f*.
vicar *n* pastore *m*.

vicarage *n* canonica *f*.
vicarious *adj* sofferto al posto di un altro.
vice *n* vizio *m*; morsa *f*.
vice-chairman *n* vicepresidente *m*.
vice-chancellor *n* rettore *m*.
vice versa *adv* viceversa.
vicinity *n* vicinanze *fpl*.
vicious *adj* maligno.
victim *n* vittima *f*.
victimize *vt* perseguitare ingiustamente.
victor *n* vincitore *m*.
victorious *adj* vittorioso.
victory *n* vittoria *f*.
video *n* video *m*.
videotape *n* videotape *m*.
vie *vi* contendersi.
view *n* vista *f*; veduta *f*; punta *f* di vista; * *vt* guardare; vedere.
viewer *n* telespettatore *m*.
viewfinder *n* mirino *m*.
viewpoint *n* posizione *f*.
vigil *n* veglia *f*.
vigilance *n* vigilanza *f*.
vigilant *adj* vigile.
vigorous *adj* vigoroso.
vigour *n* vigore *m*.
vile *adj* detestabile.
vilify *vt* diffamare.
villa *n* villa *f*.
village *n* paese *m*.
villager *n* abitante *m* di paese.
villain *n* mascalzone *m*.
vindicate *vt* scagionare.
vindication *n* scagionare *m*.
vindictive *adj* vendicativo.
vine *n* vite *f*.
vinegar *n* aceto *m*.
vineyard *n* vigneto *m*, vigna *f*.
vintage *adj* annata.
vinyl *n* vinile *m*.
viola *n* (*mus*) viola *f*.
violate *vt* violare.
violation *n* violazione *f*.
violence *n* violenza *f*.
violent *adj* violento.

violet *n* (*bot*) viola *f*; violetto *m*.
violin *n* violino *m*.
violinist *n* violinista *m/f*.
violoncello *n* violoncello *m*.
viper *n* vipera *f*.
virgin *adj*, *n* vergine *f*.
virginity *n* verginità *f*.
Virgo *n* Vergine *f*.
virile *adj* virile.
virility *n* virilità *f*.
virtual *adj* effettivo; **~ly** *adv* praticamente.
virtue *n* virtù *f*.
virtuous *adj* virtuoso.
virulent *adj* virulento.
virus *n* virus *m*.
visa *n* visto *m*.
vis-a-vis *prep* rispetto a.
viscous *adj* viscoso.
visibility *n* visibilità *f*.
visible *adj* visibile.
vision *n* vista *f*; visione *f*.
visit *vt* visitare; * *n* visita *f*.
visiting hours *npl* orario *m* delle visite.
visitor *n* ospite *m/f*; visitatore *m*.
visor *n* visiera *f*.
vista *n* vista *f*.
visual *adj* visivo.
visual aid *n* sussidi *mpl* visivi.
visualize *vt* immaginare.
vital *adj* vitale; fattale.
vitality *n* vitalità *f*.
vitamin *n* vitamina *f*.
vitiate *vt* guastare.
vitriolic *adj* caustico.
vivacious *adj* vivace.
vivid *adj* vivido.
vivisection *n* vivisezione *f*.
vocabulary *n* vocabolario *m*.
vocal *adj* vocale.

vocation *n* vocazione *f*; **~al** *adj* professionale.
vocative *adj* (*gr*) vocativo.
vociferous *adj* rumoroso.
vodka *n* vodka *f*.
vogue *n* moda *f*.
voice *n* voce *f*; * *vt* esprimere.
void *adj* nullo; * *n* vuoto *m*.
volatile *adj* volatile.
volcanic *adj* vulcanico.
volcano *n* vulcano *m*.
volition *n* volizione *f*.
volley *n* raffica *f*.
volleyball *n* pallavolo *f*.
volt *n* volt *m*.
voltage *n* voltaggio *m*.
voluble *adj* loquace.
volume *n* volume *m*.
voluntarily *adv* spontaneamente.
voluntary *adj* volontario.
volunteer *n* volontario *m*; * *vi* offrirsi.
voluptuous *adj* voluttuoso.
vomit *vt*, *vi* vomitare; * *n* vomito *m*.
voracious *adj* vorace.
vortex *n* vortice *m*.
vote *n* votazione *f*; voto *m*; * *vt*, *vi* votare.
voter *n* elettore *m*.
voting *n* votazione *f*.
vouch *vi* garantire.
voucher *n* buono *m*.
vow *n* voto *m*; * *vi* giurare.
vowel *n* vocale *f*.
voyage *n* viaggio *m* per mare.
vulgar *adj* volgare.
vulgarity *n* volgarità *f*.
vulnerable *adj* vulnerabile.
vulture *n* avvoltoio *m*.

W

wad *n* batuffolo *m*; tampone *m*.
waddle *vi* camminare come una papera.
wade *vi* camminare a fatica.
wafer *n* wafer *m*; (*relig*) ostia *f*.
waffle *vi* ciarlare; * *n* cialda *f*.

waft vt portare; * vi diffondersi.

wag vi scodinzolare; * vt dimenare.

wage vt intraprendere; ~s stipendio m.

wage earner n salariato m.

wager n scommessa f; * vt scommettere.

waggle vt dimenare.

wagon n carro m; vagone m.

wail n gemito m; urlo m; * vi gemere.

waist n vita f.

waistcoat n panciotto m.

waistline n vita f.

wait vt, vi aspettare; vi aspettare; servire; * n attesa f.

waiter n cameriere m.

waiting list n lista f d'attesa.

waiting room n sala f d'attesa.

waive vt rinunciare a.

wake vi svegliarsi; * vt svegliare; * n (mar) scia f; veglia f.

walk vt percorrere; * vi camminare; passeggiare; * n passeggiata f; andatura f.

walker n camminatore m.

walkie-talkie n walkie-talkie m.

walking n camminare m; * adj a piedi.

walking stick n bastone m da passeggio.

walkout n abbandono m.

walkover n vittoria f facile.

walkway n passaggio m pedonale.

wall n muro m; parete f.

walled adj fortificato.

wallet n portafoglio m.

wallflower n (bot) violacciocca f.

wallow vi rotolarsi.

wallpaper n carta f da pareti.

walnut n noce f; (tree) noce m.

walrus n tricheco m.

waltz n valzer m.

wan adj pallido.

wand n bacchetta f.

wander vi gironzolare; * vt girovagare per.

wane vi calare.

wanker n uomo m insulso; masturbatore m.

want vt volere; desiderare; * vi mancare; * mancanza f; miseria f; bisogno m.

wanting adj privo.

wanton adj lascivo.

war n guerra f.

ward n corsia f.

wardrobe n guardaroba m.

warehouse n deposito m.

warfare n arte f bellica.

warhead n testata f.

warily adj cautamente.

wariness n cautela f.

warm adj caldo; sentito; * vt scaldare; * vi to ~ up scaldarsi.

warm-hearted adj affettuoso.

warmth n calore m.

warn vt avvertire.

warning n avvertimento m.

warning light spia f luminosa.

warp vt deformare; * n curvatura f.

warrant n mandato m; giustificazione f.

warranty n garanzia f.

warren n tana f.

warrior n guerriero m.

warship n nave f da guerra.

wart n porro m.

wary adj diffidente.

wash vt lavare; * vi lambire; trascinare; lavarsi; * n lavata f.

washable adj lavabile.

washbasin n lavabo m.

washer n rondella f.

washing n lavaggio m; bucato m.

washing machine n lavatrice f.

washing-up n lavare i piatti.
wash-out n disastro m.
washroom n gabinetto m.
wasp n vespa f.
wastage n spreco m.
waste vt sprecare; perdere; * n spreco m; perdita f; * adj di scarto;
wasteful adj sprecone; dispendioso.
waste paper n carta f straccia.
waste pipe n tubazione f di scarico.
watch n orologio m; sorveglianza f; guardia f; * vt, vi guardare.
watchdog n cane m da guardia.
watchful adj attento.
watchmaker n orologiaio m.
watchman n guardiano m.
watchtower n torre f di guardia.
watchword n parola f d'ordine.
water n acqua f; * vt innaffiare.
water closet n gabinetto m.
watercolour n acquerello m.
waterfall n cascata f.
water-heater n scaldabagno m.
watering-can n annaffiatoio m.
waterlilly n ninfea f.
water line n linea f di galleggiamento.
waterlogged adj impregnato d'acqua; inzuppato.
water main n conduttura f dell'acqua.
watermark n filigrana f.
watermelon n anguria f, cocomero m.
watershed n spartiacque m.
watertight adj stagno; inattaccabile.
waterworks npl impianto m idrico.
watery adj acquoso.
watt n watt m.
wave n onda f, ondata f; cenno

m; * vt sventolare; salutare con un cenno della mano; * vi gesticolare.
wavelength n lunghezza f d'onda.
waver vi oscillare.
wavering adj vacillante.
wavy adj ondulato.
wax n cera f; * vt dare la cera a.
wax paper n carta f oleata.
waxwork n statua f di cera; ~s n museo m delle cere.
way n strada f; direzione f; modo m; abitudine f; * vt to give ~ dare la precedenza.
waylay vt fermare.
wayward adj ribelle.
we pron noi.
weak adj debole.
weaken vt indebolire; allentare; * vi indebolirsi.
weakling n mingherlino m.
weakness n debolezza f.
wealth n ricchezza f.
wealthy adj ricco.
wean vt svezzare.
weapon n arma f.
wear vt portare; indossare; consumare; to ~ away consumarsi; to ~ down fiaccare; to ~ out logorare; * vi durare; to ~ off non fare più effetto; * n uso m; logoramento m; usura f; abbigliamento m.
weariness n stanchezza f.
wearisome adj estenuante.
weary adj stanco.
weasel n donnola f.
weather n tempo m: * vt superare.
weather-beaten adj segnato dalle intemperie.
weather forecast n previsioni fpl del tempo.
weatherman n meteorologo m.
weathervane n segnavento m.
weave vt, vi tessere; intrecciare; * n trama f.

weaving n tessitura f.

web n tela f; ragnatela f.

wed vt sposare.

wedding n matrimonio m; nozze fpl.

wedding ring n fede f.

wedge n zeppa f; cuneo m.

Wednesday n mercoledì m.

wee adj piccolo.

weed n erbaccia f.

weedkiller n diserbante m.

weedy adj (fam) allampanato.

week n settimana f; a ~ today oggi a otto.

weekday n giorno m feriale.

weekend n weekend m; fine settimana m.

weekly adj, n settimanale m.

weep vt, vi piangere.

weeping willow n salice m piangente.

weigh vt, vi pesare.

weight n peso m.

weightlifter n pesista m.

weighty adj importante.

weird adj bizzarro.

welcome adj gradito, benvenuto; * n accoglienza f; benvenuto m; * vt accogliere.

weld vt saldare; * n saldatura f.

welfare n bene m; benessere m.

welfare state n stato m assistenziale.

well n pozzo m; * vi sgorgare; * adj, adv bene; as ~ anche.

well-behaved adj che si comporta bene.

well-being n benessere m.

well-bred adj beneducato.

well-built adj ben fatto; ben costruito.

well-deserved adj meritato.

well-disposed adj ben disposto.

well-known adj noto.

well-meaning adj ben intenzionato.

well-off adj benestante.

well-to-do adj abbiente.

well-wisher n ammiratore m.

west adj ovest, occidentale; * n ovest m; * adv verso ovest.

westerly adj di ponente.

western adj occidentale; * n (film) western m.

westward adj ovest.

wet adj bagnato; umido; piovoso; * n umidità f; * vt bagnare.

wet-nurse n balia f.

whack vt dare una manata a; * n colpo m.

whale n balena f.

wharf n banchina f.

what pron cosa; * adj che, quale.

whatever pron qualsiasi cosa.

wheat n grano m, frumento m.

wheedle vt blandire.

wheel n ruota f; * vi roteare.

wheelbarrow n carriola f.

wheelchair n sedia f a rotelle.

wheeler-dealer n trafficone m.

wheeze vi ansimare.

when adv, conj quando.

whenever adv in qualsiasi momento.

where adv, conj dove.

whereabouts adv dove.

whereas conj mentre.

whereby adv per cui.

wherever conj dovunque.

whereupon adv al che.

wherewithal npl mezzi mpl.

whet vt stimolare.

whether conj se.

which adj, pron quale; * rel pron che.

whiff n zaffata f.

while n tempo m; * conj mentre.

whim n capriccio m.

whimper vi piagnucolare; * n piagnucolio m.

whimsical adj fantasioso.

whine vi guaire; * n guaito m.

whinny *vi* nitrire.

whip *n* frusta *f*; * *vt* frustare.

whipped cream *n* panna *f* montata.

whip-round *n* colletta *f*.

whirl *vi* volteggiare; * vortice *m*.

whirlpool *n* vortice *m*.

whirlwind *n* tromba *f* d'aria.

whisk *n* frullino *m*; * *vt* frullare.

whiskers *npl* baffi *mpl*.

whisky *n* whisky *m*.

whisper *vt, vi* bisbigliare; * *n* bisbiglio *m*.

whispering *n* bisbiglio *m*.

whistle *vi* fischiare; * *vt* fischiettare; * *n* fischio *m*.

Whit *n* Pentecoste *f*.

white *adj, n* bianco *m*.

white elephant *n* oggetto *m* costoso ma inutile.

white-hot *adj* incandescente.

white lie *n* bugia *f* pietosa.

whiten *vt* sbiancare.

whiteness *n* candore *m*.

whitewash *n* bianco *m* di calce; * *vt* imbiancare.

whiting *n* merlango *m*.

whitish *adj* biancastro.

whittle away *vt* ridurre.

who *pron* chi; * *rel pron* che.

whoever *pron* chiunque.

whole *adj* intero; tutto; completo; * *n* tutto *m*.

wholehearted *adj* incondizionato.

wholemeal *adj* integrale.

wholesale *adj, adv* all'ingrosso.

wholesaler *n* grossista *m/f*.

wholesome *adj* salubre.

wholly *adv* completamente.

whom *pron* chi; * *rel, dir, obj* che.

whooping cough *n* pertosse *f*.

whore *n* puttana *f*.

whose *pron* di chi; * *rel pron* il cui.

why *adv, conj* perché.

wick *n* stoppino *m*.

wicked *adj* cattivo, malvagio, perfido.

wickedness *n* cattiveria *f*.

wicker *n* vimine *m*; * *adj* di vimine.

wide *adj* largo; ~**ly** *adv* molto.

wide-angle *adj* grandangolare.

wide-awake *adj* completamente sveglio.

widen *vt* ampliare.

wide-open *adj* spalancato.

widespread *adj* diffuso.

widow *n* vedova *f*.

widower *n* vedovo *m*.

width *n* larghezza *f*.

wield *vt* maneggiare.

wife *n* moglie *f*.

wig *n* parrucca *f*.

wiggle *vt* ancheggiare.

wild *adj* selvatico; selvaggio; furibondo.

wilderness *n* deserto *m*; giungla *f*.

wild life *n* natura *f*.

wildly *adv* violentemente.

wilful *adj* ostinato.

wilfulness *n* ostinazione *f*.

wiliness *n* scaltrezza *f*.

will *n* volontà *f*; testamento *m*; * *vt* volere; pregare; * *vi* volere.

willing *adj* volenteroso; disposto.

willingness *n* disponibilità *f*.

willow *n* salice *m*.

willpower *n* forza *f* di volontà.

willy-nilly *adv* volente o nolente.

wilt *vt* appassire.

wily *adj* astuto.

win *vt* vincere; conquistare; * *vi* vincere; * *n* vittoria *f*.

wince *vi* rabbrividire.

winch *n* argano *m*.

wind *n* vento *m*; flatulenza *f*; fiato *m*.

wind *vt* avvolgere; caricare.

windbreak *n* frangivento *m*.

windcheater *n* giacca *f* a vento.

windfall *n* bella sorpresa *f*.

winding *adj* serpeggiante.

windmill *n* mulino *m* a vento.

window *n* finestra *f*; vetrina *f*; finestrino *m*.

window box *n* cassetta *f* per i fiori.

window pane *n* vetro *m*.

windowsill *n* davanzale *m*.

windpipe *n* trachea *f*.

windscreen *n* parabrezza *m*.

windscreen washer *n* lavacristallo *m*.

windscreen wiper *n* tergicristallo *m*.

windy *adj* ventoso.

wine *n* vino *m*.

wine cellar *n* cantina *f*.

wine list *n* lista *f* dei vini.

wine-tasting *n* degustazione *f* dei vini.

wing *n* ala *f*.

winged *adj* alato.

winger *n* ala *f*.

wink *vi* ammiccare; * *n* strizzatina *f*.

winner *n* vincitore *m*.

winning post *n* traguardo *m*.

winter *n* inverno *m*; * *adj* invernale.

winter sports *npl* sport *m* invernali.

wintry *adj* invernale.

wipe *vt* pulire; * *n* passata *f*.

wire *n* filo *m*.

wiring *n* impianto *m* elettrico.

wiry *adj* magro e forte.

wisdom *n* saggezza *f*.

wisdom tooth *n* dente *m* del giudizio.

wise *adj* saggio.

wisecrack *n* spiritosaggine *f*.

wish *vt* volere; desiderare; augurare; * *vi* desiderare; * *n* desiderio *m*; augurio *m*.

whisbone *n* forcella *f*.

wishful *adj* desideroso.

wisp *n* filo *m*.

wistful *adj* nostalgico.

wit *n* intelligenza *f*; arguzia *f*.

witch *n* strega *f*.

witchcraft *n* stregoneria *f*.

witchhunt *n* caccia *f* alle streghe.

with *prep* con.

withdraw *vt* ritirare.

withdrawal *n* ritiro *m*; prelievo *m*.

withdrawn *adj* distaccato.

wither *vi* appassire.

withering *adj* raggelante.

withhold *vt* trattenere.

within *prep* dentro; * *adv* all'interno.

without *prep* senza.

withstand *vt* resistere.

witless *adj* stupido.

witness *n* testimone *m*; * *vt* autenticare; * *vi* testimoniare.

witness box *n* banco *m* dei testimoni.

witticism *n* arguzia *f*.

wittingly *adv* consapevolmente.

witty *adj* arguto.

wizard *n* mago *m*.

wobble *vi* traballare.

woe *n* dolore *m*.

woeful *adj* triste.

wolf *n* lupo *m*; mandrillo *m*; * *vt* divorare.

woman *n* donna *f*.

womanly *adj* femminile.

womb *n* utero *m*; grembo *m*.

women's lib *n* movimento *m* femminista.

wonder *n* stupore *m*; miracolo *m*; * *vt* chiedersi; domandarsi; * *vi* stupirsi.

wonderful *adj* stupendo.

won't *abbr* di **will not**.

wont *n* costume *m*.

woo *vt* corteggiare.

wood *n* legno *m*; bosco *m*.

wood alcohol *n* metanolo *m*.

wood carving *n* scultura *f* in legno.

woodcut *n* incisione *f* su legno.

woodcutter *n* tagliaboschi *m*.

wooded *adj* boscoso.

wooden *adj* di legno; impacciato.

woodland *n* zona *f* boscosa.

woodlouse *n* onisco *m*.

woodsman *n* tagliaboschi *m*.

woodpecker *n* picchio *m*.

woodwind *n* legni *mpl*.

woodwork *n* falegnameria *f*.

woodworm *n* tarlo *m*.

wool *n* lana *f*.

woollen *adj* di lana; **~s** *npl* indumenti *mpl* di lana.

woolly *adj* lanoso; vago.

word *n* parola *f*; notizia *f*; * *vt* formulare.

wordblind *adj* dislessico.

wording *n* formulazione *f*.

word processing *n* elaborazione *f* della parola.

word processor *n* word processor *m*.

wordy *adj* verboso.

work *vt* azionare; * *vi* lavorare; funzionare; * *n* lavoro *m*; opera *f*; **~s** *npl* meccanismo *m*; fabbrica *f*.

workable *adj* fattibile.

workaholic *n* lavoratore *m* accanito.

worker *n* lavoratore *m*; operaio *m*.

workforce *n* forza *f* lavoro.

working-class *n* classe *f* operaia.

workman *n* operaio *m*.

workmanship *n* fattura *f*.

workshop *n* officina *f*.

work-shy *adj* indolente.

world *n* mondo *m*; * *adj* mondiale.

worldly *adj* mondano.

worldwide *adj* mondiale.

worm *n* verme *m*; * *vt* insinuarsi.

worn-out *adj* consunto

worried *adj* preoccupato.

worry *vt* preoccupare; importunare; * *n* preoccupazione *f*.

worrying *adj* preoccupante.

worse *adj* peggiore; * *adv* peggio; * *n* peggio *m*.

worsen *vt*, *vi* peggiorare.

worship *n* adorazione *f*; **your ~** Vostro Onore; * *vt* adorare.

worshipper *n* fedele *m/f*.

worst *adj* peggiore; * *adv* peggio; * *n* peggio *m*.

worsted *adj* pettinato.

worth *n* valore *m*.

worthless *adj* inutile.

worthwhile *adj* valido.

worthy *adj* lodevole.

would-be *adj* aspirante.

wound *n* ferita *f*; * *vt* ferire.

wounded *adj* ferito.

wrangle *vi* litigare; * *n* alterco *m*.

wrap *vt* incartare; * *n* scialle *m*.

wrath *n* ira *f*.

wreath *n* ghirlanda *f*.

wreck *n* naufragio *m*; relitto *m*; * *vt* distruggere.

wreckage *n* relitti *mpl*.

wren *n* scricciolo *m*.

wrench *n* strattone *m*; chiave *m*; * *vt* strappare; (*med*) slogare.

wrestle *vi* lottare.

wrestler *n* lottatore *m*.

wrestling *n* lotta *f* libera.

wretch *n* sciagurato *m*.

wretched *adj* disgraziato; pessimo.

wriggle *vt* muovere; * *vi* agitarsi.

wring *vt* strizzare.

wrinkle *n* ruga *f*; * *vt* stropicciare.

wrist *n* polso *m*.

wristband n polsino m.

wristwatch n orologio m da polso.

writ n mandato m.

write vt, vi scrivere; **to ~ down** segnare; **to ~ off** estinguere; **to ~ up** aggiornare.

write-off n perdita f; rottame m.

writer n autore m; scrittore m.

writhe vi contorcersi.

writing n scrivere m; scrittura f.

writing desk n scrivania f.

writing paper n carta f da lettere.

wrong n torto m; male m; * adj sbagliato; ingiusto m; * vt fare torto a.

wrongful adj ingiusto.

wrongly adv erroneamente.

wry adj beffardo.

X

Xmas n Natale m

X-ray n radiografia f.

xylophone n xilofono m

Y

yacht n yacht m.

yachting n velismo m.

Yankee n yankee m.

yard n yard f; cortile m; cantiere m.

yardstick n criterio m.

yarn n filato m; racconto m.

yawn vi sbadigliare; * n sbadiglio m.

yawning n spalancato.

yeah adv sì.

year n anno m; annata f.

yearbook n annuario m.

yearling n yearling m.

yearly adj annuale.

yearn vi bramare.

yearning n desiderio m intenso; * adj bramoso.

yeast n lievito m.

yell vt, vi urlare; * n urlo m.

yellow adj, n giallo m.

yellowish adj giallastro.

yelp vi strillare; * n strillo m.

yen n yen m.

yes adv, n sì m.

yesterday adv ieri.

yet conj ma; tuttavia; * adv già; ancora.

yew n tasso m.

yield vt fruttare; cedere; * vi cedere; * n resa f.

yoga n yoga m.

yoghurt n yogurt m.

yoke n giogo m; sprone m.

yolk n tuorlo m.

yonder adv laggiù.

you pron tu, lei, voi, loro.

young adj giovane; * n prole f; **~er** adj minore.

youngster n giovane m.

your(s) pron tuo, suo, vostro, loro; **~ sincerely** distinti saluti.

yourself pron ti, si, vi, si.

youth n gioventù f; giovane m.

youthful adj giovanile.

youthfulness n giovinezza f.

yuppie n yuppy m/f.

Z

zany *adj* pazzoide.
zeal *n* zelo *m*.
zealous *adj* zelante.
zebra *n* zebra *f*.
zenith *n* zenit *m*.
zero *n* zero *m*.
zest *n* entusiasmo *m*; buccia *f*.
zigzag *n* zigzag *m*.
zinc *n* zinco *m*.
zip *n* cerniera *f*; zip *m*.

zither *n* cetra *f*.
zodiac *n* zodiaco *m*.
zone *n* zona *f*.
zonked *adj* (*fam*) distrutto.
zoo *n* zoo *m*.
zoological *adj* zoologico.
zoologist *n* zoologo *m*.
zoology *n* zoologia *f*.
zoom *vi* zumare; sfrecciare via;
  * *n* zoom *m*.

English and Italian Verbs

Verbi Irregolari en Inglese

	Preterito	Participio passato		Preterito	Participio passato
arise	arose	arisen	do [he/she/it does]		
awake	awoke	awaked,		did	done
		awoken	draw	drew	drawn
be [I am, you/we/they are, he/she/it			dream	dreamed,	dreamed
is, *gerundio* being]				dreamt	dreamt
	was, were	been	drink	drank	drunk
bear	bore	borne	drive	drove	driven
beat	beat	beaten	dwell	dwelt,	dwelt,
become	became	become		dwelled	dwelled
begin	began	begun	eat	ate	eaten
behold	beheld	beheld	fall	fell	fallen
bend	bent	bent	feed	fed	fed
beseech	besought,	besought,	feel	felt	felt
beseeched	beseeched		mistake	mistook	mistaken
beset	beset	beset	fight	fought	fought
bet	bet, betted	bet, betted	find	found	found
bid	bade,bid	bade, bid,	flee	fled	fled
		bidden	fling	flung	flung
bite	bit	bitten	fly [he/she/it flies]		
bleed	bled	bled		flew	flown
bless	blessed	blessed,	forbid	forbade	forbidden
		blest	forecast	forecast	forecast
blow	blew	blown	forget	forgot	forgotten
break	broke	broken	forgive	forgave	forgiven
breed	bred	bred	forsake	forsook	forsaken
bring	brought	brought	forsee	foresaw	foreseen
build	built	built	freeze	froze	frozen
burn	burnt,	burnt,	get	got	got, gotten
	burned	burned	give	gave	given
burst	burst	burst	go [he/she/it goes]		
buy	bought	bought		went	gone
can	could	(been able)	grind	ground	ground
cast	cast	cast	grow	grew	grown
catch	caught	caught	hang	hung,	hung,
choose	chose	chosen		hanged	hanged
cling	cling	clung	have [I/you/we/they have,		
come	came	come	he/she/it has, *gerundio* having]		
cost	cost	cost		had	had
creep	crept	crept	hear	heard	heard
cut	cut	cut	hide	hid	hidden
deal	dealt	dealt	hit	hit	hit
dig	dug	dug	hold	held	held

435

	Preterito	Participio passato		Preterito	Participio passato
hurt	hurt	hurt	shake	shook	shaken
keep	kept	kept	shall	should	-
kneel	knelt,	knelt,	shear	sheared	sheared,
	kneeled	kneeled			shorn
know	knew	known	shed	shed	shed
lay	laid	laid	shine	shone	shone
lead	led	led	shoot	shot	shot
lean	leant,	leant,	show	showed	shown,
	leaned	leaned			showed
leap	leapt,	leapt,	shrink	shrank	shrunk
leaped	leaped		shut	shut	shut
learn	learnt,	learnt	sing	sang	sung
learned	learned		sink	sank	sunk
leave	left	left	sit	sat	sat
lend	lent	lent	slay	slew	slain
let	let	let	sleep	slept	slept
lie [gerundio lying]	lay	slide	slid	slid
lain			sling	slung	slung
light	lighted,	lighted,	smell	smelt,	smelt,
lit	lit		smelled	smelled	
lose	lost	lost	sow	sowed	sown,
make	made	made			sowed
may	might		speak	spoke	spoken
mean	meant	meant	speed	sped,	sped,
meet	met	met		speeded	speeded
mow	mowed	mowed,	spell	spelt,	spelt,
		mown	spelled	spelled	
must	(had to)	(had to)	spend	spent	spent
overcome	overcame	overcome	spill	spilt,	spilt
pay	paid	paid	spilled	spilled	
put	put	put	spin	spun	spun
quit	quitted	quitted	spit	spat	spat
read	read	read	split	split	split
rid	rid	rid	spoil	spoilt,	spoilt,
ride	rode	ridden	spread	spread	spread
ring	rang	rung	spring	sprang	sprung
rise	rose	risen	stand	stood	stood
run	ran	run	steal	stole	stolen
saw	sawed	sawn	stick	stuck	stuck
say	said	said	sting	stung	stung
see	saw	seen	stink	stank	stunk
seek	sought	sought	stride	strode	stridden
sell	sold	sold	strike	struck	struck
send	sent	sent	strive	strove	striven
set	set	set	swear	swore	sworn
sew	sewed	sewn	sweep	swept	swept

	Preterito	Participio passato		Preterito	Participio passato
swell	swelled	swelled, swollen	wake	woke	woken
			wear	wore	worn
swim	swam	swum	weave	wove,	wove,
swing	swung	swung		weaved	weaved
take	took	taken	wed	wed,	wed,
teach	taught	taught		wedded	wedded
tear	tore	torn	weep	wept	wept
tell	told	told	win	won	won
think	thought	thought	wind	wound	wound
throw	threw	thrown	withdraw	withdrew	withdrawn
thrust	thrust	thrust	withhold	withheld	withheld
tread	trod	trodden	withstand	withstood	withstood
understand	understood	understood	wring	wrung	wrung
upset	upset	upset	write	wrote	written

Italian Verbs

Regular Verbs

infinitive

amare	**temere**	**partire (capire)**
to love	*to fear*	*to depart (to understand)* *

gerund

amando	temendo	partendo

past participle

amato	temuto	partito

present indicative

amo	temo	parto (capisco)
ami	temi	parti (capisci)
ama	teme	parte (capisce)
amiamo	temiamo	partiamo
amate	temete	partite
àmano	témono	pàrtono (capìscono)

imperfect indicative

amavo	temevo	partivo
amavi	temevi	partivi
amava	temeva	partiva
amavamo	temevamo	partivamo
amavate	temevate	partivate
amàvano	temévano	partvano

past absolute (or preterit)

amai	teméi (temètti)	partii
amasti	temesti	partisti
amò	temé (temètte)	part
amammo	tememmo	partimmo
amaste	temeste	partiste
amàrono	temérono (temèttero)	partrono

future

amerò	temerò	partirò
amerai	temerai	partirai
amer	temerà	partirà
ameremo	temeremo	partiremo
amerete	temerete	partirete
ameranno	temeranno	partiranno

conditional

amerèi	temerèi	partirèi
amerésti	temerésti	partirésti
amerèbbe	temerèbbe	partirèbbe
amerémmo	temerémmo	partirémmo
ameréste	temeréste	partiréste
amerèbbero	temerèbbero	partirèbbero

imperative

ama	temi	parti (capisci)
ami	tema	parta (capisca)
amiamo	temiamo	partiamo
amate	temete	partite
àmino	témano	pàrtano (capscano)

present subjunctive

ami	tema	parta (capisca)
ami	tema	parta (capisca)
ami	tema	parta (capisca)
amiamo	temiamo	partiamo
amiate	temiate	partiate
àmino	témano	pàrtano (capscano)

imperfect subjunctive

amassi	temessi	partissi
amassi	temessi	partissi
amasse	temesse	partisse
amàssimo	teméssimo	partssimo
amaste	temeste	partiste
amàssero	teméssero	partssero

* Third conjugation verbs with *-isc-* suffix include: agire, ammonire, capire, finire, obbedire, percepire, scolpire, sparire, unire.

Some third conjugation verbs can take either form, with or without the *-isc-* suffix. These include: applaudire, assorbire, inghiottire, mentire, nutrire, tossire.

Auxiliary verbs

infinitive	**avere**	**essere**		avevamo	eravamo
	to have	*to be*		avevate	eravate
				avévano	èrano
gerund	avendo	essendo	*past absolute (or preterit)*		
past participle				ebbi	fui
	avuto	stato		avésti	fosti
present indicative				èbbe	fu
	ho	sono		avémmo	fummo
	hai	sei		avéste	foste
	ha	è		èbbero	fùrono
	abbiamo	siamo	*future*		
	avete	siete		avrò	sarò
	hanno	sono		avrai	sarai
imperfect indicative				avrà	sarà
	avevo	ero		avremo	saremo
	avevi	eri		avrete	sarete
	aveva	era		avranno	saranno

439

conditional

avrèi	sarémmo
avrésti	saréste
avrèbbe	sarèbbero
avrémmo	sarèi
avréste	sarésti
avrèbbero	sarèbbesia

present subjunctive

àbbia	sia
àbbia	sia
àbbia	sia
abbiamo	siamo
abbiate	siate
àbbiano	sano

imperative

abbi	sii
àbbia	sia
abbiamo	siamo
abbiate	siate
àbbiano	siano

imperfect subjunctive

avessi	fossi
avessi	fossi
avesse	fosse
avéssimo	fòssimo
aveste	foste
avéssero	fòssero

Irregular and semi-irregular verbs

accendere (*to light*) *past participle*: acceso; *preterit*: accési, accendesti, accése, accendemmo, accendeste, accésero.

accòrgersi (*to notice*) *past participle*: accòrtosi; *preterit*: mi accòrsi, ti accorgesti, si accòrse, ci accorgemmo, vi accorgeste, si accòrsero; *auxiliary*: essere.

affliggere (*to afflict*) *past participle*: afflitto; *preterit*: afflissi, affliggesti, afflisse, affliggemmo, affliggeste, afflissero.

andare (*to go*) *present indicative*: vado, vai, va, andiamo, andate, vanno; *future*: andrò; *imperative*: va'(vai), vada, andiamo, andate, vadano; *present subjunctive*: vada, vada, vada, andiamo, andate, vadano; *auxiliary*: essere.

apparire (*to appear*) *past participle*: apparso; *present indicative*: appaio, appari, appare, appariamo, apparite, appàiono; *imperfect indicative*: apparivo; *preterit*: apparvi, apparisti, apparve, apparimmo, appariste, appàrvero; *future*: apparirò; *conditional*: apparirei; *imperative*: appari, appaia, appariamo, apparite, appaiano; *present subjunctive*: appaia, appaia, appaia, appariamo, appariate, appaiano; *imperfect subjunctive*: apparissi; *auxiliary*: essere.

appèndere (*to hang up*) *past participle*: appéso; *preterit*: appési, appendesti, appése, appendemmo, appendeste, appésero.

aprire (*to open*) *past participle*: aperto; *preterit*: apersi (aprii), apristi, aperse (apr), aprimmo, apriste, apèrsero (aprirono).

assìstere (*to assist; to be present*) see **esìstere**.

assùmere (*to assume; to*

appoint) *past participle*:
assunto; *preterit*: assunsi,
assumesti, assunse,
assumemmo, assumeste,
assùnsero.

avvòlgere (*to wind, to wrap*)
see **vòlgere**.

benedire (*to bless*) see **dire**.

bére (*to drink*) *gerund*:
bevendo; *past participle*:
bevuto; *present indicative*:
bévo, bévi, béve, beviamo,
bevete, bévono; *imperfect
indicative*: bevevo; *preterit*:
bévvi (bevéi, bevètti), bevesti,
bévve (bevé, bevètte),
bevemmo, beveste, bévvero
(bevérono, bevèttero); *future*:
berrò; *conditional*: berrei;
imperative: bévi, béva,
beviamo, bevete, bévano;
present subjunctive: béva;
imperfect subjunctive:
bevessi.

cadere (*to fall*) *preterit*: caddi,
cadesti, cadde, cademmo,
cadeste, càddero; *future*:
cadrò; *conditional*: cadrei;
auxiliary: essere.

chièdere (*to ask*) *past
participle*: chièsto; *preterit*:
chièsi, chiedesti, chièse,
chiedemmo, chiedeste,
chièsero.

chiùdere (*to close*) *past
participle*: chiuso; *preterit*:
chiusi, chiudesti, chiuse,
chiudemmo, chiudeste,
chiusero.

cògliere (*to pluck; to collect*)
gerund: cogliendo; *past
participle*: còlto; *present
indicative*: còlgo, cògli, còglie,
cogliamo, cogliete, còlgono;
imperfect indicative: coglievo;
preterit: còlsi, cogliesti, còlse,
cogliemmo, coglieste, còlsero;
future: coglierò; *conditional*:

coglierei; *imperative*: cògli,
còlga, cogliamo, cogliete,
còlgano; *present subjunctive*:
còlga, còlga, còlga, cogliamo,
cogliate, còlgano; *imperfect
subjunctive*: cogliessi.

coincdere (*to coincide*) see
decìdere.

concèdere (*to grant; to admit*)
past participle: concèsso;
preterit: concèssi. concedesti,
concèsse, concedemmo,
concedeste, concèssero.

condurre (*to lead*) *gerund*:
conducendo; *past participle*:
condotto; *present indicative*:
conduco, conduci, conduce,
conduciamo, conducete,
condùcono; *imperfect
indicative*: conducevo;
preterit: condussi, conducesti,
condusse, conducemmo,
conduceste, condùssero;
future: condurrò; *conditional*:
condurrei; *imperative*:
conduci, conduca,
conduciamo, conducete,
conducano, *present
subjunctive*: conduca,
conduca, conduca,
conduciamo, conduciate,
condùcano; *imperfect
subjunctive*: conducessi.

conòscere (*to know; to make
acquaintance of*) *past
participle*: conosciuto;
preterit: conobbi, conoscesti,
conobbe, conoscemmo,
conosceste, conòbbero.

contraddire (*to contradict*)
see **dire**.

coprire (*to cover*) see **aprire**.

corrèggere (*to correct*) see
règgere

còrrere (*to run*) *past
participle*: corso; *preterit*:
corsi, corresti, corse,
corremmo, correste, crsero;

auxiliary: avere or essere.

créscere (*to grow*) *past participle*: cresciuto; *preterit*: crébbi, crescesti, crébbe, crescemmo, cresceste, crébbero; *auxiliary*: essere; *when used transitively*: avere.

cuòcere (*to cook*) *gerund*: cocendo; *past participle*: còtto; *present indicative*: cuòcio, cuòci, cuòce, cuociamo, cuocete, cuòciono; *imperfect indicative*: cuocevo; *preterit*: còssi, cuocesti, còsse, cuocemmo, cuoceste, còssero; *future*: cuocerò; *conditional*: cuocerei; *imperative*: cuòci, cuòcia, cuociamo, cuocete, cuòciano; *present subjunctive*: cuòcia; *imperfect subjunctive*: cuocessi.

dare (*to give*) *present indicative*: do, dai, dà,, diamo, date, danno; *preterit*: diedi (detti), desti, diede, demmo, deste, diedero (dettero); *future*: darò; *imperative*: da' (dai), dia, diamo, diate, diano; *present subjunctive*: dia.

decdere (*to decide*) *past participle*: deciso; *preterit*: decisi, decidesti, decise, decidemmo, decideste, decsero.

devòlvere (*to assign*) *past participle*: devoluto

difèndere (*to defend*) *past participle*: difeso; *preterit*: difési, difendesti, difése, difendemmo, difendeste, difésero.

dipingere (*to paint*) *past participle*: dipinto; *preterit*: dipinsi, dipingesti, dipinse, dipingemmo, dipingeste, dipinsero.

dire (*to say*) *gerund*: dicendo; *past participle*: detto; *present indicative*: dico, dici, dice, diciamo, dite, dìcono; *imperfect indicative*: dicevo; *preterit*: dissi, dicesti, disse, dicemmo, diceste, dìssero; *future*: dirò; *conditional*: direi; *imperative*: di', dica, diciamo, dite, dìcano; *present subjunctive*: dica, dica, dica, diciamo, diciate, dìcano; *imperfect subjunctive*: dicessi.

dirigere (*to manage*) *past participle*: dirètto; *preterit*: dirèssi, dirigesti, dirèsse, dirigemmo, dirigeste, dirèssero.

discùtere (*to discuss*) *past participle*: discusso; *preterit*: discussi, discutesti, discusse, discutemmo, discuteste, discussero.

disdire (*to cancel*) see **dire**.

distìnguere (*to distinguish*) *past participle*: distinto; *preterit*: distinsi, distinguesti, distinse, distinguemmo, distingueste, distinsero.

divìdere (*to divide*) *past participle*: diviso; *preterit*: divisi, dividesti, divise, dividemmo, divideste, divisero.

dolére (**dolérsi**) (*to hurt; to grieve*) *present indicative*: mi dòlgo, ti duòli, si duòle, ci doliamo (dogliamo), vi dolete, si dòlgono; *imperfect indicative*: mi dolevo; *preterit*: mi dòlsi, ti dolesti, si dòlse, ci dolemmo, vi doleste, si dòlsero; *future*: mi dorrò; *conditional*: mi dorrei; *imperative*: duòliti, si dòlga, dogliamoci (doliamoci), doletevi, si dòlgano; *present* subjunctive: mi dolga, ti dolga, si dolga, ci doliamo (dogliamo), vi dogliate, si dòlgano; imperfect subjunctive: mi dolessi; auxiliary: essere.

dovére (to have to; to owe) present indicative: dèvo (dèbbo), dèvi, dève, dobbiamo, dovete, dèvono (dèbbono); imperfect indicative: dovevo; preterit: dovéi (dovètti), dovesti; future: dovrò; conditional: dovrei; present subjunctive: dèva (dèbba), dèva, dèva, dobbiamo, dobbiate, dèvano (dèbbano); imperfect subjunctive: dovessi.

emèrgere (to emerge) past participle: emèrso; emèrsi, emergesti, emèrse, emergemmo, emergeste, emèrsero; auxiliary: essere.

esìstere (to exist) past participle: esistito; auxiliary: essere.

estìnguere (to extinguish) see **distìnguere**.

evòlvere (to evolve) see **devòlvere**.

fare (to do; to make) past participle: fatto; present indicative: faccio, fai, fa, facciamo, fate, fanno; imperfect indicative: facevo; preterit: féci, facesti, féce, facemmo, faceste, fécero; future: farò; con. farei; imperative: fa' (fai), faccia, facciamo, fate, facciano. present subjunctive: faccia, faccia, faccia, facciamo, facciate, fàcciano; imperfect subjunctive: facessi.

fingere (to pretend) see **dipingere**.

fòndere (to melt; to merge)

past participle: fuso; preterit: fusi, fondesti, fuse, fondemmo, fondeste, fùsero.

giungere (to arrive; to join) past participle: giunto; preterit: giunsi, giungesti, giunse, giungemmo, giungeste, giùnsero.

godere (to rejoice; to enjoy) future: godrò; godrei.

introdurre (to introduce) see **condurre**.

invàdere (to invade) past participle: invaso; preterit: invasi, invadesti, invase, invademmo, invadeste, invasero.

lèggere (to read) past participle: lètto; preterit: lèssi, leggesti, lèsse, leggemmo, leggeste, lèssero.

méttere (to put) past participle: mésso; preterit: misi, mettesti, mise, mettemmo, metteste, misero.

mòrdere (to bite) past participle: mòrso; preterit: mòrsi. mordesti, mòrse, mordemmo, mordeste, mòrsero.

morire (to die) past participle: morto; present indicative: muoio, muori, muore, moriamo, morite, muòiono; imperfect indicative: morivo; preterit: morii; future: morrò (morirò), morrai (morirai); conditional: morrei (morirei), morresti (moriresti); imperative: muori, muoia, moriamo, morite, muiòano; present subjunctive: muòia, muòia, muòia, moriamo, moriate, muoiano; imperfect subjunctive: morissi.

muòvere (to move) past participle: mosso; preterit: mòssi, movesti, mòsse,

443

movemmo, moveste, mòssero.

nàscere *(to be born) past
participle*: nato; *preterit*:
nacqui, nascesti, nacque,
nascemmo, nasceste,
nacquero.

nascòndere *(to hide) past
participle*: nascosto; *preterit*:
nascosi, nascondesti, nascose,
nascondemmo, nascondeste,
nascòsero.

nuòcere *(to harm) past
participle*: nociuto; *present
indicative*: nòccio, nuoci,
nuoce, nociamo, nocete,
nòcciono; *imperfect
indicative*: nocevo; *preterit*:
nòcqui, nocesti, nòcque,
nocemmo, noceste, nòcquero;
imperative: nuòci, nòccia,
nociamo, nocete, nòcciano;
present subjunctive: nòccia,
nòccia, nòccia, nociamo,
nociate, nòcciano; *imperfect
subjunctive*: nuocessi.

offèndere *(to offend) see*
difèndere.

offrire *(to offer) past
participle*: offerto; *preterit*:
offersi (offrii), offristi, offerse
(offrì), offrimmo, offriste,
offèrsero (offrirono).

opporre *(to oppose) see* **porre**.

parére *(to appear) past
participle*: parso; *present
indicative*: paio, pari, pare,
paiamo, parete, paiono;
imperfect indicative: parevo;
preterit: parvi, paresti, parve,
paremmo, pareste, pàrvero;
future: parrò; *conditional*:
parrei; *present subjunctive*:
paia, paia, paia, paiamo,
paiate, paiano; *imperfect
subjunctive*: paressi;
auxiliary: essere.

pèrdere *(to lose) past
participle*: pèrso (perduto);

preterit: pèrsi, perdesti,
pèrse, perdemmo, perdeste,
pèrsero.

persuadére *(to persuade) past
participle*: persuaso; *preterit*:
persuasi, persuadesti,
persuase, persuademmo,
persuadeste, persuàsero

piacére *(to please) past
participle*: piaciùto; *present
indicative*: piaccio, piaci,
piace, piacciamo (piaciamo),
piacete, piàcciono; *preterit*:
piacqui, piacesti, piacque,
piacemmo, piaceste,
piacquero; *imperative*: piaci,
piaccia, piacciamo, piacete,
piacciono; *present
subjunctive*: piaccia, piaccia,
piaccia, piacciamo
(piaciamo), piacciate
(piaciate), piacciano;
auxiliary: essere.

piàngere *(to weep) past
participle*: pianto; *preterit*:
piansi, piangesti, pianse,
piangemmo, piangeste,
piansero.

piòvere *(to rain) preterit*:
piòvve *(impersonal)*;
auxiliary: essere *or* avere.

pòrgere *(to hold out, to offer)
past participle*: pòrto;
preterit: pòrsi, porgesti,
pòrse, porgemmo, porgeste,
pòrsero.

porre *(to place) gerund*:
ponendo; *past participle*:
posto; *present indicative*:
pongo, poni, pone, poniamo,
ponete, pòngono; *imperfect
indicative*: ponevo; *preterit*:
posi, ponesti, pose, ponemmo,
poneste, pòsero; *future*:
porrò; *conditional*: porrei;
imperative: poni, ponga,
poniamo, ponete, pòngano;
present subjunctive: ponga,

ponga, ponga, poniamo, poniate, pòngano; *imperfect subjunctive*: ponessi.

potére (*to be able*) *present indicative*: posso, puoi, può, possiamo, potete, possono; *imperfect indicative*: potevo; *preterit*: poti, potesti; *future*: potrò; *conditional*: potrei; *present subjunctive*: possa, possa, possa, possiamo, possiate, pòssano; *imperfect subjunctive*: potessi.

prèndere (*to take*) *past participle*: préso; *preterit*: prési, prendesti, prése, prendemmo, prendeste, présero.

produrre (*to produce*) *see* **condurre**.

protèggere (*to protect*) *past participle*: protètto; *preterit*: protèssi, proteggesti, protèsse, proteggemmo, proteggeste, protèssero.

règgere (*to support, to last*) *past participle*: rètto; *preterit*: rèssi, reggesti, rèsse, reggemmo, reggeste, rèssero.

rèndere (*to give back*) *past participle*: réso; *preterit*: rési, rendesti, rése, rendemmo, rendeste, résero.

resìstere (*to hold out, stand*) *see* esìstere.

rìdere (*to laugh*) *past participle*: riso; *preterit*: risi, ridesti, rise, ridemmo, rideste, rìsero.

ridurre (*to reduce*) *see* **condurre**.

rimanére (*to remain*) *past participle*: rimasto; *present indicative*: rimango, rimani, rimane, rimaniamo, rimanete, rimàngono; *imperfect indicative*: rimanevo; *preterit*: rimasi, rimanesti, rimase, rimanemmo, rimaneste, rimàsero; *future*: rimarrò; *conditional*: rimarrei; *imperative*: rimani, rimanga, rimaniamo, rimanete, rimàngano; *present subjunctive*: rimanga, rimanga, rimanga, rimaniamo, rimaniate, rimàngano; *auxiliary*: essere.

rispòndere (*to answer*) *past participle*: risposto; *preterit*: risposi, rispondesti, rispose, rispondemmo, rispondeste, rispòsero.

riuscire (*to succeed*) *see* uscire.

rivòlgere (*to turn; to address*) *see* **vòlgere**.

ròmpere (*to break*) *past participle*: rotto; *preterit*: ruppi, rompesti, ruppe, rompemmo, rompeste, rùppero.

salire (*to rise; to climb*) *present indicative*: salgo, sali, sale, saliamo, salite, salgono; *imperative*: sali, salga, saliamo, salite, sàlgano; *present subjunctive*: salga, salga, salga, saliamo, saliate, sàlgano; *auxiliary*: essere; when used transitively, avere.

sapére (*to know; to taste of*) *present indicative*: so, sai, sa, sappiamo, sapete, sànno; *imperfect indicative*: sapevo; *preterit*: seppi, sapesti, seppe, sapemmo, sapeste, séppero; *future*: saprò; *conditional*: saprei; *imperative*: sappi, sappia, sappiamo, sappiate, sàppiano; *present subjunctive*: sappia, sappia, sappia, sappiamo, sappiate, sàppiano; *imperfect* *subjunctive*: sapessi.

scégliere (*to choose*) *past participle*: scelto; *present indicative*: scelgo, scegli, sceglie, scegliamo, scegliete, scélgono; *imperfect indicative*: sceglievo; *preterit*: scelsi, scegliesti, scelse, scegliemmo, sceglieste, scélsero; *future*: sceglierò; *conditional*: sceglierei; *imperative*: scegli, scelga, scegliamo, scegliete, scélgano; *present subjunctive*: scelga, scelga, scelga, scegliamo, scegliate, scélgano; *imperfect subjunctive*: scegliessi.

scéndere (*to go or come down; to fall*) *past participle*: sceso; *preterit*: scesi, scendesti, scese, scendemmo, scendeste, scésero; *auxiliary*: essere; when used transitively, avere.

sciògliere (*to loosen; to solve; to melt*) *past participle*: sciòlto; *present indicative*: sciolgo, sciogli, scioglie, sciogliamo, sciogliete, sciòlgono; *imperfect indicative*: scioglievo; *preterit*: sciolsi, sciogliesti, sciolse, sciogliemmo, scioglieste, sciòlsero; *future*: scioglierò; *conditional*: scioglierei; *imperative*: sciogli, sciolga, sciogliamo, sciogliete, sciòlgano; *present subjunctive*: sciolga, sciolga, sciolga, sciogliamo, sciogliate, sciòlgano; *imperfect subjunctive*: sciogliessi.

sconvòlgere (*to upset*) *see* **vòlgere**

scoprire (*to discover*) *see* **aprire**.

scrivere (*to write*) *past*

participle: scritto; *preterit*: scrissi, scrivesti, scrisse, srivemmo, scriveste, scrìssero.

scuòtere (*to shake*) *past participle*: scosso; *preterit*: scossi, scotesti, scosse, scottemmo, scoteste, scòssero.

sedére (**sedérsi**) (*to sit*) *present indicative*: siedo (seggo), siedi, siede, sediamo, sedete, sièdono (sèggono); *imperative*: siedi, sieda (segga), sediamo, sedete, sièdano (sèggano); *present subjunctive*: sieda (segga), sieda (segga), sieda (segga), sediamo, sediate, sièdano (sèggano); *auxiliary*: essere.

soffrire (*to suffer*) *see* **offrire**.

sòrgere (*to rise*) *past participle*: sorto; *preterit*: sorsi, sorgesti, sorse, sorgemmo, sorgeste, sòrsero; *auxiliary*: essere.

sorrìdere (*to smile*) *see* **rìdere**.

spègnere (*to put out; to switch off*) *past participle*: spènto; *present indicative*: spengo, spegni, spegne, spegniamo, spegnete, spengono; *imperfect indicative*: spegnevo; *preterit*: spensi, spegnesti, spense, spegnemmo, spegneste, spènsero; *future*: spegnerò; *conditional*: spegnerei; *imperative*: spegni, spenga, spegniamo, spegnete, spengano; *present subjunctive*: spenga, spenga, spenga, spegniamo, spegniate, spengano; *imperfect subjunctive*: spegnessi.

spìngere (*to push*) *past participle*: spinto; *preterit*:

spinsi, spingesti, spinse, spingemmo, spingeste, spinsero.

stare (*to stay; to be situated*) *present indicative*: sto, stai, sta, stiamo, state, stanno; *preterit*: stètti, stésti, stètte, stémmo, stéste, stèttero; *future*: starò; *imperative*: sta' (stai), stia, stiamo, state, stiano; *present subjunctive*: stia, stia, stia, stiamo, stiate, stìano; *imperfect subjunctive*: stèssi, stéssi, stésse, stéssimo, stéste, stéssero; *auxiliary*: essere.

strìngere (*to squeeze*) *past participle*: stretto; *preterit*: strinsi, stringesti, strinse, stringemmo, stringeste, strinsero.

supporre (*to suppose*) *see* **porre**.

tacére (*to be silent*) *present indicative*: taccio, taci, tace, taciamo, tacete, tàcciono; *preterit*: tacqui, tacesti, tacque, tacemmo, taceste, tàcquero; *imperative*: taci, taccia, taciamo, tacete, tàcciano; *present subjunctive*: taccia, taccia, taccia, taciamo, taciate, tàcciano.

tèndere (*to hold out; to tend*) *past participle*: teso; *preterit*: tesi, tendesti, tese, tendemmo, tendeste, tsero.

tenére (*to hold*) *present indicative*: tengo, tieni, tiene, teniamo, tenete, tèngono; *imperfect indicative*: tenevo; *preterit*: tenni, tenesti, tenne, tenemmo, teneste, ténnero; *future*: terrò; *conditional*: terrei; *imperative*: tieni, tenga, teniamo tenete, tèngano; *present subjunctive*: tenga, tenga, tenga, teniamo,

teniate, tèngano; *imperfect subjunctive*: tenessi.

tògliere (*to remove*) *see* **cògliere**.

tradurre (*to translate*) *see* **condurre**.

trarre (*to pull; to attract; to fling*) *gerund*: traendo; *past participle*: tratto; *present indicative*: traggo, trai, trae, traiamo, traete, tràggono; *imperfect indicative*: traevo; *preterit*: trassi, traesti, trasse, traemmo, traeste, tràssero; *future*: trarrò; *conditional*: trarrei; *imperative*: trai, tragga, traiamo, traete, tràggano; *present subjunctive*: tragga, tragga, tragga, traiamo, traiate, tràggano; *imperfect subjunctive*: traessi.

travòlgere (*to overwhelm*) *see* **vòlgere**.

uccìdere (*to kill*) *see* **decìdere**.

udire (*to hear*) *present indicative*: odo, odi, ode, udiamo, udite, òdono; *imperfect indicative*: udivo; *preterit*: udii; *future*: udirò (udrò); *conditional*: udirei (udrei); *imperative*: odi, oda, udiamo, udite, òdano; *present subjunctive*: oda, oda, oda, udiamo, udiate, òdano; *imperfect subjunctive*: udissi.

uscire (*to go or come out*) *present indicative*: esco, esci, esce, usciamo, uscite, èscono; *imperative*: esi, esca, usciamo, uscite, èscano; *present subjunctive*: esca, esca, esca, usciamo, usciate, èscano; *auxiliary*: essere.

valere (*to be worth; to be effective, of use*) *past participle*: valso; *present indicative*: valgo, vale, vale,

valiamo, valete, vàlgono;
imperfect indicative: valevo;
preterit: valsi, valesti, valse,
valemmo, valeste, vàlsero;
future: varrò; *conditional*:
varrei; *imperative*: vali,
valga, valiamo, valete,
valgano; *present subjunctive*:
valga, valga, valga, valiamo,
valiate, vàlgano; *imperfect
subjunctive*: valessi;
auxiliary: essere.

vedere (*to see*) *past participle*:
visto (veduto); *present
indicative*: vedo; *imperfect
indicative*: vedevo; *preterit*:
vidi, vedesti, vide, vedemmo,
vedeste, vìdero; *future*: vedrò;
conditional: vedrei;
imperative: vedi, veda,
vediamo, vedete, védano;
present subjunctive: veda,
veda, veda, vediamo, vediate,
védano; *imperfect
subjunctive*: vedessi.

venire (*to come*) *past
participle*: venuto; *present
indicative*: vengo, vieni,
viene, veniamo, venite,
vèngono; *imperfect
indicative*: venivo; *preterit*:
venni, venisti, venne,
venimmo, veniste, vénnero;
future: verrò; *conditional*:
verrei; *imperative*: vieni,

venga, veniamo, venite,
vngano; *present subjunctive*:
venga, venga, venga,
veniamo, veniate, vèngano;
imperfect subjunctive:
venissi; *auxiliary*: essere.

vncere (*to win*) *past
participle*: vinto; *preterit*:
vinsi, vincesti, vinse,
vincemmo, vinceste, vìnsero.

vivere (*to live*) *past participle*:
vissuto; *preterit*: vissi,
vivesti, visse, vivemmo,
viveste, vssero; *future*: vivrò;
conditional: vivrei; *auxiliary*:
essere; *when used
transitively*: avere.

volere (*to wish, to want; to
intend*) *present indicative*:
voglio, vuoi, vuole, vogliamo,
volete, vògliono; *imperfect
indicative*: volevo; *preterit*:
volli, volesti, volle, volemmo,
voleste, vòllero; *future*: vorrò;
conditional: vorrei;
imperative: vogli, voglia,
vogliamo, volete, vògliano;
present subjunctive: voglia,
voglia, voglia, vogliamo,
vogliate, vògliano; *imperfect
subjunctive*: volessi.

vòlgere (*to turn round*) *past
participle*: volto; *preterit*:
volsi, volgesti, volse,
volgemmo, volgeste, vòlsero.